The Rights of Armenian Minorities in Lebanon and Turkey under National and International Law

Völkerrecht, Europarecht und Internationales Wirtschaftsrecht

Herausgegeben von Peter Hilpold und August Reinisch

Band 29

PETER LANG

Kyfork Aghobjian

The Rights of Armenian Minorities in Lebanon and Turkey under National and International Law

PETER LANG

Bibliografische Information der Deutschen Nationalbibliothek
Die Deutsche Nationalbibliothek verzeichnet diese Publikation in der Deutschen Nationalbibliografie; detaillierte bibliografische Daten sind im Internet über http://dnb.d-nb.de abrufbar.

Zugl.: University of Vienna, Diss., 2022

ISSN 1862-457
ISBN 978-3-631-88848-3 (Print)
E-ISBN 978-3-631-88864-3 (E-PDF)
E-ISBN 978-3-631-88865-0 (EPUB)
DOI 10.3726/b20135

Peter Lang – Berlin · Bruxelles · Lausanne · New York · Oxford

Diese Publikation wurde begutachtet.

www.peterlang.com

Zusammenfassung

Der Nahe Osten ist die Heimat vieler alter einheimischer Minderheiten, deren Machtlosigkeit dazu führt, dass ihre gegenwärtige Situation und ihr rechtlicher Status vergleichsweise unbekannt sind. Diese Dissertation untersucht die Rechte der armenischen Minderheiten im Libanon und in der Türkei aus völkerrechtlicher Perspektive. Sie zeigt auf, inwieweit das Recht der armenischen Minderheiten auf Existenz, auf eine eigene Kultur, auf das Bekenntnis und die Ausübung der eigenen Religion, auf den Gebrauch der eigenen Sprache in der Gemeinschaft mit anderen Gruppenmitgliedern und ihr Recht auf respektiert, geschützt und erfüllt werden, wie es in den von den jeweiligen Ländern ratifizierten internationalen Verträgen und im Hinblick auf andere nicht bindende internationale Instrumente gefordert wird.

Obwohl es bereits eine beachtliche Menge an Literatur über die historische, soziale und politische Entwicklung der Armenier in der Region gibt, befassen sich nur wenige aktuelle akademische Untersuchungen mit ihrem rechtlichen Status und ihrer Behandlung. Die vorliegende Arbeit versucht, diese Lücke zu schließen.

Der Libanon und die Türkei wurden ausgewählt, weil sie in einer Region liegen, die in rechtlicher, politischer, sozialer und wirtschaftlicher Hinsicht beträchtlichen Herausforderungen gegenübersteht. In dieser Arbeit wird die Lage der armenischen Minderheiten in jedem dieser Länder in verschiedenen historischen Perioden analysiert. Die Rolle der Republik Armenien bei der Förderung der Rechte der Armenier im Libanon und in der Türkei auf nationaler und internationaler Ebene wird ebenfalls kurz angesprochen.

Die Dissertation kommt zum Schluss, dass der Libanon und die Türkei ihren internationalen Verpflichtungen in Bezug auf die Achtung, den Schutz und die Verwirklichung von Minderheitenrechten nicht in vollem Umfang nachkommen, was bedeutet, dass Minderheiten nach wie vor gefährdet sind und an den Rand gedrängt werden, und dass ihr Schutz hinter den internationalen Standards zurückbleibt. Reforminitiativen erfordern einen radikalen Wandel der vorherrschenden gesellschaftlichen Mentalität und eine Änderung der offiziellen Rhetorik. Beide Länder benötigen eine Stärkung der Rechtsstaatlichkeit und der Menschenrechtsmechanismen, um das Leben der armenischen – und anderer – Minderheiten zu verbessern.

Abstract

The Middle East is home to many ancient and indigenous minority groups whose powerlessness makes their present circumstances little known – and indeed virtually hidden. This thesis examines the rights of Armenian minorities in Lebanon and Turkey under national and international Law. *It identifies the extent to which the rights of Armenian minorities to exist, to enjoy their own culture, to profess and practice their own religion, and to use their own language in the community with other members of their group as well as their right to equality and non-discrimination and to participation are respected, protected and fulfilled as it is required under international treaties ratified by the respective countries and in view of other non-binding international instruments.*

Why Armenians? Armenians have been living in the Middle East for centuries. Nowadays Eastern Turkey is the origin and historical lands of most of the Armenians living in the Middle East. They constitute a minority on four separate levels: ethnic, national, linguistic and religious. Although there is a considerable amount of literature addressing Armenians' historical, social and political development in the region, a contemporary academic research that examines the legal status and treatment of Armenian minorities under international human rights laws and national laws rarely exist or often is neglected. Therefore, the thesis tries to fill this gap.

Why Lebanon and Turkey? Lebanon and Turkey have been selected for detailed study, due to their individual complexities within a region that is itself challenging in legal, political, social, and economic terms. Human and minority rights violations and majority-minority debates are already rife in these two states. By examining the ways national and international human rights laws are enforced and protected, or violated and ignored, the thesis highlights the problems facing Armenians in Lebanon and Turkey and provides theoretical and empirical benefits which would be of great value to human and minority rights discourses. Nevertheless, tackling the question of minority rights in Lebanon and Turkey cannot be limited to an examination of laws that seek to protect minority communities. It is only by revisiting the historical social formation of the multiple geographies of the region it is possible to better understand the genesis of identity politics and legal dynamics in the area. Therefore, the thesis also analyzes the situation faced by the Armenian minorities in each of these countries during different historical stages.

In addition, the thesis studies the extent to which Armenians are aware of their rights and to what extent they are involved in human and minority rights activities both locally and internationally, hence providing a ground-level snapshot of the effectiveness of international human rights bodies and mechanisms. In this context, the thesis briefly analyzes the role the Republic of Armenia play in promoting the rights of Armenian in Lebanon and Turkey at national and international levels.

Based on the research, the thesis concludes that in Lebanon and Turkey internal tensions run high, the rule of law is not adequately established, State support for minorities is neither systematic nor sufficient and the social relationships are threatened. Subsequent governments in Lebanon and Turkey avoid or not fully comply with their international obligations in terms of respecting, protecting and fulfilling minority rights. Therefore, minorities remain vulnerable, marginalized and their status falls short of international standards.

This is the case for the Armenian minorities in both countries. Armenian identity and culture in Lebanon and Turkey – and indeed their very existence – face threats of extinction in different degrees. The reduction of the Armenian presence in the Middle East comes with the threat of the evaporation of Armenian civilization and the disappearance of its language and culture. The Armenians are a vulnerable minority and surviving as a minority in a threatening environment is only possible in the context of a strong community as well as State guarantees founded in international human rights law. Reform laws require a radical transformation of the dominant social mentality, and changes to the official rhetoric are vital when it comes to improving the rights of minorities. In order to significantly improve the lives of all minorities, including the Armenians, Lebanon and Turkey need further democratization, strengthening the rule of law and human rights mechanisms and preventing religious-conservative majoritarianism, and increasing levels of authoritarianism.

Acknowledgments

First and foremost, I am heartily thankful to my supervisor, Prof. Dr. Irmgard Marboe for her invaluable advice, continuous support, and guidance during my doctoral study. I would also like to thank my wife Ani and newly born daughter Ser Love. Without Ani's tremendous understanding and encouragement in the past few years and Ser's quiet behavior since she joined us, it would have been impossible for me to complete the thesis. Finally, as the Armenian saying goes "there is good in every evil," I would like to highlight and appreciate the fact that COVID-19 pandemic related lockdowns offered plenty of time to sit down at home and focus on the thesis.

Kyfork Aghobjian (Kevork Hagopjian)

List of Acronyms

ACHR	The Arab Charter on Human Rights
ACtHR	The Arab Court on Human Rights
AGBU	Armenian General Benevolent Union
AHRC	Arab Human Rights Committee
AKP	*Adalet and Kalkınma Partisi* (Justice and Development Party)
APCHR	The Arab Independent Permanent Committee of Human Rights
ARF	Armenian Revolutionary Federation
CC	Constitutional Court
CEDAW	The Convention on the Elimination of all Forms of Discrimination Against Women
CERD	International Convention on Elimination of all forms of Racial Discrimination
CESCR	Committee on Economic Social and Cultural Rights
CoE	Council of Europe
CoM	Committee of Ministers
CRC	Convention on the Rights of the Child
CUP	Committee of Union and Progress
CHP	*Cumhuriyet Halk Partisi* (Republican People's Party)
DP	Democrat Party
DRRP	UNESCO's Declaration on Race and Racial Prejudice
EC	European Commission
EEC	European Economic Community
ECHR	European Convention on Human Rights
ECtHR	European Court of Human Rights
ECRI	European Commission against Racism and Intolerance
ECtHR	European Court of Human Rights
ESC	The European Social Charter
EU	European Union
FCPNM	Framework Convention for the protection of National Minorities
GDF	General Directorate of Foundations
HCNM	The High Commissioner for National Minorities
HDP	*Halkların Demokratik Partisi* (People's Democratic Party)
HRC	Human Rights Committee of ICCPR

HREIT	Human Rights and Equality Institution of Turkey
HRW	Human Rights Watch
ICC	The Rome Statute of the International Criminal Court
ICCPR	International Covenant on Civil and Political Rights
ICESCR	International Covenant on Economic, Social and Cultural Rights
ILC	International Law Commission
IPMS	OHCHR Indigenous Peoples and Minorities Section
LAS	League of Arab States
MFA	Ministry of Foreign Affairs/
MoE	Ministry of Education
MP	Member of Parliament
NATO	The North Atlantic Treaty Organization
NGO	Non-Governmental Organization
OHCHR	Office of High Commissioner for Human Rights
IPMS	Indigenous Peoples and Minorities Section
OIC	The Organization of the Islamic Conference
OSCE	Organization for Security and Co-operation in Europe
OUP	Oxford University Press
PKK	Kurdistan Workers' Party
PLO	Palestinian Liberation Organization
R2P	Responsibility to Protect
SoE	State of Emergency
TPC	Turkish Panel Code
UDHR	Universal Declaration on Human Rights
UN	United Nations
UN	United Nations General Assembly
UNDP	United Nations Development Programme
UNESCO	United Nation Educational, Scientific and Cultural Organization
UNHCR	United Nations High Commissioner for Refugees
UNISEF	United Nations Children's Fund
UNSC	United Nations Security Council
UPR	Universal Periodic Review
USCIRF	The US Commission on International Religious Freedom
VCLT	Vienna Convention on the Law of Treaties
VGM	*Vakıflar Genel Müdürlüğü* (General Directorate of Foundations)
WP	Welfare Party
WWI	World War I
WWII	World War II

Contents

1. Introduction

1.1 General Background

Armenian minorities have been living in the Middle East for centuries.[1] They constitute a minority on four separate levels: ethnic, national (Armenian), linguistic (Western and Eastern Armenian languages) and religious (mainly Christian). Following the 1915 Armenian Genocide, which accounted for up to 1.5 million deaths,[2] many Armenians after being displaced from their homes took refuge in Syria and Lebanon as well as dispersed worldwide.[3] However, some Armenians remained in the homeland, in the area that became the Turkish Republic in 1923.

Nowadays, Armenian minorities exist in countries worldwide, and present-day Armenia, a country with approximately three million inhabitants,[4] has links with global diasporas that number around ten million.[5] Many Armenians settled in Middle Eastern countries immediately adjacent to their homeland, but unfortunately these countries have found themselves at the heart of the world's trouble spots, and have serious problems of their own to deal with, especially in areas related to peace, security, stability, rule of law, human rights and minority rights.

The Armenian community in Lebanon is facing profound challenges in terms of security, stability and emigration patterns, as well as difficulties in preserving its Armenian identity and collective institutional existence. In Turkey, in addition

---

1 "The first written reference to Armenians dates back to the sixth century BCE, with the majority living in areas that became part of Turkey and Iran," Tsolin Nalbantian in Armenians in the Middle East from Marginalization to Everyday in Paul S. Rowe ed., *Routledge Handbook of Minorities in the Middle East* (London. Routledge, 2019), p. 272.

2 See Chapter 4.10.2 below and Raymond Kevorkian, *The Armenian Genocide: A Complete History* (New York: I.B. Tauris, 2011) and Benny Morris & Dror Se'eavi, *The Thirty-Year Genocide: Turkey's Destruction of Its Christian Minorities*, 1894–1924 (USA: Harvard University Press, 2019).

3 Ibid.

4 "Report of Statistical Committee of Republic of Armenia, Permanent Population of the Republic of Armenia as of 01.10.2020," Republic of Armenia Statistical Committee, 01.10.2020, https://www.armstat.am/file/article/nasel_01.10.2020.pdf.

5 Monique Bolsajian, "The Armenian Diaspora: Migration and Its Influence on Identity and Politics," *Global Societies Journal*, 6 (2018), p. 30.

to what Armenians in Lebanon are encountering, Armenians are frequently subject to anti-Armenian rhetoric based on prejudice, discrimination and racial hatred. In both countries, the rights of Armenians are increasingly coming under pressure due to domestic and external disturbances and growing socioeconomic difficulties. It is worth noting that they also face linguistic restrictions, which may lead to the disappearance of their language (Western Armenian, which is spoken by majority of Armenians in Turkey and Lebanon, is on UNESCO's "definitely endangered"[6] language list). The Armenians of Lebanon and Turkey are encountering significant problems in terms of enjoying their human and minority rights.

The thesis will analyze local Statutes and practices towards Armenian minorities in Lebanon and Turkey in order to examine how the actual situation accords with national, regional, and international human rights law in both countries. The thesis will also explore the role of the Republic of Armenia in protecting and promoting the Armenians' rights in the two countries. Furthermore, the thesis will study the extent to which Armenians are aware of their rights and the degree to which they are involved in human and minority rights activities and mechanisms both locally and internationally.

Lebanon and Turkey have been selected for detailed study, due to their individual complexities within a region that is itself challenging in legal, political, social, and economic terms. Human and minority rights violations and majority-minority debates are already rife in these two States.[7] This is why the historical experiences, as well as the legal, political, and socioeconomic situation of Armenian minorities are worthy of study in both countries. By examining the ways national and international human rights laws are enforced and protected, or violated and ignored, the thesis hopes to highlight the problems facing Armenians in Lebanon and Turkey and to add value on human and minority rights discourses.

1.2 Research Question, Methodology, and Structure

The central research question addressed by this thesis will examine the extent to which the rights of Armenian minorities to exist, to enjoy their own culture, to

---

6 See the official website of UNESCO Atlas of the World's Languages in Danger, https://bit.ly/300DJYi.

7 Paul S. Rowe ed., *Routledge Handbook of Minorities in the Middle East* (London: Routledge, 2019), pp. 2–7.

profess and practice their own religion, and to use their own language in community with other members of their group, as well as their right to participation are respected, protected and fulfilled in Lebanon and Turkey.

In order to address the main research question, it is important to answer a number of sub questions:

a) Who are minorities and what are their rights under international human rights law? What is the role of international and regional human rights instruments in promoting the rights of minorities?
b) How do the legal and political systems as well as the general minority rights regime in Lebanon and Turkey function? What is the legal situation and internal organization of Armenians in Lebanon and in Turkey?
c) In what manner do the Armenian minorities exercise their rights in each country?
d) To what extent do Lebanon and Turkey respect, protect and fulfill the rights of the Armenian minorities?
e) What is the role of the Republic of Armenia in promoting the rights of Armenians in Lebanon and Turkey at national and international levels?

To address these questions posed in the most constructive and practical way, the thesis will apply the following methodology:

1) An analysis of existing legal documents, covenants, conventions, treaties, laws, and jurisprudence as well as literature regarding minority rights on international and regional levels. The thesis will study the relevant documents in international law regarding minority rights, particularly the Article 27 of ICCPR (including the case laws and General Comments of HRC) and Article 30 of the CRC as legally binding documents. After analyzing pure minority rights, the thesis will also analyze non-discrimination documents that are related to minority issues.
2) In terms of non-legally binding documents, the thesis will study the Minority Declaration, the reports of the Special Rapporteur on Minority Issues, the reports of the annual Minority Rights Forum of the Human Rights Council, the reports of the Human Rights Council, Universal Periodic Review, the Office of the United Nations High Commissioner for Human Rights, the Office of the United Nations High Commissioner for Refugees, UNESCO, and the Commission on Human Rights. By examining Armenian minorities as a case study, this thesis will explore the extent to which States adopt and apply internationally accepted human rights recommendations related to more

general minority rights, as well as the extent to which minorities in these countries benefit from these international recommendations.

3) Since Turkey and Lebanon are also part of regional human rights mechanisms, the thesis will study the minority rights both in European and Arab regions. For European region documents, the thesis will study the relevant documents such as the ECHR the FCPNM, the reports of the OSCE's High Commissioner of National Minorities, the European Charter for Regional or Minority Languages. In reference to Arab region, the thesis will examine the development and current status of minority rights in the OIC, the LAS and the Marrakesh Declaration.
4) An analysis of the current legal mechanisms and institutions for respecting, protecting, and fulfilling minority rights in each country, including the constitutional, administrative, judicial, electoral, socioeconomic, and local frameworks, and a comparison of each country's systems against the standards laid down by international law.
5) A brief analysis of the internal laws of Armenian minorities in Lebanon and Turkey. In these countries, each Armenian denomination has its own internal codes and regulations. The thesis will study these regulations, their legal validity and impacts as well as their compatibilities with human rights. In addition, it will consider the current difficulties and contradictions surrounding the application of the internal regulations and will find the gaps that need to be addressed by the current regulations for the improvement of minority rights.
6) An analysis of the historical and political developments of Lebanon and Turkey vis-à-vis the minorities. This is because addressing the question of minority rights in Lebanon and Turkey cannot be limited to an examination of laws that seek to protect minority communities. It is only by revisiting the historical/political developments of the region it would be possible to better understand the genesis of legal dynamics and understand the ways national and international human rights laws are enforced and protected or violated and ignored. Without analyzing the historical and political developments that resulted in the current legal regimes in both countries, it would be difficult (almost impossible) to answer the research questions of the thesis.

The thesis will be structured into six chapters. Following the main introduction, the second chapter will examine the nature and definition of minorities according to international law and the history of the development of minority rights. It will also analyze current minority rights legislation, legal documents and instruments that are in place to respect, protect and fulfill these rights under three headings – firstly the United Nations (UN), which will be divided into UN Documents and UN Bodies and Mechanisms, secondly European documents, bodies and mechanisms, and thirdly the existing legal documents, bodies and mechanisms in Arab and Muslim States. Looking at the conventions, treaties, frameworks, charters, directives, recommendations and legal mechanisms that have affected and impacted the treatment of Armenian minorities, will offer a better grounding for this thesis. The final section of the chapter will offer a conclusion and comparison of international and regional minority rights provisions.

The third and fourth chapters will separately address the rights of Armenians Minorities in Lebanon and Turkey. Each chapter will start with an analytical overview and analysis of the historical development, legal system as well as general human rights framework (including regional frameworks) of Lebanon and Turkey regarding minorities. After introducing what the term minority represents within each State's legal context and presenting the existing minorities and the challenges they face, these chapters will briefly look at the history and the institutional and internal structures of the Armenians. This will be followed by a thorough analyzes and examination of the Armenians' rights (the right to existence, the right to identity, the right to equality and non-discrimination and the right to participation) using relevant case laws, case studies as well as theoretical arguments. Based on the analyzes of the rights related issues Armenians face in each country, the chapters will study the Lebanese and Turkish States' obligations towards Armenians in terms of respecting, protecting and fulfilling of their rights. Before concluding each chapter, there will be analytical sections on the extent to which Armenians in Lebanon and Turkey are engaged in international and regional human rights mechanisms as well as the role of the Republic of Armenia in promoting the rights of Armenians in Lebanon and Turkey.

Before moving on to the main conclusions of the thesis, the sixth chapter will compare the Lebanese and Turkish Minority rights regimes in terms of the commonalities, differences, good practices, violations and drawbacks each legal system contains.[8]

---

8 The research phase of the thesis has stopped in March 2021. Therefore, all relevant events and developments that took place after March 2021 is not considered in the thesis.

2. Who Are Minorities and What Are Relevant Minority Rights at the International and Regional Levels?

2.1 Who Are Minorities According to International Law?

Almost all countries in the world have national, ethnic, linguistic and religious minorities. Distinctions within communities have existed throughout history, but majority and minority concepts are relatively modern in terms of international law.[9] There is still no universally agreed or legally binding definition of the word "minority"[10] due to the complexity of the minority phenomenon, the variety of situations in which minorities live and the fear States have regarding the consequences of minority recognition that might lead to secessionist movements and threaten State security.[11] In addition, some minorities live in distinct areas, separated from the dominant part of the population, whilst others are distributed throughout the country.[12] Some have a strong sense of collective identity and history, others retain only fragmented notions of common heritage.[13] Thus a definition that is too broad would be meaningless, whereas a narrower one would not apply to all minorities.

In 1950, the UN Sub-Commission on Prevention of Discrimination and Protection of Minorities drafted guidelines defining minorities:

> "a) The term minority includes only those non-dominant groups in a population which possess and wish to preserve stable ethnic, religious or linguistic traditions or characteristics markedly different from those of the rest of the population.

---

9 Judith Blau, Mark Frezzo, Sociology and Human Rights: A Bill of Rights for the Twenty-First Century (USA: Pine Forge Press, 2011).

10 "Report on Non-Citizens and Minority Rights," adopted by the Venice Commission at its 69th plenary session (Venice, 15-16.12.2006), CDL-AD (2007), para. 4 and Kristin Henrard, *Devising an Adequate System of Minority Protection: Individual Human Rights, Minority Rights and the Right to Self Determination International Studies in Human Rights* (The Netherlands: Martinus Nijhof Publishers, 2000). pp. 18-24.

11 Henrard, Devising an Adequate System, pp. 18-24.

12 UN OHCHR official website, "Minorities Under International Law," https://bit.ly/2VQd2Ru.

13 Ibid.

> b) Such minorities should properly include a number of persons sufficient in themselves to develop such characteristics.
> c) The members of such minorities must be loyal to the State of which they are nationals."[14]

This guideline was discussed but discarded, because such a general definition cannot fit every minority, since each minority group has distinct characteristics and circumstances.[15] In addition, neither numerical minimum threshold, nor the faithfulness vis-a-vis the State are requirements often to be indicated in other proposed definitions.[16] Later, while studying the implications of Article 27[17] of ICCPR, Francesco Capotorti[18] defined a minority as:

> "A group numerically inferior to the rest of the population of a State, in a non-dominant position, whose members – being nationals of the State – possess ethnic, religious or linguistic characteristics differing from those of the rest of the population and show, if only implicitly, a sense of solidarity, directed towards preserving their culture, traditions, religion or language."[19]

It is worth mentioning that Capotorti's definition has been widely accepted in academic and institutional circles dealing with minority issues.[20] However, another attempt was made by Deschenes, who had been asked by the UN Sub-Commission to define the term:

> "A group of citizens of a State, constituting a numerical minority and in a non-dominant position in that State, endowed with ethnic, religious or linguistic characteristics which

---

14 UN Economic and Social Council, Report of the Third Session of the Sub-Commission on the Prevention of Discrimination and the Protection of Minorities to the Commission on Human Rights (30.01.1950), UN Doc. E/CN.4/358 and E/CN.4/Sub.2/119.

15 Henrard, Devising an Adequate System, p. 20.

16 Ibid.

17 Article 27 of ICCPR: "In those States in which ethnic, religious or linguistic minorities exist, persons belonging to such minorities shall not be denied the right, in community with the other members of their group, to enjoy their own culture, to profess and practice their own religion, or to use their own language"

18 Francesco Capotorti is the former Special Rapporteur of the UN Sub-Commission on Prevention of Discrimination and Protection of Minorities.

19 UN Economic and Social Council, "Study on the Rights of Persons Belonging to National or Ethnic, Religious and Linguistic Minorities," 1979, UN Doc. E/CN.4/Sub.2/384/Rev.1, para. 568.

20 Antonija Petričušić, "The Rights of Minorities in International Law: Tracing Developments in Normative Arrangements of International Organizations," *Croatian International Relations Review*, 11:38-39 (2005), p. 4.

differ from those of the majority of the population, having a sense of solidarity with one another, motivated, if only implicitly, by collective will to survive and whose aim is to achieve equality with the majority in fact and in law."[21]

An interesting divergence between the two definitions above surrounds the use of "equality with the majority in fact and in law" in Deschenes' definition as a goal of minority groups, which refers to differential treatment for members of minorities, rather than to a subjective component of the definition. The subjective element is generally linked to the wish to retain separate characteristics.[22] In this context, Van Der Stoel provided useful points of reference regarding the classification of a national minority:

"The existence of a minority is a question of fact and not of definition. [...] First of all, a minority is a group with linguistic, ethnic or cultural characteristics, which distinguish it from the majority. Secondly, a minority is a group which usually not only seeks to maintain its identity but also tries to give stronger expression to that identity."[23]

What distinguishes van der Stoel's definition is the desire of minorities to retain a 'stronger expression' of identity, which might not be true or necessary for well-integrated minorities.

In the light of these different definitions and the absence of legally binding definition of the term 'minority', it can be argued that, although there is no internationally accepted definition of a minority,[24] there does seem to be some agreement regarding defining elements, even though some of these elements have different interpretations. The terms used in article 27 indicate that the persons designed to be protected are those who belong to a group and who share in common a culture, a religion and/or a language.[25] The UN Minorities Declaration, adopted by consensus in 1992, refers to minorities as based on ethnic or national, religious, cultural, and linguistic identities.[26] Article 1.1 of the Minority

21 Jules Deschenes, "Proposal Concerning a Definition of the term 'Minority'," 1985, UN Doc. E/CN.4/Sub.2/1985/31,181.

22 Henrard, Devising an Adequate System, p. 23.

23 Keynote Address of Max Van Der Stoel CSCE High Commissioner on National Minorities at the CSCE Human Dimension Seminar on "Case Studies on National Minority Issues: Positive Results," Warsaw, 1993, http://www.osce.org/hcnm/38038?download=true.

24 UNOHCHR, Minority Rights: International Standards and Guidance for Implementation (New York, Geneva: UNOHCHR Publication, 2010), p. 2.

25 HRC, "CCPR General Comment No. 23: "The rights of minorities" (Art. 27)," 08/04/94, UN Doc. CCPR/C/21/Rev.1/Add.5, para. 5.1.

26 See the preamble of the Minority Declaration.

Declaration demands from States to protect the existence and identities of national or ethnic, cultural, religious and linguistic minorities within their respective territories,[27] while Article 2.1 of the same Declaration indicates that "Persons belonging to national or ethnic, religious and linguistic minorities [...] have the right to enjoy their own culture, to profess and practise their own religion, and to use their own language, in private and in public, freely and without interference or any form of discrimination.".

In addition, the Permanent Court of international Justice states that "the existence of a minority is a question of fact before being a question of law or politics."[28] This means that any definition must include objective[29] (e.g., shared ethnicity, language or religion) and subjective (i.e., individuals identify themselves as members of a minority) criteria.[30] The subjective criteria inter-alia include the freedom to not be treated as a minority member without facing any disadvantages for their choice. FNPNM states in this regard "[e]very person belonging to a national minority shall have the right freely to choose to be treated or not to be treated as such and no disadvantage shall result from this choice or from the exercise of the rights which are connected to that choice."[31] It is now commonly accepted that recognition of minority status is not a State decision and should be based on objective and subjective criteria from minority members.[32]

Nevertheless, there are still challenges in using the term "minority" for certain communities because they identify themselves as minorities, but their host State refuses to recognize them as such.[33] On the other hand, there are cases, minorities reject being referred as such due to perceived negative connotations.[34]

---

27 Article 1.1 of Minority Declaration: "States shall protect the existence and the national or ethnic, cultural, religious and linguistic identity of minorities within their respective territories and shall encourage conditions for the promotion of that identity"

28 Permanent Court of International Justice (PCIJ), "Advisory Opinion of the Permanent Court of International Justice (PCIJ) in the Greco-Bulgarian 'communities' case," Advisory Opinion No.17, 31.07.1930, Series B.

29 HRC, "CCPR General Comment No. 23: Article 27" para. 5.1.

30 Article 3.2 of Minority Declaration: "No disadvantage shall result for any person belonging to a minority as the consequence of the exercise or non-exercise of the rights set forth in the present Declaration."

31 Article 3 of FCPNM.

32 UNOHCHR, Minority Rights: International Standards, p. 3.

33 Rita Izsák, "Report of the Special Rapporteur on Minority Issues, Human Rights Council Thirty-fourth session," 2017, UN Doc. A/HRC/34/53.

34 Ibid.

HRC's General Comment No. 23 on Article 27 of ICCPR addresses the dynamics between individual and group rights when it comes to minority rights. It states:

> "Although the rights protected under article 27 are individual rights, they depend in turn on the ability of the minority group to maintain its culture, language or religion. Accordingly, positive measures by States may also be necessary to protect the identity of a minority and the rights of its members to enjoy and develop their culture and language and to practise their religion, in community with the other members of the group."[35]

The emphasis on the individual characteristic of minority rights is central to the existing concept of human rights protection. However, minority individuals depend on the ability of their minority groups to maintain culture, language or religion and they usually exercise their rights in community with the other members of their group. In other words, as the HRC observes, Article 27 "establishes and recognizes a right which is conferred on individuals belonging to minority groups and which is distinct from, and additional to, all the other rights which, as individuals in common with everyone else, they are already entitled to enjoy under the Covenant.[36]

Regarding the positive measures aiming to protect the identity of a minority in community with the other members of the group, it should be observed that such positive measures, must respect the provisions of articles 2.1[37] and 26[38] of the Covenant both as regards the treatment between different minorities and the treatment between the persons belonging to them and the remaining part of the population. However, as long as those measures are aimed at correcting conditions which prevent or impair the enjoyment of the rights guaranteed under article 27, they may constitute a legitimate differentiation under the Covenant, provided that they are based on reasonable and objective criteria.[39]

---

35 HRC, "CCPR General Comment No. 23: Article 27" para.6.2.

36 Ibid, para.1.

37 Article 2.1 of ICCPR: "Each State Party to the present Covenant undertakes to respect and to ensure to all individuals within its territory and subject to its jurisdiction the rights recognized in the present Covenant, without distinction of any kind, such as race, colour, sex, language, religion, political or other opinion, national or social origin, property, birth or other status."

38 Article 26 of ICCPR: "All persons are equal before the law and are entitled without any discrimination to the equal protection of the law. In this respect, the law shall prohibit any discrimination and guarantee to all persons equal and effective protection against discrimination on any ground such as race, colour, sex, language, religion, political or other opinion, national or social origin, property, birth or other status."

39 HRC, "CCPR General Comment No. 23: Article 27" para.6.2.

Moreover, HRC's General Comment No. 23 is progressive in determining who can be considered a minority member, as far as it does not require that minority be nationals or citizens of the State.[40] The same General Comment elaborated this view a step further, emphasizing that minority members "need not be permanent residents"[41] to enjoy Article 27 and thus they shall not be denied the right to enjoy their own culture, practice their own religion and use their own language.

The current tendency is to adopt a more pragmatic and inclusive approach to minority definitions, rather than adhere to rigid legal definitions.[42] Nevertheless, in practice, considerable latitude is left for each State to establish a definition that applies within its own jurisdiction, and there are substantial differences between such definitions within various countries.[43] However, in doing so States must not rely on arbitrary or unjustified distinctions, which would be the source of discrimination.[44]

2.2 Brief History

International provisions for the protection of ethnic, religious, or linguistic minorities can be dated back to Augsburg (1555) and Westphalia (1648) religious peace treaties.[45] In addition, in dismantling the Napoleonic Empire, the 1815 Congress of Vienna[46] recognized some minority rights, as did the 1878 Treaty

40 Ibid, para. 5.1 - 5.2.

41 Ibid

42 "[i]t was decided to adopt a pragmatic approach, based on the recognition that at this stage, it is impossible to arrive at a definition capable of mustering general support of all Council of Europe member States." in Explanatory Memorandum on the Framework Convention for the Protection of National Minorities, para.12, reprinted in "The Council of Europe's Framework Convention for the Protection of National Minorities," Heinrich Klebes, *Human Rights Law Journal*, 16:92 (1995). UN Working Group on Minorities, Report on its third session, 10.07.1997, UN Doc. E/CN.4/Sub2/1997/18, p. 22.

43 See EU Network of Independent Experts on Fundamental Rights, Thematic Comment No.3 on "The Protection of Minorities in the EU," 25.04.2005, p. 10 and Miriam J. Aukerman, "Definitions and Justifications: Minority and Indigenous Rights in a Central/East European Context," *Human Rights Quarterly*, 22:4 (November 2000), p. 1025.

44 "Report on Non-Citizens and Minority Rights," para. 13.

45 Manfred Nowak, *UN Covenant on Civil and Political Rights: CCPR Commentary* (revised 2nd ed.) (Kehl am Rhein: Engel, 2005), p. 635.

46 Randall Lesaffer, "The Congress of Vienna (1814-1815)," *Oxford Public International Law*, 2015, http://opil.ouplaw.com/page/congress-vienna-1814-1815.

of Berlin[47] which *inter alia* required from the Ottoman Empire a guarantee for the security of the Armenians against the Circassians and Kurds. However most nineteenth century international legal-political efforts were directed towards the unification of nations based on the principle of self-determination, rather than the protection of minority groups.[48] As the nationalism grew, people outside the majority ethnic, linguistic or religious identity came increasingly under threat.[49]

By the end of the First World War, minority concerns returned to the forefront of international politics and were institutionalized by obligations set out within peace treaties, although these were generally limited to minorities in Central and Eastern Europe.[50] On an international level, the first remarkable stage towards recognizing minority rights came via a series of minority treaties adopted by the League of Nations.[51] For instance, the first of the minority treaties was the Polish treaty signed on 28 June 1919, followed by the Austrian, Czechoslovak and Yugoslavian treaties (known as Treaty of St Germain-en-Laye), the Treaty of Neuilly-sur-Seine, the Treaty of Sevres, etc.[52]

These treaties covered equality and non-discrimination and minorities' religious, cultural, charitable and educational institutions, the right to citizenship as well as the right to use one's own language in public and private. States were obliged to provide reasonable financial support to minority schools in which instruction at primary level would be in minority languages, and laws were passed protecting minorities from any subsequent discrimination.

---

47 Article 61, Treaty of Berlin 1878: "the Sublime Porte engages to carry into effect, without further delay, the improvements and reforms demanded by local requirements in the provinces inhabited by Armenians, and to guarantee their security from Kurds and Circassians." https://archive.org/details/jstor-2212670/page/n11.

48 UNOHCHR, Promoting and Protecting Minority Rights: A Guide for Advocates (New York: UNOHCHR publication, 2012), p. 2, and Chris Brown, State and Nation in Nineteen Century International Political Theory (UK: LSE Research Online, 2006), http://eprints.lse.ac.uk/745/1/Chapter8_Introduction.pdf.

49 UNOHCHR, Promoting and protecting Minority Rights, pp. 2-4.

50 Mark Mazower, "Minorities and the League of Nations in Interwar Europe," *Daedalus Human Diversity,* 126:2 (Spring 1997), p. 47.

51 Helmer Rosting, "Protection of Minorities by the League of Nations," *The American Journal of International Law*, 17:4 (Oct 1923), pp. 641-660, published online by Cambridge University Press: 04 May 2017.

52 For further insight see Carole Fink, "The League of Nations and Minority Question," *World Affairs*, 157:4 (01.04.1995), pp. 197-205 and *Defending the Rights of Others: The Great Powers, the Jews, and International Minority Protection, 1878–1938* (Cambridge: Cambridge University Press, 2004).

At the Versailles Peace Conference, the Supreme Council established the Committee on New States and for the Protection of Minorities.[53] All new successor States were obliged to sign minority rights treaties as a precondition of diplomatic recognition.[54] However, these treaties were part of the Wilsonian approach to international relations – idealistic representations that were increasingly ignored by respective governments, leading to the collapse of the system in the late 1930s. Even though the scope of minority treaties was limited (there was no agreement about the universal applicability of minority rights, and they applied only to a small number of defeated or new States) their significance should not be underestimated.[55] They had tangible consequences for minorities within States and constituted an important step in developing international minority rights and human rights law. In particular, the acceptance of the principle of international monitoring mechanisms for minorities was a breakthrough in the development of international law,[56] which largely presaged the later promotion of broader human rights by the UN.

Thus, after World War II, human rights were incorporated into the UN Charter and international human rights treaties. In its early years, the UN concentrated on universal human rights and decolonization and concluded that there was no need to include specific provisions for minorities, as long as individual human rights were protected.[57] There is no indication of minority rights *per se* in the UN Charter, although it includes many provisions on human rights. Article 1 (3) of the UN Charter indicates that one of the main purposes of the UN is international cooperation "in promoting and encouraging respect for human rights and for fundamental freedoms for all without distinction as to race, sex, language, or religion."[58]

---

53 Carole Fink, "The Minorities Question at the Paris Peace Conference," in *The Treaty of Versailles: A Reassessment After 75 Years*, Manfred Franz Boemeke, Gerald D. Feldman, Elisabeth Gläser eds. (USA: Cambridge University Press, 1998), p. 249.

54 Peter Hilpold, "The League of Nations and the Protection of Minorities – Rediscovering a Great Experiment," *Max Planck Yearbook of United Nations Law*, 17:1 (2013), pp. 87-90.

55 Fink, "The League of Nations and Minority Question."

56 UNOHCHR, *Promoting and Protecting Minority Rights*, p. 3. and Pamphlet No. 4 of the UN Guide for Minorities.

57 Manfred Nowak, "An Introduction to the UN Human Rights System," in *All Human Rights for All, Vienna Manual on Human Rights* (Vienna – Graz: Intersentia, 2012), pp. 65-66.

58 Article 1 (3) of UN Charter.

In other words, in contrast to the League of Nations, the UN took a more passive stance regarding the protection of minorities.[59] This is, as Hafner argues, because "the elaboration of specific international regimes for the protection of ethnic minorities was impeded by the fear of some States that such a regime could have a centrifugal effect, possibly threatening the stability and creating a risk of dismemberment of the affected States."[60] Therefore, the 1948 Universal Declaration of Human Rights adopted an all-inclusive approach to human rights, guaranteeing the rights of "all members of the human family [...] without distinction of any kind, such as race, colour, sex, language, religion, political or other opinion, national or social origin, property, birth or other status."[61] Rights were granted irrespective of the groups to which people belonged, which tended to blur distinctions between groups such as national minorities and migrants.

However, later on, the UN recognized the distinction of guaranteeing minority rights beside general human rights and gradually understood that under general human rights obligations it is almost impossible to address minorities and to respect, protect and fulfill their rights. This is because certain groups such as minorities need special human rights which include affirmative actions or "positive discrimination" so they can preserve and protect their existence, culture and identity and prevent gradual disappearance particularly in the light of ongoing globalization.[62] Therefore the UN gradually developed more specific mechanisms covering minority issues.

In 1960, UNESCO adopted the Convention against Discrimination in Education, recognising the rights of minority groups to undertake their own educational activities – including establishing their own schools and teaching in minority languages.[63] In 1965, the UN adopted the CERD, prohibiting

59 Nowak, UN Covenant on Civil and Political Rights, p. 636.

60 Gerhard Hafner, "Human Rights of Minorities," in *All Human Rights for All Vienna Manual on Human Rights,* Manfred Nowak et al. (Vienna - Graz: Intersentia, 2012), p. 462.

61 See the Preamble and Article 2 of UDHR.

62 Manfred Nowak et al., "Human Rights of Specific Groups," in *All Human Rights for All Vienna Manual on Human Rights,* Manfred Nowak et al. (Vienna - Graz: Intersentia, 2012), p. 420.

63 Article 5 of the UNESCO Convention against Discrimination in Education: "(c) It is essential to recognize the right of members of national minorities to carry on their own educational activities, including the maintenance of schools and, depending on the educational policy of each State, the use or the teaching of their own language, provided however: (i) That this right is not exercised in a manner which prevents the

distinctions "based on race, colour, descent, or national or ethnic origin."[64] In 1966, Article 27 of ICCPR included a specific legal provision for advancing minority rights.[65] The UN contributed further to developing principles to protect minorities with the 1981 Declaration on the Elimination of All Forms of Intolerance and of Discrimination Based on Religion or Belief.[66] In addition, it also introduced a new trend of recognizing collective rights, the most evident expression of which was the African Charter on Human and Peoples Rights.[67] But despite this, almost all minority rights related documents emphasized individual rights and avoided adding a collective dimension.[68] This is because, on one hand, minority rights are "exercised by an individual by virtue of belonging to a specific group, collective rights can only belong to a group because one individual cannot have the right realised unless all of the group has it realised."[69] On the other hand, States are still reluctant to grant collective rights to groups, since collective rights might threaten State sovereignty and "impose duties on a State that go beyond mere non-interference by requiring States to establish the conditions under which a group's autonomy can be more effectively realized."[70]

While these developments were significant, minority rights protection received more attention as the Cold War ended.[71] This is because international

---

members of these minorities from understanding the culture and language of the community as a whole and from participating in its activities, or which prejudices national sovereignty."

64 Article 1 of CERD: "In this Convention, the term 'racial discrimination' shall mean any distinction, exclusion, restriction or preference based on race, colour, descent, or national or ethnic origin which has the purpose or effect of nullifying or impairing the recognition, enjoyment or exercise, on an equal footing, of human rights and fundamental freedoms in the political, economic, social, cultural or any other field of public life."

65 See Article 27 of ICCPR.

66 See Declaration on the Elimination of All Forms of Intolerance and of Discrimination Based on Religion or Belief.

67 See African Charter on Human and Peoples Rights.

68 Jolan Hsieh, Collective Rights of Indigenous Peoples: Identity-Based Movement of Plain Indigenous People of Taiwan (New York: Routledge, 2006), p. 40.

69 European Parliament, *Workshop Expansion of the Concept of Human Rights: Impact on Rights Promotion and Protection*, Policy Department, Directorate-General for External Policies (European Parliament Publication, 2018), p. 9.

70 Richard H. Thompson, "Ethnic Minorities and the Case for Collective Rights," *American Anthropologist*, New Series, 99:4 (Dec 1997), p. 795.

71 UNOHCHR, Promoting and Protecting Minority Rights, pp. 2-3.

institutions increasingly recognized the importance of minority rights and their contribution to the stability of States especially in Central and Eastern Europe and the former Soviet Union.[72] A milestone step followed in 1992 by the adoption of the UN Declaration on the Rights of Persons belonging to National or Ethnic, Religious and Linguistic Minorities.[73]

In 1995, the Commission on Human Rights established a five-member working group to "[re]view the promotion and practical realization" of the Declaration, "[e]xamine possible solutions to problems involving minorities" and recommend "further measures, as appropriate, for the promotion and protection of the rights of persons belonging to national or ethnic, religious and linguistic minorities."[74] The Working Group on Minorities held 12 sessions between 1995 and 2006, providing a venue for minority representatives to raise issues within the UN and talk directly with State representatives.[75] The Working Group highly contributed in conceptualizing the rights of minorities and establishing good practices and other measures to promote and protect them.[76] In this context, the UN adopted the 2005 World Summit Outcome, which notes that: "The promotion and protection of the rights of persons belonging to national or ethnic, religious, and linguistic minorities contribute to political and social stability and peace and enrich the cultural diversity and heritage of society."[77]

Throughout the above developments – which on one hand were significant and somehow precedential, on the other hand they were slow and somehow fragmented[78] – a continuous challenge has been the lack of universal agreement on just what a 'minority' is.

---

72 Ibid.

73 Will Kymlicka, "The Internalization of Minority Rights," in *Global Minority Rights*, Joshua Castellino ed. (Ashgate Publishing, 2011), p. 55.

74 Human Rights Council, "Resolution 1995/24, Rights of Persons Belonging to National or Ethnic, Religious and Linguistic Minorities, ESCOR Supp. (No.4) at 92, U.N. Doc. E/CN.4/1995/24 (1995), para. 9.

75 See the documents on Working Group on Minorities here: https://bit.ly/3e85TJ0.

76 Ibid.

77 UNGA Resolution, World Outcome Summit, 16.09.2005, (A/60/L.1), Art. 130.

78 Marc Weller, Universal Minority Rights: A Commentary on the Jurisprudence of International Courts and Treaty Bodies (UK: OUP, 2007).

2.3 What Are the Rights of Minorities and Their Responsibilities?

International human rights law protects and promotes minority rights on the hypothesis that religious, cultural, and linguistic affiliations are essential human attributes.[79]

The UN Independent Expert on Minority Issues, Gay McDougall, considers that minority rights can be broken down into four broad headings:

> "1. Protecting a minority's existence [Right to Existence], including through protection of their physical integrity and the prevention of genocide;
> 2. Protecting and promoting cultural and social identity, including the right of individuals to choose which ethnic, linguistic or religious groups they wish to be identified with, and the right of those groups to affirm and protect their collective identity and to reject forced assimilation [Right to Identity];
> 3. Ensuring effective non-discrimination and equality, including ending structural or systemic discrimination [Right to Non-Discrimination and Equality]; and
> 4. Ensuring effective participation of members of minorities in public life, especially with regard to decisions that affect them [Right to Effective Participation]."[80]

2.3.1 Protection and Promotion of Right to Existence

Minorities have the right to protection in terms of their collective physical existence.[81] The Minority Declaration states that nations "shall protect the existence" of minorities "within their respective territories."[82] This includes prohibiting genocide and ethnic cleansing. As Article 2 of the Convention on the Prevention and Punishment of the Crime of Genocide (Hereafter Genocide Convention) indicates, any State intention to persecute national, ethnical, racial or religious groups "in whole or in part" is also prohibited, whether by killing members of the group or through other coercive measures devised to cause serious harm or physical destruction of the group.[83] While the Genocide Convention is not

---

79 Patrick Macklem, "Minority Rights in International Law," *International Journal of Constitutional Law*, 6:3-4 (July-October 2008), pp. 531–552.

80 UN Economic and Social Council, "Report of the Independent Expert on minority issues," Gay McDougall, 06.01.2006, UN Doc. E/CN.4/2006/74, para. 22.

81 Ibid.

82 UN Declaration on the Rights of Persons Belonging to National or Ethnic, Religious and Linguistic Minorities, 18.12.1992, UN Doc. A/RES/47/135, 92nd plenary meeting.

83 Convention on the Prevention and Punishment of the Crime of Genocide adopted by Resolution 260 (III) A of the UNGA on 09.12.1948.

limited to protecting minorities, genocides most often targets minorities in this way. ICC also prohibits the persecution of racial, national, ethnic, cultural or religious groups.[84]

General Comment No. 23 of HRC illustrates that "the existence of an ethnic, religious or linguistic minority in a given State party does not depend on a decision by that State party but [needs] to be established by objective criteria."[85] At the same time, minority existence is directly linked to how a group defines itself. The principle that belonging to a minority is a personal choice includes the right to not be treated as a minority and the notion that no disadvantage may arise from the exercise of such a choice.[86] However, as long as minorities exist and claim to be so, States are under an obligation to ensure that their existence and the exercise of the right to existence are protected against their denial or violation. Positive measures of protection are, therefore, required not only against the acts of the State party itself, whether through its legislative, judicial or administrative authorities, but also against the acts of other persons within the State party.[87]

2.3.2 Protection and Promotion of Identity

Minorities have the right to protect their identity, which entails both positive and negative obligations for the State.[88] Article 27 of ICCPR clearly indicates that minorities have the right "to enjoy their own culture, to profess and practise their own religion, or to use their own language."[89] Since the protection of these rights directly ensures the survival and sustained development of the religious, cultural and social identity of the minorities concerned, the HRC concludes that these rights "must be protected as such and should not be confused with other personal rights conferred on one and all under the Covenant. States parties, therefore, have an obligation to ensure that the exercise of these rights is fully protected, and they should indicate in their reports the measures they have adopted to this end."[90]

---

84 See article 7.1 [h] of the Rome Statute.

85 HRC, "CCPR General Comment No. 23: Article 27" (Fiftieth session, 1994), Compilation of General Comments and General Recommendations adopted by Human Rights Treaty Bodies, U.N. Doc. HRI/GEN/1/Rev.1 at 38 (1994), para. 5.2.

86 Ibid.

87 Ibid, para. 6.1.

88 Ibid, para. 6.1 & 6.2.

89 See Article 27 of ICCPR.

90 HRC, "CCPR General Comment No. 23: Article 27," para. 9.

In addition, Article 8 of the CRC secures the right of the child "to preserve his or her identity."[91] Article 29.1 [c] of CRC states that children's education should be aimed at the child's "…own cultural identity, language and values, for the national values of the country in which the child is living, the country from which he or she may originate, and for civilizations different from his or her own."[92] Meanwhile, Article 18.4 of ICCPR considers that each State should respect the freedom of parents "to ensure the religious and moral education of their children in conformity with their own convictions."[93]

Minorities cannot be prevented by restrictions or assimilation policies from celebrating their identities.[94] Assimilation policies include the denial of minorities' existence, the prohibition of minority cultural practices or vigorous State sponsored nation-building policies that exclude minority cultural or religious identity. At this point it should be underscored the differences between assimilation and integration: in short, assimilation is coerced whilst integration is voluntary.[95] Assimilation leads to the eradication of identity, whilst integration enables minority identities to flourish even as minorities become part of a broader national identity. Therefore, State integration policies should offer opportunities for minorities to feel included in society by encouraging cultural or religious expression. According to Article 4.2 of the Minority Declaration, States are also encouraged to "take measures to create favourable conditions to enable persons belonging to minorities to express their characteristics and to develop their culture, language, religion, traditions and customs."[96]

Furthermore, minorities should be free to promote their identity equally.[97] The protection of essential cultural heritage (including but not limited to religious

---

91 Article 8 of CRC: "1. States Parties undertake to respect the right of the child to preserve his or her identity, including nationality, name and family relations as recognized by law without unlawful interference. 2. Where a child is illegally deprived of some or all of the elements of his or her identity, States parties shall provide appropriate assistance and protection, with a view to re-establishing speedily his or her identity."

92 See Article 29.1 [c] of CRC and CRC Committee, "General comment No.1: Article 29 (1), The Aims of Education," 17.04.2001, UN Doc. CRC/GC/2001/1, para. 4..

93 See Article 18.4 of ICCPR.

94 UNDP, Marginalised Minorities in Development Programming: A Resource Guide and Toolkit (New York: UNDP publication, May 2010), p. 18.

95 Ibid.

96 See Article 4.2 of Minority Declaration.

97 CESCR, "General comment No. 21: Right of everyone to take part in cultural life (Art. 15, para. 1a of the Covenant on Economic, Social and Cultural Rights)," 21.12.2009, UN. Doc. E/C.12/GC/21.

places, buildings, burial sites, documents and libraries) is important and State policies may also include the recognition of some cultural autonomy for minorities in terms of education, national cultural institutions or the funding of cultural activities.[98] Therefore, it can be argued that autonomy seems to be an effective promoting and protecting tool to the right of identity.[99] The idea of autonomy as means for the administration of minority rights is far from new. History provides us with a list of examples in which minorities had enjoyed varying degrees and several forms of autonomy, ranging from the *Millet* system of the Ottoman Empire to the 1925 Law of Cultural Autonomy in Estonia.[100] Autonomy takes many forms, and the denial of appropriate forms of autonomy such as power-sharing arrangements may lead to calls for secession.

Another key factor of minority identity is education, particularly access to it, its language of instruction and its cultural content. Article 4.4 of the Minority Declaration instructs States to "take measures in the field of education, in order to encourage knowledge of the history, traditions, language and culture of the minorities existing within their territory." Minorities "should have adequate opportunities to gain knowledge of the society as a whole."[101] Education promotes non-discriminatory inter-cultural understanding and helps reduce poverty for minorities.[102] States are required to ensure equal access to education and to ensure non-discrimination in quality and content.[103] Where financial barriers exist for minority access to education, States must take measures to overcome

98 UNDP, Marginalised Minorities, p. 18.

99 Jane Wright, "Minority Groups, Autonomy, and Self-Determination," *Oxford Journal of Legal Studies*, 19:4 (Winter, 1999), p. 606.

100 See Law on Cultural Autonomy for National Minorities in Estonia, adopted in 1925. Cultural autonomy in the Republic of Estonia was enjoyed by Baltic Germans between 1925 and 1939, and by Jews between 1926 and 1940. For further information, see Kari Alenius, "The Birth of Cultural Autonomy in Estonia: How, Why, and For Whom?," *Journal of Baltic Studies*, 38:4 (Dec. 2007), pp. 445-462.

101 Article 4.4 of Minority Declaration.

102 Specific Articles relating to education rights for minorities can, for example, be found in Article 5(e)(v) of the International Convention on the Elimination of All Forms of Racial Discrimination (ICERD) which calls upon States to prohibit and eliminate discrimination in access to education.

103 See Article 13 of CESCR and CESCR, "General comment No.13: on the Right to Education, 1999, para. 6(2) of everyone to take part in cultural life (Art. 15, para. 1a of the Covenant on Economic, Social and Cultural Rights)," para. 15(B).

them. Minorities also have the right to be educated in their mother tongue and to establish their own educational facilities.[104]

In this context, Article 4.3 of the Minority Declaration indicates, "States should take appropriate measures so that, wherever possible, persons belonging to minorities may have adequate opportunities to learn their mother tongue or to have instruction in their mother tongue."[105] It is worth noting, as the phrase "where possible" in the Article 4.3 indicates, States are not legally obliged to provide mother tongue education unless they have the possibilities. In other words, large margin of appreciation is left for the States to decide whether to provide minority mother tongue education or not. Moreover, the State may require minority private education facilities to teach majority languages or the official language of the State. On the other hand, in some cases States might also provide mother tongue education in public schools.[106]

Linguistic rights are increasingly recognized as burning social issues that must be resolved if multilingual societies are to remain democratic. Governments are often hesitant to recognize minority language use in public sphere as it poses a threat to the political and social cohesion of the State.[107] However, main human rights treaties such as the ICCPR and the ECHR cover such "negative" language rights – most importantly, the right to non-discrimination based on language which can be very useful to linguistic minorities faced with repressive, assimilationist State policies.

Although ICCPR ensures that linguistic minorities can use their own languages in their community, problems often appear at national level.[108] In general States adopt a national language, and might adopt several of them, nevertheless, they cannot discriminate against minority languages that are not officially recognized. States have frequently restricted official use of minority languages because they argue that it is 'necessary' to practise only specified languages. However, these restrictions can create distinction among groups and negatively influence the identity preservation and development of Minorities. Yet it took a while for restrictions on language to be viewed as discrimination, and the linguistic

104 UNDP, Marginalised Minorities, p. 18.

105 Article 4.3 of Minority Declaration.

106 UNDP, Marginalised Minorities, p. 18.

107 Balázs Vizi, "Introduction to the Special Issue on Territoriality Language Rights and Minorities – European Perspectives," *International Journal on Minority and Group Rights*, 23 (2016), p. 424.

108 "Linguistic Rights, Minority Rights Group," Minority Rights Group, 26.08.2015, https://minorityrights.org/law-and-legal-cases/linguistic-rights/

protection afforded to minority groups is still inadequate.[109] In this context, while Article 27 of the ICCPR provides that States shall not deny members of linguistic minorities the right to use their own language, the HRC in its General comment No. 23 has indicated that: "positive measures by States may also be necessary to protect the identity of a minority and the rights of its members to enjoy and develop their culture and language [...] in community with other members of the group."[110] These positive measures should aim to correct conditions which prevent or impair the enjoyment of the rights guaranteed under Article 27, and provided that they are based on reasonable and objective criteria they might even constitute a legitimate differentiation under ICCPR.[111]

Thus, minority language rights have been increasingly recognized at international level from the 1990s and in a European context, legislation and various OSCE documents deal with specific minority language rights.[112] Yet even under these various instruments, language rights are still not accorded the status of fundamental rights under international law.[113] Support is ill-defined, and many of the useful measures have not attained the status of binding international legal principles.[114] As Robert Dunbar indicates "cases, particularly with respect to fundamental services such as education, the rights provided are subject to a range of conditions, such as sufficient levels of demand, demonstrated "real need," and the administrative and financial convenience of States themselves, all of which tend to significantly weaken the right."[115] In summary, as far as the right to identity is concerned, legislation to some extent appears to pay lip service to international law, and many trends can still be described as normative, rather than subject to legal protection and ratification.

---

109 Ibid.

110 HRC, "CCPR General Comment No. 23," para.6.2.

111 Ibid.

112 See the 1988 Council of Europe Framework Convention for the Protection of National Minorities and the 1992 European Charter for Regional or Minority Languages.

113 Robert Dunbar, "Minority Language Rights in International Law," *The International and Comparative Law Quarterly*, 50:1 (January 2001), pp. 111-112.

114 Ibid, p. 119.

115 Ibid.

2.3.3 Non-discrimination and Equality

Minorities have a right to non-discrimination and equal treatment on the basis of, among other qualities, color, language, religion, national or ethnic origin.[116] International law considers non-discrimination and equality as one of the basic and general principles regarding human rights.[117] The principle of non-discrimination in the enjoyment of human rights is expressed in the Charter of the UN and provided by customary international law as well as stipulated in the CERD, ICCPR, ICESCR, CRC, CEDAW and UDHR.[118] Here, it is important to highlight that this right guaranteed in all the above leading human rights conventions apply equally to members of minority groups.[119]

Article 26 of ICCPR[120] is a general non-discrimination clause that guarantees equality before the law and equal protection for all. As the HRC stated in its General Comment No.18. "not every differentiation of treatment will constitute discrimination, if the criteria for such differentiation are reasonable and objective and if the aim is to achieve a purpose which is legitimate under the Covenant."[121] Thus, this provision does not preclude the State from making reasonable distinctions among categories of people, such as the need to speak the official language under certain circumstances, but it prohibits any unreasonable distinction based on a person's status as a member of a minority group. Article 2 of CRC[122]

116 According to Art. 4.1 of the Minority Declaration: "States shall take measures where required to ensure that persons belonging to minorities may exercise fully and effectively all their human rights and fundamental freedoms without any discrimination and in full equality before the law."

117 Human Rights Committee, "CCPR General Comment No. 18: Non-discrimination," 10.11.1989, UN Doc. CCPR/C/21/Rev.1/Add.1, para. 1.

118 UN Economic and Social Council, "Report of the Independent Expert on Minority Issues," Gay McDougall, 2006, UN Doc. E/CN.4/2006/74, para. 20.

119 Ibid.

120 Article 26 of ICCPR: "All persons are equal before the law and are entitled without any discrimination to the equal protection of the law. In this respect, the law shall prohibit any discrimination and guarantee to all persons equal and effective protection against discrimination on any ground such as race, colour, sex, language, religion, political or other opinion, national or social origin, property, birth or other status."

121 HRC, "CCPR General Comment No. 18," para. 13.

122 Article 2 of CRC: "1. State parties shall respect and ensure the rights set forth in the present Convention to each child within their jurisdiction without discrimination of any kind, irrespective of the child's or his or her parents' or legal guardians' race, colour, sex, language, religion, political or other opinion, national, ethnic or social origin, property, disability, birth or other status. 2. "State parties shall take all appropriate

provides that the rights in the Convention must be guaranteed without discrimination on the basis of, among other qualities, race, color, language, religion, or national or ethnic origin.

CERD is the core international human rights treaty on rights to non-discrimination and equal treatment. Since it has a broad definition of the term race and 'racial discrimination', it includes ethnic and national origins and thus minorities.[123] The CERD Committee, illustrates in its report on the implementation of Article 7[124] that "although the convention applies to everyone without exception, it is concerned particularly with certain minority groups which have historically, suffered the greatest social exploration and deprivation."[125]

CERD's Article 5 demands the establishment of remedies prohibiting discrimination in the enjoyment of civil, political, economic, social and cultural rights.[126] National tribunals and other State institutions to combat discrimination shall provide "effective protection and remedies" under Article 6,[127] whilst Article 7[128] calls for public education to promote non-discrimination. Article 4[129] prohibits promotion or incitement to hatred, discrimination or acts of

measures to ensure that the child is protected against all forms of discrimination or punishment on the basis of the status, activities, expressed opinions, or beliefs of the child's parents, legal guardians, or family members."

123 Article 1 of ICERD: "In this Convention, the term 'racial discrimination' shall mean any distinction, exclusion, restriction or preference based on race, colour, descent, or national or ethnic origin which has the purpose or effect of nullifying or impairing the recognition, enjoyment or exercise, on an equal footing, of human rights and fundamental freedoms in the political, economic, social, cultural or any other field of public life."

124 Article 7 of ICERD: "State parties undertake to adopt immediate and effective measures, particularly in the fields of teaching, education, culture and information, with a view to combating prejudices which lead to racial discrimination and to promoting understanding, tolerance and friendship among nations and racial or ethnical groups, as well as to propagating the purposes and principles of the Charter of the United Nations, the Universal Declaration of Human Rights, the United Nations Declaration on the Elimination of All Forms of Racial Discrimination, and this Convention."

125 CERD Committee, Implementation of the ICERD, Article 7: "Teaching, Education, Culture and Information as Means of Eliminating Racial Discrimination (New York: United Nations, 1985,) p. 9.

126 See Article 5 of ICERD.

127 See Article 6 of ICERD.

128 See Article 7 of ICERD.

129 See Article 4 of ICERD.

violence against any group based on race, color or ethnic or other origin, and Articles 1.4 and 2.2[130] allow the State special measures in "social, economic, cultural and other fields" to promote full and equal enjoyment of human rights for groups facing discrimination.

These measures often take the form of affirmative action policies (also known as positive discrimination), for example to improve access to employment or education or learning a mother tongue by targeted development interventions.[131] These special measures cannot be treated as discriminatory under international law as long as they have a reasonable and objective justification and aim to tackle barriers posed by discriminatory practices that prevent groups from enjoying their rights.[132] Such measures are temporary and should be stopped once discrimination is not a factor anymore.[133] The question of affirmative action is also addressed by the Minority Declaration. Article 8.3 of the Minority Declaration points out that "such measures shall not prima facie be considered to be contrary to the principle of equality."[134] Additionally, the Commentary of the Working Group on Minorities explains:

> "Under normal circumstances, measures to ensure effective participation, or to ensure that minorities benefit from economic progress in society or have the possibility to learn their own language will not be a privilege vis-à-vis other members of the society. It is essential, however, that such measures do not go beyond what is reasonable under the circumstances and are proportional to the aim sought to be realized."[135]

On the other hand, discrimination is not only limited to cases in which a person or group is treated unfairly. It may also be discriminatory to treat different groups alike, which means that assimilation can mean discrimination against the minority.[136] Furthermore, the ECtHR holds that if a State takes positive measures to improve the status of a minority group (such as insuring their participation in the democratic

130 See Articles 1.4 and 2 of ICERD.

131 HRC, "General Comment No. 18," para. 10.

132 Henrard, Devising an Adequate System, pp. 198-199.

133 Ibid.

134 See Article 8.3 of Minority Declaration.

135 UN Economic and Social Council, "Commentary on the Working Group on Minorities to the UN Declaration on the Rights of Persons Belonging to National or Ethnic, Religious and Linguistic Minorities," 2005, UN Doc. E/CN.4/Sub.2/AC.5/2005/2, para. 83.

136 Pamphlet No. 7 of the UN Guide for Minorities, Minority Rights under the European Convention on Human Rights.

process), the majority cannot claim discrimination based on these measures.[137] In general, "a balance must be achieved which ensures the fair and proper treatment of minorities and avoids any abuse of a dominant position."[138] Whilst positive discrimination may appear to favor the minority in an apparent reversal of equal practice, the idea behind it is to raise those minorities to a level of equal representation as well as equal treatment.

The Minority Declaration also elaborates the principle of non-discrimination. Article 3.1[139] of the Minority Declaration makes clear that Minorities shall not be subjected to discrimination for manifesting their group identity.[140] Article 3.2[141] goes one step further and stipulates that minorities shall also not be disadvantaged in any way for choosing not to belong to the minority concerned. As the Commentary of the Working Group states:

> "This provision is directed both towards the State and the agencies of the minority group. The State cannot impose a particular ethnic identity on a given person (which is what the apartheid regime in South Africa sought to do) by the use of negative sanctions against those who do not want to be part of that group; nor can persons belonging to minorities subject to any disadvantage persons who on objective criteria may be held to form part of their group but who subjectively do not want to belong to it. While, under conventional law, responsibility for human rights compliance normally rests with the State, the Declaration in this respect implies duties - at least morally - for persons representing minorities. Furthermore, States would be under a duty to prohibit the taking of measures by minorities to impose their particular rules on any person who did not want to be part of the minority concerned and therefore did not want to exercise her or his rights."[142]

---

137 Young, James and Webster vs. The United Kingdom, application No. 7601/76; 7806/77, 1982.

138 Ibid.

139 Article 3.1: "Persons belonging to minorities may exercise their rights, including those set forth in the present Declaration, individually as well as in community with other members of their group, without any discrimination."

140 UN Economic and Social Council, "Commentary on the Working Group on Minorities," para.53.

141 Article 3.2: "No disadvantage shall result for any person belonging to a minority as the consequence of the exercise or non-exercise of the rights set forth in the present Declaration."

142 UN Economic and Social Council, "Commentary of the Working Group on Minorities," para. 54.

Also of particular importance to minorities is the principle of participation in the public sphere, without discrimination, as guaranteed by both ICCPR[143] and CERD.[144]

2.3.4 Effective Participation

The right to effective participation for minorities includes participation in public life and decision making – especially on issues that affect them – as well as the right to participate in the life of their own community, and the right to participate in the benefits of economic progress and development.[145] The right of every citizen (including minorities) to participate in public affairs is outlined in Article 25[146] of the ICCPR.[147] In addition, the General Comment No. 23 of ICCPR suggests that a State may need to ensure the "effective participation of members of minority communities in decisions which affect them,"[148] in order to guarantee full enjoyment of the right to culture.

While the above Articles as hard law put legally binding obligations on States, Article 2.2 of the Minority Declaration as soft law reiterates the same obligation by stating that "persons belonging to minorities have the right to participate effectively in cultural, religious, social, economic and public life."[149] Given that minorities are frequently excluded from public participation, Article 2.3 of the Minority Declaration states that: "Persons belonging to minorities have the right

143 See Article 25 of ICCPR.

144 See Articles 1.1 and 5 [c] of ICERD and UN Economic and Social Council, "Report of the Independent Expert on minority issues," Gay McDougall, 06.01.2006 UN Doc. E/CN.4/2006/74: para. 20.

145 UNDP, Marginalised Minorities, p. 24.

146 Article 25 of ICCPR: "Every citizen shall have the right and the opportunity, without any of the distinctions mentioned in article 2 and without unreasonable restrictions: (a) To take part in the conduct of public affairs, directly or through freely chosen representatives (b) To vote and to be elected at genuine periodic elections which shall be by universal and equal suffrage and shall be held by secret ballot, guaranteeing the free expression of the will of the electors (c) To have access, on general terms of equality, to public service in his country."

147 General Comment No. 25 of ICCPR states that "Information and materials about voting should be available in minority languages," in HRC, General Comment No. 25: The right to participate in public affairs, voting rights and the right of equal access to public service (Art. 25): 12/07/96, UN Doc. CCPR/C/21/Rev.1/Add.7, para. 12.

148 HRC, "CCPR General Comment No. 23," para. 7.

149 See Article 2.2 of Minority Declaration.

to participate effectively in decisions on the national and, where appropriate, the regional level concerning the minority to which they belong or the regions in which they live."[150]

The participation of minorities in governance is often fragile, including for minority women.[151] In many cases, minorities do not have political representation in government and/or are underrepresented within public service.[152] They may also be poorly represented in other State sponsored institutions like labor or trade unions, the academia and the media. As Rita Izsák, the former Special Rapporteur on Minority Issues, observes that there is limited, or often complete lack of minority presence in political and public offices. Therefore, she insists the urgency

> "to ensure that minorities are included in all decision-making processes, including in municipal and government structures, law enforcement bodies, the judiciary, legislative bodies, criminal justice systems and all authorities, especially when their decisions affect minorities. Without their participation, such bodies are less able to make vital decisions in a way that benefits the entire society, and they will also be less trusted by minorities, who might be reluctant to access them, or discouraged from doing so."[153]

In addition, to facilitate minority participation, Article 4.5 of the Minority Declaration reads: "States should consider appropriate measures so that persons belonging to minorities may participate in the economic progress and development in their country."[154] This is because of their limited number compared to the majority there is often a risk that minorities might be excluded, marginalized or neglected. The Commentary to the Minority Declaration calls for the integration of everyone in the overall economic development of society as a whole, while ensuring that this integration takes place in ways which make it possible for persons belonging to minorities to preserve their own identity.[155] In other words, the integration of minorities should reflect the preservation of minority identities.

---

150 See Article 2.3 of Minority Declaration.
151 UNDP, Marginalised Minorities, p. 3.
152 Ibid, pp. 51-52.
153 Rita Izsák, "Report of the Special Rapporteur on Minority Issues," 09.01.2017, UN Doc. A/HRC/34/53, para.70, https://digitallibrary.un.org/record/860596/files/A_HRC_34_53-EN.pdf.
154 Article 8.4 of Minority Declaration.
155 UN Economic and Social Council, "Commentary on the Working Group on Minorities," para. 71.

In this context, decentralization can greatly improve minority participation, because most policies concerning minorities are implemented at the local level.[156] Decentralization can take several forms. For instance, where minorities are territorially concentrated and have expressed a desire for autonomy, the creation of autonomous regions can help increase minority participation and may also include the transference of some authority to community governance.

The vital factor here is *effective* participation, and policies must be genuine and inclusive. Consultation and discussion should always foreshadow any policy decisions, and minorities should be included in this process.[157] In terms of minorities' right in effective participation, whilst international law offers legal protection both in legally binding and non-binding documents, it offers little regulation regarding practical implementation. Generally speaking, the solider the institutions and mechanisms, the more likely they are to implement and ensure the right to effective participation effectively.

2.3.5 Minority Responsibilities Vis-à-vis International Human Rights Law and the State

As the Minority Declaration states, the exercise of minority rights "shall not prejudice the enjoyment by all persons of universally recognized human rights and fundamental freedoms."[158] Minority rights are supplementary to the universally recognized rights of every person, and they should not hinder anyone to enjoy universal human rights. This boundary, although seems difficult to draw, is crucial particularly when in some cases, minority practices might violate the human rights of individuals within their community.[159] In other words, exercising minority rights must not negatively affect the enjoyment of universal human rights for persons who belong to the minority as well as for those do not belong to a minority.[160] In exercising their rights, minority communities have a responsibility to respect the human rights and fundamental freedoms of their own members and of others and they should not adopt measures which interfere with the individual human rights of any person belonging to that minority.[161] In this context,

156 UNDP, Marginalised Minorities, pp. 51-52.

157 Ibid.

158 Article 8.2 of Minority Declaration.

159 UNDP, Marginalised Minorities, p. 26.

160 UN Economic and Social Council, "Commentary to the Minority Declaration," para. 81.

161 Ibid.

the Commentary to the Minority Declaration clarifies the wordings of Article 4.2 that put some restrictions on minority practices: "except where specific practices are in violation of national law and contrary to international standards."[162] For the violation of national law, the Commentary states:

> "It is clear that the State is not free to adopt whatever prohibitions against minorities' cultural practices that it wants. If that were the case, the Declaration, and Article 4.2 in particular, would be nearly empty of content. What is intended, however, is to respect the margin of appreciation which any State must have regarding which practices it wants to prohibit, taking into account the particular conditions prevailing in that country. As long as the prohibitions are based on reasonable and objective grounds, they must be respected."[163]

On the other hand, for the meaning of the words "contrary to international standards" the Commentary states:

> "In particular, it is intended that the practices must not be contrary to international human rights standards. This, however, should apply to practices of both majorities and minorities. Cultural or religious practices which violate human rights law should be outlawed for everyone, not only for minorities. The qualification contained in the final words of Article 4.2 is therefore only a specific application of a universal principle applicable to everyone."[164]

In addition, as the Minority Declaration states, measures taken by States to ensure the effective enjoyment of minority rights "shall not prima facie be considered contrary to the principle of equality contained in the Universal Declaration of Human Rights"[165] as long as such measures (e.g., to ensure effective participation, or to have the possibility to learn minority language) do not go beyond what is reasonable under the circumstances and are proportional to the aim sought to be realized.[166]

Minorities also have responsibilities to the State and to the entire society they live in.[167] According to the Minority Declaration: "Nothing in the present Declaration may be construed as permitting any activity contrary to the purposes

162 See Article 4.2 of Minority Declaration.
163 UN Economic and Social Council, "Commentary on the Working Group on Minorities," Para. 57.
164 Ibid.
165 Article 8.3 of Minority Declaration.
166 UN Economic and Social Council, "Commentary on the Working Group on Minorities," Para. 83.
167 UNDP, Marginalised Minorities, p. 26.

and principles of the UN, including sovereign equality, territorial integrity and political independence of States."[168] Minority rights provisions neither permit nor support minorities' right to secession.[169]

Meanwhile, minorities have responsibilities of their own regarding intercultural understanding as outlined in Article 4.4 of the Declaration: "Persons belonging to minorities should have adequate opportunities to gain knowledge of the society as a whole."[170] Indeed, as the commentary to the Minority Declaration indicates:

> "this provision should counteract tendencies towards fundamentalist or closed religious or ethnic groups, which can be as much affected by xenophobia and intolerance as the majorities... The formation of more or less involuntary ghettos where the different groups live in their own world without knowledge of, or tolerance for persons belonging to the other parts of the national society would be a violation of the purpose and spirit of the Declaration."[171]

In addition, the parents of minority children, for example, must ensure that their children learn respect and tolerance for the wider society.[172] In this context, The UN CRC requires that children be prepared for "responsible life in a free society, in the spirit of understanding, peace, tolerance, equality of sexes, and friendship among all peoples, ethnic, national and religious groups and persons of indigenous origin."[173] Children's education should include the development of respect "for the national values of the country in which the child is living, the country from which he or she may originate, and for civilizations different from his or her own"[174]

2.4 Minority Rights in United Nations Documents

2.4.1 The UN Charter

The UN Charter forms the starting point for any contemporary discussion on Human Rights. The Charter is an international treaty which has been ratified

168 Article 8.4 of Minority Declaration.
169 UNDP, Marginalised Minorities, p. 26.
170 Art 4.4 of the Minority Declaration.
171 UN Economic and Social Council, "Commentary to the Minority Declaration," para. 69.
172 UNDP, Marginalised Minorities, p. 26.
173 Article 29.1 [d] of the CRC.
174 Ibid, Article 29.1 [c].

and considered as universally accepted without reservation. Universally applicable human rights principles can be derived from its provisions, even if only directly or explicitly.[175] The initial proposal made by several States that the Charter include a bill of rights analogous to most national Constitutions was dropped under pressure from the major powers.[176] Despite this, the Charter contains implicit standards for protecting and promoting human rights, including those of minorities. Its relevance to minorities lies in one of its main purposes, which is indicated in Article 3 of the Charter: "to achieve international cooperation in promoting and encouraging respect for human rights and for fundamental freedoms for all without distinction as to race, sex, language or religion."[177] Whilst the Charter does not mention the word 'minority rights' *per se*, it promotes them within the context of general human rights, emphasizing non-discrimination based on race, sex, language or religion.

2.4.2 Universal Declaration of Human Rights (UDHR)

In 1948, the UNGA adopted the UDHR, articulating human rights in much greater detail.[178] The UDHR remains one of the most important international documents and its anti-discrimination provisions (Articles 2 – 16 – 18)[179] are of vital significance to minorities. Although the UNGA failed to agree on any

---

175 William A. Schabas, *War Crimes and Human Rights: Essays on the Death Penalty, Justice, and Accountability* (London: Cameron May, 2008), p. 761.

176 William A. Schabas, *Preventing Genocide and Mass Killing: The Challenge for the United Nations* (London: Minority Rights Group International, 2000), p. 7.

177 See Article 3 of UN Charter.

178 See the full text of UDHR: https://www.un.org/en/universal-declaration-human-rights/.

179 Article 2 of the UDHR: "Everyone is entitled to all the rights and freedoms set forth in this Declaration, without distinction of any kind, such as race, colour, sex, language, religion, political or other opinion, national or social origin, property, birth or other status. Furthermore, no distinction shall be made on the basis of the political, jurisdictional or international status of the country or territory to which a person belongs, whether it be independent, trust, non-self-governing or under any other limitation of sovereignty." Article 16 states: "(1) Men and women of full age, without any limitation due to race, nationality or religion, have the right to marry and to found a family. They are entitled to equal rights as to marriage, during marriage and at its dissolution." Article 18: "Everyone has the right to freedom of thought, conscience and religion; this right includes freedom to change his religion or belief, and freedom, either alone or in community with others and in public or private, to manifest his religion or belief in teaching, practice, worship and observance."

specific formulation concerning minority rights, it did note that the UN "cannot remain indifferent to the fate of minorities."[180] In the same resolution that proclaimed the UDHR, the UN admitted that it was "difficult to adopt a uniform solution for this complex and delicate question [of minorities], which has special aspects in each State in which it arises."[181] This statement clearly expressed the complexity of minority issues, which continue to remain up until nowadays. However, following the UDHR, subsequent treaties have helped to set important legal frameworks for the protection of minority rights, which will be discussed in the following sections.

2.4.3 International Covenant on Civil and Political Rights (ICCPR)

The ICCPR[182] was intended to provide a legally binding effect to the provisions of the UDHR.[183] Its contribution to evolving laws was modest but significant.[184] Article 27 remains one of the two only binding provision for the protection of minorities (the other is Article 30 of CRC), and states:

> "In those States in which ethnic, religious or linguistic minorities exist, persons belonging to such minorities shall not be denied the right, in community with the other members of their group, to enjoy their own culture, to profess and practice their own religion, or to use their own language."[185]

In addition to the Covenant's provision for the protection of minorities beyond the general prohibition of discrimination, some issues were particularly controversial. Article 27 is ambiguous regarding individual or group rights. The draft text of Article 27 only mentions 'minorities', although this was later modified to "persons belonging to [...] minorities" which did little more than emphasizing the fact that minorities lack legal personality.[186] Here, it should be noted

180 UNGA Resolution [Part C of General Assembly Resolution 217 (III). International Bill of Human Rights] 217 C (III), Fate of Minorities, 10.12.1948, UN Doc. A/RES/3/217 C.

181 Ibid.

182 UNGA Resolution 2200A (XXI) on 16.12.1966, https://www.ohchr.org/Documents/ProfessionalInterest/ccpr.pdf

183 "What is the Universal Declaration of Human Rights?," *Australian Human Rights Commission*, 05.12.2020, https://bit.ly/2Xm2YC7.

184 Schabas, Preventing Genocide and Mass Killing, p. 6.

185 Article 27 of ICCPR.

186 Jelena Pejic, "Minority Rights in International Law," *Human Rights Quarterly*, 19:3 (1997), p. 673.

that although the Article protected individual rights, individuals depend on the ability of their minority groups to maintain culture, language or religion. Positive measures by States are therefore necessary to protect the identity of a minority and the rights of its members as a group as well as individuals.[187]

In this context, the Covenant makes a distinction between the right to self-determination and the rights protected under Article 27. The right to self-determination is expressed as a group right and is dealt with in a separate part (Part I), while Article 27 relates to individual rights and is included – like other Articles relating to personal rights conferred on individuals – in Part III of the Covenant, which is recognized under Optional Protocol I. The individualistic nature of Article 27 can be considered as the basis of a complaint before the Covenant's monitoring body, the HRC, which is authorized to address only individual, not collective, claims. This contrasts with Article 1 of the Covenant, which guarantees the right of self-determination to all "peoples." Given its collective nature, Article 1 cannot form the basis of an individual complaint. The Covenant thus affords minorities a valuable opportunity for international legal redress by allowing the HRC to interpret the protection offered by Article 27 in the context of specific disputes. However, because the HRC cannot accept claims alleging violations of the right to self-determination,[188] the Covenant's capacity to provide an institutional site for the collective rights of minorities in international law has been somewhat blunted.

In addition, the rights protected under Article 27 are distinct from the guarantees under Articles 2.1 and Article 26 of ICCPR. As HRC explains "the entitlement, under article 2.1, to enjoy the rights under the Covenant without discrimination applies to all individuals within the territory or under the jurisdiction of the State whether or not those persons belong to a minority."[189] Article 26 provides a distinct right for equality before the law, equal protection of the law, and non-discrimination in respect of rights granted and obligations imposed by the States. As HRC comments, Article 26 "governs the exercise of all rights, whether protected under the Covenant or not, which the State party confers by law on individuals within its territory or under its jurisdiction, irrespective of whether they belong to the minorities specified in article 27 or not."[190]

---

187 Ibid, p. 676.
188 HRC, "CCPR General Comment No. 23," para. 3.1.
189 Ibid, para. 4.
190 Ibid.

As far as those affected by Article 27 are concerned, the HRC expressly declared that Article 27 also applies for alien or non-citizen minorities. Article 27 confers rights on pre-existing minorities within a State, and some scholars argue that its opening phrase means that ethnic, religious, or linguistic groups must have been established within a State for a certain period and display a certain historical stability in order to qualify as minorities.[191] However immigrants – including migrant workers[192] and refugees[193] – can claim protection under this provision after a certain residency period in their new home country when they fulfill the remaining definitional criteria.[194] Some, including the drafters of the General Comment No. 23,[195] believe that given the nature and scope of the rights envisaged under the Article, it is not relevant to determine the degree of permanence that the term "exist" implies.[196] Instead, no minority should be denied the right either individually or collectively to enjoy their own culture, to practice their religion and speak their language. They need not be nationals or citizens, neither should they need to be permanent residents.

In this context, the reference to community clearly adds a collective dimension via Article 27 to individual rights established by other ICCPR Articles. In order to contextualise personal autonomy, the reference to 'community' in Article 27 of the ICCPR should imply a certain degree of organization. People belonging to minorities need enough freedom to organize themselves into associations of various kinds to pursue common aims, and notions of 'association' should include a broad spectrum of private legal entities.

The main point here is that there should be sufficient freedom for minorities to create organizations that allow personal autonomy in a group form. Not all forms of autonomy are shaped on the basis of special legislation, and the creation of minority organizations is not necessarily a top-down process.[197] The

191 Manfred Nowak, *UN Convention on Civil and Political Rights, CCPR Commentary* (revised 2nd ed. (Kehl am Rhein: Engel, 2005), p. 490.

192 Anna Michalska, "Migrant Workers as 'New' Minority. Sociological and Legal Definition of Minority," in *The Role of the Nation-state in the 21st Century: Human Rights, International Organisations, and Foreign Policy: Essays in Honour of Peter Baehr,* P. Peter R. Baehr eds. (Boston: Martinus Nijhoff Publishers, 1998), p. 142.

193 UNDP, Marginalized Minorities, p. 149.

194 Ibid.

195 HRC, "CCPR General Comment No. 23," para.5.2.

196 Ibid.

197 Markku Suksi, "Personal Autonomy as Institution Form, Focus on Europe Against the Backdrop of Article 27 of the ICCPR," *International Journal on Minority and Group Rights*, 15:2 (2008), p. 157.

grassroots creation of minority institutions can also entail a right to personal autonomy.[198] From an institutional perspective, it is important that States do not claim ownership and control of communities, and that groups should be free to expand in an organic way from the minorities themselves and have control over their affairs.[199] Article 27 therefore implies certain forms of organization as identified by the ICCPR, involving Article 22 on the freedom of association but perhaps also considering Article 21 on the right of peaceful assembly, and Article 25 on the right to participation.[200]

The obligations of Article 27 therefore require State parties to refrain from interference and to practice tolerance. The Article specifically prohibits all measures directed against or threatening the existence of ethnic, linguistic or religious minorities. However, a simple passive stance by States does not in itself guarantee the survival of minorities. Minorities are dependent on active support from their States in order to preserve their cultural, linguistic and religious identities, or they will be unable to withstand assimilationist pressures often exercised by the dominant majority.[201]

In addition, despite being formulated in negative terms Article 27 does recognize the existence of a 'right' and requires that this right is not denied. State parties are therefore under an obligation to ensure that the existence and the exercise of minority rights are not just respected but actively protected and fulfilled.[202] This means that positive measures of protection are required both against the acts of the State party itself and the acts of other persons/entities within the State party.[203] For example, the case of Lubicon Lake Band hinged on whether Canada had violated minority rights under Article 27 of the ICCPR by allowing the provincial government to sign industrial development leases on traditional native lands. The Government and the province of Alberta were accused of allowing the expropriation of the Lubicon Lake Band territory for the benefit of corporate interests. The committee observed that historical injustices, caused by both State and non-state actors, as well as more recent developments,

---

198 Ibid, p. 177.

199 Jane Wright, "Minority Groups, Autonomy, and Self-Determination," p. 697.

200 Suksi, "Personal Autonomy," p. 159.

201 Yousef T. Jabareen, "Toward Participatory Equality: Protecting Minority Rights under International Law," published online by Cambridge University Press, 19.03.2008, pp. 643-645.

202 HRC, "CCPR General Comment No.23," para. 6.1.

203 Ibid.

"threatened the way of life and culture of the Lubicon Lake Band and constitute a Violation of Art 27 as long as it continues."[204]

In some cases, governments or International Human Right mechanisms have to settle disputes between the governing authorities of a minority and its individual members. The general rule according to the HRC is that "a restriction upon the right of an individual member of a minority must be shown to have a reasonable and objective justification and to be necessary for the continued viability and welfare of the minority as a whole."[205] An example of a dispute between a minority group and its individual members in which HRC intervened is the case of Sandra Lovelace in Canada. Sandra Lovelace, a Maliseet Indian by ethnic origin, lost her legal status as an Indian under the Canadian Indian Act because of her marriage to a non-Indian, and thus her right to live on the Tobique Reserve was revoked. When she returned to the Reserve following her divorce, an expulsion order was issued against her. One question the case raised was whether she was a person belonging to the Maliseet Indians.

The Committee determined that people who are born and raised on a reserve, and who have maintained ties and want to further maintain ties to that community, are considered part of that minority group within the meaning of Article 27. By that definition, Lovelace was a member of the Maliseet Indians, because she was raised on the reservation and left only for the few years she was married.[206] The Committee also concluded that denying her recognition as a member of the Maliseet Indians was unjustifiable. The Committee also found that Ms. Lovelace's right to enjoy her culture had been disregarded as there were no communities outside of the reserve sharing the same language and culture.[207] Finally, the Committee decided that denying Lovelace access to the reserve was neither reasonable nor necessary to preserve the group's identity, and that stripping her of Indian status was a denial of her rights under Article 27 and was therefore a violation of the ICCPR.[208] The result was that Canada was compelled to amend the Indian Act. This case indicates that the factors of reasonable and objective justification as well as the necessity for either State or minority authorities'

---

204 Lubicon Lake Band v. Canada, Communication No.167/1984 (26.03.1990), UN Doc. Supp. No.40 (A/45/40) at 1 (1990).

205 Ivan Kitok v. Sweden, Communication No.197/1985, CCPR/C/33/D/197/1985 (1988), para. 9.8.

206 Sandra Lovelace v. Canada, Communication No.24/1977: Canada 30/07/81, UN Doc. CCPR/C/13/D/24/1977.

207 Ibid.

208 Ibid.

interventions play crucial role in determining whether there is a violation of Article 27 or not.

In terms of linguistic protection, it is worth mentioning that the rights of individuals belonging to a linguistic minority to use their language among themselves, in private or in public, remains distinct from other language rights protected under ICCPR, and should in particular be distinguished from the general right to freedom of expression protected of Article 19 which is available to everyone, whether they belong to minorities or not.[209] The right protected under Article 27 should also be distinguished from the right conferred by Article 14.3 (f) of ICCPR, which allows accused persons interpretation when they cannot understand or speak the language used in the courts.[210]

In this context, the issue of interference by State authorities with the use of minority languages has been raised in many cases, but in no case did the HRC find a violation of Article 27; instead it found violations of other provisions of ICCPR.[211] This underlines HRC's extremely cautious approach towards minorities' linguistic rights.[212] In *Ballantune et al v Canada,*[213] the HRC had to decide whether a prohibition under Quebec law of using any language other than French for purposes of advertising constituted a violation of the human or minority rights of English-speaking people in Quebec. Since the committee held that English speaking people in Quebec could not be considered a linguistic minority, it applied Article 27 only to justify this interference with freedom of expression. Such far-reaching interference with freedom of expression was not considered necessary "in order to protect the vulnerable position in Canada of the Francophone group," and the Committee concluded that there had been a violation of Article 19.[214]

As far as the monitoring mechanisms of State obligations towards Article 27 is concerned, the only obligatory monitoring procedure is the duty of States to submit periodic reports to the HRC on the measures they have taken to implement the obligations laid down in the ICCPR.[215] The political impact of this

209 HRC, "CCPR General Comment No. 23," para.5.3.

210 Ibid.

211 Manfred Nowak, UN Covenant on Civil and Political Rights: CCPR Commentary, pp. 662-665.

212 Ibid.

213 Ballantyne, Davidson, McIntyre v. Canada, Communications Nos. 359/1989 and 385/1989, UN Doc. CCPR/C/47/D/359/1989 and 385/1989/Rev.1 (1993).

214 Ibid, Para.11.4.

215 Pejic, "Minority Rights in International Law," pp. 666-668.

review is significant but has no immediate empirical effect. It is worth mentioning, that to this day, the interstate complaint procedure envisaged in Article 41 has not been used.[216] Due to political considerations, it is unlikely that this will happen soon. However, the HRC has been to fair extent successful in tackling alleged violations of Article 27, but its influence on minorities is often indirect. Whether States allow HRC's views to have any impact relies on their political willingness and legal culture, because HRC's decisions are not legally binding.

2.4.4 International Covenant on Economic, Social and Cultural Rights (ICESCR)

The ICESCR mentions explicitly in Article 2 (2) that:

> "The States party to the present Covenant undertake to guarantee that the rights enunciated in the present Covenant will be exercised without discrimination of any kind as to race, colour, sex, language, religion, political or other opinion, national or social origin, property, birth or other status."[217]

This Article is directly relevant for minorities, since often times they are subject to discrimination with regards to the CESCR Rights.[218] As the Committee of ICESCR explains that discrimination is "any distinction, exclusion, restriction or preference or other differential treatment that is directly or indirectly based on the prohibited grounds of discrimination and which has the intention or effect of nullifying or impairing the recognition, enjoyment or exercise, on an equal footing, of Covenant rights".[219] Discrimination also includes incitement to discriminate and harassment. States have to guarantee that the Covenant rights will be exercised without discrimination of any kind, discrimination must be eliminated both formally and substantively.[220] Articles 13[221] and

---

216 "Human Rights Bodies - Complaints Procedures, Complaining about Human Rights Violations," *UNOHCR official website*, September 2020, https://bit.ly/33Uj20H

217 See Article 2 of ICESCR.

218 CESCR, "General Comment No. 20: Non-discrimination in economic, social and cultural rights (art. 2, para. 2 of the International Covenant on Economic, Social and Cultural Rights)," 02.07.2009, UN. Doc. E/C.12/GC/20para.7.8, Para. 18.

219 Ibid.

220 Ibid.

221 Article 13: "1. The States parties to the present Covenant recognize the right of everyone to education. They agree that education shall be directed to the full development of the human personality and the sense of its dignity and shall strengthen the respect for human rights and fundamental freedoms. They further agree that education shall

14[222] set out rights to education for all and include a provision that primary education must be compulsory and free. Of particular interest to minorities is the liberty individuals and bodies have to set up and administer educational institutions, as long as these institutions conform to whatever minimum standards may be established by the State.[223]

In addition, since culture is essential part of identity, Article 15 of ICESCR[224] states that everyone has the right to take part in cultural life and to have his or her intellectual property protected.[225] Article 15's paragraph 1 (a), of the Covenant entails on States at least the obligation to create and promote an environment within which a person individually, or in association with others, or within a community or group, can participate in the culture of their choice. Paragraphs 32 of the CESCR's General comment No. 21 illustrates minorities' participation in the cultural life:

> "Article 15, paragraph 1 (a) of the Covenant also includes the right of minorities and of persons belonging to minorities to take part in the cultural life of society, and also to conserve, promote and develop their own culture. This right entails the obligation of States parties to recognize, respect and protect minority cultures as an essential component of the identity of the States themselves. Consequently, minorities have the right

---

enable all persons to participate effectively in a free society, promote understanding, tolerance and friendship among all nations and all racial, ethnic or religious groups, and further the activities of the United Nations for the maintenance of peace. 2. The States parties to the present Covenant recognize that, with a view to achieving the full realization of this right: (a) Primary education shall be compulsory and available free to all..."

222 Article 14: "Each State Party to the present Covenant which, at the time of becoming a Party, has not been able to secure in its metropolitan territory or other territories under its jurisdiction compulsory primary education, free of charge, undertakes, within two years, to work out and adopt a detailed plan of action for the progressive implementation, within a reasonable number of years, to be fixed in the plan, of the principle of compulsory education free of charge for all."

223 CESCR, "General Comment No. 13: The Right to Education (Art. 13)," UN Doc. E/C.12/1999/10 (Twenty-first session, 1999), para. 29.

224 Article 15: "1. The States parties to the present Covenant recognize the right of everyone: (a) To take part in cultural life..."

225 CESCR, "General Comment No. 17: The Right of Everyone to Benefit from the Protection of the Moral and Material Interests Resulting from any Scientific, Literary or Artistic Production of Which He or She is the Author (Art. 15, Para. 1 (c) of the Covenant)," 12.01.2006, UN Doc. E/C.12/GC/17 and CESCR, "General Comment No. 21" (2009) on cultural life.

to their cultural diversity, traditions, customs, religion, forms of education, languages, communication media (press, radio, television, Internet) and other manifestations of their cultural identity and membership."[226]

In addition, CESCR's General Comment No. 21 observes, *inter alia*, that "educational programmes of States parties should respect the cultural specificities of national or ethnic, linguistic and religious minorities"[227] and that States should "respect free access by minorities to their own culture, heritage and other forms of expression, as well as the free exercise of their cultural identity and practices."[228] This includes the right to express oneself in the language of one's choice, which is particularly important for minorities, who have the right to preserve, promote and develop their own culture and language as part of their identity.[229]

Moreover, CESCR addresses the issue of cultural integration policies affecting minorities. With this regard, CESCR's General Comment No.21 states:

"Minorities, as well as persons belonging to minorities, have the right not only to their own identity but also to development in all areas of cultural life. Any programme intended to promote the constructive integration of minorities and persons belonging to minorities into the society of a State party should thus be based on inclusion, participation and non-discrimination, with a view to preserving the distinctive character of minority cultures."[230]

In addition, while commenting on Article 12 of ICESCR regarding the right to the highest attainable standard of health,[231] CESCR Committee's General Comment No.14 enshrines the right to the highest attainable standards of health, and insists that health facilities, goods and services must be within reach of all sections of the population, especially vulnerable or marginalized groups including ethnic minorities.[232] Furthermore, such provisions must be culturally appropriate and especially mindful of the culture of minorities.[233] "States are under the obligation to respect the right to health by, *inter alia*, refraining from denying or limiting equal access for all persons, including [...] minorities, to preventive,

226 CESCR, "General Comment No. 21," para.32-33.
227 Ibid, para. 27.
228 Ibid, para. 49.
229 Ibid, para. 16(B).
230 Ibid, para. 33.
231 See Article 12 of ICESCR.
232 CESCR, "General Comment No. 14: The Right to the Highest Attainable Standard of Health (Art. 12) 11 August 2000," UN Doc. E/C.12/2000/4, para. 12(B).
233 Ibid, para. 12(C).

curative and palliative health services."[234] Thus, whilst minorities are not specifically mentioned in the ICESCR, the above Articles make the relevance of this Covenant on minorities a lot more well-defined.

2.4.5 International Convention on the Elimination of All Forms of Racial Discrimination (CERD)

Non-discrimination is a fundamental principle of international human rights.[235] A frequently used definition of discrimination is set out in Article 1 (1) of the Convention:

> "any distinction, exclusion, restriction or preference based on race, colour, descent, or national or ethnic origin which has the purpose or effect of nullifying or impairing the recognition, enjoyment of exercise, on an equal footing, of human rights and fundamental freedoms in the political, economic, social, cultural or any other field of public life."[236]

The Article uses the term "purpose or effect" to refer to legislation and/or policies which may be textually neutral but can be interpreted in a discriminatory manner. International human rights law prohibits direct and indirect discrimination. Direct discrimination concerns the treatment of people differently based on prohibited grounds with no objective reasons.[237] Indirect discrimination occurs when laws, policies or practices that appear to be neutral have disproportionate impacts on specific groups.[238] Many civil, political, economic, social and cultural rights are based on discrimination, racism and exclusion on the grounds of ethnic, religious, national, or racial characteristics. To combat this, the Committee of CERD confirms in its report on the implementation of Article 7 states: "(a) although the convention applies to everyone without exception, it is concerned particularly with certain minority groups which have historically suffered the greatest social and exploration and deprivation."[239]

States may be required to take measures to support disadvantaged racial minorities,[240] because these groups need substantive equality. To achieve this,

234 Ibid, para. 34.

235 Mpoki Mwakagali, "International Human Rights Law and Discrimination Protections, A Comparison of Regional and National Responses," *Brill Research Perspectives in Comparative Discrimination Law*, 1:2 (2018), p. 1.

236 See Art. 1 of ICERD.

237 CESCR, "General Comment No. 20," para. 10(a).

238 Ibid, para.10(b).

239 CERD Committee, "Implementation of the ICERD," Article 7, p. 9.

240 See Article 1, para. 4 of CERD.

special measures must be taken by States, although they should only remain in effect until equality is achieved. In this context:

> "the aim of the special measures is to restore the balance between the respective positions of various groups including minority groups, but the ultimate objective of the convention is uniform treatment of individuals to whatever group they belong. The fear of providing an excuse for a policy of separation prevailed over the awareness of the need for the members of different groups, especially minority groups, to in perpetuity under different regimes, based on their special characteristics."[241]

Special measures are separate from rights of certain categories of people or communities, such as the rights of persons belonging to minorities to enjoy their own culture, to profess and practice their own religion and to use their own language.[242] These rights are permanent, laid down by human rights instruments including the UN and its agencies. States must observe distinctions between special measures and permanent human rights, although those entitled to permanent rights may also enjoy the benefits of special measures.[243] In other words, different treatment is sometimes necessary to correct past injustices and to enhance equality. This affirmative action or positive discrimination is not only permissible but remains an obligation of States.

In this context, the Convention has established three mechanisms for the Committee to its monitoring functions: the early-warning procedure, the examination of inter-state complaints and the examination of individual complaints:[244] The case of the Jewish Community et al V. Norway[245] can be a good example to analyze. In this case, the CERD Committee reaffirmed that:

---

241 Francesco Capotorti, "The Protection of Minorities under Multinational Agreements on Human Rights," *Italian Yearbook on International Law*, 1976, p. 25.

242 CEDAW Committee, "General recommendation No. 25, on article 4, paragraph 1, of the Convention on the Elimination of All Forms of Discrimination against Women, on Temporary Special Measures," Thirtieth session, UN Doc. 2004, para. 16.

243 CERD Committee, "General Recommendation No. 32, The Meaning and Scope of Special Measures in the ICERD," 24.11.2009, UN Doc. CERD/C/GC/32 and para.12 of the HRC, "Recommendations of the Forum on Minority Issues on Rights to Education," UN Doc. A/HRC/10/11/Add.1 (2009).

244 CERD Committee, "Monitoring racial equality and non-discrimination," UNOHCR official website, August 2020, http://www2.ohchr.org/english/bodies/cerd/

245 In 2000, a group known as the Bootboys organized a march in commemoration of Rudolf Hess near Oslo. There was an anti-Semitic speech by the march's leader Terje Sjølie, the Nazi salute was made and there were shouts of "*Sieg Heil*." Some witnesses filed a complaint with the police, and Sjølie was charged with a violation of Section 135a of the Norwegian Penal Code (threatening, insulting, or subjecting to hatred,

"...the prohibition of all ideas based upon racial superiority or hatred is compatible with the right to freedom of opinion and expression ... [and concluded that] the statements of Mr. Sjolie, given that they were of exceptionally/manifestly offensive character, are not protected by the due regard clause, and that accordingly his acquittal by the Supreme Court of Norway gave rise to a violation of Article 4, and consequently Article 6 of the Convention."[246]

Significant conclusions also include that "the deference to Hitler and his principles and 'footsteps' must in the Committee's view be taken as incitement at least to racial discrimination, if not to violence."[247]

2.4.6 UNESCO's Convention against Discrimination in Education

In Article 5 of the UNESCO Convention, States party to the Convention agree that it is essential to recognize the right of members of national minorities to carry on their own educational activities, including the maintenance of schools and depending on the educational policy of each State, the use or the teaching of their own language. Inter alia, the Article states:

"(c) It is essential to recognize the right of members of national minorities to carry on their own educational activities, including the maintenance of schools and, depending on the educational policy of each State, the use or the teaching of their own language, provided however:
(i) That this right is not exercised in a manner which prevents the members of these minorities from understanding the culture and language of the community as a whole and from participating in its activities, or which prejudices national sovereignty;

---

persecution or contempt, any person or group of persons because of their creed, race, colour or national or ethnic origin). He was acquitted by the Halden City Court, then convicted by the Borgarting Court of Appeal, and finally acquitted again by the Supreme Court in an 11:6 decision on 17.12.2002. The Supreme Court found that penalizing the approval of Nazism would involve prohibiting Nazi organizations, which it considered would be incompatible with the right to freedom of speech. The majority held that the speech contained derogatory and offensive remarks, but that no actual threats were made, nor any instructions to carry out any particular actions. On 17.06.2003, representatives of the Jewish community and the Norwegian Antiracist Centre filed a communication before CERD. On 09.03.2005, the Committee declared the communication admissible. On 15.08.2005, it delivered the decision.

246 CERD Committee Case, Jewish Community of Oslo et al v. Norway, Communication No.30/2003, U.N. Doc. CERD/C/67/D/30/2003 (2005), (Para.10.5).

247 Ibid, Para.10.4.

(ii) That the standard of education is not lower than the general standard laid down or approved by the competent authorities; and
(iii) That attendance at such schools is optional."[248]

UNESCO's Convention against Discrimination in Education is highly relevant in terms of personal autonomy and is supplemented by public tasks and public powers.[249] According to Article 2 of the UNESCO Convention, the establishment or maintenance of private educational institutions shall not, when permitted in a State, be deemed to constitute discrimination:

"(b) The establishment or maintenance, for religious or linguistic reasons, of separate educational systems or institutions offering an education which is in keeping with the wishes of the pupil's parents or legal guardians, if participation in such systems or attendance at such institutions is optional and if the education provided conforms to such standards as may be laid down or approved by the competent authorities, in particular for education of the same level;
(c) The establishment or maintenance of private educational institutions, if the object of the institutions is not to secure the exclusion of any group but to provide educational facilities in addition to those provided by the public authorities, if the institutions are conducted in accordance with that object, and if the education provided conforms with such standards as may be laid down or approved by the competent authorities, in particular for education of the same level."[250]

It's important to note that both Articles 2 and 5 emphasize on the "optional" nature of minority members' participation in such systems or attendance at such institutions as well as meeting certain standards not lower than the ones approved by the State as a precondition not to constitute a discrimination.

2.4.7 UNESCO's Declaration on Race and Racial Prejudice (DRRP)

The DRRP was adopted in 1978 and remains a milestone and a key reference point for UNESCO in its struggle against racial intolerance. The declaration outlines standard principles, concepts and universal criteria supporting the fight for racial equality, and these principles serve as key standards for peace and social stability.[251] Article 1.2 affirms that "all individuals and groups have the right to be

248 See full text of Article 5 of UNESCO's Convention against Discrimination in Education
249 Yves Daudet, Kishore Singh, The Right to Education: An Analysis of UNESCO's Standard-setting Instruments (France: UNESCO, 2001), pp. 23-25.
250 Article 2 of UNESCO's Convention against Discrimination in Education.
251 See UNESCO's Declaration on Race and Racial Prejudice, available online at: https://bit.ly/2Oc6Bu0.

different, to consider themselves as different and to be regarded as such." while Article 1.3 indicates that "identity of origin in no way affects the fact that human beings can and may live differently, nor does it preclude the existence of differences based on cultural, environmental and historical diversity nor the right to maintain cultural identity." Article 3 lists what racism might include as follows:

> "racist ideologies, prejudiced attitudes, discriminatory behaviour, structural arrangements and institutionalized practices resulting in racial inequality as well as the fallacious notion that discriminatory relations between groups are morally and scientifically justifiable; it is reflected in discriminatory provisions in legislation or regulations and discriminatory practices as well as in anti-social beliefs and acts; it hinders the development of its victims, perverts those who practise it, divides nations internally, impedes international co-operation and gives rise to political tensions between peoples; it is contrary to the fundamental principles of international law and, consequently, seriously disturbs international peace and security."[252]

To counter the above, the DRRP obliges States to "take all appropriate steps, inter alia by legislation, particularly in the spheres of education, culture and communication, to prevent, prohibit and eradicate racism, racist propaganda, racial segregation and apartheid and to encourage the dissemination of knowledge and the findings of appropriate research in natural and social sciences on the causes and prevention of racial prejudice and racist attitudes, with due regard to the principles embodied in the Universal Declaration of Human Rights and in the International Covenant on Civil and Political Rights."[253] Furthermore, DRRP requires from States to supplement their legal actions/steps by

> "administrative machinery for the systematic investigation of instances of racial discrimination, by a comprehensive framework of legal remedies against acts of racial discrimination, by broadly based education and research programmes designed to combat racial prejudice and racial discrimination and by programmes of positive political, social, educational and cultural measures calculated to promote genuine mutual respect among groups. Where circumstances warrant, special programmes should be undertaken to promote the advancement of disadvantaged groups and, in the case of nationals, to ensure their effective participation in the decision-making processes of the community."[254]

252 Article 3 of DRRP.
253 Article 6.2 of DRRP.
254 Article 6.3 of DRRP.

2.4.8 The UN Declaration on the Rights of Persons Belonging to National or Ethnic, Religious and Linguistic Minorities (The Minority Declaration)

Although legally not binding, the 1992 UN Declaration can be considered an important soft law instrument concerning minority rights.[255] It was inspired by Article 27 of the ICCPR, and provides authoritative guidance as well as key principles and standards on the treatment of minorities.[256] It protects their existence, promotes their identity and offers them rights to effective participation, non-discrimination and equality.[257] The Declaration's prologue lays the groundwork for the protection of minority rights and it was designed to "contribute to the political and social stability of States in which they live." It will therefore "contribute to the strengthening of friendship and cooperation among peoples and States."[258] The Declaration is couched in progressive terms concerning minority participation in the State's political and economic life.[259] In contrast with earlier UNGA declarations, this did not form a prelude to more substantive treaties. Today it survives as a 'soft law', a helpful but not binding suffix to the more modest rights set out in Article 27 of ICCPR.

The Minority Declaration adds little clarification to Article 27, but its significance lies in the extra minority rights it provides. Among these is the right of minority individuals to participate effectively in cultural, religious, social, economic and public life.[260] Article 2(3) takes this participation a step further by guaranteeing individuals within minorities the right to participate in decisions taken at national and regional levels affecting them personally or in the regions where they live "in a manner not incompatible with national legislation."[261] States are also obliged to plan and implement national policies and programs with "due regard for the legitimate interests" of minority groups or individuals.[262]

---

255 See Ugo Caruso and Rainer Hofmann, eds., *The United Nations Declaration on Minorities* (Leiden, The Netherlands: Brill Nijhoff, 2015).

256 UN Economic and Social Council, "Commentary on the Working Group on Minorities," *Part I.*

257 Ibid.

258 Ibid.

259 Ibid.

260 See Articles 2.2, 2.3, 4.5 of Minority Declaration.

261 See Article 5.1 of Minority Declaration.

262 See Article 2.3 of Minority Declaration.

The Minority Declaration also grants people in minorities the right to set up and run their own associations, whilst not restricting their rights to effective participation in specific issues concerning minorities or their environment – as long as that participation is carried out in a way that conforms to national legislation.[263] Effective participation enshrines the right to association in practice, and it was therefore important that Article 2(4) was general in its possible restrictions. The Minority Declaration also lays down several contact rights for minorities, guaranteeing free and peaceful contact between group members and with those belonging to other State. It also allows cross-border contact between minorities and citizens in other States with whom they may have national, ethnic, religious or linguistic links.[264]

The negative formulation of the phrase "shall not be denied the right... " in Article 27 ICCPR (repeated in Article 30 of the CRC) was not repeated in the 1992 UNGA Minority Declaration. In this Declaration, minority rights are stated in positive rather than negative terms (for example, "States shall protect the existence and the national or ethnic, cultural, religious and linguistic identity of minorities within their respective territories..."[265]) State obligations to ensure these rights are also set out (and shall encourage conditions for the promotion of that identity... States shall adopt appropriate legislative and other measures to achieve those ends.")[266] In this context, as the Commentary to the Minority Declaration indicates, the Article 4.2[267] of the Declaration

> "calls for more than mere tolerance of the manifestation of different cultures within a State. The creation of favourable conditions requires active measures by the State. The nature of those measures depends on the situation of the minority concerned but should be guided by the purpose set forth in Article 4.2, which is twofold. On the one hand, individual members of the minority shall be enabled to express the traditional characteristics of the group, which may include a right to use their traditional attire and to make their living in their own cultural ways. On the other hand, they shall be enabled,

---

263 See Article 2.4 of Minority Declaration.

264 See Article 2.6 of Minority Declaration.

265 Article 1 of Minority Declaration.

266 Ibid, UNICEF, Implementation Handbook for the Convention on the Rights of the Child, third ed., 2007.

267 Article 4.2 of Minority Declaration: "States shall take measures to create favourable conditions to enable persons belonging to minorities to express their characteristics and to develop their culture, language, religion, traditions and customs, except where specific practices are in violation of national law and contrary to international standards."

in community with other persons belonging to the group, to develop their culture, language and traditions. These measures may require economic resources from the State. In the same way as the State provides funding for the development of the culture and language of the majority, it shall provide resources for similar activities of the minority."[268]

Overall, the Minority Declaration on Minorities is a cautious step forward from existing law. But it is still non-binding, and this limits its effectiveness as an instrument of protection. However, the effect of this is to strengthen rights; whilst they remain outside legally binding international law, they are becoming stronger as normative standards.

2.4.9 The Convention on the Rights of the Child (CRC)

The CRC included Articles that were particularly relevant to minorities: Article 2.1[269] provides that rights within the Convention could be guaranteed without discrimination on race, color, language, religion, national or ethnic origin. Article 17 encourages the media to produce and disseminate material from diverse cultural sources with "particular regard to the linguistic needs of the child who belongs to a minority group."[270] Article 20.3[271] pays due regard to children's ethnic, religious, cultural, and linguistic backgrounds, especially when children are living at a location other than the family home. Article 29[272] stresses

268 Commentary of the Working Group on Minorities, para. 56-57.

269 Article 2.1 of CRC: "State parties shall respect and ensure the rights set forth in the present Convention to each child within their jurisdiction without discrimination of any kind, irrespective of the child's or his or her parent's or legal guardian's race, colour, sex, language, religion, political or other opinion, national, ethnic or social origin, property, disability, birth or other status."

270 Article 17 of CRC: "State parties recognize the important function performed by the mass media and shall ensure that the child has access to information and material from a diversity of national and international sources, especially those aimed at the promotion of his or her social, spiritual and moral well-being and physical and mental health." Article 17(d): "…encourage the mass media to have particular regard to the linguistic needs of the child who belongs to a minority group."

271 Article 20.3 of CRC: "Such care could include, inter alia, foster placement, *kafalah* (bail) of Islamic law, adoption or if necessary, placement in suitable institutions for the care of children. When considering solutions, due regard shall be paid to the desirability of continuity in a child's upbringing and to the child's ethnic, religious, cultural and linguistic background."

272 Article 29 of CRC: "(b) The development of respect for human rights and fundamental freedoms, and for the principles enshrined in the Charter of the United Nations; (c) The development of respect for the child's parents, his or her own cultural identity,

the fundamental benefits of education and encourages education to be directed towards human rights and fundamental freedoms, the children's cultural identity, language, and values, the national values of the child's home and host countries and the values of other civilizations.

Article 30 essentially extends the ICCPR provisions of Article 27 to minority children in terms of cultural, religious and linguistic preferences and states that:

> "In those States in which ethnic, religious or linguistic minorities or persons of indigenous origin exist, a child belonging to such a minority or who is indigenous shall not be denied the right, in community with other members of his or her group, to enjoy his or her own culture, to profess and practise his or her own religion, or to use his or her own language."[273]

Despite being expressed in negative terms, Article 30 recognizes the existence of a "right" and requires that it "shall not be denied." This means that States are obliged to ensure that the right is not only respected, but also protected against denial. Positive measures of protection therefore are required, both against potential State acts – whether through its legislative, judicial, or administrative authorities – and against the acts of other persons or entities within the State.[274] Article 31.2 calls upon States to respect and promote children's rights to participate fully in cultural and artistic life.[275] However, the CRC Committee clarifies that "cultural practices provided by Article 30 of the Convention must be exercised in accordance with other provisions of the Convention and under no circumstances may be justified if deemed prejudicial to the Child's dignity, Health and development.[276]

---

language and values, for the national values of the country in which the child is living, the country from which he or she may originate, and for civilizations different from his or her own..."

273 Article 30 of CRC.

274 Javaid Rehman, *Education* (2nd ed.) (UK: Brunel University, Pearson Education, 2010), pp. 558-564.

275 Article 31.2: of CRC: "States parties shall respect and promote the right of the child to participate fully in cultural and artistic life and shall encourage the provision of appropriate and equal opportunities for cultural, artistic, recreational and leisure activity."

276 CRC Committee, "General Comment No. 11: Indigenous People and their Rights under the Convention, fifth session," 2009, UN Doc. GRC/C/GC/11, para. 22.

2.4.10 Genocide Convention

The 1948 Convention on the Prevention and Punishment of The Crime of Genocide prohibits the destruction of "a national, ethnical, racial or religious group"[277] and protects their basic rights of existence,[278] as a necessary precondition for developing a distinctive identity. Although not framed in minority terms, the Convention is still considered one of the most important multilateral agreements supporting minorities.[279] It deals with the absolute existence of certain groups, and it does require from States positive and preventive actions on their part. The Convention includes group protection factors, as the definition of genocide shows that States may intend to destroy a group either in total or in part. This Convention is intended to protect groups rather than individuals, irrespective of their size or importance.[280]

The Convention also places obligations on States, requiring that they prevent and punish genocide, which is defined as any of five specific acts that are intended to destroy national, ethnic, racial or religious groups either in part or completely.[281] States are required to enact international legislation to prosecute the perpetrators of genocide committed within their boundaries or in their territories, and to ensure criminals are punished by cooperating with extradition processes where necessary.[282] The States that proposed the recognition of genocide as an international crime sought a more strongly-worded treaty to correct what they saw as a major legal shortcoming that arose from the Nuremberg Trials.[283] The attempted extermination of the Jews of Europe had been prosecuted at Nuremberg as a 'crime against humanity', a term that first appeared earlier in the

---

277 Article 2 of the Convention on the Prevention and Punishment of the Crime of Genocide.

278 Henrard, Devising an Adequate System, p. 213.

279 Ibid.

280 Ibid, pp. 217-218.

281 Article 2 of the Convention on the Prevention and Punishment of the Crime of Genocide lists the following five acts: (a) Killing members of the group; (b) Causing serious bodily or mental harm to members of the group; (c) Deliberately inflicting on the group conditions of life calculated to bring about its physical destruction in whole or in part; (d) Imposing measures intended to prevent births within the group; (e) Forcibly transferring children of the group to another group.

282 Schabas, Preventing Genocide and Mass Killing, p. 8.

283 William A. Schabas, "Origins of the Genocide Convention: From Nuremberg to Paris," *Case Western Reserve Journal of International Law,* 40:1 (2007-2008), pp. 39-40.

century, three decades before the term 'genocide'[284] was coined by Raphael Lemkin. In May 1915, addressing the extermination of Ottoman Armenians, one of the twentieth century's first great attacks on an ethnic minority, France, Great Britain and Russia declared that:

> "[I]n the presence of these new crimes of Turkey against humanity and civilization, the allied Governments publicly inform the Sublime Porte that they will hold personally responsible for the said crimes all members of the Ottoman Government as well as those of its agents who are found to be involved in such massacres."[285]

In addition, the five cases filed before ICJ during the 1990s, all of which involve important issues of the protection of minorities.[286] The Genocide Convention thus came to stand for minority protection against the ultimate challenge to their existence. The Convention, in terms of its substantive norms, has often been described as a codification of customary international law.[287] The ICJ has also stated that the prohibition of genocide is a peremptory norm of international law (*or jus cogens*) and consequently, no derogation from it is allowed.

2.4.11 Basic Principles and Guidelines on the Right to a Remedy and Reparation for Victims of Gross Violations of International Human Rights Law and Serious Violations of International Humanitarian Law

In 2005, the UN adopted a resolution which includes principles and guidelines describing a broad range of both symbolic and material reparation mechanisms.[288] It sets out principles defining various forms, formulated on the ILC's

284 The word "genocide" was first coined in 1944 by Raphäel Lemkin in his book *Axis Rule in Occupied Europe*. It consists of the Greek prefix *genos*, meaning race or tribe, and the Latin suffix *cide*, meaning killing.

285 UN War Crimes Commission, *History of the United Nations War Crimes Commission and The Developments of the Laws of War* (London: United Nations War Crimes Commission. His Majesty's Stationery Office, 1948) (English translation) and Mahmoud Cherif Bassiouni, *Crimes against Humanity: Historical Evolution and Contemporary Application* (UK: Cambridge University Press, 25 Apr 2011) and Joseph V. Fuller, Papers Relating to the Foreign Relations of the United States, 1915, supplement (Washington: US Government Printing Office, 1928), p. 981.

286 Schabas, Preventing Genocide and Mass Killing, p. 19.

287 Erjona Ramaj, "Binding International Norms, Jus Cogens," *European Journal of Sustainable Development*, 5:3 (01.10.2016), pp. 318-324.

288 UNGA, "Basic Principles and Guidelines on the Right to a Remedy and Reparation for Victims of Gross Violations of International Human Rights Law and Serious

Articles on State Responsibility.[289] These forms cover monetary and non-monetary reparations, and can be summarized as follows.

Restitution: "...Restitution should, whenever possible, restore the victim to the original situation before the gross violations of international human rights law or serious violations of international humanitarian law occurred. Restitution includes, as appropriate: restoration of liberty, enjoyment of human rights, identity, family life and citizenship, return to one's place of residence, restoration of employment and return of property. This principle appears to include the right to restore the status of minorities or individuals, particularly where status is lost because of displacement.

Monetary 'compensation': This "should be provided for any economically assessable damage, as appropriate and proportional to the gravity of the violation and the circumstances of each case" (Principle 20). The damage may result from physical harm, mental stress or moral damage; the loss of potential in terms of employment, education and social benefits; the costs of legal representation, and medical, psychological or social services.

'Rehabilitation': Includes medical and psychological care, as well as legal and social services (Principle 21).

Satisfaction: This includes a broad range of measures, from those stopping violations to explorations of causes and underlying guilt. In more practical terms it includes that search for the missing, the recovery and the reburial of remains, public apologies, judicial and administrative sanctions, commemoration, and human rights training (Principle 22).

Guarantees of non-repetition: These guarantees generally entail broad policy measures, institutional reforms aiming to control military and security forces, strengthening judicial independence, protection for human rights personnel, and the promotion of human rights standards in public service, law enforcement, the media, industry and psychological and social services (Principle 23).

The above-mentioned forms of reparations and remedy are of direct relevance to the rights of Armenians both in Lebanon and Turkey, since they are searching

Violations of International Humanitarian Law," UNGA Resolution 60/147, 16.12.2005, Principle 19.

289 James Crawford, *The International Law Commission's Articles on State Responsibility: Introduction, Text and Commentaries,* United Nations, International Law Commission (UK: Cambridge University Press, 2002).

for justice and fairness through reparations for and recognition of their century-old Genocide for more than one hundred years now.[290]

2.4.12 Responsibility to Protect (R2P)

As indicated earlier, in 2005, the World Summit Outcome reaffirmed the importance of the UN's work, to promote and protect minority rights and to contribute to political and social stability and peace and to enrich the cultural diversity and heritage of society.[291]

The Outcome Document also declared that "each individual State has the responsibility to protect its populations from genocide, war crimes, ethnic cleansing and crimes against humanity."[292] This means that the international community was becoming aware that the increases in population movement – especially in terms of forced migration and the growing number of refugees – was coming to mean that the protection of minorities was not just a factor of local battles against prejudice, but was also becoming increasingly vital to world peace and stability.

Therefore, State responsibilities in this area are being met through appropriate diplomatic, humanitarian and other channels, and by taking collective action through the UN Security Council, 'in a timely and decisive manner',[293] if peaceful solutions cannot be found. Here it is worth mentioning, that Paragraphs 138 and 139 represent an important new political commitment by member States, and the R2P described in these paragraphs is based upon international legal obligations for States that require them to take specific actions to prevent genocide, war crimes, ethnic cleansing and crimes against humanity, and to punish perpetrators severely if they occur. The adoption of the two paragraphs at high political levels helped the development of these obligations.

In other words, R2P embodies national commitments to end persecution by narrowing the gap between member States' legal obligations and the reality faced by populations at risk of persecution.[294] The principles ultimately help States

290 See Nolwen Guibert and Sun Kim, "Compensation for the Armenian Genocide: A Study of Recognition and Reparation," in *The Armenian Genocide Legacy*, Alexis Demeridjian ed. (UK: Palgrave Macmillan, 2016), pp. 102-113.

291 UNGA Resolution, World Summit Outcome, 16.09.2005, UN Doc. A/60/L.1, para. 130.

292 Ibid, para.138.

293 Ibid, para.139.

294 See the Responsibility to Protect Website: https://bit.ly/2OkQqag.

meet their responsibilities and offer fresh opportunities for the UN system to help States prevent designated crimes against populations, including minorities. It does this by reinforcing early warning signs, and helps States construct other preventive and protective measures, rather than simply waiting to respond to danger. R2P can be seen as the end of a process leading to sovereign responsibility, rather than the idea of sovereignty as a function of power or control.[295]

In practice, however, there remain large gaps in implementation and compliance with regards to R2P.[296] The only widely recognized success of R2P was Kofi Annan's mediation in Kenya to end the post-election violence of December 2007–January 2008.[297] Repeated failures to act on R2P, as in Darfur,[298] may cast doubt on international communities' readiness to act on its responsibility.

R2P is also vulnerable to misuse.[299] In Libya in 2011, NATO's interpretation of the UNSC mandate to protect civilians alarmed many States by its potential use of R2P to accomplish regime change and made it harder to achieve consensus on a broader mandate to protect people in other crises.[300] However, R2P attracts most attention because of its provision for intervention to halt atrocities. The R2P norm is more than a mere substitute for humanitarian intervention, and entails a threefold responsibility to prevent, react, and rebuild.[301] This sets the emphasis on preventing abuses occurring in the first place, negating the need for intervention – a priority reaffirmed in the 2009 report of the UN Secretary-General on implementing R2P.[302]

---

295 Ibid.

296 UNGA & UNSC, "Implementing the Responsibility to Protect: Accountability for Prevention," UN Doc. A/71/1016 –S/2017/556. 2017, para. 1.

297 Nicholas Turner and Nanako Otsuki, "The Responsibility to Protect Minorities and the Problem of the Kin-State," Policy Brief, United Nations University, 2010.

298 Alex De Waal, "Darfur and the Failure of the Responsibility to Protect," *International Affairs* 83:6 (2007), pp. 1039–1054.

299 Mient Jan Faber, "R2P is misused," *Open Democracy*, 2011, https://bit.ly/35fC3uN.

300 Maria Banda, "Protecting R2P From Misuse," *opencanada.org*, 2014, https://bit.ly/2QqNpI8.

301 UNGA, "2005 World Summit Outcome, 16.09.2005," UN Doc. A/RES/60/1.

302 UNGA, "Implementing the responsibility to protect Report of the Secretary-General," UN. DOC. A/63/677, 2009.

2.5 The Rome Statute of the International Criminal Court (ICC)

The Rome Statute of the ICC allows the prosecution of cases covering genocide (Article 6), crimes against humanity (Article 7) and war crimes (Article 8). Any acts covering the forced transfer of populations away from the territory on which they live, as well as persecution against any identifiable group on political, racial, national, ethnic, cultural, religious, gender (Article 7) would now be considered serious breaches of the Rome Statute.[303]

The Court's Office of the Prosecutor conducts investigations either on its own initiative or through referral by individual State parties or the UNSC by gathering and examining evidence, questioning alleged perpetrators, victims and witnesses in order to determine culpability.[304] The ICC states that communication from individuals or minority groups generally cover "crimes that have been allegedly committed."[305] The prosecutor's initial task is to analyze the situation to see if it requires deeper investigation.[306] Minorities can communicate directly with the ICC, but there is no guarantee that this procedure will be fruitful. For example, the Yezidi minority of Iraq made such a complaint in 2015[307] but so far, the ICC has made no preliminary examination or authorized any investigation.

The ICC was devised by the international community as a way of fighting the world's gravest crimes that affected the most vulnerable groups in any society, but as a statutory body, the ICC will remain hostage to political considerations and the will of the international community to empower its jurisdiction.

2.6 Minorities and Customary International Law and Peremptory norms

International Human Rights laws are not limited to rights laid down in treaties, and also include the rights and freedoms that have become part of customary

303 See the Rome Statute of the International Criminal Court.

304 "Situation Under Investigation," International Criminal Court official website, 2019, https://bit.ly/2KFQvHl.

305 Constance Johnson, "Iraq/ICC: Investigation of ISIL Crimes Urged by Religious Minority," *Global Legal Monitor*, 30.09.2015, https://bit.ly/2LNbRTx.

306 ICC, "Report on Preliminary Examination Activities 2018," *International Criminal Court*, 05.12.2018, para.3, https://bit.ly/2Oievyp.

307 Johnson, "Iraq/ICC: Investigation of ISIL Crimes."

international law and are now binding on all States.[308] The HRC has indicated that the provisions in the ICCPR representing customary international law may not be the subject of reservations.[309] The HRC states that the minority rights provision does reflect such a norm and adds that:

> "A State may not reserve the right… to engage in slavery, to torture, to subject persons to cruel, inhuman or degrading treatment or punishment, to arbitrarily deprive persons of their lives, to arbitrarily arrest and detain persons, to deny freedom of thought, conscience and religion, […] to permit the advocacy of national, racial or religious hatred, to deny to persons of marriageable age the right to marry, or to deny to minorities the right to enjoy their own culture, profess their own religion."[310]

In addition, some human rights prevail over other international obligations and no derogation is acceptable under any condition. The prohibition of torture, slavery, genocide, discrimination, and crimes against humanity are now widely recognized, along with rights to self-determination as peremptory norms. These peremptory norms are reflected in ILC's draft Articles on State responsibility,[311] which does not include minority rights. However, according to the first and second Opinions of the Badinter Arbitration Committee[312] minority rights are peremptory norms of general international law.[313] There is much room for debate whether this is an accurate opinion as still many international law experts

---

308 Tawhida Ahmed and Israel de Jesús Butler, "The European Union and Human Rights: An International Law Perspective," *European Journal of International Law*, 17:4 (01.09.2006), pp. 771–801.

309 HRC, "CCPR General Comment No. 24 (52): on Issues Relating to Reservations Made upon Ratification or Accession to the Covenant or the Optional Protocols thereto, or in Relation to Declarations under Article 41 of the Covenant," 04.11.1994, UN Doc. CCPR/C/21/Rev.1/Add.6, para. 8.

310 Ibid.

311 ILC, "Draft articles on Responsibility of States for Internationally Wrongful Acts, with commentaries," 2001, UN DOC A/56/10 2:1 https://bit.ly/2KtkjnC, See paragraphs (4) to (7) of the commentary to article 20.

312 This committee was established by the European Community, in the context of the collapse of Yugoslavia, for the purpose of issuing opinions and rulings on various issues arising from that dissolution.

313 Conference on Yugoslavia Arbitration Committee, 'Opinion No. 1', 31 *International Legal Materials* (1992), p. 1496; 'Opinion No. 2', 31 *International Legal Materials* (1992), p. 1498.

do not support or are hesitant to grant minority rights the status of peremptory norm.[314]

In addition, General Comment No. 29 (2001) of the HRC adds to the previous general comments the prohibition of deportation or forced transfer of minorities and violence through advocacy of national, racial, or religious hatred.[315] However, the problem remains that in practice most minorities or their representatives lack any form of legally binding legislation as far as enforcement is concerned.

This section has discussed the legal documents, their relevant case studies and general comments brought in by the UN since its inception to protect the minorities. The abovementioned discussions will be the basis to address problems associated more specifically with the Armenian minorities in Lebanon and Turkey.

2.7 Minority Rights in UN Bodies and Mechanisms

In addition to covenants and treaties dealing with minority rights, the UN has addressed minority issues through several bodies and mechanisms based on the UN Charter. These bodies will be described in this section, and their relevance to Armenian issues will be clarified in the relevant sections accordingly. After analyzing these bodies and mechanisms, the thesis will examine the extent to which they concern Armenian minorities in Lebanon and Turkey, as well as looking at how these minorities utilize the available international mechanisms and how effective these mechanisms are in terms of protecting and promoting their rights in Lebanon and Turkey.

2.7.1 The Human Rights Council and Its Subsidiary Bodies

The establishment of the Human Rights Council in 2006 created the UN's most important intergovernmental human rights body, providing a number of avenues and possibilities through which various concerns, including minority rights, may be highlighted for UN officials and government representatives.[316]

---

314 For further details see Karen Knop, *Diversity and Self-Determination in International Law* (Cambridge: Cambridge University Press, 2002) p. 177. Matthew C.R. Craven, "The European Community Arbitration Commission on Yugoslavia," 66 *British Yearbook of International Law* (1996), p. 391.

315 HRC, "CCPR General Comment No. 29: Article 4: Derogations during a State of Emergency," UN Doc. CCPR/C/21/Rev.1/Add.11, 2001.

316 See Human Rights Council official website: https://www.ohchr.org/en/hrbodies/hrc/pages/home.aspx

Among relevant human rights mechanisms is the Forum on Minority Issues, which meets annually to discuss general minority issues; the Universal Periodic Review (UPR), which considers the human rights situation in UN member States every four and a half years; and the Complaint Procedure, under which allegation of a consistent pattern of violations of minorities' human rights can be submitted to the Human Rights Council for consideration.[317]

The Human Rights Council's main objectives are ensuring the protection of vulnerable communities, fighting discrimination and promoting equality.[318] In recent meetings on the situations in Iraq, Syria and the Central African Republic, the Council addressed violence against minorities and sectarian tensions.[319] Council resolutions have instigated Commissions of Inquiry to uncover the nature and extent of human rights violations affecting minorities, and such steps help explore the root causes of human rights violations and conflict. The Council adopts resolutions every year, and its sessions attract many observer States, UN special agency representatives, regional institutions and NGOs. Resolutions which expressing concern over or condemnation of human rights situation in a particular country are usually the subject of intense debate and State lobbying.[320] However, like many Charter-based UN bodies, the Human Rights Council's resolutions are not legally binding[321] and sometimes its decisions are politicized.

2.7.1.1 Universal Periodic Review

The UPR's mandate is to "Undertake a universal periodic review, based on objective and reliable information, of the fulfilment by each State of its human rights obligations and commitments in a manner which ensures universality of coverage and equal treatment with respect to all States."[322]

Since the Review addresses all human rights issues, minority rights are rarely at the forefront of debates. However, the minority situations have been raised many times, including Roma in Slovakia, Christians in Syria and Iraq, Kurds

317 For further information, visit UNOHCHR official website: https://bit.ly/3r8zhmj.

318 Ibid.

319 Ibid.

320 UNOHCHR, *Promoting and Protecting Minority Rights*, p. 28. and Pamphlet No.4 of the UN Guide for Minorities.

321 *The Human Rights Council: Practical Guide* (Geneva: Permanent Mission of Switzerland to the United Nations Office and to the other international organisations in Geneva, 2015).

322 UNGA Resolution 60/251, 2006, para (e).

in Turkey, Tibetans and Uyghurs in China.[323] It is therefore worthwhile for minority advocates to contribute information to State reviews. The third review cycle focuses on the implementation of any recommendations made in the first and second reviews, so information should concentrate on any recommendations on minorities and their implementation (or lack thereof). The analysis of the first UPR cycle revealed that 112 Member States issued 895 recommendations on national, ethnic, religious or linguistic minorities to 137 States. Minorities were the 9th most discussed topic at the first cycle of the UPR process and constituted 4.2 % of the total 21,353 recommendations.[324]

2.7.1.2 Forum on Minority Issues

The Forum on Minority Issues replaced the Working Group on Minorities[325] in 2007 under Human Rights Council Resolution 6/15[326] (and reaffirmed by resolution 19/23 in 2012).[327] The Forum provides a platform for issues pertaining to national or ethnic, religious and linguistic minorities, and contributes to the

---

323 Rita Izsák, "Minority Issues in the First Cycle of the Universal Periodic Review (UPR) An analysis by the UN Special Rapporteur on Minority Issues," *OHCHR*, 2014, https://bit.ly/38C7Kmv.

324 Ibid.

325 The former Working Group on Minorities was established in 1995, pursuant to Economic and Social Council Resolution 1995/31 of 25.07.1995 as a subsidiary organ of the Sub-Commission on the Promotion and Protection of Human Rights (previously called the Sub-Commission on Prevention of Discrimination and Protection of Minorities). Between 1995 and 2006, the Working Group held 12 sessions and was aimed at being a forum for dialogue. It facilitated greater awareness of the differing perspectives on minority issues and sought better understanding and mutual respect among minorities and between minorities and Governments. It also acted as a mechanism for hearing suggestions and making recommendations for the peaceful and constructive solution to problems involving minorities, through the promotion and protection of their rights. A wealth of work was undertaken by the Working Group not only on conceptualization of the rights of persons belonging to minorities but also good practices and other measures for the promotion and protection of minorities. Numerous papers on topics such as multicultural and intercultural education, recognition of the existence of minorities, participation in public life including through autonomy and integrative measures, inclusive development and conflict prevention were prepared and submitted for consideration by the Working Group.

326 UN Human Rights Council Resolution 6/15, Forum on Minority Issues, 28.09.2007.

327 UN Resolution adopted by the Human Rights Council, Forum on Minority Issues 18/23, 10.04. 2012 UN Doc. A/HRC/RES/19/23.

work of the Special Rapporteur on minority issues. Each session considers a specific theme. The Forum's mandate is to "identify and analyse best practices, challenges, opportunities and initiatives for the further implementation of the Declaration."[328] It aims to offer specific outcomes in the form of thematic recommendations relevant to all stakeholders. Since the Forum is the only annual UN meeting dedicated to minority issues and their rights, it provides a unique platform for engagement and dialogue with representatives of member States, UN specialized agencies, human rights treaty bodies, intergovernmental and regional organizations, NGOs, representatives of civil society, national human rights institutions, minority representatives, academics, and experts.[329]

2.7.1.3 The Special Rapporteur on Minority Issues

The Special Rapporteur's mandate on minority issues was established by resolution 2005/79 of the UN Commission on Human Rights[330] in 2005, and subsequently renewed by the Human Rights Council, most recently in 2017.[331] The mandate is explicitly designed to implement the Minority Declaration through consultation with governments, based on existing international standards and national legislation concerning minorities, and to examine ways of overcoming existing obstacles to fully and effectively realize the rights of minorities.[332]

The substantive reports submitted by Special Rapporteurs to the Human Rights Council and UNGA address specific minority issues and provide timely and reliable information to the Human Rights Council. They provide a solid basis for promoting minority rights and protecting and improving the situations of minority groups worldwide. As Ella argues "Sometimes information contained in their reports and the evidence provided by civil society is an essential early warning to the international community that we must be better at listening

---

328 See official website of Forum on Minority Issues, UNOHCHR, https://bit.ly/2O9pkGB.

329 Graham Fox, "The United Nations Forum on Minority Issues and its Role in Promoting the UN Declaration on the Rights of Persons Belonging to National or Ethnic, Religious and Linguistic Minorities," in *The United Nations Declaration on Minorities an Academic Account on the Occasion of Its 20th Anniversary (1992-2012)*, Ugo Caruso and Rainer Hofmann eds. (The Netherlands: Brill, Nijhoff, 2015).

330 UN Commission on Human Rights, "Resolution 2005/79: Rights of persons belonging to national or ethnic, religious and linguistic minorities," 21.04.2005, UN Doc. E/CN.4/RES/2005/7921.

331 The official website of the Special Rapporteur on Minority Issues, UNOHCHR, 2020, shorturl.at/BCGP2

332 Ibid.

and responding."[333] This somehow indicates that the international community is not paying serious attention and care to the reports and the recommendations produced by the Special Rapporteur.

2.7.2 The Office of the UN High Commissioner for Human Rights (OHCHR)

The High Commissioner for Human Rights has the lead responsibility within the UN system for implementing UN human rights programmes through public statements, direct dialogue with governments, cooperation with the UN and other bodies, and by ensuring that human rights, including minority rights, remain an integral part of the UN's work.[334] The High Commissioner offers a voice to minorities facing discrimination. The OHCHR services the main UN human rights bodies and ensures that minority issues are regularly placed on the international human rights agenda.[335]

The Office works through its global network of more than 50 field offices, and the section most concerned with minority rights issues is the Indigenous Peoples and Minorities Section, based in Geneva. OHCHR field offices enable direct communication with UN staff, and participate in programming, training and monitoring activities. The OHCHR features minority issues in its involvement with the UN Human Rights Council and its special procedures, as well as human rights treaty bodies and the UPR process.[336]

Moreover, the OHCHR is focused on standard-setting, monitoring and evaluation.[337] It develops international norms to advance human rights protection and entitlements, ensuring that these standards are implemented in practice by finding early-warning signs of crises and deteriorating situations, and wherever is possible offering technical support to States by deploying staff and resources to contribute to the prevention of human rights violations. The OHCHR leads inter-agency work on minorities. It coordinates the UN Network on Racial

333 Statement by H.E. Baudelaire Ndong Ella, President of the Human Rights Council, Geneva, OHCHR, 25.11.2014, "Preventing and addressing violence and atrocity crimes targeted against minorities."

334 UNOHCHR official website: https://www.ohchr.org/EN/pages/home.aspx.

335 UNOHCHR, Minority Rights: International Standards, pp. 8-11.

336 Ibid.

337 "What We Do," OHCHR official website, https://bit.ly/2YyrqVT.

Discrimination and protection of Minorities[338] established by the Secretary-General in 2012 to advance system-wide collaboration in human rights areas.[339]

2.7.3 OHCHR Indigenous Peoples and Minorities Section (IPMS)

The OHCHR's Indigenous Peoples and Minorities Section[340] is specifically tasked with protecting and promoting the rights of persons belonging to minorities.[341] The IPMS aims to have main human rights standards (particularly the Minority Declaration and the Declaration on the Rights of Indigenous Peoples) reflected more consistently in law, policy and practice, and in the UN's programmes and activities. To do this, IPMS builds national capacity through human rights training for members of the civil society, conducts research and analysis, and provides input for the Special Rapporteur on Minority Issues and the Forum on Minority Issues. It engages with the wider community to form partnerships, to raise awareness about the Minority Declaration and other key standards and to mobilize support for anti-discrimination measures through legislation, policies and programmes. The Section also coordinates the Inter-Agency Group on Minority Issues[342] which has been meeting since 2004 and supports field offices and UN country teams in their efforts to promote minority rights.

---

338 The Network aims to enhance dialogue and cooperation between relevant UN Departments, Agencies, Programmes and Funds and is currently, *inter alia*, developing guidance for the UN System on how to address racial discrimination and protection of minorities in line with the Universal Declaration of Human Rights and other key standards. The Guidance Note was endorsed by the Secretary General on 06.03.2013. It contains 19 recommendations for the UN system on how to address racial discrimination and protection of minorities in line with the Universal Declaration of Human Rights, the UN Declaration on Minority Rights and other key standards, drawing from effective practices. The Guidance Note sets out guiding principles and framework for UN action with a view to ensuring a comprehensive and coherent UN approach from headquarters to regional and country presences.

339 For more information see official website of UNOHCHR: http://www.ohchr.org/EN/pages/home.aspx.

340 See the official website of the OHCHR's Indigenous Peoples and Minorities Section https://bit.ly/3e1gCF6.

341 UNOHCHR, Promoting and Protecting Minority Rights, p. 11.

342 Ibid, p. 5.

2.7.4 The UN High Commissioner for Refugees (UNHCR)

Many of the world's refugees and asylum seekers are members of minority groups with specific protection.[343] The UNHCR is mandated by the UN to administrate and coordinate international action to protect refugees and to find durable solutions for the future.[344] The UNHCR is sensitive to age, gender and diversity and pays particular attention to groups with specific needs, including minorities, seeking to promote the equal rights of disenfranchised groups, among others.[345] UNHCR provides specific protection and assistance activities for minority groups.[346]

2.7.5 The UN Children's Fund (UNICEF)

UNICEF's work is conducted by the provisions and principles of the CRC. Its mission is to advocate for children's rights and needs and to help them reach their full potential.[347] As a human rights-based organization, UNICEF's involvement in the promotion and protection of minority children is not a choice but an obligation. Its mission statement says that "UNICEF is non-partisan, and its cooperation is free of discrimination. In everything it does, the most disadvantaged children and the countries in greatest need have priority."[348] Given that minority children are often the most vulnerable members of society, UNICEF seeks to strengthen its capacity to prevent and protect children from violence, exploitation, abuse, neglect and conflict by increasing awareness on child protection rights. Coupled with relevant advocacy initiatives for minority communities, UNICEF facilitates the development of tailored initiatives to meet children's needs. Its specialized area of work is a vital factor in ensuring the safety and security of minority children.

---

343 Ibid. p. 67.

344 See Pamphlet No. 12 of the UN Guide for Minorities: "Protection on Refugees who belong to Minorities: The UN High Commissioner for Refugees."

345 Ibid.

346 For more details on such initiatives see the official website of the OHCHR: https://www.unhcr.org/.

347 "What We Do," UNICEF Official Page, 2019, at https://www.unicef.org/.

348 See UNICEF's mission statement at https://www.unicef.org/about/who/index_mission.html

2.7.6 The UN Educational, Scientific and Cultural Organization (UNESCO)

UNESCO undertakes a wide range of initiatives that may be relevant to minority culture, religion and in particular education helping to combat racism, discrimination and intolerance.[349] Members of minorities can submit complaints under a confidential UNESCO procedure if rights falling within UNESCO's mandate have been violated. Article 1 of UNESCO's constitution defines its purpose as being:

> to contribute to peace and security by promoting collaboration among the nations through education, science and culture in order to further universal respect for justice, for the rule of law and for the human rights and fundamental freedoms which are affirmed for the peoples of the world, without distinction of race, sex, language or religion by the Charter of the UN.[350]

UNESCO has protected "intangible cultural heritage" since 1989, pursuant to Recommendations on the Safeguarding of Traditional Culture and Folklore.[351] Intangible cultural heritage includes oral heritage, languages, performing arts and festive events as well as social and environmental practices, knowledge systems and beliefs.[352] This is because for minority populations, intangible cultural heritage is an essential source of identity.

In recent years, important conventions on the promotion of the cultural rights were adopted by UNESCO. The 2003 UNESCO Convention for the Safeguarding of the Intangible Cultural Heritage promotes practice, representation, expression, knowledge, and skills which communities, groups, and in some cases individuals, recognize as part of their cultural heritage.[353]

The 2005 UNESCO Convention on the Protection and Promotion of the Diversity of Cultural Expressions[354] encourages States to incorporate into national

---

349 See Pamphlet No.11 of the UN Guide for Minorities The protection of the Rights of Minorities and the UN Educational, Scientific and Cultural Organization.

350 "UNESCO's Constitution," UNESCO Official Page, 2019, https://bit.ly/2JeAfMz.

351 For further information see UNESO Document, "Recommendations on the Safeguarding of Traditional Culture and Folklore," 15 November 1989 and Janet Blake, *Intangible Cultural Heritage - Working definitions* (Italy: UNESCO, March 2001).

352 See Article 2 of Convention for the Safeguarding of the Intangible Cultural Heritage 2003.

353 See Convention for the Safeguarding of the Intangible Cultural Heritage, 2003, https://bit.ly/2pAIqt1.

354 UNESCO's Convention on the Protection and Promotion of the Diversity of Cultural Expressions https://bit.ly/3mhUhVr.

and international development strategies and adopt measures aimed to protect and promote a wide range of cultures within their territory. The Convention emphasizes the importance of respect for all cultures, including minority ones, and requires States to create environments in which minority cultures can thrive. The Convention's prologue recognizes the importance of minority or indigenous cultures, and Article 2 (3) stresses the cultural dignity of minorities.[355]

Most of UNESCO's human rights work is promotional, but as mentioned earlier, it has had a complaints procedure in place since 1978 regarding alleged violations of human rights.[356] The procedure applies only to human rights violations within UNESCO's fields of competence, namely education, science, culture and information.[357] Most minority concerns relate to language, culture and education, and in theory it should be simple to identify issues that fall within the jurisdiction of UNESCO. Individuals, groups and NGOs may complain to UNESCO concerning human rights violations if they are the victims themselves, or if they have only reliable knowledge of relevant violations. All communications are examined in private by the Committee on Conventions and Recommendations of the Executive Board, a group of Government representatives which meets twice each year. The Committee may ask the State concerned to provide more information or answer questions on the problem. The Committee is not an international tribunal and will attempt to resolve the problem before it goes any further to achieve a mutually satisfactory settlement, rather than to decide whether or not a violation has occurred. The Committee reports to the Executive Board, offering decisions or recommendations, and the complainant and the State concerned are informed of the Committee's decisions.

2.7.7 The UN Development Programme (UNDP)

There are marginalized minorities in all countries where the UNDP operates.[358] The experience shows that minority members make a fundamental contribution to human development as strategic partners.[359] Therefore, the inclusion of

355 Article 2.3 states: "The protection and promotion of the diversity of cultural expressions presuppose the recognition of equal dignity of and respect for all cultures, including the cultures of persons belonging to minorities and indigenous peoples."

356 Klaus Hüfner, *How to File Complaints on Human Rights Violations, A Manual for Individuals and NGOs* (German Commission for UNESCO and the United Nations Association of Germany, 2010), pp. 144-159.

357 Ibid.

358 UNDP, Marginalised Minorities, p. 2.

359 Ibid.

minorities further improves UNDP efforts to achieve fair and sustainable human development for all. Minorities have different perspectives on development, and their input helps find sustainable and effective solutions to development challenges. The UNDP analzses the situation in each minority group setting, examining the root causes and impacts of marginalization and exclusion. It reviews State policy frameworks for protecting minorities and identifies areas that need work or improvement, contributing to electoral reforms, decentralization, policing and democratic governance.[360]

To summarize, the two sections above have discussed in detail the relevant UN legal documents as well as several UN human rights bodies and mechanisms that protect the world's minorities. Its specific relevance to Armenian minorities will be discussed in the appropriate chapters, but it is against this background that the UN and other international bodies strive to protect all minorities. The fact that many initiatives set out under the mandates discussed above eventually fail is both disappointing and worrying. The example of Syria proves that there are many different interpretations of the norms, laws and responsibilities laid down by the UN. Armenian minorities in different countries - particularly in Lebanon and Turkey - who may be struggling for their rights to existence, identity, non-discrimination, and equality as well as effective participation, tend to achieve varying degrees of success under the above-mentioned laws and mechanisms, depending on the countries in which these rights are exercised.

2.8 Minority Rights in Europe

This section will address minority rights in the contexts of CoE, the Organization for Security and Co-operation in Europe (OSCE) and the European Union (EU). This is mainly because Turkey is a member State to CoE and OSCE with subsequent legal obligations and is also a candidate for full membership to the EU.

2.8.1 The Council of Europe (CoE)

Protecting national minorities has always been high on the CoE's agenda. The Council's actions are based on the idea that protecting minorities is part of the more universal protection of human rights.[361] Its focus is on setting standards, encouraging intergovernmental co-operation, and introducing activities for the

360 Ibid, pp. 3-4.
361 Geoff Gilbert, "The Council of Europe and Minority Rights," *Human Rights Quarterly*, 18:1 (February 1996).

development and consolidation of State stability and national confidence. This agenda reaches many related policy fields, involving the co-operation of various national and international bodies. Relevant CoE documents and mechanisms include the ECHR, the FCPNM, the European Charter for Regional or Minority Languages, the European social charter which will be discussed accordingly.

2.8.1.1 The European Convention on Human Rights (ECHR)

The Convention includes no specific provisions on minorities, although several ECHR rights are relevant for minority rights. This can explain, why ECtHR has been dealing with plenty of cases involving minorities. The only specific reference to minorities is to be found in Article 14 of the ECHR:

> "The enjoyment of the rights and freedoms set forth in this Convention shall be secured without discrimination on any ground such as sex, race, colour, language, religion, political or other opinion, national or social origin, association with a national minority, property, birth or other status."[362]

With regards to the right of minorities to protect and promote their identity, the ECtHR *inter alia* has considered for example the registration of a minority within a State. In this context, the leading case is *Sidiropoulos v. Greece,*[363] which is considered by many authors as ushering in a new legal attitude to minority rights.[364] In this case, the applicants belonged to the northern Greek Macedonian minority founded an association called "the Home of Macedonian Civilisation."[365] They complained when the Greek authorities refused to register the association, saying it had separatist intentions. The Strasbourg judges ruled unanimously that any assertion that the applicants' association represented a danger to Greece's territorial integrity was mere suspicion, and there was no justification to restrict the association's freedom. Perhaps the most relevant factor in this judgment was the Court's reference to OSCE Documents allowing the formation of associations to protect minority groups' cultural and spiritual identity. This helps interpret the Convention, because in deciding whether different treatment is reasonably justified, the ECtHR stresses trends that reflect, amongst

362 Article 14 of ECHR.

363 Sidiropoulos and Others v. Greece (57/1997/841/1047), 10.07.1998, Case no 26695/95.

364 Roberta Medda-Windischer, "The European Court of Human Rights and Minority Rights," *Journal of European Integration*, 25:3 (2003), p. 250.

365 Sidiropoulos and Others v. Greece.

other things, the commitments States have undertaken through the adoption of international instruments.

Another aspect that the Court recognized is that freedom of association is important for minority populations, and that as laid down in the preamble to the FCPNM: "A pluralist and genuinely democratic society should not only respect the ethnic, cultural, linguistic and religious identity of each person belonging to a national minority, but also create appropriate conditions enabling them to express, preserve and develop this identity."[366]

In this context, the case of *Sidiropoulos v. Greece* (presented above) confirms this approach. Upon examining the alleged violation of Article 11 ECtHR found a violation. It did not accept Greece's submissions, and concluded that:

> "Territorial integrity, national security and public order were not threatened by the activities of an association whose aim was to promote a region's culture, even supposing that it also aimed partly to promote the culture of a minority; the existence of minorities and different cultures in a country was a historical fact that a "democratic society" had to tolerate and even protect and support according to the principles of international law."[367]

From this it can also be concluded that forming an association in order to express and promote minority identities may be instrumental in helping minorities to preserve and uphold their rights. However, The Court has never recognized any right to the protection of cultural and natural heritage and stated in a recent decision that "the applicant has failed to point to any case of this Court where it has held that Article 8 gives rise to a general right to protection of cultural heritage of the nature contended for in the present case."[368]

However, in its judgment on the case of *Kozacıoğlu v. Turkey*, the Court held that failing to consider the unique architectural or historical characteristics of a listed building when assessing compensation for its expropriation amounted to a violation of Article 1 of Protocol No.1, as far as it imposes a disproportionate burden on the applicant.[369] Thus, the Grand Chamber underlined the necessity of protecting cultural heritage when assessing the legitimate aim of the interference.[370]

---

366 See the Framework Convention for the Protection of National Minorities, https://bit.ly/2pxc1mZ.

367 Sidiropoulos and others v. Greece, para. 41.

368 Syllogos Ton Athinaion v. The United Kingdom (Dec.), Application No.48259/15, 31.05.2016.

369 Kozacıoğlu v. Turkey [GC], Application No.2334/03, 19.02.2009 para. 82.

370 Ibid, para. 53.

Freedom of assembly (Article 11 of the ECHR) also protects the rights of minorities to hold peaceful meetings, such as those held in commemoration of specific and significant cultural or religious events. In the case *Barankevich v. Russia*,[371] the town authorities based on a 1988 decree applicable at that time, refused to allow a minority religion (Christ's Grace Church of Evangelical Christians) to hold a religious service in a public park, this is because that service would provoke public disorder within the majority, who practiced other religions.[372] The Court stated that there was no justification for interfering with the rights of the followers of a religion merely because they were a minority group. In addition, The Court also noted that there was no indication that those participating in the service would incite or resort to violence, nor any indication that the local authorities had considered adopting measures necessary for neutralizing the threat of a violent counter-demonstration and allowing the assembly to take place peacefully; instead they had "den[ied] the applicant the possibility of exercising his rights to freedom of religion and assembly."[373] Consequently, the ECHR found violations of Article 11 of the ECHR interpreted in the light of Article 9.

Individual rights to freedom of religion (Article 9) represent another essential element of identity and includes the right to manifest and celebrate religion. In the case of *Kokkinais V. Greece*, the defendant was convicted for proselytism contrary to Greek law. The Court found a breach of Article 9 and held that:

> "As enshrined in Article 9, freedom of thought, conscience and religion is one of the foundations of a 'democratic society' within the meaning of the Convention. It is, in its religious dimension, one of the most vital elements that go to make up the identity of believers and their conception of life... While religious freedom is primarily a matter of individual conscience, it also implies, inter alia, freedom to "manifest [one's] religion." Bearing witness in words and deeds is bound up with the existence of religious convictions."[374]

According to Article 9, freedom to manifest one's religion is not only exercisable in community with others, "in public" and within the circle of those whose faith one shares but can also be asserted "alone" and "in private". Furthermore, Article 9 includes in principle the right to try to convince one's neighbor, for example

371 Barankevich v. Russia Final, Application No.10519/03 Final, Eur. Ct. H.R., 26.10. 2007.

372 Ibid, para.35.

373 Ibid, para. 33.

374 Kokkinakis v. Greece, Application No.14308/88, 25.05.1993, Para. 31.

through "teaching" which is in line with, "freedom to change [one's] religion or belief," enshrined in the Article.[375]

In addition, allowing a minority the required degree of control over community religious issues is another aspect of freedom of religion.[376] The Court holds that the State must not interfere in the internal affairs of the religious communities.[377] The case of *Hasan and Chaush v. Bulgaria* concerns the autonomy of religious groups, and came about because of the forced replacement by the Bulgarian authorities of the Muslim community leadership. The applicants asserted that protection against unjustified State interference is an essential aspect of religious freedom. The Court upheld this assertion, concluding that freedom of religion would become vulnerable if the organizational life of the community was not protected by Article 9 of the Convention.[378] In other words, the State may limit manifestation of a minority's religious matters only if it is "prescribed by law," directed at one or more of the legitimate aims in paragraph 2 of Article 9 and "necessary in a democratic society" for achieving them.[379]

With regards to the freedom of expression, the Court holds that historical truth is an integral aspect of freedom of expression, protected by Article 10 of the Convention. Minorities should be at liberty to explore their heritage, although it is not the court's role to arbitrate on underlying historical issues, which remain subject to historical interpretation (See *Chauvy and Others v. France*).[380] In addition, the Court supports State efforts to debate their own histories openly and dispassionately (See *Monnat v. Switzerland*).[381] The Court will however examine issues relating to established historical facts such as the Holocaust.[382] The

375 Ibid.

376 Laura-Maria Crăciunean, "The European Court of Human Rights' approach to cultural rights and cultural diversity," *Revista Română de Drept Comparat*, 2, (2013), pp. 236-237.

377 Hasan and Chavush v. Bulgaria, Application No.30985/96, 2000.

378 Ibid, para.62.

379 Article 9.2: "Freedom to manifest one's religion or beliefs shall be subject only to such limitations as are prescribed by law and are necessary in a democratic society in the interests of public safety, for the protection of public order, health or morals, or for the protection of the rights and freedoms of others."

380 Chauvy and Others v. France, Application No.64915/01, 29.06.2004, para.69.

381 Monnat v. Switzerland, Application No.73604/01, 2006, para. 64.

382 Paolo Lobba, "Holocaust Denial before the European Court of Human Rights: Evolution of an Exceptional Regime," *The European Journal of International Law*, 26:1 (2015), pp. 235-237.

negation or revision of the Holocaust was removed from the protection of Article 10 by Article 17 which prohibited the abuse of rights (See *Lehideux and Isorni v. France*,[383] and *Garaudy v. France* (dec).[384] The Court states:

> "There can be no doubt that denying the reality of clearly established historical facts, such as the Holocaust, as the applicant does in his book, does not constitute historical research akin to a quest for the truth. The aim and the result of that approach are completely different, the real purpose being to rehabilitate the National-Socialist regime and, as a consequence, accuse the victims themselves of falsifying history. Denying crimes against humanity is therefore one of the most serious forms of racial defamation of Jews and of incitement to hatred of them. The denial or rewriting of this type of historical fact undermines the values on which the fight against racism and anti-Semitism are based and constitutes a serious threat to public order. Such acts are incompatible with democracy and human rights because they infringe the rights of others. Their proponents indisputably have designs that fall into the category of aims prohibited by Article 17 of the Convention."[385]

Such aspects are highly relevant to the freedoms of expression granted or denied in Turkey and other CoE member States – not only to Armenians, but also to others as well in reference to the case of the recognizing or denying Armenian Genocide[386] and its consequences.

Linguistic rights are also protected under rights to freedom of expression guaranteed by Article 10. For instance, in *Ulusoy and Others v. Turkey*,[387] the Court found that the ban on a Kurdish play in municipal buildings breached freedom of expression, and a ban on Kurdish language newspapers in Turkish prisons amounted to a violation of Article 10 (*Mesut Yurtsever and Others v. Turkey*).[388]

The ECtHR has also dealt with different linguistic rights guaranteed by the Convention. For instance, the right to spell names in minority language formats falls within the remit of Article 8, which guarantees respect for private and family life.[389] However the Court can set up certain restrictions favoring

383 Lehideux and Isorni v. France, 55/1997/839/1045, 1998, para.59.
384 Garaudy v. France, Application No.65831/01), 24.06.2003.
385 Ibid.
386 See Perinçek v. Switzerland, Application No. 27510/08, 15.10.2015.
387 Ulusoy and others v. Turkey, Application No. 34797/03, 03.05.2007.
388 Mesut Yurtsever and others v. Turkey, Application Nos. 14946/08, 21030/08, 24309/08 20.01.2015.
389 See Guide to Article 8 of the European Convention on Human Rights, the Right to Respect Private and Family Life, Home and Correspondence, updated on 31.08.2019, p. 58.

contracting States in view of historical, linguistic, religious and cultural barriers unique to each country in the absence of a common European denominator (see *Mentzen v. Latvia* [dec.][390]; *Bulgakov v. Ukraine*[391]; *Baylac-Ferrer and Suarez v. France* [dec.][392]). The court recalled that linguistic freedom as such is not one of the rights and freedoms governed by the Convention,[393] and confirmed that the Convention per se does not guarantee the right to use a particular language in communications with public authorities or the right to receive information in a language of one's choice.[394]

States in principle have liberty to regulate and impose the use of their official language or languages in identity papers and other official documents, for the purposes of linguistic unity. However, in *Güzel Erdagöz v. Turk*ey,[395] the Court found a breach of Article 8 on the ground that the Turkish courts had refused the applicant's request for rectification of the spelling of her forename according to its Kurdish pronunciation (she claimed to be called "Gözel," not "Güzel"). The breach was based on the fact that Turkish law did not clearly explain the extent and manner in which authorities used their discretion with regards to imposing restrictions on and rectifying forenames.[396] This will be another important issue, as members of the Armenian minority in Turkey have been forced to change their names over the past decades.

Another aspect to minority identity which can also be protected is the education of children (Article 2, Protocol 1) belonging to minority groups. However, there is no right to education in minority languages under the ECHR, unless it is a pre-existing right that the State attempts to withdraw.[397] Refusing to approve schoolbooks written in the minority's home State may in some circumstances count as a breach of the right to freedom of expression.[398] Even when the home State's books impart a different view of history and culture to that of the host State, the government must show that the undisputed censorship or blocking

390 Mentzen v. Latvia, Application No. 71074/01, 2004.

391 Bulgakov v. Ukraine, Application No. 59894/00, 2007, para.43-44.

392 Baylac-Ferrer and Suarez v. France, Application No. 27977/04, 25/09/2008.

393 "Cultural rights in the case-law of the European Court of Human Rights," Council of Europe, Research Division of ECtHR, p. 23.

394 Ibid.

395 Güzel Erdagöz v. Turkey, Application No.37483/02, 21.10.2008.

396 Ibid.

397 Pamphlet No. 7 of the UN Guide for Minorities, Minority Rights under the European Convention on Human Rights, p. 3.

398 Ibid.

of the books was done in accordance with law and pursued a legitimate aim, for instance the prevention of disorder. Then, it would be for the respondent government to demonstrate that the censorship measures were necessary in a democratic society.[399] This is another very interesting aspect of the relationship between the Armenian minority and the Turkish State which will be discussed in the respective sections below.

With regards to rights on non-discrimination and equality, the ECtHR traditionally focuses on the legitimacy of differential treatments.[400] The Court's judgments were based on formal conceptions of equality, from which analogous situations could be treated identically.[401] The Court indicated in the 1968 Belgian Linguistics case that prohibiting discrimination does not prevent States from treating groups differently in order to correct factual inequalities.[402] Moreover, the Court in the *Sejdic and Finci v Bosnia* case even added that "in certain circumstances a failure to attempt to correct inequality through different treatment may, without an objective and reasonable justification, give rise to a breach"[403] of prohibitions on discrimination. However, it was the *Thlimmenos* judgment that was considered the landmark case in establishing duties of treatment under the prohibition of discrimination.[404] *Thlimmenos* was a Jehovah's Witness who studied to become a chartered accountant, but who was unable to obtain a license because of convictions for refusing to serve in the military for religious reasons. He argued that Greek law on the licensing of chartered made no distinction between convictions due to fundamental religious rights and other convictions, and that the Greek State was thus discriminating against him on religious grounds. The Court followed this line of reasoning and concluded that:

> "...the right under Article 14 not to be discriminated against on religious grounds guaranteed under the Convention is violated when States treat people in analogous situations differently without providing objective or reasonable justifications.... However, the Court also concluded that this was not the only facet of the prohibition of

399 Ibid.

400 Kristin Henrard, "The European Court of Human Rights, Ethnic and Religious Minorities and the Two Dimensions of the Right to Equal Treatment: Jurisprudence at Different Speeds," *Nordic Journal of Human Rights*, 34:3 (2016), p. 166.

401 Ibid.

402 Relating to Certain Aspects of the Laws on the Use of Languages in Education in Belgium v. Belgium, Application no 1474/62, (23.07.1968), para. 7.

403 Sejdic and Finci v Bosnia and Herzegovina, Application Nos 27996/06 and 34836/06, 22.12.2009, para. 44.

404 Thlimmenos v Greece, Application No.34369, 1997.

> discrimination in Article 14. The right not to be discriminated against in enjoying the rights guaranteed under the Convention is also violated when States fail to treat differently people whose situations are significantly different without an objective and reasonable justification."[405]

In reference to the rights of Minority groups to participate effectively in political, cultural, religious, social, economic and public life, as Coraddetti indicates "the formal or *de facto* exclusion from participation in the political processes of the State is contrary to democratic principles."[406] It is part of the democratic process to allow diverse political projects to be proposed and debated – even those that call into question the way a State is organized, as long as they do not undermine democracy or human rights.[407]

In the case of *Sejdic and Finci v. Bosnia and Herzegovina*[408] the applicants (one Roma, one Jewish) complained that they had been prevented from standing for State elections. The Constitution of Bosnia and Herzegovina – drawn up after the Dayton Peace Agreements of 1995 – distinguished two categories of citizens: so-called "constituent peoples" (Bosnians, Croats and Serbs) and "others" (Jews, Roma and other minorities, together with those who did not declare any group affiliation). It was declared that political representatives must belong to the three constituent peoples, thereby excluding ethnic minorities. The Court agreed that this system – which was put in place during a fragile ceasefire, pursued the legitimate aim of restoring peace. However, the situation in Bosnia and Herzegovina had since improved considerably and the Court concluded that the applicants' continued ineligibility to stand for election to the House of Peoples of Bosnia and Herzegovina lacked reasonable justification.[409]

To sum up this sub-section, the above argument offers ways in which the ECHR can protect minority rights – although it is not the Convention's primary task. The Convention could be accused of addressing only a narrow range of rights, and claims may be dismissed as lying beyond the scope of the Convention. Furthermore, even when a violation is found, it is still up to the State involved to provide legal remedies to avoid future violations, such as amending any offending legislation. The Court is not an appellate court for domestic decisions

---

405 Ibid, para. 44.

406 Claudio Corradett, *Philosophical Dimensions of Human Rights: Some Contemporary Views* (Rome: Springer Science & Business Media, 29 Oct 2011), p. 256.

407 Ibid.

408 Sejdic and Finci v. Bosnia and Herzegovina.

409 Ibid.

and is only able to consider whether a State has fulfilled its obligations under the Convention, not whether it might have adopted different policies or laws.[410] Therefore, it is important to study how (or if) Turkey fulfills its obligations in terms of offering reparation or adopting new policies regarding the treatment of its Armenian minority.

2.8.1.2 The Framework Convention for the Protection of National Minorities (FCPNM)

The FCPNM represents the first legally binding instrument for the protection of national minorities.[411] The FCNM's Preamble highlights that the protection of national minorities "is essential to stability, democratic security and peace."[412] It emphasizes the components of a pluralist and genuinely democratic society and identifies the necessity for tolerance and dialogue to enrich society.[413] The Convention considers that "the protection of national minorities and of the rights and freedoms of persons belonging to those minorities forms an integral part of the international protection of human rights, and as such falls within the scope of international co-operation."[414] The word "Framework" indicates the scope for member States to translate the Convention's provisions to their specific country situation through national legislation and appropriate governmental policies.[415]

The FCPNM sets out principles and goals to ensure the protection of minorities. It contains mainly programme-type provisions setting out objectives that States must fulfill.[416] Member States undertake to promote full and effective

410 Pamphlet No. 7 of the UN Guide for Minority Rights under the European Convention on Human Rights.

411 Rainer Hofmann, "The Framework Convention for the Protection of National Minorities: An Introduction," in *The Rights of Minorities in Europe, A Commentary on the European Framework Convention for the Protection of National Minorities*, Marc Weller ed. (New York: OUP 2007), p. 3.

412 The Preamble of FCPNM.

413 Ibid.

414 Article 1 of FCPNM.

415 See CoE, Factsheet on the Framework Convention for the Protection of National Minorities, CoE official website, https://www.coe.int/en/web/minorities/fcnm-factsheet.

416 These provisions are State obligations, not individual or collective rights, leaving the States a measure of discretion in the implementation of the objectives. See. Alan Phillips, *the Framework Convention for the Protection of National Minorities: A Policy Analysis* (London: Minority Rights Group International, September 2002), p. 3.

equality for national minorities in the fields of economic, social, political, public, and cultural life, together with conditions allowing them to express, preserve and develop all cultural traditions. States must ensure freedom of assembly, association, expression, thought, conscience, religion and access to media. The Convention also provides guidelines for minorities' linguistic freedom and education rights.[417]

Moreover, the provisions of the FCPNM cover the use of the minority language in public and private, and sometimes in dealings with administrative authorities.[418] It protects the use of personal names, private information and topographical names in the minority language. The FCPNM does not define the term national minority, but rather adopts "a pragmatic approach, based on the recognition that at this stage, it is impossible to arrive at a definition capable of mustering general support of all CoE member States."[419] Each member State is therefore left with some degree of autonomy in assessing which groups are covered by the Convention within their territory. Such decisions must be made in good faith (Article 2)[420] and in accordance with fundamental principles of international law (Article 2.1),[421] including principles of self-identification (Article 3).[422] Individuals can decide whether they wish to be treated as belonging to a national minority, but their decision must be based on relevant objective criteria such as religion, language, traditions and cultural heritage.[423]

The Committee of Ministers carries out the evaluation of the implementation of the FCPNM by the party States, assisted by the Advisory Committee. States are required to submit a report summarizing legislative and other measures

---

417 Hofmann, "The Framework Convention," pp. 3-5.

418 Ibid.

419 See CoE, "Explanatory Report for the Framework Convention for the Protection of National Minorities European Treaty Series - No.157," Strasbourg, Council of Europe Publication, 1.II.1995, para. 12.

420 Article 2: "The provisions of this framework Convention shall be applied in good faith, in a spirit of understanding and tolerance and in conformity with the principles of good neighbourliness, friendly relations and co-operation between States."

421 Article 2.1: "This provision stresses the importance of the fundamental principles of international law and specifies that the protection of persons belonging to national minorities must be in accordance with these principles."

422 Article 3: "Every person belonging to a national minority shall have the right freely to choose to be treated or not to be treated as such and no disadvantage shall result from this choice or from the exercise of the rights which are connected to that choice."

423 See CoE, "Explanatory Report for the Framework Convention," para. 13.

taken to comply with the principles of the FCPNM within one year of the entry into force. Additional reports need to be submitted on a periodical basis and whenever the Committee of Ministers requests. If the State does not submit the reports, the Committee of Ministers can authorize the Advisory Committee to start the monitoring process.[424]

The Advisory Committee examines State reports and generally conducts country visits to dialogue constructively with both authorities and civil society. Following its close examination of the situation in the country, the Advisory Committee[425] adopts an Opinion,[426] which becomes the basis for a resolution[427] adopted by the Committee of Ministers with conclusions and recommendations in respect of the State concerned. Follow-up activities are promoted for the implementation of the recommendations. This monitoring mechanism has contributed to improving dialogue between governmental agencies and national minorities and prompted the adoption of new laws for the protection of national minorities and assisted States to enhance their non-discrimination legislation and practice.[428]

Some authors on the other hand claim that The FCPNM's impact is greatly diminished by a weak enforcement mechanism comprised of state authored compliance reports and non-binding recommendations from the FCPNM's monitoring body, the Advisory Committee, and the Committee of Ministers.[429]

---

424 CoE, Factsheet on the Framework Convention for the Protection of National Minorities.

425 Over the years, the Advisory Committee's Opinions have emerged as a central reference in the work of other international bodies, such as the OSCE HCNM and the EU's Agency for Fundamental Rights (FRA). See CoE, Factsheet on the Framework Convention for the Protection of National Minorities.

426 The Opinion is transmitted to the authorities concerned who have an opportunity to submit comments on this Opinion within four months after which time the comments and the Opinion are made public. Ibid.

427 The preparation of this resolution provides an opportunity for other states, including non-state parties to express themselves on the situation in the state concerned. This resolution is made public upon its adoption. See CoE, Monitoring the implementation of the Framework Convention for the Protection of National Minorities, CoE official website, https://www.coe.int/en/web/minorities/monitoring.

428 CoE, Factsheet on the Framework Convention for the Protection of National Minorities.

429 Lauren C Baillie, "Protection of Religious Minorities in Europe: The Council of Europe's Successes and Failures," *American University International Law Review*, 23:3 (2007), p. 621.

The political nature of the monitoring bodies (not judicial), the state-driven compliance system, and the incapability of other States, individuals, and groups to invoke the protection of the FCPNM hinders its efforts to ensure better protection of minorities.[430]

Nevertheless, as Henrard argues, although States are granted a wide margin of appreciation in minority sensitive areas and its monitoring/supervisory mechanism seems to be weak and politicized, the actual practice developed in such a way that the extensive state discretion has been gradually but surely circumscribed through its not legally binding mechanisms focusing on constructive and ongoing dialogue with the State authorities.[431] In addition, The FCPNM puts duties on the States beyond merely prohibiting discrimination by requesting from them to foster an environment in which minorities can flourish.[432] FCNM confirms that interpreting prohibition of discrimination and (other) general human rights in line with substantive equality and identity considerations, has the potential to achieve an adequate minority protection.[433] At the end, the FCPNM narrows the gap left by general Human Rights Conventions through acknowledging that minority protection requires not only expanded protections, but also affirmative duties of member States so minorities might flourish. Since Turkey at the time of writing this thesis neither signed nor ratified the FCNM, further analyzes will not be provided.

2.8.1.3 The European Charter for Regional or Minority Languages (the Language Charter)

CoE's European Charter for Regional or Minority Languages signed in 1992 and effective since March 1998 is the first international instrument focused exclusively on the question of language – suggests that the situation of linguistic rights is changing at least on European level.[434] The Charter sets out measures promoting the use of minority languages in public and private life, protecting and promoting minority languages in education (Article 8), judicial and

---

430 Baillie, "Protection of Religious Minorities in Europe," p. 635.

431 Kristin Henrard, "The Added Value of the Framework Convention for the Protection of National Minorities; the Two Pillars of an Adequate System of Minority Protection Revisited," in *The Framework Convention for the Protection of National Minorities: A Useful Pan-European Instrument?* (Antwerp: Intersentia, 2008), p. 115.

432 Baillie, "Protection of Religious Minorities in Europe," p. 635.

433 Henrard, "The Added Value of the Framework Convention for the Protection," p. 116.

434 Dunbar, "Minority Language Rights in International Law," p. 90.

administrative authorities and public service (Articles 9 and 10), access to media (Article 11), and cultural, economic and social activities (Article 12 and 13).[435]

The Charter goes beyond minority protection and anti-discrimination, requiring its State parties to promote the benefits of minority languages.[436] The CoE monitors the implementation of the Charter, and each party accepts the application of a minimum of thirty-five paragraphs or sub-paragraphs selected from the measures, some of which are obligatory.[437] Each party must specify the regional or minority language to which the chosen paragraphs shall apply.

Enforcement of the Charter is controlled by a committee of experts which periodically examines reports presented by the parties. Many provisions consist of several options of varying degrees of rigidity, one of which must be chosen "according to the situation of each language"[438] in policy, legislation and implementation. For example, States may choose to offer education in regional or minority languages or to provide only for the teaching of these languages.

The Charter's most important role is its legally binding State obligations to ensure minority language rights. The threat posed to minority languages is due "at least as much to the inevitably standardizing influence of modern civilization and especially of the mass media as to an unfriendly environment or a government policy of assimilation."[439] In this context, the Charter recognizes that linguistic tolerance is not enough for minority language communities, a point which is recognized explicitly in the explanatory report: "Having regard to the present weakness of some of the historical regional or minority languages of Europe [...] the mere prohibition of discrimination against their users is not a sufficient safeguard."[440] Nevertheless, the main criticism of the Charter that each State can determine for itself the languages to which the charter will apply and select their obligations "a la carte."[441] Here it is worth noting that although keen to be an active member of the CoE, Turkey as it is the case for the FCPNM, has not yet signed up the Language Charter.

---

435 See the full text of the Charter: http://www.coe.int/en/web/conventions/full-list/-/conventions/treaty/148.

436 Dunbar, "Minority Language Rights in International Law," p. 108.

437 Ibid, p. 113.

438 Article 7.1 of the Charter.

439 CoE, Explanatory Report to the European Charter for Regional or Minority Languages, European Treaty Series No.148. Strasbourg, CoE Publication, 5.11.1992.

440 Ibid.

441 Henrard, Devising an Adequate System, p. 215.

2.8.1.4 *The European Social Charter (ESC)*

The ESC is a CoE treaty that guarantees "fundamental social and economic rights as a counterpart to the European Convention on Human Rights, which refers to civil and political rights."[442] The revised ESC guarantees fundamental social and economic rights, *inter alia* protecting minorities in social and economic fields. Part V. of Article E indicates: "The enjoyment of the rights set forth in this Charter shall be secured without discrimination on any ground such as race, colour, sex, language, religion, political or other opinion, national extraction or social origin, health, association with a national minority, birth or other status."[443] Article 24.3 of ESC notes that race, color, sex, marital status, family responsibilities, pregnancy, religion, political opinion, national extraction or social origin are not valid reasons for termination of employment.[444]

The Charter imposes obligations in respect of cultural rights as they apply to the cultural rights of minorities,[445] and enshrines the right of collective complaint[446] under its provisions. It is collective in two senses. Firstly, only certain categories of trades unions, employers' organizations and NGOs may bring complaints; individuals may not. Secondly, the complaint may concern only a general situation and not an individual case.[447] The Committee's decision, which is not legally binding, is passed to the CoE's Committee of Ministers, who must adopt a resolution which may include a recommendation to a State calling upon it to take certain action, although again this is not legally binding. The collective complaints procedure strengthens the role of social partners and NGOs by enabling them to apply directly to the European Committee for Social Rights for rulings on possible non-implementation of the Charter in States which have accepted its provisions and the complaints procedure. Furthermore, complaints may be lodged before domestic remedies have been exhausted and without the claimant organization necessarily being a victim of relevant violations.[448]

---

442 See the official website of the European Social Charter: https://bit.ly/306Ak8l.

443 See the full text of the European Social Charter: shorturl.at/ruwG2.

444 Ibid.

445 David J. Harris, "Collective Complaints under the European Social Charter: Encouraging Progress?," in *International Law and Power: Perspectives on Legal Order and Justice. Essays in Honour of Colin Warbrick*, K.H. Kaikobad and M. Bohlander eds., (2009), p. 5.

446 The Collective Complaints procedure was introduced by the Additional Protocol providing for a system of collective complaints adopted in 1995.

447 Harris, "Collective Complaints under the European Social Charter," p. 5.

448 Ibid.

In addition to European social partners, certain international non-governmental organizations (INGOs) holding participatory status with the CoE and social partners at national level are entitled to lodge a collective complaint, and States may grant representative national NGOs within its jurisdiction the right to lodge complaints against it.[449] However, States can agree on which NGOs are allowed to bring collective claims, which may distort the purpose of the ESC as States might avoid granting rights to NGOs that criticize them. As of 1 May 2016, only Finland has allowed the NGOs within its jurisdiction the right to complain against it.[450] Generally speaking, when States grant this right, they may not distinguish between the national NGOs, which may only lodge complaints in respect of matters in which they have been recognized as having particular competence.[451] This means that minority rights groups or institutions can bring collective claims to the ESC once they have been given permission to do so. This process weakens the collective claims procedure since it is dependent on the State's willingness to grant or withhold this permission.

2.8.1.5 European Commission against Racism and Intolerance (ECRI)

ECRI also makes an important contribution to the fight against discrimination. The ECRI[452] combats racism, discrimination, xenophobia, antisemitism, and intolerance in Europe from a human rights perspective based on ECtHR rulings, additional protocols and related case-law.[453] Its objectives are to review the effectiveness of member States' anti-racism legislation and policies, to propose further action at local, national and European level, to work with member States in the formulation of general policy recommendations and to study as well as if necessary to reinforce international legislation.

The ECRI provides CoE States with advice on tackling racism and intolerance. It examines in each country's legal framework on combating discrimination, supports independent bodies to assist victims of racism and intolerance, and studies the situation of vulnerable groups in education, employment, housing, health, and access to goods and services. It considers political and public debate

449 Ibid.

450 Collective complaints procedure - European Social Charter (CoE, 2017), p7.

451 Ibid.

452 See the full text of the European Commission against Racism and Intolerance (ECRI): https://bit.ly/2DG00Q2.

453 Article 1 of ECRI's Statute.

surrounding relevant issues for these groups and monitors situations within States where potential trouble spots could occur.[454]

2.8.2 Organization for Security and Co-operation in Europe (OSCE)

An important breakthrough for Europe came in 1990, when a review of the Conference on Security and Co-operation in Europe – now the Organization for Security and Co-operation in Europe (OSCE) – adopted a declaration on human rights, democracy, the rule of law and minority rights. The Copenhagen Document commits now the 57 participating OSCE States to a range of minority rights.[455] Its impact has been significant and has helped pave the way for the FCPNM which was adopted by the CoE in 1994.[456]

The Copenhagen Document compels States to protect the ethnic, cultural, linguistic and religious identity of minorities within their borders and promote their identities.[457] As a tool to protect ethnic identity the Document contains the first reference to autonomous administrations in any international agreement.[458] Several Articles affirm the rights of minorities to use their mother tongue in public and private, to receive instruction in their mother tongue and to use it before public authorities. One key provision (Article 30) establishes clear links between minority rights and the law, affirming that democracy and an independent judiciary are prerequisites for resolving rights-related problems, meaning that rights can be used, not merely held.

454 ECRI Mandate, see https://bit.ly/2R9ufH4.

455 See Document of the Copenhagen Meeting of the Conference on the Human Dimension of the CSCE: https://bit.ly/2P3rMv4.

456 Hofmann, "The Framework Convention for the Protection of National Minorities," pp. 2-3.

457 Paragraph 33: "Participating States will protect the ethnic, cultural, linguistic and religious identity of national minorities on their territory and create conditions for the promotion of that identity," in Document of the Copenhagen Meeting of the Conference on the Human Dimension of the CSCE.

458 Paragraph 35: "The Participating States note the efforts undertaken to protect and create conditions for the promotion of the ethnic, cultural, linguistic and religious identity of certain national minorities by establishing, as one of the possible means to achieve these aims, appropriate local or autonomous administrations corresponding to the specific historical and territorial circumstances of such minorities and in accordance with the policies of the State concerned."

In other words, the minority rights instruments of the OSCE goes beyond the ICCPR and ECHR to set rigid legal obligations on States regarding the protection of all minorities and their languages. There are negative and positive obligation to these rulings. Negative aspects involve guarantees of freedom from assimilation. Article 32 provides that: "Persons belonging to national minorities have the right freely to express, preserve and develop their ethnic, cultural, linguistic or religious identity and to maintain and develop their culture in all its aspects, free of any attempts at assimilation against their will."[459]

While a number of OSCE field operations focus on positive aspects of the Copenhagen Document, these include better protection and integration of minorities into public life, educational reform and training, enhancing equitable representation and strengthening the use of minority languages, building confidence among communities and fostering regional networks for minorities to protect their rights.[460]

In this context, post of the OSCE High Commissioner on National Minorities, established in 1992, is important. Since that year, the High Commissioner's recommendations have provided guidelines and clarifications to help define the domestic policies of participating States (including Turkey) and maintain peace between majorities and minorities. Implementing the commitments of the Copenhagen Document remains high on the OSCE agenda.

The High Commissioner aims to de-escalate tensions involving minorities, especially where such tensions could lead to conflict.[461] The High Commissioner addresses inter-ethnic tension and considers long-term structural concerns to prevent it, alerting the OSCE if a situation threatens to exceed diplomatic containment. In other words, the High Commissioner's role is conflict prevention, although the HCNM frequently reminds States of their obligations to minorities; failure to respect them provides significant ethnic tensions that may lead to conflict.[462] So far the HCNM has issued two "early warnings" as defined in the mandate: on the former Yugoslavian Republic of Macedonia in 1999 and on Kyrgyzstan in 2010.[463] The High Commissioner can become involved in minority issues without the approval of the Permanent Council or the State concerned.

---

459 Article 32 of OSCE's Copenhagen Document.

460 Dmitri Alechkevitch, "The Copenhagen Document and minority rights in 20 years of the Copenhagen Document," *OSCE Magazine* 2 (2010), p. 29.

461 See the official website of the OSCE High Commissioner on National Minorities, http://www.osce.org/hcnm.

462 Ibid.

463 See the Mandate of OSCE: http://www.osce.org/hcnm/107878.

The HCNM's policy represents an active approach in comparison to judicial or monitoring processes, which are more limited and seek legal remedies for rights issues. However, political and legal approaches to minority protection complement each other to provide a more comprehensive response to protect OSCE member States' minorities. Thus, the HCNM can play a role in assisting Turkey to move towards full implementation and compliance with current standards of the protection and promotion of minority rights which will be discussed accordingly in the relevant sections below.

2.8.2.1 The Bolzano/Bozen Recommendations on National Minorities in Inter-State Relations & Explanatory Notes

These are a set of recommendations by the HNCM on national minorities in inter-state relations based on HCNM experiences and the advice of international experts. They seek to provide OSCE participating States with guidelines on how best to manage inter-state issues concerning national minorities.[464] The recommendations cover general principles and State obligations to national minorities based on multilateral and bilateral agreements and other mechanisms. The Recommendations are accompanied by a set of explanatory notes which define with greater clarity how States can pursue their own interests as well as those of national minorities abroad without jeopardizing peaceful relations with other, usually neighboring States.[465] The Recommendations are elaborated in the Explanatory Notes, guided by principles of international law and extensive HCNM experience. They are intended to clarify State mechanisms to support and extend benefits to their national minorities residing in other countries in ways that do not conflict with inter-ethnic or bilateral relations. The recommendations underline the dual responsibility of States to protect and promote the rights of minorities under their jurisdiction whilst acting as a responsible member of the international community regarding minorities under the jurisdiction of another State.

The Recommendations (nineteen in total) are divided into four sections: general principles, State obligations to national minorities, benefits accorded by States to persons belonging to national minorities abroad, and multilateral and bilateral inter-state recommendations.[466] They offer both practical and

---

464 OSCE, The Bolzano/Bozen Recommendations on National Minorities in Inter-State Relations & Explanatory Note. OSCE Publication, June 2008.

465 Ibid.

466 Ibid.

normative guidance in accordance with sovereignty, human and minority rights and international responsibility principles. The Recommendations' main tenets stipulate that under international law, the host State is responsible for the protection of minority rights, although home States and other countries with whom minority groups are linked or with which they share a common cultural heritage also have some interest.[467] However, home States have no right under international law to exercise jurisdiction over people residing in other States.[468] In other words, the Recommendations distinguish rights from interests. States can only pursue interests in extending benefits to minorities abroad via consultation with the host State of residence, with due respect being paid to principles of territorial integrity, sovereignty and good relations. In addition, States should ensure that policies regarding their national minorities abroad do not affect the rights or safety of host States or fuel separatist tendencies.

States may extend benefits to citizens residing abroad, but only by respecting these aforementioned principles. Benefits may include cultural and educational opportunities, work permits, etc., but these should be provided on a non-discriminatory basis.[469] The host State should not obstruct such benefits, as long as they are consistent with international law.[470] This is particularly important in respect of the Armenian minority in Turkey. Armenia and Turkey are both member States to OSCE, although there are no diplomatic relations between the two countries. Turkey now hosts more fifty thousand of Armenian economic migrants[471] who retain their Armenian citizenship and their status as a minority group. This will be dealt with in more detail in the relevant section of the thesis.

2.8.2.2 The Lund Recommendations on the Effective Participation of National Minorities in Public Life

This set of HCNM recommendations on the effective participation of national minorities in public life was based on the experiences of the OSCE and the advice of internationally recognized experts. The Lund recommendations[472] offered

467 Francesco Palermo and Natalie Sabanadze eds., *National Minorities in Inter-State Relations* (Boston: Brill, Nijhoff, 2011), pp. 216-220.

468 Ibid.

469 OSCE, The Bolzano/Bozen Recommendations on National Minorities.

470 Ibid.

471 Gabriele Rasuly-Paleczek and Maria Six-Hohenbalken, *Migration and Its Impact on Armenia A Field Practice* (Vienna: University of Vienna, 2017), p. 6.

472 OSCE, The Lund Recommendations on the Effective Participation of National Minorities in Public Life (OSCE Publication, 1999).

guidance to participating States on encouraging the participation of national minorities within their States. The recommendations cover principles such as participation in decision-making at central, regional and local levels, elections and consultative bodies, self-governance in terms of territory, and guarantees covering legal and constitutional safeguards. The recommendations encourage States on how best to alleviate national and minority tensions; they are accompanied by a set of explanatory notes, but they remain advisory and there are no powers to enforce conflict prevention.

2.8.2.3 The Hague Recommendations Regarding the Education Rights of National Minorities

The Hague Recommendations, adopted in 1996, are another set of HCNM's Recommendations focusing on the education rights of national minorities. The 21 recommendations provide guidance to OSCE participating States on how best to ensure the education rights of national minorities within their borders. They cover the spirit of international instruments, measures and resources, decentralization and participation, public and private institutions, minority education at primary and secondary levels, minority education in vocational schools, minority education at the tertiary level and curriculum development. The Recommendations are accompanied by a set of explanatory notes.[473] Inter alia, the explanatory notes argues that regardless of the level of education access afforded by States, it should not be established in an arbitrary fashion. States should consider the needs of national minorities as communicated and expressed by the communities in question. On the other hand, national minorities should ensure that their demands are reasonable, legitimate and proportional for their own numerical strength, their demographic density in any given region (or regions), as well as their capacity to contribute to the durability of these services and facilities over time.[474]

2.8.2.4 The Oslo Recommendations Regarding the Linguistic Rights of National Minorities.

These recommendations adopted in 1998, seek to provide guidance to OSCE participating States on how best to ensure the linguistic rights of national minorities

473 OSCE, The Hague Recommendations Regarding the Education Rights of National Minorities & Explanatory Notes (OSCE Publication, October 1996).

474 Ibid, pp. 10-11.

within their borders. These 21 recommendations cover names, religion, community life and non-governmental organizations, the media, economic life, administrative authorities and public services, independent national institutions, the judicial authorities and deprivation of liberty.[475] The recommendations are accompanied by a set of explanatory notes which *inter alia* clarifies that:

> "The Oslo Recommendations Regarding the Linguistic Rights of National Minorities must be seen in a balanced context of full participation in the wider society. The Recommendations do not propose an isolationist approach, but rather one which encourages a balance between the right of persons belonging to national minorities to maintain and develop their own identity, culture and language and the necessity of ensuring that they are able to integrate into the wider society as full and equal members."[476]

The Oslo Recommendations are useful reference to develop State policies and laws that contribute to a successful implementation of the language rights of persons belonging to national minorities, particularly in the public domain.

2.8.2.5 The Graz Recommendations on Access to Justice and National Minorities

Adopted in 2017, relatively new set of recommendations try to fill the gap on the little work that has been done so far on access to justice for persons belonging to national minorities from a conflict prevention perspective.[477] This is because access to justice for national minorities is relevant to conflict prevention within and between States. The Graz Recommendations include the principles underpinning access to justice for national minorities (i.e., rule of law, non-discrimination, and equality, including gender equality, the right to a fair hearing within a reasonable time and by an independent and impartial body established by law, the right to legal assistance and the right to effective remedy).[478] In addition, Graz Recommendations cover the scope of access to justice; language and cultural considerations; legal assistance; reflecting diversity in institutions related to justice (Recommendation No.5); trust between law-enforcement agencies and minority communities; enforcing the law in an impartial and non-discriminatory manner (Recommendation No.8); ensuring victim support services and witness

475 OSCE, Oslo Recommendations Regarding the Linguistic Rights of National Minorities (OSCE Publication, February 1998).

476 Ibid. pp. 13-14,

477 OSCE, The Graz Recommendations on Access to Justice and National Minorities (OSCE Publication, November 2017).

478 Recommendation No.1 of the Graz Recommendations.

protection measures are sensitive to minority needs; executing court orders and judgments effectively, impartially and within a reasonable time (Recommendation No.8); treating minorities in detention or prison with respect (Recommendation No.10); and providing effective redress in cases of human rights violations as a result of inter-ethnic conflict (Recommendation no 10).

In this context, as Zannier says:

> "The Graz Recommendations construe the concept of access to justice as being something much broader than merely access to courts. For this reason, they encourage States to also establish effective and independent human rights institutions, such as Ombudspersons and similar, whose mandate could efficiently complement that of the judicial bodies in ensuring access to justice for all members of society. The Recommendations also touch upon the composition of courts, tribunals, prosecution offices and law-enforcement bodies, and emphasize that in order for these State bodies to be representative of all segments of society, and to enjoy wide legitimacy and everyone's trust, they must reflect the diversity of society, and therefore also employ persons of minority background among their personnel."[479]

In other words, the more well established and independent human rights institutions are developed within a State, the more effective access to justice for minorities can be achieved. In addition, 'adequate representation' of minorities in different justice related bodies, seems to be crucial to ensure diversity within the justice system of the state.

2.8.3 The European Union (EU)

The European Union used to have a limited role in protecting minorities and has relied on general international human rights law and the general principles common to the traditions of its member States.[480] However as Gabriel Toggenburg chooses to term a 'de-economization' moment of European integration which started in the 1990s[481] has changed this situation. While the political relevance of protecting national minorities remained high, there was no provision

---

479 Lamberto Zannier, Keynote Speech by OSCE High Commissioner on National Minorities on the occasion of the launch of the Graz Recommendations on Access to Justice and National Minorities, OSCE, Austria, 14.11.2017, https://bit.ly/2Rbxxtc.

480 Daniel Šmihula, "National Minorities in the Law of the EC/EU," *Romanian Journal of European Affairs*, 8:3 (September 2008), pp. 51-52.

481 Gabriel N. Toggenburg, "A Rough Orientation through a Delicate Relationship: The European Union's Endeavours for (its) Minorities," *European integration Online Papers 4* (2000), p. 3.

in primary law on minority rights until the Amsterdam Treaty – apart from the general prohibition of discrimination – that would have guaranteed minorities specific rights and protection.[482] Article 2.7 of the Amsterdam Treaty, although it does not refer to minorities per se, enables the European Council to "take appropriate action to combat discrimination based on sex, racial or ethnic origin, religion or belief, disability, age or sexual orientation."[483] Based on this Article the European Council adopted Council directive 2000/43/EC implementing equal treatment in principle between persons irrespective of racial or ethnic origin.[484]

However, during the adoption of EU's Charter of Fundamental Rights,[485] member States abandoned the variant suggested by the European Parliament, which included specific minority rights that would go beyond non-discrimination into the EU's fundamental rights.[486] As a result there are only two Articles dealing with minority issues in the Charter: Article 21 prohibiting discrimination on the basis of membership of a national minority, and Article 22 which stipulates that the EU respects cultural, religious and linguistic diversity.[487] In this context, the Commission has no powers as regards minorities, and has no legislative powers relating to their recognition.[488] EU countries retain the power to take decisions about minorities, but must guarantee that fundamental rights are protected in accordance with international law.[489]

---

482 Claudia Tavani, *Collective Rights and the Cultural Identity of the Roma: A Case Study of Italy* (Boston: Martinus Nijhoff Publishers, Sep 2012), p. 77.

483 Treaty of Amsterdam amending the Treaty on European Union, the Treaties establishing the European Communities and certain related acts - Contents, Official Journal C 340, 10/11/1997.

484 See European Council Directive 2000/43/EC of 29.06.2000 implementing the principle of equal treatment between persons irrespective of racial or ethnic origin, https://bit.ly/35V2fuN.

485 See the full text of the EU Charter of Fundamental Rights: https://bit.ly/2YTtR2b.

486 Guido Schwellnus, *Much ado about nothing? Minority Protection and the EU Charter of Fundamental Rights* (Web papers on Constitutionalism & Governance beyond the State, 2001, No 5), p. 7.

487 Discussions of the reasons for this lie beyond the remit of this thesis, but it is possible that European legislators recognized that Europe has so many different minority groups (and may come to contain more in time) that positive legislation may invite problems in the future.

488 Viktors Gusevs, Petition 0714/2013 (Latvian) on Personal problem, European Parliament Document, 31.03.2014, https://bit.ly/35XrLzy.

489 Ibid.

Nevertheless, currently, there is a strong trend in Europe towards improving minority rights, an approach that is reflected in Article 2 of the EU Treaty which stresses that "Respect for the rights of persons belonging to minorities"[490] is one of the values of the EU. This approach can be clearly seen in external relations and in conditions set out for cooperation with or accession to the EU.[491] In order to join the EU, aspirant countries must reach certain benchmarks on their treatment of minorities.[492] Turkey's longstanding attempts to join the EU have not yet proved successful,[493] partly because of its record in the treatment of its minorities – including the Armenian minorities which form the focus of this thesis.

In summarizing the European laws on respecting, protecting and fulfilling minority rights, it can be argued that despite the complexity of organizations and entities which deal with minority rights and the mechanisms which are already in place, member State parties in EU, CoE and OSCE still enjoy a wide margin of discretion in determining their laws and policies towards minorities. However, European monitoring mechanisms seems to be better than existing international ones, but they are still far from being ideal in terms of protecting minorities and fulfilling their rights.

2.9 Minority Rights in the Arab Region

The following section will address the minority rights within the Arab region and Muslim majority States by analyzing the Organisation of the Islamic Conference and the LAS and its relevant bodies. This is because Lebanon and Turkey are OIC member States and therefore undertake relevant commitments derived from the OIC charter, while for the LAS and its relevant bodies, Lebanon is a

490 Treaty on European Union - Title I: Common Provisions - Article 2, *Official Journal* 115, 09/05/2008.

491 Bruno De Witte and Eniko Horvath, "The Many Faces of Minority Policy in the European Union," in *Synergies in Minority Protection: European and International Law Perspective*, Kritin Henrard and Robert Dunbar eds. (UK: Cambridge University press, 2008), p. 377.

492 Sergio Carrera et al., *Towards a Comprehensive EU Protection System for Minorities* (Policy Department C: Citizens' Rights and Constitutional Affairs European Parliament, 2017), Abstract, p. 1.

493 See Communication from the Commission to the European Parliament, the Council, the European Economic and Social Committee and the Committee of the Regions 2019 Communication on EU Enlargement Policy, p. 6, https://bit.ly/2JJDkDF.

member State and has treaty obligations derived from the Charter of LAS and its subordinate bodies' Statues.

Before starting the section, since almost all Arab region States are Muslim majority countries, it is worth mentioning that the first relevant document about minorities in the Islamic history is the Charter of Medina,[494] a constitutional contract consisting of 47 chapters[495] between the Prophet Muhammad and the people of Medina, which guaranteed the religious liberty of all, regardless of faith; dates back to 622 CE.[496] The Charter of Madina mainly administers the coexistence of Madina's multi-tribal inhabitants[497] contained provisions on a number of the principles of constitutional contractual citizenship, including justice and equality before the law, property ownership, freedom of movement, mutual solidarity and defence.[498] When it comes to minority rights arguments, many Muslim scholars refer to the Charter of Medina as the foundation and the first document dealing with minorities in Muslim majority countries.[499] Even the recent "Marrakesh Declaration" (elaborated below) is based on the Charter of Medina to provide an authentic model of citizenship.

2.9.1 The Organization of the Islamic Conference (OIC)

The OIC is the second largest international and inter-governmental organization after the UN, and as of 2017 has a membership of 57 States.[500] The Organization has a permanent delegation to the UN, and supports the Universal

494 See, Saïd Amir Arjomand, "The Constitution of Medina: A Sociolegal Interpretation of Muhammad's Acts of Foundation of the Umma," *International Journal of Middle East Studies*, 41:4 (2009), pp. 555-575.

495 Muhasyaroh, "Da'wah Model of Prophet Muhammad in Madina," *Qudus International Journal of Islamic Studies*, 2:1 (01.08.2016), pp. 54-57.

496 See Harry Munt, *The Holy City of Madina: Sacred Space in Early Islamic Arabia* (New York: Cambridge University Press, 2014).

497 Arjomand, "The Constitution of Madina."

498 See the Executive Summary of the Marrakesh Declaration on the Rights of Religious Minorities in Predominantly Muslim Majority Communities 25-27.01.2016, https://bit.ly/3eAY9hd.

499 Mohammed Raissouni, "Rights of Minorities in Islam, Report of the 9th Regular Session of the OIC Independent Permanent Human Rights Commission," OIC, 2016, p. 46. https://bit.ly/3lkPOAR.

500 Majid Bozorgmehri, "The Human Rights in OIC, A Gradual Movement but in Progress," *Journal of Politics and Law*; 10:2 (2017).

Islamic Declaration of Human Rights (adopted in 1981),[501] Cairo Declaration on Human Rights in Islam (adopted in 1990)[502] and the Beirut Declaration of Regional Protection of Human Rights (adopted in 2003)[503] as guidance for member States on the subject of human rights and their compliance and compatibility with Shari'a Law.[504]

OIC have no jurisdiction or even concrete proposals concerning minority rights in the member States, but their focus is more on protecting Muslim minorities in non-Muslim Countries. Article 1(16) of the OIC charter States that the OIC's purpose is "to safeguard the rights of Muslim communities and minorities in non-Member States and to assist Muslim minorities and communities outside Member States to preserve their dignity, cultural and religious identity."[505] Ironically the OIC is more focused and interested to promote Muslim minorities and their rights within non-member States than it is to minorities living within its own member States. Nevertheless, this reality has started to change gradually in many Muslim majority countries and the "Marrakesh Declaration on the Rights of Religious Minorities in Predominantly Muslim Majority Communities" (Marrakesh Declaration) adopted in January 2016 by more than 300 Muslim religious leaders, heads of States, and scholars is a good example of the new approach.

2.9.2 Marrakesh Declaration

The Marrakesh Declaration on the Rights of Religious Minorities in Predominantly Muslim Majority countries, also known as "Marrakesh Declaration," is relatively new document in the field. In the aftermath of several incidents brutally targeting minorities in predominantly Muslim countries, in 2016, King Muhammad VI. of Morocco hosted a conference "Religious Minorities in Muslim Lands: It's Legal Framework and a Call to Action" in Marrakesh organized by the

501 See the full text of the Universal Islamic Declaration of Human Rights, 19.09.1981, https://bit.ly/3p7uJfe.

502 See the full text of the Cairo Declaration on Human Rights in Islam, OIC, 05.08.1990, https://bit.ly/3n5GnFP.

503 See the Full text of the Beirut Declaration on the Regional Protection of Human Rights published by the Cairo Institute for Human Rights Studies and the Association for the Defence of Human Rights and Liberty, Beirut, Lebanon, 2003, https://bit.ly/354ATEY.

504 Bozorgmehri, "The Human Rights in OIC."

505 See the Charter of OIC: https://www.oic-oci.org/page/?p_id=53&p_ref=27&lan=en.

Ministry of Endowments and Islamic Affairs of the Kingdom of Morocco and the Forum for Promoting Peace in Muslim Societies, based in the U.A.E.

Prominent Muslim scholars, ministers, muftis, governmental officials and representatives of religious minorities in the Arab world attended the conference to deeply examine what entails the rights of religious minorities in Muslim world theoretically and practically.[506] The conference focused on "grounding the discussion surrounding religious minorities in Muslim lands in Sacred Law utilizing its general principles, objectives, and adjudicative methodology; exploring the historical dimensions and contexts related to the issue; and examining the impact of domestic and international rights."[507] The conference resulted in a declaration "providing full protection for the rights and liberties to all religious groups in a civilized manner that eschews coercion, bias, and arrogance."[508] In addition, the declaration *inter alia* calls upon:

> "Muslim scholars and intellectuals to develop a jurisprudence of the concept of citizenship which is inclusive of diverse groups. Such jurisprudence shall be rooted in Islamic tradition and principles and mindful of global changes, urge Muslim educational institutions and authorities to conduct a courageous review of educational curricula that addresses honestly and electively any material that instigates aggression and extremism, leads to war and chaos, and results in the destruction of our shared societies; call upon politicians and decision makers to take the political and legal steps necessary to establish a constitutional contractual relationship among its citizens, and to support all formulations and initiatives that aim to fortify relations and understanding among the various religious groups in the Muslim World."[509]

The Marrakesh Declaration was welcomed by many scholars[510] and international organizations[511] and considered a progressive step towards recognizing

506 See the official website of the Marrakesh Declaration: http://www.marrakeshdeclaration.org/about.html.

507 Ibid.

508 See the Executive Summary of the Marrakesh Declaration.

509 Ibid.

510 Around 300 scholars participated in the conference, giving gave consensus to the Marrakesh Declaration, see "On the Marrakesh Declaration and Freedom of Religion or Belief," United States Mission to OSCE, 03.03.2016, https://osce.usmission.gov/on-the-marrakesh-declaration-and-freedom-of-religion-or-belief-statement-at-the-pc/.

511 See Susan Hayward, "Understanding and Extending the Marrakesh Declaration in Policy and Practice," *United States Institute of Peace*, September 2016, https://bit.ly/381tkyv and "KAICIID Secretary General Welcomes Declaration on the Protection of Religious Minorities from Marrakesh Conference," KAICIID International Dialogue Center, 27.01.2016, https://bit.ly/2U6qqm0.

and protecting the rights of religious minorities in Muslim and Arab majority countries. Nevertheless, many commentators rightly demanded that tangible legal actions should follow the Declaration.[512] In addition, it is worth mentioning, that the Marrakesh Declaration deals only with religious minorities and does not consider the rights of national, ethnic and linguistic minorities. This is another indicator that national, ethnic and linguistic minorities in Muslim and Arab majority countries still need full recognition and consideration.

2.9.3 The League of Arab States

LAS is the first regional intergovernmental organization of independent Arab States officially established in 1945 by seven newly independent Arab States.[513] Currently, 22 Arab States are member to LAS. Its Charter does not specify any criteria for membership except that the State needs to be an independent Arab State – without defining what an Arab country is. As Rishmawi argues:

> "the founding Charter reflects the fact that it was created by newly independent Arab States that, at the time, did not want a super-organization that replaced or overshadowed their own States. They sought a balance between maintaining strong individual independent States, on the one hand, and the desire for a pan-Arab formation, with the possibility of bilateral or multilateral inter-Arab States formations, on the other."[514]

Article 2 of LAS States that its purpose is: the strengthening of the relations between the member States, the coordination of their policies in order to achieve cooperation between them and to safeguard their independence and sovereignty; and a general concern with the affairs and interests of the Arab countries.[515] The same Article identifies cooperation in six areas: economic and financial affairs; communications; cultural affairs; nationality, passports and visas; social affairs; and health affairs. It is important to highlight that the inclusion of provisions on the protection of human rights as one of LAS' founding principles remains one of the fundamental pending amendments to its Charter.[516]

---

512 Ayman Ibrahim, "History suggests Marrakesh Declaration no guarantee of religious freedom," *Religious News Service*, 01.02.2016, https://bit.ly/32lGchG.

513 Egypt, Iraq, Transjordan (which became Jordan in 1946), Lebanon, Saudi Arabia, Syria and North Yemen (which became Yemen after its unification with South Yemen).

514 Mervat Rishmawi, "The league of Arab States Human Rights Standards and Mechanisms," *Open Society Foundation*, 2015, p. 9.

515 Article 2 of LAS Charter.

516 The draft, which is pending adaptation by LAS member States, integrates recognition of human rights protection as one of the Arab League's founding principles.

This section will examine the Arab Independent Permanent Commission of Human Rights, The Arab Charter on Human Rights, The Arab Human Rights Committee as well as The Arab Court on Human Rights and their relevance to minority rights within Arab States.

2.7.3.1 *The Arab Independent Permanent Committee of Human Rights (APCHR)*

The APCHR was created in 1968 to stablish rules of cooperation among Arab States in the domain of human rights, to draft human rights related treaties, to provide recommendations and to promote the implementation of human rights agreements.[517] The APCHR is a body made up of representatives of Arab League Member States (similar to the Human Rights Council of the UN).[518] However, the internal regulations of the APCHR makes no reference on dealing with internationally agreed human rights when they are incompatible with Islamic values.[519] Many human rights organizations, and academics believe that the Permanent Committee is more of a political body,[520] and its narrow mandate prevents it from effectively engaging in human rights. The Permanent Committee can study matters referred to it by the LAS Council, the Secretary General or member States, and its recommendations are not binding.[521]

The Permanent Committee has no mechanism for considering the human rights situation in member States (like the Universal Periodic Review Mechanism of the UN Human Rights Council, for example).[522] It is unable to make resolutions against Arab States in which human rights are not respected, neither does it have any special procedures such as Special Rapporteurs, experts or working groups.[523] For these reasons, the Permanent Committee has proved ineffective

517 Internal Regulations of the APCHR adopted by Resolution 6826, Regular Session 1285 of the Council of Ministers of Foreign Affairs, September 2007.
518 Rishmawi, "The league of Arab States Human Rights Standards and Mechanisms." pp. 27-28.
519 Internal Regulations of the APCHR.
520 Joshua Castellino and Kathleen A. Cavanaugh, *Minority Rights in the Middle East* (UK: OUP, 2013), p. 75.
521 Rishmawi, "The league of Arab States Human Rights Standards and Mechanisms."
522 ibid.
523 "The Arab League and Human Rights: Challenges Ahead," Regional Seminar held in Cairo on 16-17.02.2013, (Open Society Foundations-Arab Regional Office, the Swedish International Development Cooperation Agency (SIDA), Irish Aid and the Norwegian Ministry of Foreign Affairs, May 2013), https://bit.ly/3p8KnqE.

in addressing human rights concerns in the Arab region.[524] The lack of human rights enforcement mechanisms in the LAS needs critical addressing.[525]

2.7.3.2 The Arab Charter on Human Rights & the Arab Human Rights Committee

The Arab Charter on Human Rights (ACHR) – and the treaty body established to supervise its implementation, the Arab Human Rights Committee (AHRC)[526] – is a comparatively unknown mechanism.[527] There are no provisions in its Charter for individual or State complaint mechanisms,[528] and the Committee focusses instead on monitoring the Charter's implementation by State parties through national reports, comments and recommendations, and interpreting its provisions during the course of this process.[529]

the 1994 version of the Charter fell far short of international standards and was widely criticized.[530] In 2001, the APCHR recommended revisions to the 1994 Charter,[531] which had never entered into force.[532] In March 2003 the LAS Council agreed and gave the modernization task to the APCHR.[533] In 2004 the APCHR offered an improved version,[534] which represented an effort to 'modernise' the LAS,[535] but it was still inconsistent with international human rights law – despite the fact that all LAS member States are party to at least one UN human rights treaty.[536] This effectively meant that agreeing to a regional treaty

524 Ibid.

525 Wael Allam, "The Arab Charter on Human Rights: Main Features," *Arab Law Quarterly*, 28:1 (2014), p. 62.

526 Article 45 & 48 of the ACHR.

527 Rishmawi, "The Arab Charter on Human Rights and the League of Arab States," *Human Rights Review*, 10:1 (2010), pp. 169-178.

528 Wael Allam, "The Arab Charter on Human Rights: Main Features."

529 Ibid.

530 Rishmawi, "The Arab Charter on Human Rights and the League of Arab States."

531 The Charter was adopted by the LAS Council, Resolution No. 5437 in 1994. See the Arab Charter of Human Rights of 1994: https://bit.ly/2rfgBri.

532 LAS Council Resolution No. 6089, 12.03.2001.

533 LAS Council Resolution No. 6302, 24.03.2003.

534 See the full text of the League of Arab States, Arab Charter on Human Rights, 22.05.2004, reprinted in 12 Int'l Hum. Rts. Rep. 893 (2005), entered into force on 15.03.2008.

535 See Hassiba Hadj Sahraoui, "Modernising the Arab Charter on Human Rights," *Yearbook of the International Commission of Jurists*, (2004), pp. 339-348.

536 Rishmawi, "The Arab Charter on Human Rights and the League of Arab States."

with standards below the UN's universal human rights values would be inconsistent with States' obligations under international human rights law.

The latest ACHR consists of a preamble and 4 sections, including 53 Articles covering all civil, political, economic, social and cultural rights and implementation mechanisms.[537] It covers individual rights, State obligations, supervisory mechanisms and State reports, as well as ratification procedures and enforcement.[538] Article 1 details the aims of the Charter, which sets human rights at the "centre of the key national concerns" of Arab States, focusing on the concept that all human rights are universal, indivisible, interdependent and interrelated.[539] State parties must ensure that the rights contained in the Charter are put into effect nationally via legislative or advisory measures.[540]

With regards to minority rights, the ACHR States in its Article 25 that:

> "Persons belonging to minorities shall not be deprived of their right to enjoy their culture to use their language or to follow the teachings of their religions. The enjoyment of these rights is regulated by law."[541]

The negative formulation of the Article indicates that the States should refrain from interfering to the rights of minorities to enjoy their culture or to practice their religion. No positive obligations in terms of protecting and fulfilling these rights are mentioned. In addition, interestingly, the Article does not refer to specific minority groups, such as national or ethnic, religious and linguistic minorities and leaves the door open for interpretations, although "to follow the teaching of their religions" implicitly might be referred to religious minorities. Moreover, as Muller argues: "the addition of "the exercise of these rights shall

537 Konstantinos D Magliveras, "Completing the Institutional Mechanism of the Arab Human Rights System, The Arab Court of Human Rights," *International Human Rights Law Review*, 6 (2017), pp. 37-38.

538 Ibid.

539 Article 1 of ACHR inter-alia states: "The present Charter seeks, within the context of the national identity of the Arab States and their sense of belonging to a common civilization, to achieve the following aims: 1. To place human rights at the centre of the key national concerns of Arab States, making them lofty and fundamental ideals that shape the will of the individual in Arab States and enable him to improve his life in accordance with noble human values."

540 Article 44 of ACHR of 2004 states: The States parties undertake to adopt, in conformity with their constitutional procedures and with the provisions of the present Charter, whatever legislative or non-legislative measures that may be necessary to give effect to the rights set forth herein."

541 Article 25 of ACHR of 2004.

be governed by law" sets out the task for States to embody these within national laws... [and] leaves the exact regulation of these rights up to national legislation, which – depending on the actual implementation – poses a risk to the effectiveness of this right."[542]

There is also an important affirmation of international human rights in which the rights of minorities are mentioned. Article 43 provides that:

> "Nothing in this Charter may be construed or interpreted as impairing the rights and freedoms protected by the domestic laws of the States parties or those set forth in the international and regional human rights instruments which the States parties have adopted or ratified, including the rights of women, the rights of the child and the rights of persons belonging to minorities."[543]

Nevertheless, some problematic provisions still exist within the Charter.[544] Many economic and social rights, such as the right to work (Article 34), the right to free basic health care (Article 39.1), and the right to free education at the primary and basic levels (Article 41.2) are only granted to citizens, rather than all people coming under the jurisdiction of the State. Meanwhile, other rights contained in the Charter depend upon interpretations of Islamic Shari'a law. For example, Article 3.3 provides that "[m]en and women are equal in respect of human dignity, rights and obligations within the framework of the positive discrimination established in favour of women by the Islamic Shari'a, other divine laws and by applicable laws and legal instruments."[545]

Article 30 also allows the imposition of limitations on freedom of thought, conscience and religion, if these are "provided for by law,"[546] ratifying the possibility of limitations which UN and EU charters have already overcome. Article 18 of the ICCPR distinguishes between freedom of thought, conscience and religion, and the manifestation of religious beliefs. Only this second aspect may be subject 'to such limitations as are prescribed by law and are necessary to protect public safety, order, health, or morals or the fundamental rights and freedoms of others.[547]

---

542 Hanna Siebenrock, *The Enforceability of Human Rights in the States of the Arab League* (Diploma-Thesis, Institut für Europa- und Völkerrecht, 2018).

543 Article 43 of the ACHR of 2004.

544 Magliveras, "Completing the Institutional Mechanism of the Arab Human Rights System," pp. 38-39.

545 Article 3(3) of The ACHR of 2004.

546 Article 30 of the ACHR of 2004.

547 Article 18.3 of ICCPR.

While the 2004 Charter reflects a larger degree of acceptance of international human rights law and standards,[548] the reluctance of certain Arab States is demonstrated by their reservations regarding UN human rights treaties.[549] In terms of minorities and their freedom of thought, culture, religious and ethnic preferences, it is obvious that the Charter lags behind UN and EU initiatives in the area, and such discrepancies will have severe effects on minorities living in majority Muslim and Arab States. In addition, one of the biggest challenges that AHRC members may face in the immediate future is how willing they are to free themselves from the perception that the Arab States represent an autonomous religious and cultural specificity rather than a more ambitious global region, and that they – as a Committee – must frame their comments, conclusions and recommendations on human rights accordingly.

2.8.2.3 The Arab Court on Human Rights (ACtHR)

In 2014 September, the Council of the LAS, Ministers of Foreign Affairs, set up the ACtHR under its Statutes.[550] Although the court has not yet opened,[551] it has been receiving considerable criticism for its inaccessibility and lack of impartiality or effectiveness.[552]

Restricted access is one of the main criticisms.[553] Article 19 of the Statute states that Court access is only available to State parties, and gives member States

548 Konstantinos D. Magliveras and Gino Joseph Naldi, "The Arab Court of Human Rights: A Study in Impotence," *Revue Québécoise de droit international*, 29:2 (2016), p. 153.

549 For further details see Ratification of 18 International Human Rights Treaties, https://indicators.ohchr.org/.

550 The Council of Ministers of Foreign Affairs of LAS, Decision No. 7790, 07.09.2014.

551 It was opened for ratification in November 2014 through the LAS (press release, 04.11.2014), and in 2016 Saudi Arabia was the first country to ratify the statute (see "Arab League Secretary General Welcomes Saudi Arabia's Ratification on the Statute of Arab Court for Human Rights," *Saudi Press Agency*, 24.06.2016, https://bit.ly/2NTKzwj.

552 "Arab League's Human Rights Court will not bring justice to victims of violations," International Commission of Jurists, Press Release, 2014, https://bit.ly/2I7rTWF and "Proposed Arab Court of Human Rights: An empty vessel without substantial changes to the draft statute," Human Rights Watch, 06.06.2014, https://bit.ly/356JDuf.

553 International Commission of Jurists, *The Arab Court of Human Rights: A Flawed Statute for an Ineffective Court* (Switzerland: International Commission of Jurists, 2015), pp. 26-27.

the discretionary option of allowing registered and state-approved Civil Society Organizations to present cases on behalf of individuals.[554] It does not grant individuals the right of direct access to the Court – a right that is fundamental to the functioning of any court that seeks to protect individual rights.[555] This severely hampers the Court's effectiveness, as experience from other human rights bodies shows that States rarely employ complaints mechanisms against each other in issues relating to human rights.[556] Political considerations tend to prevent States from acting on behalf of victims of other States.[557]

Many international and regional NGOs have expressed their concerns that the Statute is "a gross departure from the human rights courts established in other regions of the world."[558] The Court Statute contains provisions that would seriously reduce the Court's ability to perform as a guarantor of rights.[559] It is therefore very important that the Statute Articles relating to accessibility/admissibility criteria are amended, as well as those relating to the provisions of the draft Statute, the independence of the Court and its judges and the applicable law and jurisdiction of the Court. These amendments might help to meet international human rights standards and serve as an effective judicial process.[560]

The journey towards human rights protection in the Arab world has been a long one. There remains a strong and valid argument that regional instruments and mechanisms for human and minority rights are still not well established and crystalized within the Arab and Muslim worlds.[561] Populations in many Arab

554 Article 19: "The right to access the Court 1: The State Party whose citizen claims to be a victim of a human rights violation has the right to access the Court, provided that both the claimant State and the Defendant State are party to this Statute, or they have accepted the jurisdiction of the Court as determined by Article 20 of the Statute." 2: State parties can accept, when ratifying or acceding to the Statute or at any time later, that one or more NGOs that are accredited and working in the field of human rights in the State whose subject claims to be a victim of a human rights violation has access to the Court.

555 International Commission of Jurists, *The Arab Court of Human Rights*, p. 6.

556 Ibid, p. 5.

557 Ibid.

558 Human Rights Watch, "Proposed Arab Court of Human Rights: An empty vessel."

559 Ibid.

560 International Commission of Jurists, "The Arab Court of Human Rights: A Flawed Statute," pp. 26-27.

561 Fida Hammami, *The Arab Charter on Human Rights: The Task Still Unfinished* (Master's Thesis, Irish Centre for Human Rights National University of Ireland Galway, 2013), p. 7.

and Muslim States continue to struggle for the recognition of their fundamental civil rights – and this is without even beginning to consider the rights of minorities within those States. The struggles have their roots in social injustice, marginalization and lack of rights protection. These factors have an obvious effect on the treatment of Armenian monitories in predominantly Islamic and Arab States, which this thesis will exemplify using Turkey and Lebanon as case studies.

2.10 Concluding Remarks on Minority Rights under International, as well as Europe and Arab Regions

Currently, minority rights at international and regional levels are mainly clustered under four rights: the right to existence, the right to identity, the right to equality and not discrimination and the right to participation. Although rights to existence, equality and non-discrimination are firmly rooted in legally binding international conventions and treaties, discrimination and lack of adequate protection remain a widespread challenge to minorities in all regions of the world.[562] For the right to existence, international law requires States to prevent and punish attacks on racial, ethnic and religious minorities as well as to provide protection beyond the basic duty not to destroy or deliberately weaken them. It also demands respect for and protection of their religious and cultural heritage, and other essential aspects of their group identity, including buildings such as libraries, churches, mosques, temples and synagogues.[563] Minority protection confirms that religious, cultural, and linguistic affiliations are essential features of what it means to be human.[564]

Regarding the preservation of minority identities, as well as fulfilling minorities' rights to equality, non-discrimination and effective participation, it can be argued that these rights help shape minority identities and interrelate them with other human rights to construct an adequate system of minority protection. All implementing instruments of non-discrimination principles are highly relevant to minorities.[565] Positive measures are required –in order to identify minority

562 UN Document, Guidance Note of the Secretary-General on Racial Discrimination and Protection of Minorities, 2013, http://www.ohchr.org/Documents/Issues/Minorities/GuidanceNoteRacialDiscriminationMinorities.pdf.

563 Human Rights Council, "Note by the Special Rapporteur on Minority Issues, Rita Izsák, on preventing and addressing violence and atrocity crimes targeted against minorities," UN Doc. A/HRC/FMI/2014/2 https://bit.ly/2RlhtFr

564 Macklem, "Minority Rights in International Law."

565 Henrard, Devising an Adequate System, pp. 8-11.

needs and terminate inequality. Additionally, creating conditions conducive to the effective participation in the political, social, economic and cultural life of the State serves to prevent conflict and facilitate development, peaceful coexistence and democratic governance.[566]

The arguments described in this chapter lead to conclude that legal frameworks on minority rights are firstly essential and secondly insufficient. UN and European frameworks lack legally binding implementation mechanisms, and Arab States' own frameworks are insufficient, ill-focused and misapplied. Resolute and specialized institutional legal mechanisms need to be put in place at all levels to facilitate legislative and policy development and the design, implementation and monitoring of minority-related programmes. The soft approach exemplified by international or regional organizations such as OSCE emphasizing partnership, dialogue, and cooperation is a way forward in what is an extremely troublesome issue in the realm of minority rights, but sometimes there is no alternative to hard law.[567]

In the final analysis, as long as the implementation of minority rights at the universal level is subject to many escape clauses, weak monitoring mechanisms and only to quasi-judicial review, it seems political pressure remains one of the most effective avenues for addressing minority grievances and improving their record on minority protection.[568] There is no one-size-fits-all solution to minority issues. Each country has a unique set of historical and contemporary circumstances that create different conditions and opportunities for addressing the problems of minorities. This is true of Lebanon and Turkey. Each has its unique historical and contemporary conditions and contexts that will be discussed at length in the relevant chapters. Their treatment of Armenian minorities will shed a great deal of light on the issues discussed theoretically in this chapter. The many different charters and frameworks that have been set up under three spheres of influence – the UN, the CoE, the OSCE, the EU, and the Arab & Islamic States have been discussed at length here as a necessary prerequisite that sets the scene for the Armenian experience. The following chapters will investigate the unique problems facing the Armenians based on their historical context and their treatment in modern society and the Middle East in general and by virtue of empirical case studies in Lebanon and Turkey in particular.

---

566 Human Rights Council, Report of the independent expert on minority issues, Gay McDougall, Thirteenth Session, 07.01.2010, UN Doc. A/HRC/13/23.

567 Jane Wright, "Minority Groups, Autonomy, and Self-Determination," p. 629.

568 Ibid.

3 The Rights of Armenian Minority in Lebanon

3.1 Lebanese Legal and Political Regimes

3.1.1 Brief History

Lebanon was established in 1920 and gained independence in 1943.[569] Despite its autonomy since the sixteenth century, Mount Lebanon, the base that underpins the Lebanese State, was an integral part of Syria under Ottoman empire, and its status as a separate entity was only established in 1920 in favor of Lebanon under the French mandate.[570]

Ottoman rulers manipulated local religious elites to maintain power over the province.[571] Ruling through powerful Druze families, although quasi-independent Druze and Maronite regions remained beyond governmental control. Later Ottoman mismanagement, European reforms and rivalries between Druze and Maronites brought ruthless conflict between the two communities in Mount Lebanon.[572] After local battles during the 1860s, the Maronites gained autonomy under European powers.[573] Christian domination in Mount Lebanon was challenged by a well-established Druze community that played a significant role in the history of the Mountain. The dynamic between the Maronites and Druze in Mount Lebanon made Lebanon different from other Middle Eastern mandated territories.

After the WWI, Rowe argues that Lebanon "was effectively created for Christians by the French colonial Mandate."[574] The confessional system "privilege[d]

569 Fawwaz Traboulsi, *A History of Modern Lebanon* - Second Edition (UK: Pluto, 2012), p. 88-89.

570 Castellino and Cavanaugh, *Minority Rights in the Middle East*, p. 339.

571 "Religion and Conflict, "Case Study Series Lebanon: The Persistence of Sectarian Conflict," Berkley Center for Religion, Peace, and World Affairs, 2013, https://bit.ly/3l74eEx.

572 Ibid.

573 Judith Harik, "Shaykh al-'Aql and the Druze of Mount Lebanon: Conflict and Accommodation," *Middle Eastern Studies*, 30:3 (July 1994), pp. 461-486.

574 Paul Rowe, "The Sheep and the Goats? Christian Groups in Lebanon and Egypt," in *Nationalism and Minority Identities in Islamic Societies*, M. Shatzmiller ed. (Montreal: McGill-Queens UP, 2005), p. 94.

the Christian populations and created a political system that was secular and sectarian."[575] As a minority rights model, Lebanon owes much to this system, which rooted identity politics. Although the system endured, the entrepreneurial power of elites within sectarian communities maintained it, as it does with the system itself.[576] The sectarianism of Lebanese history has become part of the national project upon which Lebanon was built as a State comprising different communities (*Tai'fs*).[577] Sectarianism remains integral to Lebanese politics.

From Lebanon's perspective, modern consociationalism is a modern manifestation of the *Millet* system,[578] and the modern State appears to have had little impact in shaping its unified national identity. The system resulted from inter-sectarian bargains between Lebanon's minority elites and anchored to Lebanon's political system under the 1943 National Pact.[579] Through this system, groups developed their identities further, retaining customs and practices with an autonomy characterizing Ottoman rule, creating community-oriented identities that were guaranteed and legitimized throughout French colonial rule.[580] Some Muslim communities sought closer association with the Arabism of Syria, while others accepted a multi-confessional Lebanese polity, hence creating a tension.

However, the National Pact directed tension into politics rather than violence, and competing communities involved themselves in national stability. This phenomenon continued until Jamal Abdel Nasser's pan-Arabism unrest swept the region, a US-led intervention in 1958 supported Lebanon's government, but by the late 1960s, the National Pact had become outmoded, and Lebanon suffered regional instability.[581] Demographics were changing due to a decline in Maronite numbers and political compromise under the National Pact became ineffective. Meanwhile Palestinian nationalism, waves of refugees and external violence from the Israeli-Palestinian conflict were making themselves felt.[582]

By the 1970s, the system was breaking down, and armed Christian militias fought attempts by the PLO to seize Lebanon. These militias were united under the Lebanese Forces umbrella in 1976. The PLO was determined to establish a

575 Ibid.
576 Ibid.
577 Ussama Makdisi, "The Modernity of Sectarianism in Lebanon," *Middle Ease Report Middle East Research and Information Project*, 200 (1996), p. 25.
578 Ibid.
579 Castellino and Cavanaugh, *Minority Rights in the Middle East*, p. 336.
580 Ibid.
581 Traboulsi, *A History of Modern Lebanon*, pp. 129-138.
582 Ibid.

Lebanese sanctuary to avoid repeating the Jordanian Black September in 1970[583] which resulted in expulsion from Jordan. In this radicalized climate, Sunni leaders attempted to use the PLO's presence to increase their political power. Lebanese Sunni groups armed themselves, competing against Christians and each other. Armed groups targeted rival religious civilians and civilians from their own community who rejected the militia's views.[584]

The Lebanese Civil War began in 1975, when a Maronite armed group opened fire on a bus full of civilians in response to the attempted assassination of a Maronite militia leader by PLO-affiliated people. Sectarian tensions were running high, due to the arrival of hundreds of thousands of PLO-related refugees in southern Lebanon. To avoid a PLO takeover, Syria entered the conflict in June 1976, resulting in a division of Lebanon into zones controlled by Syria, the PLO and Maronite militias.[585] The civil war continued until 1990, resulting in over 100,000 deaths[586] and the destruction of Lebanese infrastructure.[587] Under Syrian pressure, a quorum of Lebanese deputies from the 1972 Parliament met in Tai'f (Saudi Arabia) in 1989, agreeing new formula to replace the National Pact. The Tai'f Agreement proposed reducing the Maronite presidency to a titular power, vesting executive power with the half-Muslim, half-Christian cabinet and the Prime Minister, enlarging the Chamber of Deputies, ensuring a 50:50 Christian/Muslim split and abolishing political confessionalism. The Tai's agreement entrenched Syrian influence in Lebanon.[588] It did not repair a divided society. Arab intervention and war-weariness ended the conflict, but the Tai'f Agreement rectified representational groups that had become unbalanced through gerrymandering.[589]

In this context, population demographics are controversial because of the historical premise negotiated by the first Lebanese Constitution of 1926. Later, under French rule, Lebanon's informal constitution 'The National Pact' was based on its official census of 1932.[590] Of a population of 785,543, Christians

583 For further information see: "Fifty years ago: Black September for PLO," *France24*, 15.09.2020, https://bit.ly/2OcSzsf.

584 Religion and Conflict, "Case Study Series Lebanon," 2013, p. 5.

585 Ibid.

586 Castellino and Cavanaugh, *Minority Rights in the Middle East*, p. 343.

587 Sune Haugbolle, "The Historiography and the Memory of the Lebanese Civil War," *SciencesPo*, online paper, 2011, https://bit.ly/2SXX0Vi.

588 "World Directory of Minorities and Indigenous Peoples - Lebanon," *Minority Rights Group International*, June 2008, https://bit.ly/2QbwKb8.

589 Makdisi, "The Modernity of Sectarianism in Lebanon," p. 26.

590 Castellino and Cavanaugh, *Minority Rights in the Middle East*, p. 350.

comprised 52 % (Maronites 29 %, Greek Orthodox 10 %, Greek Catholics 6 %, Armenians 4 %, Latins, Protestants and others 3 %) and Muslims 48 % (Sunnis 22 %, Shias 19 %, Druze 7 %).[591] The territorial changes made by the French to Mount Lebanon augmented the country's territorial dimension and influenced population dynamics. Here the population was mostly Christian and Druze, but coastal towns such as Tripoli, Tyre, Sidon and the Beqaa Valley included large segments of Sunni Muslims. Beirut had a Shia, Greek Orthodox and an Armenian population.

Meanwhile, many refugees from persecution in neighboring States immigrated to Lebanon, including Kurds, Shia and Chaldeans from Iraq and Coptic Christians from Egypt and Sudan. Currently, there are no official records, although a study conducted by 'Statistics Lebanon', a Beirut-based private research firm, found that Lebanon's population now numbers 6,229,794 million[592]; Muslims make up around 54 % (27 % Sunni, 27 % Shia). Christians have declined to 41 % (21 % Maronites, 8 % Greek Orthodox, 5 % Greek Catholic, 6.5 % others). Druze make up approximately 5.6 % of the population, and Alawites number between 40,000 and 120,000.[593]

Demographically, Lebanon can be considered as a melting-pot for minorities, in which all religions and sects are regarded as minorities, with 18 officially recognized religious sects/groups including four Muslim, twelve Christian, Druze and Judaism.[594] The Lebanese have therefore created a power-sharing political system that is consociational. The polarized Tai'f Agreement calls for cross-community power sharing between Christian and Muslim groups, vetoes to ensure that significant decisions will only be made with their agreement, proportionality rules applied throughout government and the civil service and a

591 Minority Rights Group International, "World Directory of Minorities and Indigenous Peoples – Lebanon."

592 "Lebanon Demographics Profile 2019," Index Mundi, online resource, 2019, https://bit.ly/2AhnVVa

593 Leila Nicolas, "Minority Rights in Arab Levant: Between Extremism and the Envisioned Future Regional System," Fordham University, NY, June 2016, p. 17.

594 According to Law No. 553 dated 24 July 1996 which amended Annex 1 of Decision No. 60 Law and Regulation of 13 March 1936 on Religions in Lebanon, the recognized religious sects in Lebanon are: 1-Alawite, 2-Armenian Catholic, 3-Armenian Orthodox, 4-Assyrian Church of the East, 5-Chaldean Catholic, 6-Copts, 7-Druze, 8-Greek Catholic, 9-Greek Orthodox, 10-Isma'ili, 11-Jewish, 12-Maronite, 13-Protestant, 14-Roman Catholic, 15-Sunni, 16-Shi'a, 17-Syriac Catholic, 18-Syriac Orthodox.

high level of cultural and legal autonomy for the eighteen officially recognized religious communities.[595]

3.1.2 The Power Sharing System in Lebanon

Lebanon is a parliamentary democratic republic.[596] To preserve the balance among the 18 religious and confessional communities, legislature seats are traditionally pre-allocated to specific numbers from each community.[597] The 2017 electoral law prescribes that seats in the country's 128-member legislature should be divided equally between Christian and Muslim deputies.[598] The same law pre-allocates the 64 Christian seats to pre-specified numbers of Maronites, Greek Orthodox, Greek Catholics, Orthodox Armenians, Armenian Catholics and Evangelicals (Protestants). The remaining Christian communities are allocated a single minority parliamentary seat.[599]

The executive, the distribution of government portfolios and the Council of Ministers are not strictly defined, but are agreed proportionally to the number of seats held by various religious sects.[600] Unlike standard presidencies, the incumbent Maronite politician who acquires presidency is not elected, but must gain the support of a weighted majority of two-thirds of the Chamber of Deputies (72 representatives).[601] The president then nominates a Sunni candidate as Prime Minister, and both must then consult the Chamber of Deputies and win support from the Shi'a Speaker of Parliament prior to confirming the appointment.[602] Since the Speaker is also subject to parliamentary approval,[603] the result is that

---

595 David Russell and Nadim Shehadi, "Power Sharing and National Reconciliation: The Case of Lebanon," in *Power Sharing: New Challenges for Divided Societies* (London: Pluto Press 2005), pp. 138-152.

596 Lebanese Constitution Preamble Paragraph (C): "Lebanon's Constitution of 1926 with Amendments through 2004," translated by Fouad Fahmy Shafik (constitution), and Abed Awad (Law No.462), OUP. Constitution Prject.org, https://bit.ly/36RL7HK.

597 See Article 24 of the Lebanese Constitution.

598 See 2017 Parliamentary Electoral law of Lebanon, International Foundation for Electoral System, 2018, https://bit.ly/2X19jTl.

599 Ibid.

600 Michael. C. Hudson, "Trying Again: Power-Sharing in Post-Civil War Lebanon," *International Negotiation, 2:1* (1997), pp. 103–104.

601 Article 49 of the Lebanese Constitution.

602 Ibid, Article 53.

603 Ibid, Article 44.

only those politicians who appeal for support across political lines and the communal divide stand a chance of being elected to the top three posts.[604]

3.1.3 The Lebanese Constitution, the National Pact and the Tai'f Agreement

3.1.3.1 The Constitution

According to the 1926 Constitution, amended on 21 August 1990: "Lebanon is a parliamentary democratic republic based on respect for public liberties, social justice and equality of rights and duties among all citizens without discrimination."[605] In most countries, rights derive from the constitution, but in Lebanon it is important to understand the inter-sectarian National Pact or Pact of Coexistence, based on the results of the 1932 official census.[606] The prominence of the National Pact is specified in the constitution, which states: "There is no constitutional legitimacy for any authority which contradicts the 'pact of communal coexistence'."[607]

A chapter of the Lebanese Constitution is dedicated to defining citizens' rights and duties.[608] Articles 7–15 guarantee the State's obligation to protect basic rights and freedoms, particularly equality before the law in terms of civil and political rights, personal liberty, freedom of belief, education, expression (oral or written), and assembly and association.[609] As the rights and duties of citizens, these Articles amount to a constitutional bill of rights.

The Constitution guarantees equality for all citizens regardless of religious or denominational affiliation, ethnicity or political views.[610] Article 7 stipulates that: "All Lebanese shall be equal before the law, shall enjoy equal civil and political rights and shall be bound, without any distinction among them, by public obligations and duties."[611] Equality is defined in general terms and it covers all forms of discrimination on grounds of race, color, descent, national or ethnic origin.[612] However, defining equality in 'general terms' within the constitution

---

604 Hudson, "Trying Again: Power-Sharing," pp. 103–104.
605 Lebanese Constitution Preamble, Paragraph (C).
606 Castellino and Cavanaugh, *Minority Rights in the Middle East*, p. 350.
607 Lebanese Constitution Preamble [j].
608 Ibid. (Part A, chapter II.).
609 Ibid, Chapter II.
610 Ibid, Preamble Paragraph (C).
611 Ibid, Article 7.
612 "Committee on the Elimination of Racial Discrimination considers the report of Lebanon, "UN OHCHR official website, Geneva, 11.08.2016, https://bit.ly/3geVdsY.

requires articulating it in clear terms and codifying it by law, which is not the case.[613] Article 12 emphasizes that: "Every Lebanese shall have the right to hold public office."[614] Under Article 9 of the Constitution:

> "Freedom of belief is absolute. In homage to Almighty God, the State shall respect all religions and creeds and shall ensure and protect freedom of religious observance provided that such is not prejudicial to public order. The State shall also ensure respect for the personal status and religious interests of the population regardless of the religious community to which they belong."[615]

Article 9 declares freedom of conscience and seems to offer legal recognition to religions or creeds.[616] From a human rights perspective, rights holders are people, as individuals and as part of a community. Article 9 requires the State to respect all religions and denominations and guarantees respect for the status and faith of every citizen. Personal status laws therefore fall under the jurisdiction of religious communities and their courts.[617]

Meanwhile Article 13 stipulates that: "Freedom to express opinion orally or in writing, as well as freedom of the press, freedom of assembly and freedom of association, shall be guaranteed within the limits of the law."[618]

Article 10 is very relevant for minorities. This Article – on education and confessional schools – states that education shall be free unless it contravenes public order and morals or affects the dignity of any religion or sect.[619] All religious communities may run schools provided they follow the State rules regulating public instruction.[620] This provision has considerably fewer qualifications than most States, where religious education is not state-funded or is only funded for majority communities.[621]

The Lebanese Constitution recognizes other fundamental rights and freedoms, including respect for personal liberty. Article 8 of the Constitution states: "Personal freedom is guaranteed and protected by the law. No one can

---

613 Ibid.

614 Article 12 of the Lebanese Constitution.

615 Ibid, Article 13.

616 Human Rights Council, "Report of the Special Rapporteur on Freedom of Religion or Belief on His Mission to Lebanon," 30.11.2015, UN Doc. A/HRC/31/18/AD/add.1, para.10.

617 Ibid.

618 Article 13 of the Lebanese Constitution.

619 Article 10 of the Lebanese Constitution.

620 Ibid.

621 Castellino and Cavanaugh, *Minority Rights in the Middle East*, p. 356.

be arrested, jailed or suspended except according to the rules of the law." No offense can be determined, and no penalty can be imposed except according to the law. Respect for privacy is defined by Article 14 of the Constitution, which states that: "Private homes shall be inviolable and shall not be entered except in the circumstances and the manner prescribed by law." Respect for private property comes under Article 15: "Private property rights shall be protected by law. No one's property may be expropriated except on grounds of the public interest in the circumstances prescribed by law and provided that fair compensation has been paid in respect thereof."

Article 95 of the 1926 Constitution read: "As a temporary measure, and for the sake of justice and concord, the communities shall be equitably represented in public employment and in the composition of the Cabinet, such measures, however not causing prejudice to the general welfare of the State."[622] This was amended in November 1943 to read: "As a provisional measure, and for the sake of justice and amity, they shall be equitably represented in public employment and in the composition of the Ministry, provided such measures do not harm the general welfare of the State."[623] The significance of this change impacted upon the abrogation of Article 96 on 21 January 1947, which stated: "According to Article 22 and 95, the seats of the senate shall be distributed among the sects as follows: 5 Maronites; 3 Sunnis; 3 Shias; 3 orthodox; 1 catholic; 1 Druze; 1 minorities."[624]

The Article was amended after the Tai'f Agreement, stipulating that the Chamber of Deputies elect Muslims and Christians equally and abolish political confessionalism.[625] A National Council would be formed, headed by the President and including the Chamber of Deputies' President and the Prime Minister, with leading political, intellectual and social figures as members. The Council's initial tasks were to study alternatives and propose how to abolish confessionalism.[626] Meanwhile, sectarian groups should be fairly represented in the Cabinet, although confessional representation in public service and military positions would be canceled.[627] Confessional representation was to be replaced by expertise and competence. Grade one posts were excepted from this rule and

622 Lebanese Constitution of 1926, Article 95.
623 Lebanese Constitution of 1943, Article 95.
624 Lebanese Constitution of 1943, Article 96.
625 Tai'f Agreement Text, Paragraph G, Political Reform, https://bit.ly/34Pmutr.
626 Ibid.
627 Ibid, Paragraph G-a.

distributed equally between the major Christian and Muslim communities regardless of denominational affiliation.[628]

The abolition of political confessionalism thus became a national goal entrusted to a national committee. According to this formula, a constitutionally determined proportional representation system would have been established, at least as an interim measure, until an undivided Lebanon could be realized. With the abrogation of Article 96, the formula for mutual co-existence now exists beyond the Constitution in the Tai'f Agreement. However, no deadline was set, and little progress has been made in removing confessional divisions from public life, reflecting the persistence of geographic division of faith-based communities.[629]

In terms of linguistic rights, Article 11 of the Constitutions stipulates that The Arabic language is the official national language. The conditions under which the French language is to be used are determined by law."[630] No linguistic rights of minorities are considered or guaranteed by the Constitution, while the influence of the French mandate explains the reason for mentioning French.[631] Other Articles address the Lebanese system of guaranteeing minority rights to establish institutions, including those covering the Constitutional Council. The President, the Speaker of the Chamber of Deputies, the Prime Minister or any group of 10 or more Deputies are entitled to consult the Constitutional Council concerning matters of legal constitutionality.[632] Legally recognized confessional leaders can also consult the Council on matters of personal status, freedom of belief, religious practices and freedom of religious education.[633] The Council provides religious leaders the right to petition on issues pertaining to personal status, which means that community elites can directly impact the legislative agenda of the State, preventing its infringement of personal status laws.[634]

---

628 Ibid.

629 Mark Latimer, "Minority Participation and New Constitutional Law," *International Journal on Minority and Group Rights,* 12 (2005), p. 331.

630 Article 11 of the Lebanese Constitution.

631 For further information, Ballais JL et al, "The Place of the French Language in Arabic-Speaking Mediterranean," in *Handbook of the Changing World Language Map,* S. Brunn & R. Kehrein, eds. (Cham: Springer, 2018).

632 Article 19 of the Lebanese Constitution.

633 Ibid.

634 Castellino and Cavanaugh, *Minority Rights in the Middle East,* p. 357.

3.1.3.2 The National Pact

When Lebanon achieved independence in 1943, Maronite President Bishara Al-Khoury and Sunni Prime Minister Riyad Al-Sulh devised an unwritten National Pact, incorporating a confessional split that preserved the presidency for Maronites, the premiership for Sunnis, and position of speaker for Shiites.[635] The Pact distributed parliamentary seats, cabinet posts and administrative and military positions at all levels on a sectarian basis.[636] This distribution of political power still provides the framework of national and local government. The chamber was to be composed of six Christians to every five Muslims, ensuring a slight Christian majority.[637] It was a fragile basis for consensus, even if birthrates in all communities remained proportional. The National Pact was an accommodation that intensified political controversies rather than producing consensus, resulting in vertical cleavages that eventually became obstacles to the development of horizontal stratification.[638] Central cultural values were replaced by communal values.[639] The pact internally renewed consociational agreement to regulate access to public positions in a form that respected proportional representation, and externally strove to preserve a distinctive Lebanese Arab identity within the larger framework of Arab States.

3.1.3.3 The Tai'f Agreement

The first steps in Lebanon's political reconstruction were taken in October 1989 with the adoption of the Tai'f Agreement (Officially the Document of National Accord – *Wasiketh al Mithaq Al Watany*). The agreement, reached while hostilities were still raging and ratified by what remained of the 1972 Lebanese parliament, offered a formula to end the civil war.[640] Its core confirmed the

635 Thomas Collelo, *"The National Pact" in Lebanon: A Country Study (Washington*: GPO for the Library of Congress, 1987), https://bit.ly/34OYKWs.

636 Roupen Avsharian, "The Tai'f Agreement and the Lebanese Armenians," in *Armenians of Lebanon: From Past Princesses and Refugees to Present-Day Community*, Aida Boudjikian, ed. (Haigazian University and the Armenian Heritage Press, Beirut, 2009), p. 387.

637 Ibid, p. 389.

638 Castellino and Cavanaugh, *Minority Rights in the Middle East*, p. 367.

639 Ibid.

640 Nicola Migliorino, (Re)Constructing Armenia in Lebanon and Syria Ethno-Cultural Diversity and the State in the Aftermath of a Refugee Crisis (USA: Berghahn Publications, 2008), p. 180.

re-establishment of the National Pact, reproducing its twin propositions: Lebanon's independent identity and its pace in the wider Arab family.[641] The Agreement, and the political understandings that complemented it, also provided for the re-establishment of a consociational political system based on confessional affiliations.[642] In a recreation of the 1943 National Pact, confessionalism was declared a temporary arrangement, and its abolition a national objective. However, as Picard indicates: "the most salient feature of Lebanon's post-war political system [was] the solidification of political communitarianism."[643] Post-war consociationalism adjusted the balance, giving Christians and Muslims equal representation, reinforcing the cabinet's executive powers at the expense of the President's.[644]

The Tai'f Agreement provided a legal framework encompassing domestic change and identifying principles of national identity.[645] One of the issues the Agreement addressed was identity which is essentially Arabic.[646] The Tai'f Agreement determines Lebanese society as one that comprises communities united by a desire to live together.[647] This principle was considered vital, since there was a war to be ended – but it remains at odds with the Lebanese Constitution, which stresses the elimination of the confessional system. In this context, another principle fights separatism by expressing a commitment to maintaining a unitary State.

The confessional solution remains temporary, and the Agreement foresaw electoral laws without communal reference.[648] Meanwhile, parliamentary seats would be distributed equally by community, proportionally within the two confessional blocks and between regions.[649] In other words, those who drafted and

---

641 Ibid.

642 Ibid.

643 Elizabeth Picard, *Lebanon, a Shattered Country* (New York and London: Holmes, 1996), p. 156.

644 For further details see Deirdre Collings ed., *Peace for Lebanon? From War to Reconstruction (*London: Lynne Rienner, 1994).

645 Sami. A. Ofeish, "Lebanon's Second Republic: Secular Talk, Sectarian Application," *Arab Studies Quarterly*, 21:1 (1999), pp. 97–116.

646 Castellino and Cavanaugh, *Minority Rights in the Middle East*, p. 351.

647 Joseph Maila, Prospects for Lebanon: The Document of National Understanding: A Commentary (Lebanon: Centre for Lebanese Studies, 1992), p. 17.

648 Point 5 of Chapter II of the Tai'f Agreement: "Until the Chamber of Deputies passes an election law free of sectarian restriction, the parliamentary seats shall be divided according to the following bases."

649 Castellino and Cavanaugh, *Minority Rights in the Middle East*, p. 352.

negotiated the Agreement knew that the only way to provide stability was by dismantling the system, but although this was made clear, no time limit was set, and the agreement simply adjusted previous mechanisms while hoping for future dismantling.

3.1.4 The Justice System and Minorities in Lebanon

The structure of the judiciary in Lebanon reflects the historical developments of its legal institutions and the diversity of its legal sources. It was mainly influenced by the French model for both civil and administrative courts, while for religious ones it has largely maintained the existing structures inherited from Ottoman law.[650] In other words, Lebanon's judiciary is based on a combination of Civil Law, Islamic, and Ottoman legal principles, and the laws of the Lebanese legislature. The Lebanese Constitution states that the judiciary is an independent entity, subject merely to the law.[651] Decree Law No. 7855 of 1961, the Judicial Organization Law, regulates the structure and function of the judiciary.

There are three types of courts: ordinary, special and religious. The ordinary courts are divided into hierarchical courts – civil, criminal and administrative.[652] The special courts include the High Court of Justice, responsible to try Presidents and Ministers of the Republic, the Justice Council as well as the Military tribunals. Lebanon has no civil code regulating personal status.[653] Instead, there are fifteen separate personal status laws for each recognized religious community, administered by separate religious courts.[654] These courts are not part of Lebanese State's judicial structure. They decide on matters related to marriage,

650 Maya W. Mansour and Carlos Y. Daoud, *Lebanon - The Independence and Impartiality of the Judiciary* (Denmark: Euro-Mediterranean Human Rights Network, 2010), p. 13.

651 Article 20 of Lebanese Constitution: "The Judicial Power is vested in the Courts at various levels and jurisdictions, within a system prescribed by the law which provides the necessary guarantees to the Judges and litigants. Conditions of judicial guarantee and its limits are prescribed by the law. Judges are independent in exercising their functions. Decisions and judgments are issued by all the courts and are executed in the name of the Lebanese People."

652 "Legal Research Guide: Lebanon, Introduction to Lebanon's Legal System," Library of US Congress, 2015, https://bit.ly/2Miq1II.

653 In 1936 a decree established Lebanon's personal status order which allowed religious groups to apply their own laws to their communities and offered every citizen the right to choose their religious affiliation, or to choose not to affiliate with any religion and be subject to a civil code on personal status matters at least theoretically.

654 Library of US Congress, "Legal Research Guide: Lebanon,"

divorce, child custody and alimony without having jurisdiction over successions since successions of non-Muslims come under the jurisdiction of civil courts.[655]

Religious authorities promote this judicial pluralism to protect Lebanon's religious diversity. Religious court's Judgments are not rendered nor enforced in the name of the People of Lebanon. This contradicts Article 20 of the Lebanese Constitution which states that: "All rulings and decisions by all courts shall be rendered and enforced in the name of the People of Lebanon."[656] Nevertheless, the Court of Cassation has considered that "the pronouncement of a judgement which is not in the name of the People of Lebanon, but rather in the name of the religious tribunal that rendered it, does not constitute a violation of a fundamental public order principle."[657] This multiplicity of laws means that Lebanese citizens are treated differently when it comes to key aspects of their lives, including marriage, divorce and custody of children.[658] In addition, It is important to emphasize that religious authorities do not have enforcement powers, and the religious courts' decisions should be submitted to the enforcement departments in accordance with civil laws in place.[659]

The Lebanese Court of Cassation is Lebanon's highest court, the final arbiter of disputes. The Court of Cassation put forward certain principles as public order principles which must be respected by religious courts. The principles include provisions regarding the composition of courts,[660] the confirmation of damages[661] and the rights of the defence.[662] In case these principals are not respected by the religious courts, their judgments can be annulled. In other words, the Court of Cassation is responsible for examining the compatibility of religious codes with the public order.[663] However, it has long interpreted this responsibility as being limited to examining jurisdictional and procedural religious rules.[664] The Court of Cassation used to have a limited power over religious court proceedings and decisions,[665] resulting in a lack of supervision or accountability.

655 Mansour and Daoud, Lebanon - The Independence and Impartiality, p. 15.
656 Article 20 of Lebanese Constitution.
657 Decision No. 9/91 of Court of Cassation of Lebanon (Plenary assembly).
658 Human Rights Watch, Unequal and Unprotected Women's Rights under Lebanese Personal Status Laws (USA: Human Rights Watch, 2015), p. 25.
659 Mansour and Daoud, Lebanon - The Independence and Impartiality, p. 16.
660 Decision No. 7/85 and Decision No. 25/96 of Court of Cassation of Lebanon.
661 Decision No. 9/91 of Court of Cassation of Lebanon (Plenary assembly).
662 Decision No. 9/91, Decision No. 5/97 of Court of Cassation of Lebanon (Dissenting Opinion of Judge Mounah Mitri).
663 US. Library of Congress, "Legal Research Guide: Lebanon."
664 Ibid.
665 Human Rights Watch, *Unequal and Unprotected*, p. 5.

Recently, however, the Court of Cassation has challenged religious court decisions when they conflicted with child protection measures. On July 7-th, 2009, it rejected challenges to orders from juvenile courts by applying a cross confessional child protection law – Law No. 422 on Protection of Children in Conflict with the Law or at Risk – ordering that a child remain in the mother's care for protection despite the fact that a religious court had transferred custody to the father.[666]

Essentially it seems important to amend Article 95 of the Code of Civil Procedure to give the plenary assembly of the Court of Cassation authority to overturn religious court judgments if they violate human rights. In this context, the Court of Cassation recognizes that Article 25 of Decree 60LR[667] permits Lebanese nationals to marry in foreign countries and that marriages are governed by the laws of the country of the marriage, and Lebanese courts must respect those laws in disputes between married parties.[668] The Court of Cassation has also ruled that if a couple holds civil and religious ceremonies, the marriage is subject to religious law.[669]

In this context, courts and religious laws comply with the Lebanese Constitution, but the Christian courts are administratively and financially independent, while Muslim courts – although affiliated to and funded by the State – operate independent of State institutions.[670] This reflects a limited understanding of fundamental public order doctrines insofar as it only includes trial procedures that guarantee the right of defence, excluding from its supervision the substance of religious court judgments whether they are consistent with human rights and constitutional guarantees or not.

In terms of commitments under human rights law, Lebanon entered reservations to Articles 9 and 16 of the CEDAW. These Articles address State obligations to eliminate discrimination against women and their children based on nationality (Article 9) and in marriage (Article 16). In 1994, the CEDAW committee expressed its alarm at:

---

666 Fawzi Khamis and Fadi Al-Aridi, *Protecting Children at Risk in Light of the Law and Jurisprudence in Lebanon,* 2nd edition (Lebanon: Lebanon Friedrich Ebert Stiftung, 2011).

667 Decree 60 Law and Regulations of 1936.

668 Ibid.

669 Baz, Court of Cassation, 25.06.1965, p. 117; al-`Adl, 2001, ruling of 29.03.2001, p. 73.

670 Human Rights Watch, *Unequal and Unprotected*, p. 5.

> "the number of State parties which have entered reservations to the whole or part of Article 16, especially when a reservation has also been entered to Article 2, claiming that compliance may conflict with a commonly held vision of the family based, *inter alia*, on cultural or religious beliefs or on the country's economic or political status."[671]

> "States parties should resolutely discourage any notions of inequality of women and men which are affirmed by laws, or by religious or private law or by custom, and progress to the stage where reservations, particularly to Article 16, will be withdrawn."[672]

The committee asked State parties to "progress to the stage where reservations, particularly to Article 16, will be withdrawn."[673] The reservations question Lebanon's commitment to advancing women's rights, especially equality in marriage and divorce. Speaking to Lebanon in 2005, the CEDAW committee pointed out that Lebanon's reservations contravened the Convention's objectives and purpose and urged it to withdraw them. Lebanon was also urged to "adopt a unified personal status code which is in line with the convention and would be applicable to all women in Lebanon, regardless of religious affiliation."[674] The committee renewed its calls in following reports, expressing regret that Lebanon had made no progress towards the unified code.[675] The CEDAW committee called Lebanon to:

> "(a) To withdraw its reservation made upon accession to the Convention regarding Article 9 (2), repeal Decree No. 15 of 1925 on Lebanese Nationality and adopt legislation to ensure women equal rights with men to pass on their nationality to their foreign spouses and children;
>
> (b) To withdraw its reservation made upon accession to the Convention regarding Article 16 (1) (c), (d), (f) and (g);
>
> (c) Initiate a dialogue with the leaders of religious communities and religious scholars, taking into consideration best practices in the region, with a view to overcoming the resistance to the withdrawal of its reservations to the Convention."[676]

---

671 CEDAW Committee, "General Recommendation No.21, Equality in Marriage and Family Relations" 1994, UN Doc. HRI/GEN/1/Rev.9, para. 41.

672 Ibid, para. 44.

673 Ibid, para. 43.

674 CEDAW Committee, "Concluding Observations of the UN Committee on the Elimination of Discrimination against Women, Lebanon," 33rd session, July 2005, UN Doc. CEDAW/C/LBN/CO/2, para. 24.

675 CEDAW Committee, "Concluding Observations and Recommendations Report of the Republic of Lebanon," 2015 UN Doc. CEDAW/C/LBN/CO/4-5, para. 46.

676 Ibid, para. 16.

Lebanon responded that it could not lift the reservations or implement a unified family code as "each Lebanese is subject to the laws, regulations and courts of his or her own religious community."[677] The government's reservation remains inconsistent with Lebanon's international obligation under CEDAW Article 2 to work towards taking "all appropriate measures, including legislation, to modify or abolish existing laws, regulations, customs and practices which constitute discrimination against women."[678] Lebanon continues to use these norms to justify human rights violations against women. Therefore, immediate substantive steps to ensure equality in procedural and personal status laws are needed.

3.1.5 Electoral Law

Since independence, Lebanon has been dominated by majoritarian, first-past-the-post systems with multi-candidate districts and open electoral lists. Adjustments made through 13 parliamentary elections have focused on the size of electoral districts and the number of candidates in each, with gerrymandering playing a prominent role.[679] By 2004, despite the Tai'f Agreement establishing communal coexistence (*al-aysh al-mushtarak*) between Lebanon's different sects and political representation (*sihat al-tamsil al-siyasi*) as the objectives of post-war electoral law, both goals remained elusive. Instead of solidifying peace and helping ethnic moderation, post-war Lebanese electoral laws have hardened ethnic loyalties. After Syrian troops withdrew in 2005, elections were held under the same system as in 2000, known as the Ghazi Kanaan Law after the Syrian high commissioner who had helped design the changes.[680] In the run-up to the elections, Christians expressed frustration because even though Syrian troops had withdrawn from Lebanon, elections were arranged according to the very law they perceived was designed to marginalize the Christians. However, political alliances shifted, and the anti-Syrian opposition managed to gain a substantial majority.[681]

---

677 CEDAW Committee, "Consideration of Reports Submitted by States Parties under Article 18 of the Convention on the Elimination of All Forms of Discrimination Against Women, Third periodic report, Lebanon," 07.07.2006, UN. Doc. CEDAW/C/LBN/3.

678 Article 2 of CEDAW.

679 Saleh El Machnouk, "Electoral System Reform in Lebanon: Dilemmas of a Consociational State," *Ethnopolitics*, 17:1 (2018), p. 2.

680 Ibid, p. 5.

681 Ibid.

After three years of political crisis pitting the anti-Syrian majority against Hezbollah and culminating in armed clashes in May 2008, Lebanese leaders went to Qatar, for negotiations intended to break the deadlock. In the Doha Agreement,[682] Lebanese leaders addressed Christian grievances by returning to the 1960 Law which included 26 smaller districts, each with two to ten seats, giving Christians more say in electing members of parliament.[683] While the 2000 law gave Muslims the decisive vote on electing 35 Christian MPs, the recycled 1960 Law reduced that to 23.

Reilly argues that "the most powerful electoral systems for encouraging accommodation are those that make politicians reciprocally dependent on voters from groups other than their own."[684] The non-independence of Muslim politicians on Christian votes rendered the process of cross-voting counterproductive, and instead of promoting inter-ethnic accommodation, the law fueled ethnic grievances and promoted fears of "majority tyranny."[685]

After years of discussion, politicians have realized that this electoral system is inappropriate for a twenty-first century democracy. Given that majoritarian systems have lost their standing among political parties and the broader public, proposed alternatives range from mixed-member proportional to purely proportional systems with varying district schemes.[686] Most prominent alternatives are the Boutros Commission proposal, the 'Orthodox Gathering' proposal and the single-district 'Proportional Representative' (PR) adopted by the Amal Movement, small secular parties and civil groups. The May 6, 2018 elections tested a new and contentious electoral law which was finally passed in June 2017, reducing the number of Lebanon's districts and introducing PR, adding complicated elements to the electoral process. Seats were to be allocated proportionally

682 "Doha Agreement on the Outcome of the Meeting of the Lebanese National Dialogue," *UN Security Council Report*, UN Doc. S/2008/392, https://bit.ly/355LwY1.

683 Natalia Nahas Calfat argues that "The 2008 Doha Agreement, while correcting major sectarian imbalances and readjusting disproportionalities in representation, has once again ratified this system and institutionalised political representation based exclusively on a religious sectarian basis." in "The Frailties of Lebanese Democracy: Outcomes and Limits of the Confessional Framework," *Contexto Internacional* 40:2 May/Aug 2018, p. 275.

684 Benjamine Reilly, "Electoral systems for divided societies," *Journal of Democracy*, 13, (2002), p. 157.

685 El Machnouk "Electoral System Reform in Lebanon," p. 6.

686 Arend Lijphart, Patterns of Democracy: Government form and Performance in Thirty-six Countries (New Haven, CT: Yale University Press, 2012).

according to candidate lists. Seventy-seven lists were drawn up in a tangled web of contradictory alliances, while each ballot included a preferential vote, or *sawt tafdili*, a compromise that preserved Lebanon's winner-takes-all system and broke from proportional models.[687]

3.1.6 Incorporation of International Law in Lebanese Domestic Law

Lebanon has a comprehensive legal framework ratifying most international human rights treaties, including the ICCPR, ICESCR, CEDAW and the CRC.[688] The Constitution's preamble stipulates Lebanon's commitment to the UN Charter and the UDHR.[689] Lebanon's Constitutional Council considers that the ICCPR and ICESCR complement the UDHR.[690] International treaties have been integrated into domestic law after ratification or accession procedures by which automatic incorporation takes effect upon the treaty's publication in the *Official Gazette*. Customary international law is also binding.[691] As it was mentioned in Section 3.1.4 above, Lebanon maintains reservations to several Articles of CEDAW: Article 9 (2) (equal rights with regard to nationality) 16 (1) (c) (d) (f) (g) (equal rights in marriage and family life) and 29 (1) (related to the administration of the convention; arbitration in the event of a dispute). More than a few of these Articles contain provisions that are central to the purpose of the convention and the CEDAW Committee stated that: "…reservations to Article 16, whether lodged for national, traditional, religious or cultural reasons, are incompatible with the Convention and therefore impermissible…"[692]

---

687 Asma Ajroudi and Alia Chughtai, "Lebanon Elections 2018: Politics as Usual," *Al Jazeera*, 02.05. 2018, https://bit.ly/2I9Q98U.

688 UNOHCHR official website, the Ratification Status of Lebanon, September 2019: https://bit.ly/2S3hy1v.

689 Article B of the Lebanese Constitution's Preamble.

690 Decisions of the Constitutional Council, dated 07.08.1994, 18.09.1995, and 10.05.2001 and National report submitted in accordance with Paragraph 15 (a) of the annex to Human Rights Council Resolution 5/1 Lebanese Republic, UN Doc. A/HRC/WG.6/9/LBN/1 2015 para. 12.

691 Human Rights Council, "Report of the Special Rapporteur on freedom of religion," 30.11.2015, UN Doc. A/HRC/31/18/Add.1, para. 18.

692 International Human Rights Instruments, Compilation of Guidelines on the Form and Content of Reports to be Submitted by States Parties to the International Human Rights Treaties, Addendum, May 2003," UN Doc. HRI/GEN/2/Rev.1/Add.2, para. 5.

In addition, The Lebanese Republic while accepted the inquiry procedure under the Convention Against Torture, it has not accepted any individual complaints procedures for the covenants and treaties ratified by the State.[693] There are still no developments in this regard.[694] The relevant authorities prepare the treaty reports, emphasizing Lebanon's commitment to the responsibilities it assumed by acceding to these instruments.[695]

International treaties and conventions constitute an important part of Lebanon's international obligations and are accorded a higher authority than domestic law.[696] If a conflict between domestic and international law occurs, Lebanon's Civil Code recognizes the supremacy of international treaties. Lebanese courts apply international treaties in their jurisprudence, and the Court of Appeal has exclusive competency to interpret international treaties in cases involving individual rights and freedoms.[697] No other court can declare a law invalid if it contravenes the Constitution or international conventions.[698] In addition, Lebanon ratified the Arab Charter on Human Rights[699] adopted by the Arab Summit in May 2004, although it has not yet ratified the Statutes of the Arab Court of Human Rights.

---

693 The official website of UNOHCHR, UN Treaty Bodies Database, the ratification status by country or by treaty, Lebanon, 06.01.2021, https://bit.ly/3gRrxCZ.

694 UNOHCHR official website, "The Ratification Status of Lebanon."

695 "Lebanese National report submitted in accordance with paragraph 15 (a) of the annex to Human Rights Council," para. 14.

696 Human Rights Council, "Report of the Special Rapporteur on Freedom of Religion," para. 18.

697 Ibid.

698 Article 2 of the Code of Civil Procedure: "The courts shall adhere to the principle of the hierarchy of legal materials. When the provisions of international treaties are inconsistent with the provisions of ordinary law, the former shall have precedence over the latter. The courts may not declare the invalidity of the work of the legislative authority on the grounds that ordinary laws do not apply to the Constitution or international treaties."

699 Ratification status of the Arab Charter of Human Rights, https://bit.ly/2REAuEg.

3.1.7 Protection and Promotion of Human Rights; General Framework

Lebanon claims to have a long history of human rights protection.[700] It participated in drafting the Charter of the United Nations and the UDHR and is recognized as a secure refuge for oppressed minorities in the Middle East.[701] It has hosted half a million Palestinian refugees since 1948 and currently hosts more than 1.5 million displaced Syrians, a number equivalent to almost half its own population. Lebanon was the first Arab State to ratify the Optional Protocol to the Convention against Torture and Other Cruel, Inhuman or Degrading Treatment or Punishment.[702] Lebanon also hosts the Regional Office of the OHCHR.[703]

Human rights and governance in Lebanon have slightly improved over recent years, but an urgent need for more progress remains. Most Lebanese laws seek to protect human rights, but their implementation is problematic. Although Lebanon is party to many human rights treaties, gaps persist between legal obligations and empirical practice. Lebanon has tried to improve its human rights situation. In 2012, the National Human Rights Plan was launched.[704] Lebanon has taken steps and introduced initiatives to protect human rights at institutional and legislative levels. At structural level, a directorate general of human rights has been established.[705] The Internal Security Forces have also established a Human Rights Section in the Office of the Inspector General and a Strategic Planning and Human Rights Committee composed of Internal Security Forces' officers.[706] Moreover, the National Human Rights Action Plan 2014–2019 and the adoption of a bill establishing an independent National Human Rights Institution by the Human Rights Committee and the Committee on Administration

700 Human Rights Council, National report submitted in accordance with paragraph 5 of the annex to Human Rights Council Resolution 16/21, Lebanese Republic, 25.09.2015, UN Doc. A/HRC/WG.6/23/LBN/1.
701 Ibid.
702 UNOHCHR official website, "The Ratification Status of Lebanon."
703 See the official website of the Regional Office of the Middle East and North Africa of OHCHR, https://www.ohchr.org/EN/Countries/MenaRegion/Pages/MenaRegion20122013.aspx.
704 See the National Action Plan for Human Rights in Lebanon 2014-2019, https://bit.ly/2K7yezy.
705 Ibid, p. 27.
706 Ibid.

and Justice of the Chamber of Deputies on 8 April 2014 reflect the State's commitment to guaranteeing civil and political rights.[707]

In October 2016, the Lebanese Chamber of Deputies adopted Act No.62/16 establishing an independent National Human Rights Commission including a Committee on the Prevention of Torture. The Ministry of Human Rights and the Ministry of Women's Affairs were also established, and Act No.28 on access to information was adopted in February 2017.[708] In May 2018 the Cabinet selected ten members to form a National Human Rights Institution (NHRI).[709] However, there is no indication of any minority rights in the 2014–2019 action plan.[710] The word 'minority' is missing. This might be because Lebanon considers majorities and minorities regardless of their size as 'communities' and even legally recognized minorities they do not perceive themselves 'minorities' per se, considering that admitting to being part of a minority is like being considered a marginalized, second-class member of society.[711] This will be discussed in greater depth in the next section.

The main challenge is promoting equal participation and equal opportunities in civil, cultural, economic, political and social life, as well as gender equality and the right to a safe and healthy environment. Women suffer more discrimination in certain issues such as divorce, custody of children and inheritance.[712] In denominationally mixed marriages, the husband's religious affiliation usually determines the legal regime of the marriage, and the religious socialization of the children. As the 62nd CEDAW report indicated "It was regrettable that the State party continued to maintain that personal status matters should be left exclusively to the sectarian system to regulate."[713] The Committee recommends the adoption of a unified personal status code, but the government effectively

707 HRC, "Consideration of Reports Submitted by States Parties under Article 40 of the Covenant," 28.12.2016, UN Doc. CCPR/C/LBN/3.

708 HRC, "Concluding Observations on the Third Periodic Report of Lebanon," 09.05.2018, UN Doc. CCPR/C/NBN/CO/3.

709 "UN Welcomes Appointment of Members of the National Human Right Institution," Office of the UN Special Coordination for Lebanon, 22.05.2018, https://bit.ly/2Lkrdub.

710 See National Action Plan for Human Rights in Lebanon 2014-2019.

711 Personal interview with Dr. Ara Sanjian, Lebanese Armenian historian, lecturer at Michigan University, the interview was held online on 8.10.2018.

712 Lana Asfour, "Lebanon's divorce and child custody laws 'discriminate against women,'" *The New Arab*, 19.01.015, https://bit.ly/2IjpYhF.

713 CEDAW Committee, "Summary record (partial), of the 1346th meeting," 06.11.2015, UN Doc. CEDAW/C/SR.1346, para. 34.

relinquishes its obligations. Judicial pluralism was considered essential for protecting religious diversity, but the multiplicity of laws resulted in discrimination against women within sects and inequality among women belonging to different sects in key aspects of their lives.[714]

3.2 What Does It Mean to Be a Minority in Lebanon? Are Armenians a Minority?

"There is not a single resident in Lebanon who cannot, in one sense or another, truthfully claim to belong to a minority."[715] Lebanon is a country whose population is so pluralistic that every ethno-religious group or sect can be considered a minority.[716] Religious diversity is compounded by ethnic and/or linguistic diversity, given that for example Armenian or Kurdish Lebanese citizens may have multiple religious and linguistic affiliations.[717]

In Lebanon, it is difficult to determine who should be considered a minority, which means it becomes increasingly difficult to understand what rights should be offered, and to whom. Demographics are controversial, and there has been no census since 1932.[718] The Lebanese State does not consider the Tai'f Communities (Sunnis, Shia, Druze, Maronite, Catholics, Greek Orthodox and Armenians) as minority communities, but as national communities. It is challenging to stipulate the nature of these communities. Although in principle, each individual is free to belong to the creed that they feel is in conformity with their religious beliefs, in the vast majority of cases membership of a community is the result of coming from a family registered as part of a particular creed. Legally recognized minorities include only six Christian sects: Syriac Orthodox, Syriac Catholics, Latin Catholics, Assyrian Catholics, Chaldean Catholics and Coptic Orthodox. Combined, these groups have only one of the national parliament's 128 seats.[719] In addition, legally speaking, non-citizen minority members (e.g., migrants – refugees coming from minority backgrounds) are not entitled or protected by any minority rights. This means that the legal definition of minorities in Lebanon does not reflect Capotorti's definition and is not inclusive to

714 Ibid.

715 Castellino and Cavanaugh, *Minority Rights in the Middle East*, p. 345.

716 Avsharian, "The Tai'f agreement and the Lebanese Armenians," p. 387.

717 Human Rights Council, "Report of the Special Rapporteur on freedom of religion or belief," para. 19.

718 Castellino and Cavanaugh, *Minority Rights in the Middle East*, p. 345.

719 See Lebanon's 2017 Parliamentary Electoral Law.

all segments of the society who meet both subjective and objective criteria of being a minority. In other words, although, there are several groups numerically inferior to the rest of the population in Lebanon, who are in a non-dominant position and possess ethnic, religious or linguistic characteristics different from Lebanon's rest of the population and express a sense of solidarity to preserve their culture, traditions, religion or language,[720] they are not legally recognized or considered as minority. While acknowledging the protection extended to some minority groups, the CESCR regrets the lack of clarity on Lebanese minority laws, and is worried about the obstacles to the recognition of the Dom and Bedouins.[721] Indeed, certain religious (Buddhists, Hindus and unregistered Protestant Christians) and national, ethnic groups (Syrians, Palestinians, Kurds) lack official legal recognition, and their members do not qualify for certain government positions and cannot own land or property collectively.[722] No seats are allocated for the Baha'i confession, and Baha'is cannot run for Parliament, nor can they hold senior government positions.[723] Some unregistered religious groups are considered under the recognized religions; some Baha'is, for example, are registered as Shia Muslims, and as such may run for office and occupy a seat allocated to the Shia community. Similarly, some Mormons are registered under the Greek Orthodox faith.[724]

To address this issue, the Committee on Economic Social and Cultural Rights recommends:

> "the State party ensure that the legal framework on the rights of ethnic minorities, as well as their recognition, protection and promotion, complies with international standards. It also recommends that the State party protect and promote the cultural rights of all ethnic minorities, including the Dom and Bedouins, without discrimination. The Committee refers the State party to its General Comment No. 21 (2009) on the right of everyone to take part in cultural life."[725]

---

720 See Capotorti's definition for minorities in Section 2.1 above.

721 CESCR, "Concluding Observations on the Second Periodic Report of Lebanon," 24.10.2016, UN Doc. E/C.12/LBN/CO/2, para. 64.1.

722 "2011 Report on International Religious Freedom - Lebanon," United States Department of State, 30.07.2012, https://bit.ly/2NyCZ7b.

723 Ibid.

724 Human Rights Council, "Report of the Special Rapporteur on Freedom of Religion or Belief," para. 44.

725 CESCR, "Concluding Observations on the Second Periodic Report of Lebanon," para. 64.2.

It is in this context and due to historical misperceptions surrounding the notion of "being minority," many Armenians do not consider themselves a "minority" but rather a Tai'f "community."[726] They have joint Lebanese and Armenian identities, with associated rights and obligations. Armenians consider most of Lebanon's population as coming from a minority group.[727] Armenians are one of Lebanon's seven largest religious communities, and each community is a minority vis-à-vis the others. There are no religious majorities in Lebanon and minorities see themselves as different communities.[728] However, they are recognized only as a religious community and not as an ethnic, national and linguistic community. This attitude identifies the complexity of defining minorities in the Lebanese context.

Although legally speaking Armenians are not recognized by the Lebanese legal system as minority group per se, they are undoubtedly a minority group meeting both subjective and objective criteria of being a minority. Therefore, Armenians should be entitled to minority rights under international law regardless of State recognition as such. Being a minority is a fact rather than a definition, and minorities are defined as groups with separate linguistic, ethnic or cultural characteristics who seek to maintain and emphasize their identity. The Permanent Court of International Justice states that "the existence of a minority is a question of fact before being a question of law or politics."[729] This applies to the Armenian Minority in Lebanon.

3.3 Existing Challenges

Lebanon's sectarian political system challenges the organization of political power and various group interests. Lebanese politics are built on the Tai'f Agreement which ended the country's civil war in 1990 but instead of demolishing, entrenched sectarianism and a system of patronage.[730] While different groups have co-existed quite peacefully since the war, Lebanon's pluralism sparks debate over

726 Personal interview with Ms. Arsho Balian, editor of *Aztag* newspaper, the interview was held online in 05.08.2018.

727 Ibid.

728 "Minorities and Indigenous People in Lebanon," Minority Rights Group International, May 2019, https://bit.ly/3n3Xh7D.

729 Permanent Court of International Justice, "Advisory Opinion in the Greco-Bulgarian communities' case, advisory opinion No. 17," 31.07.1930, Series B.

730 Martin Patience, "Lebanon protesters' euphoria gives way to despair," *BBC*, 16.10.2020, https://bbc.in/2NXaZx7.

what political system is best. All parties agree that war should be prevented, but some argue in favor of erasing sectarian cleavages while others promote the current representational quota system. Sectarian lines could be erased by organizing Lebanon into fewer and larger constituencies, or even one single constituency. Others consider Lebanon a special case and believe that a majority democracy would ignore the interests of certain groups.[731] The Tai'f Agreement reduced the worst manifestations of sectarian violence, but deepened communal divisions, especially at political levels.[732] In the years that have passed since the Agreement, little progress has been made from the sectarian political system.

Any explanation of Lebanese politics must consider the role of religious attitudes and organizations, and much of the organization of government officially reflects the country's religious structure.[733] Lebanon is a multicultural and multi-judicial complexity. Until recently it was impossible for two people of different faiths to marry, and such marriages took place outside the country, usually in Cyprus. A Christian cannot inherit from a Muslim, or vice versa.[734] In this context, because religious balance is such a sensitive issue, a national census has not been conducted since 1932 – before the founding of the modern Lebanese State. Consequently, there is little accurate data on the percentages of population belonging to major religions. Most observers believe that Muslims make up the majority, but Lebanon's Muslims are not a homogenous group.[735]

Meanwhile, the destructive impact of combined economic, demographic and security challenges facing Lebanon as a consequence of conflict in and around the country have brought other major problems. A mass influx of roughly 1.5 million Syrian refugees as well as 500,000 Palestine refugees has resulted in debilitating social and economic costs to Lebanese society, bringing a sharp increase in poverty and unemployment. Health, education and infrastructure are

---

731 Hilde Torhaug, "Lebanese Political Identity Exploring Sovereignty and Democracy in Lebanon through Norm Socialisation Processes" (Master Thesis, Institute for Statsvitenskap, University of Oslo, 2004), p. 121.

732 Hudson, "Trying Again: Power-Sharing in Post-Civil War Lebanon," p. 117.

733 This has been the case for the last 8 decades. See Ralph E. Crow, "Religious Sectarianism in the Lebanese Political System," *The Journal of Politics*, 24:3 (Aug 1962), p. 489.

734 Klaus Wivel, *The Last Supper: The Plight of Christians in Arab Lands* (New York: New Vessel Press, 2013), p. 138.

735 Rania Maktabi, "The Lebanese Census of 1932 Revisited. Who Are the Lebanese?," *British Journal of Middle Eastern Studies*, 26:2 (1999), pp. 219-241.

overstretched, and the security situation is deteriorating, exacerbated by sectarian conflict and changes in the size of various groups.[736]

The resulting political deadlock prevents the enactment of laws and measures to promote and protect minority rights. There is also insufficient support from the international community to alleviate the economic burden on Lebanon and share the costs of the humanitarian response.[737] There are concerns about the rise of religious conservatism and sectarian divisions in the country's pluralist society.[738] Sectarianism is now being referred to as the "dark deviant underside of the nationalist narrative."[739]

In addition, Lebanon struggles with is its failed economy. According to the UN Economic and Social Commission for Western Asia, 55 % of the population in Lebanon lives below the poverty line, a triple increase from 2019.[740] Lebanon has a national debt of $92 billion – nearly 170 % of its GDP – one of the highest debt ratios in the world.[741] Unemployment is high, and the Lebanese struggle to earn enough to survive. According to the *Economist* "Annual GDP growth was 8 % in 2010, before neighbouring Syria plunged into civil war. Since then, it has averaged less than 2 %."[742]

People have long been angered by the government's inability to provide even basic services. Residents must deal with daily power cuts, a lack of safe drinking water, absent of an adequate public healthcare and weak internet connections. In late 2019, a plan to tax WhatsApp calls spilled over into mass protests against economic turmoil and corruption, which eventually led to the then Saad Hariri's

736 Anchal Vohra, "Lebanon Is Sick and Tired of Syrian Refugees," *Foreign Policy*, July 2019, https://bit.ly/36Ovelf.

737 "Lebanon Events of 2018," Human Rights Watch, Online Report, https://bit.ly/338B8vy.

738 CEDAW Committee, "Concluding Observations on the Combined Fourth and Fifth Periodic Reports of Lebanon," UN Doc. CEDAW/C/SR.1345 and 1346, 2015, section C, para. 10.

739 Castellino and Cavanaugh, *Minority Rights in the Middle East*, p. 343.

740 "ESCWA Warns: More Than Half of Lebanon's Population Trapped in Poverty," UN Economic and Social Commission for Western Asia, 19.08.2020, https://bit.ly/3ikj4Xt.

741 "Beirut Explosion," Center for Disaster Philanthropy, 08.01.2021, https://bit.ly/380VDP7.

742 "When the Music Stops: Lebanon's Economy Has Long Been Sluggish. Now a Crisis Looms," *Economist*, 30.08.2018, https://econ.st/2FD0tVY.

governments resignation. Although Covid-19 pandemic[743] had curbed the protests, the financial fall continued and 2020 August's Beirut port blast,[744] which came on the heels of multiple other crises in Lebanon, was seen by many as the deadly result of years of corruption and mismanagement.

In terms of corruption, Lebanon is the 137th out of 180 countries (180 being the worst) on Transparency International's 2019 Corruption Perceptions Index.[745] In his resignation speech after the Beirut blast, prime minister Hassan Diab criticized

> "a system of corruption... deeply-rooted in all the functions of the State…One of the many examples of corruption exploded in the port of Beirut, and the calamity befell Lebanon…But corruption cases are widespread in the country's political and administrative landscape; other calamities hiding in many minds and warehouses, and which pose a great threat, are protected by the class that controls the fate of the country."[746]

The BBC referring to a report published by Transparency International claims that corruption in Lebanon "permeates all levels of society" with the police, political parties and Parliament perceived as "the most corrupt institutions of the country."[747] In addition, it argues that the "very system of sectarian power-sharing which is fuelling these patronage networks and hindering Lebanon's system of governance."[748] This explains why the recent public anger was directed at the same ruling elite who have dominated politics for decades and accumulated their own wealth while failing to address the basic needs of the people. The people taking part in the demonstrations were demanding accountability not just from the government as a whole, but the leaders of their own sects. "All of them means all of them," is one of the main slogans adopted by protesters.[749]

---

743 As of December 30, 2020, Lebanon had nearly 180,000 COVID-19 cases, an increase of nearly 36 times the number of cases that were confirmed when the blast took place. See Worldometers.info, https://bit.ly/3b4f7nU.

744 The massive explosion killed almost 200 people, injured 6,000 others, and caused as much as $4.6bn of physical damage and $3.5bn of economic damage. See "Lebanon crisis: Saad Hariri returns as PM a year after protests," BBC, 22.10.2020, https://www.bbc.com/news/world-middle-east-54630150.

745 "Corruption Perceptions Index," Transparency International Global Coalition against Corruption, 12.12.2020, https://www.transparency.org/en/cpi/2019/results/lbn.

746 "Lebanon: Why the country is in crisis," BBC, 05.08.2020, https://bbc.in/3r9xbCI.

747 Ibid.

748 Ibid.

749 "'All of them means all of them': Lebanon protest slogans," *France 24*, 21.10.2019, https://bit.ly/2PthuIz.

The above-mentioned problems are increasing uncertainty and hopelessness among Lebanese people and leading to emigration. This is not to a historical interest in emigration, but because Lebanon is no longer a viable place to live in dignity. As Roula Ibrahim argues "a country with no production, no economy growing, no clean environment, no health insurance system, no decent free education for all, no welfare system... is an expelling country for its people."[750] All these developments impact the Armenians as much as other Lebanese communities.

3.4 The Armenians in Lebanon

The Armenians are one of eighteen religious communities in Lebanon, and they are also one of the seven large communities whose long historical roots are recognized by Tai'f Agreement.[751] There are no official statistics on the size of Lebanon's Armenian population. In the 1932 official census Armenians were 32,000. In the following decades, this number increased to more than 200,000 because of natural growth and inflows from Damascus in 1930s, the Sandjak of Alexandretta in 1939 and Palestine in 1948 as well as constant arrivals from insecure neighboring countries.[752] They are scattered across the country and in Mount Lebanon, as well as Beirut, Tripoli, Anjar, Zahle, Batroun and Jbeil. The largest concentration of Armenians is in Beirut.[753] It is safe to assume that the number of Armenians has at least halved from a pre-civil-war high of 200,000. Ara Sanjian estimated Armenian voters in Lebanon in the 2000 parliamentary elections at 116,214,[754] but this included absentees, so a safe estimate would be somewhere between 60,000 and 80,000.[755] The number is still declining,

---

750 Roula Ibrahim, *"Arman Lebnan Yankaridoun,"* (Armenians of Lebanon are Becoming Extinct), *Al-Akhbar* newspaper, 13.10.2018, https://bit.ly/2RWMgsJ.

751 Mustafa Tayfun Ustun, "The History of the Armenian Community in Lebanon: From 'Refugee Camps' to 'Neighbourhoods," *International Journal for Social Sciences*, 5:9 (2017), p. 95.

752 Antranig Dakessian, "Lebanon," Armenian Diaspora Survey, 2019, https://bit.ly/3q4dRoV.

753 Arda Jebejian, "Patterns of Language Use among Armenians in Beirut," *Haigazian Armenological Review*, 31:1, 2011, p. 455.

754 Ara Sanjian, "Armenians and the 2000 Parliamentary Elections in Lebanon," Armenian New Network, Groong, Review and Outlook, September 2000, https://bit.ly/3k2T0iU.

755 Asbed Kotchikian, "Between (Home) land and (Host)land: Lebanese-Armenians and the Republic of Armenia," in *Armenians of Lebanon: From Past Princesses and Refugees to Present-Day Community*, Aida Boudjikian, ed. (Beirut: Haigazian University and the Armenian Heritage Press, 2009), p. 476.

and the Armenian community has mostly lost interest in retaining the community that once mattered so much to them.[756]

Just as Lebanon's population is the most varied in the Middle East, so its Armenian community is the most religiously eclectic in the Armenian diaspora. Counting 80 % Apostolic, 15 % Catholics, and 5 % Protestants, Lebanon's Armenian population is quite diverse.[757] Its Catholic population was once the Armenian diaspora's largest, while Protestant Armenians have an influence and visibility in Lebanon far beyond their modest numbers.[758] Religion is not the only element that accounts for the Lebanese Armenians' diversity, and Lebanese Armenians follow various political ideologies. The ARF (hereafter *Tashnagtsutioon*) was the hegemon of Lebanese Armenian politics from the late 1950s until the 1972 Lebanese parliamentary election, although the *Ramgavar* and *Hunchagian* parties remained part of the scene throughout as Lebanon became the hub of international Armenian institutions.[759]

The measure of communal autonomy Lebanese Armenians enjoy is quite unique. According to Asbed Kotchikian "The Lebanese confessional system has given the various sects a level of autonomy to run their internal affairs, which gave the Armenians in Lebanon the ability to build, strengthen and develop institutions that are similar to a state within a state."[760] Although the community is integrated into the Lebanese system, it has a life of its own, speaking its own language alongside Arabic, reading, watching and listening to its own press and organizing itself through social, sport and cultural institutions. The following section will examine the historical account as well as the religious, political, educational, cultural and judicial institutions of Lebanese Armenians.

3.4.1 Historical Account of the Armenians in Lebanon

Armenian presence in Lebanon dates to the fourteenth century.[761] After the dissolution of Cilicia,[762] Lebanon was a main destination for Armenian emigrants.

---

756 Ibid.

757 Scott Abramson, "Lebanese Armenians; A Distinctive Community in the Armenian Diaspora and in Lebanese Society," *the Levantine Review*, 2:2 (Winter 2013), p. 204.

758 Ibid.

759 Ibid.

760 Agnieszka Pikulicka-Wilczewska, "No "Velvet Revolution" for Lebanese Armenians," Open Democracy, 2018, https://bit.ly/34giNfZ.

761 Ustun, "The History of the Armenian Community in Lebanon," p. 95.

762 For more historical insights see Robert Lee Wolff and Harry Williams Hazard eds., "*XVIII* The Kingdom of Cilician Armenia," in The later Crusades, 1189-1311(Madison, Wisconsin: University of Wisconsin Press, 1969), pp. 630-659.

Interactions between Armenians and the Crusaders were helped mobilize Armenians towards the Middle East, but although many Armenian families lived in Lebanon since the 1300s, the community's recognition as a Lebanese minority is relatively recent.[763] After the Armenian Genocide, waves of Armenian refugees settled in Lebanon. Settlers were of low socioeconomic status but raised their living standards through hard work to become self-sufficient.[764] When Lebanon became independent, Armenians obtained citizenship under the French mandate were recognized and offered rights and privileges associated with their status as a Lebanese community.[765]

3.4.1.1 Armenian Refugee Flux

The Lebanese Armenian community bears traces of each wave of refugees that has settled in the land, from the late seventeenth century Catholic refugees to the present influx of Syrian Armenian refugees.[766] Lebanese Armenians were overwhelmingly Catholic until the 1880s, fleeing persecution in the Armenian homeland.[767] The community changed dramatically as Apostolic Armenian refugees fleeing the Hamidian Massacres began arriving in Lebanon and setting up sectarian institutions after 1894. During and after the 1915 Genocide, Armenians from Cilicia, the six vilayets of Ottoman Armenia and elsewhere flooded Lebanon. In the 1920s, refugees from Soviet Armenia, Syria and Turkey settled in Lebanon, adding variety to the country's already diverse Armenian population. By the 1930s, the Lebanese Armenian community was a crucible for Armenians of three different denominations (Armenian Orthodox, Armenian Catholic, Armenian Protestant), four different language groups (Armenian – Turkish – Arabic – French) not mentioning the dialectal differences, and innumerable different points of origin. Refugee camps contained peasants, villagers, mountaineers, urbanites, elites – Armenians from every background brought together by the twentieth century's first Genocide.[768]

A further influx of homogenous Armenian refugees from the same province settled in Lebanon a few years later. In the late 1930s, thousands of Armenians

763 Ustun, "The History of the Armenian Community in Lebanon," p. 95.

764 Ibid.

765 Tsolin Nalbantian, "Going Beyond Overlooked Populations in Lebanese Historiography: The Armenian Case," in *History Compass*, 11:10 (October 2013), pp. 821–832.

766 Abramson, "Lebanese Armenians; A Distinctive Community," pp. 189-192.

767 Ibid.

768 Ibid, p. 205.

fled to Lebanon and other countries from the Sanjak of Alexandretta. As Turkey stood poised to annex the Sanjak – an autonomous province within the French mandate's *États du Lebanon* since 1921 – Armenians feared a reprise of Turkish atrocities. The French authorities gave the newcomers farmland in the Beqaa Valley, where they built an entirely Armenian community on a former marsh. Anjar quickly grew into a town of several thousand, and the French Mandatory authorities gave citizenship to the villagers of Anjar.[769]

Armenian refugees continued to come to Lebanon during the following years. Palestinian Armenian refugees from the First Arab Israeli War[770] and Syrian Armenians fleeing repression and instability all took shelter in Lebanon.[771] Unlike Armenians who took refuge in Europe as individuals, those who came to Lebanon took refuge as a nation. In Lebanon, a multitude of nations and *Millets* awaited them.[772]

3.4.1.2 Lebanese Armenians from 1915 to the End of French Mandate

If the massacres instigated by Sultan Abdul Hamid II produced a trickle of Armenian refugees, the Armenian Genocide of 1915 generated a flood.[773] Thousands of deported Armenians fled to Lebanon, but far from finding the sanctuary that their predecessors enjoyed, they encountered a country in turmoil. In 1915, as the Armenian Genocide unfolded, Jamal Pasha, commander of the Ottoman Fourth Army, abolished the autonomy of the *Mutasarrafiya* and levied a blockade against Lebanon.[774] The resulting famine was exacerbated by Lebanon's economic disruption and a plague of locusts. By 1918, one third of Lebanon's population had perished.[775] It was against this backdrop of anguish and privation that Armenians who had escaped the Genocide arrived in Lebanon. Thousands of

---

769 Ibid.

770 Michael W. Suleiman, Political Parties in Lebanon: The Challenge of a Fragmented Political Culture (New York: Cornell University Press, 1967), p. 186.

771 Shahan Kandaharian, "Around 10,000 Syrian Armenians moved to Armenia and 8,000 to Lebanon," *News.am*, 2013, https://bit.ly/2NyTKza and Deniz Oz, "Armenians Fleeing Syria Say it is Like Another Genocide," *Ahval*, 2018, https://bit.ly/2Q4xC1q.

772 Maron Salhani, "The Armenian 'Signifier' in the Culture and Arts of the Land of the Cedars," in *Haygagan Inknutian Khntirner 21-rt Tarum* (Issues of Armenian Identity in 21 Century), (Yerevan: Yerevan State University, 2014), p. 139.

773 Abramson, "Lebanese Armenians; A Distinctive Community," p. 204.

774 Ibid, p. 191.

775 Melanie Tanielian, The War of Famine: Everyday Life in Wartime Beirut and Mount Lebanon (1914-1918) (UC Berkeley: University of California, 2012), p. 108.

incoming survivors were interned in tents and quarantined.[776] Armenians heard anti-Armenian propaganda voiced in areas of Beirut, with chants of "Beware of Armenians, stay away from Armenians…Armenians want to steal your bread and throw you out of your homes." As well as calls to avoid employing Armenians and media talk of "Armenian gangs" and "foreign thieves."[777] This antagonism led to clashes between refugees and Lebanese demonstrators.[778]

After the First World War, Ottoman territories in the Middle East were occupied by French and British armies under the Sykes-Picot Agreement. Southern Eastern Provinces and western Mesopotamia (Syria and Lebanon) were taken by France, so most Armenians in Lebanon found themselves living under the French mandate.[779] In the early 1920s, Lebanese Armenians were largely a community of refugees, detached from Lebanese society. In the two decades that followed the First World War, Armenian refugees set down roots in areas that would become Lebanon's main Armenian enclaves, considering their residence in Lebanon as temporary pending their restoration to the Armenian homeland.[780]

Political machinations soon warned refugees that their stay in Lebanon might not be as temporary as they had supposed. The Allied powers and the Ottoman Empire concluded the Treaty of Sevres, promising an independent republic covering much of historic Armenia, but instead the Allies acceded to the creation of Turkey and signed the Treaty of Lausanne,[781] confounding the hopes of Armenian refugees aspiring for repatriation and changing their status in their host countries too. Among the Treaty's provisions was the stipulation that refugees from Eastern provinces in former Ottoman territories be granted citizenship there.[782]

For the French authorities in Lebanon and their Maronite protégés – who hoped to augment Lebanon's Christian sector, this clause was providential, and on 31 August 1924, despite opposition from Lebanon's Sunni Muslims, Lebanese Armenians were naturalized *en masse*.[783] The French and their allies then

776 Hilmar Kaiser, "The Armenians in Lebanon during the Armenian Genocide," in *Armenians of Lebanon: From Past Princesses and Refugees to Present-Day Community*" Aida Boudjikian, ed. (Beirut: Haigazian University & Armenian Heritage Press, 2009), p. 37.

777 Salhani, "The Armenian 'Signifier,'" p. 141.

778 Ibid.

779 Ustun, "The History of the Armenian Community in Lebanon," p. 98.

780 Abramson, "Lebanese Armenians; A Distinctive Community," pp. 191-192.

781 Ibid, p. 193.

782 Ibid.

783 Migliorino, (Re)Constructing Armenia in Lebanon and Syria, pp32-34.

"reinforced and expanded the political spaces reserved for the Armenians in the new confessional system being established in Lebanon."[784] Lebanese Christians defended the Armenian presence in Lebanon, considering it "a significant factor for the preservation of their dominant political power in the country."[785] This was criticized by some Lebanese Muslims because the Armenians helped sustain a Christian predominance in Lebanese society.[786]

As time passed, the hostile attitude of the Muslims and the native population's prejudices diminished as the Armenians participated in post-War reconstruction and pursued a policy of least interference in Lebanese internal confessional politics, adopting pro-government policies.[787] In 1925 the Armenian community abandoned any posture of independence and involved itself in Lebanese affairs by voting to renew Lebanon's Representative Council (an advisory elected body under the French High Commission). In 1929, Abdullah Ishaq became the first Armenian parliamentarian in Lebanon's Chamber of Deputies. A Catholic, unrepresentative of the overwhelmingly Apostolic Armenian community, he represented minorities in general, not just Armenians. In 1934, one Lebanese parliamentary seat was earmarked for an Apostolic Armenian, and the first Armenian deputy Vahram Leilekian was elected.[788] An official Armenian representative has been returned in every election since.[789]

Two further factors contributed to the importance of Lebanese Armenians in diaspora. In 1928, the Armenian Catholic Church moved its headquarters from Constantinople to Lebanon, which hosted the Armenian Catholics' largest community. In 1930 the Catholicosate of Cilicia also relocated from Sis (Kozan in modern Turkey) to Antelias, north of Beirut, where it has since remained. The relocation of such a venerable and influential institutions to Lebanon transformed the country into a spiritual center for many diasporic Armenians.[790]

---

784 Ibid, p. 55.

785 Ibid, pp. 32-34.

786 Ohannes Geukjian, "From Positive Neutrality to Partisanship: How and Why the Armenian Political Parties Took Sides in Lebanese Politics in the Post-Tai'f Period (1989–Present)," *Middle Eastern Studies*, 45:5 (September 2009), p. 740.

787 Ibid.

788 Zaven Messerlian, *Armenian Participation in the Lebanese Legislative Elections, 1934-2009* (Lebanon: Haigazian University press, 2014), pp. 47-49.

789 Abramson, "Lebanese Armenians; A Distinctive Community," p. 193.

790 Ibid.

3.4.1.3 *The Post Mandate Era*

By the time the French left Lebanon in 1946, Armenians were no longer an alien presence.[791] Many still lived in camps at the edge of towns and spoke no Arabic, but their presence in Lebanon had become a *fait accompli* and the community had integrated itself into Lebanon's economy and society.[792] By 1946, the network of Armenian associations was transforming and expanding. The role of these Armenian associations developed steadily, becoming part of most Armenian families' daily lives through social welfare schemes, sporting or cultural events and structures of self-help, socialization and cultural preservation, as well as efforts to solve housing problems.[793]

The Armenians became an identifiable minority player in the Lebanese political arena, although the community's existence as a diverse ethno-cultural group in a newly independent country came under doubt. The approach newly independent Lebanon adopted to ethno-cultural diversity – particularly the impact independence would have on Armenian strategies of cultural preservation – could not be separated from the broader debate on new, post-Mandate institutions in Lebanon.[794]

Lebanon emerged as a semi-liberal oligarchic republic dominated by large landowners, clan leaders and urban notables, but over the following two decades the post-Mandate order was repeatedly challenged. Key policy issues were foregrounded, including the relationship between State and religion, public education, the economy and social services and women's roles in society and public life. Lebanon's oligarchy drew from the legacy of the Ottoman era and the French mandate, providing an ideal environment for the Armenian reconstruction internally, within the community. The relationship between the State and the Armenians related to conflict over the identity of the State itself. The struggle over Lebanon's identity saw little participation from the Armenians, whose role in shaping Lebanon's politics in the mid-1940s and beyond was negligible.

3.4.1.4 *Civil War*

The Armenian community adopted a position of positive neutrality during the 16-year civil war in Lebanon between 1975 and 1991.[795] Christians saw the

791 Ibid.
792 Migliorino, (Re)Constructing Armenia in Lebanon and Syria, p. 126.
793 Ibid.
794 Ibid, p. 90.
795 Geukjian, "From Positive Neutrality to Partisanship," p. 743.

Armenians as being on their side, but Muslims sought their allegiance too, and because the Armenians chose neutrality sometimes they were persecuted, kidnapped and killed by both sides.[796] In addition to targeting Armenian individuals, Armenian neighborhoods and the Armenian Genocide memorial in Bikfaya was bombed in the 1970s.[797] Militant Lebanese Christians resented Armenians' reluctance to fight in what they saw/assume as a Muslim-Christian battle.[798] Nevertheless, Armenian decision makers distanced themselves from the two warring Lebanese parties, but the three Armenian political parties managed to cooperate and take a united stance due to similar outlooks on policy issues.[799]

Armenian politicians condemned violence, seeking national solidarity among all Lebanese and appealing for reconciliation.[800] Despite their neutrality, Armenians considered it wise to involve themselves in certain key decisions concerning cultural, political and socio-economic rights.[801] The Armenian community was a factor of the Lebanese political structure and their parliamentarians met with various parties to mediate a ceasefire, worried that the war would cause immense damage. They called for dialogue between conflicting parties.[802] In addition, Armenian community leaders sought unity and consensus to resolve disputes peacefully, especially contested national issues such as the constitution, the structure of government, the institutions and the political system.

Proponents of positive neutrality, Armenian deputies – particularly Babikian – involved themselves in the negotiations of the Tripartite Committee created by the LAS at its 1989 Casablanca Summit. Babikian was a prominent associate of the six-member Bekerki Committee created by Patriarch Sfeir of Lebanon's Maronite church to negotiate with the Tripartite Committee. This Committee, which included King Fahed Bin Abdul Aziz of Saudi Arabia, King Hasan II of Morocco

796 Vera Choulhadjian Yacoubian, "The Politics of the Armenians in Lebanon: 1975-1989" (Master Thesis, Lebanese American University, 2003), pp. 51-52 and personal interview with Mr. Vicken Avakian, director of Radio Voice of Van, former school principal, Zarehian Seminary teacher, writer, member of Homenetmen Central Committee, the interview was held online on 15.09.2018.

797 Ibid.

798 Jebejian, "Patterns of Language Use among Armenians in Beirut," p. 454.

799 Geukjian, "From Positive Neutrality to Partisanship," p. 743.

800 *Aztag* newspaper, 23.10.1975.

801 Avsharian, "The Tai'f agreement and the Lebanese Armenians," p. 396.

802 Melkon Eblighatian, *Kaghtagayanen Khorertaran,* (From the Refugee Camp to Parliament), Vol. II (Aleppo: Cilicia Publishing House, 2005), p. 16.

and President Al-Shadhili Bin Jdid of Algeria, aimed to reach a ceasefire by 29 August 1989.

It can be concluded that the Armenian policy of positive neutrality was not an attempt to avoid participating in the decision-making processes of internal Lebanese politics. Armenian leaders pursued elective communication, consultation and negotiation at State and party levels to establish sustainable peace. While Armenian efforts did not lead to an immediate ceasefire, they helped prevent further deterioration in relationships between the Armenians and the warring sides. Presumably, had the Armenian political leadership taken a side in the war, Armenian material and human losses would have been much greater.[803]

3.4.1.5 Tai'f Agreement onwards

After the September 1989 ceasefire, 63 of the 99 members of the 1972 Parliament gathered in Tai'f in Saudi Arabia.[804] Three Armenian deputies – Babikian, Eblighatian (Armenian Apostolic) and Manougian (Armenian Evangelical) – attended.[805] The deliberations were aimed at reforming Lebanon's political system, phasing out confessionalism and establishing a new system offering numeric parity to Christians and Muslims. In October 1989, an opening agreement was reached towards reconstructing post-war Lebanon,[806] which the Armenians signed and to which they pledged support. Some of the success resulted from the Armenian policy of positive neutrality. The Tai'f Agreement re-established consociational power-sharing and institutionalized sectarian affiliations. A confessional balance between Christians and Muslims was established in parliament, revamping executive authority at the expense of the Maronite President. The Tai'f did not alter the confessional affiliations of the Prime Minister (Sunni) or the Speaker (Shiia), and the Armenians lost no privileges within the readjusted balance.

Hagop Pakradouni argues that Tai'f recognized the Armenian community as "one of the seven main communities of the country, rather than the seventh one."[807] In the pre-Tai'f period, the Armenians participated in Lebanese politics but were not recognized by the system as a community equal to the six predominant ones (Maronites, Sunnis, Shiias, Druze, Greek Orthodox and Greek

803 Geukjian, "From Positive Neutrality to Partisanship," p. 760.
804 See the Tai'f Agreement.
805 Yacoubian, "The Politics of the Armenians in Lebanon: 1975-1989," p. 68.
806 Avsharian, "The Tai'f agreement and the Lebanese Armenians," p. 403.
807 Ibid.

Catholics). Pakradouni stresses that in the post-Tai'f period the Armenians had to defend all their communal rights with no concessions. Armenians were assigned one ministerial post in any Cabinet formed by at least 14 members, and at least two portfolios in Cabinets comprising 28 members or more.

The confessional distribution of government posts was maintained for the public administration, although only for the civil service's upper echelons and without pre-assigning specific posts to any community. The Tai'f Agreement specified that:

> "The following shall be done during the interim period [...] Abolish the sectarian representation base and rely on competence and specialization in public jobs, the judiciary, the military, security, public, and mixed institutions, and in the independent agencies, in accordance with the dictates of national accord, excluding the top-level and equivalent posts which shall be shared equally by Christians and Muslims without allocating any particular post to any confession."[808]

The first category included 256 positions to be divided equally between Christians and Muslims; the Armenian quota, from the Christian half, amounted to six or seven appointments. In terms of parliamentary seats, Electoral Law No.154 awarded Armenians a sixth seat, while Armenian Evangelicals were also allowed to contest the Protestant seat in Beirut. In the post-Tai'f period Armenians could potentially win seven seats, an unprecedented number. Armenian representation was improved through various State structures, but the three Armenian parties continued to nominate candidates along partisan lines.[809]

The 1990s and early 2000s ware periods of uncertainty for Armenian cultural diversity in Lebanon. The slow post-war recovery of Lebanon took its toll on the Armenian community, questioning the financial sustainability of Armenian communal institutions.[810] Armenian leadership lacked unity or a clear strategy, despite fully accepting the temporary restoration of the Lebanese consociational agreement.

808 See the Tai'f Agreement, Section (G).
809 Geukjian, "From Positive Neutrality to Partisanship," p. 744.
810 Migliorino, (Re)Constructing Armenia in Lebanon and Syria, p. 179.

3.5 The Institutional Structure of the Armenians in Lebanon

3.5.1 Religious Institutions

The Lebanese Constitution demands that communities identify themselves by their religious affiliations,[811] and the Armenians have three. However, only Christianity is legally recognized as the Armenian religion. Non-Christians and atheists have no recognition, and the government must abide by religious court decisions in matters of personal status. Based on the Ottoman model, the Armenian Orthodox and Catholic churches are recognized as separate communities by the Lebanese government.[812] Protestant Armenians are not recognized separately, but as Lebanese Protestants. Most Lebanese Armenians belong to the Armenian Orthodox community under the Catholicosate of Cilicia and the Prelate of the Armenian Church in Lebanon. The rest are distributed between Catholic and Evangelical faiths.[813]

3.5.1.1 The Armenian Apostolic (Orthodox) Church

The administration and internal affairs of the Armenian Apostolic Church are still regulated by the Armenian National Constitution (hereafter 'National Constitution'), which in Ottoman Turkish is referred to as the (*Nizamname*) "Regulation of the Armenian Nation."[814] This is a document that was written in 1860 by Armenian Patriarchy of Constantinople and approved by the Ottoman Empire in 1863.[815] This system offer people from different backgrounds the opportunity to get involved in communal affairs in one of the sub-organizations (such as financial, judicial and educational bodies) or by being elected to its own parliament.[816] The church has schools and institutions, and plays a central role in preserving Armenian identity in Lebanon.[817] The church also retains authority in

811 Ibid.

812 Ara Sanjian, "Armenians and the 2000 Parliamentary Elections in Lebanon."

813 Geukjian, "From Positive Neutrality to Partisanship," p. 741.

814 Fehmi Akın, The Approach of the Ottoman Empire to Armenians within the Context of The Regulation of the Armenian Nation Dated 1864 (Turkey: Marmara University, 2008), https://bit.ly/2lSQRyd.

815 Ibid

816 Ibid.

817 Vahram Ter-Matevosyan et al., "Institutions and identity politics in the Armenian diaspora: the cases of Russia and Lebanon," *Diaspora Studies*, 10:1 (2017), p. 76.

family law issues (marriage, divorce, fosterage and alimony), and exists as an important center of social life, managing schools, charities and cultural activities. These institutions, which include laymen and clergy, have national assemblies, religious committees and family tribunals as well as an executive committee and sub-committees for secular issues.

Lebanon hosts the headquarters of the Holy See of Cilicia of the Armenian Apostolic Church, providing a unique significance for the Armenian diaspora. Apostolic Armenians in Lebanon, Syria, Iran, Greece, Cyprus, and several parishes in the West are subject to the Holy See of Cilicia's jurisdiction.[818] One of the prelacies of the Holy See of Cilicia is the Armenian Prelacy of Lebanon which as of 2021 runs sixteen churches and five schools across Lebanon,[819] and most parishes provide Sunday schools for children.[820]

3.5.1.2 The Armenian Catholic Church

One supreme Patriarch exercises jurisdiction over the world's Armenian Catholic dioceses from his cathedral in Ashrafiyeh, Beirut.[821] The Patriarchate was established in 1743 by Apraham Bedros I Ardzivian. The Bzoummar monastery was built in 1749,[822] the church in 1771 and the theological seminary in 1810. The Patriarchate has enjoyed good relations with Maronite and other Lebanese Patriarchates since 1741, which helped settle Armenians in Lebanon in 1921–2.[823] The Lebanese Armenian Catholic community and its courts are administered by ecclesiasts. The seven local churches are administered by a priest, who

---

818 Since the eleventh century, the Apostolic Church has had two main administrative centres, known as Catholicosates. The Catholicos of Etchmiadzin was located in the Caucasus, while the Catholicos of Cilicia was in Turkey. The Genocide wiped out church institutions in Cilicia, and its Catholicos fled to Syria's Aleppo first, then to Lebanon, where the American Committee for Relief in the Middle East leased the Catholicos an orphanage in Antelias, allowing the reestablishment of the Apostolic Church and making Antelias one of the most important global centres for Apostolic Armenians.

819 Four Armenian national schools were recently combined under a school called United Armenian College.

820 "Sunday Schools," Armenian Catholicosate of Cilicia, 2019, https://bit.ly/2X2rBDJ.

821 Hratch Bedoyan, "The Social, Political, and Religious Structure of the Armenian Community in Lebanon," *The Armenian Review*, 32:2 (1979), p. 121.

822 Bzoummar administrates Armenian Catholics globally, functioning as an intellectual centre with a seminary and a library of rare Armenian manuscripts.

823 Messerlian, *Armenian Participation*, p. 14.

appoints laymen for religious or educational needs, and the Patriarchate controls the priests.[824]

Other Armenian Catholic institutions liaise with the Patriarchate but are directly responsible for their activities to their Abbot in Venice and Prioress in Rome. These are the Vienna Mekhitarists, who run an institution in Bikfaya, and the Immaculate Conception of Armenian Sisters in Beirut, who run two schools in Fanar and Bourj Hamoud and an orphanage in Bzommar for girls, where they also have a retirement home for nuns.[825]

3.5.1.3 The Armenian Protestant Church

Lebanese Protestants, including the Armenian Evangelicals, are considered as a single community whose member churches are represented by the Supreme Council of the Lebanese and Syrian Evangelical Council.[826] This council safeguards its political interests but does not interfere in the internal affairs of its churches. The Armenian Evangelical communities of Lebanon and Syria are each represented by four delegates[827] covering a decentralized community with no specific administrative center. Instead, there are several geographically based Armenian Evangelical Unions. Lebanon is important because the executive committee of the Union of the Near East is based there. Today there are six Protestant Armenian churches in Lebanon. Haigazian University in Beirut is biggest Protestant Armenian College in Lebanon, and the only higher educational institution in the entire diaspora. Haigazian University was established in 1955 as a classical school and became a university in 1966.[828]

3.5.2 Political Institutions

In the early 1900s, Armenians established political institutions in Lebanon. *Tashnagtsutioon* which was founded in Tbilisi in 1890 and in Lebanon in 1904, is a socialist and nationalist party. The Social Democratic *Hunchagian* party (initially founded in 1885 in Geneva), established in Lebanon in 1912 and considers itself Marxist with nationalist elements, and the Democratic Liberal *Ramgavar*

824 Ibid.

825 Ibid.

826 See the official website of the Supreme Council of the Lebanese and Syrian Evangelics: www.scevanchurch.org evangelical council https://bit.ly/324JuCX.

827 Messerlian, *Armenian Participation*, p. 16.

828 See the official website of Haigazian University, 2020, http://www.haigazian.edu.lb/.

party, established in 1921, advocates the application of democratic principles. All three parties gradually emerged with sophisticated cadres and leaders, and function until today in other countries including Republic of Armenia and the wider Armenian diaspora. No independent Armenian groups have challenged the leadership or play active roles in the community. Armenian communists did not establish their own party, but in 1925 helped establish the communist party of Lebanon.[829]

3.5.3 Educational, Social and Cultural Institutions

The Constitution allows all communities to establish schools[830] and teach their own history and language.[831] In 1924, *Nor Piunik,* the first Armenian newspaper in an Arab-defined country, went to press, and by 1944 fifty-seven Armenian publications were available in Lebanon,[832] playing an important role in the political and humanitarian areas and maintaining the Armenian language. The first long-lasting Armenian language daily, *Aztag*, was established in 1924 by Hagop Balian, and was transferred in 1927 to *Tashnagtsutioon*. *Zartonk* newspaper dates from October 1937 as an organ of the *Ramgavar* Party, while *Ararad* newspaper was established in November 1937 by the *Henchag* party. Unions such as *Marsh, Hadjin, Ourfa* and *Zeitoun*, named after placed worst affected by Armenian Genocide maintain charitable organizations, but many lack legal registration and State support.[833]

There are also dozens of monthly and quarterly journals, in-house magazines and newsletters from organizations, churches, schools, and centers.[834] Only the party-sponsored press survived the civil war but are now under severe pressure because of the economic crisis in Lebanon has hit advertising revenues and the younger generations see them as old fashioned.[835] Social media helps Lebanese Armenians to communicate more easily. There are no statistics, but web pages, social groups or blogs published through Lebanese networks are widespread.[836]

829 Migliorino, (Re)Constructing Armenia in Lebanon and Syria, p. 56.
830 See Article 10 of Lebanese Constitution.
831 Ter-Matevosyan et al., "Institutions and identity politics in the Armenian diaspora," p. 70.
832 Migliorino, (Re)Constructing Armenia in Lebanon and Syria, p. 123.
833 Messerlian, *Armenian Participation*, p. 14.
834 Jebejian, "Patterns of Language Use among Armenians in Beirut," p. 454.
835 Migliorino, (Re)Constructing Armenia in Lebanon and Syria, p. 212.
836 Ibid.

Two Armenian stations, Radio *Van* and Radio *Sevan* (established in 1986 and 2007 respectively) offer the Armenian communities in Lebanon and the diaspora 24-hour broadcasts, reporting on political, social and cultural issues in Lebanon and Armenia. The stations promote Armenian culture, language and music. Art exhibitions are organized in different art galleries, including *Luci Tutunjian* and *Noah's Ark*,[837] while political and cultural institutions have their own sporting, educational, cultural and youth associations.[838] *Tashnagtsutioon*'s sister organizations include *Homenetmen*, a sport and scouting association, *Hamazkayin*, an educational and cultural association running theater, dance, painting and music classes, the Armenian Relief Cross and the Lebanese Youth and *Zavarian* Student Associations. Similar institutions are also run by the Armenian General Benevolent Union Lebanon as well as by the other two political parties *Henchag* and *Ramgavar*.[839]

There have been attempts to broadcast Armenian television programmes in Lebanon. The first was broadcast in 1996 on the private network ICN and lasted eight months. In 2000, with parliamentary elections approaching, Rafiq Al-Hariri offered an Armenian news programme on his 'Future' Television network, and in April 2003 a new programme produced by the Armenian Catholic Patriarchate began broadcasting from Lebanon on *Nour Sat*, a satellite channel controlled by the Christian television network *Télé-Lumièr'*. In 1999 *Al-Mustakbal* 'Future' and in 2009, 'Orange' television stations started broadcasting daily 30-minute Armenian news programs.[840]

The first Armenian school in Lebanon was the eighteenth-century catholic seminary in *Bzoummar* Abbey, which still functions. The number of Armenian schools and kindergartens has increased in mid-twentieth century, and by 1948 fifty-nine Armenian schools served nearly eleven thousand pupils in Lebanon,[841] rising to 66 by 1975 and boasting a combined 21,000 students. However, emigration and the civil war reduced numbers, and by 1991 only 42 as well as 5 vocational schools remained. At present there are only 26 functioning Armenian schools in Lebanon, serving 8,000 students.

---

837 "Armenian Community in Lebanon," Embassy of Armenia to Lebanon, 2019, https://bit.ly/2K8TOni.

838 Ter-Matevosyan et al., "Institutions and identity politics in the Armenian diaspora," p. 69.

839 See the official website of AGBU Lebanon, http://agbulebanon.org/ and the official website of *Ramgavars*: http://ragmamoul.net/en/.

840 Jebejian, "Patterns of Language Use among Armenians in Beirut," p. 455.

841 Abramson, "Lebanese Armenians; A Distinctive Community," p. 203.

3.5.4 Judicial Institutions

Personal Law issues are generally managed by Lebanon's religious courts. The Judicial Acts of the Armenian Apostolic Church are performed according to procedural laws of the Armenian Church of Lebanon's Procedural Rights Courts, based on the Lebanese Republic Law of 2 April 1951 – the "Law on the Rights of Christian and Jewish Communities' Religious Authorities"[842] – approved by the Armenian Orthodox Church and the Catholicosate of Cilicia. The political and religious National Assembly appoints a judicial council consisting of three clergy and three laymen.[843] The Chairman of the Council is a bishop, who participates in meetings of the presiding board individually or through a representative. Judicial Council meetings are chaired by an elected representative from the secular assembly and may invite a specialist lawyer to conduct its proceedings. The Court of Appeal comprises three religious and three secular members elected by the National Assembly's Board of Directors, and the chairperson runs this position personally or through an intermediary.[844]

The heads of the First Instance Armenian Orthodox courts are usually civilians, often with no legal background. Panos Manjian, a former Lebanese Army general, was the head of the first instance court at the time of writing this thesis. The court of the appeal is headed by a bishop, who also has no legal background.[845] According to Aram I:

> "The only problem that I see is the absence of legal experts in our courts. To address the issue, the president of the court asks the intervention or the legal opinion of legal experts. To be on the safe side the bishop, who is the president of the court, offers some confidence and moral authority to the court which is very important."[846]

The evangelical courts have a similar structure. The Union has its headquarters in Lebanon, and its central executive council appoints judges, clerics and laymen for personal matters in Lebanon's Armenian Evangelical Community, first

842 Law of 2 April 1951 – the "Law on the Rights of Christian and Jewish Communities' Religious Authorities".

843 See Article 45 of the Code of Armenian Prelacy of Lebanon, www.armprelecylb.org, https://bit.ly/2Wy57dJ.

844 Ibid, Article 46-47-48.

845 Personal interview with Maître Simon Khederian, lawyer at the Armenian Orthodox Religious Court, the interview was held online on 26.08.2018.

846 Personal interview with His Holiness Aram I, Catholicos of the Armenian Orthodox Church, Holy See of Cilicia, the interview was held in Antelias on 21.09.2018.

instance court, judicial court and court of appeal.[847] The evangelical courts employ legal counsels, through whom all cases pass to ensure that laws and regulations are respected.[848] Since Armenian Evangelists have no separate religious court, Rev, Haidostian points out that attempts are sometimes made to appoint non-Armenian judges to the upper court. Such attempts have so far failed, but non-Armenian appointments may be made in the future to ensure transparency and justice.[849]

Catholic Armenians follow the same system as the entire Catholic denominations in Lebanon. There is a unified first instance tribunal for the entire Lebanese territory and only one court of appeal. It is however possible to appeal first instance decisions directly before the Rota courts in Vatican. The cassation appeal can be presented either before the Court of Cassation (Civil Chamber) or before the Rota in the Vatican.[850]

It seems Armenian denominations' religious courts in Lebanon do not necessarily meet internationally accepted standards and procedures.[851] According to Aram I "Unfortunately our courts do not reflect up-to-date standards in terms of personal or international laws." The quality of the courts is controversial, and this author notes that all interviewees are aware of their imperfections. Interviewees mentioned that political/religious interventions and favoritism plays a negative role during trials of family cases. In addition, equality is not emphasized in the 'National Constitution' inherited from the Ottomans. Then there is the question of mentality. "We are in the Middle East and it's a Patriarchal system. In our case because we are in a daily contact with western societies, we are much more sensitive to the issue of equality between men and women. We are very careful to preserve this equality as much as possible" comments Aram I.[852] For example, according to Dr. Sanjian, in one divorce case, the verdict gave custody of a divorced couple's child to the grandmother from the father's side because the

847 Messerlian, *Armenian Participation*, p. 16.

848 Personal interview with Rev. Dr. Paul Haidostian, president of Haigazian University, community and religious leader of Armenian Protestant Community in Lebanon, the interview was held in Beirut on 17.09.2018.

849 Ibid.

850 Mansour and Daoud, Lebanon - The Independence and Impartiality, p. 15.

851 Personal interview with Rev. Dr. Paul Haidostian, (17.09.2018).

852 Personal interview with His Holiness Catholicos Aram I, (21.09.2018).

mother was a Jehovah's Witnesses.[853] This is unlawful and unacceptable. There is little accountability, and public reports on court conduct is rare.

The situation in Armenian religious courts reflects other Lebanese religious courts, which are incompatible with International Law and eschew internationally accepted standards and procedures, often violating human and minority rights (Article 26 of ICCPR and Article 3.2, Article 4.2 and 8.2 of the Declaration). Addressing this issue at national level is of the utmost importance.

3.6 Armenian Minority Rights in Lebanon

Four basic rights will be discussed in this section, and a detailed analysis will be provided on the rights to existence, identity, equality and non-discrimination, and effective participation. Since there is no sufficient literature or legal research on the rights of Armenians in Lebanon from a legal perspective, this section also includes and reflects upon interviews the author undertook with various Lebanese Armenian citizens from a variety of backgrounds and backed up the research on legal issues and existing literature.

3.6.1 The Right to Existence

The right to collective existence of Lebanese Armenians within the Lebanese territory is protected by law and politics as a recognized community by Tai'f Agreement.[854] This does not mean that there are no threats to the existence of Armenians. Political unrest, lack of security, economic problems, regional wars, continuing lack of opportunities, corruption, the dangers of assimilation, the absence of the rule of law, uncertainty about the present and the future are among the factors that directly threatens the physical and collective existence of Armenians in Lebanon.

While minorities have a right to protection and continued existence under UN general assembly Resolution 47/135/1992[855] and inter alia its Article 1.2 requires that "States shall adopt appropriate legislative and other measures to achieve those ends,"[856] there are no specific protection mechanisms for

853 Personal interview with Dr. Ara Sanjian, Lebanese Armenian historian, lecturer at Michigan University, the interview was held online on 10.10.2018.

854 See Tai'f Agreement.

855 Article 1.1 of Minority Declaration: "States shall protect the existence and the national or ethnic, cultural, religious and linguistic identity of minorities within their respective territories and shall encourage conditions for the promotion of that identity."

856 Article 2.1 of Minority Declaration.

minorities, including Armenians or to any other constituent of Lebanese society. The nature of the Lebanese system and the resources police and security forces or other State institutions have cannot provide an effective protection of Lebanese citizens regardless of their background.[857]

This might be one of the reasons, why almost all Lebanese communities have self-defence militias, and many – including the Armenians – work with State security forces to defend their communities.[858] As Kothchikian argues "Minimum guarantees are provided. You may have the will, but you may not have sufficient resources and abilities to comply with the international standards. The will is there but the means are not. The State is highly fractured and State institutions are weak."[859]

In addition, the temptation to leave for the West and Armenia is powerful, especially for educated young people. They identify the need to free themselves from doubtful regimes and the sense of being regarded as incomplete citizens, and from their own communities, which many consider close-knit and restrictive. The erosion of the Armenian middle class encourages migration, further weakening the Armenian presence in Lebanon.[860]

Financial problems surrounding Armenian institutions and organizations is causing decreasing enrolment in primary and secondary schools.[861] While Armenian institutions continue to function, activity levels have declined to the extent that Lebanese Armenians no longer feel they live in the capital of the Armenian diaspora which influences to their collective existence.[862]

Nevertheless, compared to other Middle Eastern states, it can be argued that the right to existence for Armenians is well established in Lebanon. However, Armenians feel uneasy whenever Lebanon faces external threats. Conflicting

---

857 "Lebanon: Situation of Christians, including treatment by society and authorities; treatment of Christians by Hezbollah and Al-Qaeda; State protection (2011-2013)," Canada: Immigration and Refugee Board of Canada, 16.01.2014, LBN104728.E, https://bit.ly/2NElbYF.

858 Personal interview with Prof. Asbed Kotchikian, senior lecturer, Global Studies, Boston University, the interview was held online on 10.10.2018.

859 Ibid.

860 Migliorino, (Re)Constructing Armenia in Lebanon and Syria, p. 199.

861 Varduhy Hyusisyan, "Armenians in Lebanon After Israeli Invasion in 2006: A Community Under Threat of Vanishing" (Master Thesis, American University of Armenia, 2008), p. 20.

862 Salhani, "The Armenian 'Signifier,'" p. 143.

parties demand that Armenians take a side, and when they refuse to do so they become targets for all sides.[863]

> "Every time Lebanon loses its balance, we feel that our basic right to existence is threatened. Therefore, we should not examine the right to existence in the peaceful times of Lebanon, but rather during its tensions and conflicts."[864]

In times of conflict, many Armenians fear being targeted or expelled. According to one inhabitant of Anjar:

> "We often ask ourselves what we are doing here. This is not our land. We cultivate it, but when the political currents turn against us, we will be deported again. After all, not long ago, we were forcefully uprooted from our historical homeland. How can we be sure we would be left in peace in Lebanon, which is not our historical homeland? We may be deported any time despite our Lebanese citizenship. We do not know what is going to happen to Lebanon, and the future is rather uncertain."[865]

> "I do not see any threat towards the official existence of Armenians, but psychologically I feel threatened. The same applies to all Christians and sometimes to all Lebanese people. Often the Lebanese State tries to show more sympathy towards Armenians because we are respected as good citizens who add value to society."[866]

In this context, a recently published Article in the local media seems to indicate that "Armenians of Lebanon are becoming extinct"[867] (*Arman Lebnan Yankaridoun*). The Article says:

> "The last (2018) parliamentary elections revealed radical changes affecting the Christian community in general and the Armenian community in particular. Perhaps these changes concern the emigration of Armenians to America and European countries.... The majority of those who remain today belong to the older generation, which raises more than one question about the existence of an entire community that is threatened with extinction."[868]

---

863 Ohannes Geukjian, "An Ignored Relationship: The Role of the Lebanese Armenian Diaspora in Conflict Resolution (1975–90)," *Middle Eastern Studies*, 50:4 (2014), p. 554.

864 Personal interview with Rev. Dr. Paul Haidostian, president of Haigazian University, Community and Religious leader of Armenian Protestant Community in Lebanon, the interview was held in Beirut on 17.09.2018.

865 Sima Aprahamian, "Armenian Identity: "Memory, Ethnoscapes, Narratives of Belonging in the context of the Recent Emerging Notions of Globalization and its Effect on Time and Space," *Feminist Studies in Aotearoa Journal*, 60 (1999), p. 7.

866 Personal interview with Rev. Dr. Paul Haidostian, (17.09.2018).

867 Ibrahim, "Armenians of Lebanon are Becoming Extinct."

868 Ibid.

The Article offers some statistics to back up its argument:

> "In comparison to the religious and sectarian distribution of voters between 2009 and 2018, the Armenian Orthodox population recorded a decline in numbers across Lebanon from 91290 voters to 87679 voters, and from 20709 Armenian Catholic voters to 19566 voters in 2018. This is equivalent to an Orthodox decline of 3.96 % and a Catholic decline of 5.52 %."[869]

The recent drop in voter numbers and the wave of emigration by Lebanese Armenians towards Armenia or the West may threaten the existence of the community in the long term. According to the *Ararad* daily newspaper:

> "If the Genocide was a red massacre, aiming at extirpating Armenians, the white massacre is the life we are living. The white massacre is the transfer of Armenians into foreign places, migration, assimilation, forgetting national customs and traditions little by little. This is an issue that should bother Armenians all over the world and make them decide on proper ways of addressing this issue."[870]

In other words, Armenians have profound concerns for their continuing existence,[871] and only feel comfortable in areas where they are numerous, where they can raise collective defence mechanisms in the face of weak State institutions. When ISIS was a threat, Armenians living in Christian areas felt safer than those who lived in Tripoli and Anjar, but in the face of conflict a trend has been established to move to Armenia or the West to find new opportunities.[872]

The extent to which the Lebanese government can meet its obligations to protect the Armenians' right to existence will be discussed at greater length in the chapter on State obligations. Although there are currently no serious or immediate threats to the Armenians' physical security in Lebanon, the factors discussed above might eventually result in imminent threats to their existence as an organized community.

3.6.2 The Right to Identity

Many historians see the Armenian community in Lebanon as a success story for identity preservation and active involvement in national causes.[873] The identity

869 Ibid.

870 "Why Do They Migrate from Motherland?," *Ararad Daily newspaper*. 2-8.07.2006.

871 Hyusisyan, "Armenians in Lebanon After Israeli Invasion in 2006," p. 20.

872 Personal interview with Dr. Ara Sanjian, Lebanese Armenian historian, lecturer at Michigan University, the interview was held online on 10.10.2018.

873 Ter-Matevosyan et al., "Institutions and identity politics in the Armenian diaspora," p. 73.

of Lebanese Armenians cannot be understood outside the historical and cultural circumstances within which it was negotiated. The Armenian community has followed cycles of identity preservation, redefinition and renegotiation. While the community's formative years in the 1920s and 1930s were conditioned by traumas of the Genocide, it was soon integrated into the Lebanese fabric economically, politically and socio-culturally.[874] One of the main indicators of this integration was that during the heaviest fighting in the Lebanese Civil War, many local Armenians did not flee the country and pursued a policy of non-involvement based on self-preservation and dedication to their adoptive homeland.[875] The war has eroded the trust of many Lebanese Armenians, encouraging migration and generating a sense of disillusion about life in Lebanon, particularly among the young.[876] On the other hand, for some, the war has reinforced a sense of belonging to Lebanon. The shared experience, communal self-help and self-governance have been significant experiences shared by the disparate population of a common country. The trend towards further "Lebanonization" has encouraged marginal elements to adopt assimilationist approaches, but for the majority of Armenians the war has revived the shift from being a nation in exile to being a permanent transnational diaspora.[877]

Migliorino argues that the debate over Armenian identity has taken place in the context of Lebanese reconstruction that started in 1989–1990.[878] This reconstruction questioned the organization of relations between the State and ethno-cultural groups, which was using the consociational formula that offered the Armenians the chance to preserve their cultural diversity. The relationship between the Armenians and the Lebanese State today depends on whether the new version of consociationalism and the re-establishment of the 'Lebanese model' still serves the Armenian community's needs and aspirations.[879]

In this context, the meaning of Armenian identity has been influenced by one crucial event: the inception of the Republic of Armenia in September 1991, seventy one years after the first Republic of Armenia fell in 1920. Independence, and the Nagorno Karabagh (Artsakh) crisis[880] between 1988 and 1994, have

874 Kotchikian, "Between (Home)land and (Host)land," p. 475.
875 Ibid.
876 Ibid.
877 Migliorino, (Re)Constructing Armenia in Lebanon and Syria, p. 179.
878 Ibid.
879 Ibid, p. 180.
880 For more information see Heiko Krüger, *The Nagorno-Karabakh Conflict: A Legal Analysis* (London: Springer, 2010).

become symbolic for exiled Armenian nationals, reinforcing the dominance of Armenian concerns. By facilitating a dramatic increase in interaction between Armenia and its diasporas, independence has dispelled myths about Armenian nationalism and helped to underscore Armenian identity.[881] A study of Statutes and charts shows that all Armenian organizations in Lebanon pursue the strengthening of Armenian national identity within Lebanon.[882] *Tashnagtsutioon* believes that preserving Armenian history, language and culture is of utmost importance to the diaspora,[883] while ensuring that Armenians remain loyal and dutiful citizens in Lebanon.

The Armenian Genocide is a common cause that mobilizes Armenians and represents vital factor to Armenian identity.[884] To be Armenian is to be concerned with all Armenian issues, including participation in annual commemorations on April 24, remembering the 1.5 million victims of the Genocide, advocating for the Artsakh cause and enhancing relations between Armenia and Lebanon.[885] The Lebanese Parliament has recognized the Armenian Genocide twice,[886] while many facets of the Turkish government still refuse to.[887] Moreover, being Armenian means following a liturgical calendar and celebrating Christmas on January 6. It means speaking a unique language and keeping traditions alive.[888]

On the other hand, to be Armenian in Lebanon according to some locals is:

> "…to carry within yourself the anguish of all the times where you felt different, when you *were* different, when you were not a part of the Lebanese identity. Either because so many Armenians did not speak Arabic properly for so long (a language completely

---

881 Migliorino, (Re)Constructing Armenia in Lebanon and Syria, p. 180.

882 See Homenetmen & Hamazkayin Statutes as well as AGBU Mission.

883 "*Dzrakir Hay Heghapokhagan Tashnagtsutian* (1998)." (ARF Programme,) Published by the 27 General Assembly of ARF.

884 Anthonie Holslag, *The Transgenerational Consequences of the Armenian Genocide: Near the Foot of Mountain Ararad* (Swiss: Palgrave Macmillan, 2018), pp. 241-243 and Agnieszka Pikulicka-Wilczewska and David B. MacDonald, *Identity Politics in the Age of Genocide* (New York: Routledge, 2007), p. 119.

885 Maral *Dikran* Boyadjian, "Ethnic Identity and Psychological Well-Being among Fourth-Generation High School Students in Lebanon" (MA Thesis, Beirut, American University of Lebanon, 2005), p. 30.

886 Lebanon, Chamber of Deputies, Resolution – 03.04.1997, and Lebanon, Chamber of Deputies, Resolution – 11.05.2000.

887 Richard Hovannisian, Ed., *Remembrance and Denial: The Case of the Armenian Genocide*, (Detroit: Wayne State University Press, 1999).

888 Boyadjian, "Ethnic Identity and Psychological Well-Being," p. 30.

> unfamiliar to your grandparents on their arrival) or even because, despite your presence on this land, you arrived at a later period in history, and will always be a foreigner.... It's the agonizing memories you've carried around for so many years when your Lebanese classmates made fun of your name as a result of attending a non-Armenian school."[889]

In most Armenian homes the mother tongue is still spoken, "Even now in the Middle East we cannot envisage an Armenian who does not speak Armenian" argues Sanjian.[890] Most Armenians live in Armenian areas, preserving their identity alongside other Armenians who live and work in the same area.[891]

Religion is another crucial aspect of identity:

> "In Lebanon you are born, you get married, get divorced, inherit, die and are buried based on your religious sect [...] In this part of the world religion is not an option; you can't do much without a religious passport [...] You are given your own little niche and you do whatever you want as long as it is permissible."[892]

Religion emphasizes identity and allows Armenians political representation and participation.[893] As mentioned above, the relocation of religious centers to Lebanon has also contributed positively to developing the Armenian community.[894]

It should be highlighted that for most of Lebanese Armenians, preserving the Armenian identity did not prevent them from integrating into the Lebanese society, Many Armenians living in Lebanon feel fully integrated:

> "Let's face it, we are very much part of the local fabric. We have no anxieties about knowing where we are or where we belong. We feel we belong here, which is why we never thought of leaving Lebanon during the war years. We lived the hardships of the war just like our Lebanese neighbours. We were threatened by the same bombs, endured the same misfortunes."[895]

While working on this thesis, all interviewees firmly agreed that Armenians should perfectly learn the Arabic language, culture and history of Lebanon. The

---

889 Ibid, p. 32.

890 Personal interview with Dr. Ara Sanjian, Lebanese Armenian historian, lecturer at Michigan University, the interview was held online on 10.10.2018.

891 Ter-Matevosyan et al., "Institutions and identity politics in the Armenian diaspora," p. 75.

892 Myriam Sfeir, "Arda Arsenian Ekmekji, An Armenian-Lebanese Academician Recounts," *Al-Raida*, Volume 20:101-102 (Spring/Summer 2003), p. 71.

893 See Arpine Papikian, "The Impact of Religion on the Preservation of Armenian Identity in Lebanon" (Thesis Georg-August-Universität Göttingen, Göttingen, 2017), p. 5.

894 Ustun, "The History of the Armenian Community in Lebanon," p. 99.

895 Sfeir, "Arda Arsenian Ekmekji," p. 71.

problem is that acculturation weakens traditional definitions of Armenian identity,[896] and since the line between preserving Armenian identity and assimilation is thin, challenges are growing. According to Pakradouni:

> "Agreeing on the elements of the Armenian identity is challenging. Are not speaking Armenian, not going to Armenian schools, marring non-Armenians, becoming disconnected with Armenian institutions, assimilation within other cultures threats to the Armenian identity? Is receiving Armenian State citizenship helpful to preserving Armenian identity? Some argue that 'feeling Armenian is enough to preserve identity. However, experience shows that those who followed an assimilationist approach in earlier centuries are fully assimilated and can only admit to Armenian origin."[897]

Although Lebanon's communal autonomy favors the preservation of Armenian identity, the spectre of assimilation, whether voluntary (as in the US and France) or imposed (as in Turkey) does not threaten all Lebanese Armenians equally.[898]

In other words, in the last two decades, assimilation has become a real challenge for Lebanese Armenians and will continue to progress.[899] Soon, little will remain of the Armenian communities in Lebanon and other Middle Eastern countries.[900] In preserving the Armenian identity, the challenges the community in Lebanon faces include the loss of language and the problem of mixed marriages. There is a reduction in the number of the people speaking Armenian, and a growth in mixed marriage. Struggling with assimilation, the Armenian community emphasizes the activities of its organizational structures and contests assimilation, demographic change and emigration, but the Armenian discourse no longer mobilizes new generations.

> "We are becoming more Lebanese. The decrease in identity awareness is leading the Armenians to seek solutions for their daily life problems before addressing challenges to their identity. People are being bribed to vote for non-Armenians, and because

896 Ibid.

897 Personal interview with Mr. Hagop Pakradouni, Armenian Member and Secretary of Lebanese Parliament and chairperson-representative of the Central Committee of the Armenian Political Party ARF-Tashnagtsoutioon in Lebanon, the interview was held in Beirut in 19.09.2018.

898 Abramson, "Lebanese Armenians; A Distinctive Community," p. 199.

899 Hagop Doghramadjian, "Diaspora Focus: Lebanon," *The Armenian Weekly*, 2017, https://bit.ly/2PGoeB4.

900 Neil Hauer, "Middle East's Armenians in Retreat," *Asia Times*, 2019, https://bit.ly/2Wx73mO.

of the economic hardship, people are putting their identity aside and voting for non-Armenians."[901]

In this context, Associations contribute to the preservation of Armenian identity when it is threatened by war and economic crisis. They help limit migration and invest resources in Armenian education or other cultural activities. Associations have played a direct role in promoting Armenian culture.[902] However, this has become increasingly difficult, and the Armenian self-help network itself now appears to be under stress. Fundraising is largely insufficient, and voluntary work and financial support from richer global diasporas has become increasingly important.[903] In Lebanon, the right of association is still grounded in Article 13 of the Constitution,[904] regulated by the 1909 Ottoman law,[905] but modern practices reveal legal inadequacies and ambiguities, particularly regarding associations' official registration and licensing, and the range the governmental control. Many Armenian institutions continue to operate without registration.[906] Episodes of restrictive government legal interpretations expose the fragility of the associations' position under current regulatory frameworks.[907]

Nevertheless, identity preservation binds the loyalty of the Armenian community to its institutions, be they schools, political parties, patriotic organizations, churches or media.[908] In this context, Armenian political parties play a key role in consolidating Lebanon's Armenians, acting as the institutional infrastructure around which Lebanon's Armenian community is organized.[909] Nevertheless,

901 Personal interview with Mr. Hagop Pakradouni, (19.09.2018).

902 Migliorino, (Re)Constructing Armenia in Lebanon and Syria, p. 200.

903 Ibid, p. 201.

904 Article 13 of the Lebanese Constitution: "The freedom to express one's opinion orally or in writing, the freedom of the press, the freedom of assembly, and the freedom of association shall be guaranteed within the limits established by law."

905 See the Ottoman Law on Associations, provided and translated by the International Center for Not-for-Profit Law: https://bit.ly/327oX0B.

906 Migliorino, (Re)Constructing Armenia in Lebanon and Syria, p. 202.

907 In 1992 the government withdrew the registration of 138 associations, claiming they were engaging in political activities. The political inconsistency of this approach encourages the view that the law was interpreted to accommodate Syrian agendas dominance in Lebanese political life.

908 Ter-Matevosyan, et al "Institutions and identity politics in the Armenian diaspora," p. 71.

909 Khatchig Der Ghoukassian, "Lebanon in My Mind. The Civil War and the Centrality of the Lebanese-Armenian Community in the Making of the Armenia Diaspora

they do not strategize integration or delay assimilation. They also lack a united vision/strategy on addressing the common challenges the community is facing.

There are concerns on insufficient means to preserve Armenian identity. Membership of Armenian political parties and affiliated organizations and attendance at Armenian schools are "no more than pain relievers."[910] People talk about these issues, but they remain talks, they are rarely transferred into actions. For example, launching a Fund for Strengthening National Identity in 2017 by *Tashnagtsutioon*,[911] aimed to address these challenges and to help young Armenian couples with marriage expenses, baptism expenses for Armenian children as well as to provide a Family Rejuvenation Fund for families with three or more children and a Student Foundation to support Armenian students.[912]

To sum up, according to scholars like Geukjian, the Lebanese socio-political communal structure contributed to the preservation of Armenian national identity.[913] Although the Lebanese State's weakness has proved its Achilles' heel, Lebanese Armenians cherish the latitude offered and run their own private schools, while clergy from all three denominations regulate personal issues in their religious courts – all without government intrusion. So congenial has the Lebanese system been to Armenian self-sufficiency that "nowhere in the Middle East did the concept of the *Millet* system take such hold and nowhere in the area did the Armenians flourish so well under it as in the Republic of Lebanon."[914] This argument may have been true for the last century, but the challenges discussed above have weakened Armenians' identity, and institutions will not survive without State support. This is because the influence of Armenian institutions decreases, the threats to Armenian identity rise accordingly. Armenians are abandoning institutions, and the more this happens, the more rapidly their identity will weaken, and their rights and guaranties will deteriorate.

Nationalism," in *Armenians of Lebanon: From Past Princesses and Refugees to Present- Day Community*, A. Boudjikian ed., (Beirut: Haigazian University, 2009), pp. 411-429.

910 Hyusisyan, "Armenians in Lebanon after the Israeli Invasion In 2006," p. 37.

911 *Aztag* newspaper, 28.03.2017.

912 "From May 2017 to June 2018, 270 Armenians benefited from the "Strengthening National Identity," in *Aztag* newspaper, 04.08.2018, http://www.*Aztagdaily*.com/archives/403838.

913 Geukjian, "From Positive Neutrality to Partisanship," p. 741.

914 Robert H. Hewsen, *Armenia: A Historical Atlas* (Chicago: University of Chicago Press, 2001), p. 268.

3.6.2.1 Right to Education and Mother Tongue

The Lebanese school regulatory framework allowed Armenians to develop autonomous education and cultural preservation.[915] The post-independence policy continued the principles expressed in the 1926 constitution, namely the freedom of education. The consociational political system renounced the concept of the education as an instrument of state-building, and the lion's share of Lebanon's educational needs were met by the private sector and the Ministry of Education simply bridged the gaps left by communities.[916]

Armenian schools in Lebanon were covered by Ministerial Decree 1436 (1950) regulating the private sector, and the 1956 Law setting rules for teaching bodies. Armenian schools are mainly affiliated to the Armenian Churches (Apostolic, Catholic and Evangelical), the political parties (*Tashnagtsutioon*, *Hunchagian, Ramgavar*) and the AGBU. Mergers or closures of schools could easily assume the significance of political events, altering balances within the community. The current struggle is not preserving one network of Armenian schools but preserving several.[917]

In 1960, Armenian elementary schools taught most subjects in Armenian, but efforts were made to adapt programs to national curricula, so that Armenian students could develop a sense of belonging to their 'second motherland' and to obtain diplomas for universities and careers.[918] Many Armenians who settled in Lebanon after the Genocide opted to learn western languages, especially French and English, before Arabic, as Arabic and the power of the Lebanese government were in dispute under the French mandate. Self-imposed residential segregation kept the Armenian community insulated and made the need for Arabic unnecessary or basic, while French and English were important for travel and commerce.[919] Students wishing to pursue Armenology could study at the American University of Beirut or the Université Saint-Joseph, each of which boasted a chair of Armenian studies. Lebanon was a religious educational center for Apostolic and Catholic Armenian communions. Apostolic Armenian ordinands came to study at the Cilician See's seminary in Antelias, while Catholic Armenian clergy from the diaspora came to receive instruction in the Bzoummar seminary.[920]

---

915 Migliorino, (Re)Constructing Armenia in Lebanon and Syria, p. 114.
916 Ibid.
917 Ibid.
918 Ibid, p. 117.
919 Jebejian, "Patterns of Language Use among Armenians in Beirut," p. 460.
920 Abramson, "Lebanese Armenians; A Distinctive Community," p. 203.

The 1989 Tai'f Agreement instigated educational reform, creating a new curriculum promoting national unity.[921] The propositions of the Tai'f Agreement on education – criticized by some as vague and subject to misinterpretation – potentially marked a turning point in the relationship between State and private education, although the reinforcement of control over private schools failed to materialize.[922] The regulatory follow-up, a "New framework for education in Lebanon" (*Haykaliya jadida li al-ta'lim fi lubnan*, 1995)[923] and a revision of the curriculum (completed in 1997) updated national educational programs but avoided challenging private schools' autonomy. The main goals of the new curriculum were "building the individual's personality and establishing citizenship."[924] The 1997 curriculum emphasized citizenship, education and reconciliation, and included a new compulsory subject, National and Civic Education, taught one hour per week from Grades 1 to 12.[925]

In 2010 Lebanon began further reforms, revising the citizenship curriculum and textbooks.[926] New reforms considered the extent to which the 1997 curriculum addressed components promoting social cohesion and reconciliation.[927] Language rights were considered basic to pluralistic democratic societies and part and parcel of human rights.

The Armenian language is an important expression of Armenian identity, maintaining social relationships and preserving historical links. Lebanon is one of the few native language speaking centers for Western Armenian in the Armenian diaspora.[928] With regard to mastering the language, a study conducted by Jebejian with students showed that 87.2 % considered Armenian to be their first language while 90.3 % of parents spoke Armenian as the first language at home. 9 % considered Arabic as their first language, as opposed to 7.9 % of parents. Fourth-generation Armenian students are therefore less proficient in Armenian,

---

921 Maha Shuayb, "Human Rights and Peace Education in the Lebanese Civics Textbooks," *The Centre for Lebanese Studies*, 10:1 (2015), pp. 135 –150.

922 Ibid.

923 "*Haykaliya jadida li al-ta'lim fi lubnan*," (New Structure for Education in Lebanon), Ministry of Education Publication, 1995.

924 "General Objectives of the Curricula and their Details," Educational Centre for Research and Development, Beirut, 1997, p. 3.

925 Shuayb, "Human Rights and Peace," p. 135.

926 Ibid.

927 Ibid, p. 136.

928 Hourig Attarian, Armenian Schools and Education in Lebanon: Fostering a New Culture of Learning, Teaching and Practice (Lisbon: Gulbenkian Foundation, 2014), p. 5.

and in certain circles Armenian is losing prominence. A small percentage of the sample (1.3 %) did not speak the language at all or spoke it poorly (6.3 %), but this should not be surprising, as almost 90 % of the students in the sample attend Armenian schools. The results indicate assimilation, considering that 7.4 % of students do not know how to read Armenian at all, 11.6 % read Armenian poorly, 8 % cannot write in Armenian at all and 17 % write Armenian poorly.[929] Teachers of Armenian language, literature and history expressed concern that their courses are not sufficient to perpetuate Armenian culture. Such courses are subject to government policies and regulations.[930] One principal pointed out:

> "The curriculum has to be approved by the Lebanese government. The students must be prepared for the Lebanese governmental exams, and as a result we must give priority to subjects in these exams. Armenian language, literature and history are not part of the programme. They are given over and above the required courses. Hence, some students do not take these courses seriously."[931]

This might suggest that the educational system in Lebanon endangers cultural and linguistic proficiency for the new generations of Armenian community. Before entering the university, students must pass the government Baccalaureate examinations, which test proficiency in Arabic language, literature and history. This requirement automatically makes these subjects mandatory in all Armenian schools, while the Armenian community believes that safeguarding Armenian culture and identity is their responsibility alone.[932]

Western Armenian language is declining, the current generation of teachers is aging, and there are no clear plans for a generational transfer. "Our roots have started to dry up," one educator commented, "the only long-term solution to save Western Armenian is to invest in teacher education, to have qualified teachers in Armenian-related subjects, both locally and transnationally."[933] There are many factors affecting language. The first is the negative impact of decreasing school enrolment. Fewer students mean fewer formal learners contributing to linguistic atrophy. There is no unified approach to Armenian classes in primary and secondary schools. Classes are being reduced to prioritize exam-related subjects, and the lack is felt strongly when it comes to financial support.[934]

---

929 Jebejian, "Patterns of Language Use among Armenians in Beirut," p. 466.

930 Aprahamian, "Armenian Identity: Memory, Ethnoscapes, Narratives of Belonging," p. 8.

931 Ibid, p. 9.

932 Ara Sanjian, "The Armenian Minority Experience in the Modern Arab World," *Bulletin of the Royal Institute for Inter-Faith Studies*, 3:1 (2001), p. 152.

933 Attarian, Armenian Schools and Education in Lebanon, p. 16.

934 Ibid.

Despite conditions of freedom and autonomy that many consider ideal for Armenian education, Armenian schools in Lebanon have not recovered since the war, and numbers of both schools and students have been dropping since 1990.[935] Between 1991/2 and 2001/2 the number of schools fell from 45 to 33 and decreased to 26 in 2019[936] with just 8,000 students compared to nearly 12,000 in 1991/2.[937] All schools face deficits.[938] The crisis is explained by a combination of factors, the first of which is the overcapacity of the Armenian educational system. The population decrease caused by war and emigration had a delayed effect on schools.[939] A second factor concerns the effects of post-war and current economic crisis on school enrolment. Lebanese incomes have been reduced by economic factors, and families can no longer afford private education.[940]

Other explanations for falling enrolment are reflected in changes in attitude toward the importance of Armenian education. Some higher income families prefer non-Armenian private colleges, believing they offer a better education and more opportunities. Families believe that Armenian schools place excessive burdens on students, preparing students for national examinations by adopting an extended curriculum combining national curriculum subjects with Armenian subjects.[941] As tuition fees fund private schools, falling enrolment results in closure. Boards respond to this by closing or merging schools. Schools call for increased support from local community support structures and the diaspora, producing only partial success due to the economic crisis and decreasing support for the Armenian community and the lack of financial or substantive State support.

Most Armenians live under no illusion that the State could intervene to support Armenian schools.[942] They receive little assistance from the government, and usually balance their budgets using donations from wealthy Armenians in their communities or the West.[943] For Armenian schools

---

935 Ibid, p. 12.

936 "Armenian Community in Lebanon," Embassy of Armenia to Lebanon, 2019, https://bit.ly/2SYq9Cz.

937 Jirayr Tanielian, *Lipananahay Tebrotze: Tiver yev Mdoroumner* (The Armenian Schools in Lebanon, Some Data and Some Ideas), (Lebanon, 2002).

938 Attarian, Armenian Schools and Education in Lebanon, p. 16.

939 Migliorino, (Re)Constructing Armenia in Lebanon and Syria, p. 202.

940 Ibid, p. 203.

941 Ibid.

942 Ibid, p. 205.

943 Hyusisyan, "Armenians in Lebanon after the Israeli Invasion In 2006," p. 29.

to survive and thrive, targeted reforms and State support seems to be inevitable.[944]

3.6.3 The Right to Equality and Non-discrimination

Before the civil war of 1975, the State was ruled by Maronites, who also controlled Lebanon's economic power.[945] Some argue that it was this inequality between Muslims and Christianity that led to the civil war.[946] The Tai'f Agreement confirmed Muslims and Christian equality, at least constitutionally.[947] Even if the number of Christians become fewer than the Muslims, the agreement would remain in terms of the power-sharing relationship.[948]

The UN concluded that Lebanon's diverse personal status laws and confessional system differentiated citizens, and the access to power was based on factional affiliation.[949] In Lebanon, citizenship is inherited only through a male relative (father or husband). A woman cannot pass citizenship neither to a child born to a non-Lebanese father nor to her non-Lebanese husband.[950] Under a market-oriented economy, lawlessness thrived, and confessional networks organized employment and services.[951] Political and administrative careers depends on confessional community membership, while most of Lebanese religious authorities are also political actors, intervening in political debates.[952] The amended Constitution of 1990 recommended abolishing religious affiliation as a criterion for government positions, but few practical steps have been taken to accomplish this.[953]

---

944 Attarian, Armenian Schools and Education in Lebanon, p. 5.

945 Personal interview with Mr. Yeghia Tashjian, expert in political relations and research, founder of New Eastern Politics Bloc, the interview was held online on 08.09.2018.

946 Robert Nicholson, "Lebanon's Discontent Has Religious Roots," *Wall Street Journal, 2019,* https://on.wsj.com/2NElkvf.

947 Ohannes Geukjian, *Lebanon after the Syrian Withdrawal: External Intervention, Power-Sharing and Political Instability* (New York: Routledge, 2016), p. 42.

948 Joseph Bahout, "Lebanon's Tai'f Agreement: Limits of Sect-Based Power Sharing," Carnegie Endowment for International Peace, 2016, https://bit.ly/2C3zhMy.

949 Human Rights Council, "Compilation prepared by the Office of the High Commissioner for Human Rights in accordance with paragraph 15 (b) of the annex to Human Rights Council Resolution 5/1," 02.09.2010, A/HRC/WG.6/9/LBN/2, para. 17.

950 UNDP, *Lebanon Gender Justice & The Law* (USA: UN Publication 2018), p. 8.

951 Human Rights Council, "Compilation prepared by the Office of the High Commissioner for Human Rights," para. 17.

952 Migliorino, (Re)Constructing Armenia in Lebanon and Syria, p. 194.

953 Castellino and Cavanaugh, *Minority Rights in the Middle East,* p. 352.

To evaluate the status of Armenians in relation to equality and discrimination, the issue should be situated in the larger context described. Are there discriminatory policies towards Armenians compared to other communities? Many interviewees believe that there is no discrimination towards Armenians. "In the beginning we faced discrimination because we were newcomers, and we were seen as a danger to the opportunities of others."[954]

The Lebanese State avoids discrimination based on ethnic, religious or linguistic affiliations,[955] but inequality still prevails because the State is built on the confessional consensus. In other words, it seems that inequality is somehow accepted to maintain the balance among communities. In this context Armenians often hold secondary cabinet positions. In addition, as diplomat Vartanian says "Because our community is not strong enough, I cannot become an ambassador in any G20 country, even though I have the qualifications and the experience."[956] Armenians cannot become the head of the Army, Foreign Minister, Interior Minister or Prime Minister because of unwritten customs. Ironically enough this custom is not seen by many as discrimination *per se* because of the power sharing system of Lebanon. Moreover, public sector opportunities are limited for Armenians; for every 100 vacancies only 2 Armenians can be appointed.[957]

In addition, some interviewees believe they are being discriminated against,[958] with a general impression that Christians, as an ever-decreasing minority throughout the Middle East, are despised, secretly or otherwise, by the majority Muslim population.[959] In addition, like all ethnic groups, especially urban cultural minorities, Lebanese Armenians are stereotyped by the Lebanese.[960] "If you are an Armenian you are supposed to eat *basterma*, speak broken Arabic and live in Bourj Hammoud, mixing genders in speech because the Armenian language is gender-neutral."[961]

---

954 Personal interview with Mr. Vicken Avakian, director of Radio Voice of Van, former school Principal, Zarehian Seminary teacher, writer, member of Homenetmen Central Committee, the interview was held online on 15.09.2018.

955 See Lebanese Constitution's Preamble Para. C.

956 Personal interview Mr. Shant Vartanian, newly appointed Lebanese diplomat, the interview was held in Beirut, on 15.09.2018.

957 Ibid.

958 Ibid.

959 Arda Arsenian – Ekmekji, "Revisiting Artin in Beirut How Armenians are Viewed in Lebanon," Arab Stereotyping Conference, Haigazain University, November 2001, https://bit.ly/38KlnQN.

960 Ibid.

961 Sfeir, "Arda Arsenian Ekmekji, An Armenian-Lebanese," p. 72.

There is not any State intervention to counter hate speech. Armenians sometimes lack awareness and community leaders are not able to control abuse on social media channels. One example of hate speech and racial abuse concerns basketball matches in Lebanon. Tensions between the *Homenetmen* and *Riyadi* teams have been high since 2017, when Turkish flags raised at the January 8 match between the clubs sparked controversy. Photographs of the flags circulated on social media networks after the game as a targeted attack against the *Homenetmen* players and fans, since *Riyadi* is not a Turkish club. Online comments included "If you want to stop us raising the Turkish flag at the stadium, then stop them from singing the Armenian national anthem at their stadium."[962] Mohammed Khoder, a Riyadi supporter, tweeted "Tonight we'll be raising the Turkish flag in the basketball game against the Homenetmen Armenian Lebanese team! BURNNN!"[963]

Riyadi responded with an official statement on its Facebook page, denouncing the raising of the Turkish flag and condemning provocation.[964] Several *Riyadi* fans were criticized for similar actions during 2019 seven-game series. The Prime Minister, Saad Hariri, condemned the fans' actions. But hate speech incidents do not result formal complaints. In general, club officials apologise on behalf of their fans and the incident is considered closed. To understand the context better, hate speech also occurs in other games. For example, pro-Syrian sport groups might chant "Syria! Syria!" at anti-Syrian opposition. Other clubs raise Hezbollah's or Iran's flag to anti-Iranian clubs to provoke them. Spreading hate speech is not just used towards Armenians, and there are no legal mechanisms to prevent such incidents.

In this context, many community representatives believe that the anti-Armenian discourse is made under the Turkish influence.[965] Khederian believes that "the anti-Armenian discourse does not reflect most of the Lebanese communities. We should not forget that Turkey, and particularly Erdogan, influences them in the region and hence they prefer to show loyalty to Turkey by targeting Armenians."[966] Vartanian similarly argues that "anti-Armenian statements tend

962 "Turkish Flags Spark Controversy at Homenetmen Lebanon Basketball Game," *The Armenian Weekly*, 10.01.2017, https://bit.ly/3bY7Bdo.

963 Ibid.

964 Ibid.

965 "Anti-Armenian Protests Continue in Beirut," *Azernews*, 2019, //bit.ly/2C8kGzo.

966 Personal interview with Maître Simon Khederian, lawyer at the Armenian Orthodox Religious Court, the interview was held online on 26.08.2018.

to take place on a very narrow level, and are made by small numbers of groups motivated by Turkish influence and policies in certain areas of Lebanon."[967]

Community representatives believe that the weaker and fewer the Armenians become, the more anti-Armenian sentiments they will face. Anti-Armenian incidents generally increase during election times, with Armenians being described as 'temporary residents' and told to go home if they don't like Lebanese political policies or procedures.[968] These sentiments are common to Christians and Muslims in Lebanon, but regardless of their timing, such statements may eventually be translated into real existential threats as Armenian presence in Lebanon diminishes.

In Lebanon it is vital to adopt anti-discrimination laws.[969] Without them, there are no effective guarantees. For example, Armenians who are fired or not hired because of their ethnic or religious background have no effective and well-established mechanism of recourse. In general, there is a lack of trust towards rule of law in combatting discrimination. Discrimination cases do not come to court in Lebanon, and there are no laws protecting minorities from hate speech or hate crimes. It is possible to file a case on the grounds of defamation, but no such cases have gone to court so far, because of the long and complicated judicial process and the possibility of provoking tension within the communities. With no specific law governing hate speech, everything is based on mutual respect. Armenians emphasize tolerance, mutual respect and dialogue, but this approach is spiritual, moral and political, rather than legal. The culture of equality and non-discrimination embodied in the constitutions of many developed countries has not yet materialized in Lebanon.

3.6.4 The Right to Participation

> "Lebanon is a country of communities. Everything in Lebanon is based on communities."[970]

Once Lebanese Prime Minister Saad Hariri stated: "Lebanese Armenians are considered to be instrumental in public life - in labour relations, production, culture,

---

967 Personal interview with Mr. Shant Vartanian, (15.09.2018).

968 Personal interview with Hagop Pakradouni, (19.09.2018).

969 Nadim Houry, "Time for an Anti-discrimination Law," Human Rights Watch, 16.12.2012. https://bit.ly/2IEsFdY.

970 Personal interview with His Holiness Catholicos Aram I, Catholicos of the Armenian Orthodox Church, Holy See of Cilicia, the interview was held in Antelias on 21.09.2018.

education and arts."[971] Armenians enjoy full rights in the political, economic and social spheres, consolidated in the constitution.[972] However, as Pakradouni argues, the Lebanese State does not always offer opportunities for participation, and large communities do not offer opportunities for smaller communities to participate in public life.[973] The preservation of the 1926 Constitution and the formula of coexistence reinforced political and juridical bases for participation, offering the reconstruction of an Armenian institutions in Lebanon, but the requirements for public participation remain fairly limited.[974]

Historically, the *National* Accord (*Mithaq Al-Watani)* resulted from negotiations between Bishara Al-Khouri and Riad Al-Solh, leading representatives of the Christian Maronite and Sunni Muslim communities.[975] No Lebanese communities were collegially involved in the pact, although Armenians were counted *ex officio* in the Christian group, and their numbers were used to help forge a balance in which Christians were offered a preeminent position.[976] The ratio of Christian to Muslim-Druze parliamentary representatives remained at 6 to 5. For the Armenians, their inclusion in the National Pact gave the blessing of the newly independent State to their continued presence in Lebanon. The Armenian community strove to cope with this, trying to impose itself in Lebanon and be recognized as a religious sect, consolidating communal distinctiveness by identifying with the Armenian Church.[977]

The following sub-sections will analyze the participation of Armenians in Lebanese political, economic, social and public life, and their involvement in decision-making processes.

---

971 "Speeches by Karen Karapetyan and Saad Hariri during the official dinner given in honour of RA Prime Minister," the official website of the Government of Republic of Armenia, Armenia, 13.03.2018, https://bit.ly/3bwR95j.

972 Article 7 of the Lebanese Constitution: "All Lebanese shall be equal before the law. They shall equally enjoy civil and political rights and shall equally be bound by public obligations and duties without any distinction."

973 Personal interview with Hagop Pakradouni, Armenian Member and Secretary of Lebanese Parliament and chairperson-representative of the Central Committee of the Armenian Political Party ARF-Tashnagtsoutioon in Lebanon, the interview was held in Beirut in 19.09.2018.

974 Migliorino, (Re)Constructing Armenia in Lebanon and Syria, p. 203.

975 Ibid, p. 93.

976 Ibid, pp. 93-94.

977 Avsharian, "The Tai'f agreement and the Lebanese Armenians," *p. 387.*

3.6.4.1 Political Participation

Growing activism in Lebanon's political processes is a relatively novel feature of the post-Genocide Armenian diaspora.[978] After the 1923 Lausanne Treaty, Armenians realized that their diasporic existence appeared more permanent, leading to active involvement in Lebanese politics. They hoped that this involvement would help them integrate with their hosts and pursue local and international causes close to their hearts through the legislatures of their host countries.[979] The Armenian political community was well represented in the first Republic of Lebanon, and since that time with different proportionalities.[980]

Armenian participation in Lebanese Parliament was not encouraging, particularly before the Tai'f Agreement.[981] Participation began in 1929 when Abdallah Ishaq, an Armenian Catholic, became the first elected Member of Parliament.[982] Deputy Vahram Lelekian was elected even before Lebanon gained independence from France, while Hrachia Shamlian and Movses Der-Kalousdian represented the Armenians after independence.[983] Thirteen different Lebanese Armenian individuals were elected to the Lebanese Parliament between 1927 and 1991, with inconsistent numbers and varied percentages. The Tai'f Agreement set a fixed percentage on Armenian representation, and only six seats are now allocated to the Armenians.[984] The law prescribes that of 64 Christian deputies, five should be Armenian Orthodox and one Armenian Catholic.[985] All Evangelicals are considered as members of one common *Millet*.[986] Armenian Evangelicals have no pre-allocated seat, and Armenian and non-Armenian Evangelicals compete for a single seat, which is considered to represent the entire Evangelical community in the legislature.[987]

---

978 Ibid.

979 Abramson, "Lebanese Armenians; A Distinctive Community," p. 193.

980 Avsharian, "The Tai'f agreement and the Lebanese Armenians," p. 388.

981 Ibid.

982 Geukjian, "From Positive Neutrality to Partisanship," p. 743.

983 Avsharian, "The Tai'f agreement and the Lebanese Armenians," p. 388.

984 Ibid.

985 See Electoral Law of Lebanon.

986 Personal interview with Rev. Prof. Paul Haidostian, president of Haigazian University, Community and Religious leader of Armenian Protestant Community in Lebanon, the interview was held in Beirut on 17.09.2018.

987 See Electoral Law of Lebanon.

In 1960 the Armenian community became entitled to a minister in the Lebanese government.[988] The Tai'f Agreement codified the postbellum political order, prescribing that Armenians receive a second portfolio if there are thirty or more members in a cabinet.[989] This changed Armenian representation in all subsequent Lebanese governments. Of 12 post Tai'f Agreement governments, Lebanese-Armenians were represented with a 9.7 % share.[990] According to Michael Hudson, 'the Percentage game' governed interaction between religious sects, affecting the Armenian community negatively.[991]

Lebanese Armenians were not politically united throughout the decades. Internal divisions from the 1950s continued in the post-Tai'f period. The Armenian parties failed to reach a compromise over political representation of the Armenian community, and the *Hunchags* and *Ramgavars* rejected to give the *Tashnagtsutioon* a monopoly to control Armenian deputies to maintain an Armenian bloc inside Parliament and hence to have a united position to defend Armenian communal concerns. From the *Tashnagtsutioon* perspective, the Armenian bloc demonstrated political strength and bargain power with Lebanese groups during election campaigns, as well as exerting significant influence on government.[992]

> "We can consider the Armenian bloc as an institutional group expressing the interest of the community and having direct access to policymakers. Our block proposes ministers in the cabinet because we are the real representatives of the Armenians. A fragmented representation in Parliament could not effectively serve Armenian communal interests."[993]

In this context, Armenian political parties mobilized their electorate efficiently. Once support had been won, they delivered Armenian votes at the polling stations.[994] Pre-election periods in Lebanon, particularly since the Civil War, have proved a mixed blessing for the Armenian minority. Armenians form about 4 %

988 Christine Babikian, *L'identité Arménienne: Le cas Libanais [The Armenian identity: The Lebanese case]*. Paper presented at the Présence de L'arménie [The presence of Armenia] conference. Retrieved 14.01.2003, from Saint Joseph University (Beirut: History Department, Lebanon, 2003), pp. 1-8.
989 Avsharian, "The Tai'f agreement and the Lebanese Armenians," p. 404.
990 Ibid.
991 Ibid.
992 Geukjian, "From Positive Neutrality to Partisanship," p. 739.
993 Personal interview with Hagop Pakradouni, (19.09.2018).
994 Geukjian, "From Positive Neutrality to Partisanship," p. 739.

of the country's electorate, and their votes are significant in the constituencies of Beirut and the district of Metn, including the suburb of Bourj Hammoud.[995] In recent years, Armenian participation has lagged behind the average because of mass migration.

The first post-war Lebanese parliamentary elections were characterized by continuing the dominance of *Tashnagtsutioon*. In 1992 and 1996, the *Tashnagtsutioon* maintained its position within the Armenian sector and led Armenian lists including *Tashnagtsutioon*, *Hunchagian* and *Ramgavar*/AGBU figures. Armenian coalitions sided with the Syrian-supported government in charge.[996] The political scene became more complex in 1998 after President Emile Lahoud was elected.[997] By 2000, antagonism between Lahoud and Hariri forced the Armenian parties to choose between supporting the government or siding with Rafiq Hariri in his attempted political comeback. The disastrous policy that still haunts the Armenian Lebanese community began in 2000, when Hariri's government changed parliamentary election laws and stripped the Armenian Lebanese majority (75 %) of its right to elect representatives.

In the run up to the elections, the unity of the Armenian camp was shattered by Hariri's determination to create a support base within the community. In a campaign to boost his image, Hariri opened offices in Armenian neighborhoods, dispensed aid to needy families, and introduced a fifteen-minute news service in Armenian on his television network, *Al-Mustaqbal*. As the elections approached, Hariri ignored the traditional leading role of the *Tashnagtsutioon* and picked his own candidates. For the *Tashnagtsutioon*, negotiations to join the Hariri list failed when it became apparent that they could only join on Hariri's conditions – renouncing the candidacy of an Armenian for the Protestant seat and the longstanding maintenance of an Armenian bloc of deputies in parliament. The vote marked a political revolution: the *Tashnagtsutioon* managed to obtain most of the Armenian vote, but Hoss lost the elections. As a result, for the first time in decades, *Tashnagtsutioon* hegemony was defeated. The *Tashnagtsutioon* scored a modest victory in the Metn, where minister and incumbent MP Sebouh Hovnanian was re-elected. New MPs obtained their seats with only a handful of

---

995 Sanjian, "Armenians and the 2000 Parliamentary Elections in Lebanon."
996 Migliorino, (Re)Constructing Armenia in Lebanon and Syria, p. 186.
997 Fida Nasrallah, "Syria after Tai'f: Lebanon and the Lebanese in Syrian Politics," in *Contemporary Syria: Liberalization between Cold War and Cold Peace*, E. Kienle ed., (London: British Academic Press, 1994), pp. 132–138.

Armenian votes, and 20 % of the Armenians that sided with Saad Hariri received 4 seats out of 6.[998]

The 2000 elections underlined the weakness of the Armenian position in Lebanon, exemplifying the limitations of the Lebanese system in producing fair representation and well-established political participation. The State took no action to stop the intervention of Hariri, nor did it protect the rights of the Armenians to fair and equal elections.[999]

The 2008 Doha agreement[1000] ending the Sunni-Shiite conflict in Beirut only partially re-instated the Armenian Lebanese majority's right to representation. The Doha agreement placed three Armenian Lebanese parliamentary seats in Beirut. Here, Armenians were outnumbered by the Sunni Lebanese and non-Armenian Christian Lebanese voters.[1001] This is why, during the 2009 election, the hijacking of four out of six Armenian seats raised eyebrows in Lebanon and around the world.[1002] These Hariri-controlled seats were filled by Armenians hand-picked by Saad Hariri. They received only 15–20 % of the Armenian votes in their respective districts yet were still elected.[1003]

The last Lebanese elections were held on May 6, 2018, for the first time in nine years.[1004] The three Armenian parties nominated eight candidates. *Tashnagtsutioon* won an additional seat in Parliament to secure three MPs, but the *Hunchags* lost their representative. The *Ramgavar* Party was unsuccessful in reclaiming the seat it lost in 2009.[1005] *Tashnagtsutioon*'s three winning candidates had a total of 13,009 votes combined.

> "Personally, I am not satisfied with the outcome of the recent elections. It was expected that there would have been more than 14,000 Armenian votes, but the number of the voters did not exceed 10,000. Political participation is going out of the political party's

---

998 Sanjian, "Armenians and the 2000 Parliamentary Elections in Lebanon."

999 Ibid.

1000 The Doha Agreement was reached by rival Lebanese factions on 21.05.2008 in Doha, Qatar. This agreement ended an 18-month-long political crisis in Lebanon.

1001 See A. Sanjian, "Armenians and the 2009 Parliamentary Elections in Lebanon," Armenian News Network / Groong, 29.06.2009.

1002 Appo Jabarian, "Hariri Hijacks Armenian Seats in the Lebanese Parliament," USA Armenian Life Magazine, 30.06.2019, https://bit.ly/36EfLox.

1003 Ibid.

1004 Ayda Erbal, "Expanded Version: Lebanese Elections and Lebanese-Armenian Politics," *The Armenian Mirror-Spectator*, 17.05.2018, https://bit.ly/32B5sxN.

1005 Ibid.

control. The NGOs and youth are not happy with the policies of the traditional political parties."[1006]

The lack of participation in recent parliamentary elections sent many messages. The voters lacked understanding of electoral laws, and lists were closed with voters only having one choice. Sevag Hagopian, *Ramgavar*'s international central board secretary and editor-in-chief of *Zartonk*, credited its loss to a "combination of the [new] law, bribery and delays in reaching an agreement between the three [Armenian] parties to form a unified block."[1007]

In this context, it is very important to mention that non-affiliated Armenian deputies won a plurality of mandates in every parliamentary election since 1992. They are *de jure* Armenian representatives who do not represent the Armenians. Paula Yacoubian, who ran with the Sabaa party, won an Armenian Orthodox seat in Beirut with 2,500 votes[1008] despite having no relationship with the Armenian community. Jan Tallouzian represents the Armenians without knowing Armenian (something very uncommon in the Lebanese context). Armenians have occasionally joined non-Armenian parties and ascended to leadership positions in them. Joseph Chader, a Catholic Armenian, was former vice-president of the Maronite Kataeb party and its first parliamentarian in the Chamber of Deputies.[1009] According to Avakian, since the number of Armenians and other Christians have declined, it is natural that Christians will not be the true representatives of their respective communities because they are elected by other community groups.[1010]

The gap between theory and practice within the confessional system was even more pronounced in the composition of cabinets. Amid protests from the Armenian community, Rafiq Hariri's October 2000 cabinet included only one Armenian minister instead of two, despite consisting of thirty members. The April 2003 government reshuffle failed to address this problem – in fact, the situation

---

1006 Personal interview with Mr. Yeghia Tashjian, expert in political relations and research, founder of New Eastern Politics Bloc, the interview was held online on 08.09.2018.

1007 Gasia Trtrian, "Tashnag: Last Armenian Party Left Standing in Vote Aftermath," *Daily Star*, May 2018, https://bit.ly/36SFRnm.

1008 Ibid.

1009 Abramson, "Lebanese Armenians; A Distinctive Community," p. 203.

1010 Personal interview with Mr. Vicken Avakian, director of Radio Voice of Van, former school principal, Zarehian Seminary teacher, writer, member of Homenetmen Central Committee, the interview was held online on 15.09.2018.

took an ironic turn when Kataeb party leader Karim Pakradouni was appointed Minister for Administrative Reform. Pakradouni, an Armenian Orthodox by birth, had virtually no political connections with the Armenian community. Protests against his appointment as an Armenian minister achieved no result. Aram I noted that:

> "Unfortunately, the rights of our community have been neglected recently. [...] The Lebanese State is based on the rights of the communities and their participation in public affairs, and we insist on respect for rights and participation. Therefore, we must differentiate between automatic membership of a given community through an identity card and an effective membership which confers real representation."[1011]

In other words, the State could not protect or address this violation of rights.

After the 2018 parliamentary elections discussions were held to exclude one Armenian minister from the cabinet and offer the position to another minority community. The three Armenian parties met on October 18, 2018, to discuss Armenian community representation. The participants welcomed efforts being made to form a government and hoped they would help lead the country from its political crisis. The meeting stressed party consensus to maintain sectarian balances and respect the customs as stipulated in the Tai'f Agreement. Participants expressed commitment to the community right of representation by two ministers.[1012] Armenian MP Hagop Pakradouni, acting Minster of Tourism Avedis Gidanian and Catholicos Aram I for the Catholicosate of Cilicia rejected the discussion to exclude one Armenian minster from the new government. "It is impossible to make any mistakes about this" said Pakradouni. Gidanian emphasized "the principle of respecting the full rights of Lebanese Armenians."[1013] Eventually, when the government was finally formed in 2019, two Armenians were included in the cabinet as Ministers of Tourism and Social Affairs.[1014]

Post-Tai'f governments marginalized the Armenians for several reasons. The first was that the Armenian parties lacked unified strategies and could not influence Lebanese decision makers or the Syrian authorities in Lebanon.[1015]

1011 Migliorino, (Re)Constructing Armenia in Lebanon and Syria, p. 184.

1012 *Aztag* newspaper, *Haghortakrutioon* (Statement), 18.10.2018.

1013 "*Aram Gatoghigos yev Pakradouni Ge Merjen Lipanani Hamyanki Iravunke Khlelu Portse,*" (Aram Catholicos and Pakradouni Reject the Attempts to Violate the Rights of Armenian Community), *Asbarez* Newpaper, 19.10.2018, https://bit.ly/2KaAzd1.

1014 Presidential Decree 4340, 31.01.2019, the official website of the Presidency of Council of Ministers of Lebanon, https://bit.ly/36WOvkO.

1015 Meguerditch Bouldoukian, "Armenian Business in Lebanon," *The Armenian Review, 32:2 (1979)*, p. 132.

Secondly, community demographics were altered by large-scale emigration.[1016] Armenian voter numbers fell year-on-year in the 1992, 1996, 2000, 2005, 2009 and 2018 elections. Low turnouts demonstrate a lack of interest by Armenians, and much the Armenian electorate had emigrated. The third reason for marginalization was the crisis between party leaders and younger Armenians who seem to be not happy with the traditional parties and are not voting for them.[1017] The fourth reason is the inability of the Lebanese State institutions to respect the laws and customs in managing political participation due to the sectarian nature of the political domain and the need for constant bargains and compromises to form governments and ensure their functionality.

3.6.4.2 Economic Participation

Armenians have prospered as much from the Lebanese economy as they have contributed to it. One observer noted in 1975 that "Armenians form approximately eight percent of the Lebanese population, but their contribution to the national income of Lebanon is fifteen percent."[1018] The per capita income of Armenians was forty percent above the Lebanese average. Armenians thrived as artisans, merchants and professionals, winning a reputation for industriousness and honesty. Government employment held little appeal for them, so much so that Armenians scarcely reached their quotas in Lebanon's confessionally divided public sector.[1019] Armenians went from pauperized refugees in the 1920s to a prosperous community within a few decades, due to the synergy between the Armenians' business acumen and the liberal Lebanese economy. Lebanon was especially conducive to the Armenians' talents in business,[1020] and Armenians rapidly became part of Lebanese economic life, to the extent that some MPs believed that if the Armenians left the Industry Association, for example, it would go bankrupt.[1021] There are also Armenian physicians, dentists, lawyers, engineers and other professionals who are actively engaged in the economic life of Lebanon.[1022] The current reality is different. Armenians suffer as much

---

1016 Ibid.

1017 Geukjian, "From Positive Neutrality to Partisanship," p. 746.

1018 Migliorino, (Re)Constructing Armenia in Lebanon and Syria, p. 133.

1019 Ibid.

1020 Hewsen, Armenia: A Historical Atlas, p. 268.

1021 Personal interview with Ms. Arsho Balian, editor of *Aztag* newspaper, the interview was held online in 05.08.2018.
Ibid.

1022 Messerlian, *Armenian Participation*, p. 36.

as other Lebanese communities from the lack of economic opportunities and high rates of unemployment. Several Armenian owned businesses are shot down recently due to lack of State support or intervention in times of financial and Covid-19 pandemic related crises.

3.6.4.3 Social Participation

Throughout the 20-th century, Armenians led an insular lifestyle in which they could spend their lives as 'outsiders'.[1023] Despite rapidly establishing economic ties, Armenians perceived social and cultural relations with non-Armenians as inimical to their survival. "Centuries of persecution have deepened the sense of paranoia toward outsiders – *odars* – who are sometimes regarded with apprehension lest they marry Armenians, thereby hastening the community's assimilation[1024]

Although uncommon, intermarriage between Armenians and Lebanese Christians did happen more frequently over time.[1025] Many Lebanese, mainly from Muslim backgrounds, though initially were antagonistic towards the Armenian refugees, gradually thawed to them.[1026] Armenians embraced their fellow Christian and Muslim citizens,[1027] so when Lebanese statesman Raymond Eddé spoke of "Armenians of the Lebanese family,"[1028] he voiced genuine Armenian sentiments.[1029] Using the heritage left from the mandate period, Armenians established cultural and social institutions. Today, as Ustun argues "It could be considered that fourth generation Armenian youngsters overcame difficulties in using Arabic and integrated into Lebanese society in contrast to their ancestors. Visibility of Armenians has increased quantitatively and qualitatively."[1030]

1023 Arda Jebejian, Changing Ideologies and Extralinguistic Determinants in Language Maintenance and Shift Among Ethnic Diaspora Armenians in Beirut (UK: School of Education University of Leicester, 2007), p. 84.

1024 Hrayr Dekmejian, "The Armenian Diaspora," in *The Armenian People: From Ancient to Modern Times*, Richard G. Hovannisian ed., Vol. 2 (New York: St. Martin's Press, 1997), p. 439.

1025 Aghop Der Karabetian and Emma Oshagan, "Ethnic Orientation of Armenians in Lebanon," *The Armenian Review*, 30:2 (1977), p. 164.

1026 Bedoyan, "The Social, Political, and Religious Structure," p. 120.

1027 Karabetian and Oshagan, "Ethnic Orientation of Armenians in Lebanon."

1028 Bedoyan, "The Social, Political, and Religious Structure."

1029 Tsolin Nalbantian, "Fashioning Armenians in Lebanon, 19461958" (PhD Dissertation, Columbia University, New York, 2011), p. 295.

1030 Ustun, "The History of the Armenian Community in Lebanon," p. 105.

The legacy of the Genocide and the fear of losing Armenian identity should not become obstacles to further integration. Lebanon's Armenian Community participates in charitable, cultural and sporting endeavors, constituting an important part of Lebanese society and sometimes represent Lebanon in regional and international arenas. Community organizations (AGBU, *Hamazkayin*, Lebanese Armenian Relief Cross, *Homenmen, Homenetmen*) sometimes even compete between themselves, which has a positive impact on the level of activities in their spheres.

3.6.4.4 Participation in Public Life

On the seventy-fifth anniversary of the *Homenetmen*, Hraoui,[1031] who delivered the keynote address, stressed Armenians' constructive role in Lebanon, declaring: "State institutions, including the army, police and internal security forces are open for you to join."[1032] He reiterated that no State policy marginalized Armenians, and that the State was ready to embrace the community because its members had demonstrated loyalty to Lebanon.[1033] The Armenians have traditionally avoided the Lebanese public sector, and the quota for Armenians is limited. The same holds true for the Army,[1034] but this has not prevented some Armenians from working in State administration. There are Armenian Director Generals, ambassadors and senior soldiers in the Lebanese army.[1035] Although Armenians were hesitant to involve themselves in the public domain, the new generation is different and more proactive.

The Goguikian Foundation,[1036] established in 2008, aims to "help the Armenian community in Lebanon to integrate into the fabric of society and take part in the governance of the country through encouraging its brilliant young men and women to work in the public sector."[1037] In this context Vartanian says:

> "People think that if you want to become a civil servant you have to have connections, since nepotism and favouritism play a role. However, in some posts this is not true. Based on my personal experience, my recruitment to the Ministry of Foreign Affairs

---

1031 Elias Hraoui, President of Lebanon from 1989 to 1998.
1032 *Aztag* newspaper, special issue, January 1994, p. 92.
1033 Ibid.
1034 Messerlian, *Armenian Participation*, p. 36.
1035 Geukjian, "From Positive Neutrality to Partisanship," p. 743.
1036 See the official website of Goguikian Foundation: https://www.goguikianfoundation.org/
1037 Messerlian, *Armenian Participation*, p. 36.

> was free of such things. Lebanese citizens can be hired as civil servants through the Civil Service Council."[1038]

On the other hand, Khederian believes that:

> "Although the constitution is clear in terms of the distribution of posts of first level State officials between Muslim and Christian and the rest on the basis of equality and qualifications, the reality is different, from the minister's driver to the high-ranking State positions which are distributed on a sectarian basis."[1039]

It seems that favoritism depends on the power and influence of the community.[1040] "We literally fight to appoint an Armenian in the State university as a lecturer," Pakradouni comments.[1041]

Although the Armenians view the Tai'f Agreement positively, its practice during the 1990s and early 2000s has been less well-received. There is a widespread perception that the representation of the Armenian community is not respected, and Armenians hold fewer public positions than they should under Tai'f Agreement.[1042] In November 2002 only four first category civil servants were Armenians (out of the six or seven that the community should have). The current situation is worse; the Armenians have two director generals, one ambassador and a deputy central bank director. At second category and lower levels Armenians are even less well-represented.[1043] If this could be ascribed to a matter of choice, the same cannot be said for the upper echelons, where underrepresentation results from the community's political weakness.

Religious membership is deeply interwoven into the fabric of society, and many are obliged to use religion as a 'ticket' to access certain services or posts.[1044]

1038 Personal interview with Mr. Shant Vartanian, newly appointed Lebanese diplomat, the interview was held in Beirut on 15.09.2018.

1039 Personal interview with Maitre Simon Khederian, lawyer at the Armenian Orthodox Religious Court, the interview was held online on 26.08.2018.

1040 Bilal Malaeb, *State Fragility in Lebanon: Proximate Causes and Sources of Resilience* (UK: University of Oxford and University of Southampton, 2017), p. 10.

1041 Personal interview with Hagop Pakradouni, Armenian Member and Secretary of Lebanese Parliament and chairperson-representative of the Central Committee of the Armenian Political Party ARF-Tashnagtsoutioon in Lebanon, the interview was held in Beirut in 19.09.2018.

1042 Migliorino, (Re)Constructing Armenia in Lebanon and Syria, p. 184.

1043 Personal interview with Hagop Pakradouni, (19.09.2018).

1044 Human Rights Council, "Report of the Special Rapporteur on Freedom of Religion," para. 66.

Individuals with different beliefs thus face a dilemma: they either have to go against their convictions or risk forfeiting certain opportunities. This violates Article 3.2 of Minority Declaration[1045] as not belonging or not participating to any religious community/practices might result in disadvantage or unjustified restrictions, loss of opportunities and limits to practice and enjoy the right to participation to public life. Disentangling opportunities from religious belonging would be in the interest of religious freedom, and would help create an open, inclusive society based on common citizenship and without discrimination.[1046]

Although Armenian Community leaders protest that the law should allow Armenians to participate in public life, sometimes they lack the capacity to occupy such positions. It can be argued that there is a reduced influence for Armenians in Lebanese public life due to lack of legal guarantees ensuring the right to participation. The Armenians' participation, like that of other communities, depends on political consensus and power.

3.6.4.5 Participation in the Decision-making Processes

While Armenians are consulted and elected to many local councils, they sometimes feel that their voices are not heard because problems outweigh their influence in solving them. A good example is the case of the Turkish peacekeepers. Around 260 Turkish soldiers arrived in Lebanon in October 2006 as part of the UN peacekeeping mission, raising concerns among Lebanese Armenians for historical reasons.[1047] The Armenians urged the government to reject Turkish troops, stating that all Lebanese communities should be respected equally.[1048] Catholicos Aram I released a statement denouncing Turkish presence as morally unacceptable. *Tashnagtsutioon* met with Lebanese Prime Minister Fuad Siniora, explaining that collective opposition signalled a community-wide consensus. Siniora replied that there were not enough international forces available to fulfill the needs of the international peacekeeping force and that the Armenian position was not sustainable. The Lebanese officials explained this kind of action was in the Lebanese interest. Another serious political

1045 Article 3.2 of Minority Declaration: "No disadvantage shall result for any person belonging to a minority as the consequence of the exercise or non-exercise of the rights set forth in the present Declaration."

1046 Ibid.

1047 "Turkish Peacekeepers Arrive for Mission in South Deployment Comes Despite Vocal Opposition from Armenian Community," *The Daily Star*, 21.10.2006.

1048 Hyusisyan, "Armenians in Lebanon After Israeli Invasion in 2006," p. 39.

setback for the Armenians was the naming of a square after Sultan Abdul Hamid[1049] in 2006.[1050] it seems that it resulted in a sense of betrayal among the Armenian community.

Similarly, Armenians were officially included in Lebanon's recent electoral laws, but felt marginalized. After helping construct electoral law, Hagop Pakradouni was left out of the committee, and other groups managed to tailor the new laws according to their own needs and interests.[1051] The situation is better at municipal level, where Armenians represent Bourj Hamoud, Mezher, Antelias and Anjar and are part of the decision-making processes. The Mayors of Bourj Hamoud[1052] and Anjar[1053] are Armenians.

To sum up, the right to participation gives Armenians less influence in modern Lebanon, reflecting their dwindling numbers and forming a vicious circle in which Armenian rights matter less, leading to emigration, reducing Armenians' inclusion in higher levels of State and marginalising them. Educated Armenians believe that a more principled stand on socio-political issues will help them assert their influence in local society and politics. In addition, preserving the Armenian identity in Lebanon underlines the importance of increased active involvement in broader national activities and national structures.[1054]

1049 The name "Sultan Abdul Hamid" has extremely negative connotation among Armenians as during his reign from 1894-1896 the *Hamidian* massacres were carried out against the Armenians. For information see: "Hamidian massacres, Ottoman and Armenian History," Britanica.com, 2020, https://www.britannica.com/topic/Hamidian-massacres.

1050 "Tripoli Decides to Name Square after Sultan Abdul Hamid," *Asbarez* Newspaper, 2006, https://bit.ly/2X1hr6B.

1051 "The Armenian Electorate Proved its Strength. Three of the Four ARF nominees - Hagop Bagratuni, Hagop Terzian and Alexander Matossian - Were Elected," *Diaro Armenia*, 2018, https://bit.ly/328lJd6.

1052 See the official website of Bourj Hamoud Municipality: https://www.bourjhammoud.gov.lb/ar.

1053 Arsho Balian, "*Marash Taghamasi Norokutian Dzrakire Shudov Girakordzevi*," (The Marash District Renovation Project Will Be Implemented Soon), *Aztag* newspaper, 16.01.2019 and 09.07.2016, http://www.*Aztagdaily*.com/archives/423401.

1054 Vahram Navoyan, "On the Modern Challenges the Armenian Community Faces in Lebanon," *Noravank* Foundation, 2013, https://bit.ly/2WZX2ie.

3.7 The Lebanese State's Obligations towards Armenian Minority Rights

By ratifying international instruments, Lebanon "assumes obligations and duties under international law to respect, protect and fulfill human rights,"[1055] including minority rights. "The obligation to respect means that States must refrain from interfering with or curtailing the enjoyment"[1056] of these rights. "The obligation to protect requires States to protect individuals and groups against human rights abuses"[1057] or violations. "The obligation to fulfil means that States must take positive action to facilitate the enjoyment of basic human rights."[1058] This section examines Lebanese State obligations to its Armenian minority.

3.7.1 Respecting the Rights of Armenian Minority in Lebanon

> "Much as we preserved our identity, we are integrated into Lebanese society. The State has never interfered or put obstacles in front of the preservation of Armenian identity."[1059]

Lebanon has granted all necessary freedoms to its communities,[1060] and many Armenians believe that the Lebanese State's attitude is positive, even 'extraordinary.'[1061] Lebanese Armenians are granted freedoms without hindrance.[1062] In reality, policies reflect the Lebanese confessional system. As long as national laws are respected, the State allows Armenian schools to teach Armenian language, history, religion and culture.[1063] The State does not interfere to the Armenian educational curricula. In addition, the director of Radio Van states that there is no interference in Armenian media,[1064] although censorship exists in Lebanon.[1065]

1055 UNOHCHR Official Page, International Human Rights Law, 2019, https://bit.ly/3pRq1V6.

1056 Ibid.

1057 Ibid.

1058 Ibid.

1059 Personal interview with Ms. Arsho Balian, editor of *Aztag* newspaper, the interview was held online in 05.08.2018.

1060 See Sections 3.1.2 and 3.1.3 above.

1061 Personal interview with Mr. Vicken Avakian, director of Radio Voice of Van, former School Principle, Zarehian Seminary Teacher, writer, member of Homenetmen Central Committee, the interview was held online on 15.09.2018.

1062 Joanne Randa Nucho, "Becoming Armenian in Lebanon," in *Middle East Report*, No. 267, Christians: Egypt, Iraq, Lebanon, Palestine (Summer 2013), pp. 32-36.

1063 Article 10 of Lebanese constitution.

1064 Personal interview with Mr. Vicken Avakian, (15.09.2018).

1065 For example, in 2010, Eileen Khatchadourian's music video '*Zartir Vortyag*' which touches on Armenian topics is reported to have been banned by the Lebanese General Security. See "Lebanon: Song touching 'The Armenian question' banned,"

The Armenian Christmas Day (January 6) is a national public holiday out of respect to the Armenians,[1066] Every 24 April, with prior authorization, Armenians organize demonstrations, vigils, or marches. The State remained neutral when Turkey sued the *Ramgavar's* and *Tashnagtsutioon's* dailies, *Zartonk* and *Aztag*, for publishing "false and defamatory" Articles.[1067] Although no similar charges were leveled at *Ararat*, the *Hunchagians* joined the other parties in mobilizing the Armenian public against this Turkish lawsuit. An estimated 20,000 Armenians assembled outside the Palais de Justice after the first hearing in May 1970. The Turks did not send a representative to the trial, so the judge postponed until July, by which time Turkey had withdrawn the suit.[1068]

There are no guarantees that non-intervention will continue. The press once endured censorship, and front pages of Armenian newspapers in the 1950s had blank sections where articles had been repressed or redacted.[1069] Nowadays there is little censorship, the State does not translate Armenian media into Arabic. But if the National Media Commission wants to censor Armenian media, there is nothing prevents it from doing so. For example, if relations with Turkey improve, Lebanese authorities could impose limitations on Armenian media, despite constitutional guarantees of freedom of speech.

The Lebanese State does not interfere in the personal affairs of Armenian communities, each of which has its own religious courts.[1070] Unlike Muslim judges, Christian judges are not paid by the government, but rather by community/church funds, because community members believe that if the State pays the judges, then they will intervene in the trials which is something not preferable for many as they prioritize non-intervention from the State.[1071] Armenian legal decisions are only rubber-stamped by State authorities. If a mistake has

---

Freemuse Artsfreedom Online Platform, 03.05.2010, https://freemuse.org/news/lebanon-song-touching-the-armenian-question-banned/.

1066 Decree No.15215, 27.9.2005 and its amendments, the Appointment of Holidays and Official Occasions.

1067 Zohrap Teokmechian, "*Trkakan Despanatan Batsats Date*," (The lawsuit filed by the Turkish Embassy,) *Zartonk* newspaper, 20.05.2016, p. 3.

1068 Personal interview with Ara Sanjian, Lebanese Armenian historian, lecturer at Michigan University, the interview was held online on 10.10.2018.

1069 *Aztag* newspaper, 03.04.1956.

1070 Article 9 of the Lebanese constitution.

1071 US Department of State "2016 Report on International Religious Freedom – Lebanon," 15.08.2017, https://bit.ly/36VAG5O.

been made, the right to appeal in front of Court of Cassation exists and only in this case the government can intervene, but this is rare.[1072]

Citizens are not required to show religious affiliations on their passports or identity cards,[1073] but they do exist in official registry extracts (*ikhraaj qaid*). The Government complies with citizens' requests to reflect new religious statuses, but Lebanese citizens wishing to marry, divorce, adopt or register births or deaths must refer to courts run by their own religious community.

Finally, at least in the recent decades, there are no records indicating Lebanese State's intervention in the process of electing/appointing religious leaders for all three Armenian denominations (Orthodox, Catholic, Evangelic) in Lebanon.

3.7.2 Protecting the Rights of Armenian Minority in Lebanon

Camille Chamoun, Lebanese president from 1952 to 1958, told the Armenians: "You should consider yourself in your own home, since it is without exaggeration when I say Lebanon is a second Armenia."[1074] This statement from country's highest leader indicates the willingness of the State to protect the Armenians.

Such attitudes change in times of crises, however. During the civil war, despite the Armenian community's policy of positive neutrality Armenians armed themselves to protect their neutrality when the Lebanese State failed to provide security for them.[1075] The efforts of each group to enhance its own security resulted in a dilemma in which each group undermined the security of the others.[1076] Armenian paramilitary formations maintained order in Bourj Hammoud, Khalil-Badaoui and Hadjin,[1077] which were considered neutral zones by the warring parties. The Armenians maintained their armed neutrality, except for a few violations in Khalil-Badaoui before its occupation, where Armenian

---

1072 See Section 3.1.4. above.

1073 US Department of State, "2016 Report on International Religious Freedom."

1074 Abramson, "Lebanese Armenians; A Distinctive Community," p. 212.

1075 Ohannes Geukjian, "The Policy of Positive Neutrality of the Armenian Political Parties in Lebanon during the Civil War, 1975-90: A Critical Analysis," *Middle Eastern Studies,* 43:1 (January 2007), p. 68.

1076 *Aztag* newspaper, 09.01.1976 and 17.01.1976.

1077 *Aztag* newspaper, 8. 10.1975;13.10.1975; 23.10.1975, p. 1. Later, the *Hunchak* quarters of Khalil-Badaoui and Hadjin were occupied by National Liberals, followed by Phalangist militiamen.

communists fired at Phalangist positions in Beirut's Ashrafieh quarter. These acts were condemned by the Armenian political leadership.[1078]

Since the State institutions has been weak or not able to provide effective protection, the degree to which the Armenian parties involved themselves in the lives of Lebanese Armenians are extraordinary.[1079] Party affiliations influenced employment, schooling, homes and friendships. As Schahgaldian noticed, "parties controlled most religious, educational, administrative, sporting and professional structures in the community."[1080] An official from *Tashnagtsutioon* liaising between the party and the Lebanese police revealed that incidents involving Armenians in Bourj Hammoud are sometimes referred to the party.[1081] The same applies to Anjar village, where villagers do not rely totally on State security forces:

> "We villagers never rely on State security. We always notice that whenever tension increases in any community, the Lebanese Army withdraws. In Anjar, two Army points ensure further security for the village. Their presence gives us confidence. However, a couple of years ago when extremists crossed the border through the mountains, our villagers protected the village and arrested them. We believe that first and foremost we need to defend our self and then we should rely on the State security forces."[1082]

Even 30 years after the end of the Civil War, Armenians do not feel they can rely on the Lebanese government for their protection, which is an indication of State's inability to protect its own communities, including the minorities.

In addition, there is no information on legal cases brought by or against the Armenian community, except the Anjar property case, which will be discussed in more detail later. As lawyer Khederian commented: "In Lebanon we try to solve our issues through intercommunity communications, negotiations and bargains."[1083] The Catholicosate of Cilicia, which has the right to apply to the constitutional Council if Armenian rights are violated, has never used this

1078 Geukjian, "The Policy of Positive Neutrality of the Armenian Political," *p. 68.*

1079 Ibid.

1080 Nikola Schahgaldian, The Political Integration of an Immigrant Community into a Composite Society: The Armenians in Lebanon, 19201974 (New York: Columbia University, 1979), p. 61.

1081 Migliorino, (Re)Constructing Armenia in Lebanon and Syria, p. 187.

1082 Personal interview with Mr. Yesayi Havatian, member of the Legal Committee of Anjar land dispute, the interview was held in Anjar on 05.102018.

1083 Personal interview with Maître Simon Khederian, lawyer at the Armenian Orthodox Religious Court, the interview was held online on 26.08.2018.

right: "I cannot recall any legal case between the Armenian community and the State" says Aram I.[1084]

Another issue is the commemoration of April 24 as a National Holiday. Undermining the Armenian Genocide or denying it harms the Armenians on individual and collective levels. The Lebanese State recognizes the Armenian Genocide,[1085] but does not commemorate it, and does not prohibit its denial. The number of people denying the Armenian Genocide is rising, and Anti-Armenian protests are taking place supporting Turkey and denying Armenian Genocide.[1086] In similar cases, State officials respond with statements of support and participate in events commemorating anniversaries of the Genocide, sending a clear message about Lebanon's official stand on the matter.

With reference to protecting minorities, including the Armenians against discrimination, it should be noted that Lebanon has not yet adopted any law containing a definition of racial discrimination and the related rules of evidence. The Lebanese courts use the definition contained in ICERD until such a law is adopted.[1087] Acts that constitute racial discrimination are criminalized particularly by the Criminal Code, the Press Act and the Television and Radio Broadcasting Act.[1088] As it's indicated in the Lebanese State report submitted to CERD Committee:

1084 Personal interview with His Holiness Catholicos Aram I, Catholicos of the Armenian Orthodox Church, Holy See of Cilicia, the interview was held in Antelias on 21.09.2018.

1085 Lebanon, Parliament Resolution – 11.05.2000: On the occasion of the 85th anniversary of massacres perpetrated by the Ottoman authorities in the year 1915, as a result of which 1.5 million Armenians fell victim, the Lebanese Chamber of Deputies recognizes and condemns the Genocide perpetrated against the Armenian people and expresses its complete solidarity with demands of its Armenian citizens. Furthermore, it believes that the international recognition of this Genocide is a necessary condition for the prevention of similar crimes that may occur in the future. Another similar Resolution was also adopted by the Parliament in 1997.

1086 "Anti-Armenian Protests Continue in Beirut," *Azernews*, 02.05.2019, https://bit.ly/2UHIVxP.

1087 According to Article 2 of the Lebanese Code of Civil Procedure, the provisions of the treaties to which Lebanon has acceded must be applied and that the treaties have primacy over domestic laws in the event of conflict between them.

1088 CERD Document, "Combined twenty-third and twenty-fourth periodic reports submitted by Lebanon under article 9 of the Convention, due in year 2018, 29 January 2019, UN Doc. CERD/C/LBN/23-24.

"in general terms, any act promoting or seeking to promote sectarianism or racism or to incite conflict among religious denominations or the various components of society is an offence punishable by law. Affiliation with a group established for that purpose and the broadcasting of material designed to promote sectarianism or racism also constitute an offence. Rhetoric designed to trigger sectarian conflict is also considered an offence."[1089]

Regarding the rules of evidence, the general rules of evidence used in the criminal and civil law apply to all acts that fall within the scope of racial discrimination. Public prosecutors act whenever they receive a complaint or report of any act or written or oral communication that is intended to instigate racial bigotry or hate crime.[1090]

The Lebanese Criminal Code prohibits "causing tension between religious communities."[1091] Articles 317 and 318 partially satisfy the requirements of Article 4 of CERD[1092] by targeting acts that threaten the State, but do not prevent discrimination against individuals. There are other gaps in the legislation, such as the lack of criminalization for the dissemination of ideas of racial superiority or organizations that promote them. CERD is concerned at the lack of definition of racially aggravated behavior and the prohibition of racist expressions. There are records of arrest of individuals accused of hate crimes, but racist hate speech, stereotyping and expressions of intolerance, prejudice and stigmatization against minorities, migrants and refugees have gone unpunished.[1093] The CERD Committee recommends the prohibition of insults, ridicule or slander, hatred or contempt on the grounds of race, color or ethnic origin. The Committee urges the State to condemn hate speech and statements against migrants and refugees.[1094] The absence of complaints or legal action by victims indicates lack of legislation or insufficient willingness by the authorities to prosecute.[1095] Armenians

---

1089 Ibid, para 10.

1090 Ibid. para. 119-121.

1091 Articles 474-475 of Lebanese Panel Code, Legislative Decree No. 340, 1943-03-01.

1092 See Article 4 of CERD.

1093 CERD Committee, "Concluding Observations on the Combined Eighteenth to Twenty-Second Periodic Reports of Lebanon," 05.10.2016, CERD/C/LBN/CO/18-22, Para. 11.

1094 Ibid.

1095 CERD Committee, "Consideration of Reports Submitted by State Parties Under Article 9 of the Convention: Concluding Observations of the Committee on the Elimination of Racial Discrimination Lebanon," 28.04.2004, UN Doc. CERD/C/64/CO/3.

could be better protected when it comes to discrimination, hate speech and hate crime. The case of the Riyadi fans' statements towards the Armenians (introduced above) shows the lack of legal protection mechanisms and remedies for such incidents.

Lebanese Armenian women face similar challenges. The CEDAW Committee urges Lebanon to adopt a unified personal status code in line with the Convention, applicable to all Lebanese women, regardless of religious affiliation.[1096] The Arab Human Rights Committee stated in 2015 that the Lebanese political system allows discrimination and exclusion, and recommends that Lebanon "takes legal and institutional measures to ensure equality and equality of opportunity on the basis of citizenship."[1097] The CEDAW Committee also urged the government to ensure that women are treated equally in issues related to child custody, inheritance and divorce, and to criminalize domestic violence and prosecute perpetrators.[1098]

After visiting Lebanon in March 2015, the UN Special Rapporteur on freedom of religion stated that religious family laws had become a publicly contested area in which religious freedom and gender-related discrimination largely overlapped.[1099] The Rapporteur expressed concern about the lack of civil marriage laws, noting that allowing civil marriage would test diversity further.[1100] The Rapporteur praised Lebanon's tradition of religious diversity and urged the Lebanese to protect and preserve it. Some Lebanese openly declared themselves agnostics or atheists and expressed critical views on religion in general. In such instances the Special Rapporteur expressed concern that non-believers still had to refer to their religion of origin when applying for certain posts in society.[1101]

Another disadvantage of the system, from the viewpoint of the CERD Convention, is that it does not provide for persons who do not wish to disclose their

1096 CEDAW Committee, "Concluding Observations of the UN Committee on the Elimination of Discrimination against Women, Lebanon," 33rd session, July 2005, para. 24.

1097 CEDAW Committee, "Concluding Observations and Recommendations Report of the Republic of Lebanon," 2015, UN Doc. CEDAW/C/LBN/CO/4-5, para. 46.

1098 Human Rights Council, "Report of the Special Rapporteur on Freedom of Religion or Belief," para. 61.

1099 Human Rights Council, Compilation prepared by the Office of the United Nations High Commissioner for Human Rights in accordance with paragraph 15 (b) of the annex to Human Rights Council Resolution 5/1 and paragraph 5 of the annex to Council Resolution 16/21, 31.08.2015, A/HRC/WG.6/23/LB/N/2.

1100 Ibid, para. 47.

1101 Ibid, para. 55.

descent, ethnic origin or religious faith in order to participate in public life which is an impediment to the freedoms of those individuals who do not wish to identify themselves with a particular group. The Lebanese State tries to justify this reality by indicating that "This is in keeping with Article 1, paragraph 4, of the Convention, which makes the measures that it authorizes provisional, and with Article 95 of the Lebanese Constitution, under which, as early as 1926, the equitable representation of the communities in public employment and in the composition of the Government was to be transitional in nature."[1102] In addition, the State argues that:

> "The societal diversity of Lebanon is linked to the nature of the personal status system, which is reflected in the political system and in the continued allocation of certain public positions to specific denominations. It enables all denominations to live together and ensures their participation in governance and administration until such a time as political confessionalism is abolished according to a transitional plan, in accordance with paragraph H of the preamble to the Constitution and with Article 95 of the Constitution."[1103]

Nevertheless, considering that there is neither a concrete plan nor a timeline to end confessionalism, Lebanese State's arguments seem to be invalid and not convincing.

The constitution guarantees equality,[1104] but Lebanon needs to reform its laws to ensure protection from discrimination and provide equality for all[1105] this is because on the ground and in real life inequality still prevails as the State institutions and participation in political and public life are still built on the confessional consensus.

1102 CERD Document, "Reports Submitted by States Parties Under Article 9 of The Convention, Sixteenth Periodic Reports of States Parties due in 2002," UN Doc. CERD/C/383/Add.218 November 2003, para. 19.

1103 CERD Document, "Combined twenty-third and twenty-fourth periodic reports submitted by Lebanon under article 9 of the Convention, due in year 2018," 29.01.2019, UN Doc. CERD/C/LBN/23-24, para 17.

1104 See Lebanese Constitution's Preamble Para. C.

1105 CRC Committee, "Consideration of Reports Submitted by States Parties under Article 44 of the Convention," UN. Doc. CRC/C/LBN/4-5.

3.7.2.1 The Elections of Cilicia Catholicos in 1956

The early 1950s were characterized by intra-Armenian political conflict.[1106] Political parties fought for political control of diasporic institutions, specifically the Apostolic Church. The *Tashnagtsutioon* justified his actions to prevent Soviet influence, stating that: "Soviet authorities [intended] to use [the See of] Holy Etchmiadzin as an instrument to control the Armenian communities in the diaspora."[1107] In 1953 the *Tashnagtsutioon*-controlled *Armenian Review* wrote that Armenian churches must be rescued from Soviet agents, stressing that the Cilician Catholicosate must be occupied by a capable and courageous, independent-minded leader free from Soviet influence.[1108] The struggle began in 1952, when the Catholicos of Cilicia, Karekin I, died. Armenian political parties could not agree on his successor and all elections failed. Soviet interference was clarified in February 1956 when the Catholicos of All Armenians from Etchmiadzin, Vazken I, traveled to Beirut and became involved in the electoral process.[1109] The *Tashnagtsutioon* obtained the support of President Camille Chamoun. Political co-operation was not new: in the 1953 elections the party joined the government's list and contributed to its victory.[1110] Levels of co-operation increased by the mid-1950s, with the *Tashnagtsutioon* calling for cooperation and alliance with all anti-Soviet forces.

On February 19, 1956, it became obvious that the *Tashnagtsutioon* candidate – Bishop Zareh of Aleppo – would win. Catholicos Vazken I. asked Chamoun to suspend the election. Chamoun responded by deploying the gendarmerie in the Catholicosate to allow the vote to proceed. Bishop Zareh's election marked a victory for the *Tashnagtsutioon* but broke the unity of the Apostolic community and radicalized intra-Armenian confrontation. Anti-*Tashnagtsutioon* groups denounced the election, and a coalition of *Hunchags*, *Ramgavars*, independents

---

1106 Yeghia Tashjian, "The Origin, Success and Failure of The Lebanese-Armenian "Third Force" during the Intra-Communal Cold War (1956-1960)," *New Eastern Politics*, 2018, https://bit.ly/2PHZrMY.

1107 Seta Dadoyan, *The Armenian Catholicosate from Cilicia to Antelias* (Antelias: Armenian Catholicosate of Cilicia, 2003), p. 95.

1108 Roupen Darbinian, "In Retrospect: A Glance at the Last Thirty Years," *Armenian Review*, 6 (3–23), 1953, p. 62.

1109 Tsolin Nalbantian, "Articulating Power through the Parochial: The 1956 Armenian Church Election in Lebanon," *Journal of Middles East and North Africa Migration Studies*, 1:2 (2013), p. 42.

1110 Messerlian, *Armenian Participation*, pp. 192–214.

and others challenged the authority of the new Catholicos, seeking official recognition from the Lebanese government as an independent community.[1111]

Tension, violence and Armenian collaboration with Arab political groups reached a peak in 1957 and 1958, when the intra-Armenian struggle overlapped with a Lebanese national institutional crisis.[1112] In the 1957 Lebanese parliamentary election, the Armenians were split between *Tashnagtsutioon* allied with Chamoun and the Kataeb, and an anti-*Tashnagtsutioon* front siding with opposition leaders including Abdullah Yafi and Saeb Salam. The run-up to the election saw the Armenians participating in demonstrations with the national opposition. On 30 May 1957, security forces opened fire against opposition demonstrators, killing eight and arresting five hundred; twelve of those arrested were Armenians. Meanwhile, Chamoun's Armenian supporters obtained recognition when Falangist Joseph Chader became the first Armenian in the Lebanese cabinet. When the crisis developed into insurrection in May 1958, the Armenian quarters of Beirut became a theater of armed confrontation between opposing Armenian sides. Hostilities in the Armenian quarters continued and an agreement between the parties was not achieved until December 1958 through the new Minister of the Interior, Raymond Eddé.[1113] Meanwhile the Lebanese government seized the monastery of Bikfaya and handed it to the Catholicos of Cilicia.[1114]

The above-mentioned incidents demonstrate how the State protected the official institutions residing within the country, enabled the community to hold the election of the Catholicos and prevented further escalation of intra-Armenian violence.

3.7.2.2 The Case of Anjar's Property Rights

Anjar is a village in the Beqaa Valley in Lebanon. The main residents (2,500–3,000 people) are Armenians, and the village council is composed exclusively of Armenians. Agriculture is the main activity, although the construction sector has developed recently.[1115] The area was resettled in 1939 by 5,000 Armenian

1111 Migliorino, (Re)Constructing Armenia in Lebanon and Syria, p. 101.

1112 Ibid, p. 102

1113 Seta Kalpakian, "The Dimensions of the 1958 inter-communal Conflict within the Armenian Community in Lebanon" (Thesis, American University of Beirut, 1983), pp. 91-92.

1114 Messerlian, *Armenian Participation*, p. 218.

1115 Karine Bennafla, "A Land Appropriation Conflict that Reveals and Produces Borders: The Case of Anjar (Lebanon, Bekaa plain)," *Cultures & Conflicts*, 73:1 (2009).

refugees from the Musa Dagh area of Turkey. Its six neighborhoods are named after Musa Dagh villages.[1116]

In 1939, the French acceded and Alexandrette, including the villages of Musa Dagh had become part of Turkey.[1117] Since Armenian had long memories with Turks, most of them refused to live under Turkish rule.[1118] With French help, Armenians had been relocated to Lebanon's Beqaa valley.[1119] Movses Der Kalousdian, the Armenian leader in Musa Dagh, negotiated with the French to locate the Armenians in Anjar.[1120]

A hill located between Anjar and communal lands as well as other properties have become a bone of contention between Armenian and the Muslim authorities,[1121] which deserves attention because it relates directly to Armenian rights in Lebanon. The French originally bought[1122] the land with Armenian philanthropists and the Calouste Gulbenkian foundation in 1939.[1123] Islamic authorities immediately filed a suit claiming rights to the lands. Nevertheless, a representative attended the trial and sold the property rights, signing a declaration that the Islamic authorities had no further claim on the land or its properties. This step was confirmed by the Administrative Council of Damascus.[1124]

Two more areas were later purchased, making a total of 3,257 properties.[1125] Twenty-five further properties were placed at the disposal of the municipality for investment.[1126] In 1940 the French authorities transferred ownership of these

---

1116 Vahram L Shemmassian, "The Settlement of Musa Dagh Armenians in Anjar, Lebanon, 1939-1941," *Asbarez* newspaper, Special Issue, 02.01 2015, https://bit.ly/2CzUv50.

1117 Avedis K. Sanjian, "The Sanjak of Alexandretta (Hatay): Its Impact on Turkish-Syrian Relations (1939-1956)," *Middle East Journal*, 10:4 (Autumn, 1956), pp. 379-382.

1118 Ibid.

1119 Shemmassian, "The Settlement of Musa Dagh Armenians in Anjar."

1120 Ibid.

1121 Bannafla, "A land appropriation," p. 85.

1122 Decision No.176 of French High Commissioner of 1939/8/19.

1123 Vicken Cheterian, *Open Wounds: Armenians, Turks and a Century of Genocide* (UK: OUP, 2015), p. 225 and Patrick J. Mcdonnell, "Armenians in Lebanon Keep Their Culture, Memory of Heroic 1915 Battle Alive," Los Angeles Times, 24.04.2015, https://lat.ms/2Q7xJsU.

1124 Intervention Request Submitted by Municipality of Anjar to the Court of First Instance in Bekka, 01.10.1997.

1125 Ibid.

1126 Decision No. 1811 of French High Commissioner, May 1940.

properties to the Armenians,[1127] but due to bureaucratic errors and the WWII the transfer was not made official, and the concept of "*Jumhury*" (Republican) lands was born.

"*Jumhury*" lands are French authority territories unofficially transferred to Armenians, so they remained part of the Lebanese State when the French left in 1956. Lebanon did not pay for the land, but the State registry indicates that the land belongs to the Lebanese Republic "*Jumhuriye Libnaniye*."[1128] The lands have no deeds,[1129] and the properties comprise of 423 lots, 200 of which are municipal land, while the rest belong to villagers.[1130] The legal problem caused by the lack of official ownership was exploited by the Islamic authorities, although almost half of the lots had changed ownership since 1939 without records being updated. Many of Anjar's inhabitants have no deeds of ownership, and these lots were the first targeted by the Islamic Endowment, which identifies relevant plots through informants in the land registry.

A second attempt to take over the lands was made after WWII, when Armenians immigrated to Soviet Armenia.[1131] In 1963 the State confirmed the legitimate property rights of the Armenians in these "*Jumhury*" Lands, and called for a committee to solve the issue.[1132] No committee has been formed, and a note in the registration statements started indicating that the plots "can only be registered to those who can prove ownership from the Armenian refugees of Musa Dagh."[1133] However, during the Lebanese Civil War, the second part of the sentence was removed from the statement leaving "They can be registered only to those who can prove ownership,"[1134] which meant that anyone who could prove ownership could own the land. On this basis, the *al-Awkaf al Islameih* started claiming lands from Anjar,[1135] while Nazem Al-Adry, a former MP from the

---

1127 Decision No.355 of French High Commissioner, 1940/12/18.

1128 See Financial Agreement between France and Lebanon of 1948-01-24, in the *Intervention Request*.

1129 Intervention Request Submitted by Municipality of Anjar to the Court of First Instance in Bekka, 01.10.1997.

1130 Ibid.

1131 Legal Committee of Anjar Land Dispute, "*Aynjari Hoghayin Hartsin Himnagan Hankrvannere*" (The Main Stages of Anjar Land Dispute), Lebanon, 2007.

1132 Law No. 40/63, 02.11.1963.

1133 Legal Committee of Anjar Land Dispute, "*Hagirj Deghegutioon Aynjari Hoghayin Hartsin Veraperyal*," (Summary Information of Anjar Land Dispute), Lebanon, a summary report, 2007.

1134 Legal Committee of Anjar Land Dispute, (The Main Stages of Anjar Land Dispute).

1135 Ibid.

area, confiscated two large areas of land - and put them under a 90-year lease. The court nullified Nazem's actions, but 30 years later the ownership has not reverted to the municipality and the properties on the land are still being used by Nazem.[1136]

Meanwhile, imitating the Mufti of the Beqaa, in 1998 supported by the Lebanese Sunni Prime Minister, Anjar City Council members tried to activate sectarian solidarity, not at populist or local levels, but at the highest national authority – the president of the Lebanese Republic, Emile Lahoud. In 2000, Lahoud set up a commission to examine the disputed lots of land in Anjar and establish official title papers on a case-by-case basis. More than 100 cases were filed, so far without result.[1137] According to the Armenians, Committee decisions were blocked by one of its Sunni members. Six months later, the Commission's mandate expired with nothing resolved.

Thus, the Anjar question took another dimension and became an instrument of internal political struggle between Lahoud and Prime Minister Rafic Hariri, as the latter became increasingly critical of Syrian interference in Lebanon, unlike Lahoud, who according to many observers, is committed to the authorities in Damascus. Internal dissensions paralyzed the Lebanese government, which was unable to adopt a clear position on the conflict.[1138] In 2003, President Lahoud told Armenian emissaries that he could do nothing while Rafik Hariri remained Prime Minister. Faced with uncooperative Lebanese authorities, the Armenians of Anjar turned to the Syrian authorities, then appealed to the government of Damascus. The establishment of the Syrian Forces Headquarters at Anjar favored foreign intermediation, and General Ghazi Kanaan negotiated between the two sides, alerting the Lebanese head of State to his role in the conflict. In 2001, Kanaan convinced the Armenians to abandon the hill to the Islamic Endowment in exchange for certificates of ownership of disputed lots located on the remaining communal territory. The conciliation attempt was dismissed by the Muslims and was never implemented.[1139] The withdrawal of the Syrian army and military intelligence services from Lebanon in 2005 marked a turning point in the conflict. The Lebanese army replaced the Syrian military at the two control checkpoints installed in the commune and now acts as a buffer between

1136 Legal Committee of Anjar Land Dispute, (Summary Information of Anjar Land Dispute), 2007.

1137 Ibid.

1138 Bannafla, "A land appropriation," p. 103.

1139 Ibid.

the Islamic and Armenian residents.[1140] From 2006 onwards, the atmosphere in Anjar has once again become pessimistic.

Anjar's problems exemplify the inaction and inability of the Lebanese authorities to stem the escalation of tensions between minorities. In Anjar, there are inheritances and different legal conceptions of boundaries: those of the Ottoman period, those of the French mandate and those of the Lebanese State.[1141] Over the years, the spatial claims on the town of Anjar have widened. In 1998, the Islamic Endowment of Barr Elias called for ownership of the top of the hill where ruins stood, but then claimed the entire hill. In 2002, their claim extended to the orchards surrounding the hill, and by 2004 half of the village, the cemetery, the Umayyad ruins and the communal water source had been included in the list of claims.[1142]

With tensions escalating, Armenian residents faced provocation, harassment and intimidation. The first incident came in 2001, when 300 fruit trees were cut down by activists close to the Barr Elias Committee, eight of whom were arrested.[1143] Targeting the trees symbolized an attack on development by the Armenians. In December 2002, a rebuilt mosque was blown up,[1144] generating tensions against the Armenians. By April 2004, incidents between the Armenians and Muslims became almost daily, and one altercation between an Armenian farmer and members of the Islamic Endowment degenerated into a riot. About 200 Sunni Muslims threatened the Armenians with imminent expulsion. Syrian soldiers stopped the exchange, but it marked an escalation into real clashes, with poisoning and stones thrown at cars carrying municipal officials.[1145] A written threat was distributed in the village, and during Islamic feasts, religious figures publicly threatened the Armenians.[1146]

The ownership conflict led to the development of two different discourses. The Islamic Endowment played the religious card, while the Armenians promoted

---

1140 Ibid, p. 105.

1141 Khaled Arar, "The Armenians and the Awqaf Confirm that they Have Documents Proving the Ownership of Anja," *Al-Diyar* newspaper, 04.10.1997, https://bit.ly/36M3ldA.

1142 Bannafla, "A land appropriation," p. 97.

1143 Ibid.

1144 "Reports on Religious Freedom: Lebanon,2003," Jewish Virtual Library, 2003, https://bit.ly/3pxSc9F.

1145 Bannafla, "A land appropriation," p. 98.

1146 Personal interview with Mr. Yesayi Havatian, member of the Legal Committee of Anjar land dispute, the interview was held in Anjar on 05.102018.

their right to existence and property, based on the legal purchase made by the French authorities and their role in agricultural development since their exile. Anjar's problems are fueled by juridical and administrative confusion over the status of the land, as well as Lebanese cartographic uncertainties relating to the boundaries of communal constituencies and border plots.

Local residents complain that protecting their rights is a challenge. Armenians find themselves having to defend their rights, despite being the legal owners of the land. Villagers with land are not allowed to use it, and after almost 30 years of jurisdictional prevarication, the case is postponed every six months.[1147] One resident comments: "I believe this conflict requires political settlement, rather than a judicial/legal one, since judicial verdicts can be not implemented because it is very difficult to execute the legal verdict on the ground. The blatant example of this is the verdict for Nazim Adri, in which he still uses the lands illegally."[1148]

Armenian politicians in the Lebanese Parliament are technically responsible for following up this issue, but they argue that they must wait for proper political circumstances.[1149] Therefore, it can be concluded that Anjar land dispute highlights the lack of rule of law in Lebanon, as well as a lack of practical clarity or jurisdiction, representing communitarian friction and identity strategies, the establishment of a local border and a conflict of memories. The way the dispute has been managed emphasizes the complexity of Lebanon's political system, the relationship between competing sides and the inability to control situations at a practical level.[1150] Anjar's example highlights the current weaknesses in the Lebanese political and legal system,[1151] and the conflict will continue to test the ability of the Lebanese authorities to govern and protect their minorities.

3.7.3 Ensuring the Rights of the Armenian Minority in Lebanon

The existence of an Armenian community in Lebanon is recognized, and this can be considered part of guaranteeing their right to existence. When it comes to

---

1147 Ibid.

1148 Ainteblian, Khajag. member of the Board of Trustees for the Armenian "Haratch Kalousd Gulbenkian" school in Anjar, the interview was held in Anjar on 05.10.2018.

1149 Personal interview with Hagop Pakradouni, Armenian Member and Secretary of Lebanese Parliament and chairperson-representative of the Central Committee of the Armenian Political Party ARF-Tashnagtsoutioon in Lebanon, the interview was held in Beirut in 19.09.2018.

1150 Bannafla, "A land appropriation," p. 102.

1151 Ibid.

fulfilling minority rights, Vartanian's statement seems to be more pragmatic: "I believe the Lebanese State respects the rights of the Armenians, but maybe it is unable to ensure them."[1152] This statement indicates the lack of legal mechanisms to ensure the rights of Armenians. Tashjian's words back this conclusion:

> "I do not believe that the Lebanese government puts all its efforts into ensuring the rights of the Armenians. Armenians are always considered secondary communities. In almost every sphere, the lion's share goes to Sunnis, Shias and the Maronite communities. Other communities get whatever is left, because we do not have enough power demographically and we are too easily satisfied with what we have."[1153]

The Lebanese State plays no direct role in the preservation of Armenian identity, since all Lebanese communities try to preserve their identity independently with rare direct State support. However, this implies a severe financial burden on the community. When it comes to social services, since the State institutions are not well established, each community member – including the Armenians – refer to their own communities' social institutions when seeking help and support. During the war, when State institutions were absent, Armenian institutions and parties met Armenian needs, and Armenians felt safe within their neighborhoods.[1154] Even recently, after the Beirut blast, instead of relying on the State institutions for systematic rehabilitation and reconstruction work, Armenians formed cross-denominational and cross-party 'Lebanese-Armenian Rehabilitation Commission' to address the damages and the socioeconomic consequences of the Beirut blast.[1155]

Armenians are a well-organized community, but some believe that this distances them from Lebanon's other State institutions, giving elites sufficient leverage to mobilize the community to support their candidates.[1156] In the weeks preceding polling day Armenians expect favors from the government of the day as it seeks Armenian support. This period offers Armenians a rare opportunity to

---

1152 Personal interview with Mr. Shant Vartanian, newly appointed Lebanese diplomat, the interview was held in Beirut on 15.09.2018.

1153 Personal interview with Mr. Yeghia Tashjian, expert in political relations and research, founder of New Eastern Politics Bloc, the interview was held online on 08.09.2018.

1154 Ibid.

1155 "The Lebanese Armenian Rehabilitation Commission Was Created," Catholicosate of Cilicia Antelias – Lebanon, 10.08.2020, https://www.armenianorthodoxchurch.org/en/archives/37522.

1156 Sanjian, "Armenians and the 2000 Parliamentary Elections in Lebanon."

promote their own agendas, arguing that bloc voting attracts Lebanon's power-hungry politicians, especially incumbent candidates.[1157]

In terms of ensuring linguistic rights, there is no direct support for the preservation of the Western Armenian language, or the Musa Dagh dialect used in Anjar and there is no legal obligation to teach in any specific language.[1158] Official documents or laws are not translated into Armenian by the authorities and Armenians cannot apply or submit documents in Armenian to government institutions. For example, there are no formal application forms for any official submission in Armenian. This prevents the language to be integrated within the larger society and keeps its usage only internally, within the Armenian community. Using Armenian, on the other hand is a common practice in public spaces where there is a noticeable Armenian presence (e.g., on shop signs – banners – posters -etc.) and during Armenian public events (e.g., election campaigns – public celebrations – festivals- etc.).

Accreditation efforts concerning Western Armenian took place in Lebanon several years ago during reforms in the Lebanese education system, and a proposal was tabled to have a third elective language option besides Arabic, French or English as part of the official Baccalaureate programme. However, the plan has not moved forward and there is little hope that it will be revived by the government.[1159] In theory, language accreditation for Western Armenian in Lebanon would be ideal, changing attitudes towards the language and improving the status of Armenian teachers. Given its potential impact, the issue should be re-examined to include the possibility of a unified assessment programme at the end of primary (grade 6) and secondary (grade 12) cycles across Armenian schools.[1160]

The State also offers cultural support. For example, on the centennial of Armenian Independence, a street was named "*Mayis* 28" (May 28) the date of Armenian Independence in 1918.[1161] Local municipalities support smaller Armenian

---

1157 Ibid.

1158 Anaid Donabedian-Demopoulos, "Middle East and Beyond - Western Armenian at the crossroads: A sociolinguistic and typological sketch." in *Linguistic Minorities in Turkey and Turkic-Speaking Minorities of The Periphery*, Christiane Bulut ed., (Harrazowitz Verlag, 2018), p. 91.

1159 Ibid.

1160 Attarian, Armenian Schools and Educations in Lebanon, p. 34.

1161 "*Hayasdani Hanrabedutian 100 Amyagin Nvirvadz Mayis28 Boghodayin Anvanagotchutioon yev Houshartsani Patsum*," (Dedicated to the 100th Anniversary of the Republic of Armenia - "May 28" Avenue Naming and Monument Opening?, *Aztag* newspaper, 17.07.2018, http://www.*Aztagdaily*.com/archives/401264

institutions by offering financial support, but it does for all existing institutions and not because certain institutions require more attention and support.[1162] The Lebanese State may also waive annual fees or taxes or allow them to be made in instalments. Churches, monasteries, their properties, and other recognized institutions are tax free and do not pay utility fees.[1163] However as Balian believes, "if *Aztag* runs out of financial resources and is in a danger of ceasing publication, I do not think that the Lebanese State would support the newspaper, since four Arabic daily newspapers have already shut down. If the State cannot help Arabic newspapers, I do not believe that it would be fair to support the Armenian ones."[1164]

According to informants, other Lebanese communities should worry about Armenian decline, because it affects the State's demographic balance. Entire Christian communities, with no policies in place, are threatened with decline. There is no plan to stop Armenian emigration because Lebanon has more urgent political, economic and social issues to deal with, and ensuring basic needs of the citizens. The Lebanese State has no policy on preserving the identity of its diverse communities and this contradicts Article 4.2 of the Minority Declaration.[1165] This means that there is no systematic or sustainable policy level approach, although State authorities often show flexibility to the Armenian schools in terms of social taxes, indirectly helping to lessen the growing financial deficit of the schools. However, the State cannot offer any substantial and systematic support to the challenges faced by the education sector.[1166]

In many countries, a minority problem would turn into a national crisis that required a quick resolution, but Lebanese crises usually relate to internal sectarian problems rather than national concerns. The current Armenian crisis must become a national issue before it is resolved, and its treatment would involve the

1162 Marwa Boustani et al, "Responding to the Syrian Crisis in Lebanon: Collaboration between Aid Agencies and Local Governance Structures," Working Paper September, IIED's Human Settlements Group, 2016, p. 5.

1163 US Department of State, "Lebanon 2018 International Religious Freedom Report, Bureau of Democracy, Human Rights, and Labor," 2018, https://bit.ly/36T6gRI.

1164 Personal interview with Ms. Arsho Balian, editor of *Aztag* newspaper, the interview was held online in 05.08.2018.

1165 Article 4.2: "States shall take measures to create favourable conditions to enable persons belonging to minorities to express their characteristics and to develop their culture, language, religion, traditions and customs, except where specific practices are in violation of national law and contrary to international standards."

1166 Migliorino, (Re)Constructing Armenia in Lebanon and Syria, p. 209.

State and major communities.[1167] Lebanon's migration problem is a general one, and the disappearance of Armenian family records applies to members of other communities – although to a lesser extent. There is a general reduction in the Lebanese population, not just because of emigration, but because it is hard to live comfortably in Lebanon. The country has no production, no economic growth, no environmental protection, no health insurance, and no welfare state. It is a country whose people are abandoning it.[1168]

State institutions are not well established. Lebanon is governed by communities and sects rather than State institutions, which have little political, economic or social vision and billions of dollars in debt. Local communities must take the initiative to determine their destiny and future, and each community establishes its own mechanisms of self-governance. Some are connected to Saudi Arabia, others to Iran or France, while the Armenians remain loyal to Armenia.[1169]

Successful efforts to preserve Armenian identity and culture largely depend on Lebanese national evolution, but integration is dictated by Lebanon's own socio-political needs, rather than by the value of ethno-cultural diversity or minority rights protection *per se*.[1170] The State has no alternative but to take proper steps to address the challenges it faces, but the lack of support means that Armenians must be creative to ensure their basic needs are met and their rights respected. Such support must reflect State interests as well as those of the minority.

In other words, guarantees surrounding the continued Armenian existence depend on the power of State institutions. The more central government holds on to power and authority, the better the rights of the Armenians will be. However, it seems that Lebanese central government has as much power as its elements agree to concede, and loyalty lies with community (sometimes feudal) leaders rather than the State and its instructions.

1167 Ibrahim, "Armenians of Lebanon are Becoming Extinct."

1168 Ibid.

1169 Personal interview with Mr. Vicken Avakian, director of Radio Voice of Van, former School Principle, Zarehian Seminary Teacher, writer, member of Homenetmen Central Committee, the interview was held online on 15.09.2018.

1170 Anna Martirosyan, "A Review of: "(Re)Constructing Armenia in Lebanon and Syria: Ethno-Cultural Diversity and the State in the Aftermath of a Refugee Crisis. Nicola Migliorino," *Journal of Immigrant & Refugee Studies*, 7:1 (2009).

3.8 Armenians in Lebanon and International/Regional Human Rights Mechanisms

After conducting empirical research through numerous interviews, it seems that Lebanese Armenians lack awareness of international human rights mechanisms and are not involved in monitoring or promoting mechanisms at international or regional levels. There is almost no documentation on the involvement of Lebanese Armenian institutions in international human rights mechanisms/instruments, and more than 80 % of interviewees representing the Armenian leadership were unaware of the Human Rights Treaty Bodies-Committees, Universal Periodic Review, the mandates of the several UN Human Rights Special Rapporteurs, or the annual Forum for Minority Issues organized by the UNOHCHR. Arab or Islamic Human Rights mechanisms are also ineffective, and the State does not promote international mechanisms or encourage communities and civil society organizations to involve themselves. The Lebanese media seldom mention human rights mechanisms or reports on any relevant recommendations and resolutions.

Many interviewees mentioned that several Armenian institutions in Lebanon have a negative perception of non-Armenian or international NGOs, and do not officially collaborate with non-Armenian local or international NGOs promoting human rights. For decades Armenians remained aloof from international mechanisms, concentrating instead on internal affairs, although younger Armenians are currently working with human rights organizations and NGOs. According to Pakradouni, Armenians in Lebanon have little faith in international human rights mechanisms due to their historical experiences throughout the twentieth century and will not complain to international bodies. They solve their issues internally and reporting to international institutions is considered contrary to principles of loyalty to Lebanon.[1171] Although Anjar and Bourj Hamoud have implemented joint initiatives with UNDP and other UN agencies (mainly on humanitarian and development projects),[1172] there is still no record of any UN agency working with Lebanese Armenians on minority rights.

1171 Personal interview with Mr. Hagop Pakradouni, (19.09.2018).

1172 Balian, "The Marash District Renovation Project Will Be Implemented Soon."

3.9 The Role of Republic of Armenia in Promoting the Rights of Armenians in Lebanon

Since its independence in September 1991, the Republic of Armenia has increased its engagement with the diaspora,[1173] enhancing the efficiency and broadening the scope of interactions between Armenia and the diaspora to promote the rights of Armenian minorities globally.[1174] In 2005 the Armenian constitution was amended, allowing diasporic Armenians to obtain citizenship.[1175] The importance of Armenia's diaspora was underlined in the National Security Strategy of 2007,[1176] which established the Ministry of Diaspora in 2008.[1177]

Lebanese Armenians have participated enthusiastically in events organized in Armenia. Strong and big delegations from Lebanon participated in the pan-Armenian games, youth gatherings, festivals and other events organized in Armenia.[1178] The Lebanese Armenian community maintains close relations with Armenia, inviting cultural representatives for visits of varying length. In September 2009, Haygazian University signed a memorandum of understanding with Yerevan State University,[1179] while Lebanese Armenian radio stations co-operate with stations in Armenia to broadcast programmes in both States. Armenia supports the Lebanese community by printing textbooks for diasporic Armenians throughout the Middle East.[1180] To overcome language problems and teacher shortages, the Armenian State occasionally organizes teacher training implemented via the Ministries of Education and Diaspora. Other joint programs aim to protect and enhance the Armenian language, history and literature.[1181] Although these initiatives are not funded or supported by the Lebanese

---

1173 Gabriele Rasuly-Paleczek and Maria Six-Hohenbalken, *Migration and Its Impact on Armenia A Field Practice* (Vienna: University of Vienna, 2017), p. 11.

1174 "Republic of Armenia National Security Strategy," (approved at the session of National Security Council at the RA President office on 26.01.2007), https://www.mfa.am/filemanager/Statics/Doctrineeng.pdf.

1175 Article 13 of 2005 'Armenian Constitution': "Armenians by national origin shall acquire the citizenship of the Republic of Armenia through simplified procedure."

1176 "Republic of Armenia National Security Strategy."

1177 The ministry of Diaspora was closed in 2019 and replaced by an Office of High Commissioner for Diaspora affairs linked to the Prime Minister of Armenia.

1178 See the official website of Embassy of Armenia to Lebanon, http://lebanon.mfa.am/en/community-overview/.

1179 Ibid.

1180 Ibid.

1181 Hyusisyan, "Armenians in Lebanon after the Israeli Invasion In 2006," p. 50.

State, the Armenian community enjoys the full respect of the Lebanese government on such matters, in line with international requirements on host State relationships towards minority rights.

In the context of inter-state relations and minority rights, one disadvantage is Lebanon's electoral laws. Article 60.3 of Lebanon's new electoral law states that "It is strictly prohibited for the candidate or the list to accept or receive contributions or assistance issued by a foreign country or by a non-Lebanese person, whether natural or legal, directly or indirectly."[1182] The Armenian State cannot therefore legally support Armenian candidates – which is also in line with Article 8.4 of Minority Declaration: "Nothing in the present Declaration may be construed as permitting any activity contrary to the purposes and principles of the United Nations, including sovereign equality, territorial integrity and political independence of States."[1183]

Political and diplomatic relations between Armenia and Lebanon were established on March 4, 1992.[1184] They were set up in an atmosphere of friendship and confidence, and high-level mutual visits remain common. Lebanon's Armenian community has since improved relations further,[1185] with more than 40 agreements and Memorandums of Understanding coming into effect on various issues including the economy, trade, education, culture and sport.[1186] Before the Covid-19 pandemic there were almost daily flights between Yerevan and Beirut as tourism between the two countries was flourishing.[1187] Armenian products are easily available in Lebanese markets, and vice versa as Lebanon promotes a friendly relationship with Armenia, supporting all initiatives that improve relations between them. Lebanese investments are among the seven largest in Armenia, while the Armenian Government includes Lebanon in the list of countries with which Armenia has the best economic relations.[1188]

1182 See Lebanon's 2017 Parliamentary Electoral law.

1183 Article 8.4 of Minority Declaration.

1184 Official website of Embassy of Armenia to Lebanon.

1185 Hyusisyan, "Armenians in Lebanon after the Israeli Invasion In 2006," p. 50.

1186 Official website of Embassy of Armenia to Lebanon.

1187 Aneta Harutyunyan, "Lebanese People Love Armenia through Local Armenian Community and Definitely Want to See the Country – Minister," *Armenpress*, 2018, https://bit.ly/2UvWhwT.

1188 Grace Hovsepian, "Embassy of Lebanon in Armenia Celebrates the Diplomatic Relations Between Both Countries," *the 961 Online resources*, 2017, https://bit.ly/2X1UkbU.

In his visit to Lebanon in October 2018, Armenian Prime Minister Nikol Pashinyan pointed out that the Armenian people have special gratitude towards Lebanon for accommodating the refugees escaping the Armenian Genocide. "Lebanon is the only country in the region that has officially recognized the Armenian Genocide, which is important not only for preserving the historical memory but also preventing its recurrence," Pashinyan stressed.[1189] Saad Hariri noted that Lebanon appreciates its ongoing cooperation with Armenia in terms of the role played by the Lebanese-Armenian community in his country's development, as well as the furtherance of Armenian-Lebanese ties.[1190] Nikol Pashinyan and Saad Hariri agree that a strong political dialogue exists between the two countries, and that vigorous efforts should be made to upgrade the economic component of their interaction.[1191]

In this context, in late 2014, 33 Armenian peacekeepers were deployed in the UN Interim Force in Lebanon (UNIFIL) occupying a demilitarized zone created by the UN in 1978 to confirm Israeli withdrawal from Lebanon and help Lebanon restore its authority in the area.[1192] The former defence minister of Armenia commented: "Our compatriots have lived on the Mediterranean coast in Lebanon for many years side by side with peoples of various religious. It is extremely important to maintain peace there."[1193] According to former Armenian president Serge Sarkisian:

> "We are deeply grateful to the people and leadership of Lebanon for their caring attitude towards our compatriots who have become fully-fledged citizens of Lebanon, preserving their national identity, and of course we are grateful to the authorities of Lebanon, including the parliament, for recognizing the fact of the Armenian Genocide. This is a very important contribution."

There are positive aspects of Lebanese State's attitude in terms of respecting the relationship between Armenia and Armenians in Lebanon.

1189 "Pashinyan Visits Lebanon Meets with Leadership," *The Armenian Mirror Spectator*, 25.10.2018, https://bit.ly/2O2EGZI.

1190 "Nikol Pashinyan and Saad Hariri discuss Armenia-Lebanon ties," *News.am*, 20.10.2018, https://bit.ly/2CBnxAU.

1191 Ibid.

1192 UNIFIL Mandate, the official website of UNIFEL, 01.10.2020, https://unifil.unmissions.org/unifil-mandate.

1193 Sisak Gapreilian, "Armenian Troops Start Lebanon Mission," Radio Freedom, 27.11.2014, https://bit.ly/2K7f2Sj.

3.10 Concluding Remarks on the Rights of Armenians in Lebanon

The recognition of religious communities in Lebanon as legal bodies is an Islamic law and Ottoman legacy, connected to a system of rules and practices traditionally applied to deal with Christian and Jewish diversity.[1194] But the recognition of groups also reflects the political needs and priorities of the French colonial authorities during the Mandate period in the context of the creation of Lebanon in 1920. In other words, Lebanon's legal and constitutional recognition of groups is deeply rooted in regional religious tradition and connected with the circumstances surrounding the establishment of the Lebanese state.[1195]

It also relates to traditional practices of coexistence, conflict resolution and compromise which have marked the history of Lebanese traditions, arguably renewed in spirit by the National Pact of 1943 and Tai'f Agreement of 1989.[1196] In addition, the diversity of Lebanon's population has precluded any sect from gaining absolute power or from imposing itself on other sects, but militating against any disturbance to the status quo of communal autonomy has been the perennial weakness of Lebanon's central government.[1197]

It is in this context that the Lebanese system offers the Armenian community opportunities and restrictions to enjoy their minority rights.[1198] Lebanese Armenians are aware of the benefits of the Lebanese consociational system. Official statements from the community's political and religious authorities and interviews with Lebanese Armenians reflect a sense of appreciation for a context in which they feel "100 % Armenian and 100 % Lebanese at the same time."[1199]

There are many examples of opportunities the Lebanese system has offered Armenians and of the positive role these opportunities played toward the preservation of a distinct Armenian identity and culture in Lebanon. Political confessionalism and political formulas (the constitution, National Pact and the Tai'f

---

1194 Benjamin Braude, ed., Christians and Jews in the Ottoman Empire: The Abridged Edition (USA: Lynee Rienner, 2014), p. 16.

1195 Nicola Migliorino, "The Lebanese System and Armenian Cultural Diversity," in *Armenians of Lebanon: From Past Princesses and Refugees to Present-Day Community*, Aida Boudjikian, ed. (Beirut: Haigazian University and the Armenian Heritage Press, 2009), pp. 481-482.

1196 Ibid.

1197 Abramson, "Lebanese Armenians; A Distinctive Community," p. 196.

1198 Migliorino, "The Lebanese System and Armenian Cultural Diversity," p. 481.

1199 Ibid, p. 482.

Agreement) offer the Armenian community participation, seats in Parliament and ministerial quotas, and roles in local administration and public service as well as autonomy to manage the internal and family affairs of the community.[1200] The autonomy under which Armenians manage their affairs (religious, educational, cultural, family, etc.) and the context that encourages communal political representation provide pillars upon which Armenian cultural distinction has been constructed since the 1920s.[1201]

However, these spaces of communal autonomy are closely connected to weaknesses at the Lebanese State's core.[1202] The Lebanese State takes only a minimal role in protecting and ensuring Armenian rights; if an Armenians find themselves in an adverse situation, they often seek help from Armenian institutions first, rather than the State. There are insufficient State institutions to guarantee the rights, safety and security of minorities as defined by international law.

Another consequence of Lebanon's innate instability is that constitutional recognition of groups in Lebanon results from an incomplete extension of State sovereignty rather than the affirmation of minority rights in line with international human rights law.[1203] This explains the absence of systematic support for minority identities. The price of autonomy is that the State cannot provide support to a community. The burden of the preservation of identity thus falls on the shoulders of the community itself.[1204] The preservation and development of Armenian identity – and the financial burden of maintaining a vast cultural apparatus of schools, clubs and social institutions – has been sustained by the Armenians or by diasporic communities.[1205] But what if the community was unable to sustain itself? This is no longer just a simple hypothesis in Lebanon; it is the reality on the ground. The economic crisis affecting the country since the civil war has taken its toll on average Armenian family budgets, severely limiting their ability to contribute to the maintenance of Armenian identity. It is doubtful that the State will support Armenian culture in the current context of economic hardship, but if confessionalism were to be reformed, some form of synthesis could be found, reconciling the need to preserve cultural autonomy for

1200 Ibid.
1201 Nalbantian, "Fashioning Armenians in Lebanon, 1946-1958," p. 57.
1202 Migliorino, "The Lebanese System and Armenian Cultural Diversity," p. 482.
1203 Ibid, p. 482-483.
1204 Ibid.
1205 Ibid.

Armenians while endowing the Lebanese State with sufficient powers of intervention to support Armenian identity and traditions.[1206]

Consociational systems are fragile, and power sharing formulas are subject to renegotiation and amendment.[1207] New agreements are difficult to achieve, and consociational democracy in ethnoculturally diverse societies is often unable to represent or accommodate social change,[1208] as exemplified by the delay in forming a new government due to lack of consensus on cabinet distribution. The recent election took place in May 2018, but there was still no government by January 2019. Similarly, after the Beirut blast and upon widespread public demonstrations blaming the government for negligence and corruption Hassan Diab's government resigned in August 2020[1209] and Saad Hariri was reappointed to form a government. By January 2021, the government was still not formed due to lack of agreements among the political parties. These are indicators of the inability and dysfunctionality of the political and legal systems of Lebanon to address the ongoing crises. In this context, despite many repeated demands from the international community for Lebanon's leaders to reform the system, it seems it has been largely business as usual for the country's political class despite the ongoing crises related to the free-fall of economy, Covid-19 pandemic, unemployment, Beirut blast consequences and other persisting social and political challenges.[1210]

In terms of protecting minority rights under international law, the Lebanese State takes a passive stand and does not do enough in protecting and ensuring them. Armenians need to be proactive, prepared and organized to claim their rights locally and internationally, and fight attempts to undermine those rights.

When it comes to analyzing international human rights organizations' recommendations, several issues remain unsolved regarding minority rights. Personal status consistent with CEDAW needs to be developed to ensure women are treated equally in issues related to child custody, inheritance and divorce.[1211]

1206 Ibid.

1207 Matthijs Bogaards, "Formal and Informal Consociational Institutions: A Comparison of the National Pact and the Tai'f Agreement in Lebanon, Nationalism and Ethnic Politics," *Nationalism and Ethnic Policies*, 25:1 (2019), pp. 37-38.

1208 Ibid.

1209 "Lebanese PM Announces Government's Resignation Over Beirut Blast," *France 24*, 10.08.2020, https://www.france24.com/en/20200810-live-lebanese-pm-announces-government-s-resignation-over-beirut-blast.

1210 Patience, "Lebanon Protesters' Euphoria Gives Way to Despair."

1211 Human Rights Council, "Report of the Working Group on the Universal Periodic Review-Lebanon," 22.12.2015, UN Doc. A/HRC/31/5.

The State also has an obligation to protect minority rights under legal frameworks.[1212] Lebanon must ensure that legal frameworks on the rights of ethnic minorities comply with international standards. The Lebanese government also needs to take steps to progressively develop and apply appropriate indicators on the implementation of economic, social and cultural rights in order to facilitate the assessment of progress.[1213]

In addition, Lebanon lacks a sustainable or consistent model to ensure equality and non-discrimination as outlined in CERD and other international human rights instruments. Lebanon must reform structural discrimination in religious family courts.[1214] The government needs to introduce civil marriage as an option to all Lebanese citizens.[1215] In accordance with the Tai'f Accords, the government needs to gradually overcome political confessionalism in favor of a common Lebanese citizenship and prevent religion from being used as an "entry ticket" to societal recognition or political positions.[1216]

However, these recommendations face several challenges. The country is in economic collapse, followed by the Covid-19 pandemic and then, in August 2020, the devastating Beirut blast, which uncovered the corrupt, ineffective and incompetent core of the Lebanese State institutions.[1217]

Many Lebanese citizens have no trust in State institutions and still rely on their community to solve their issues. For the Armenians, several community representatives believe that the more the community is united, the easier it will be to address the challenges.[1218] But what if someone does not want to be part of the community? Or if community leaders do want to support specific community members? There are no mechanisms in place to address such issues.

In addition, freedom of choice is restricted because seats are predetermined according to communities, and voters must choose candidates from Muslim and Christian groups. In other words, those in power may not represent the opinions of the community they represent and may even be returned to power by an electoral majority from another community, raising the difficult issue of democratic

1212 CESCR, "Concluding Observations on the Second Periodic Report of Lebanon," 24.10.2016, UN Doc. E/C.12/LBN/CO/2, para. 64.

1213 Ibid.

1214 Human Rights Council, "Report of the Special Rapporteur on Freedom of Religion."

1215 Ibid.

1216 Ibid.

1217 Patience, "Lebanon Protesters' Euphoria Gives Way to Despair."

1218 Hagop Ladoian, "*Entunely Che*," (Not acceptable), *Aztag* newspaper, 2018, https://bit.ly/34UgNul.

representation. Therefore, Lebanon's structural difficulties make it very hard to accommodate social change within the system of confessional representation or to participate in the political, economic and social life of the State. It could be argued that Lebanon's fate lies more in the realm of political negotiation, rather than in legal prescription.

The third challenge in addressing recommendations of international human rights monitoring bodies is the way laws are implemented in Lebanon, which is driven by two main factors. The first relates to internal and regional political developments, while the second covers religious balance and sensitivities. This means that laws might not necessarily be based on international human rights law if they might shake the existing religious balance of the country. In this context, many Armenian officials interviewed think that readdressing the Tai'f Agreement would bring serious challenges.[1219] One of the reasons is the current wave of religious extremism in the Middle East which raises concerns that without formal or informal quotas, majority rule could possibly erode the State's legacy of religious tolerance. Such worries are understandable, but unqualified majority rule is not the only viable alternative to political confessionalism. Many contemporary democracies have complex institutional arrangements in place to ensure that fundamental rights are guaranteed without discrimination.[1220]

Replacing a quota-based system with a more consistently implemented rights-based approach to promoting diversity may offer a promising way of preserving Lebanon's legacy of multi-ethnic and multi-religious coexistence.[1221] The Lebanese consociational formula of representing the people of Lebanon appears to be not sustainable and the democratic gap in the current representation of the Armenian community and Lebanon's inability to guarantee democratic processes between communities and within the same community are clear examples of current limitations.[1222]

In other words, it seems that communal power-sharing has become inseparable from the maintenance of the post-conflict environment and that Lebanese State institutions find it hard to implement international obligations on human and minority rights. This is because communities are more polarized,

1219 Personal interviews with Mr. Hagop Pakradouni and Rev. Prof. Paul Haidostian, (September 2018).

1220 Human Rights Council, "Report of the Special Rapporteur on Freedom of Religion," para. 67.

1221 Ibid.

1222 Migliorino, (Re)Constructing Armenia in Lebanon and Syria, p. 222.

religious or ethnic differences have dominated State institutions and political organizations, even when their abolition was agreed as a national goal.[1223] While democracy is offered as a panacea, the inclusiveness of institutions is a better gauge of the extent to which such societies can survive.[1224] Issues of institutional design in fractured societies center on devising structures and processes that can capture the will of the entire people and provide conditions to reinstitute a national consensus. Seeing the issue this way emphasizes divided loyalties and their susceptibility to rearrangement and transformation through institutional engagement.[1225]

In this context, although there has been a modest improvement in human rights provision and good governance in Lebanon, there is still a pressing need for further progress, as there are many shortcomings in its implementation.[1226]

Based on these considerations, the successful preservation of Armenian existence and identity in Lebanon so far can be considered as a result of Lebanon's unresolved search for a solution to the political problems raised by its varied societies, or as a temporary condition in its search for legitimacy. It seems that minority rights are not legally well founded and ethno-cultural diversity exists not for its own sake, but because the stability of the State cannot be maintained without it until a more solid form of legitimacy, based on cross-cultural allegiances and cleavages, can be found. How long this temporary condition can last, and how legal and institutional change might affect the future of the Armenian communities in Lebanon is hard to tell. In the meantime, the Armenian minority while still enjoys the non-interference of the State and freedoms to maintain identity, it faces gross challenges in terms of collective and institutional existence. It urgently needs systematic State protection and promotion of its rights to existence, preserving identity, equality and non-discrimination as well as participation in the political, social and economic life of the State.

1223 Mark Lattimer, "Minority Participation and New Constitutional Law," *International Journal on Minority and Group Rights, 12:* 2-3 (2005), p. 231.

1224 Castellino and Cavanaugh, *Minority Rights in the Middle East*, p. 368.

1225 Ibid.

1226 CESCR, "List of issues in relation to the second periodic report of Lebanon," 20.07.2016, UN Doc. E/C.12/LBN/Q/2/Add.1.

4. The Rights of Armenian Minority in Turkey

4.1 Introduction

The Ottoman Empire's cultural variety was not reflected in a multicultural system, nor was the Empire a federation of ethnic communities.[1227] It represented majority's acceptance of ethnic attributes to preserve peace and maintain sovereignty, in which legal, economic and social status varied by groups.[1228] The *millet* system divided subjects on the basis of religion: Muslims, regardless of ethnic origin, were considered a single dominant Muslim community, with non-Muslims as dominated communities.[1229]

Turkey as the "continuing" State or at least the legal successor of the Ottoman Empire,[1230] has a demographic composition of interethnic, interreligious and

1227 Samim Akgönül, *The Minority Concept in the Turkish Context*. Practices and Perceptions in Turkey, Greece and France, trans. Sıla Okur (Boston, Brill, 2013), p. 70.

1228 Ibid.

1229 Gözde Yilmaz, Minority Rights in Turkey: A Battlefield for Europeanization (New York: Routledge, 2017), p. 29.

1230 As Dumberry argues, "under international law Turkey should be considered as the 'continuing' state of the Ottoman Empire. Thus, changes related to a state's territory, its government, and its population do not affect its identity and the continuity of its international legal personality per se…One relevant criterion to examine when discussing issues of state identity is whether what is left of a state's territory (following a significant reduction in its size) is the nucleus of the state (its essential part). The application of this important objective criterion strongly supports the conclusion that there is an identity of State between the Ottoman Empire and the Republic of Turkey. This conclusion is also supported by one subjective criterion: other states' refusal to recognise Turkey's claim to be a new state. In fact, such refusal ultimately prevented Turkey's claim of discontinuity from having any effectiveness. Thus, several provisions of the Lausanne Treaty support the conclusion of continuity between the Ottoman Empire and the Turkish Republic. Similarly, the sole arbitrator in the 1925 arbitration case of the Ottoman Public Debt (1925) concluded that Turkey was the continuing State of the Ottoman Empire. The same conclusion was also reached by the French-Greek Arbitral Tribunal in the 1956 Lighthouse Arbitration case as well as by the District Court of Amsterdam in the 1925 case of Roselius. Therefore, the analysis of both objective and subjective criteria shows that post-1923 Turkey was not a new state under international law." For further details see Patrick Dumberry, "Is Turkey the 'Continuing' State of the Ottoman Empire under International Law?,"

confessional links that grew during the Ottoman Empire's expansion.[1231] Ethnic diversity peaked in the nineteenth century, after which Muslim and non-Turkish ethnic groups migrated to Eastern Turkey and historical Armenian highlands (*Haygagan Lernashkhar*), increasing the region's diversity and the proportion of Muslims in the population.[1232] The process continued in the twentieth century, accompanied by a deterioration of diversity due to the mass expulsion, population exchange, relocation, emigration and massacres of non-Muslims including Armenians and Greeks.[1233]

After WW1, minority rights became securitized as minorities were thought to be destroying the Turkish State.[1234] The legal system helped create a discourse of Turkish nationalism, treating minority identities as a threat to the official order. From 1923 onwards, minority policies were largely shaped by ethnic homogenization and Turkification.[1235] Despite forced assimilation, Turkey remains home to a multi-ethnic, multi-religious society, and since the 1990s, non-Turkish

---

Netherlands International Law Review, 59: 2 (Aug 2012), pp. 235-262. In addition, Oktem presents several other factual elements to support his position that Turkey continued the legal personality of the Ottoman Empire: 1- Turkey acquired all the embassies and consulates inherited from the Ottoman Empire; 2- Turkey acquired all weaponry, warships, and other military assets of the Ottoman Empir. 3-Turkey inherited from the Empire its bureaucratic and military elite as well as 'most of its institutions, including its administration and its legal structure, as well as the parliamentary experience and the educational and financial systems, without major changes' (pp. 577-578). See Emre Oktem, "Turkey: Successor or Continuing State of the Ottoman Empire?" *Leiden Journal of International Law*; Cambridge 24:3 (Sep 2011), pp. 561-583.

1231 Mehmet Bardakci et al., Religious Minorities in Turkey Alevi, Armenians, and Syriacs and the Struggle to Desecuritize Religious Freedom (UK: Palgrave Macmillan, 2017), p. 59.

1232 According to Roderic Davison, the late nineteenth century Ottoman population was divided as follows: "In the Empire, Turkish population was only around 35 percent… whereas Arabs constituted 13.8 percent, Romanians 11.4 percent, Bulgarians 7.8 percent, Serbo-Croatians 7 percent, Armenians 6.5 percent, Greeks 5.5 percent, Albanians 3.1 percent, Kurds 2.6 percent and Circassians 2.6 percent," Roderic Davison, "Nationalism as an Ottoman Problem and the Ottoman Response," in *Nationalism in a Non-national State: The Dissolution of the Ottoman Empire* (William W. Haddad & William Ochsenwald eds. (Columbus: Ohio State University Press, 1979), p. 31.

1233 Bardakci et al., Religious Minorities in Turkey, p. 60.

1234 Derya Bayır, *Minorities and Nationalism in Turkish Law* (UK: Ashgate Publishing, 2013), p. 5.

1235 Bardakci et al., Religious Minorities in Turkey, p. 11.

identities have been strengthened through partial liberalization and ethnic revival because of internal and regional political changes and Turkey's EU candidacy granted at the Helsinki Summit in 1999.[1236]

In this context, a contentious history shapes Armenian minority rights in Turkey. Under the Ottoman Empire, Armenians represented a semi-autonomous *millet*, enjoying religious and civil autonomy but discriminated against in public employment, education and taxation. Universal citizenship was granted in 1876 to end discrimination as nationalist uprisings in the Balkans and the Middle East threatened the Empire's integrity, and Ottomanism gave way to the Turkist movement, aiming to construct a homogenous national community.[1237] The Ottoman policy of dealing violently with Armenians fueled the ongoing notion of an Armenian enemy.[1238]

4.2 Historical Development of Minority Regimes in Turkey

4.2.1 The *Millet* System and Minorities in the Ottoman Empire

Under the *Millet* System of the Ottoman Empire, Non-Muslim subjects enjoyed some autonomy in religious and cultural practices, education, finance, and law.[1239] Each group was organized into a *millet,* electing its own leader and running its own courts. The State recognized the highest religious leader of each group and gave them a place in State protocols, granting responsibilities such as tax collection, military recruitment and ensuring public order. Religious leaders governed communities at various levels,[1240] but non-Muslims had an inferior status.[1241] Only Muslims could testify against Muslims in court, and there were

---

1236 Ibid, p. 12.

1237 Bahar Rumelili & Fuat Keyman, "Enacting multi-layered citizenship: Turkey's Armenians' struggle for justice and equality," *Citizenship Studies*, 2016, 20:1, p. 70.

1238 "Why Hafiza Merkezi," *Hafiza Merkezi Website*, https://hakikatadalethafiza.org/en/why-hafiza-merkezi/.

1239 Cemal Eren Arbatli, Gunes Gokmen "Minorities, Human Capital and Long-Run Development: Persistence of Armenian and Greek Influence in Turkey," (CESIFO Working Paper No.6268 Category 12.12.2016), p. 12.

1240 Günay Göksu Özdoğan and Ohannes Kılıcdagı, Hearing Turkey's Armenians: Issues, Demands and Policy Recommendations, Turkish Economic and Social Studies Foundation (Turkey: Tesev Publication, 2012), p. 13.

1241 Baskin Oran, "The Minority Concept and Rights in Turkey: The Lausanne Peace Treaty and Current Issues," in *Human Rights in Turkey*; Zehra F. Kabasakal Arat ed. (Philadelphia, PA: University of Pennsylvania, 2007), pp. 35–56.

restrictions on clothing and homes and houses of worship.[1242] Non-Muslims paid tax (*jizya*), and the State ensured their safety and security[1243] in a system that was both multicultural and discriminatory.[1244]

During the nineteenth century the Ottoman Empire's position deteriorated, resulting in negative impacts on minorities. Ethnic independence movements and wars resulted in the loss of Ottoman territory, and the Ottomans attempted to modernize. The *Tanzimat* reforms improved minority rights in 1839, and the reform of 1856 (*Islahat Fermanı*) abolished the *Dhimmi*[1245] status and the *millet* system, granting subject rights to faith-based group members. The reforms created equality for all residents irrespective of religious affiliation[1246] and were elaborated in the first Ottoman constitution in 1876.[1247] The Sultan suspended this constitution in 1878 because of anti-Ottoman uprisings, the Turkish-Russian war of 1877–1878 and the Berlin Congress negotiations in 1878.[1248] The impending collapse created a negative view of minorities, producing suspicion about their loyalty as many rebelled to establish independent states.[1249] Ottoman society perceived minorities as a threat and a tool for international powers to infiltrate the Empire.[1250]

1242 Özdoğan & Kılıçdağı, *Hearing Turkey's Armenians*, p. 13.

1243 David D. Grafton "Religious minorities in the diversity of Islamic thought," in *Routledge Handbook of Minorities in the Middle East*; Paul S. Rowe ed. (London: Routledge, 2019), pp. 27-28.

1244 Ilhan Dogan and Osman Can "Minorities in Turkey and in the EU," in *Deutsch-türkisches Forum für Staatsrechtslehre III*, Otto Depenheuer, ed. (Münster, LIT Verlag, 2006), pp. 49–54.

1245 Non-Muslims under the protection of Muslim law. Adult male dhimmis were required to pay tax on their income and sometimes on their land. Restrictions and regulations on dress, occupation and residence were often applied. In return, Islam offered dhimmis security of life and property, defence against enemies, communal self-government and freedom of religious practice.

1246 Türkay Salim Nefes, *Political Roots of Religious Exclusion in Turkey* (Oxford: OUP, Parliamentary Affairs, 2017), p. 3.

1247 Rumelili & Keyman, "Enacting multi-layered citizenship," p. 70.

1248 Bayır, Minorities and Nationalism, p. 35.

1249 Nefes, *Political Roots*, p. 3.

1250 Ioannis Grigoriadis, "On the Europeanization of Minority Rights Protection: Comparing the Cases of Greece and Turkey," *Mediterranean Politics,* 13:1 (March 2008), p. 34.

4.2.2 Young Turks Era

Concerned for the fate of the Empire, the Young Turk's CUP[1251] staged a coup in 1908, seizing power from the Sultan.[1252] In the wake of the coup, the CUP moved from nationalism to Ottomanism 'to make terms with non-Turkish groups they had previously refused to work with'.[1253] In the 1908 elections, CUP candidates won by a slim margin, and the Parliament was composed of Turkish, Arab, Albanian, Kurdish, Greek, Armenian, Slavic and Jewish deputies. The CUP programme centered on reforms, freedom and unity.[1254] Although the reform-oriented agenda sought to reinstitute a constitutional framework and to unify all *millets* under an Ottoman identity, it settled for national homogenization. Traumatized by losing European provinces, Ottomanism was abandoned in favor of Turkish ethnicity and promoted nationalism to sustain territorial integrity. Islamist ideology sought a Muslim nation ruled by ethnic Turks, marking the start of exclusionary views about non-Muslim communities in Turkey.[1255]

European claims to hegemony, exercised on the pretext of protecting Ottoman minorities,[1256] along with the humiliation of the Balkan Wars (1912–1913) and WWI contributed to form a perception among Muslims that Christian minorities were disloyal and deceitful. Disillusioned non-Muslims lost hope for peaceful co-existence under Ottoman rule,[1257] and the CUP gained control of the government after a coup in 1913. The new regime led the Empire into WW1 as Germany's ally. The situation seemed ripe for a more assertive form of Turkish nationalism under a pan-Turkish empire,[1258] and the regime offered little to the Empire's minorities. The CUP encouraged Turkish and Muslim immigration to increase the Muslim population while encouraging policies to decrease

---

1251 For further information on the Young Turks and CUP see Hasan Kayalı, "The Young Turks and The Committee of Union and Progress," in *The Routledge Handbook ff Modern Turkey*, Metin Heper & Sabri Sayarı eds. (Abingdon: Routledge, 2012).

1252 Arbatli & Gokmen, "Minorities, Human Capital," p. 20.

1253 Şükrü M Hanioğlu, Preparation for a Revolution: The Young Turks (1902-1908) (Oxford: OUP, 2001), p. 296.

1254 Bayır, Minorities and Nationalism, p. 49.

1255 Nefes, *Political Roots*, p. 3.

1256 UNGA, "Elimination of all Forms of Religious Intolerance, Note by the Secretary General," 11.08.2000, UN Doc. A/55/280/Add.1, para. 62.

1257 Arbatli & Gokmen, "Minorities, Human Capital," p. 12.

1258 Ömer Taşpinar, Kurdish Nationalism and Political Islam in Turkey: Kemalist Identity in Transition (New York and London: Routledge, 2004), p. 48.

non-Muslim numbers and banning non-Muslim immigration.[1259] Population exchange policies allowed the CUP to reduce the non-Muslim population, and the CUP promoted the first international population exchange agreement with Bulgaria in 1913.[1260]

The most drastic measure, the Deportation *(Tehcir)* Law of 27 May 1915, gave the army powers to resettle villages and towns on the basis of espionage risks during WW1.[1261] This law affected various minorities, but there were special conditions for the resettlement of Armenians, effectively ordering a mass deportation towards Syria, which become an early stage of the Armenian Genocide.[1262]

4.2.3 The Republican Era

After WWI, the Ottoman Empire lost the Arab territories of the Empire and the Treaty of Sèvres, which was signed by the Ottoman Sultan, became an important symbol of Turkish distrust of the West and minorities, turning into a form of collective paranoia known as "Sevres Syndrome" over the course of time.[1263] Turkey saw itself as facing external and internal threats.[1264] The Treaty was opposed by the Ottoman military and resistance groups led by Mustafa Kemal Ataturk. In 1923 Ataturk successfully concluded Turkey's War of Independence, contributing to the non-ratification of the Sevres Treaty by forcing different borders on the international community through the 1923 Treaty of Lausanne.[1265] The Treaty of Lausanne recognized the Republic of Turkey in 1923 and was put under the guarantee of the League of Nations.[1266] Ataturk wanted to create a

1259 Hande Sözer, *Managing Invisibility: Dissimulation and Identity Maintenance among Alevi Bulgarian Turks* (Boston: Brill, 2014), p. 75.

1260 Ibid.

1261 Paul Bartrop, Steven Leonard Jacobs, *Modern Genocide: The Definitive Resource and Document Collection [4 volumes]* (Oxford: ABC-Clio, 2015), pp. 106-107.

1262 Bayır, Minorities and Nationalism, p. 62.

1263 Türkay Salim Nefes, "Understanding Anti-Semitic Rhetoric in Turkey Through the Sèvres Syndrome," *Turkish Studies*, 16:4 (2015).

1264 Yilmaz, Minority Rights in Turkey, p3.

1265 David Romano, "The Kurds in the Middle East," *in Routledge Handbook of Minorities in the Middle East,* Paul S. Rowe ed. (New York: Routledge, 2019), p. 257.

1266 Fatma Zeynep Özkurt, "The Impact of EU Conditionality on Democratisation in Turkey: Institutional Transformation and Policy (Re)formation of Minority Rights, Freedom of Expression, the Military and the Judiciary" (PhD thesis, University of Nottingham, 2013), p. 126.

State with institutions and laws which would enable a homogeneous society,[1267] and only recognized Armenian, Jewish and Greek Minorities, agreeing to grant them some minority rights.[1268]

Meanwhile, Local resistance groups met at the Erzurum Congress of July 1919 and the Sivas Congress of September 1919.[1269] Article 5 of The Erzurum Congress's final resolution demanded that local resistance groups respect the rights of all Christian elements,[1270] affirming the status quo for non-Muslims. The resolution opposed the formation of any 'Greek and Armenian [entity]' *(Rumluk ve Ermenilik)*, but reaffirmed their respect for non-Muslim elements, and documents suggest that the relationship between resistance groups and non-Muslims was defined along conventional lines.[1271] Article 2(2) states that "The security of [Non-Muslims] possessions, life, honour is the exigency of our [Muslim] religion, national tradition *(an 'anat-ı milliye)* and the essence of our law." In other words, as Chilingirian argues, the State arguably continued a republicanized version of the *millet* system, preserving elements of the *millet* system, but systematically ignoring all rights pertaining to the internal life of minority communities, including some of the rights derived from the Treaty of Lausanne which will be discussed in detail in the subsequent sub-section.[1272]

Turkish *etnie* and Sunni Islam subsequently remained a factor of Turkish identity, and Turkification became the authorities' goal.[1273] The new republic aspired to create a homogeneous nation State whose citizens were Muslim, spoke Turkish and possessed Turkish culture. Religion and religious affiliations were misused for political calculations. Nevertheless, the Muslim majority was not homogeneous, but were considered first-class citizens, while non-Turkish

---

1267 Mehmed S. Kaya, "Turkey's Vain Struggle to Create a Homogeneous Nation," *Middle East Policy*, Middle East Policy Council, 25:2 (Summer 2018), p. 122.

1268 Samim Akgönül, "Religious Minorities," in *The Routledge Handbook of Turkish Politics*, Alpaslan Özerdem & Matthew Whiting eds. (New York: Routledge, 2019), p. 329.

1269 Bayır, Minorities and Nationalism, pp. 67-68.

1270 Ibid.

1271 Ibid.

1272 Hratch Tchilingirian, ""The 'Other' Citizens": Armenians in Turkey Between Isolation and (Dis)Integration," *Journal of the Society for Armenian Studies*, 25 (2016), p. 126.

1273 Ayşe Kadıoğlu, "The Twin Motives of Turkish Nationalism," in *Symbiotic Antagonisms Competing Nationalisms in Turkey*, Ayşe Kadıoğlu & E. Fuat Keyman eds. (Salt Lake City: University of Utah Press, 2011), p. 40.

Muslims such as Kurds and Lazes were not assimilated.[1274] Non-Muslims, such as Christians and Jews, were unwanted and were subjected to segregationist policies. Turkishness was open only to non-Turkish Muslims.[1275]

Minorities were subject to discriminatory practices during this period.[1276] From June 1923, the government restricted travel for all non-Muslim minorities. Travel was also restricted for Greeks and Armenians until 1930 and 1932 respectively, while non-Muslim minorities were also "forbidden to exercise property rights outside their place of residence."[1277] These restraints were not lifted until 1932.[1278] In 1926 the government made Turkish the only language for business transactions, while Turkish descent became a precondition for public employment, lasting until 1965.[1279] Meanwhile in 1931, the 'Citizen, Speak Turkish!' campaign was initiated,[1280] and in 1939, non-Muslim males were conscripted into the Turkish army as menial laborers, even if they had already completed their service.[1281] The deadliest of these measures were the Dersim Massacres on 1937–1938, through a military campaign in the province of Tunceli supressing an uprising of Alevi Zazas who were rebelling against the government.[1282]

Turkification was also manifested in changing place names. Article 2(D) of Law 5442 permitted the Ministry of Internal Affairs to change non-Turkish names of cities, villages and geographical features.[1283] People were forced to adopt Turkish names, demonstrating that non-Turkish cultures no longer had a place within the State and reinforcing the impression that 'national culture' referred only to the culture and language of the Turkish *ethnie*.[1284] In 1952, the

---

1274 Rifat Bali, "Politics of Turkification During the Single Party Period," in *Turkey Beyond Nationalism: Towards Post-Nationalist Identities*, Kieser Hans Lukas ed. (UK: London I.B. Taurus, 2006).

1275 Ibid.

1276 Yilmaz Çolak, "Language Policy and Official Ideology in Early Republican Turkey," *Middle Eastern Studies,* 40:6 (2004), pp. 67-91.

1277 Banu Eligür, "Ethnocultural Nationalism and Turkey's Non-Muslim Minorities during the Early Republican Period," *British Journal of Middle Eastern Studies*, 46:1 (2019), p. 13.

1278 Ibid.

1279 Ibid.

1280 Rumelili & Keyman, "Enacting multi-layered citizenship," p. 70.

1281 Bayır, Minorities and Nationalism, p. 103.

1282 Ozlem Goner, Turkish National Identity and Its Outsiders: Memories of State Violence in Dersim (New York: Routledge, 2017).

1283 Law No. 5442, 10.06.1949, Provincial Administration Law in Turkey.

1284 Bayır, Minorities and Nationalism, p. 12.

'Name Changing Specialized Board' *(AdDeğiştirme İhtisas Kurulu)* was established, and changing non-Turkish place names is still on the State's agenda.[1285]

Under the pretext of securing finance during WWII, a special 'Wealth Tax' *(Varlik Vergisi)* was levied disproportionately on non-Muslim citizens, and those unable to pay were sent to forced labor camps in Ashkale.[1286] The wealth tax became an instrument that eliminated non-Muslim minorities from the market.[1287] The principal executor of the Wealth Tax Law Faile Ölcte described it as one of "the most embarrassing events in the financial history of Turkey."[1288] Alexandris describes the tax as "a small scale bloodless financial massacre" of non-Muslim groups.[1289]

The securitization of minority rights continued after WWII,[1290] and the CHP and DP liberalized policies toward recognized minorities[1291] due to foreign affairs considerations and election campaign strategies· However, internal strategy documents and non-official directives prove that opinion mostly stood against non-Muslims. They were not accepted as members of the Turkish nation and considered disloyal traitors and threats to the State, leading to their economic and social marginalization.[1292] The minority policy pursued by the DP was motivated only by the desire to gain electoral support, many important pledges were not kept, and liberal and tolerant regulations were replaced by more rigid measures. The situation for non-Muslims deteriorated again after 1953 and got even worse with the Cyprus conflict in 1954.[1293] In addition, on 6-7 September 1955, pogroms took place in the ongoing conflict between Turkish and Greek Cypriot communities.[1294] Reacting to a false report that Atatürk's house in Thessaloniki had been bombed, thousands gathered in Istanbul to protest, directing their anger against property owned by Greeks and other minorities.[1295] After

1285 Ibid, p. 107.

1286 Ayhan Aktar, *Varlik Vergisi ve Turklestirme Politikalari* (Capital Levy and "Turkification" Policies), (Istanbul: Iletisim Yayınlari, 2000).

1287 Ibid.

1288 Bayır, Minorities and Nationalism, p. 125.

1289 Alexis Alexandris, *The Greek Minority of Istanbul and Greek-Turkish Relations (1918-1974)* (Athens: Center for Asia Minor Studies, 1994), p. 220.

1290 Back then, approximately one-third of the eligible voters in Istanbul are non-Muslim.

1291 Bardakci et al., *Religious Minorities in Turkey*, pp. 73-74.

1292 Ibid.

1293 Ibid.

1294 Cheterian, Open Wounds: Armenians, Turks and a Century of Genocide, p. 254.

1295 Ibid. More than 4000 residences, more than 1000 shops, 73 churches and 26 schools were attacked.

the incidents, emigration of the Greek community increased, and 12,562 Greeks were expelled as a security threat to Turkey.[1296]

Increased violence against Christians between 1975 and 1979 led to a decline in the Christian population.[1297] Increasing tension led Ankara to impose a series of restrictions on minority groups. All private universities in Ankara, including the seminaries, were closed,[1298] and the state-imposed restrictions on properties belonging to minority foundations. On May 8, 1974, the Supreme Court claimed minority institutions as 'foreign' and decided that their ownership of property was dangerous.[1299] Civil war in the southeast between the PKK and the Turkish military claimed more than 30,000 lives,[1300] since fighting began in 1984.[1301] More than a million Kurds and Assyrians were displaced in the Southeast as violence became a part of minorities' daily lives,[1302] while a 10 % electoral threshold prevented minority parties from entering the Parliament and being part of succeeding governments.[1303]

Developments in domestic politics after the military putsch of 1980 and new political, social and economic conditions at global level strengthened the desire for political liberalization – especially the fall of communism and the democratization of former Soviet States.[1304] These changes affected State policies from the mid-1980s onwards and gathered pace during the 1990s.[1305] Newly established

---

1296 Bardakci et al., Religious Minorities in Turkey, p. 75.

1297 Tessa Hofmann, Armenians in Turkey Today: A Critical Assessment of the Situation of the Armenian Minority (Brussels: The Forum of Armenian Associations in Europe, 2002), p. 17.

1298 Ramazan Kilinç, Alien Citizens: The State and Religious Minorities in Turkey and France (UK: Cambridge University Press, 2019), p. 54.

1299 Ibid, p. 59.

1300 Mneesha Gellman, Democratization and Memories of Violence: Ethnic minority rights movements in Mexico, Turkey, and El Salvador (New York: Routledge, 2017), pp. 90-91.

1301 Turkey justified its militarism based on the territorial integrity norm and maintained Turkish State maintained a state of emergency in the south-east until 2002 to prevent the formation of an independent Kurdistan.

1302 Hofmann, Armenians in Turkey Today, p. 44.

1303 Yilmaz, Minority Rights in Turkey, p. 331.

1304 Bardakci et al., Religious Minorities in Turkey, p. 25.

1305 Turgut Özal, prime minister from 1983 to 1991, advocated a political solution to the conflict with the Kurds in the form of modest democratization. Based on his economically neoliberal, neoconservative and pro-Islamic orientation, Özal considered that the ailing Turkish economy could only be revived by democratic reform and integration into global processes.

NGOs in Turkey started to work on the improvement of human rights,[1306] and politicians recognized the Kurdish problem.[1307] The ban on the Kurdish language was lifted in 1991,[1308] although efforts were undermined by the CC, which questioned the legitimacy of a party founded on a particular ethnic identity.[1309]

Since the 1990s there has been an increase of ethnically motivated cultural activity throughout the south-east of Turkey.[1310] In this context, the rise in political Islam[1311] during the 1990s[1312] increased the legitimacy of the Alevi in the State apparatus and the public sphere.[1313] Alevis demanded equal treatment by the Directorate of Religious Affairs attached to the Prime Minister's office.[1314] These developments did not make life much easier for the Armenians,[1315] who continued to be viewed through the prism of Kemalist nationalism, stigmatizing them as enemies of the State.[1316]

It was not until Turkey's EU candidacy that human and minority rights improved and a shift became visible in Turkey's understanding of citizenship.[1317]

1306 Hofmann, Armenians in Turkey Today, p. 44.

1307 Yilmaz, Minority Rights in Turkey, p. 20.

1308 Bayır, Minorities and Nationalism, p. 178.

1309 Ayhan Kaya, "Multiculturalism and Minorities in Turkey," in *Challenging Multiculturalism Book Subtitle: European Models of Diversity* Raymond Taras eds. (UK: Edinburgh University Press, 2012), pp. 305-306.

1310 Gellman, Democratization and Memories of violence, p. 25.

1311 In 1996 after Centre-right coalition's defeat, WP leader Necmettin Erbakan headed first pro-Islamic government since 1922. The WP demanded for the exercise of Islamic law, the segregation of the sexes in social life, religious education and the headscarf issue. The military/bureaucratic state-elite made it clear that the WP's Islamist demands could not be tolerated. In January 1998 a CC decision ordered the WP to be banned. The WP and other Islamist forces challenged the Republican and secular regime by suggesting to adopt a legal framework allowing each legally recognized community to be governed according to its own religious rules. It also tried to undermine the secular order by stressing a religious and Islamic way of life in politics. In Kaya, "Multiculturalism and Minorities in Turkey," pp. 303-304.

1312 Bardakci et al., Religious Minorities in Turkey, p. 56.

1313 Ibid, p. 104,

1314 Kaya, "Multiculturalism and Minorities in Turkey," p. 305.

1315 As it will be discussed in detail in the following chapters, in 1990s several threats and attacks against the Armenian community centres in Istanbul and against some of its members were organized overwhelmingly by the far right "*Ülkü oçaklari.*"

1316 Bardakci et al., Religious Minorities in Turkey, p. 63.

1317 Ibid, p. 77.

4.3 Contemporary Era and Existing Challenges

A new era for Turkey started when Recep Tayib Erdogan's AKP took power in 2002. Before then, Turkey had no legal documentation on minority rights other than the Lausanne Treaty.[1318] Reforms to restrictive policies began in the early twenty-first century.[1319] Under the AKP, neo-Ottomanism has gradually replaced Turkish secular nationalism, and Sunni Islam became a key feature of the AKP's restoration of Turkish society.[1320] The AKP invoked the term 'new Turkey' to revise tenets of Republican citizenship,[1321] claiming that language courses and the return of properties to Greek and Armenian foundations showed Turkey as a more democratic and multicultural country.[1322] Party leaders consistently espoused a 'great restoration', making Turkey a regional power and global player.[1323] These openings were justified, as AKP politicians argue that more religious tolerance existed in the Ottoman Empire.[1324]

In 2004, the Directorate General for Religious Affairs established a Minority Issues Review Board to address minority issues,[1325] and the AKP encouraged the construction and restoration of churches and synagogues. In 2006, a Turkish Protestant church was opened – a first for Turkey.[1326] In 2010, Erdogan issued a circular[1327] allowing non-Muslim minorities to exercise their cultural rights, stressing the necessity to implement existing rights. The AKP reforms constituted a radical break from previous State policies.[1328] However, many Alevi

---

1318 Yilmaz, Minority Rights in Turkey, p. 412.

1319 Ibid.

1320 Tunç Aybak, "Geopolitics of Denial: Turkish State's 'Armenian Problem'," *Journal of Balkan and Near Eastern Studies*, 18:2 (2016), p. 133.

1321 Şener Aktürk, "One Nation under Allah? Islamic Multiculturalism, Muslim Nationalism and Turkey's Reforms for Kurds, Alevis, and non-Muslims," *Turkish Studies*, 19:4 (2018), p. 539.

1322 Ibid.

1323 Kenan Çayır, "Citizenship, nationality and minorities in Turkey's textbooks: from politics of non-recognition to 'difference multiculturalism'," *Comparative Education*, 51:4 (2015), p. 530.

1324 Aktürk, "One Nation under Allah?" p. 539.

1325 Lacin Idil Oztig and Kenan Aydın, "The AKP's Approach toward Non-Muslim Minorities: Constructivist and Rationalist Insights," *Alternatives: Global, Local, Political*, 42:2 (2017), p. 61.

1326 US Department of State, "2007 Report on International Religious Freedom - Turkey," 14.09.2007, https://www.refworld.org/docid/46ee679269.html.

1327 Official Gazette 2010: No.27580, 13 May.

1328 Aktürk, "One Nation under Allah?" p. 523-524.

organizations were not considered legitimate interlocutors, and Kurdish socialist organizations affiliated with the PKK were treated as problematic, reflecting ambiguity concerning the selective nature of these reforms and question the motives of the Turkish government.[1329]

The Gezi Park Protests[1330] are considered a turning point for the AKP's behavior, and the situation worsened after the 2013 bribery case.[1331] In July 2015, after a two-year ceasefire,[1332] conflict between PKK and the government resumed, bringing significant casualties to both sides. Reports told of shelling and destruction of towns, resulting in civilian deaths and up to 500,000 people displaced by early 2017.[1333] In addition, Erdogan continued to tighten his grip on power since the failed coup in July 2016.[1334] Turkey derogated its obligations under the ECHR and the ICCPR.[1335]

During the SoE the government circumvented the rule of law,[1336] and Erdogan used the SoE powers to amend laws, "substantially modifying the legal and administrative structures of the State."[1337] Emergency powers have been used

---

1329 Ibid.

1330 In June 2013, the Turkish government's plans to transform an Istanbul park into a shopping mall produced an unexpected result. The activism of opposition groups triggered a revolt involving tens of thousands of people, who occupied the park for weeks. The protests resulted in eight deaths and thousands of serious injuries due to the police response. See Ayşe Parla and Ceren Özgül, "Property, Dispossession, and Citizenship in Turkey; Or, the History of the Gezi Uprising Starts in the *Surp Hagop* Armenian Cemetery," *Public Culture*, 28 (2016), pp. 617–653.

1331 Mahmut Cengiz, "How the Corruption Investigations of 2013 Still Shape Turkey's Bleak Future," *Vocal Europe*, 21.12. 2017, https://bit.ly/2JnWEYq.

1332 "Kurdish leader Abdullah Ocalan declares ceasefire with Turkey," *The Guardian*, 21.03.2013, https://www.theguardian.com/world/2013/mar/21/pkk-leader-ocalan-declares-ceasefire.

1333 "Turkey, Current Issues," Minority Rights Group International, 2020 https://minorityrights.org/country/turkey/.

1334 A State of Emergency (SoE) was declared on 21.07.2016 in accordance with Article 120 of the Turkish Constitution and Article 3 of State of Emergency Law.

1335 Human Rights Council, "National report submitted in accordance with Paragraph 5 of the annex to Human Rights Council Resolution 16/21," Turkey, UN Doc. A/HRC/WG.6/35/TUR/1.

1336 Henry Barkey, "One Year Later, the Turkish Coup Attempt Remains Shrouded in Mystery," *Washington Post*, 14.07.2017, https://wapo.st/3uRyit5.

1337 UN OHCHR, "Report on the Impact of the State of Emergency on Human Rights in Turkey, Including an Update on the South-East: January-December 2017," March 2018, para. 39.

to “stifle any form of criticism or dissent vis-à-vis the Government,”[1338] while a set of constitutional amendments passed in a flawed referendum on 16 April 2017 set the stage to transform Turkey to a presidential government. The June 2018 Parliamentary elections marked the transformation of Turkey’s political system, giving it extensive presidential powers, limited parliamentary oversight and reduced judicial independence.[1339]

According to the Venice Commission, the new system puts “an excessive concentration of power in the hands of the President and the weakening of parliamentary control of that power”[1340] and “curtails the independence of the judiciary vis-à-vis the president.”[1341] Although Turkey’s SoE ended in July 2018, according to HRW the constitutional amendments “in practice make permanent many of the emergency powers the president has already assumed.”[1342] UN experts consider that Turkey does not have carte blanche to ignore obligations under the Covenant.[1343]

Many of Turkey’s emergency decrees contained provisions ignoring human rights safeguards.[1344] The Special Rapporteur on freedom of expression stated that these decrees gave the authorities power to ignore human rights obligations.[1345] In Turkey, the rights to believe, not to believe and to change beliefs are legally protected, although there are widespread reports of pressures on people with beliefs other than Islam.[1346] For atheists, Christian converts, Alevis and other non-Muslim minorities, channels of redress are often ineffective,[1347]

1338 Ibid, para. 42.

1339 OSCE Document, “Turkey, Early Presidential and Parliamentary Elections,” Office for Democratic Institutions and Human Rights (ODIHR), 24.06.2018, Final Report, 21.09.2018.

1340 European Commission for Democracy Through Law, “Opinion on the amendments to the constitution adopted by the Grand National Assembly on 21 January 2017 and to be submitted to a national referendum on 16 April 2017,” 10-11.04.2017, para. 47.

1341 Ibid, para. 113.

1342 “Questions and Answers:” Turkey’s Constitutional Referendum,” HRW, 2018, https://bit.ly/2ViHcPA.

1343 UNOHCHR “Report on Turkey,” UN Doc. A/HRC/WG.6/35/TUR/2, sec. III., para. 7.

1344 Ibid, para. 8.

1345 Ibid.

1346 Norwegian Helsinki Committee Freedom of Belief Initiative, “2019 Report Pursuing Rights and Equality: Monitoring Report on the Right to Freedom of Religion or Belief in Turkey,” 2019, para. 4.1.

1347 Ibid.

and exclusions and attempts to render minorities invisible mean that tensions rise whenever a clash occurs. However, when there are positive developments in bilateral or multilateral relations, the conditions for minorities improve. Both situations prove that minorities are regarded as external elements, possibly explaining why the 'aliens within' concept is frequently cited,[1348] such as when Turkish ultranationalist group the Alperen Hearths protested Israel's restrictions on access to the Al-Aqsa compound in 2017 in front of the main synagogues in Istanbul.[1349] Choosing the Turkish Jews places of worship instead of the Israeli Embassy shows how they view both as the same and see Turkish Jews as foreigners.[1350]

Moreover, the process of granting rights to minorities is not accompanied by legal provisions, and it was accompanied by unease on the part of the Turkish bureaucracy. A set of institutions continues to function in Turkey with ultra-conservative attitudes towards secular education, religious services and minorities' issues.[1351] A decade ago, many thought that the practice of destroying non-Muslim minorities in Turkey has ended."[1352] However, "the State's tight grip on society is legitimized by rallying people around the nation-state."[1353] In other words, Turkey has suffered significant democratic setbacks in the past five years.[1354] Of all the world's democracies, El Salvador, Guatemala, Haiti and Turkey have the lowest low levels of access to justice.[1355] More than half of the world's imprisoned journalists are in five countries, and Egypt and Turkey together hold 38 % of them.[1356] Meanwhile, the blocking and erasing of online content continues and many media workers have been laid off.[1357]

1348 Samim Akgönül, *The Minority Concept in the Turkish Context*, p. 86.

1349 Anne-Christine Hoff, "Turkey Turns on Its Christians," *Middle East Quarterly*, Summer 2018, Middle East Forum online platform, https://www.meforum.org/7243/turkey-turns-on-its-christians.

1350 Nefeș, *Political Roots*, p. 13.

1351 Vahram Ter-Matevosyan, "The Armenian Community and the AK Party: Finding Trust under the Crescent," *Insight Turkey*, 12:4 (2010), p. 97.

1352 Tchilingirian, "The 'Other' Citizens," p. 154.

1353 Doğu Ergil, "Identity Crises and Political Instability in Turkey," *Journal of International Affairs*, 54.1 (Fall 2000), pp. 58-59.

1354 "Global State of Democracy 2019," International Institute for Democracy and Electoral Assistance, 2020, www.IFEA.com.

1355 bid.

1356 Ibid.

1357 European Commission, "Progress Report on Turkey, SWD (2019) 220," Brussels, 29.5.2019, https://bit.ly/3qk3v5Y p. 32-33.

By 2018, Turkey had become a weak democracy, and the only European country showing statistically significant declines in four of the five 'Global State of Democracy' attributes: Fundamental Rights, Checks on Government, Impartial Administration and Participatory Engagement.[1358] Restrictions on freedom in the face of an independent and impartial judicial system are at the core of these criticisms.[1359] Human rights defenders face intimidation, prolonged arbitrary detention and ill-treatment leading to a shrinking space for civil society.[1360] Meanwhile, anti-terrorism legislation and the Criminal Code contradict European standards.[1361] Criminal legislation allows prison sentences for insulting the President, while legislation on hate speech is not in line with ECtHR case law.[1362] Hate speech and threats, including in the media against minorities, remain a serious problem.[1363] School textbooks need to be revised, and attacks on minority places of worship need to be investigated properly so perpetrators can be brought to justice. State subsidies for minority schools have also fallen considerably.[1364]

The Erdogan government pursues minority rights but uses policy instrumentally. Activities in favor of minorities end when values and norms of the minorities contradict Erdogan's conservative worldview.[1365] While restrictions on religious freedom and religious persecution have increased since 2016,[1366] State media discriminates against minority religions, deeming them agents of the West and the government suggests minorities were involved in the coup.[1367] As Kaya argues, the AKP's apparent shift in discourse to diversity has not changed

1358 Global State of Democracy 2019.

1359 Serkan Demirtaş, "Justice Minister Vows Greater Freedoms through New Human Rights Action Plan," *Hurriyet Daily News*, 20.12.2019, https://bit.ly/3qe0mEx.

1360 Commission Staff Working Document final, p. 220.

1361 Ibid.

1362 Ibid.

1363 In 2006, a Catholic priest in Trabzon was murdered, in 2007, three Protestants in Malatya were murdered, and Hrant Dink, editor of the bilingual Turkish-Armenian newspaper *Agos* and human rights defender was also murdered. See *Turkey in Transit - Democratisation in Turkey* (New York: Freedom House, 2008), p. 15.

1364 European Commission, "Progress Report on Turkey, SWD (2019) 220," p. 32.

1365 Bardakci et al., Religious Minorities in Turkey, p. 216.

1366 US Department of State, "Report on International Religious Freedom: Turkey, International Religious Freedom Report for 2019," 2019, https://bit.ly/3qgyC23.

1367 UN OHCHR Report on Turkey, /HRC/WG.6/35/TUR/3, 12.11.2019, para. 31.

the Sunni-Turkish majority' attitude towards minorities and their ethno-cultural and religious diversity.[1368]

4.4 Turkish Legal and Political Regimes vs. Minorities

Turkish nationalism relies on the indivisibility of the State: "The Turkish State, with its territory and nation, is an indivisible entity."[1369] The 1928 citizenship law gave citizenship to those residing within the republic, but since 1931, the inclusive citizenship which was defined on the basis of *jus soli* had become exclusively ethno-cultural, based on *jus sanguinis*.[1370] This approach was exclusive and restrictive, denying the existence of minorities and their rights other than those translated from the Lausanne Treaty by the Turkish authorities.[1371] As a result citizenship as an ethnically defined concept of Turkishness, implying that citizens are Sunni Muslim Turks, was framed within civic republican borders and a rhetoric of universal values.

The indivisibility of Turkish State also refers to the territorial integrity, a prominent feature of Turkish national identity and nationalism which denotes the preservation of the State and the immutability of its borders.[1372] Stressing the focus on territorial indivisibility and the potential enemies targeting it, is a perpetual survival concern continues to be the defining feature of nationalism, the credo 'Turks have no friends but Turks', which gives birth to a thriving industry of conspiracy theories and a laborious process of inventing enemies.[1373]

In this context, the primacy of religion in Turkey was a legacy of Ottoman rule, in which religion determined legal status, rights and obligations.[1374] The main reason for the prevalence of religion in Turkish citizenship practices is that since the early nineteenth century religion has become the language of various

---

1368 Ayhan Kaya & Ece Harmanyeri, *Tolerance and Cultural Diversity Discourses in Turkey* (Turkey: European Institute Istanbul Bilgi University, 2010), p. 21-22.

1369 Article 3 of Turkish Constitution.

1370 Yilmaz, Minority Rights in Turkey, p. 30-31.

1371 Ibid.

1372 Kadıoğlu, "The Twin Motives of Turkish Nationalism," pp. 42-43.

1373 Umut Özkırımlı, "The Changing Nature of Nationalism in Turkey Actors, Discourses, and the Struggle for Hegemony," in *Symbiotic Antagonisms: Competing Nationalisms in Turkey*, Ayşe Kadıoğlu & E. Fuat Keyman eds. (Salt Lake City, UT: The University of Utah Press, 2011), p. 94.

1374 Lerna Ekmekcioğlu, *Recovering Armenia, The Limits of Belonging in Post-Genocide Turkey* (UK: Stanford University Press, 2016), p. 97.

events that led to the demise of the Ottoman Empire. For instance, Balkan movements for independence used Christianity as their cause, and the Great Powers used the language of Christianity to justify their protection of formed Ottoman subjects, leading the Sublime Porte to view such gestures as intervention in its domestic affairs. These processes and the devastating experience of WW1, Genocide and divided loyalties made it almost impossible for Turkish citizens to detach religion from national identity. The Lausanne Treaty's minority clauses reinforced the unacceptability of separating religion from national identity by reserving minority status for non-Muslims, thus maintaining the relevance of religion for citizenship and belonging.

The legal framework surrounding religious issues is centered around the *Diyanet*, the Presidency of Religious Affairs, first established in 1924 and first recognized in the 1961 Constitution, responsible for "the delivery of service to citizens without discrimination."[1375] Until the 1980s, the *Diyanet* was used to justify and consolidate the State's secularist character and oversee State hegemony over religious practices.[1376]

Turkey's legal system is based on equality before the law, which assumes that everyone benefits from rights and has uniform duties.[1377] Anything that transcends this status has been condemned as privilege and demonized. Since the application of formal equality principles is seen as a *sine qua non*, minority rights requiring different treatment are considered incongruous. Equality within the citizenship framework mostly equates to national homogenization within the Republican tradition, with diversity seen as a 'threat' by the authorities. Accordingly, concepts of national uniformity left no room for embracing ethnic, linguistic and religious differences within society.[1378]

In other words, equality is conceptually blind to difference on racial, ethnic, religious, or linguistic grounds, so the legal system assumes that no specifically different configurations can be penalized. The State considers that the principle of equality before the law is sufficient to establish and maintain public peace and order, and to prevent discrimination or racism in society.[1379] The principle of

1375 See the official website of Presidency of Religious Affairs: https://www.diyanet.gov.tr/tr-TR/Kurumsal/Detay//3/diyanet-isleri-baskanligi-temel-ilke-ve-hedefleri.

1376 Ahmet Erdi Ozturk, "Turkey's Diyanet under AKP Rule: From Protector to Imposer of State Ideology?," *Southeast European and Black Sea Studies,* 16:4 (2016), p. 620.

1377 Bayır, Minorities and Nationalism, p. 221.

1378 Yilmaz, Minority Rights in Turkey, pp. 30-31.

1379 Bayır, Minorities and Nationalism, p. 221.

equality in Turkish legal law has been accepted into Turkish identity and culture, which effectively requires a transformation of diverse groups into a single form of Turkishness dictated by State ideologies. Equality as construed in Turkish law therefore does not construct a right to equal concern and respect to all of Turkey's diverse groups but is used to negate demands for the protection of differences.[1380]

The Turkish authorities claim that the Law 6701[1381] prohibits discrimination on the grounds of sex, race, color, language, religion, faith, sect, political or other opinion, ethnicity, property, birth, marital status, state of health, disability and age. It lists forms of discrimination that fall under the scope of the law: Segregation or isolation, giving instructions to discriminate against someone and following such instructions, multiple, direct or indirect discrimination, mobbing, not providing reasonable accommodations for persons with disabilities, harassment and discrimination. All persons and public and private entities providing services to the public are prohibited from discriminating against persons who wish to use such services. Law 6701 also imposes an obligation on all public and private entities to take necessary measures to terminate discrimination, provide compensation, prevent repetition, and pursue legal and administrative remedies against it.

However, there is no definition of racial discrimination in law. Although judicial bodies can use Article 216(1) of the 2004 Turkish Penal Code to penalize acts and speech motivated by hatred, there is also no clear definition for hate speech. According to CERD, this represents an important obstacle to the "adequate application of relevant legislation prohibiting such discrimination".[1382] However, racism as a political ideology is prohibited by Turkey's legal system. The idea of prohibiting racism in the political sphere was introduced in the now defunct Article 90 of the Political Parties Law of 1965, which referred to the 'prohibition of regionalism and racism'.[1383] With this provision, establishing a political party on grounds of race and region was also banned, as were parties seeking to make one

1380 Ibid.

1381 See Law on Turkish Human Rights and Equality Institution. Law No.6701, published in the Official Gazette dated 20/4/2016 numbered 29690.

1382 CERD Committee, "Concluding Comments on Turkey 2009," 24.03.2009, UN Doc. CERD/C/TUR/CO/3.para. 11.

1383 Law No.648, 13.07.1965.

race 'dominant and privileged' over others.[1384] Despite its heading, the provision did not criminalize racist acts *per se.*[1385]

Political party closure judgments are grounded in two main claims which are considered the major dilemmas of Turkish modernity. The first is the violation of laicism and the second is the violation of the 'State's indivisible integrity with its territory and nation'.[1386] While the first dilemma is clearer, the second demands further scrutiny. Here, according to CC, the State's indivisible integrity principle firstly prevents the creation of minorities, secondly prevents regionalism and racism, and thirdly protects the principle of equality. The CC has objected to political formations which defend cultural diversity and the protection of differences because it considers them as *creating* minorities and treats their ideas as racism and against egalitarianism. These principles are used to legally justify ignoring minorities and their rights.[1387] The CC closed minority parties on the grounds of race and language, claiming that they promoted non-Turkish cultures and languages, impairing the unity of State and its territory and nation, reinforcing the idea of race *(irk).*[1388]

4.4.1 The Turkish Constitution

The Turkish Constitution 'solves' the question of minorities without addressing it. There is no reference in the Constitution to the word 'minority', not even the Lausanne Treaty minorities.[1389] Ideology is encapsulated in the unamendable Articles of the constitution, which entrench secularism and loyalty to the nationalism of Atatürk (Article 2), the indivisibility of the State, and a single State language (Article 3). More specifically, the Turkish Republic's first Constitution in 1921 contained no provision for the status of non-Muslims. In Contrary, as Çağaptay states, during the Independence War, Turkish nationalists fueled

1384 The establishment of an organization using the name of a race or religion with the aim of publicizing them has been prohibited since 1909 with the CUP's *Cemiyetler Kanunu* (Association Law).

1385 Bayir, Minorities and Nationalism, p. 249.

1386 Ibid, p. 190.

1387 Ibid.

1388 For example, in Emek Party (Labour Party)-1997 case, the CC accused the EP of 'racism', for claiming that differences exist between Kurds and Turks, and that discrimination against the Kurds was taking place, Emek Partisi vs. *Yargıtay Cumhuriyet Başsavcılığ* Official *Gazete*: 26.6.1998/23384.

1389 Yilmaz, Minority Rights in Turkey, p. 29.

antipathy towards Christians,[1390] as illustrated by the speech by Izmir deputy Mahmut Esat (Bozkurt) during the talks on the 1921 Constitution:

> "I speak as a person who believes that the Christian group does not have any rights in this country. They have abdicated from citizenship of this country, and [they] are the ungrateful children of Ottoman history and they do not have any rights left in this country. In this country […] they are the spies of the imperialists and they are the traitorous children of this land, they do not have a place in this Assembly."[1391]

As Derya argues, Non-Muslims, who were now the 'ungrateful children of Ottoman history', became 'minorities' under the Lausanne Treaty, excluded from the Turks' nation-state, a theme that recurs throughout the history of the Republic.[1392] The 1961 CC was established to review legal constitutionality, but by the mid-1990s, it became an obstacle to a more pluralistic democracy by closing political parties that attempted to bring excluded identities, into Turkish politics.[1393] Effectively, the CC sees references to ethnicity in the preamble – 'Turkish national interests', 'the Turks' existence and 'the spiritual values of Turkishness' – as the founding principles of the Constitution.[1394] This means that diverse social, cultural, moral and political ideas are prevented from entering the political realm and a single national formation has represented Turkish ethnic identity and culture for decades, at least before AKP came to power. In other words, the CC has participated in the homogenization of society by applying official ideology strictly. Limiting the political realm to 'Turkishness' and 'Turks' is incompatible with the principle of neutrality and liberal statehood that Turkey has somewhat contradictorily aimed to establish since WWII.[1395]

In this context, every Constitution secured Turkish as the country's only official language by declaring its status 'unchangeable'.[1396] In 2001, Parliament

1390 Soner Çağaptay, Islam, Secularism and Nationalism in Modem Turkey: Who Is a Turk? (London: Routledge 2005), p. 28.

1391 *Türkiye Büyük Millet Meclisi Zabıt Ceridesi* (Turkish Parliament Minutes Journal), 18.11.1920, p. 437.

1392 Bayır, Minorities and Nationalism, p. 70.

1393 Belge Ceren, "Friends of the Court: The Republican Alliance and Selective Activism of the Constitutional Court of Turkey," *Law and Society Review*, 40:3 (2006), pp. 654-655.

1394 Bayır, Minorities and Nationalism, p. 189.

1395 Ibid.

1396 Article 4 of the Turkish Constitution: "The provision of Article 1 regarding the form of the State being a Republic, the characteristics of the Republic in Article 2, and the provisions of Article 3 shall not be amended, nor shall their amendment be proposed."

amended the 1982 Turkish Constitution, removing the sentence "No language prohibited by law can be used to express and diffuse thoughts" from the Constitution.[1397] However, further restrictions are added by the Article 42 of the Constitution that states:

> "No language other than Turkish shall be taught as a mother tongue to Turkish citizens at any institution of education. Foreign languages to be taught in institutions of education and the rules to be followed by schools conducting education in a foreign language shall be determined by law. The provisions of international treaties are reserved."[1398]

Article 66 of the Constitution reads "everyone bound to the Turkish State through the bond of citizenship is a Turk."[1399] The principle established a unique basis for the nation to avoid granting privileges to ethnic groups who formed it. Here, the CC claims that 'Turk' has no racial meaning, and that citizenship and national identity do not mean the denial of ethnic roots. What is prohibited is their utilization to create minorities within Turkey to undermine national unity or to create a new State on that basis.[1400]

No part of the Constitution legislates against discrimination *per se,* but 'equality before the law' is combined with a 'specific distinctions ban' (*ozgul ayrımlar yasağı*), legislation against the 'recognition of privileges', and a resolution to benefit equally from uniform fundamental rights and freedoms. Article 10[1401] of the Constitution enshrines equality for all before the law and states that administrative bodies and State organs must treat all citizens according to these principles.

However, conceptualizing equality within these boundaries has serious legal consequences for minority rights and differences. The principle of non-discrimination has not been interpreted as recognising differences; instead, it is used to silence demands for the recognition of differences applying the logic that non-discrimination demands non-differentiation.[1402] The failure of this formula to create equality and non-discrimination becomes apparent in the case of

---

1397 European Commission, "Progress Report on Turkey, SEC (2001) 1756," Brussels, para. 25.

1398 Article 42 of Turkish Constitution.

1399 Article 66 of Turkish Constitution.

1400 Decision No: 94/2 of 16.6.1994, in Official Gazette, 30.06.1994).

1401 Article 10 of the Turkish Constitution: "Everyone is equal before the law without distinction as to language, race, colour, sex, political opinion, philosophical belief, religion and sect, or any such grounds."

1402 Bayır, Minorities and Nationalism, pp. 225-226.

obtaining a government office. Since 1960, restrictions on public sector employment have been lifted. and 'every Turk' can enter public service. The Constitutions have provided that no distinction *(ayrım)* except qualification for the office concerned is to be taken into consideration for recruitment into the public service.[1403] However, the absence of non-Muslims as judges, soldiers and bureaucrats shows that the equality clause has no impact on discriminatory practices within society and State.[1404]

Meanwhile, Religious freedom has been constitutionally recognized since the 1924 Constitution. Article 24[1405] of the Constitution protects freedom of religion and conscience. Acts of worship and religious ceremonies should be conducted freely, provided they do not violate Article 14.[1406] No one shall be compelled to worship, participate in religious ceremonies, disclose religious beliefs or be

---

1403 Article 58 of the 1961 Constitution; article 70 of the 1982 Constitution, Article 70 of current constitution "Every Turk has the right to enter public service. No criteria other than the qualifications for the office concerned shall be taken into consideration for recruitment into public service."

1404 Ibid.

1405 Article 24 of the Turkish Constitution: "Everyone has the freedom of conscience, religious belief and conviction. Acts of worship, religious rites and ceremonies shall be conducted freely, as long as they do not violate the provisions of Article 14. No one shall be compelled to worship, or to participate in religious rites and ceremonies, or to reveal religious beliefs and convictions, or be blamed or accused because of his religious beliefs and convictions. Religious and moral education and instruction shall be conducted under State supervision and control. Instruction in religious culture and morals shall be one of the compulsory lessons in the curricula of primary and secondary schools. Other religious education and instruction shall be subject to the individual's own desire, and in the case of minors, to the request of their legal representatives. No one shall be allowed to exploit or abuse religion or religious feelings, or things held sacred by religion, in any manner whatsoever, for the purpose of personal or political interest or influence, or for even partially basing the fundamental, social, economic, political, and legal order of the State on religious tenets."

1406 Article 14 of the Turkish Constitution: "None of the rights and freedoms embodied in the Constitution shall be exercised in the form of activities aiming to violate the indivisible integrity of the State with its territory and nation, and to endanger the existence of the democratic and secular order of the Republic based on human rights. No provision of this Constitution shall be interpreted in a manner that enables the State or individuals to destroy the fundamental rights and freedoms recognized by the Constitution or to stage an activity with the aim of restricting them more extensively than stated in the Constitution. The sanctions to be applied against those who perpetrate activities contrary to these provisions shall be determined by law."

accused on religious grounds. Instruction in religious culture and morals is a compulsory lesson in primary and secondary schools. Other religious is subject to the individual's own wishes, and for minors at the request of their legal representatives. No one can exploit or abuse religion or religious sensitivities, or anything held sacred for personal or political interest, and no fundamental, social, economic, political or legal order of State could be based on religious tenets.

The 1982 Turkish Constitution has undergone several amendments, with successive governments reforming various issues and changing Articles.[1407] For example, the 2004 Constitutional Reform adopted an amendment in Article 90 concerning the ratification of international agreements to the Constitution.[1408] The amendment confirmed that if a conflict between a domestic and international convention on human rights occurs, the latter takes precedence. Such a clause protects minorities, bypassing any domestic law.[1409]

One positive development following the September 2010 referendum was that the CC gained the authority to issue final judgments on individual applications, and Turkish law gained a new avenue for the pursuit of legal remedies.[1410] Individuals can now make individual applications to the CC in the event of a violation of any fundamental right guaranteed under the Constitution and included in the ECHR. When the CC rules that a fundamental right has been violated, it can order a retrial or provide compensation. The CC specifies the measures to be taken to remedy any violation.[1411]

1407 Eduard A. Bulut, *Minorities in Constitution Making in Turkey* (UK: Cambridge Scholars Publishing, 2017), p. 1.

1408 Secretariat General of the Turkish Republic for EU Affairs, *Political Reforms in Turkey* (Ankara: MFA Turkey, 2007), p. 19.

1409 Yilmaz, Minority Rights in Turkey, p. 38.

1410 The official website of MFA of Turkey, Human Rights, 2020, https://bit.ly/3tPuR5m.

1411 This legal remedy was included in the legal structure through the changes made to Articles 148 and 149 of the Constitution after the 12.09.2010 referendum, and by decree for the Constitution's Provisional Article 18. The Law on the Establishment and Rules of Procedure of the Constitutional Court of Turkey, No.6216, particularly Articles 45–51, further solidify these Constitutional decrees. Moreover, the CC Rules of Procedure published in the Official Gazette, 12.07.2012 – 28351, contains very detailed directions on the functioning of the application process.

4.4.2 The Turkish Penal Code

Throughout the Republic era, it seems that Turkish Legal system has been keen to protect ethnic Turks by penalizing 'insulting Turkishness'.[1412] The provision has been used to suppress ethnoreligious minorities, and 'insulting Turkishness' was first encoded in Article 159 of the now-defunct 1926 panel code.[1413] After being amended several times, Article 159 was replaced by the current Article 301 in 2004's TPC.[1414] In the early years of the Republic, the provision was used against non-Muslims, prosecuting them for 'insulting Turkishness', offering a serious threat against non-Muslims.[1415]

Increasing pressure from the EU following the assassination of Armenian journalist Hrant Dink[1416] questioned the legitimacy of this aspect of the penal code. The Article was amended in 2008 and 'Turkishness' was replaced by 'Turkish nation', which was deemed an ethnically neutral concept, and prosecution was made conditional on authorization by the Minister of Justice.[1417] Despite the change, problems remain as to the criteria used to define the 'Turkish nation' because according to the explanatory note of the amending law the "nation is a community which consists of people who have lived together since times past (*gecmişten beri*), who have the belief, desire and determination to live together, and have the same homeland; who have a culture, history and unity of ideals."[1418] This means the criteria to define the nation is not the citizenship, but rather unity in culture, history and ideals which cannot be the case for minorities who have different culture, history and ideals.

The Turkish legal system also legislates against assaults on religious freedom. Article 153 penalizes attacks upon graveyards and places of worship with one to three years imprisonment, considering such desecration as a hate crime.[1419] If the commission of such attacks is accompanied by the intention to insult *(tahkir)*, such insults are considered as aggravated circumstances.[1420] In addition, Article 125(3)(b) allows increased sentences for insulting someone for expressing or

1412 Bayır, Minorities and Nationalism, pp. 244-245.
1413 Ibid.
1414 See Article 301 of TPC of 2004, Law No.5237 Official Gazette, 12/10/2004 No.:25611.
1415 Bayır, Minorities and Nationalism, p. 223-225.
1416 See section 3.11.1.3 below.
1417 Article 1 of Law No.5759, 30.04.2008.
1418 Bayir, Minorities and Nationalism, p. 246.
1419 See Article 153 of TPC, Law No.5237 Official Gazette, 12/10/2004 No.:25611.
1420 Ibid, Article 153(3).

practising his/her religious or philosophical views, or if the insult is committed by referring to the individual's religious values.[1421]

The 2004 TPC penalizes Genocide (Article 76) and crimes against humanity (Article 77) for the first time with no limitation period. Furthermore, establishing an organization with the aim of committing Genocide or a crime against humanity, or being members or leaders of such an organization is penalized under Article 78. Article 216(1) demands one to three years' imprisonment for "publicly inciting hatred and hostility against a segment of the populace."[1422] In addition, the concept of group defamation entered the Turkish legal system. Article 216(2) of the 2004 TPC, penalizes publicly degrading "a section of the public on grounds of social class, race, religion, sect, gender or regional differences."[1423] Article 216(3) is specifically designed to protect religious freedom. Thus to "publicly degrade the religious values of a section of the public" is punishable by imprisonment "if the action amounts to impairing the public peace."[1424]

Article 216(1) directly recognizes the existence of different groups in Turkey referring to such groups as having 'different particularities'. Nonetheless, should hatred and animosity are provoked on grounds which are not included in the Article, this Article is not applicable.[1425] For example, inciting hatred against people's ethnicity, nationality, sexual orientation, culture, are not protected under this Article. In addition, having the clause of only "if a clear and present danger to public security occurs as result" indicates that the State is more concerned in protecting public security, rather than the peace and security of diverse groups. The explanatory note of the Article states:

> "...the 'incitement' should be beyond abstract disrespect and denial; it should be objectively appropriate to develop enmity or to intensify these kinds of behaviour. The perpetrator subjectively should have sought this aim and incited people to develop hatred and enmity. In this regard, to break off relations with someone, behaving or using remarks in a manner of abstract rejection or disrespect is not sufficient to amount to this crime. For an act to amount to this crime there should be a serious and intense existence of incitement to develop a hatred and enmity against a definite part of the society."[1426]

1421 Ibid, Article 125 (3)(b).

1422 Ibid, Article 216 (1).

1423 Ibid, Article 2016(2).

1424 Ibid, Article 216 (3).

1425 See CERD Committee, "Concluding Comments on Turkey 2009," para. 11, for its criticism regarding the lack of 'national and ethnic origin' as 'prohibited grounds under article 10 of the 1982 Constitution.

1426 Bayir, Minorities and Nationalism, pp. 241-242.

In other words, the 'abstract disrespect and denial' of a group is not considered a punishable action hence potentially leaving a very wide discretion to prosecutors and the judiciary as to what the Article actually penalizes.[1427]

In line with the official State ideology, the Supreme Court also denies the existence of discrimination in Turkish society because declaring equality before the law is considered to have eradicated discrimination in Turkey.[1428] In this context, despite the inclusion of "Hatred and Discrimination" in Article 122 in the current TPC,[1429] Turkey's practice of attaching reservations to provisions concerning discrimination in international treaties casts doubt about their legal effectiveness. The EC has also noted that despite changes to the TPC, Turkey remains out of step with EU directives on discrimination, the implementation of which would considerably improve the country's legal architecture against discrimination.[1430]

4.4.3 The Treaty of Lausanne

The 1923 Treaty of Lausanne inter-alia established the legal status of minorities in Turkey. Allied powers, while aiming to protect Christians in Turkey, tried to introduce a broad definition of the concept of *minority* based on ethnicity, religion and language as was the case in other minority treaties in Europe.[1431] This would result in granting some non-Turkish Muslim communities (e.g., Kurds, Circassians and Arabs) a minority status. The Turkish delegation opposed this, asserting that Turkey had no minorities other than non-Muslim minorities.[1432] The Treaty limited its definition to non-Muslims. Turkey regarded not all non-Muslims, but only Greeks, Armenians and Jews as non-Muslim minorities,

---

1427 Ibid.

1428 Ibid, pp. 229-233.

1429 "Any person who (a) Prevents the sale, transfer or rental of a movable or immovable property offered to the public, (b) Prevents a person from enjoying services offered to the public, (c) Prevents a person from being recruited for a job, (d) Prevents a person from undertaking an ordinary economic activity on the ground of hatred based on differences of language, race, nationality, colour, gender, disability, political view, philosophical belief, religion or sect shall be sentenced to a penalty of imprisonment for a term of one year to three years."

1430 European Commission, "Progress Report on Turkey, SEC (2005) 1426," Brussels, p. 96.

1431 Eligür, "Ethnocultural nationalism and Turkey's non-Muslim minorities," pp. 6-7.

1432 Yeşim Bayar, "In Pursuit of Homogeneity: The Lausanne Conference, Minorities, and the Turkish Nation," *Nationalities Papers*, 42:1 (2014), p. 114.

leaving other communities (Nestorians, Chaldeans or Assyrians) unrecognized and unprotected.[1433]

Lausanne was a diplomatic victory for Kemalists, but the Turkish delegation met fierce criticism from Parliament as MPs expressed their dissatisfaction with minority clauses, especially because the League of Nations would supervise Turkey. Dr. Rıza Nur, assistant head of the Turkish delegation and the main participant in Lausanne's minority commissions, pointed to the ineffectiveness of the League, saying that "although Bulgaria and Romania had also agreed on minority protection and League of Nations' supervision, they recently mistreated their Jews badly and the League did nothing about it [...] That's why all these supervisions are only in words."[1434]

Ottomans had a history of Great Powers using Christians inside the Empire to intervene in domestic affairs,[1435] so minority protections were problematic for Turkish politicians. This affected those same minorities the protection clauses aimed to protect. The fact that minorities, especially Armenians and Greeks, were given what Turkish State actors saw as 'privileges' by the Lausanne Treaty problematised the already fraught relationship between the Turkish majority and the country's minorities.

Articles 37 to 45 of Treaty of Lausanne deal with minority protection. Article 37 sets the provisions contained in Articles 38 to 44 into law, meaning that no regulation or official action may contradict or overrule them. However, recognized minorities are affected by a juridical void and by legislation, regulations, jurisprudence and internal practice inconsistent with the Treaty.[1436] Under Article 38, all Turks can exercise any faith or belief, providing it is compatible with public order and morality. Article 39 guarantees non-discrimination and permits to use any language in any setting. Article 40 guarantees non-Muslims the right to create, manage and supervise any charitable, religious or social institution or school using their own language and to exercise their religious freedom in such institutions. Article 41 obliges Turkish Government to provide adequate facilities ensuring that in the primary schools the instruction shall be given to

---

1433 Eligür, "Ethnocultural nationalism and Turkey's non-Muslim minorities," p. 7.

1434 Ekmekcioğlu, *Recovering Armenia*, p. 107.

1435 Ntina Tzouvala, "'These Ancient Arenas of Racial Struggles': International Law and the Balkans, 1878–1949," *European Journal of International Law*, 29:4 (November 2018).

1436 UNGA Document, "Legal Interim report of the Special Rapporteur of the Commission on Human Rights on the elimination of all forms of intolerance and of discrimination based on religion or belief," UN Doc. A/55/280/Add.1, August 2000, para. 141.

the children of non-Muslim citizens through the medium of their own language in those towns and districts, where a considerable proportion of them are resident.[1437] In addition, these minorities shall be assured an equitable share in the enjoyment and application of the sums which may be provided out of public funds under the State, municipal or other budgets for educational, religious, or charitable purposes.

Article 42 gives minorities the right to settle family issues or personal status in accordance with their own customs. Meanwhile, the Government must protect minority places of worship, provide full facilities to minority religious foundations and charitable establishments, and to approve the creation of new establishments.[1438] Article 43 prohibits to compel non-Muslims to perform any act which constitutes a violation of their faith or religious observances and placing them under any disability by reason of their refusal to attend Courts of Law or to perform any legal business on their weekly day of rest.[1439]

In this context, the collective nature of the *millet* system had been in decline since 1839 and was finally annulled by the Lausanne Treaty. Henceforth, minority protection would have to be sought individually within a secular European-model legal system.[1440] While confirming the new Turkish nation-state, the Treaty determined minority status within it. It promised everybody the same rights, replacing the *millet* rights of non-Muslim communities.[1441]

Implementing the Treaty was a different matter. The rights were restrictive, and implementation was problematic.[1442] The Articles set up a commission of minority representatives to reach a consensus. Disagreements between the government and the commission supposed to be settled through the Council of International Commission, a worrying imposition for the Government. However, the minority commissions (Greek, Jewish and Armenian) were abrogated when

1437 This provision will not prevent the Turkish Government from making the teaching of the Turkish language obligatory in the said schools.

1438 See Article 40 of Treaty of Lausanne.

1439 This provision, however, shall not exempt non-Muslims from such obligations as shall be imposed upon all other Turkish nationals for the preservation of public order.

1440 Marcie J. Patton, "Constitutionalism and Political Culture in Turkey," *In Political Culture and Constitutionalism: A Comparative Approach*, Daniel P. Franklin & Michael J. Baun eds. (Armonk, NY and London, 1995), pp. 138-58.

1441 Bayir, Minorities and Nationalism, p. 79.

1442 Samim Akgönül, *The Minority Concept in the Turkish Context*, p. 78.

each minority committee penned collective petitions (*Mahzars*),[1443] to renounce the Lausanne rights on family and civil matters, which were then replaced with the 1926 secular Civil Code. Despite the provisions guaranteed in Article 42, the minority commissions ended the process of supervision by the League of Nations.[1444] In other words, certain provisions of the Treaty conflicted with the institutions of the Turkish State, which pressured non-Muslim communities to abrogate certain rights to enjoy equal citizenship at national levels.[1445]

The adoption of the secular Civil Code in 1926 pressured non-Muslim communities into ceding rights to civil self-governance. In addition, the 1923 Unity in Education Law subjected minority schools to the Ministry of National Education in curricular and governance affairs.[1446] The Treaty's minority protection 'survived' the 1945 abrogation of the League of Nations minority protection system as well as all progress in human rights and minority protection law. It remained almost unaffected by new minority protection law in the European context and resisted any attempt to amend it.[1447]

Articles 37–44 of the Treaty were implemented only through political considerations towards national interests. For example, the Treaty provides for minority language education, but after the 1950s minority schools became bilingual due to Turkey's desire to strengthen the official language.[1448]

Here, it is important to highlight the Article 45 of the Lausanne Treaty, which reads, "The rights conferred by the provisions of the present Section on the non-Moslem minorities of Turkey will be similarly conferred by Greece on the Moslem minority in her territory"[1449] has been interpreted by Turkey as a reciprocity Article, which made Greek Muslim rights dependent on non-Muslim

1443 *Mahzar* was a distinctive Ottoman diplomatic term used to frame a demand, complaint or commitment, bearing the signatures of more than one person. For further information see Betül Açıkgöz & Erdoğan Keskinkılıç "The Renunciation of Minority Rights and the Making of the 1926 Civil Law: *Mahzars* Penned by Non-Muslim Minorities," *Middle Eastern Studies*, 54:1 (2018), pp. 68-93.

1444 Akgönül, The Minority Concept in Turkish Context, p. 75.

1445 Rumelili & Keyman, "Enacting multi-layered citizenship," p. 71.

1446 Ibid.

1447 Konstantinos Tsitselikis "A Surviving Treaty: The Lausanne Minority Protection in Greece and Turkey," in *The Interrelation between the Right to Identity of Minorities and their Socio-economic Participation Studies*, Kristin Henrard ed. (Boston: Brill Publishing, 2013), pp. 287-313.

1448 Ibid.

1449 Article 45 of Lausanne Treaty.

rights in Turkey.[1450] However, the word 'reciprocity' is not used in the Article, and the Article simply indicates that undertakings made for non-Muslims in Turkey would be applied to the Muslims in Greece. The reciprocity-based interpretation[1451] is considered invalid in human rights treaties because reciprocity cannot be applied under Article 60(5) of the VCLT of 23 May 1969.[1452] Moreover, as established in ECtHR's case law, Turkey's reciprocity claims are unjustified.[1453]

Subsequent chapters will argue that the Turkish concept of minorities derives from the Lausanne Treaty. However, restricted State policies along with limited interpretations of the Treaty in the past reveal Turkey's negative approach to minority rights.[1454] The Treaty is still binding in Turkey, which falls behind in incorporating current international standards on minority rights.[1455] There are disparities between legally established minority rights and their implementation.[1456]

4.5 Incorporation of International and Regional Laws in Turkish Domestic Law

According to Article 90 of the Turkish Constitution, international agreements have the force of law, and no objection of unconstitutionality can be raised against these agreements.[1457] In the case of conflict, the provisions of international agreements shall prevail.[1458] No information exists of instances when an international convention has been directly invoked in local courts. Turkey is party to sixteen UN human rights conventions, and compliance with UN conventions

---

1450 Bayir, Minorities and Nationalism, pp. 92-93.

1451 Ibid.

1452 Article 60 of VCLT.

1453 See the cases of Apostolidi and Others v. Turkey (no.45628/99, § 64, 27.03.2007), Nacaryan and Deryan v. Turkey (no.19558/02 and27904/02, § 30, 08.01.2008) and Fokas v. Turkey (no.31206/02, § 30, 29.09.2009).

1454 Gözde Yılmaz & Diğdem Soyaltın, "Zooming into the 'Domestic' in Europeanization: Promotion of Fight against Corruption and Minority Rights in Turkey," *Journal of Balkan and Near Eastern Studies*, 16:1 (2014), p. 14.

1455 Dilek Kurban, *A Quest for Equality: Minorities in Turkey* (UK: Minority Right Group International 2007).

1456 Bülent Aras and Sule Toktas "The EU and Minority Rights in Turkey," *Political Science Quarterly*, 124:4 (December 2009), p. 702.

1457 The official website of MFA of Turkey: http://www.mfa.gov.tr/%C4%B0nsan-haklar%C4%B1.en.mfa.

1458 Ibid.

are reviewed by relevant treaty-based committees.[1459] Since 2001, Turkey has extended standing invitations to special procedures. Special Rapporteurs visit Turkey within this framework.[1460] Turkey ratified the 1965 UN CERD in 2002, and ICCPR (with reservations to Article 27) and ICESCR in 2003. Turkey is party to 121 of the 225 CoE conventions and claims to maintain close cooperation with human rights bodies covering various areas including racism, discrimination, prevention of torture and ill-treatment.[1461] Since 2006, Turkey has been a party to the First Optional Protocol of ICCPR, giving the HRC jurisdiction on individual complaints concerning possible derogations.[1462]

Turkey's foreign policy on international treaties aims to ensure that only non-Muslims are given legal recognition and protection. The policy on minority rights is one of non-signature, as it is the case for the FCPNM. If the treaty entails provisions granting minorities rights, then the policy is signed with reservations on these provisions. The Turkish Constitution and foreign policy ensure that Turkey remains in compliance with the Lausanne Treaty without granting non-Muslims minority status in the constitution and preventing the expansion of protection to other minorities.[1463]

In its reservation to Article 27 of the ICCPR in September 2003, Turkey: "reserves the right to interpret and apply the provisions of Article 27 in accordance with the related provisions and rules of the Constitution of the Republic of Turkey and the Treaty of Lausanne of 24 July 1923 and its Appendixes."[1464] Turkey's reservation purports to subsume the interpretation of Article 27 to the provisions of the Turkish constitution and the Treaty of Lausanne. The reference to the Treaty is further explained in Turkey's response: "According to this Treaty, Turkish citizens belonging to non-Muslim minorities fall within the scope of the term 'minority'. Turkish legislation which is based on the Lausanne

---

1459 UNOHCHR official website of Turkey, https://bit.ly/3gnZ1qs.

1460 The official website of MFA of Turkey: http://www.mfa.gov.tr/%C4%B0nsan-haklar%C4%B1.en.mfa.

1461 Ibid.

1462 Martin Scheinin, "Turkey's Derogation from Human Rights Treaties– An Update," *Ejil Talk Blog of the European Journal of International*, 18.08.2016, https://bit.ly/3qpkFhm.

1463 Yilmaz & Soyaltın, "Zooming into the 'Domestic'," p. 14.

1464 See The Reservation of Turkey to Article 27 of ICCPR in the official website of UNOHCHR, https://bit.ly/3pgLeVq.

Peace Treaty contains the term 'non-Muslim minority' only."[1465] The reference to Turkish legislation indicates Turkey's interpretation of the Treaty of Lausanne. In other words, as Thomas argues, the Treaty of Lausanne *positively* identifies non-Muslims as minorities, whereas Turkish legislation *negatively* excludes all other candidates from minority status.[1466]

Here it is important to examine the invalidity of Turkey's reservation to Article 27 of ICCPR. Article 19 of the VCLT states:

> "A State may, when signing, ratifying, accepting, approving or acceding to a treaty, formulate a reservation unless:
>
> (a) the reservation is prohibited by the treaty;
>
> (b) the treaty provides that only specified reservations, which do not include the reservation in question, may be made; or
>
> (c) in cases not falling under sub-paragraphs (a) and (b), the reservation is incompatible with the object and purpose of the treaty"[1467]

To assess Turkey's reservation to Article 27 with the object and purpose of the ICCPR, it is crucial to consider that the reservation refers to an entire body of Turkey's domestic law without clearly specifying the content of the reservation. The reference to the Turkish constitution *per se* does not necessarily invalidate treaty reservations considering they are compatible with the object and purpose of the treaty,[1468] but the problem is in the vague or general formulation of the reservation. According to Guideline 3.1.5.2 of the ILC's report a reservation "shall be worded in such a way as to allow its meaning to be understood, in order to assess in particular its compatibility with the object and purpose of the treaty".[1469]

Turkey's reservation has considerable degree of vagueness. The provisions of domestic law to which it refers are complex and dynamic, and it is hard to understand the full extent of the Article 27 obligations accepted by Turkey by reading the text of its reservation alone. As the ILC underscores, this situation damages

1465 HRC, "Initial Reports of States Parties: Turkey," 13.04.2011, UN Doc. CCPR/C/Tur/1, para. 409.

1466 Thomas James Phillips, "The (In-)Validity of Turkey's Reservation to Article 27 of the International Covenant on Civil and Political Rights," *International Journal on Minority and Group Rights,* 27 (2020), pp. 90-92.

1467 Article 19 of VCLT.

1468 ILC, "Guide to Practice on Reservations to Treaties," UN Doc. A/66/10/Add.1, Guideline 3.1.5.5; Commentary para. 7.

1469 *Ibid.*, Guideline 3.1.5.2.

the consensual nature of the law of treaties as the uncertain meaning of the reservation makes it difficult or impossible for other parties to the treaty to accept or object to it on its own terms.[1470]

Turkey's reservation nevertheless includes a core meaning, which is relatively clear and easily understood by States[1471] as well as treaty monitoring bodies. For instance, the CERD Committee in its Concluding Observations to periodic reports of Turkey, noted that "the Treaty of Lausanne does not explicitly prohibit the recognition of other groups as minorities" and that Turkey should consider recognising other groups, such as Kurds and Alevis as minorities.[1472] The very limited number of minorities recognized by Turkey, and the arbitrary way in which they are identified might lead Turkey to discriminate against minorities other than particular non-Muslim minorities by excluding all other minorities from the scope of application of Article 27. Therefore, the reservation provides a relatively clear core meaning leading to an argument that it is invalid.

In addition, as the ILC Guidelines indicate, three elements should be considered while assessing the compatibility of a reservation with the object and purpose of a treaty containing numerous interdependent rights such as the ICCPR: a- the *interdependence* of the rights and obligations; b- the *importance* that the provision has within the general tenor of the treaty; and c- the extent of the *impact* that the reservation has on the treaty.[1473]

The element of the interdependence of the rights and obligations aims to ensure that the treaty does not disintegrate into bundles of obligations, "the individual, separate realisation of which would not achieve the realisation of the object of the treaty as a whole".[1474] ICCPR's preamble recognizes the "equal and inalienable rights of all members of the human family...,"[1475] while its object and purpose as defined by the HRC, is "to create legally binding standards for human rights by defining certain civil and political rights and placing them in a framework of obligations which are legally binding for those States which ratify ..."[1476]

1470 *Ibid.*, Guideline 3.1.5.2; Commentary para. 3.

1471 Finland and Sweeden have formally objected to Turkey's reservation to Article 27 of ICCPR. See the official website of UN Treaty collections: https://treaties.un.org/Pages/ViewDetails.aspx?chapter=4&clang=_en&mtdsg_no=IV-4&src=IND

1472 CERD Committee, "Concluding Observations on the Combined Fourth to Sixth Periodic Reports of Turkey," 2016, UN Doc. CERD/C/tur/CO/4–6, para. 14.

1473 ILC, "Guide to Practice on Reservations to Treaties," Guideline 3.1.5.6.

1474 *Ibid.*, Commentary para. 7.

1475 See the Preamble of ICCPR.

1476 HRC, General Comment No. 24, para. 7.

Considering that minority rights, as expressed in Article 27 and elaborated by Thomas, "are aimed at allowing minority groups to maintain and develop their very existence as minority groups (i.e. to protect them from unwanted assimilation), it could be argued that serious reservations to that Article undermine the interdependence of ICCPR rights and obligations, in that without access to those rights there can be no substantial relationship of equality between the minority group and the majority of the population."[1477]

With regard to the importance of minority rights, considering that certain rights protected by human rights treaties are less essential than the non-derogable ones,[1478] they shall be assessed according to the "general tenor" of the treaty. which as described by ILC is "balance of rights and obligations which constitute its substance or the general concept underlying the treaty."[1479] Minority rights' importance is distinctly expressed in several regional and international instruments (See Chapter 2 above) and Turkey's reservation limiting those rights to only a selected subset of religious minorities is not compatible with international and regional human rights instruments' positioning on the importance of minority rights. Furthermore, in General Comment No. 24, the HRC underscored the particular importance of non-derogable ICCPR rights and highlighted that "a State has a heavy onus to justify such a reservation"[1480] adding that even though Article 27 is not a non-derogable right,[1481] it is nevertheless "of profound importance".[1482]

In reference to the impact of the reservation, it is explained by the ILC that, "even in the case of essential rights, reservations are possible if they do not preclude protection of the rights in question and do not have the effect of excessively modifying their legal regime."[1483] Turkey's reservation to Article 27 precludes protection of the right for entire categories of people and therefore excessively

1477 Philips, "The (In-)Validity of Turkey's Reservation," p. 79.

1478 ILC, "Guide to Practice on Reservations to Treaties," Guideline 3.1.5.6; Commentary, para. 8.

1479 *Ibid.*, Guideline 3.1.5.6, Commentary para. 14(ii) and Alain Pellet, 'The ILC Guide to Practice on Reservations to Treaties: A General Presentation by the Special Rapporteur," *European Journal of International Law*, 24 (2013), p. 1081.

1480 HRC, General Comment No. 24, para. 10

1481 HRC states that "elements" of minority rights are non-derogable. *See* HRC, "General Comment No. 29," UN Doc. CCPR/C/21/Rev.1/Add.11, para. 13(c).

1482 HRC, General Comment No. 24, para. 10

1483 ILC, "Guide to Practice on Reservations to Treaties," Guideline 3.1.5.6, Commentary para. 9.

modify the legal regime. Based on this assessment, it can be argued that Turkey's reservation to Article 27 is incompatible with the object and purpose of the ICCPR. Moreover, as discussed in section 2.6 above, Article 27 might reflect both a norm of a customary law and a peremptory norm (jus cogens)[1484] which enhances the argument that Turkey's reservation is incompatible with the object and purpose of the ICCPR.

Last but not least, CERD Committee noted in 2009 "[t]he application of restrictive criteria to determine the existence of ethnic groups, official recognition of some and refusal to recognise others, may give rise to differing treatment for various ethnic and other groups."[1485] This might result to *de facto* discrimination in the rights and freedoms referred to in Articles 2 and 5 of CERD. Therefore, Turkey's refusal to grant minority rights to anybody except particular non-Muslim groups was unjustifiable, leading HRC to conclude that it would lead to discrimination:

> "The Committee is of the opinion that the international protection of the rights of persons belonging to minorities includes elements that must be respected in all circumstances. This is reflected in the prohibition against Genocide in international law, in the inclusion of a non-discrimination clause in Article 4 itself (paragraph 1), as well as in the non-derogable nature of Article 18."[1486]

The HRC (General Comment No. 31: 26 May 2004) remarked that:

> "...the beneficiaries of the rights recognized by the covenant are individuals...rights of members of minorities (Article 27) may be enjoyed in community with others - States parties are required on ratification to make such changes to domestic laws and practices as are necessary to ensure their conformity with the covenant.-A failure to comply with this obligation (Article 2, to take steps to give effect to the covenant rights is unqualified and of immediate effect) cannot be justified by reference to political, social, cultural or economic considerations within the State."[1487]

1484 See section 2.6 above.

1485 CERD Committee, "Concluding Observations on the Combined Fourth to Sixth Periodic Reports of Turkey," 2016, UN Doc. CERD/C/tur/CO/4–6, para. 12.

1486 HRC, "CCPR General Comment No. 29," para. 13(C).

1487 HRC, "CCPR General Comment No. 31: The Nature of the General Legal Obligation Imposed on States Parties to the Covenant," 26.05.2012, UN Doc. CCPR/C/21/Rev.1/Add. 13.

To summarize the arguments above, under the VCLT[1488] and ILC guidelines,[1489] it can be stated that Turkey's reservation to Article 27 of ICCPR is null and void. because it contradicts the purpose of the Treaty. Moreover, Turkey cannot exclude or modify Article 27, the object of which is to create legally binding standards for human rights in a framework of obligations.[1490] By limiting the scope of Article 27, minority groups are denied rights as individuals or as members of a group. This undermines the interdependent rights in the ICCPR, thus undermining the recognition of those rights.[1491] Finally, the impact of the reservation may involve Turkey violating the *jus cogens* norm of non-discrimination, even if Article 27 *per se* does not reflect a peremptory norm.

Turkey has been criticized by HRC for restrictions on minorities, affecting their right to enjoy their culture and use their language (Articles 2 and 27), commenting that:

> "The State party should ensure that all persons belonging to ethnic, religious or linguistic minorities are effectively protected against any form of discrimination and can fully enjoy their rights. To this regard, the State party should consider withdrawing its reservation with respect to Article 27 of the Covenant."[1492]

A clear decision on the invalidity of Turkey's reservation would be meaningful. International law has sufficient ideological force[1493] to legitimise struggles for emancipation,[1494] and the identification of certain groups in Turkey as minorities helps claims for rights. Elevating such claims to international law would force Turkey to address them, and failure to meet these demands would be a matter of breaking the law, thus significantly legitimizing and strengthening minority rights in Turkey.[1495]

1488 Articles 19 to 23 of VCLT.

1489 Pellet, 'The ILC Guide to Practice on Reservations to Treaties: A General Presentation," p. 1078.

1490 Phillips, "The (In-)Validity of Turkey's Reservation," pp. 90-92.

1491 Ibid.

1492 HRC, "Concluding Observations on the Initial Report of Turkey adopted by the Committee at its 106th session" (15 October - 2 November 2012) UN Document CCPR/C/TUR/CO/1, 2012, para. 9.

1493 For more insight on International Legal ideological forces, see Susan Marks, *The Riddle of All Constitutions: International Law, Democracy, and the Critique of Ideology* (UK: OUP, 2003).

1494 Philips, "The (In-)Validity of Turkey's Reservation," p. 92.

1495 Ibid.

Turkey has issued similar reservations to other international instruments, such as the CRC. Here, Turkey purports to exempt itself from upholding the rights of children from groups other than Greek, Armenian and Jewish communities. This includes the obligation to ensure that children's education shall be directed towards the child's cultural identity and language.[1496] The CRC Committee is concerned about Turkey's reservations to Articles 17, 29 and 30 of the Convention, noting that in terms of education, freedom of expression and the right to enjoy one's own culture and language, these reservations have a negative impact on children belonging to ethnic groups, particularly Kurdish children:

> "The Committee encourages the State party to consider withdrawing its reservations to Articles 17, 29 and 30 of the Convention in order to provide better protection and opportunities to all groups of children, in particular children of Kurdish origin, who are not recognized as a minority under the Turkish Constitution and the Treaty of Lausanne of 1923."[1497]

Turkey still has not ratified the optional protocol to the International Covenant on Economic, Social and Cultural Rights, while CERD encouraged Turkey to consider ratifying the Domestic Workers Convention of 2011.[1498] UNESCO, meanwhile, encouraged ratification of the Convention against Discrimination in Education.[1499]

In addition, after Turkey's ratification of the 2005 UNESCO Convention on the Protection and Promotion of the Diversity of Cultural Expressions, in 2017, the Ministry of Culture and Tourism contributed to the work of the Convention's National Committee, but measures for its implementation have not taken properly.[1500]

1496 See Turkey's Reservation to CRC and Article 29(C) of CRC: https://bit.ly/2TsuZu8.

1497 Consideration of reports submitted by States Parties under Article 44 of the Convention Concluding Observations: Turkey, UN Doc. CRC/C/TUR/CO/2-3, 2012.

1498 UNOHCHR Document, "Compilation on Turkey Report of the Office of the UNHCHR," UN. Doc. A/HRC/WG.6/35/TUR/2, 12.11.2019, para. 3.

1499 UNESCO, Submission for the Universal Periodic Review of Turkey, para. 15. Contribution of UNESCO to Compilation of UN information (to Part I. A. and to Part III - F, J, K, and P): Turkey, 2015, Universal Periodic Review (21st session), para. 15, https://www.refworld.org/docid/54c109484.html.

1500 European Commission, "Commission Staff Working Document, Turkey 2019 Report Accompanying the document Communication from the Commission to the European Parliament, the Council, the European Economic and Social Committee and the Committee of the Regions 2019 Communication on EU Enlargement Policy," p. 92.

Furthermore, in 1965, Turkey signed the 1954 Hague Treaty on the Preservation of Cultural Monuments during War and in 1969 it signed the International Treaty for the Preservation of Cultural Monuments, which included provisions for the preservation of minority monuments. The dire situation of the Armenian cultural and historical monuments (which will be discussed below) illustrates the extend of Turkey's commitment to meet its international obligations.

Lastly, Turkey fails to cooperate closely with the OSCE's HCNM, and has not signed the CoE's FCPNM nor the European Charter for Regional or Minority Languages. Turkish authorities have repeatedly stated that the Charter opposes Articles 3 and 42 of the Turkish Constitution[1501] which includes the Turkish-only provision in educational institutions.[1502]

4.6 Turkey's National Human Rights Mechanisms

The HREIT[1503] and the Ombudsman[1504] are the main official human rights institutions in Turkey. The main difference in the scope of both institutions is the individual application procedure. While the Ombudsman deals only with complaints against the actions of the public administration, the HREIT rejects applications that are within the sphere of the Ombudsman.

The Ombudsman Institution was established by Act 6328 in 2012. Attached to the Turkish Grand National Assembly, the Ombudsman has a separate budget and is based in Ankara to establish an independent and efficient complaint mechanism regarding public services and the investigation of actions of the administration in terms of human rights.[1505]

1501 Article 3 of Turkish Constitution: "The State of Turkey, with its territory and nation, is an indivisible entity. Its language is Turkish."; Article 42 of Turkish Constitution: "No language other than Turkish shall be taught as a mother tongue to Turkish citizens at any institution of education. Foreign languages to be taught in institutions of education and the rules to be followed by schools conducting education in a foreign language shall be determined by law. The provisions of international treaties are reserved."

1502 "Turkey Criticized for not Signing Charter on Minority Languages," *Zaman* newspaper, 23.06.2010.

1503 The official website of HREIT: http://ennhri.org/our-members/turkey/.

1504 The official website of Ombudsman of Turkey: https://www.ombudsman.gov.tr/English/index.html.

1505 For further information see the official website of the Ombudsman Institution in Turkey: https://www.ombudsman.gov.tr/English/index

The HREIT act of 2016, under which the Turkish National Human Rights Institution became the Human Rights and Equality Institution, weakens the monitoring mandate as the institution will now investigate human rights violations upon application only,[1506] and the Act does not fully comply with the Paris Principles.[1507]

The founding law of the HREIT was revised to cover anti-discrimination and equality, and now it protects and improves human rights, ensuring equal treatment and preventing discrimination against rights and freedoms. Decree Law No.703 (July 2018) brought about this restructure, adding that the President selects all 11 members of the HREIT's decision-making body (Article 149 of Decree Law No.703). HREIT is now affiliated to the Ministry of Justice and has legal personality and administrative and financial autonomy. This restructuring has weakened the HREIT's independence.[1508]

Meanwhile, CERD, CEDAW and the Committee against Torture recommended ensuring the functional, structural and financial independence of the HREIT, with guarantees that the appointment of its members complies fully with the Paris Principles. Turkey should also ensure that the HREIT fulfills its mandate as a national preventive mechanism, with a dedicated structure and adequate resources.[1509] It seems that neither institution is independent.[1510] So far, the HREIT has no accreditation with the relevant International Coordinating Committee of National Institutions for the Promotion and Protection of Human Rights. Turkey is under obligation to ensure that human rights violations cases

---

1506 Committee on the Protection of the Rights of All Migrant Workers and Members of Their Families, "Concluding Observations on the Initial Report of Turkey," 2016 UN Doc. CMW/C/TUR/CO/1, para. 29(b).

1507 Human Rights Council, "Summary of Stakeholders' Submissions on Turkey. Report of the Office of the UNHCHR," UN. Doc. A/HRC/WG.6/35/TUR/3, 12.11.2019, para. 9.

1508 ECRI, "Conclusions on the Implementation of the Recommendations in Respect of Turkey Subject to Interim Follow-Up," adopted 03.04.2019, Published 06.06.2019, p. 1.

1509 Human Rights Council, "Working Group on the Universal Periodic Review, Thirty-fifth session 20–31 January 2020 Compilation on Turkey, Report of the Office of the United Nations High Commissioner for Human Rights," UN Doc. A/HRC/WG.6/35/TUR/2, Para. 6.

1510 Ibid.

are effectively dealt with and processed, and that both bodies comply with the Paris Principles and EC Recommendation on Standards for Equality Bodies.[1511]

An action plan is being drawn up by the CoE and civil society to boost democracy and human rights in Turkey which was announced in March 2021.[1512] The plan is based on "harmonization of legislation," "awareness-raising and training" and "institutional capacity building on human rights."[1513]

4.7 Turkey's EU Accession Process and Minority Rights

Relations between Turkey and the EU have been problematic as far as prospective membership is concerned. Turkey's 1959 application to the EEC meant that relations became closer. In 1963, the Ankara Agreement signed to stablish a Customs Union between the parties, and in 1987 Turkey applied for full EC membership.[1514] The EEC recommended sticking to the Agreement with Turkey rather than adopting an accession perspective, and the Customs Union Agreement was signed in 1995.[1515] The 1999 Helsinki Summit[1516] declared Turkey a candidate State and provided a roadmap for wide ranging reforms in areas including minority rights. The EU made the protection of minorities an explicit criterion for accession,[1517] which has been problematic. Onar and Özgüneş consider the European minority regime is a "flawed model of best practice for at least three reasons": there is no consensus on what constitutes a minority; a gap exists between directives to members and candidates and there is a "discrepancy between the EU's compelling normative thrust and lack of concrete guidelines."[1518]

1511 European Commission, "Progress Report on Turkey," SWD (2019) 220, p. 28. https://bit.ly/3qk3v5Y.

1512 Cetin Kaya, "Turkey Announces Human Rights Reform," Lexology, 03.03.2021, https://bit.ly/33jlmPZ.

1513 Human Rights Council, "Working Group on the Universal Periodic Review," para. 28.

1514 Meltem Müftüler-Baç and Lauren McLaren, "Enlargement Preferences and Policy-Making in the European Union: Impacts on Turkey," *International Journal on Minority and Group Rights,* 17(1) (2010), p. 129.

1515 Decision No 1/95 of the EC-Turkey Association Council Of 22 December 1995 on Implementing the Final Phase of The Customs Union (96/142/Ec).

1516 See Helsinki European Council 10 And 11 December 1999 Presidency Conclusions, https://www.europarl.europa.eu/summits/hel1_en.htm

1517 Bardakci et al., Religious Minorities in Turkey, p. 17.

1518 Nora Fisher Onar & Mehmet Özgüneş, "How Deep a Transformation? Europeanization of Greek and Turkish minority policies," *International Journal on Minority and Group Rights,* 17:1 (2010), p. 121.

Nevertheless, tailor-made guiding principles for minority protection are set up for each candidate country.[1519]

In March 2001, the EU adopted the EU-Turkey Accession Partnership (revised in 2003, 2006, and 2008), and Turkey approved its first National Program for the Adoption of the *Acquis*. In December 2002, the Copenhagen summit[1520] concluded that the EU would open accession negotiations with Turkey if Turkey fulfilled the Copenhagen criteria for membership: democracy, the rule of law, human rights and protection of minorities. In the meantime, EU leaders agreed to offer Turkey increased pre-accession financial assistance. Between 1999 and 2014, EU demands from Turkey included the ratification of the CoE FCPNM, eliminating bans on broadcasting and education in languages other than Turkish and the limited interpretation of the Lausanne Treaty that restricted minority definitions to Armenians, Greeks and Jews.

In addition, the EU demanded the resolution of cultural and socio-economic problems in southeast Turkey relating to refugees and the Kurdish issue, granting property rights and removing bans on training clergy and eliminating problems relating to the Alevis.[1521] Specific measures prioritized by the EU included the abolition of the requirement to specify religion on ID cards, solving difficulties experienced by non-Muslims minorities in acceding to administrative and military positions and eliminating discriminatory language in schoolbooks.[1522]

After 2008, the EU provided a more detailed roadmap for minority protection in Turkey. The focus shifted to implementation problems and issues left unresolved such as the elimination of restrictions on using languages other than Turkish in political life.[1523] Roma and their rights were foregrounded in this period, along with the elimination of hate speech and hate crimes from 2011 onwards.[1524] The EU also focused on the Kurdish problem following the launch of the Kurdish peace process by the Turkish government.[1525]

1519 Şule Toktaş, "EU Enlargement Conditions and Minority Protection: A Reflection on Turkey's Non- Muslim Minorities," *East European Quarterly,* 40:4 (2006), pp. 489–518.

1520 See Copenhagen European Council 12 And 13 December 2002 Presidency Conclusions, https://www.consilium.europa.eu/media/20906/73842.pdf.

1521 European Commission, "Progress Reports on Turkey: 1999, 2005a, 2006a, 2007, 2008, 2009, 2012, 2013, 2014."

1522 European Commission, "Progress Reports on Turkey: 2005, 2007."

1523 European Commission, "Progress Reports on Turkey: 2009, 2012."

1524 European Commission, "Progress Reports on Turkey: 2011, 2013, 2014, 2015."

1525 European Commission, "Progress Reports on Turkey: 2008, 2009, 2010, 2013, 2015."

Turkey's response to the EU requirements was a massive reform process referred to by many as a 'silent revolution'.[1526] The 1999–2002 period was more of a preparation phase to establish necessary institutions like the Secretariat General for EU Affairs and agreements with the EU.[1527] In 2001, the Turkish Parliament adopted over 30 amendments to meet the Copenhagen criteria. In 2002 it passed further reforms to meet EU human rights criteria, including the lifting of bans on Kurdish-language education and broadcasting.[1528] After the 2002 elections, the reform process in minority rights accelerated under the AKP government. Eight reform packages passed through Parliament by 2004, including amendments of minority rights laws and measures to improve minority protection. Difficulties in property rights for non-Muslim foundations were relatively eased, and an amendment to Article 2 of the Law on Construction allowed the construction of places of worship for all denominations.[1529]

In 2004, broadcasting and teaching in languages other than Turkish began.[1530] 2005 and 2006 saw a new penal code, a new Ombudsman office, and the improvement and implementation of earlier reforms.[1531] A new Foundations Law was adopted in 2008 providing non-Muslim representation in the Foundations Council and giving further property rights.[1532] In October 2011, Article 11 of the Foundations Law regulating the conditions for applications for properties and compensation payments was amended.[1533] In 2013, an amendment allowed campaigning in non-Turkish languages used by political parties and candidates, removing the ban on using those languages in political life.[1534] In March 2014, an amendment to the Criminal Code increased penalties for hate crimes.[1535]

1526 Bardakci et al., Religious Minorities in Turkey, p. 3.

1527 Yılmaz, Minority Rights in Turkey, p. 37.

1528 Bardakci et al., Religious Minorities in Turkey, p. 78.

1529 Official Gazette No. 25173, 19.07.2003, Amendment to the Law on Construction in Turkey.

1530 Yılmaz, Minority Rights in Turkey, p. 40.

1531 Ibid. p. 43.

1532 Thomas Hammarberg, Review Report on Human Rights of Minorities, CoE, CommDH, 2009, p. 11.

1533 CERD Committee, "Reports Submitted by States Parties under the Article 9 of the Convention Combined Fourth to Sixth Periodic Reports of States Parties due in 2013 Turkey," 10.02.2013, UN. Doc. CERD/C/TUR/4–6., para. 27.

1534 European Commission, "Progress Report on Turkey 2914," p. 62.

1535 Ibid, para. 60.

In 2013, the introduction of questions on Islam in university entrance and secondary school examinations was followed by a declaration on questions for non-Muslim students.[1536] Children without Turkish citizenship can attend courses as guest students.[1537] Dialogue with minority representatives intensified between 2008 and 2014, and the Turkish Parliament invited minority representatives to listen to their views on the new 2011 Constitution.[1538] Discussions also included making peace with the PKK.[1539] This initiative represented further progress in the protection of minorities by extending cultural and linguistic rights to the Kurdish minority.[1540]

Throughout this process, Kemalism, as the State ideology of Turkey, was challenged. Kemalist ideology embraces secularism and reinforces a single Turkish identity causing problems for other ethnicities.[1541] As Ulusoy notes, reforms challenged "the whole political project upon which the Republic was established in 1923."[1542] The number of minority associations rose significantly, and there is now more information on them available, with more members of minorities lodging cases with the Turkish courts and the ECHR.[1543]

The EU has played a significant role in promoting minority rights in Turkey, and Turkey's new political environment seemed to allow questioning the exclusivist notions of Turkish citizenship, by removing some hurdles to the free exercise of minority rights.[1544] Although Turkey has made progress, there is still plenty of room for improvement. Turkey has not signed the CoE FCPNM, the Language Charter, or eliminated its restrictive interpretation of the Lausanne Treaty; it has not adopted an action plan for Roma and IDPs and has published no regulation on election procedures in non-Muslim foundations.[1545] The same applies to the implementation of the adopted reforms, due to lack of strong

---

1536 European Commission, "Progress Report on Turkey 2013," para. 54, 61.

1537 European Commission, "Progress Report on Turkey on 2013," para. 62.

1538 Yılmaz & Soyaltın, "Zooming into the 'Domestic,'" p. 14.

1539 Ibid, p. 22.

1540 Ibid, p. 16.

1541 Posch Walter, "Crisis in Turkey: Just Another Bump on the Road to Europe?" *Institute for Security Studies Occasional Paper 67*, (2007), p. 10.

1542 Kıvanç Ulusoy, "Turkey's Reform Effort Reconsidered, 1987–2004," *Democratization*, 14:3 (2007), p. 477.

1543 Bardakci et al., *Religious Minorities in Turkey*, pp. 236-237.

1544 Ibid.

1545 European Commission, "Progress Report on Turkey 2012, para. 31, 2014 paras. 16, 18, 2015: Paras. 68–9".

monitoring mechanisms, which represent a tremendous step for the Europeanization process. The legislative scope of the action plans does not cover all rights and relevant ECtHR case-law.[1546] Compliance has fluctuated over time, despite positive developments.[1547]

Moreover, declining EU membership prospects in response to several human rights violations, the tense geopolitical EU-Turkey relationship and the refugee crises and shifting AKP priorities threaten the status of minority rights.[1548] These factors might explain why there have been no significant recent improvements in Minority Rights in Turkey, and the accession process seems unlikely to improve the situation for minorities in the immediate future. In addition, given the EU's obvious reluctance, accession no longer seems credible to Turkey, and EU conditionality is no longer a powerful motivating force. As Turkey's chances of EU membership diminish, Turkey's reforms towards more minority rights have lost pace and are being reversed.[1549]

4.8 Turkey - ECtHR Relations

The ECtHR constitutes an important factor in cooperation between Turkey and CoE. In 1987, Turkey accepted the right to individual applications to the court for a review based on the ECHR. Turkey recognized the compulsory jurisdiction of the ECtHR in 1990,[1550] and is ranked first in the number of ECHR violations in the over 60-year history of the ECtHR.[1551] Turkey, with 3,224 judgments, is by far the largest violator in terms of "judgments finding at least one violation."[1552] This fact is just another indicator on the concerning situation of general human rights issues in Turkey and highlights the need to address these violations systematically so the rights protected by ECHR are guaranteed by law and practice.

1546 Ibid, 2016, para. 2.4.

1547 For further details, Gözde Yilmaz "Exploring the Implementation of Minority Protection Rules in the 'Worlds of Compliance': The Case of Turkey," *Perspectives on European Politics and Society*, 13:4 (2012), p. 412.

1548 Bardakci et al., Religious Minorities in Turkey, p. 18.

1549 Onar & Özgüneş, "How deep a transformation?," p. 123.

1550 Official website of Turkish MFA: http://www.mfa.gov.tr/%C4%B0nsan-haklar%C4%B1.en.mfa.

1551 Violations by Article and by State, ECHR Official page, 2020, https://bit.ly/3a7KNIl.

1552 "Statistics Show that Turkey is the Top Violator of European Rights Charter," Stokholm Center for Freedom, 10.04.2020, https://bit.ly/3i7dbgc.

The CC also stated that the ECHR has become a part of domestic law within Article 90 of the Constitution.[1553] The provisions of the Convention are binding which means that the ECHR and the ECtHR case-law are acknowledged among the sources of the Turkish legal system.[1554] However, serious backsliding is now occurring in terms of fundamental human rights, especially in freedom of expression, assembly, association and procedural and property rights. While the legal framework includes guarantees of respect for rights, it still requires to be aligned with the ECHR and case law of the ECtHR. No legislative changes were made after the SoE was lifted in 2018, which eliminated safeguards protecting activists, human rights defenders, journalists, and academics. Enforcement of rights is impeded by the lack of independence and fragmentation of public institutions responsible for protecting rights and freedoms and by the lack of an independent judiciary.[1555]

The 2015 Progress Report on Turkey stresses harmonization with ECtHR rulings, emphasizing rulings on exemption from compulsory religious classes, the indication of religious convictions on identity cards, legal conditions of religious bodies and work and residence permits for foreign clergy.[1556] There only was limited implementation of the 2014 action plan to prevent ECHR violations. Implementation reports are not made public, limiting the accountability of Turkish institutions.[1557] In addition, the Turkish Government did not implement the 2016 action plan relating to ECtHR decisions on *Cem* Houses and compulsory religion classes. School textbooks must be revised to remove discriminatory elements against other faiths. No steps were taken to open the Halki (Heybeliada) Greek Orthodox Seminary, and concerns remain regarding the protocols on the delivery of educational tasks of the Ministry, while the work of the Religious Affairs Presidency (Diyanet) increased throughout public life.[1558] Turkish attitudes to minorities have progressed considerably, but many reforms are needed before the country's practices reach international standards. Minority groups still experience repression in Turkey, and the government still only recognizes Armenians, Jews and Christians as minorities.

1553 Official website of Turkish MFA: http://www.mfa.gov.tr/%C4%B0nsan-haklar%C4%B1.en.mfa.

1554 Ibid.

1555 European Commission, "Key findings of the 2019 Report on Turkey, European Commission - Countries insights, Brussels," 29.05.2019.

1556 Bardakci et al., Religious Minorities in Turkey, p. 46.

1557 European Commission, Progress Report on Turkey, 2019, SWD (2019) 2020.

1558 Ibid, p. 32.

4.9 What Does It Mean to Be a Minority in Turkey?

Despite its founders' intentions to create a homogenous nation-state, Turkey remains diverse. Capotorti's (1979) definition[1559] of minorities indicates that many minority groups exist in Turkey, although there is no official recognition for many of them.[1560] This is because these groups are citizens numerically inferior to the rest of Turkey's population, they are in a non-dominant position and possess ethnic, religious or linguistic characteristics different from rest of the population and express a sense of solidarity to preserve their culture, traditions, religion or language. According to Kaya, Turkey is a multi-ethnic and multi-religious State with approximately 50 different minority groups living in it[1561] Accurate numbers of minority groups remain unknown, and quantitative data need to be read cautiously.[1562]

Before 1990, censuses had a question on native language, this information was no longer disclosed. The only official information on minorities in Turkey can be derived from the census of 1965, which is out of date and inaccurate.[1563] The term 'minority' is recalled as one of the main sources of the fall of the Ottoman Empire.[1564] They are considered "enemies of the State, agents of foreign powers, people harmful to society, traitors, and dangerous to Turkey's territorial integrity,"[1565] and minorities are still characterized accordingly in State textbooks, media, and public speeches.[1566]

Turkey still believes in possible collaboration among foreign powers and minorities to break up the country as the Ottoman Empire was broken up.[1567] The narrow definition of national identity on the grounds of homogeneity and indivisibility of State and nation has been the primary reason behind Turkey's restrictive minority approach.[1568] Minority rights are considered a threat to national unity, leading to social fragmentation on the basis of demands for

1559 See Capotorti's definition of minorities in Section 2.1 above
1560 Yilmaz, Minority Rights in Turkey, p. 24.
1561 Ayhan Kaya, *Europeanization and Tolerance in Turkey: The Myth of Toleration* (England, Basingstoke: Palgrave Macmillan 2013), P. 47.
1562 Yilmaz, Minority Rights in Turkey, p. 28.
1563 Kurban, A Quest for Equality: Minorities in Turkey, p. 11.
1564 Kaya and Harmanyeri, Tolerance and Cultural Diversity, p. 2.
1565 Bardakci et al., Religious Minorities in Turkey, p. 67.
1566 Ibid.
1567 Ibid.
1568 Ibid.

autonomy and secession, especially with Kurdish issue.[1569] In the CC's view, minority status "impairs the State's integrity, leads to violence, and creates hate and animosity among the people."[1570] It claims that speaking about ethnic, linguistic and cultural differences amounts to expressing "ideas based on race" *(ırk temeline dayanan duşunce).*[1571]

There are several approaches to categorizing Turkish minorities. They can be grouped by religious, ethnic and linguistic differences. Turkey has historically housed various religious groups, including Alevis, Caferis, Armenians (belonging to mainly three Christian denominations), Jews, Greek Orthodox Christians and Assyrians. Precise numbers are unknown, but totals seem to be between 10 % and 33 % of the country.[1572]

Turkey also contains different ethnic and linguistic minorities, including Kurds, Arabs, Armenians, Caucasians, Roma and Laz, totaling 10–23 % of the population.[1573] According to the authorities, over 3.5 million Syrian refugees[1574] also live in Turkey. Another approach to categorizing minority groups is by legal recognition. There are legally recognized non-Muslim minorities (Jews, Armenians, Greeks), non-recognized non-Muslim Minorities (Assyrians, Protestants, Chaldeans, Georgians, Maronite Christians, Bahais), non-recognized ethnic minorities: Arabs, (Sunni, Alevi, Christian), Laz, Kurds (Sunni, Alevi, Caferi, Yezidi), Circassians, Georgians, Bosnians, Roma, non-recognized religious/sectarian minorities: Alevis (Turks, Kurds), Nusayris (Arab), Caferis, and unrecognized linguistic/ethnic minorities (Zaza).[1575]

Until the 1920s, non-Muslim elements were never referred to as 'minorities' in any official Ottoman State documents.[1576] This changed with the *'Ahd-ı Milli Beyannamesi'*, the so-called National Pact *(Misak-i Milli)* passed on 17 September 1920. Article 5 of the Pact read:

> "The rights of minorities *(akalliyetler)* as defined in the treaties concluded between Allied Powers and their enemies and certain of their associates shall be confirmed and

1569 Yilmaz, Minority Rights in Turkey, p. 32.
1570 Bayir, Minorities and Nationalism, p. 206.
1571 Ibid.
1572 Kurban, A Quest for Equality: Minorities in Turkey, pp. 11-14.
1573 Yilmaz, Minority Rights in Turkey, p. 28.
1574 See Operational Portal Refugee Situation: https://data2.unhcr.org/en/situations/syria/location/113.
1575 Bayir, Minorities and Nationalism, p. 3.
1576 Ibid, p. 68.

> assured by us in reliance on the belief that Muslim minorities in neighbouring countries will also have the benefit of the same rights."[1577]

Referring to non-Muslims as 'minorities', the document conditioned the protection of their rights upon the rights of Muslims in neighboring countries. For the Ottoman Empire, the idea of reciprocity was brought into the management of diversity.[1578] In addition, minorities' rights were defined and legitimated through international treaties which mean that the rights of communities, which had been observed for many centuries, were being annulled.[1579]

Legally speaking, the concept of minority in Turkey simply means 'non-Muslim' citizens. The concept derives from the Lausanne Treaty, which is cited by many as the source of official policy regarding minority rights, with the 'non-Muslim' phrase interpreted as 'prominent non-Muslim communities' (Armenians, Greeks and Jews), minorities under the protection of the League of Nations when the Treaty was signed.[1580] Turkey still rejects the international definition(s) of minorities on the basis of race, language or religion, and denies many minorities, including Kurds or Alevis their rights.[1581]

Closer examination of the Lausanne Treaty demonstrates no references to Armenians, Jews, or other non-Muslim groups. Apart from Greeks, other groups do not appear in the Treaty, despite presenting submissions to the conference. However, Article 42(3) of the Lausanne Treaty mentions the protection of 'churches, synagogues [and] cemeteries', implying that non-Muslim places of worship are protected. It remains difficult to explain the Turkish State's selective approach towards some non-Muslims.[1582] Official minority status was denied to eastern provinces' Christians (such as Assyrians) and to the new Christian communities such as Protestants.[1583] These unrecognized groups became the main targets of homogenization under discourses of 'equal citizenship'.[1584]

1577 Bayir, Minorities and Nationalism, p. 68.

1578 Ibid.

1579 Ibid.

1580 Marcus Dressler, "Historical Trajectories and Ambivalences in Turkish Minority Discourse," *New Diversities*, 17:1 (2015), p. 16.

1581 Yılmaz, Minority Rights in Turkey, p. 28.

1582 Bayir, Minorities and Nationalism, p. 90.

1583 Esra Özyürek, "Convert Alert: German Muslims and Turkish Christians as Threats to Security in the New Europe," *Comparative Studies in Society and History*, 51:1 (2009), pp. 91–116.

1584 Mesut Yeğen, "Citizenship and Ethnicity in Turkey," *Middle Eastern Studies*, 40:5 (2004), pp. 682–708.

Following the terms of the Treaty, a notation of 'Islam' as a person's religion came to connote Turkishness, and having made this connection, the registers refused to recognize ethnic and sectarian differences within the Muslim majority.[1585] The CC has only ever defined 'minorities' in the TEP-1980 judgment, as "citizen groups who [are different] from the majority in terms of language, religion, race, etc. and who have the legal rights to pursue their [different] being."[1586] In the CC's view, the minority definition has two components: firstly objective differences and, secondly the recognized status of a minority.[1587] In addition, as the CC judgment indicates, non-citizen minority members residing in Turkey (e.g. Syrian refugees) are not legally recognized as minority and they cannot claim or enjoy minority rights.

While recognizing ethnically or religiously different groups in a country, the CC considers that the mere existence of such groups is not sufficient to grant them differentiated special rights. The CC makes clear that being different in ethnicity, religion and language, or being smaller than the majority, does not qualify a group as a minority. The CC has added another dimension to the recognition of a minorities by asserting that rules on minorities in Turkey are governed by international treaties, so minority status cannot be granted by domestic law alone. In the CC's opinion, other than those mentioned in the Lausanne Treaty no other minority groups exist in Turkey.[1588]

These "Lausanne" communities have a long-standing history in modern Turkey as well as distinct characteristics they want to preserve that the Additional protocol on the Rights of Minorities to the European Convention on Human Rights define as a "national minority."[1589] They remain present and active

---

1585 Ceren Özgül, "Legally Armenian: Tolerance, Conversion, and Name Change in Turkish Courts," *Comparative Studies in Society and History*, 56:3 (2014), p. 634.

1586 Constitutional Court Verdict TEP (*Türkiye Emekçi Partisi*, Proletarian Party of Turkey), 08.05.1980.

1587 Bayir, Minorities and Nationalism, p. 203.

1588 Ibid.

1589 Article 1 of Additional protocol on the Rights of Minorities to the European Convention on Human Rights: For the purposes of this Convention (1) The term "Convention" in this text refers to the Convention for the Protection of Human Rights and Fundamental Freedoms., the expression "national minority" refers to a group of persons in a State who: a. reside on the territory of that State and are citizens thereof; b. maintain longstanding, firm and lasting ties with that State; c. display distinctive ethnic, cultural, religious or linguistic characteristics; d. are sufficiently representative, although smaller in number than the rest of the population of that State or of a region of that State; e. are motivated by a concern to preserve together that which

today, although their populations have dwindled for various reasons.[1590] Students belonging to non-Muslim minorities can attend minority schools where they learn about their own culture while taking national curriculum classes. As of the 2018–2019 school year, 59 minority schools carry out educational activities.[1591] There are 387 non-Muslim places of worship, including 87 churches.[1592] Recognized minorities can carry out activities through foundations and associations they have established in Turkey and can acquire movable and immovable property. There are currently 167 community foundations.[1593]

Although the AKP has brought openness to Turkish politics regarding minority rights, the government promotes a careful approach rather than *de jure* recognition of minorities.[1594] The AKP has not radically changed the rhetoric of official minority policy in terms of legal recognition. Erdogan clarified the AKP's position on minorities: "Minorities in our country are evident, and they are defined by the Lausanne Treaty. There are no other minorities than these in our country."[1595] The same approach is applicable for indigenous people: "the Republic of Turkey declare[d] that no community exists on its territory that can be deemed an 'indigenous people' under the [UNESCO] convention."[1596] According to Aras and Toktaş "[T]he Turkish State does not seem willing to extend minority rights beyond the Lausanne regime and has made it clear that it will

constitutes their common identity, including their culture, their traditions, their religion or their language.

1590 Allison S. Block, "Judicialization and Implementation of Religious Minority Rights in Turkey: Case Studies from the European Court of Human Rights," (Postdoctoral Thesis, Johnson-Shoyama Graduate School of Public Policy, 2018), p. 95.

1591 Working Group on the Universal Periodic Review, Thirty-fifth session 20–31 January 2020 National report submitted in accordance with paragraph 5 of the annex to Human Rights Council Resolution 16/21, Turkey, UN Doc. A/HRC/WG.6/35/TUR/1, para. 71.

1592 ECRI Report, "Appendix: Government's Viewpoint, Observations of The Turkish Government on ECRI's Fifth Report on Turkey," 2016, para. 36.

1593 Directorate General of Foundation in Turkey official website: https://www.vgm.gov.tr/foundations-in-turkey/foundations-in-turkey/cemaat-community-foundations.

1594 Yilmaz, Minority Rights in Turkey, p. 103.

1595 AKP political Group 2007. Prime Minister and Chairman of the AKP Recep Tayyip Erdoğan's Speech to his Political Group. 13.11.2008, Ankara.

1596 Convention on the Protection and Promotion of the Diversity of Cultural Expressions - see Tulay Cetingulec, "Does Turkey care about cultural diversity?" *Al-Monitor Turkey Pulse*, 17.08.2015, https://bit.ly/3qcQbzd.

handle this issue through improvements in three realms: elimination of discrimination, cultural rights, and religious freedom."[1597]

Based on the above legal and historical contexts the following sections argue the situation of the Armenian minority in Turkey.

4.10 The Armenians in Turkey

Most Armenians in Turkey originated in today's eastern Turkey, and differ from Turks in terms of ethnicity, religion, language and culture. Turkey's Armenians can be divided into three groups: Christian Armenians, recognized by the Lausanne Treaty, Armenian Migrants from Armenia (most of them live illegally), and Hidden Armenians (Islamized, Crypto Armenians).[1598] The latter group are registered as Muslims, and does not have the legal status of an 'Armenian minority' nor minority rights. The same absence of rights applies to migrant Armenians. In the 1990s Turkey's national office of statistics estimated that, out of a total of 82,000 Armenian citizens in Turkey, eight to ten thousand were living abroad, predominantly in Germany, the Netherlands and Belgium. Of the 72,000 left, only 5 % (3,600 people) live outside Istanbul.[1599] The Armenian community in Turkey estimates its own numbers at about 60,000 to 65,000,[1600] while a Yerevan based expert gives an even lower estimate of 35,000 - 50,000.[1601] Others estimate the number of Christian Armenians with Turkish citizenship living in Turkey is between 40,000 and 70,000, but there are up to 170,000 Armenian economic migrant, some of whom already have integrated socially.[1602]

Furthermore, there is a large group of Muslim Armenians[1603] whose ancestors were forced to convert to Islam to escape displacement and death in the Armenian

1597 Bülent Aras, Sule Toktas and Bulent Aras, "The EU and Minority Rights in Turkey," p. 716.

1598 Hrag Papazian, "*Türkiye'deki üç farklı Ermeni kimliği*," *Agos* newspaper, 2016, http://www.*Agos*.com.tr/tr/yazi/16758/turkiye-deki-uc-farkli ermeni-kimligi.

1599 Ibid, p. 9.

1600 Personal Interview with His Beatitude Patriarch Sahak II Mashalian, Armenian Patriarch of Constantinople, the interview was held in Istanbul in 16.02.2020 and US Department of State, "Annual Report on International Religious Freedom 2008," 2008 http://www.state.gov/g/drl/rls/irf/2008/108476.htm.

1601 Tessa Hofmann, One Nation, Three Sub-Ethnic Groups: The Case of Armenia and Her Diaspora (Yerevan, 2011), p. 83.

1602 Bardakci et al., Religious Minorities in Turkey, p. 135.

1603 Ibid.

Genocide. There are also some Armenian Crypto-Christians in eastern provinces, who keep their identities secret and practice Islam in the public sphere. The number of Islamized Armenians and Crypto-Armenians, which are sometimes called "Dönme" ("returnee" or "convert"), is difficult to estimate; sources estimate numbers from 30,000 to several million people.[1604]

In addition, the origin and ethnicity of the *Hemşinli* group is still disputed.[1605] Their language is a dialect of Armenian, and their formerly Christian ancestors probably converted to Islam from the fifteenth century onwards.[1606] The Number of Armenians cannot be validated as there is no official way of enumerating them. Turkey's Armenian Orthodox/Apostolic community is the country's largest Christian group,[1607] and several Armenians belong to Armenian Catholic Church, Armenian Protestant Church, free evangelical churches or they are non-believers. Rather strikingly, Turkey's official census shows virtually no increase in the Armenian population since 1935, when official records gave a figure of 57,000, compared to 58,000 for 1965.[1608] Armenian Catholic numbers shrank from 5,000 to under 2,000 by 1999. The number of Armenian Protestants is estimated at 500.

Armenians mainly live in Istanbul. However, there are 500 in Ankara, 300 in Iskenderoun, 70 in Sepastia, 50 in Malatia, and 20 families in Kharpert.[1609] The village of Vakıfli (*Vakif Köyü*) near Samandağ (*Mousa Ler*), with its 120 inhabitants, is the only village in Turkey inhabited only by Armenians.[1610]

Some Istanbul Armenians prefer not to be identified as minority members.[1611] Kalayci states: "We are not a group that migrated to this land and became minority. We have been living in these lands for thousands of years, we had our

---

1604 Altuğ Yılmaz, *Müslümanlaş(tıril)mış Ermeniler* (Islamized - Islamatized Armenians) (Istanbul: Hrant Dink Vakfı Yayınları, 2015).

1605 For further information, see Hovann Simonian ed., *The Hemshin: History, Society and Identity in the Highlands of Northeast Turkey* (New York: Routledge, 2007).

1606 Bardakci et al., Religious Minorities in Turkey, p. 136.

1607 US Department of State, "2016 Report on International Religious Freedom – Turkey." Bureau of Democracy, Human Rights, and Labor 15.08.2017, https://www.refworld.org/docid/59b7d82a13.html.

1608 Committee for Monitoring Minority Rights, Minorities in Turkey, *Human Rights Association-Turkey*, (Istanbul), 02.06.1996, p. 3.

1609 Harut Sassounian, "Istanbul Armenians Document Violations of Minority Rights in Turkey," *Asbarez* newspaper, 04.03. 2011, https://bit.ly/2ZjM0pO.

1610 Bardacki, Religious Minorities in Turkey, p. 136.

1611 Özdoğan & Kılıçdağı, *Hearing Turkey's Armenians*, p. 28.

kingdoms and statehood in these lands, we have a thousand-year-old civilization developed on these lands."[1612] At first glance, there is little contrast between being a minority and being an autochthonous element; but being a minority in Turkey has negative connotations, such as being a foreigner, an enemy within or a traitor. However, Haddejian provides the counter argument:

> "We, as a minority due to the Treaty of Lausanne and the Mother Constitution [*Anayasa*] of Turkey, have rights that give us special privileges; they give us certain rights of being a minority. In my view, saying you are not a minority means giving up the responsibility of upholding those rights. Obviously, we have issues with the government, we have limitations and, until recently, many injustices, confiscation of our properties, all these exist. But first of all, we should protect what we already have. […] We have an enormous heritage, it is both historical and living heritage, both above the soil and under the soil. We are the preservers of all these by remaining here. Of course, along these treasures and rights, we have limitations […].[1613]

Alternative concepts proposed are being counted as a constitutive element or equal citizen, as opposed to being a 'minority'. Here, 'constitutive element' refers to being Turkish, with rights and a voice. Moreover, Armenians who remained inside what became Turkey do not consider themselves as diaspora, since they remained on their own land. Even Istanbul, which historically never was part of Armenia, had Armenian presence back to the 6-th century.[1614] Armenians see their Istanbul community as the remnant of the largest part of the Armenian nation, the Western Armenia. In other words, the mass movement from rural areas to Istanbul – a displacement within the homeland, as Suciyan calls it – represents a desire to live on the land of one's ancestors, where a unique civilization was developed over 26 centuries.[1615] Moreover, although the Republic of Armenia borders Turkey to the east, but most Armenian citizens of Turkey are not exiles or immigrants, but aboriginal descendants of Armenians from today's eastern Turkey.[1616] Together with other Armenian diasporas, Turkey's Armenians consider themselves heirs of the culture and civilization destroyed by the Armenian Genocide and as a truly indigenous population in a what used to be a Western Armenia.

1612 Personal Interview with Maître Arno Kalayci, lawyer, founding member of *Nor Zartonk* Foundation, the interview was held in Istanbul on 17.02.2020.

1613 Tchilingirian, "The 'Other' Citizens," p. 128.

1614 Hofmann, *One Nation*, p. 42.

1615 Talin Suciyan, The Armenians in Modern Turkey: Post-Genocide Society, Politics and History (London: I. B. Tauris, 2016), p. 33.

1616 Gellman, Democratization and Memories of violence, p. 116.

4.10.1 The Armenians in the Ottoman Empire until WWI

The *millet* system meant that Armenians were given some rights in running their own community and were able to reach a significant position within the Empire.[1617] Some Armenians were employed in the political arena as ministers or diplomats. Due to their loyalty to the Ottomans, they were recognized as *millet-i sadika* (a loyal nation) by the Ottomans.[1618] Nevertheless, for nearly four centuries, Armenians in the Armenian parts the of Ottoman Empire (i.e., East of today's Turkey) were oppressed under the Ottoman rule.[1619]

Conflict between Ottomans and Armenians began to intensify in the late nineteenth century and is based on a mixture of social and political tensions. In March 1878, with the advocacy of Armenian Patriarch Nerses Varjabedian and others, at the end of the Russo-Turkish War, Article 16[1620] was inserted into the Treaty of San Stefano, stipulating that the Russian forces occupying the Armenian provinces would withdraw only with the full implementation of reforms improving the lives of the Armenians. The 'Armenian Question' became a common term among diplomatic circles and the popular press after the Congress of Berlin in 1878, referring to Europe's involvement with the Armenian subjects of the Ottoman Empire. Great Britain's refusal to Russia to hold so much Ottoman territory forced Russia and Turkey into new negotiations under the Congress of Berlin. Article 16 was modified so that all mention of the Russian forces remaining in the provinces was removed. Instead, the Ottoman government was periodically to inform the Great Powers of the progress of the reforms. In the Treaty of Berlin, Article 16 was transformed into Article 61, which read:

> "The Sublime Porte undertakes to carry out, without further delay, the improvements and reforms demanded by local requirements in the provinces inhabited by Armenians, and to guarantee their security against the Circassians and Kurds. It will periodically make known the steps taken to this effect to the powers, who will superintend their application."[1621]

1617 Bardakci et al., Religious Minorities in Turkey, p. 137.

1618 Ibid.

1619 For further information, See Mesrob K. Krikorian, *Armenians in the Service of the Ottoman Empire: 1860-1908* (New York: Routledge, 2018), first published in 1978.

1620 Though not as explicit, Article 16 of the Treaty of San Stefano read: "For the purpose of preventing oppressions and atrocities which have occurred in the Ottoman Empire's European and Asiatic provinces, the Sultan guarantees, in agreement with the Czar, to grant administrative local self-government to the provinces inhabited by Armenians and to guarantee their security against the Kurds and Circassians.

1621 See Treaty of Berlin, https://archive.org/stream/jstor-2212670/2212670_djvu.txt.

An Armenian delegation headed by Fr. Khrimian traveled to Berlin to present the case of the Armenians and demand their rights, but his requests were ignored.[1622]

In this context, the development of Turkish and Armenian nationalism played a crucial role through the emergence and spread of nationalism or nationalist movements across Europe and the expansionary ambitions by several European great powers towards the Ottoman Empire. Several escalatory factors overlapped and reinforced each other in the course of the nineteenth and the beginning of the twentieth century.

Thus, Ottoman-Armenian relations were influenced by wars in the Balkans and the Caucasus in the 1870s and the Berlin congress in 1878. Ottomans considered the demand for Armenian autonomy was meaningless for demographic reasons,[1623] and the Berlin Treaty failed to provide any enforceable solution to the "Armenian Question." Increasing nationalism among Armenians in the international arena fueled the government's distrust for Armenian elements.[1624] As a result of increasing tension and the lack of political concessions by the Ottoman State, Ottoman Armenians became further nationalized, created Armenian political parties and partisan groups aimed at achieving more rights or independence.[1625] The best-known of these were the *Armenagan* Party, *Hunchagian* Party and the *Tashnagtsutioon* Party (ARF).

As the State failed to deliver promised administrative reforms, things got worse.[1626] Armed resistance by Armenian forces against local officials and Kurdish chieftains intensified Abdul Hamid's fears of large-scale uprisings in the eastern provinces. He sided with the Kurdish chieftains and formed armed regiments of Kurdish militia to carry out local massacres in the east between 1894 and 1896 of Armenians and Assyrians.[1627] With the encouragement and guidance of the Hamidian administration, around 300,000 Armenians were killed in Trabzon, Erzurum, Muş, Bitlis, and the Sason region.[1628] The Armenian parties, mostly the *Tashnagtsutioon*, acted against the Abdul Hamid regime.

1622 Hamo Bedrosian, "*135 Dari Arach – Khrimian Hayrign u Berlini Vehajoghove,*" (135 years ago, Khrimian Hayirg and Berlin Conference, *Asbarez* newspaper, 02.01.2014, https://hairenikweekly.com/2014/01/02/16507.

1623 Bardakci et al., Religious Minorities in Turkey, p. 138.

1624 Arbatli & Gokmen, "Minorities, Human Capital," p. 17.

1625 Bardakci et al., Religious Minorities in Turkey, p. 138.

1626 Özdoğan & Kılıçdağı, *Hearing Turkey's Armenians*, p. 15.

1627 Arbatli & Gokmen "Minorities, Human Capital," p. 19.

1628 Ibid, p. 101.

The re-proclamation of the constitution in 1908 resulted to some extent from this action, and the formation of a national assembly gave hope to the Armenians and other peoples who desired a more liberal and democratic country. During the 1908, 1912 and 1914 parliaments, Armenians held 14, 13, and 14 seats respectively.[1629] With this new hope, *Tashnagtsutioon* continued the effort to cooperate with the CUP.[1630] However, within a few years, it became clear that the CUP's policy and anti-Armenian stand was similar to Abdul Hamid's approach. In April 1909, anti-Armenian pogroms in Adana vilayet killed up to 30,000 Armenians.[1631]

With the Ottomans defeated at Tripolis,[1632] an agreement with Russia on 8 February 1914 was signed to further pro-Armenian reforms supervised by European officials in the eastern provinces of the Ottoman Empire,[1633] but the Ottoman Turks rarely complied with the terms of these agreement and other international obligations they had back then (e.g., the Treaty of Berlin of 1878 and The Hague II Convention on Laws and Customs of War on Land of 1899). In contrary they escalated the persecution of the Armenians under the pretext that Armenian volunteers are supporting the Russians.

The Young Turks' nationalism became even more radical than before. Although most Armenian civilians, political parties and the military had remained loyal to the Ottoman Empire during WWI, the government now blamed them for military losses. A sense of willingness to solve the 'Armenian Question' through expulsion and extermination grew in early 1915.[1634] The Armenians constituted a racial, demographic, and geographic obstacle to unification with the Turkish people of the South Caucasus and Central Asia – a main aim of the

1629 Michael B. Bishku, "The Interactions and Experiences of Armenians and Jews in the Ottoman Empire and Republic of Turkey from the Young Turk Revolution of 1908 to the Present," *Nationalism and Ethnic Politics*, 23:4 (2017), p. 435.

1630 Feroz Ahmad, The Young Turks: The Committee of Union & Progress in Turkish Politics, 1908–1914 (Oxford: OUP, 1969), p. 155.

1631 Arbatli & Gokmen, "Minorities, Human Capital," p. 24.

1632 Bardakci et al., Religious Minorities in Turkey, p. 139.

1633 The agreement was signed by the Ottoman Grand Vizier Said Halim and the Russian chargé d'affaires Konstantin Gulkevich and included reform project for seven Ottoman eastern provinces that covered roughly half of Asia Minor. This agreement often is called 'Armenian Reforms'. For further information see: Kieser Hans-Lukas et al, "Reform or cataclysm? The agreement of 8 February 1914 regarding the Ottoman eastern provinces," Journal *of Genocide Research,*17:3 (2015).

1634 Bardakci et al., Religious Minorities in Turkey, p. 139.

Pan-Turanism ideology propagated by the Young Turks.[1635] These factors paved the way for State led Genocide towards the Armenians.

4.10.2 The Armenian Genocide

4.10.2.1 Neither the Term "Genocide" nor the Genocide Convention Existed in 1915

The term "Genocide" did not exist until 1944, when Raphael Lemkin, combined the Greek word for race or tribe, "geno," with "-cide," from the Latin word for killing. He coined the term partly in response to the systematic killings of Jewish people conducted by the Nazis.[1636] But Mr. Lemkin said he also had the killings of Armenians in mind. In an interview conducted in 1949 Mr. Lemkin said: "I became interested in genocide because it happened so many times. It happened to the Armenians, and after the Armenians, Hitler took action."[1637] Lemkin repeatedly stated that early exposure to newspaper stories about Ottoman crimes against Armenians was key to his beliefs about the need for legal protection of groups.[1638] In other words, the origin of the term "Genocide" and its codification in international law have their roots in the mass and systematic murder of Armenians in 1915.

As briefly mentioned in section 2.4.10 above, the Genocide Convention did not create a new offense in international criminal law,[1639] but it codified the prohibition of massacres, which was already binding international law. In its 1951 Advisory Opinion, the ICJ stated that "the principles underlying the Convention are principles which are recognized by civilized nations as binding on all States, even without any conventional obligation."[1640] Additionally, the U.N.

1635 Ibid, p. 140.

1636 See the official website of the UN Office on Genocide Prevention and the Responsibility to Proters, UN, 2021, https://bit.ly/3pTGjfr.

1637 "Raphael Lemkin, creator of word "Genocide", referring to Armenian Genocide," Youtube, 29.04.2020, https://www.youtube.com/watch?v=F57pgpr_jdw.

1638 "The Armenian Genocide (1915-16): Overview," United States Holocaust Memorial Museuem, 2021, https://bit.ly/3pdbDqa.

1639 Nehemiah Robinson, *The Genocide Convention: A Commentary* (New York, NY, USA: Institute of Jewish Affairs, 1960); Leo Kuper, *International Action Against Genocide* (London, UK: Minority Rights Group, 1984).

1640 "Reservations to the Convention on the Prevention and Punishment of the Crime of Genocide," May 28, 1951, Advisory Opinion, International Court of Justice, ICJ Reports 1951, pp. 15-69.

Commission on Human Rights noted in 1969 that "It is therefore taken for granted that as a codification of existing international law the Convention on the Prevention and Punishment of the Crime of Genocide did neither extend nor restrain the notion of genocide, but that it only defined it more precisely."[1641] Even the Genocide Convention which does not have a retroactive effect,[1642] refers to past genocides in the preamble:

> Recognizing that at all periods of history genocide has inflicted great losses on humanity, and being convinced that, in order to liberate mankind from such an odious scourge, international co-operation is required.[1643]

What is crucial to affirm here is that the State Responsibility for the Armenian Genocide did not originate neither with the creation of the term Genocide nor with the adoption of Genocide Convention. The term and the Convention merely confirmed existing international law and thereby strengthened the pre-existing rights of Armenian victims. Armenian claims derive from the doctrine of State responsibility for crimes against humanity, and that this international liability pre-dated the entry into force of the Genocide Convention. For example, Article 3 of the 1907 Hague Convention IV on land warfare stipulates: "A belligerent party which violates the provisions of the said Regulations shall, if the case demands, be liable to pay compensation. It shall be responsible for all acts committed by persons forming part of its armed forces"[1644] In addition, the Ottoman Empire made several international commitments to protect the Christian minorities within the empire in a series of international treaties in the 1800s.[1645]

1641 U.N. Commission on Human Rights, "*Report of the Ad Hoc Working Group of Experts on Southern Africa*," February 28, 1969, UN Doc. (E/CN.4/984/Add.18).

1642 The ICJ has stated that "the substantive provisions of the Convention do not impose upon a State obligation in relation to acts said to have occurred before that State became bound by the Convention." See Application of the Convention on the Prevention and Punishment of the Crime of Genocide (Croatia v. Serbia), Judgment, I.C.J. Reports 2015, p. 46, para. 100. In addition, Article 28 of the VCLT prohibits the retroactive application of treaties "unless a different intention appears from the treaty or is otherwise established," which is not the case in the Genocide Convention.

1643 The Preamble of Genocide Convention.

1644 Convention [IV] Respecting the Laws and Customs of War on Land, Article 3, in James Brown Scott (ed.), The Hague Conventions and Declarations of 1899 and 1907 [New York, NY, USA: OUP, 1915], pp. 100-106 at 103.

1645 On the peace treaties between the Ottoman Empire and the European Powers, see generally Karl Heinz Ziegler, "The Peace Treaties of the Ottoman Empire with

Article 61 of the Treaty of Berlin, which superseded the Treaty of San Stefano, requested the Ottoman authorities to:

> carry out, without further delay, the improvements and reforms demanded by local requirements in the provinces inhabited by the Armenians, and to guarantee their security against the Circassians and Kurds. It will periodically make known the steps taken to this effect to the Powers, who will superintend their application.[1646]

Thus, as Roscini argues, Armenians were placed under the explicit protection of the international law of contract, and under the control of the Great Powers which acquired the right to receive periodic reports, assess the measures adopted and supervise their application. The natural obligations of the Government to all its subjects have become, as regards the Armenians, strict engagements with the States which are parties to the Treaty of Berlin.[1647] In other words, the Armenian question was not just an internal affair anymore since 1878, but also a matter of international obligation. The acts of the Ottoman authorities therefore towards the Armenian minority, constituted an internationally wrongful act as they breached treaty obligations.[1648] Although some might argue that the Treaty of Berlin only obliged the Ottoman Empire to protect the Armenians, and did not provide an obligation not to commit certain harmful actions against them, the ICJ clarified in the Bosnian Genocide case in relation to genocide that

> "[i]t would be paradoxical if States were ... under an obligation to prevent, so far as within their power, the commission of genocide by persons over whom they have a certain influence, but were not forbidden to commit such acts through their own organs, or

---

European Christian Powers," in *Peace Treaties and International Law in European History*, Randall Lesaffer ed. (Cambridge University Press, Cambridge, 2004) pp. 338-364.

1646 Article 61 of Treaty of Berlin. Treaty between Great Britain, Germany, Austria, France, Italy, Russia, and Turkey for the Settlement of Affairs in the East: Signed at Berlin, July 13, 1878.

1647 Marco Roscini, "Establishing State Responsibility for Historical Injustices: The Armenian Case," International *Criminal Law Review* 14(2) (2014), pp. 291-316.

1648 See Article 1 and Article 2 of the 1930 Articles adopted in first reading by the Third Committee of the Conference for the Codification of International Law (*Yearbook of the International Law Commission*, 1956, Vol. II, p. 225). The Ottomans denounced the 1878 Berlin Treaty only in late 1916 invoking, *inter alia*, the violation of those treaties by the European Powers and the fundamental change of the circumstances in which the treaties were signed (the text of the communication containing the denunciation is in 5 *Current History: A Monthly Magazine of The New York Times* (February 1917) pp. 822-824).

> persons over whom they have such firm control that their conduct is attributable to the State concerned under international law."[1649]

The systematic deportations and mass killings of Armenian have been often qualified as 'genocide'. In the *Reservations to the Genocide Convention* proceedings before the ICJ, for instance, the United States argued that "the Turkish massacres of Armenians" were one of the "outstanding examples of the crime of genocide".[1650] Today, thirty-two countries,[1651] most Genocide scholars[1652] and number of international bodies – including the European Parliament, the CoE, and the Catholic Church – have made official proclamations recognising the Genocide, but Turkey does not acknowledge the events as such.[1653] The Association of Genocide Scholars is unequivocal that the events of 1915 merit the label of Genocide.[1654] Genocide remains a contested term in Turkey, where words such as massacre, deportation, or catastrophe are preferred. Turkish politicians, society and academia admit that there were hundreds of thousands of Armenian casualties during that period, but deny the deliberateness of the Genocide, depicting the deportations as necessary protective measures to maintain security in an emergency situation or as defence in times of war.[1655]

4.10.2.2 The Main Phases of the Armenian Genocide

In the main phase of the Armenian Genocide (1915–1923), the CUP attempted to 'Turkify' the remaining empire that roughly remined in Asia Minor. The perpetrators systematically murdered up to 1.5 million Armenians, forcefully uprooted the Armenian population from their historical lands and expropriated

1649 Application of the Convention on the Prevention and Punishment of the Crime of Genocide (Bosnia and Herzegovina v. Serbia and Montenegro), 26 February 2007, ICJ, Merits, I.C.J. Reports 2007, para.
166.

1650 Written statement of the Government of the United States of America, "Reservations to the Convention on the Prevention of Genocide," 28 May 1951, ICJ, Advisory Opinion, *I.C.J. Pleadings*, p. 25.

1651 The official website of MFA of Armenia: https://www.mfa.am/en/recognition/.

1652 "How Genocide denial warps Turkish politics," *Economist*, 7.11.2019, https://econ.st/3dfScYq.

1653 The official website of MFA of Armenia: https://www.mfa.am/en/recognition/.

1654 Gellman, Democratization and Memories of violence, p. 114.

1655 Bardakci et al., Religious Minorities in Turkey, p. 140.

virtually all Armenian owned land, property and assets.[1656] The CUP effectively removed the Armenian presence from its 2,500-year-old Armenian homeland in eastern Asia Minor.

The main phase of the Genocide was planned and directed by the CUP using the apparatus of the Ottoman-Turkish State, from government administrators, national police and the Ottoman Army to local police and administrators.[1657] The CUP leadership created and directed killing squads comprised of released criminals to commit killing, rape and torture. The government encouraged members of the local populations, including Turks and Kurdish tribal groups, to participate in various aspects of the destruction of Armenians.[1658]

1656 For general accounts of the main phase of the Armenian Genocide, see for example, Raymond Kevorkian ed., *The Armenian Genocide: A Complete History* (New York, NY, USA: I.B. Taurus, 2011); Henry Morgenthau, *Ambassador Morgenthau's Story* (Reading, UK: Taderon Press/Gomidas Institute, 2000), pp. 193-257; Richard G. Hovannisian, "The Historical Dimensions of the Armenian Question, 1878-1923," *The Armenian Genocide in Perspective* G. Hovannisian ed. (New Brunswick, NJ, USA: Transaction Books, 1986), pp.19-34; Vahakn Dadrian, *The History of the Armenian Genocide* (New York: Berghahn Books, 2003- first published in 1995), pp. xviii-355; Grigoris Balakian, *Armenian Golgotha: A Memoir of the Armenian Genocide, 1915-1918*, Peter Balakian and Aris Sevag (trans.) (New York, NY, USA: Albert A. Knopf, 2009); Matthias Bjørnlund, "'A Fate Worse Than Dying': Sexual Violence During the Armenian Genocide," in *Brutality and Desire: War and Sexuality in Europe's Twentieth Century*, Dagmar Herzog ed. (New York, NY, USA: Palgrave Macmillan, 2009), pp. 16-58; Katharine Derderian, "Common Fate, Different Experience: Gender-Specific Aspects of the Armenian Genocide, 1915-1917," *Holocaust and Genocide Studies* 19:1 (2005): pp. 1-25; Asya Darbinyan and Rubina Peroomian, "Children: The Most Vulnerable Victims of the Armenian Genocide," in *Plight and Fate of Children During and Following Genocide*, Samuel Totten ed., *"Genocide: A Critical Bibliographic Review"* book series, 10 (New Brunswick, NJ, USA: Transaction Publishers, 2014), pp. 57-83; Vahakn N. Dadrian, "Children as Victims of Genocide: The Armenian Case," *Journal of Genocide Research* 5:3 (2003) pp. 421-437. For comprehensive sets of primary US and German government documents on the Genocide, see Wolfgang Gust ed., *The Armenian Genocide: Evidence from the German Foreign Office Archives, 1915-1916* (New York, NY, USA: Berghahn Books, 2014); Ara Sarafian (comp.), *United States Official Records on the Armenian Genocide, 1915-1917* (Princeton, NJ, USA: Gomidas Institute, 2004). For presentation and analysis of representative survivor accounts of the Genocide, see Donald E. Miller and Lorna Touryan Miller, *Survivors: An Oral History of the Armenian Genocide* (Berkeley, CA, USA: University of California Press, 1993).

1657 Ibid.

1658 Ibid.

The first and main phase of the Armenian Genocide was carried out in a four-part process. Firstly, in early 1915, roughly 250,000 Armenian men in the Ottoman Army were disarmed and either worked to death as slaves or simply massacred. Secondly, on the night of April 23–24, 1915, hundreds of Armenian political, religious, and cultural leaders were rounded up in Istanbul, and most were murdered. Thirdly, based on a State adopted (*Tehjir*) Deportation Law, remaining Armenians were sent on death marches into the Syrian desert. Often the deportations began with massacres, torture and rape, which continued during the deportations. Young Armenian men and teenage boys were separated from the others, marched out of their homes and killed. Women, children and the elderly were force-marched for weeks at a time. Children were stolen and girls and women converted to Islam and pushed into forced 'marriages' or sexual slavery.[1659] Numerous eyewitnesses – Western missionaries, US consular officials and others – recorded the horrors in consistent and comprehensive detail.

Lastly, Armenians' immovable and movable property was confiscated or looted.[1660] The Regulation of 10 June 1915 consisting of thirty-four Articles, regulated how property and goods left behind by deported or murdered Armenians would be impounded by the State.[1661] The Temporary Law of 26 September 1915 and the Regulation of 8 November 1915 provided important steps toward the appropriation of Armenian cultural and economic wealth and how the aforementioned law would be implemented.[1662]

1659 Ibid.

1660 The exact extent of confiscated properties during this period is unknown. According to the private documents of Talaat Pasha, the Ottoman interior minister and chief architect of the confiscation legislation, 20,545 buildings and 267,536 acres of land were confiscated by the government, as well as 76,942 acres of vineyards, 703,941 acres of olive groves and 4,573 acres of mulberry gardens, in Ümit Uğur Üngör, "The Armenian Genocide: A Multi-Dimensional Process of Destruction" *Global Dialogue* 15:1 (Winter 2013) pp. 97–106. In addition, During the 1919 Paris Peace Conference, an Armenian delegation estimated the worth of material losses suffered by the Armenian Church at $3.7 billion (about $51 billion today) in Vahagn Avedian, "State Identity, Continuity, and Responsibility: The Ottoman Empire, the Republic of Turkey and the Armenian Genocide." *European Journal of International Law* 23:3 (2012), 797–820.

1661 For more information, see Taner Akçam & Umit Kurt, *The Spirit of the Laws: The Plunder of Wealth in the Armenian Genocide* (New York: Berghahn Books, 2015).

1662 Ümit Kurt, "The Plunder of Wealth through Abandoned Properties Laws in the Armenian Genocide," *Genocide Studies International*, 10:1 (Spring 2016), pp. 39-40.

The second phase of the Genocide took place between 1918 and 1923 by Turkish ultranationalist forces under Kemal Ataturk.[1663] The nationalist army conquered the lands in today's eastern Turkey in 1918.[1664] They murdered thousands of Armenians who attempted to return to their homes and drove out tens of thousands more who had remained throughout earlier Genocide. The most obvious case was the destruction of Smyrna, where a sustained Armenian presence would have undermined the results of the first phase of the Genocide, namely the "Turkification" of Asia Minor. The ultranationalists minimized any attempt to hold perpetrators accountable through military trials, prematurely ending the judicial process that begun in 1919.[1665]

The laws designed to legitimize the appropriation of Armenian property marked one of many key continuities between the late Ottoman Empire and the Turkish Republic.[1666] These laws were a "structural element of the Genocide and continue to constitute the essence of the Republican legal system."[1667] Based on Akçam and Kurt's analysis, the "institutionalized erasure of Christian-Armenian presence"[1668] through the erasure of property ownership represents just another approach to the expulsion and annihilation of a multi-ethnic, multireligious population by homogenizing the population.[1669] Despite the secrecy surrounding the Armenian Genocide, the international community and the press reacted to

1663 For Further information, see Levon Marashlian, "Finishing the Genocide: Cleansing Turkey of Armenian Survivors, 1920-1923," in *Remembrance and Denial: The Case of the Armenian Genocide,* Richard G. Hovannisian ed. (Detroit, MI, USA: Wayne State University Press, 1999), pp. 113-145; Hovannisian, "The Historical Dimensions," pp. 33-38; Dadrian, *The History of the Armenian Genocide*, pp. 356-374. Although it's not specifically about the Genocide, Richard G. Hovannisian, *The Republic of Armenia*, 4 vols. (Berkeley, CA, USA: University of California Press, 1971-1996) offers much on the impact of the Genocide on Armenians in the 1918 Republic and the continuation of mass violence against Armenians, leading to significant destruction in and an end to the 1918 Republic (see especially Vol. 1, "The First Year, 1918-1919," pp. 126-155 and Vol. 4, "Between Crescent and Sickle: Partition and Sovietization," pp. 180-292, respectively).

1664 Ibid.

1665 Ibid.

1666 Akçam and Ümit. *The Spirit of the Laws*, p. 13.

1667 Ibid.

1668 Ibid.

1669 Ayşe Parla and Ceren Özgül, "Property, Dispossession, and Citizenship in Turkey; or, The History of the Gezi Uprising Starts in the *Surp Hagop* Armenian Cemetery," *Public Cultures*, 28:3 (80), 01.09.2016, p. 623.

the ongoing massacres. On May 24, 1915, Britain, France and Russia, jointly issued a statement explicitly charging for the first time ever another government of committing a crime against humanity.[1670]

4.10.3 The Armistice Period and the Returning Armenians

After WWI, the CUP government resigned. The first new cabinet was established by Ahmet Isset Pasha on 11 October 1918, and eleven governments held office between then and November 1922.[1671] These governments initiated legal proceedings against the CUP members and allowed surviving Armenians to return.[1672] By December 1918, 2,552 Muslims, 19,695 Greeks and 23,420 Armenians returned and had been resettled. The most important step was taken on 4 November 1918, when the Deportation Law was found to be contrary to the Constitution and rescinded.[1673]

The biggest question concerning the repatriates was how their movable and immovable property should be returned to them. Rulings on the return of abandoned properties was issued on 12 January 1920. They contained thirty-three Articles stating how Armenian properties were to be returned, with Article 13 revoking the Liquidation Law of September 1915 and the Regulation of November 1915.[1674] The most important point of the regulation was the fact that all properties would be immediately returned to their original owners and the practices of the CUP period were revoked. The return of usurped Armenian properties began but was not without problems.

Later, the Ottoman government and the Nationalist movement worked to legally prevent the return of Armenians remaining outside borders drawn by the 1918 Mondros Armistice.[1675] The fifth and sixth Articles of the 1869 Law of Citizenship regulating how Ottoman citizens could acquire citizenship in

---

1670 See Section 2.4.10 above.

1671 Ümit Kurt, "Legal and Official Plunder of Armenian and Jewish Properties in Comparative Perspective: The Armenian Genocide and the Holocaust," *Journal of Genocide Research, The Armenian Genocide After 100 Years: New Historical Perspectives,* 17:3 (2015), pp. 313-315.

1672 Ümit Kurt, "The Political Micro-Economy of the Armenian Genocide, 1915-1922," *Journal of Balkan and Near Eastern Studies*, 20:6 (2018), pp. 624-625.

1673 Taner Akçam, A Shameful Act: The Armenian Genocide and the Question of Turkish Responsibility (New York: Metropolitan Books, 2006), p. 275.

1674 Ümit Kurt, "Legal and official plunder," pp. 313-315.

1675 Ibid.

other countries, were significant here. According to Article 5, an Ottoman citizen could only acquire a different country's citizenship with the permission of the Ottoman government. Without this permission, such a procedure would be invalid. According to Article 6, a person acquiring the citizenship of another country without permission could, if the State wished, have his Ottoman citizenship revoked and be refused from re-entering Ottoman territory. This Law was thus used to prevent the return of the Armenians who had been forcibly removed from their homes, and to stop them regaining their properties.[1676]

In the beginning of Republic era, the Turkish government began issuing new confiscation laws.[1677] in April 1923, A new regulation amending the Law of Abandoned Properties of 1922 demanded the seizure of all possessions of Armenians no longer living in Turkey.[1678]

4.10.4 The Armenians and the Treaty of Sèvres

The Treaty of Sèvres (August 10, 1920), abolished the Ottoman Empire and obliged Turkey to renounce all rights over Arab Asia and North Africa. The Treaty provided for an independent Armenia, an autonomous Kurdistan and Greek control over the Aegean islands commanding the Dardanelles. The relevant Articles of the Treaty with regards to Armenians were Articles 88-89-90-148-144-230[1679] as well as the Arbitral Award on Turkish-Armenian boundary

---

1676 Ibid, p. 311.

1677 For more information see Akçam & Kurt, *The Spirit of the Laws.*

1678 For more information Nevzat Onaran, *Cumhuriyet'te Ermeni ve Rum Mallarinin Turklestirilmesi (1920-1930) Emvali Metrukenin Tasfiyesi – II,* (Turkification of Armenian and Greek Properties in the Republic (1920-1930) Liquidation of Abandoned Property – II,) (Turkey: Evrensel Publications, 2013), pp. 135-138.

1679 **Article 88:** Turkey recognizes Armenia as a free and independent State. **Article 89:** Turkey and Armenia, as well as the other High Contracting Parties, agree to submit to the arbitration of the President of the USA the question of the frontier between Turkey and Armenia, and to accept his decision thereupon, as well as any stipulations he may prescribe regarding access for Armenia to the sea, and as to the demilitarization of Turkish territory adjacent to the said frontier. **Article 90:** Turkey hereby renounces as from the date of such decision all rights and title over territory transferred to Armenia. **Article 148:** In towns and districts with a considerable proportion of Turkish nationals belonging to racial, linguistic or religious minorities, these minorities shall be assured an equitable share in the enjoyment and application of any sums provided by the State, municipal or other budgets for educational or charitable purposes. These sums shall be paid to qualified representatives of the communities. **Article 144:** The Turkish Government recognises the injustice of the

by Woodrow Wilson.[1680] Turkey never ratified the Treaty of Sèvres, and the Allies did not apply sufficient political and economic pressure on Turkey to ensure its ratification and implementation.[1681] Such failure was attributable to the political disarray following WWI, the rise of the Soviet Union, the withdrawal of the British from Turkey, US isolationist policies, the demise of the Young Turk regime and the rise of Kemalism in Turkey and their victory in the independence war 1919–1923.[1682]

The International Criminal Tribunal envisaged in Article 230 of the Treaty was never established. A new peace treaty, the Lausanne Treaty, eventually emerged between Kemalist Turkey and the Allies (Britain, France, Italy, Japan, Greece, and Romania). The Treaty of Lausanne did not confirm the Sèvres Treaty to punish the perpetrators of the Armenian Genocide, to draw the border between Turkey and Armenia or the commitment to grant reparations to Genocide survivors or the recognition of a free Armenian State.[1683]

4.10.5 Armenians at the Lausanne Treaty

The Armenians lacked a representative government at Lausanne because Armenia had already been part of the Soviet Union. Nonetheless, a continuation of the former delegation that had been working in Paris since the beginning of the Paris Peace Conference went to Lausanne to lobby the Allies' representatives to

---

law of 1915 relating to Abandoned Properties and declares them null and void. **Article 230:** The Turkish Government undertakes to hand over to the Allied Powers the persons responsible for the massacres committed during the war on territory which formed part of the Turkish Empire on 01.08.1914, in Treaty of Sevres: https://wwi.lib.byu.edu/index.php/Section_I,_Articles_1-260.

1680 The first Armenian Republic was established in 1918. On April 26, 1920, the WWI Allied Powers submitted an application to US President Woodrow Wilson asking him to determine the border between Armenia and Turkey. On 17.05.1920, the President agreed to act as arbitrator. Article 89 of the 20.08.1920 Treaty of Sèvres confirmed the referral to the arbitration of President Wilson, fixing the border between Turkey and Armenia in the vilayets (provinces) of Erzerum, Trebizond, Van and Bitlis, which required transfer of territory to Armenia in order to provide Armenia with access to the sea.

1681 Henry C. Theriault et al, "Resolution with Justice Reparations for the Armenian Genocide: The Report of the Armenian Genocide Reparations Study Group," *Armenian Genocide Reparations*, March 2015, p. 50, www.armeniangenocidereparations.info.

1682 Ibid, p. 52-53.

1683 Ibid.

get a hearing. Despite the Turkish delegation's protests, they received a hearing at a Minorities Sub-Committee meeting.[1684] The Turkish government had been initially persistent about including Armenians into the exchange agreement and had pushed İsmet Pasha to adopt this course. Despite the Turkish government's persistence in wanting to include all non-Muslim minorities in the population exchange, Pasha tried to stop an Armenian exchange by warning the government of the reaction of the international community towards such a declaration; insisting that an exchange of Armenians could be perceived as another 'exile'. This would risk the status quo by reopening discussions on the eastern border with the Allied powers and would also have required a review of the Moscow Treaty of Brotherhood between Turkey and Bolshevist Russia, which recognized Turkey's borders.[1685] However, at the Lausanne Conference, Ismet Inönü, representing Turkey, allowed no discussion on the return of Armenian refugees, arguing that such a return would constitute a national security threat.[1686]

The Turkish side refused to consider a national home for Armenians where they could live and maintain their race, language and culture under Turkish rule or in Turkish territory.[1687] Turkey also refused any undertaking to accept Armenian refugees from the WWI. These efforts by the Turkish delegation were made to actualize a more homogenous population in line with their nation-state ideal.[1688] The Republic also attempted to realize that ideal through various denationalization laws in the second half of the 1920s excluding the return of non-Muslim subjects who had fled the country during the war. The most vulnerable of these subjects were the Armenians.[1689]

On 15 April 1923, just before the Treaty of Lausanne, Turkey enacted the Law of Abandoned Properties, confiscating the property of any Armenian who was not present on their property, regardless of the reason. For Turkish Armenians it was also important that the Lausanne Treaty amnestied all war-related crimes between August 1, 1914, and November 20, 1922.[1690] The amnesty statement declared that they were "desirous to cause the events which have troubled the

1684 Ömer Turan, "The Armenian Question at the Lausanne Peace Talks," in *The Armenians in the Late Ottoman Period*, Turkkaya Ataov, ed. (Ankara: Turkish Historical Society, 2001).

1685 Bayir, Minorities and Nationalism, p. 81.

1686 Parla & Özgül, "Property, Dispossession, and Citizenship."

1687 Bayir, Minorities and Nationalism, p. 83.

1688 Ibid.

1689 Ibid.

1690 Ekmekcioğlu, *Recovering Armenia*, p. 95.

peace in the East to be forgotten."[1691] Effectively, the Allies pardoned the perpetrators of the Armenian Genocide, a major blow particularly those Armenians who survived the Genocide.

Many perpetrators of the Genocide and usurpers of Armenian property became ministers, parliamentarians and powerful State actors in the Republic of Turkey.[1692] However, by Treaty of Lausanne, the Armenians were explicitly recognized as a minority within the Turkish Republic in 1923, and were granted certain rights to develop their own culture, language, and identity as a religious group and to maintain institutions including schools, hospitals, and cemeteries[1693]

4.10.6 The Relationship between the Treaty of Sèvres and the Treaty of Lausanne

The Treaty of Lausanne is often considered as the replacement for the unratified Treaty of Sèvres,[1694] but this claim is not correct. Although the Treaty of Sèvres did not enter into force, it was signed by "High Contracting Parties," which are states that agree to be bound by the provisions of a treaty whether or not the treaty enters into force.[1695] According to international law, Treaty of Sèvres is an "unperfected treaty."[1696]

As codified by the VCLT,[1697] any treaty can be amended, terminated, or withdrawn from only by agreement of all contracting states according to the procedures defined in the treaty itself or according to customary international law.[1698]

1691 Treaty of Lausanne VIII: Declaration of Amnesty, www.mfa.gov.tr/viii_-declaration-of-amnesty.en.mfa.

1692 Ekmekcioğlu, *Recovering Armenia*, p. 95.

1693 Bardakci et al., Religious Minorities in Turkey, 142.

1694 See for example, Adam Augustyn," Treaty of Sèvres," *Britannica*, February 2021, https://www.britannica.com/event/Treaty-of-Sevres

1695 Article 2 (1) (f) of the 1969 VCLT: "a contracting State means a State which has consented to be bound by the treaty, whether or not the treaty has entered into force."

1696 Theriault et al., "Resolution with Justice Reparations for the Armenian Genocide," p. 53.

1697 Article 40 (2) of the VCLT: "Any proposal to amend a multilateral treaty as between all the parties must be notified to all contracting States, each one of which shall have the right to take part in: (a) the decision as to the action to be taken in regard to such proposal [and] (b) the negotiation and conclusion of any agreement for the amendment of the treaty."

1698 United Nations, *Final Clauses of Multilateral Treaties: Handbook* (New York, NY, USA: United Nations, 2003), p. 95.

The Lausanne Conference cannot be treated as an act of amendment or modification of the Treaty of Sèvres. This is because no official notification for amendment was communicated to each State party of the treaty. the Treaty of Lausanne was concluded by only 7 signatories (the British Empire, France, Greece, Italy, Japan, Romania, and the Government of the Grand National Assembly of Turkey) of the 13 who signed the Treaty of Sèvres (Armenia, Belgium, the British Empire, Czechoslovakia, France, Greece, Italy, Japan, Poland, Portugal, Romania, the Serb-Croat-Slovene State, and Turkey). In other words, the Treaty of Lausanne cannot legally have amended the Treaty of Sèvres because it was not a treaty of all the parties of the Sèvres Treaty. Moreover, the Treaty of Lausanne had and has no legal effect and did not create neither obligations nor rights for the States who signed the Treaty of Sèvres but were not party to the Treaty of Lausanne.[1699]

The absence of legal obligation for Armenia deriving from the Lausanne Treaty was highlighted by Avetis Aharonian, President of the Sèvres Delegation of the Republic of Armenia on behalf of the Republic of Armenia, in an August 8, 1923 letter addressed to the Foreign Ministers of the Allied Powers:

> "the delegation which signed the Sèvres Treaty for Armenia reserves and insists upon all the rights which the powers, during and since the war, solemnly recognized and which were duly embodied in the Sèvres Treaty and reincorporated and reaffirmed by decisions of subsequent conferences."[1700]

In addition, the termination of a treaty or the withdrawal of a contracting state from a treaty may take place only by consent of *all* parties.[1701] This means that Turkey cannot unilaterally break out from the obligations derived from by the Treaty of Sèvres without consent of the other parties, including Armenia. No such consent has been given so far.

Beside the difference in signatory parties to Sèvres and Lausanne Treaties, the scope, objectives, and context of the two treaties were also different and further disqualify any claim that the Treaty of Lausanne was meant to or could replace the earlier. First, as argued above, the Treaty of Sèvres was signed by

1699 Article 40 (2) of the VCLT: "A treaty does not create either obligations or rights for a third State without its consent."

1700 "Armenia Denounces Lausanne Treaty; Note to the Powers Formally Reserves All Grants Under the Treaty of Sèvres," *The New York Times*, September 12, 1923, p. 30.

1701 Article 54 of the VCLT: "The termination of a treaty or the withdrawal of a party may take place:(a) in conformity with the provisions of the treaty; or (b) at any time by consent of all the parties after consultation with the other contracting States."

"High Contracting Parties," which are states that agree to be bound by the provisions of a treaty whether or not the treaty enters into force, while the Lausanne Treaty was not signed by "contracting states" and thus had no status until ratified. Second, Sèvres was signed between the "Allied and Associated Powers" and Turkey meant to end the part of World War I that concerned Turkey and to establish peace.[1702] On the other hand, the Lausanne Treaty meant to address the Greek-Turkish conflict of 1919–1922 and was signed by individual parties with interests in the region.

Last but not least, the Lausanne Treaty fixed the Turkish border with Bulgaria, Greece, Iraq and Syria,[1703] but it did not fix Turkish-Armenian border. However, Article 16 of the Lausanne Treaty indirectly reconfirmed the title and rights of the Republic of Armenia by virtue of the renunciation of the title and rights of Turkey over the boundaries of Armenia set up through the arbitration of U.S. President Wilson pursuant to the Sèvres Treaty, typically referred to as "Wilsonian Armenia." Article 16 of Treaty of Lausanne states:

> "Turkey hereby renounces all rights and title whatsoever over or respecting the territories situated outside the frontiers laid down in the present Treaty and the islands other than those over which her sovereignty is recognised by the said Treaty, the future of these territories and islands being settled or to be settled by the parties concerned… The provisions of the present Article do not prejudice any special arrangements arising from neighbourly relations, which have been or may be concluded between Turkey and any limitrophe countries."

Nevertheless, Treaty of Lausanne's silence on the Turkish-Armenian border somehow meant that there was no enforcement of the Wilsonian arbitration pursuant to the Sèvres Treaty, practically accepting the actual situation, with Turkey militarily invading and conquering that part of Armenia that had already been incorporated into the 1918 Armenian Republic.

1702 As stated in the Preamble of Treat of Sèvres: Whereas the Allied Powers are equally desirous that the war in which certain among them were successively involved, directly or indirectly, against Turkey, and which originated in the declaration of war against Serbia on July 28, 1914, by the former Imperial and Royal Austro-Hungarian Government, and in the hostilities opened by Turkey against the Allied Powers on October 29, 1914, and conducted by Germany in alliance with Turkey, should be replaced by a firm, just and durable Peace.

1703 (Article 2 [1], [2], Article 3 [1] of Treaty of Lausanne.

4.10.7 The Situation of the Armenians in the Turkish Republic

When the Republic of Turkey was declared in 1923, the Armenian population had been cut by over 90 %, but the new Republican administration had to decide how to deal with the Armenians who remained.[1704] The 1863 Armenian Constitution became *de facto* void in the Republic era. The government and media praised this, seeing it as the adaptation of the Armenian community to the new secular administration. The State curbed or eliminated communal rights and organizations in the name of egalitarianism and secularism.

Having eliminated Article 42[1705] of the Lausanne Treaty and the 1863 Armenian Constitution, it became obvious that this was aimed at abolishing the legal basis of treating Armenians and other non-Muslims as communities with group rights. The Republic created and maintained an ambiguity on this issue, sometimes treating Armenians as individual citizens and sometimes as members of a group.[1706] This inconsistency was possibly created deliberately, since it offers the State flexibility in the treatment of these groups. Treating non-Muslims as collectivities and recognizing group rights would improve their situation, so the State has rejected this as it would contradict with the secular character of the

1704 Ohannes Kılıcdagˇ "Social and Political Roles of the Armenian Clergy from the Late Ottoman Era to the Turkish Republic Istanbul Bilgi University, Istanbul, Turkey," *Philosophy and Social Criticism* 43:4-5 (2017), p. 544.

1705 Article 42 of the Lausanne Treaty states: "The Turkish Government undertakes to take, as regards non-Moslem minorities, in so far as concerns their family law or personal status, measures permitting the settlement of these questions in accordance with the customs of those minorities These measures will be elaborated by special Commissions composed of representatives of the Turkish Government and of representatives of each of the minorities concerned in equal number. In case of divergence, the Turkish Government and the Council of the League of Nations will appoint in agreement an umpire chosen from amongst European lawyers. The Turkish Government undertakes to grant full protection to the churches, synagogues, cemeteries, and other religious establishments of the above-mentioned minorities. All facilities and authorisation will be granted to the pious foundations, and to the religious and charitable institutions of the said minorities at present existing in Turkey, and the Turkish Government will not refuse, for the formation of new religious and charitable institutions, any of the necessary facilities which are guaranteed to other private institutions of that nature."

1706 Arus Yumul, "'*Azınlık Mı Vatandas¸ Mı?*'," (Minority or Citizen?), in *Turkiyede Cogunluk ve Azınlık Politikaları: AB Surecinde Yurttaslık Tartısmaları* (Majority and Minority Politics in Turkey: Citizenship Debates in EU Process) (Istanbul: TESEV Yayınları 2005), pp. 101–21.

State and has instead implemented a continuous policy of discrimination based on group identities.

In August 1926, the Turkish Government publicly declared that it would keep all property confiscated before the Treaty of Lausanne, and in May 1927 it authorized the exclusion of Turkish nationality to anyone who had not taken part in the War of Independence or who had remained abroad between 24 July 1923 and 27 May 1927. This negated any Armenian claims for confiscated property. Protests to the League of Nations by the Central Committee for Armenian Refugees from 1925 to 1928 were rejected by Turkey and never acted on.[1707] For Atatürk, all those who lived within the borders of the country – Christians, Jews, and Muslims (including Kurds) alike – were Turks and had to accept Turkish as the official language as well as dominant Turkish culture.[1708] In the subsequent decades, the Turkish government has used legal, administrative, and practical measures to undermine and violate the rights of minorities, who became the targets of discriminatory policies, assimilatory Turkification and ethnic homogenization.[1709]

As other non-Muslim Minorities Armenians' foundations were placed under the 2762 Law of 1935.[1710] The Law also paved the way for the seizure of non-Muslim minority foundation properties by the GDF, the Treasury, or the National Real Estate. Minority private schools also had to follow the State curriculum.[1711] Only civil marriages were recognized by the State, and religious officials were prohibited from wearing their vestments in public, except on special occasions such as funerals.[1712]

In this context, to show loyalty to the State, in 1935, a number of Greeks and Armenians formed the Turkish Association of Secular Christians in order to promote Turkification among their communities.[1713] But Turkey's non-Muslim minorities' conciliatory policies towards Turkification failed to protect them from being targeted by the elite's own Turkification policies.[1714] Violent attacks led to deaths or forced expropriation of the properties owned by Christian

1707 Bishku, "The Interactions and Experiences of Armenians," p. 449.

1708 Umit Ungor Uğur & Mehmet Polatel, *Confiscation and Destruction: The Young Turk Seizure of Armenian Property* (UK: Bloomsbury Publishing, 2011), p. 59.

1709 Bardakci et al., *Religious Minorities in Turkey*, p. 144-146.

1710 Law No. 2762 for Foundations passed on: 05.06.1935.

1711 Mine Yildirim, The Collective Dimension of Freedom of Religion: A Case Study on Turkey (New York: Routledge, 2017), p. 177.

1712 Bishku "Interactions and Experiences of Armenians," p. 441.

1713 Soner Çağaptay, Islam, Secularism, and Nationalism – Who is a Turk?, p. 60.

1714 Eligür, "Ethnocultural nationalism and Turkey's non-Muslim minorities," p. 19.

communities, schools, and private citizens. Armenian properties were occupied, while security forces, authorities, and courts refused to work for the Armenians, who were discriminated against by the public sector. There were allegations against Armenians in the press, which depended on political interests. The looting and destruction of religious and cultural buildings or their misuse as warehouses or sports halls, and demands for refurbishment of Armenian properties were refused resulting in the emigration of thousands of Armenians to Syria as well as the forced resettlement of the Armenian population from rural areas to larger towns and cities (especially Istanbul) in 1934, and in the replacement of nearly all Armenians from the Alexandretta region after its integration into Turkey in 1939 to Lebanon (Particularly Anjar). Another group of Armenians abandoned Turkey in 1945–46 after a repatriation campaign by the Soviet Union to Armenia.[1715]

The late 1940s and early 1950s represented a period of comparative ease for the Armenians.[1716] Things worsened after the creation of four foreign Armenian militant underground organizations from 1975 onwards, and their attacks on Turkish institutions and diplomats in the 1970s and 1980s for the recognition of the Armenian Genocide and Armenian Cause in general, which resulted in 79 deaths from the Turkish side. The Armenians in Turkey again became the target of retaliation, with the bombing of Armenian religious and cultural institutions in Istanbul between 1977 and 1979.

The right-wing military coup in 1980 fueled an increase in Turkish nationalism, while armed conflict with the Kurds reinforced the political and public stigmatization of minority groups and left the remaining Armenians in eastern provinces at the mercy of the PKK, the Turkish army and other Kurdish actors. The 1980 military coup was followed by a series of show trials. Father Manuel Yergatian is one example and Armenian Protestant preacher Hrant Güzelyan another case who unlawfully charged with training Armenian militants at Camp Armen and sentenced to fifteen years in prison.[1717] The government sealed off the camp and closed the church in Gedikpasa. The military prosecutors accused Güzelyan of "bringing orphaned Turkish children to Istanbul and indoctrinating them with Armenian nationalism."[1718] Güzelyan did initiate a relocation

1715 Bardakci et al., Religious Minorities in Turkey, p. 143.

1716 See Section 4.2.3 above.

1717 Tchilingirian, "The 'Other' Citizens," pp. 144-146.

1718 "*Hrant Küçükgüselyan'ın yargılanmasına başlandı*" (The trial of Hrant Kucukguselyan has begun), *Cumhuriyet* newspaper, 03.10.1981.

program, reasoning that an Armenian community concentrated in Istanbul could be cared for more easily, more cheaply and more intensively than a minority scattered across Turkey.[1719] In addition, in late 1980s there were public campaigns via the media against several clergymen, among them Bishop Mesrob Mutafyan (later a Patriarch), who at the time was an outspoken young Chancellor of the Patriarchate. Mutafyan was predictably accused of supporting "terrorist acts against Turks."[1720]

In this context, on 11 June 1986, the laws concerning 'abandoned' Armenian properties were abrogated, and in 2001, the Land Registry issued an order effectively transferring any unclaimed properties to the government. The order also forbade the disclosure of information regarding the title or the documentation of the properties, so owners or their heirs could not make claims on the property since had become property of the Sate.[1721]

This overall situation and the political and social pressure it brought increased Armenians' vulnerability, encouraging those few who remained in rural areas to resettle abroad or in Istanbul. According to the Armenian Patriarchate, approximately 25,000 Armenians left Turkey, and up to 20,000 migrants moved to Istanbul between 1955 and late 1980s.[1722]

Moreover, the conflict that erupted between Nagorno Karabagh, Armenia and Azerbaijan in 1988 increased anti-Armenian sentiment in Turkey.[1723] Turkey had declared itself protector of Turkish-Azeri interests in the Eastern Transcaucasus in 1988, and joined Azerbaijan's embargo against Armenia in 1993, even though the latter had stated repeatedly that Nagorno Karabakh, not Armenia, was a party to the conflict. Graffiti appeared on Armenian schools and churches in Istanbul in 1992 after Karabakh Armenian units took over Khodjalu, at the end of 1992, causing violent and often racist reactions in the Turkish media. Anonymous hate mail and threats were made against Armenian institutions, including the Apostolic Armenian Patriarchate.[1724]

An anti-Armenian campaign provoked by Turkish media and politicians created disadvantages for Armenians in professional and business life. The Armenian daily newspaper *Marmara* reported on 9 March 1994 that hostility was being

1719 Tchilingirian, "The 'Other' Citizens," pp. 144-146.
1720 *Marmara* newspaper, January 23, 25, and 28, 1988 issues.
1721 Ibid.
1722 Bardakci et al., Religious Minorities in Turkey, p. 144.
1723 Ibid.
1724 Hofmann, Armenians in Turkey Today, p. 20.

generated against members of minorities, particularly Armenians and Jews. Members of Trade associations received anonymous letters demanding: "Don't do business with Jews and Armenians!."[1725] All five Armenian cemeteries in Istanbul were vandalized between April 1993 and August 1994. At least twenty facilities belonging to the Apostolic Armenian church were attacked, in some cases repeatedly.[1726] There are only two reports of offenders being caught after attacks against Armenian institutions. In March 1994, 'Islamic terrorists' were blamed for the attacks on Narlikapi church.[1727] This is surprising since the attacks are most probably attributable to perpetrators from the extreme right nationalist MHP party. The second incident reported in the Armenian press in Turkey concerned the arrest of 'thieves' who were charged with looting an Armenian church in August 1994.[1728]

To sum up, it can be argued, that the Republic's minority policies were based on harassment, discrimination, intimidation, suppression, attacks on places of worship, oppression, assimilation through Turkification policies, and domination,[1729] resulting in the gradual destruction of the Armenian population and culture throughout the Republican period.

4.10.7.1 The Present Situation of Armenians in Turkey

It can be argued that the contemporary Armenian era began with the assassination of Hrant Dink in 2007.[1730] After this murder by Turkish nationalists, the Armenian community received more public attention than ever before.[1731] Declarations of sympathy came from Turkish politicians (including Erdogan) and the media – which called the murder an act of treason and an attack against the whole of Turkey.[1732] The killing seemed to trigger an awakening of conscience in Turkish society, leading to stronger support and acceptance. Armenian culture and history became popular topics of the media, specialist literature and

1725 Ibid.

1726 Ibid.

1727 *Marmara* newspaper, 26.3.1994.

1728 Hofmann, Armenians in Turkey Today, p. 22.

1729 Uğur Umit Ungor, "'Turkey for the Turks' Demographic Engineering in Eastern Anatolia, 1914–1945," in *A Question of Genocide,* Ronald Grigor Suny, Fatma Müge Göçek, & Norman M. Naimark eds. (UK: OUP, 2011), p. 290.

1730 See Section 4.11.1.3 below.

1731 Bardakci et al., Religious Minorities in Turkey, p. 145.

1732 Ibid.

conferences, leading to a stronger awareness of the Genocide, conquering one of the biggest political and social taboos.[1733] These developments also effected an ethnic and religious revival within Islamized Armenians.[1734]

Social and political improvements also occurred from the 2000s because of Turkey's EU accession process, and there has been small scale government support for schools and media, more approvals for renovations of historic Christian buildings, a return of expropriated goods to Armenian churches.[1735] Nevertheless, current State policies represent a mix of moderate improvements and delays as well as constant interventions of the internal affairs of the Armenian community. Some problems remain unaddressed, and others have only partially been solved.[1736]

One problem is that Christian communities have no legal status. Following an expropriation campaign that has lasted several decades, Christian groups in today's Turkey remain deprived of their property and now only own a fraction of the churches, monasteries and land they owned before the foundation of the Turkish Republic. The implementation of legal changes is slow and remains incomplete. Due to a lack in priests and churches, the Armenian churches are unable to meet increasing spiritual needs beyond Istanbul, which depend on visits by traveling priests.[1737] This is related to acknowledgment and registration problems for converted Armenian Christians.

Armenian schools face ideological and financial problems due to the strict control the State. Financial discrimination, arbitrarily school closures and difficulties in training Armenian teachers persist, resulting in declining attendances and difficulties in preserving Armenian culture, language, and identity.[1738] Furthermore, many Armenians intellectuals still feel restricted in their freedom

1733 An important milestone here was the 2005 conference held at Bilgi University in Istanbul, where the pogroms were discussed publicly within an academic environment for the first time in Turkey.

1734 For further information see Altuğ Yılmaz, *Müslümanlaş(tırıl)mış Ermeniler* (Islamized-Islamatized Armenians) (Istanbul: Hrant Dink Foundation, 2015) and Ayse Gul Altinay, *The Grandchildren: The Hidden Legacy of 'Lost' Armenians in Turkey* (New York: Routledge, 2017).

1735 Bardakci et al., Religious Minorities in Turkey, p. 146.

1736 Ibid, pp. 147-178.

1737 Ibid, p. 148.

1738 Christoph Giesel, "Status and Situation of the Jews in Turkey: Historical Lines of Development and Contemporary Circumstances in the Context of Socio-political Transformations," *Electronic Journal of Political Science Studies*, 5:2 (2014), pp. 1–32.

of expression, based on the regular use of the controversial Article 301 of the Turkish Criminal Code against them.[1739] These restrictions are particularly apparent in politics, administration, the legal and medical professions, education, defence and security. While some non-Muslims obtain low-grade work in these areas, there are no equal opportunities for career advancement compared to their Muslim peers. Many Armenians still complain of harassment, insults, hate speech and mistreatment by colleagues and superiors during military service.[1740]

The Armenian community's cautious embrace of the AKP is understandable. The AKP Government initially provided a relief from the shackles of the 'Deep State' which had dominated the community through constant court cases, administrative restrictions, penalties and psychological pressures. Currently, property expropriations by the State are among the most contentious issues. For instance, one morning in 1974 bulldozers drove onto land belonging to *Surp Pırgic* Hospital in Zeytinburnu and confiscated the valuable piece of real estate because it had no registered owner. The land was appropriated by the Istanbul Metropolitan Municipality. It was given back in 2014 after a long court case, but the Municipality appealed in 2016. The case remains pending.[1741]

Since the AKP's third election victory in 2011, Armenians have become increasingly sceptical due to the latest political developments.[1742] These include an increase in authoritarian nationalism, Islamist elements within AKP's policies, setbacks in the democratization process, increased unlawful interference in the internal affairs of the Armenian community, increased hate speech towards Armenians, the deterioration of the EU/Turkey relationship and failure of constitutional reform. Meanwhile, the reform of minority rights and the expansion of Turkey's relationship with Armenia have stagnated.

External factors in the treatment of Armenians in Turkey are still playing a role. For example, Turkey supports Azerbaijan and influenced by its pressure in the negotiations and peace process of Nagorno-Karabakh conflict. Another factor is the recognition of the Armenian Genocide by other States or entities, which are still accompanied by anti-Armenian incidents. These included Erdogan's threat in 2010 to expel all economic migrants from Turkey in response to the Armenian government's efforts to have the events of 1915/1916 recognized

1739 Bardakci et al., Religious Minorities in Turkey, p. 177.
1740 Ibid, p. 146.
1741 Tchilingirian, "The 'Other' Citizens," p. 143.
1742 Bardakci et al., *Religious Minorities in Turkey*, p. 150-151.

by the international community.[1743] To sum up, the accumulation of restrictions, the arbitrariness with which changes occur and legal uncertainty determine the daily life of Turkey's Armenian community.

4.10.8 Armenian Institutions

After the 1856 Reform, the State asked each community to prepare a Statute regulating their internal affairs, providing an opportunity for liberal Armenian intellectuals.[1744] Following negotiations, in 1863, a text of considerable complexity, called the 'National Constitution' by the Armenians and the Code of Regulations (*Nizamname*) by the State was adopted.[1745] According to the Armenian Constitution, an Armenian National Assembly was to be established, which would convene every two years to elect Spiritual and Civil Councils which would run the community's affairs.[1746] The National Assembly was given the duty of electing a Patriarch from the candidates nominated by the Councils. The Patriarch was subordinated to the Armenian National Assembly but was head of the community and the intermediary between the Ottoman State and Armenian society.[1747]

Historical institutions were considered community foundations (*vakıf*) and lost their Ottoman era autonomy under Republican period laws. Meanwhile, waiver from specific rights on personal matters granted to non-Muslims was ensured by State pressure on Armenian and Greek Patriarchates and the Jews.[1748]

1743 Antoine Blua, "Turkey Threatens to Expel Armenian Immigrants Amid Genocide Row," *Radio Liberty*, 17 March 2010, https://bit.ly/3scSG6B.

1744 For further information, Vartan Artinian, *Osmanlı Devleti'nde Ermeni Anayasasının Doğuşu, 1839-1863*, (The Birth of the Armenian Constitution in the Ottoman State 1839-1863) (Istanbul: Aras Publish House, 2004).

1745 For further information, Murat Bebrioghlu, *Osmanli Devletinde Gayrimulslim Nizamnameleri* (Non-Muslim Regulations in the Ottoman Empire) Cahit Klukeci ed., (Istanbul: Kişisel Yayinlar, 2008).

1746 Rumelili & Keyman, "Enacting multi-layered citizenship," p. 70.

1747 The Constitution had problems. The complex administrative structure brought disagreements, and public interest in the elections failed to reach expected levels. The State suspended the implementation of this code between 1866 and 1869, but it was adopted again in 1869 and implemented smoothly until 1891, when the Assembly was closed due to tensions in State relations because of the Armenians' demand for reform in Eastern Anatolia. The code became void in 1891.

1748 Özdoğan & Kılıcdağı, *Hearing Turkey's Armenians*, p. 51.

Today, the main Armenian Institutions in Turkey are the Armenian Patriarchate, community foundations, Hrant Dink Foundation, 18 schools[1749] and their alumni associations, more than 40 churches, two Istanbul hospitals two orphanages, three newspapers with 2 Armenian language dailies (*Jamanak* and *Nor Marmara*) and one weekly magazine in Turkish and Armenian (*Agos*), couple of journals, and couple of newly stablished youth led associations.[1750] In addition, *Lraper* is the official organ of the Armenian Apostolic Patriarchate, *Surp Pergic* is issued by the hospital of the same name, and there is the satirical magazine *Jbid*, as well as the periodicals *Kulis*, *Şoğagat* and *Norsan*. In addition to the online versions of the periodicals mentioned, online information gateways in Turkish and Armenian have recently been established by Armenian organizations (*bolsohays.com* and *hyetert.com*).[1751] Aras Publishing was established in 1993 in Istanbul, adopting a publishing policy as "the window to Armenian literature."[1752] With books in Turkish and Armenian, it became one of the few publishing houses in Turkey to publish in two languages.

4.10.9 Armenian Schools

Until 1924, Armenian schools were controlled by the Patriarchate, which helped with funding, appointed staff, and provided textbooks. After the 1924 Unification of Education Act,[1753] Armenian minority schools were put under the MoE. Minority schools were soon required to hire a percentage of Turkish teachers.[1754]

1749 With nationalist provocation, many Armenian schools were opened in a short space of time in the mid-1800s with support from France. In 1859, there were 42 Armenian schools in Istanbul. In 1894, 183 Armenian schools were active in Elazıg with the support of the French government. See Emrah Dolgunsöz, "Language Policies and Multilingual Education in Minority Schools in Ottoman Empire: Outcomes and Future Insights," Idil, 3.12,2014, p. 103.

1750 The official website of *Jamanak* http://www.jamanak.com/ and the official website of *Marmara* newspaper http://www.normarmara.com/.

1751 The official websites of *Bolsahay.com* and *Hyetert.org*.

1752 Mark Williams "Turkey-based Armenian publisher Aras Publishing takes Publishing House of the Year award, 2019," *The New publishing Standard*, 26.01.2019, https://bit.ly/3tYJuDI.

1753 Act No.430 of March 3, 1340 (1924) on the Unification of the Educational System in Turkey.

1754 Ekmekcioğlu, *Recovering Armenia*, p. 124.

Turkish literature, geography, and history had to be taught by Turkish teachers, and the vice principals had to be Turks.[1755]

Armenian minority schools have no specific laws and are accepted as institutions operating under the Lausanne Treaty – yet they are subject to National Education Law No.1739, which regulates education in general, and Law no 5580 on Private Education Institutions. There are significant differences in how private and Armenian schools operate. Because of their social and cultural roles, schools cannot turn down a student who wants to enrol. Children of families who are unable to cover education costs are accepted, and as it is not possible to turn away any students.[1756] In practice, these schools operate much like public schools, although the State does not accept them as such, and Armenian and other non-Muslim schools have characteristics and requirements that differ in legal definitions from other foreign and private schools.

Despite all their inadequacies, the State adopted two regulations concerning Armenian schools in1976: The Regulation on Private Greek and Armenian Minority Primary Schools, and the Regulation on Private Armenian High Schools and Secondary Schools.[1757] Both regulations are today effectively defunct, having become distanced from changes taking place in the education system. Armenian migrants attend an illegal school on a daily basis called after 'Hrant Dink'. Church basement serves as informal primary schools, and Turkish authorities turn a blind eye, allowing the schools to follow the State curriculum of Republic of Armenia.[1758]

4.10.10 Religious Institutions

The Armenian Apostolic Church is the largest Christian community in Turkey. Its head is the Armenian Patriarchate of Constantinople in Istanbul. The Armenian Catholic Archdiocese of Constantinople and the Protestant community[1759]

1755 Lerna Ekmekcioğlu, "Republic of Paradox: The League of Nations Minority Protection Regime and the New Turkey's Step-Citizens," *Int. Journal for Middle East Studies*, 46 (2014), pp. 670-671.

1756 Özdoğan & Kılıçdağı, *Hearing Turkey's Armenians*, p. 36.

1757 Ibid, p. 38.

1758 Baruyr Kuyumciyan, "Hrant Dink School Students Dream of a Real Classroom," *Agos* newspaper, 13.03. 2015, http://www.*Agos*.com.tr/en/article/10865/hrant-dink-school-students-dream-of-a-real-classroom.

1759 The Catholic Armenians were recognised in 1830, and the Protestant Armenians in 1850 as separate *Millet*s, i.e., separate groups with specific autonomy, by the State.

play a minor role within the Armenian community, and the Armenian community only uses 43 orthodox/apostolic, 12 catholic, and 3 protestant churches, most of which are in Istanbul.[1760]

The Armenian Patriarchate was not originally established by the Armenian Church, but by Sultan Mehmet II following the Conquest of Constantinople to counterbalance the Greek Orthodox Patriarchate.[1761] The Patriarchate assumed responsibility for the Armenians' spiritual and civil matters under the *millet* system, but in 1863 the Patriarchate's authority was restricted and an autonomously elected assembly was established to take decisions on the community's civil issues. Turkey refused to adopt this system of self-governance during the Republican era, subjecting Armenian institutions to national laws in 1934, leaving only the Patriarchate and the Religious Council as autonomous institutions, creating a vacuum concerning civil and social matters.[1762] Although the authority of the Patriarchate was confined to spiritual matters, the State approached the Armenian Patriarchs, encouraging them to take on civil responsibilities.[1763] Since the founding of the Republic of Turkey, the Patriarchate has no legal entity; and no new bylaws have been introduced covering Patriarchal elections.[1764]

Although the inter-community organization model has been abolished, the general State view of non-Muslims in general and Armenians in particular considers them as 'communities' and wants their representation to be through their spiritual leaderships. There is a consensus that the Patriarchs have acted as civil

---

See Arestakes Simavoryan, "Armenian Catholics in Turkey," *Noravank Foundation*, 01.03. 2010, https://bit.ly/2Zh8DeD.

1760 Bardakci et al., Religious Minorities in Turkey, p. 152.

1761 The official website of the Armenian Patriarchate in Istanbul, http://www.turkiyeermenileripatrikligi.org/site/.

1762 Rumelili & Keyman, "Enacting multi-layered citizenship," p. 73.

1763 According to some accounts no book in Armenian could be published without patriarchal permission until 1865. They could try, jail or banish community members breaking spiritual rules and customs. Nevertheless, these punishments could only be enforced by confirmation of the State. The ultimate basis of such acts was the authority they took from the State. Armenian patriarchs and prelates were even given the authority to practice corporal punishment. However, in the nineteenth century this right was abolished. Armenian clerics during this period also supervised the conscription of Armenian youth into the Ottoman army. Related government orders were distributed to provincial Armenian communities through prelacies. The political and social roles of Armenian clerics were thus legitimized in the eyes of government and society.

1764 Özdoğan & Kılıçdağı, *Hearing Turkey's Armenians*, p. 151.

leaders during the Republican period, particularly after 1950. The Ottoman system gave the Patriarch the power of head of the *millet (milletbaşı)*; and today the State accepts the Patriarch as its interlocutor.[1765]

4.10.11 Foundations and Associations

The community foundations are non-Muslim institutions established by decrees (*fermans*) of the Ottoman Sultans to facilitate community's religious, financial and charitable services.[1766] The *fermans* did not – unlike a new foundation today – clarify what the objectives or rules of governance (such as for elections) are for the community foundations.[1767] They have a special legal status in the Turkish Republic, based on the special protection given to the then-existing non-Muslim communities under the 1923 Lausanne Peace Treaty.[1768]

These community foundations do not provide legal entity status for the communities themselves. Their existence does not address the central problem that no religious community is allowed to have legal status and so to as themselves among other things legally govern and administer their own community life and property.[1769] These foundations still operate, providing substantial financial support to Armenian churches. In 1912, under Law 1328, religious, charitable and educational foundations acquired legal entity and the right to register their immovable properties in their own names.[1770] When the Turkish Republic was founded, the framework for regulating non-Muslim communities was established through foundations, which could own houses of worship, educational buildings, orphanages, hospitals, and other similar institutions.[1771]

With the passage of Law 2762 in 1935, the governance of foundations was transferred to the GDF. The following year, under the '1936 Declarations', the government demanded that foundations declare their purpose, as well as their assets and income to formalize the national land registry. Foundations were required

1765 Ibid, 53.
1766 Kilinç, *Alien Citizens*, p. 47.
1767 Ibid.
1768 Mine Yildirim, "Turkey: Minority Foundations Still Cannot Hold Elections," Forum 18, 05.03.2019, http://www.forum18.org/archive.php?article_id=2459.
1769 Ibid.
1770 Dilek Kurban & Kezban Hatemi, The Story of an Alien(ation): Real Estate Ownership Problems of Non-Muslim Foundations and Communities in Turkey (Istanbul: TESEV Publications, 2009), pp. 9-10.
1771 Ibid, p. 14.

to submit property deeds to prove ownership, but because they had acquired the properties by *ferman* under Ottoman rule, they did not have these deeds.[1772] As a result, the GDF determined that only submitted documents would serve for each foundation. From the 1960s, these declarations were used against the foundations to seize their properties.[1773] This was justified by the false claim that non-Muslim minorities were non-Turks with no right to purchase land.[1774] In addition, the establishment of a foundation to support a certain community was not permitted according to the Turkish Civil Code. The establishment of a new community foundation is therefore legally impossible.

Article 3 of Foundations Law No. 5737 defines community foundations as foundations which have a legal entity as per Foundations Law No. 2762, and which belong to non-Muslim communities in Turkey whose members are citizens of the Republic of Turkey regardless of whether they have a foundation certificate charter or not. Such foundations comprise special legal entities as per Article 4 of the same law separately and are conducted by the Foundations Council elected by their members. Selections for the Foundations Council are performed by members themselves according to relevant provisions of the Foundations Law.[1775]

Beside the foundations, Armenian school alumni associations play important role in community life. These associations dated back to the late Ottoman period or were established by Getronagan alumni in 1947, became more widespread in the 1950s and 1960s. With the abolition of the ban on Armenian theaters in 1946,[1776] some of these associations performed plays. Today, there are 14 active alumni associations in Armenian society. The Associations Law of December 2004 began a new era where organization within civil society became relatively free. More recently, new associations were established by architects and art

---

1772 See Ayşe Ozil, "Whose Property Is It? The State, Non-Muslim Communities, and the Question of Property Ownership from the Late Ottoman Empire through the Turkish Nation State," *Journal of the Ottoman and Turkish Studies Association*, 6:1 (Spring 2019), pp. 211-235.

1773 Mine Yildirim, "The Collective Dimension of Freedom of Religion or Belief in International Law: The Application of Findings to the Case of Turkey" (Dissertation, Abo, Finland: Abo Akademi, 2015), pp. 227-228.

1774 Ibid.

1775 Official website of Directorate of General Foundation in Turkey, https://www.vgm.gov.tr/foundations-in-turkey/foundations-in-turkey/cemaat-community-foundations.

1776 Özdoğan & Kılıçdağı, *Hearing Turkey's Armenians*, p. 82.

historians and Armenians from Sasoun, Malatya and Dersim. These civic formations led by the younger generation shows that new organizational models began to be adopted in Armenian society.[1777]

Under Turkey's legal system religious or belief community members (but not communities themselves) can come together to gain legal status as associations, a route followed by some Protestants and Jehovah's Witnesses. In theory such associations have legal personality and can own property in their own name, though this does not mean that religious communities as such own the property.[1778]

Generally speaking, the activities of non-religious organizations are much more diverse than those of religious groups, with different political orientations and a wide array of ideologies and affiliations. One critically oriented and socio-politically active organization is the Hrant Dink Foundation, which defines the development of dialogue, empathy and peace in all its activities.[1779] It was founded in 2007 and has since organized studies, publications, conferences, public discussions, workshops, cultural events and Turkish-Armenian exchange programs to combat discrimination on ethnic and religious grounds and develop cultural relations in Turkey, Armenia, and Europe.

4.11 Armenian Minority Rights in Turkey

Armenians have been subjected to limited minority rights granted by the 1923 Lausanne Treaty. Traditionally a closed, depoliticized community, the Armenian minority has become increasingly differentiated over decades.[1780] Armenians in Istanbul have focused on defending their rights from the Turkish State.[1781] They

1777 The Faith and Social Solidarity Association of the Armenians of Dersim, founded in October 2010 in İstanbul, signalled a new type of organization. Before founding these new associations, civil activist groups began to raise their voices during the second half of 1990s. One such group was the Hay-Gin platform, founded in 2001 by young Armenian women of Istanbul focusing on gender equality, gender-based role models and female identity. Another group was *Nor Zartonk* (New Awakening), a civic organisation formed by a young Armenians activist group after the brutal murder of Hrant Dink in January 2007. Its purposes include "strengthening the intellectual capacities of all peoples of Turkey, starting from the Armenian Society of Turkey." See official website of *Nor Zartonk Foundation*: https://www.norzartonk.org/.

1778 Yildirim, "Turkey: Minority foundations."

1779 The official website of Hrant Dink Foundation, https://hrantdink.org/en/about-us/vission-mission.

1780 Rumelili & Keyman, "Enacting multi-layered citizenship," p. 67.

1781 Gellman, Democratization and Memories of Violence, pp. 116-117.

have used the EU accession process and the ECtHR to create greater space for their rights in Turkey, but these are questioned through State rhetoric.[1782] Turkey lacks basic multicultural policies (e.g. educational policies), and any account that portrays the incorporation of minorities as unproblematic not only conceals the official denial of the Armenian Genocide but also disavows the urgency of contemporary minority rights claims.[1783]

4.11.1 The Right to Existence

> "As members of a minority, we are like ice melting in hot water. According to statistics, for every 12 new-born Armenian babies we have 26 people dying. This is very dangerous in terms of our long-term existence. We are slowly moving towards extinction."[1784]

Armenians limited their existence and activities for decades to the framework of their church, with language and culture officially tolerated only in the narrow context of religious practices. Turkey's nation-building denied or repressed the identities of non-Turkish ethnic communities, and the Armenians were one of the first groups whose existence was regarded as a threat to the Ottoman State. Later, Republican nationalists attempted to pursue Turkish national identity by demographic engineering, reinventing history, ethnic cleansing and suppression of non-Turkish people.[1785] Akçam goes one step further and explains this erosion of Armenian identity at a deeper level. According to him "to acknowledge 1915 is to acknowledge the existence of 'them,'... on this soil, which is virtually to announce our own nonexistence."[1786]

Today, outside Istanbul, Armenians possess six churches, no monasteries and no schools. However, at the 1919 Paris Peace Conference, the heads of the Armenian delegations listed 1860 Armenian churches, 229 monasteries, 1439 schools, 29 high schools and seminaries and 42 orphanages.[1787] Later scholars based their data on unpublished archives of the Armenian Patriarchate of Constantinople

1782 Ibid, p. 119.
1783 Parla and Özgül, "Property, Dispossession, and Citizenship," p. 6.
1784 Personal interview with His Beatitude Patriarch Sahak II Mashalian, Armenian Patriarch of Constantinople, the interview was held in Istanbul on 16.02.2020.
1785 Tunç Aybak, "Geopolitics of Denial: Turkish State's 'Armenian Problem,'" p. 125.
1786 Laure Marchand and Guillaume Perrier, "Önsöz," (Introduction) in *Türkiye ve Ermeni Hayaleti: Soykırımın I · zinde Adımlar* (Turkey and the Armenian Ghost: On the Trail of the Genocide), (Istanbul: İletişim Yayınevi, 2014), pp. 9-18.
1787 Dickran Kouymjian, "Confiscation and Destruction: A Manifestation of the Genocidal Process," *Armenian Forum*, 1:3 (Autumn, 1998), pp. 1-12., p. 5.

for 1913–1914, listing 2538 churches, 451 monasteries and 1996 schools.[1788] Eastern Turkey is the historical Armenia, which was emptied in the Genocide and cleansing operations in the following decades.[1789]

In other words, Armenians were almost totally erased from the eastern Provinces where they had lived for thousands of years. In 1820, non-Muslims constituted 40 % of the total Ottoman population. By the beginning of WW1, this had declined to 19 %, and by 1927 to 12.5 %.[1790] Armenians made up 7 % of the entire Ottoman Empire's population in 1914, dropping to 0.5 % of the population by 1927. Many converted to Islam due to security concerns or by force.[1791] The Armenian population and culture continued to dwindle throughout the Republican period, leading to the social and economic collapse of Armenian centers such as Adana, Sivas, Yozgat, Diyarbakir, Harput, Malatya and Bitlis.[1792] Parishes outside Istanbul have shrunk significantly since 1964, and none of them retains its own priest.[1793]

During the 1972–73 school year there were 32 Armenian schools with 7,336 students, but by the 1999–2000 school year, numbers had reduced to 18 schools with 3,786 students. Within three decades, the number of schools had been reduced by 50 % and the number of students by 60 %.[1794] Today, there are 18 schools with around 3000 students.[1795] The success of ideological indoctrination and the reduction of the Armenian population to a silent and invisible minority (some Armenians used to be afraid to wear crosses or any other signs relating to Christianity or Armenianness[1796]) have erased the memory of Armenians as native citizens, turning them into foreigners who are more easily demonized.[1797]

1788 Raymond Kevorkian and Paul Paboudjian, *Les Arméniens dans l'Empire ottoman à la veille du Génocide,* (Armenians in the Ottoman Empire on the eve of the Genocide) (Paris: Arhis, 1992), pp. 57-60, synoptic table for all 17 Ottoman provinces with populations statistics.

1789 Hofmann, Armenians in Turkey Today, p. 6.

1790 Rumelili & Keyman, "Enacting multi-layered citizenship," p. 71.

1791 Özdoğan & Kılıçdağı, *Hearing Turkey's Armenians*, p. 16.

1792 Ibid, p. 18.

1793 Hofmann, Armenians in Turkey Today, p. 10.

1794 Özdoğan & Kılıçdağı, *Hearing Turkey's Armenians*, p. 37.

1795 Personal interview with His Beatitude Patriarch Sahak II Mashalian, Armenian Patriarch of Constantinople, the interview was held in Istanbul on 16.02.2020.

1796 Personal interview with Ms. Tatevik Sargsyan, journalist, historian based in Turkey, the interview was held in Istanbul on 19.02.2020.

1797 Edhem Eldem, "A Shameful Debate? A Critical Reassessment of the 'Torossian Debate,'" *Journal of Genocide Research*, 19:2 (2017), p. 268.

Arno Kalayci, a young lawyer from Istanbul, illustrates the situation most Armenians often find themselves:

> "Every day I need to prove that I am not an alien, that I am not a foreigner. I feel sick and tired of it all. I want to leave, but at the same time I know that I am from these lands. One day I went to the land registry and the officer told me, "You do not look like an Armenian." "What are Armenians supposed to look like?" I replied. "Do they have tails?"[1798]

However, due to trends towards democratization stimulated by the EU accession process, it has become easier for the Armenian community to have their voices heard by the Turkish State and society.[1799] The difference between the 1990s and the present is striking. Nevertheless, the Armenians have been threatened and targeted several times.[1800] The killing of Sevag Balıkçı while doing military service and the murder of Hrant Dink, then Chief Editor of *Agos* newspaper, led Celina Doğan, an Armenian attorney who was elected to Parliament on the CHP list, to comment that "none of us feel safe in such an atmosphere of violence."[1801]

In terms of educational institutions, minorities no longer have religious seminaries, preventing them from renewing the ranks of their clergy. Today, the Patriarchate has only 27 priests to minister to an estimated population of more than 200,000 Armenians (both citizens and migrant Armenians) 43 churches all over Turkey.[1802] The Armenian Patriarchate no longer has a seminary.[1803]

In addition, since the early 1990s, hundreds of citizens claiming Armenian descent have submitted petitions to Turkey's secular legal authorities to change their name and religion in the public records. The 'voluntary' conversion of

1798 Personal interview with Maître Arno Kalayci, lawyer, founding member of *Nor Zartonk* Foundation, the interview was held in Istanbul on 17.02.2020.

1799 Bardakci et al., Religious Minorities in Turkey, p. 19.

1800 The torture and killing of 3 people in a raid on "Zirve Yayınevi" (Zirve Publishing house), a publishing house engaged in missionary activities, was one of the most painful examples of this oppression, as was the murder of a Catholic priest in February 2006 in Trabzon. Roman Catholic bishop Luigi Padovese, the apostolic vicar of Anatolia and the Vatican's representative in eastern Turkey, was stabbed to death outside his home in 2010. An assassination plot was also revealed against Armenian Patriarch Mesrob Mutfayan.

1801 Tchilingirian, "The 'Other' Citizens," p. 112.

1802 Armenian Patriarchate in Istanbul, *Official Calendar booklet of the Armenian Patriarchate* (2019 Publication).

1803 USCIRF 2012 Annual Report, p. 8, https://bit.ly/3pO2Byw.

Armenians points to the Armenian Genocide that is still largely unmentionable.[1804] Regaining visibility has become of similar relevance as has the Armenian diaspora's insistence on Genocide acknowledgment. According to Turkish-Armenian lawyer Fethiye Cetin: "If people hide their origin or religious stripe because of fear, threat or isolation, if they try to prove that they belong to the majority then such an atmosphere contradicts global values, human rights, democracy and nature. Hiding and rejecting your roots under pressure, threat, or because fear, is first of all inhuman."[1805] This means that to protect their existence, Armenians chose to perform submissive loyalty to ensure their security.

Although multilateral treaties theoretically guaranteed the preservation of these differences, in practice they remain a constant site of negotiation between the State and the Armenians of Istanbul (*Bolsahay*) elite. Those who remained in Istanbul have had to find a balance between integrating with the larger society and disappearing as Armenians.[1806] One of the most tangible strategies Armenians use to hide their Armenian identity is to use a "Turkish" name in the public domain.[1807]

Regarding Armenians as 'religion-based communities' means denying their existence as ethnic identities and cultures, as well as implying a dehistorization, a removal from history. In 1994, the paper "Armenian International Magazine" quoted an Armenian in Istanbul saying: "We are guests here. If they say we have to leave, there is nothing we can do about it."[1808] In June 2002, an Armenian woman described the relations of the Armenian minority with the Turkish State: "We are hostages in their hands. Sure, they allow us to pray in our churches. And we are also allowed to pay for our schools. But that is all. They do what they please with us."[1809] The Armenians of Istanbul have been there for many centuries and their presence dates back to Byzantine times.[1810] Their heritage has been deliberately

1804 Ceren Özgul, "From Muslim Citizen to Christian Minority: Tolerance, Secularism and Armenian Return Conversions in Turkey" (Dissertation, The City University of New York, 2013), p. 2.

1805 Rouben Melkonyan, "Armenia did not seem to be strange to me…": Interview with Fethiye Cetin," *Noravank Foundation*, 04.05.2009, http://www.noravank.am/en/?page=theme&thid=1&nid=1793.

1806 Ekmekcioğlu, *Recovering Armenia*, p. 160.

1807 Personal interview with Ms. Tatevik Sargsyan, journalist, historian based in Turkey, the interview was held in Istanbul on 19.02.2020.

1808 Armenian International Magazine, August-September 1994, p. 61.

1809 Hofmann, Armenians in Turkey Today, p. 43.

1810 Nareg Seferian, "The Final Frontiers: The Various Borders between Armenia and Turkey," *Turkish Review*, Kerim Balci ed., 3:3 (2013), p. 262.

neglected or destroyed, and their existence remains mostly unacknowledged in the teaching of history to Turkey's people.[1811]

In terms of the current physical existence of Armenians in Turkey, Armenian NGO worker Hrant Kasparyan commented: "There are funerals but no weddings." In 2015 there were 253 baptisms against 569 funerals in the community. The Patriarch also highlights the disparity between birth and death rates in the community. Other contentious challenges threatening the existence of the Armenians are mixed marriages, migration and the impact of globalization,[1812] combined with the following problems which will be discussed below.

4.11.1.1 Anti-Armenianism as a Threat to the Existence of Armenians in Turkey

> "Anti-Armenian discourse is like a stick of dynamite that could explode at any moment. In addition, it justifies discrimination. In other words, it is OK to do whatever you want to people you consider to be inferior. Because of Anti-Armenian sentiment, people think that they can do whatever they want to us. They can take our property; they can discriminate against us and we cannot rely on the authorities."[1813]

Armenophobia has been an inseparable part of the Turkish identity for decades.[1814] Turkish identity is generally authority-oriented and state-centered, demonstrating a hostile attitude towards 'outsiders'.[1815] In Turkey, calling someone 'Armenian' is an insult, reflecting discrimination against religious and national minorities.[1816] When you say someone is 'Armenian' they reply God Forbid *(Hasha)*. An opposition MP accused former president Gül of having an Armenian mother. Gül considered the accusation an insult and initiated legal action against the MP.[1817]

In this context, the Armenian Genocide was a taboo subject, narrated only through the official line that the Armenians had betrayed their country in the war. It was even claimed that Armenians had killed Turks en masse. Such Turkish

---

1811 Ibid.

1812 Personal interview with His Beatitude Patriarch Sahak II Mashalian, Armenian Patriarch of Constantinople, the interview was held in Istanbul on 16.02.2020.

1813 Ibid.

1814 Özdoğan & Kılıçdağı, *Hearing Turkey's Armenians*, p. 23.

1815 Ibid.

1816 Cheterian, Open Wounds: Armenians, p. 4.

1817 Alaettin Çarıkcı, "The Art of Memory: The Remembrance of the Armenians in Turkey," (Dissertation, University of Leiden, 2016), p. 25.

official declarations continue today. Turkish Deputy Prime Minister Emrullah Ishler, in a televised interview, announced that Armenians who had committed Genocide against Turks and had killed "over one million Turks."[1818]

In a survey of Turkish people who are not Armenian, 30 % of respondents believed that "the Armenians living in Turkey today came to Turkey after the disintegration of the Soviet Union," while a further 30 % had no idea where Armenians come from.[1819] In a 2011 survey, 73.9 % of respondents admitted to having negative opinions of Armenians.[1820] Armenians are often associated with the ASALA [the Armenian Secret Army for the Liberation of Armenia], whose attacks on Turkish diplomats in Europe from 1975 to 1986 encouraged the ostracizing of Armenians living in Turkey.[1821] These figures indicate severe lack of knowledge and awareness about Armenians among Turkish society.

In 2012, as part of an anti-Armenian hate campaign the ultra-nationalist ASIM-DER group targeted Armenian religious and educational institutions.[1822] After huge street rallies took place in 2012 to mark the fifth anniversary of Hrant Dink's death, an anti-Armenian protest was held at Taksim Square that included hate speech directed against Armenians.[1823] In February 2014, a group of protestors carrying a banner that said, "Long live the Ogun Samasts[1824]! Down with Hrant Dink!" marched in front of an Armenian school in Istanbul and the *Agos* newspaper, where Hrant Dink was assassinated in 2007.[1825]

Another scandal involving President Erdogan took place in Trabzon, where a crowd gathered during his speech and started chanting anti-Armenian chants. Instead of silencing or reprimanding the crowd, Erdogan continued his speech, smiling along with colleagues at the chants.[1826] More concerning for the

---

1818 Cheterian, "The Last Closed Border of the Cold War: Turkey–Armenia," *Journal of Borderlands Studies*, 32:1 (2017), p. 81.

1819 Özdoğan & Kılıçdağı, *Hearing Turkey's Armenians*, p. 25.

1820 Tarik Işık, "*Türk Halkı Bir Tek Kendini Sever*" (Turkish People Only Love Themselves), *Radikal* newspaper, 02.05.2011.

1821 Bishku, "The Interactions and Experiences of Armenians," p. 444.

1822 "Ultra-nationalist group targets Turkey's Armenians" *Zaman* newspaper, 28.11.2012. Retrieved 31.05.2013.

1823 Seferian, "The Final Frontiers," p. 262.

1824 Ogun Samasts is the murderer of Hrant Dink.

1825 "*Agos'un önüne ırkçı pankart* (Racist banner in front of *Agos*)," *Dinken.com*, 23.2.2014, https://bit.ly/38dpBzl.

1826 "Erdogan Supporters Chant Anti-Armenian Slogan at Rally in Turkey," *PanArmenian net*, 17.10.2016, https://www.panarmenian.net/eng/news/223362/.

Armenian community is the increasing nationalist and racist discourse of AKP politicians. In the past it was the Kemalist State that engaged in framing and labeling the Armenians, but now it is the AKP, led by Erdogan. In August 2014, Erdogan complained: "Excuse me, they have called me Armenian, but I am a Turk, from my grandfather's, my father's and all sides."[1827]

Anti-Armenian sentiments and incidents are common phenomena during Armenian related external developments. For example, during the recent 2020 September war in Nagorno-Karabakh (Artsakh), Turkish ultranationalists storm Armenian neighborhoods in Istanbul,[1828] protests have broken out directed at Armenians in general and in particular the Armenian community of Istanbul.[1829]

Anti-Armenian discourse can also be seen in broader anti-Christian sentiments, and anti-Christian hate speech has increased in Turkey in social and conventional media.[1830] Things came to a head during the abortive July 15, 2016, coup when the regime ordered the imams to go to their mosques and urge the faithful to take to the streets to quash the attempted revolt. Not surprisingly, this Islamist-nationalist reassertion was accompanied by numerous anti-Christian actions. Targeting churches increased dramatically after the coup attempt.[1831]

USCIRF also noted that some Turkish textbooks contained antagonistic statements towards minorities in the form of educational material reconstructing the history in line with the denial policies of the government, portraying the Armenians as a threat to the sovereignty and identity of modern Turkey.[1832] The demonization of the Armenians in Turkish education is a State policy to reinforce the denial discourse.[1833] In other words, anti-Armenian campaigns remain a part of the denialist practice in Turkey to silence the victims and their successors who

1827 "*Erdoğan: Bana çok daha çirkin şeyler söyleyenler oldu, Ermeni dediler*!" (Erdogan: they said even uglier things to me, they said [I am] Armenian!) *Cumhuriyet* newspaper, 06.08.2014, https://bit.ly/34gaDXC.

1828 Djamel Belayachi, "Turkish ultranationalists storm Armenian neighbourhoods in Istanbul as fighting rages in Nagorno-Karabakh," *France 24*, 15.10.2020, https://bit.ly/3c2u4Gr.

1829 Murat Yildiz, "'They are scared': Armenians flee Istanbul amid anger over Nagorno-Karabakh," *Middle East Eye*, 11.11.2020, https://bit.ly/3uQEcut.

1830 Hoff, "Turkey Turns on its Christians."

1831 In Malatya, for example, a gang chanting "Allahu Akbar" broke the glass panels of the front door of a Protestant church. See Hoff, "Turkey Turns on its Christians."

1832 "Religious Minorities in Turkey: 'An Endangered Species'?," *The Armenian Weekly*, 12.04.2012, https://bit.ly/30gfwNK.

1833 Aybak, "Geopolitics of Denial: Turkish State's 'Armenian Problem,'" p. 137.

remained in Turkey and to reproduce the official historiography.[1834] Armenians are regularly targeted by campaigns in which the media and political elites whip up public fear, resentment and anger toward an urban minority now representing less than 0.1 % of the country's population.[1835]

4.11.1.2 Assimilation as a Threat to the Existence of Armenians in Turkey

One of the main dilemmas for Armenians in Turkey is assimilation. Assimilation is based on an idea of a dominant culture that aims to produce homogeneity by getting minorities to abandon their culture. Kymlicka and Norman mention two form of assimilation, distinguished by the degree of coercion. The more coercive form would include banning: "Associations and publications that seek to foster or reproduce a minority identity or compel all citizens to stop using surnames that reflect a minority background... [while the State] rewrote history in the attempt to assimilate minority groups into the larger nation."[1836] The less coercive kind respects citizens but refuses to accord recognition to minority languages and cultures. This form still insists that schools, public institutions, street signs and public holidays reflect the dominant language and culture.[1837]

Turkish policy on diversity have always stressed assimilation and this has not changed significantly. Assimilation is a serious problem for the Armenians, as Turkey's sociological dynamics seem to work towards the destruction of Armenian culture and identity.[1838] In the last 40 years, the decrease in the number of schools and students represents a devastating blow for Armenians.[1839] The situation for any remaining Armenian families in eastern provinces is particularly difficult. For them, likelihood of assimilation and losing identity is higher, as they have no access to local ethno-religious networks, so their opportunities for linguistic, cultural and religious development are limited.[1840]

1834 Nazan Maksudyan, Book Review: The Armenians in Modern Turkey: Post-Genocide Society, Politics and History, Talin Suchiyan, ed. (London: Tauris, 2016), in Global affairs, 2:2 (2016), pp. 234-236.

1835 Hofman, Armenians in Turkey Today, p. 16.

1836 Will Kymlicka and Wayne Norman, "Citizenship in Culturally Diverse Societies: Issues, Contexts, Concepts," in *Citizenship in Diverse Societies*, Will Kymlicka & Wayne Norman eds. (Oxford and New York: OUP, 2000), p. 14.

1837 Bayir, Minorities and Nationalism, p. 7.

1838 Özdoğan & Kılıçdağı, *Hearing Turkey's Armenians*, p. 32.

1839 Ibid.

1840 Bardakci et al., *Religious Minorities in Turkey*, p. 156-157.

The dominant language of communication for Armenians in Turkey is Turkish because of continuing restrictive regulations and the influence of modern media.[1841] The Armenian language is declining, and to prioritize a secure and economically successful life for themselves, some Armenians seem to accept the loss of their religion, history, language, culture and heritage in order to assimilate into Turkey's mainstream society.[1842]

This tendency particularly affects the younger generation. According to a research conducted by Bardakci et al., when compared sense of their groups' collective identities, Armenians show stronger tendencies to assimilation than Syriacs and Alevis. This might be surprising, as an assumption that a Muslim minority would be more prone to actively integrate in Turkey, while the Armenians, would be developing a more pronounced sense of distinction. The opposite seems to be the case.[1843] Assimilation is considered more than a survival mechanism and represents a tool for upward mobility.[1844] It seems that Armenians assimilate in order to access their rights as citizens of Turkey.[1845]

4.11.1.3 Hrant Dink's Murder

Hrant Dink was an Armenian citizen of Turkey who spent his life as a writer and intellectual addressing issues within the Armenian community from the Armenian community's social cohesion and civil society strength to the memory politics of 1915.[1846] In 1996, Dink founded *Agos*, the first newspaper to be published in both Armenian and Turkish languages to engage Armenians who had linguistically assimilated and form a platform to share Armenian issues with a State level audience.[1847] Dink was prosecuted three times for 'denigrating Turkishness' in his editorials, receiving death threats from ultra-nationalists and threats from the Istanbul governor and agents of the National Intelligence Agency (MIT).[1848] Dink had asked for but did not receive police protection. He was about to take

1841 Hofmann, *One Nation*, p. 100.
1842 Bardakci et al., Religious Minorities in Turkey, p. 156.
1843 Ibid, p. 234.
1844 Gellman, Democratization and Memories of Violence, p. 100.
1845 Ibid, p. 781.
1846 For further information, see Tuba Candar, *Hrant Dink: An Armenian Voice of the Voiceless in Turkey* (New York: Routledge, 2017).
1847 See the official website of *Agos* newspaper: http://www.*Agos*.com.tr/en/home.
1848 Fatma Müge Göçek, "The 2007 Assassination of Hrant Dink through the Lenses of History," *Memory and Emotions*, 70:2 (2018), p. 149.

his legal case to the ECtHR when he was assassinated on 19 January 2007 in front of the *Agos* office in Istanbul.[1849] The murder, carried out by Ogun Samast,[1850] an unemployed teenager from Trabzon who has been linked to ultra-nationalists, was connected to a wider web of paramilitary repression against minorities and leftists.[1851] Samast confessed his crime proudly by saying, "I shot the Armenian because he had insulted Turkishness."[1852] During Dink's funeral, about 200,000 protestors took to the streets chanting "We are all Hrant, we are all Armenians."[1853] In the decade since Dink's death, State and government officials that planned the assassination have still not been tried or sentenced properly.

Transcending ethnic boundaries, people honored Dink's life while challenging deep State violence.[1854] The presence of so many Turks allowed Armenians to protest the State's behavior and inspired personal commitment to action by some Armenian intellectuals. Aris Nalcı, then a journalist at *Agos*, described how this turning point affected him personally: "I lost my fear in 2007. If I speak, I can be killed, if I don't speak, I can be killed, so why not speak?"[1855] For Armenians living with this mindset, Dink's assassination proved the danger in trying to stir the conscience of the State. Dink's assassination proved to the older generation that their way of thinking to be passive and not visible was right, namely that the State is incapable of respecting and protecting the rights of non-Muslims, and it is dangerous to advocate for them.[1856] Nevertheless, and more importantly, Dink's assassination transformed Armenians' struggle for justice into an internal debate within Turkey. Dink succeeded in raising awareness about the Armenian existence and their search for justice within Turkey.[1857]

1849 Ibid.

1850 In contrast, Dink's assassin Ogun Samast was treated like a hero at the police station where he was taken after his arrest; officers there posed alongside Samast, who was made to hold a Turkish flag. See "Turkish police 'treated alleged killer as a hero'," *Irish Examiner*, 03.02, 2007, https://bit.ly/3tXatiV.

1851 *Ergenekon Is Our Reality* (Ankara: Young Civilians and Human Rights Agenda Association, 2010), pp. 47-49.

1852 Çarıkcı, "The Arts of Memory," p. 24.

1853 Alice Von Bieberstein, "Surviving Hrant Dink Carnal Mourning under the Specter of Senselessness in Post-Ottoman Topologies: The Presence of the Past," in *The Era of the Nation-State*, Nicolas Argenti ed. (New York: Berghahn Books, 2019), p. 64.

1854 Mneesha Gellman, "Remembering violence: the role of apology and dialogue in Turkey's democratization process," *Democratization*, 20:4 (2013), p. 786.

1855 Gellman, Democratization and Memories of Violence, p. 124.

1856 Ibid, p. 126.

1857 Cheterian, *Open Wounds: Armenians*, p. 312.

4.11.1.4 Migrants from Armenia

The presence of Armenian immigrants is purposely 'overlooked' by the Turkish administration. For example, Turkey so far allows the continuity of not authorized Armenian School called after 'Hrant Dink' to organize classes in the basement of an Evangelical Church for migrant Armenians' children.[1858] It uses the presence of illegal Armenian immigrants as a threatening card whenever there is an international pressure regarding the recognition of Armenian Genocide or Turkey-Armenian relationship in general. In October 2000, when the US Congress brought up the Armenian Genocide, Tansu Çiller, Turkey's opposition leader, suggested deporting Armenian citizens in retaliation. In March 2010, Prime Minister Erdogan said to the BBC:

> "There are 170,000 Armenians in my country. 70,000 of them are my citizens. But the rest, we turn a blind eye. But it turns out that I may tell them 'Off you go,' sooner or later. Why will I do this? They are not my citizens. I don't have to keep them in my country. We approach them with understanding, but they keep pushing us with this attitude and they don't know it."[1859]

In other words, minorities and those who are "not of us" can be sacrificed to other interests.[1860] The following year, Erdogan once again threatened to expel Armenian immigrants when Germany passed an Armenian Genocide resolution.[1861] Even more dramatic are the consequences of Turkey's refusal to establish diplomatic relations with Armenia. To this day, children of immigrants who are born in Turkey remain stateless. Children of migrant workers encounter difficulties in accessing State education as they face barriers in obtaining support for disadvantaged or minority students.[1862]

4.11.1.5 The Legal Existence of Armenian Religious Institutions

The State's attitude to the Armenian Patriarchate is another revealing example. The State receives the Patriarch as *de facto* representative of the community on many occasions and offer him symbolic privileges such as wearing a gown and bearing a sceptre in public places.[1863] However, since the establishment of the

---

1858 Kuyumciyan, "Hrant Dink School students."
1859 Akgönül, The Minority Concept in the Turkish Context, p. 82.
1860 Ibid, p. 83.
1861 "Erdoğan Threatens Armenian Citizens Once Again," *Agos* newspaper, 04.06.2015), https://bit.ly/38dQGBG.
1862 Committee on the Protection of the Rights of All Migrant Workers, para.67(g).
1863 Ibid, p. 57-58.

Republic, the Patriarchate has never enjoyed a legal existence as an institution. It simply does not exist in Turkey's legal system.[1864] It cannot take administrative or legal action in court, it cannot even open a bank account, own property, buy or rent real estate receive revenues and must only act through foundations, which have legal status.[1865] There is no law or Statute defining Patriarchate's authority, responsibilities or the election of Patriarchs.[1866]

In addition, it is not allowed to worship in historical churches that are not under jurisdiction of the church, but rather confiscated by the State. The Patriarchate has no say regarding these churches and is banned from undertaking clerical education.[1867] The non-recognition of Patriarchate's authority as a legal entity has created other problems in daily life. For instance, any repair and maintenance work in the Patriarchate is subject to special authorization. The State, while recognizing the Patriarch as a person, refuses to recognize the Patriarchate as an institution. It is a contradiction that a historical institution with a history of more than 5 centuries cannot legally exist.[1868] If the status of the Patriarchate is recognized, the scope of the status must be discussed in Armenian society and then agreed by the Turkish government.

1864 The Patriarch (not the patriarchate) is recognized by the authorities, and when the Patriarch was elected the Turkish Government sent a letter to the Patriarch allowing him to wear religious habits in public (the Hat Law and the Law relating to Prohibited Garments of 1934 emphasized that religious clothing should not be worn outside religious places). This was, nevertheless, merely de facto recognition, with no legal effect.

1865 *Nufusumuz Hizla Azaliyor* (Our Population Is Declining Rapidly), *Agos* newspaper, 07.02.2020, and Personal interview with His Beatitude Patriarch Sahak II Mashalian, Armenian Patriarch of Constantinople, the interview was held in Istanbul on 16.02.2020.

1866 Kılıcdagi, "Social and political roles of the Armenian clergy," p. 545.

1867 Özdoğan & Kılıçdağı, *Hearing Turkey's Armenians*, p. 59.

1868 Ibid.

4.11.1.6 *Transforming Surp Khach (Holy Cross Church) into Akdamar Museum*

After two years of renovation, the opening ceremony of the *Surp Khach*[1869] on Aghtamar island as the Akdamar Museum[1870] took place in March 2007. An enormous Turkish flag was draped over one of the spurs to demonstrate Turkish hegemony, and the Minister of Tourism and Culture in his opening speech did not mention the Armenians or the Armenian heritage, demonstrating the State policy of ignoring the existence of Armenians.[1871] The renovation was presented as a political achievement for Turkey's recognition of minority rights. Traditionally, the rituals of the Armenian Church require a religious site to be consecrated before its opening, but this was not allowed for the *Surp Khach* on the grounds that it was a museum. Turkish officials also refused to allow a cross on the church, although one was added later.[1872] The church was not renovated to recognize the Armenians, but to showcase the Turkish government's engagement with religious differences. Meanwhile, the Armenians had no legal claims on the church. Given the legal landscape described above, the church was an 'abandoned property' and there were no legal grounds to contest the government's decisions about the restoration.[1873]

4.11.1.7 *The Destruction of Armenian Historical Monuments*

Once the decision was carried out to rid the Armenian homeland of its population, the logical consequence was to complete the Genocide by removing any association of the Armenian people. Thus, the name 'Armenia' was dropped from all Turkish maps and documents; when it inadvertently surfaced in textbooks or

---

1869 The Cathedral of the Holy Cross is one of the most famous and iconic of all Armenian churches, a high point of Armenian architecture of the Armenian kingdom of Vaspurakan. It was completed in 921 and was the seat of an Armenian Catholicosate for several centuries. See Der Nersessian and Vahramian, *Aght'amar* (Millan: Oemme Edizioni, 1974).

1870 The Island was historically named Aghtamar (Աղթամար) after the hero of the Armenian legend Tamar, while Akdamar (Pure vein) in Turkish is the manipulated/altered version of the name in Turkish.

1871 Çarıkcı, "The Arts of Memory," pp. 112-114.

1872 Ibid.

1873 Christopher Sheklian, "Promises of Property: Religious Foundations and the Justice and Development Party's Ambiguous Attitudes towards Religious Minorities," *Turkish Studies*, 20:3 (2019), p. 9.

popular literature, the book was confiscated and destroyed. The Turkish government has gone to great lengths to efface all traces of Armenian civilization. In the 1950s it changed the names of towns and villages in the eastern provinces.[1874]

Another policy that continues to cause a real threat to the existence of the Armenians is the destruction of their Historical sites and monuments. Thousands of Armenian historical monuments are being destroyed or left to decay, obliterating the memory of Armenian presence in eastern provinces.[1875] In some cases, monuments have been protected as examples of "Seljuk architecture"[1876] while others have been transformed into mosques. One particularly sensitive issue is the cathedral at Urfa, in which 300 Armenians were burned alive in 1895, an event witnessed by American missionary Corinna Shattuck. The cathedral has been used as a fire station by the local fire brigade since the extermination of the Armenians of Urfa in 1915 and was transformed into a mosque in 1993.[1877]

> "Destructive restoration," the pretence of archaeological excavation and amateurish restoration are especially deserving of criticism. The Armenian origin of monuments is never mentioned. Instead, they are described as Byzantine or Turkish monuments, without a mention of Armenian ethnic affiliation.[1878] According to 1974 UNESCO data, 464 of 913 buildings that remained after the 1915 Genocide were destroyed, 252 were left ruins and 197 are in dire need of reconstruction. In an August 2000 study, Armenian lawyer Anahid M. Ugurlayan concluded that "Thousands of Armenian cultural monuments are subject to a policy of wilful neglect on the part of Turkey."[1879]
> To sum up, as a consequence of emigration, circular migration, and assimilation, the number of Turkish Armenians tends to decrease. When the Turkish Republic was founded in 1923, the Armenian community of Turkey numbered 300,000 among a population of approximately 13 million. Ninety-seven years later, the population of Turkey had increased to 82 million, but the Armenian community had declined to around 60,000.[1880]

1874 Dickran Kouymjian, "The Destruction of Armenian Cultural Monuments: Its Significance for World Heritage Preservation." in *Noah's Country A Roadtrip through Post-Genocide Armenia*, Judith Crispin ed. (Sydney: T&G Publishing, 2015).

1875 Ibid.

1876 The best-known examples are the tenth century churches of Aght'amar and Kars, which were built before the Seljuk Turks entered history.

1877 Hofmann, Armenians in Turkey Today, p. 39

1878 Ibid, p. 40.

1879 "Neglecting Armenian Monuments, Turkey Violates Lausanne Treaty," *Armenian Forum*, 17.08.2000.

1880 Tchilingirian, "The 'Other' Citizens," p. 127.

The enormous loss and decline of Armenian heritage and cultural production over the decades, is largely due to the state-imposed restrictions, limitations and violations of minority rights. The existence of the Armenians decreased so much that many current Armenians in Istanbul believe that the State no longer considers the Armenians inside Turkey as 'threat'.[1881] In contrary, some think Turkish State prefers to maintain the existence of the Armenians so they can show to the outside world how diverse and multicultural Turkey is.[1882]

4.11.2 The Right to Identity

Under the provisions of the Treaty of Lausanne, Armenians are seen as a religious minority. Their rights to identity therefore mainly encompass the maintenance of the Armenian language to the extent that it remains part of the Armenian Apostolic or Uniate Armenian rites.[1883] For most of the twentieth century, the question of Turkey's Armenian community has been considered as mainly a state-security concern. It was never taken into serious consideration as a question within the context of the minority rights and particularly the right to identity.[1884] There are several reasons to explain the prejudiced interpretations of the Lausanne Treaty's clauses and the principles and ideological features of Kemalism. With the passage of time and the application of rigid forms of laicism, the Armenians' religious and ethnic identity seriously jeopardised. The Armenians have long been treated as 'local foreigners with Turkish citizenship'.[1885] Turkey's bureaucracy continues to be guided by a nationalist and unitary concept of society, denying and neglecting the existence of ethnic identities. As expressed in Gellman's work, "Being an Armenian in Turkey is very dangerous. Only if you accept assimilation you are allowed to be a citizen, but minorities want to be accepted as citizens with their own identities. We need to create a new "we."[1886]

1881 Personal interview with Ms. Silva Kouyoumdjian, principal of *Getronagan* Armenian High School Armenian in Istanbul, the interview was held in Istanbul on 16.02.2020.

1882 Personal interview with Ms. Celina Doğan, former member of Turkish Parliament, current member of Shishli Municipality Council in Istanbul, the interview was held in Istanbul on 18.02.2020.

1883 Vahram Ter-Matevosyan, "The Armenian Community and the AK Party," p. 97.

1884 Ibid.

1885 Gabriel Goltz, "The Non-Muslim Minorities and Reform in Turkey," in *Turkey Beyond Nationalism: Towards Post-Nationalist Identities*, Hans Lukas Kieser ed. (London: I. B. Tauris, 2006), p. 175.

1886 Gellman, Democratization and Memories of Violence, p. 114.

The pressure and discrimination stemming from the State and society play an important role in shaping the perceptions Armenians have about themselves. There is a traditional attitude that Armenians in Turkey should not draw attention to themselves or to Armenian society in general. They must be "twice as hard-working, twice as honest, twice as courageous and twice as peace-loving as everyone else."[1887] One result of the prevailing situation is that multiple or hybrid identities have emerged.

Armenian schools and churches play a significant role in sustaining Armenian identity. Schools teach Armenian language, literature and music, but are not allowed to teach Armenian history in general, specifically the Genocide and its consequences.[1888] This situation diminishes social memory and alienates Armenians from their own identities. Armenian students can only learn Turkish history through standard textbooks distributed by the MoE which depict minorities as enemies.[1889] This causes the Armenians somehow to be reluctant to preserve and enjoy their identity particularly in public and social life. In addition, this limitation also makes them reluctant to accept Islamised Armenians, Crypto Armenians, Armenians from mixed marriages and migrants from Armenia as part of the traditional Armenian society.[1890] It seems that a society of prejudice builds and encourages prejudice, even within the minorities who are victims of prejudice. As Sevan argues "Armenians are imprisoned within the traditional boundaries of identity and do not accept other Armenians"[1891] According to the prevailing Armenian mentality in Turkey, identity is a quasi-religious term, and the community revolves around the church, even for non-believers.[1892]

The perception of Armenians in Turkey is usually limited to the visible community in Istanbul. Having largely lost their linguistic identity, religion remains a key identifier, with the Patriarchate of Istanbul as the focus of religious and cultural life.[1893] More recent AKP discourse and policies have encouraged a new Ottoman-Islamic Turkish identity, which Armenians find hard to accept, and

1887 Özdoğan & Kılıçdağı, *Hearing Turkey's Armenians*, p. 28.
1888 Ekmekcioğlu, *Recovering Armenia*, p. 125.
1889 Ibid.
1890 "Interview with Istanbulate Armenian Sevan Degirmenjian," *Aztag newspaper*, 03.01.2018.
1891 Ibid.
1892 Ibid.
1893 Hofmann, *One Nation*, p. 84.

respond by embracing their Christian identity.[1894] Recently, re-constructing multiculturalism and multi-ethnicity have risen in Turkey's agenda. For Armenians in particular, such a public discussion is new, as their identity had been shaped by other's actions.[1895] Today, the Armenian Apostolic Church still dominates, but Armenian identity is not reduced to adherence to it. Armenian identities in Turkey have been shaped by the recent history of Turkey.[1896] In this context, the impact of the Armenian Genocide on shaping the identity of Armenians in Turkey is worth examining in more detail.

4.11.2.1 The Impact of Armenian Genocide on the Rights to Identity for Armenians in Turkey

Debates over naming the violence perpetrated against Armenians continue to shape policies that affect their descendants.[1897] The events of the 1915 Genocide are a traumatic memory. Compared to diasporic Armenians, those in Turkey were not able to raise the subjects as they continued to live State oppression and were even deprived of the opportunity to mourn the Genocide. 1915 is the root cause of why Armenians today are scattered throughout the world, why the number of Armenians in Turkey is so low today, and why their culture has been destroyed. The Armenians have lost their people, their accumulated knowledge, their history, their arts and their intellectual wealth, and have been uprooted from their homeland.

Turkey still refuses to take responsibility for the annihilation of the Armenians and imposes this denialism on remaining Armenian communities.[1898] Turkey censors any discussion about the Genocide and continues to destroy any remaining signs of the Armenian past. Scholarly debate on the Genocide only began in the 1980s.[1899] Human rights NGOs began to appear in the 1990s, and academics have initiated a debate on formerly taboo issues, particularly the Genocide. This has broken Turkey's monopoly of opinion on the interpretation of

---

1894 "Interview with Istanbulate Armenian Sevan Degirmenjian," *Aztag newspaper*, 03.01.2018.

1895 Hofmann, *One Nation*, p. 81.

1896 Ibid.

1897 Özgül, "Legally Armenian," p. 627.

1898 For further details, See, Talin Suciyan, *The Armenians in modern Turkey*.

1899 Vicken Cheterian, "Book review, The Armenians in Modern Turkey: Post-Genocide Society, Politics and History, by Talin Suciyan," *International Affairs*, 93:4 (July 2017), pp. 972–973.

history, which had been guarded by the Turkish Historical Society (*Turk Tarih Kurumu*), established in 1931 on the orders of Mustafa Kemal.[1900]

However, this development does not counterbalance the state-sponsored historical propaganda. The official denial policies are an extension of the official State ideology as a nation-building process. Turkish governments characterize the events as 'widespread partisan fighting' in which Turks and Armenians were killed, and identifying the acts of 1915 as Genocide was prosecuted under Article 301 of the Turkish penal code.[1901] Although the law was amended in 2008 as part of EU accession reforms, the revised iteration still can be used to prosecute any acknowledgment of the Genocide as insulting Turkish nation.[1902] In essence, denial functions as a 'double killing' that reconstructs history and degrades the memories of the victims.[1903] In other words, institutional denial has tangible public consequences for the victims and their successors through the negation of their experiences.[1904] The denial of a fundamental historical event means that Armenians in Turkey today must downplay their ethnic identities. Just as the victims of the Genocide disappeared from the map, the survivors have been forced into the shadows.

Denial policies remain at the heart of the Turkish foreign policy and the 'Armenian problem' has been included into Turkey's neo-Ottomanist grand strategy.[1905] The recognition of the Armenian Genocide is still regarded as a threat to Turkish national identity and security. Instead of pursuing a policy and mentality that acknowledges the pain, sees the injustice and respects the dead, Turkey is leading a campaign to argue that the real villain was actually the victim,[1906] while Turkish museums of local history in Van and Erzurum have sections about the alleged extermination of Turks and Muslim population by the Armenians. On the border with Armenia in the vicinity of Iğdır, a 45-metre monument was dedicated to the alleged Turkish victims of Armenian Genocide on October 5, 1999.[1907]

The rigid divergence in naming what took place in 1915 highlights potential roadblocks to Armenians, while a century of State denial has allowed Armenians

1900 Hofmman, Armenians in Turkey Today, p. 44.
1901 Özgül, "From Muslim Citizen to Christian Minority," p. 101.
1902 Ibid.
1903 Aybak, "Geopolitics of Denial: Turkish State's 'Armenian Problem,'" p. 131.
1904 Ibid.
1905 Ibid.
1906 Özdoğan & Kılıçdağı, *Hearing Turkey's Armenians*, p. 95.
1907 Hofmann, Armenians in Turkey Today, p. 32.

to employ memory as a rallying concept.[1908] Genocide denial has major repercussions for identity development. Invalidating culturally formative memories inhibits the incorporation of minorities as full citizens with their legitimate right to preserve, develop and enjoy their own identities.[1909] It is worth pointing out that Armenians in Turkey are often critiqued for not pushing hard enough for Genocide recognition, but their narratives are more restricted than those same memories in the diaspora. In this context, it is exceedingly difficult for Armenians to create an acceptable narrative within Turkey.[1910] However, Armenian Genocide commemorations have been taking place in Istanbul and sometimes other cities since 2005. Several intellectuals, NGOs and Armenian MPs have been advocating for the recognition of the Genocide.[1911] In the Parliament, for example Garo Paylan requested an inquiry from the Parliament and made the following statement in the occasion of commemoration the 105 anniversary of the Armenian Genocide:

> "Armenian Genocide has been debated at dozens of parliaments around the world, it has been recognized as a Genocide. But none of them has healed the wound of Armenian people…As a member of the Grand National Assembly of Turkey, I know that the only Parliament that will heal the wound of the Armenian people is the Grand National Assembly of Turkey."[1912]

4.11.2.2 Islamized Armenians

The voice of the 'Islamized' Armenians, who are growing in numbers, reveals a long-hidden dimension of the destruction, coercion and devastation created by the events of 1915. The choice of these people creates unease within Armenian society as it may exacerbate the discrimination against Armenians.

Descendants of forcibly Islamized Armenians render the entanglements of religion and ethnicity in Turkey, even if the numbers of such reconverts are

---

1908 Gellman, Democratization and Memories of Violence, p. 115.

1909 Ibid, p. 123.

1910 Ibid.

1911 According to Arno Kalayji, in the last two years it has been very difficult to get permission to hold Armenian Genocide commemorations. In 2019, the government gave permission for a gathering only in an insignificant place, rather than in the main squares where previous commemorations used to take place.

1912 Siranush Ghazanchyan, "Garo Paylan submits inquiry to Turkish Parliament on 105th anniversary of Armenian Genocide," *Public Radio of Armenia*, 24.04.2020, https://bit.ly/2KN0nza.

small.[1913] Questions on identity have ambiguous and conflicting answers, and the definition of Armenian-ness is elusive and uncertain. Many Islamized Armenians face severe challenges to preserving and promote their identities, and are excluded from the Armenian community, which accuses them of acting out of economic motives.[1914] Many clergy members believe that "These issues are political issues. We don't like to talk about them."[1915] Some other Armenians are afraid of being accused of motivating Islamized Armenians to convert back to Christianity.[1916] Beside the conservative Armenians, the State also does not provide free and safe spaces to allow Islamised Armenians to return to their roots and identities.[1917]

The pivotal issue here is how to assess Armenian-ness; should it be through religion, culture, or said ethnic roots? Since the early 2000s Turkish law no longer adjudicates conversion, simplifying the process, but claiming Armenian ethnicity for those Islamised Armenian converts from Islam to Christianity still requires the stamp of approval from the Patriarchate.[1918] Without Armenian Patriarchate's approval conversion is not recognized and it also demands proof of sincerity of convert's claims for their act of conversion.[1919]

Legally, for the converts claiming Armenian ancestry does not establish belonging to the Armenian community; it requires baptism certificate from the church. To get acceptance for baptism application, a documentation as well as convincing the Patriarchate about the sincerity of conversion (which is very subjective) is required. The main document required is the certificate of civil registry (*vukuatli nufus kayit ornegi*). This document consists of the postulant's lineage on his or her father's side and details birth and death dates and places, as well as the religious affiliation of all of one's fore-parents born after 1831, when the first official census was conducted by the Ottoman Empire. After obtaining this document confirming the Armenian ancestry, converts need to pass a course organized by the clerics and after convincing the clerics about their intends of

1913 Özgül, "Legally Armenian" p. 629.
1914 Özgül, "From Muslim Citizen to Christian Minority," p. 13.
1915 Ibid, p. 189.
1916 Personal interview with Mr. Yetvart Danzikyan, chief editor of *Agos* newspaper, the interview was held in Istanbul on 19.02.2020.
1917 Personal interview with Mr. Sevan Degirmendjian, teacher, journalist, activist and the manager of member of Turkish Parliament Garo Paylan, the interview was held in Istanbul on 18.02.2020.
1918 Özgül, "From Muslim Citizen to Christian Minority," p. 110.
1919 Ibid, pp. 113-114.

conversion, they get baptized. In some cases, some applicants are being refused to get baptized because of their ideological or political views which might oppose the government.[1920]

In other words, the Patriarchate's control over baptism and thus its authority over the boundaries of Armenianness is a second layer of control after the registrar's office and the State legislative apparatus. Although the Patriarchate is reluctant to assume this role because the Turkish State denies the 1915 Genocide, today it administrates conversion appeals on the basis of an authority it no longer possesses, while its administration relies on official records and subjective/arbitrary decisions.

4.11.2.3 Name Change Cases

Many citizens claiming Armenian descent have submitted petitions to change their name.[1921] It is important for converted Armenians to adopt Armenian names, because it's part of their identity and a Muslim name might lead to the assumption that the Muslim name carrier is a Muslim. Changing one's name is a legal procedure[1922] which is a real challenge in the face of State reluctance to accept name change cases. In 2007, a plaintiff stated that although the civil registers (*kütükte*) recorded his name as Mehmet, he had converted to Christianity and wanted to take the Armenian name he had been given at his baptism, Agop, as his new first name. The lawyer argued that the plaintiff was born in an Armenian village in eastern provinces that converted to Islam.[1923]

However, the plaintiff converted from Islam to Christianity to return to his own religion. The court rejected Agop's request, but his petition was different from many regular name change cases.[1924] The lawyer challenged the court,

---

1920 Personal interview with Maître Arno Kalayci. lawyer, founding member of *Nor Zartonk* Foundation, the interview was held in Istanbul on 17.02.2020.

1921 Hans J. Trenz, "Reconciling Diversity and Unity - Language Minorities and European Integration," *Ethnicities,* 7:2 (2007), pp. 157-185.

1922 Name Change falls under the category of "*kayıtdüzeltme*" (corrections of the records) in Turkey's Civil Procedure Law. Any person over eighteen can adopt any name provided that he or she can demonstrate just cause. Applicants must demonstrate – with support from at least two witnesses – that they have already been known in public by the name they want to use and must vow to take on that name permanently. The name cannot be offensive (including racial slurs, for example). The court may also reject the applicant's petition on the basis of failure to provide just cause.

1923 Decision of the Beyoğlu Civil Court (3. Asliye Hukuk Mahkemesi), Esas No: 2007/106, Decision No: 2007/197.

1924 Ibid.

arguing that her client had not simply converted to Christianity but had converted *back* to Christianity. Thus, she reasoned, his case should be considered as a return to his original religion lost during State violence against Armenians. By defining religion as an element of ethnic belonging, the lawyer challenged the clear-cut boundaries between religious and ethnic identification. The court rejected the petition, citing failure to provide a just cause.[1925] The redefinition of religion for Armenian converts links religion to historical episodes of ethnic violence. Return converts indirectly also force the courts to recognize the 1915 Genocide.[1926]

Name-change cases bring up undesirable and illegal topics, including first and foremost the Armenian Genocide. Designated subjects of tolerance remain undesirable issues that defy the established limits for name-change.[1927] The emergence of Islamized Armenians triggers legally sanctioned resentment vis-à-vis Armenian claims regarding the fate of their ancestors. The conversion of Armenians back to their ancestors' religion therefore perceived as a threat to Turkish homogeneity. The fact that some Turkish Muslims are of Armenian or Christian origin worries nationalist decision makers. In 2006, the national security service (MIT) and the armed forces invoked the threat of Christian separatism and changes in identity within the population. MIT warned that the Christians' aimed to increase the Christian population to 10 % by 2020.[1928] The reality is different, however, by the end of 2020, the number of Christians in Turkey, continues to decrease.

4.11.2.4 Western Armenian: An Endangered Language

Today, Armenian speakers in Turkey are a minority within a minority. According to UNESCO Western Armenian is an endangered language.[1929] Armenians in Turkey feel historically connected to their language. According to Paylan: "You call yourself an Armenian because you feel it, but if you don't speak Armenian, if you don't speak your language, you lose your identity."[1930] The Armenian language may become less of a marker of identity, but speaking it still holds

1925 Ibid.

1926 Özgül, "Legally Armenian," p. 630.

1927 Özgül, "From Muslim Citizen to Christian Minority," p. 104.

1928 Hofmann, *One Nation*, p. 32.

1929 The official website of UNESCO, UNESCO Atlas of the World's Languages in Danger, 2020, http://www.unesco.org/languages-atlas/index.php.

1930 Gellman, Democratization and Memories of Violence, p. 118.

weight.[1931] In Istanbul, Armenian children speak Turkish on the street and daily interacting. Armenian is considered their grandparents' language.[1932] Armenian language teaching in Armenian schools is also declining rapidly and has become a 'textbook language' rather than an accepted means of communication.[1933]

There is no united strategy to address the decline of the Western Armenian Language. The dire situation of the Armenian language has come about because of State pressure. Meanwhile, there is a need for modernized Armenian Language and Literature textbooks at primary and secondary levels. Armenian language education suffers from a lack of learning materials, qualified teachers and money. Armenian schools must gain government approval for textbooks, drastically extending the timeline and cost for new material, as texts must be translated into Turkish for prior review.[1934] The government needs to remove this prohibition or streamline administration.

In addition, there is a lack of qualified teachers capable of teaching subjects in Armenian because Turkish universities have never offered subject-specific curriculum/programmes in the language.[1935] Another factor working against the use of Armenian is that for every Armenian language activity, texts must be translated into Turkish and then submitted for approval at district or province level.[1936] Moreover, the number of hours per week for teaching Armenian has reduced steadily since 1972 and is now only 5, one of which is dedicated to religion.[1937] The newspaper *Marmara* commented in January 2000: "The teaching of subject matters in Armenian is a right our schools enjoy. If all subjects are to be taught in Turkish, then what is the point of spending so much to maintain and preserve our Armenian schools?"[1938]

Language rights are on Armenian activist agendas as Armenian schools deteriorate and young Armenians leave school with low levels of fluency.[1939] The Armenian language, though still spoken, has suffered in the face of Turkification. Yet the language has its champions willing to pressure the State to support

1931 Ibid.
1932 Ibid.
1933 Özdoğan & Kılıçdağı, *Hearing Turkey's Armenians*, p. 41.
1934 Ibid.
1935 Gellman, Democratization and Memories of Violence, p. 117.
1936 Ibid.
1937 Personal interview with Ms. Silva Kouyoumdjian, principal of *Getronagan* Armenian High School Armenian in Istanbul, interview was held in Istanbul on 16.02.2020.
1938 Hofmann, *One Nation*, p. 27.
1939 Gellman, Democratization and Memories of Violence, p. 179.

its commitment to multiculturalism.[1940] The Hrant Dink Foundation aims to protect Western Armenian as a living language, transmitting it to new generations through teaching techniques adapted to a changing world, preparing new teaching materials and organizing seminars on Armenian history, culture and language.[1941]

In Turkey, language rights lie within a larger package of cultural rights that minority communities demand. Language is not the only way in which ethnic identity is preserved and passed on, but it has long been accepted as a key marker of culture.[1942] The loss of Armenian as a living language strikes at the core of Armenian identity.[1943] The preservation of Armenian identity – let alone new developments and cultural enrichment – has been difficult, and elements of Armenian identity have already been lost.

4.11.3 The Right to Equality and Non-discrimination

> "Turkish nationals belonging to non-Muslim minorities will enjoy the same civil and political rights as Muslims. All the inhabitants of Turkey, without distinction of religion, shall be equal before the law. Differences of religion, creed or confession shall not prejudice any Turkish national in matters relating to the enjoyment of civil or political rights, as, for instance, admission to public employments, functions and honours, or the exercise of professions and industries."[1944]

Despite the obligation under this international Treaty, the laws and policies of the Republican era have generally restricted the rights stipulated in the Treaty of Lausanne. There is a problem of inequality between religious and ethnic groups in Turkey, and discrimination occurs because of this situation. Turkish laws emphasize equality, but the problem lies in practice and the prevailing mentality.[1945] Inequality and discrimination are problematic for minority policy, and Turkish twentieth century history is marked by many instances of persecution and repression, displaying systematic discrimination towards Armenians in particular.

Discrimination by the State has been institutionalized and structured over the decades.[1946] A major source of discrimination against Armenians is the current

1940 Ibid, p. 128.
1941 Hrant Dink Foundation, Western Armenian Program, 2020, https://hrantdink.org/en/activities/projects/western-armenian-program/246-bati-ermenicesi-programi-2.
1942 Gellman, Democratization and Memories of Violence, p. 106.
1943 Ibid, p. 119.
1944 Article 39 of the Lausanne Treaty.
1945 Özdoğan & Kılıçdağı, *Hearing Turkey's Armenians*, p. 23.
1946 Tchilingirian, "The 'Other' Citizens," p. 153.

Constitution of the Republic, which does not recognize minorities and thus fails to protect and guarantee their rights.[1947] While in theory the Constitution promotes equality, the State has failed as a safeguard of cultural diversity.[1948] Instead, the Turkish culture and ethnicity have been imposed over other cultures, resulting in the elimination of cultures left unprotected.[1949] Meanwhile the media and some Muslim clerics also take a role in the establishment of the discriminatory language, using anti-Armenian expressions like "Do not befriend Christians" or "Do not do business with Armenians."[1950]

Research conducted by Bardakci et al. illustrates areas of discrimination in descending order. Armenians experienced discrimination in freedom of expression (69 %), history (65 %), education (60 %), the military (49 %), ethnicity (49 %), basic rights (46 %), culture (4 %), legal matters (41.5 %), state affairs (41.5 %), society (29 %), the press (28 %), television (23 %), professional life (14 %), and economic areas (12 %).[1951] All these areas directly affect minorities' cultural life and identity. There are many different reasons and pretexts for discrimination. Bardakci and his colleagues also asked about elements of minority group identity that provoke discrimination. Armenians cited Christianity (80 %), historical events (75 %), ethnic origin (71 %), Armenian language (48 %), Armenian culture (45 %), and the Muslims' social and economic fears (35 %).[1952]

Hence, the Republican regime has created conditions that directly discriminated minorities. The most important case of official discrimination was the so-called Wealth Tax (*Varlık Vergisi*) during WWII, that in practice targeted non-Muslim minority groups, including Armenians, with exorbitant rates levied on them to Turkify wealth and capital in Turkey.[1953] In addition, the State directly discriminated against Armenian community foundations. The primary threat to community foundations is the seizure of their properties within the framework of the Foundations Law and the fact that 'foreign' legal entities cannot own immovable properties. Armenian community foundations have had to fight Turkey

---

1947 Özdoğan & Kılıçdağı, *Hearing Turkey's Armenians*, p. 30.

1948 CESCR, "The Right to Take Part in Cultural Life: Comments / Submitted by the International Labour Organization," 09.05.2008, UN Doc. E/C. 12/40/12, para. 2.

1949 Bayir, Minorities and Nationalism, p. 13.

1950 Özdoğan & Kılıçdağı, *Hearing Turkey's Armenians*, p. 31.

1951 Bardakci et al., Religious Minorities in Turkey, p. 212.

1952 Ibid.

1953 John M. Vander Lippe, *The Politics of Turkish Democracy: Ismet Inonu and the Formation of the Multi-Party System, 1938-1950* (New York: State University New York Press, 2005), pp. 83-85.

in courts for return of seized immovable, and this struggle has continued in recent years at the ECtHR.[1954]

Meanwhile, non-Muslim religious groups do not enjoy the same status or the same rights as Sunni Muslims. Turkish Christians pay the same taxes as Turkey's Muslim citizens, but the State excludes Christian communities from tax-funded initiatives that are accessible to Muslims. This support enables Sunnis to build and run mosques with the State paying for repairs and personnel. Muslim cultural or charitable organizations, institutions, activities, projects, and publications are also funded or co-funded by the State.[1955] For instance, the State provides training for Muslim clerics while restricting other religious groups from training clerics within Turkey.[1956] Another example of inequality is illustrated by Sevan: "As a citizen I pay taxes. When I die, I will have to pay the church for my funeral, while other citizens' funerals are organized by the municipality free of charge. This is inequality."[1957]

Armenians are exposed to rights violations and subject to practices that violate the understanding of positive rights protecting non-Muslim minorities. The existence of the secret Minorities Sub-Commission (*Azınlıklar Tali Komisyonu*) for decades shows that minority communities are seen as threats to national security. The rearrangement of this commission as the Minority Issues Review Board (*Azınlık Sorunları Değerlendirme Kurulu*) in 2004 may be considered a positive development, but the Board ironically has no Armenian representatives.

Last but not least, In Article 4 of the Law on Civil Servants dated 1925, being ethnically Turkish was stipulated as a condition for eligibility for recruitment as a public employee.[1958] Although the Law on Civil Servants adopted in 1965 changed the stipulation to "being a citizen of the Republic of Turkey" and although there are no provisions preventing the Armenians or other non-Muslims from becoming civil servants, it is not possible to see a non-Muslim in the middle and top tier of the bureaucracy. "You might be elected, but very rarely appointed as civil servant, if you are an Armenian, you even cannot become a street cleaner

1954 Özdoğan & Kılıçdağı, *Hearing Turkey's Armenians*, p. 86.

1955 Bardakci et al., Religious Minorities in Turkey, p. 161.

1956 US Department of State, "2016 Report on International Religious Freedom -Turkey," 15.08.2017, https://www.refworld.org/docid/59b7d82a13.html.

1957 Personal interview with Mr. Sevan Degirmendjian, teacher, journalist, activist and the manager of member of Turkish Parliament Garo Paylan, the interview was held in Istanbul on 18.02.2020.

1958 Özdoğan & Kılıçdağı, *Hearing Turkey's Armenians*, p. 26.

employed by the municipality," says Seropian.[1959] Civil servant recruitment is seen by Armenians as discriminatory,[1960] and thus as an indication of inequality, violating the Treaty of Lausanne (Article 29(2)).[1961]

When it comes to equality and non-discrimination in Armenian schools and education, one problem is the State appointment of vice-principals at Armenian schools, who are identified as 'Turkish' vice-principals, an emphasis that reflects the State's view of Armenian institutions. Both vice-principals and teachers who teach Turkish subjects are appointed by the MoE from staff with a 'national consciousness' and 'national sentiments'.[1962] These are breaches of the Treaty of Lausanne's minority protection clauses. In other words, the appointment of vice-principals and teachers somehow shows that Armenians are not seen as full citizens and that they must be put under the charge of a 'pure Turk'.[1963]

In this context, it is also important to highlight another discriminatory restriction - that lasted for decades and just eased recently - related to the enrolment process to Armenian schools. If 'legal' Armenian parents do not baptise their children, they cannot enrol their kids in Armenian schools. This is not acceptable, since being Armenian does not necessarily and automatically mean to be a Christian faithful believer. If someone is not practicing Christianity or any religion, then they should not have to pretend to be practicing in order to register their kids at a particular school.[1964]

Another example of discriminatory practices towards Armenians is the need for authorization to organize Armenian cultural events – a process that is not required for other non-Turkish language activities – for example English cultural activities. This is an indication of how the State regards the Armenians and the Armenian language.[1965] Moreover, the security and education authorities

---

1959 Personal interview with Mr. Vagharshag Seropian, secretary at the Armenian Patriarchate in Istanbul, interview was held in Istanbul, on 15.02.2020.

1960 Özdoğan & Kılıçdağı, *Hearing Turkey's Armenians*, p. 27.

1961 Hofmann, Armenians in Turkey Today, p. 31.

1962 Mehmet Deri, *Türkiye'de Azınlıklar ve Azınlık Okulları: Rum-Yahudi Ve Ermeni Cemaatleri* (Minorities and Minority Schools in Turkey: Greek-Jewish and Armenian communities) (Istanbul: IQ Kültür Sanat Yayıncılık, 2009), pp. 169–171.

1963 Özdoğan & Kılıçdağı, *Hearing Turkey's Armenians*, p. 39.

1964 Personal interview with Mr. Sevan Degirmendjian, teacher, journalist, activist and the manager of member of Turkish Parliament Garo Paylan, the interview was held in Istanbul on 18.02.2020.

1965 Personal interview with Ms. Silva Kouyoumdjian, principal of *Getronagan* Armenian High School Armenian in Istanbul, the interview was held in Istanbul on 16.02.2020.

prohibit any child not recognized as 'legally' Armenian from attending Armenian schools. On the other hand, the High School Placement System, introduced in 2018, contains 10 questions related to 'Religious Culture and Ethics' courses. Students registered in minority schools answer alternative questions, but minority students who are not enrolled in minority schools are not given these alternative questions. Their scores are calculated using exam performance on other courses. Despite complaints from parents that this creates an unfair situation, the MoE has not changed the evaluation criteria.[1966]

In the Military, Armenians are often subject to discriminatory and degrading treatment from fellow soldiers and from superiors during their military service. "They are insulted as 'infidels' or as 'dirty Christian pigs who won't even let themselves be circumcised'."[1967] Armenians also experience discrimination at the social level. Armenian names often evoke confusion, questions about origin, and stigmatization, and Armenians often adopt an additional Turkish name to use in social interactions.[1968]

4.11.3.1 Coding Minorities

> "We are coded. We are stigmatized and blacklisted. And our records are secretly kept and saved."[1969]

In 2013, a news story became topical in Turkey's agenda.[1970] A lady with Turkish citizenship wanted to return to the religious and ethnic identity of that her parents and ancestors. She fulfilled all the religious requirements, was baptized in accordance with Armenian Church creeds and revealed her religious and ethnic identity. She applied to the Civil Registry Office to change the religion on the back of her ID card, asking for Christianity to be written there instead. Later she went to enrol her child in an Armenian nursery school, but the school asked for supporting documentation in the form of a certificate of approval issued by the MoE. The Provincial Directorate of National Education in Istanbul issued the

1966 "Pursuing Rights and Equality Monitoring Report on the Right to Freedom of Religion or Belief in Turkey," Norwegian Helsinki Committee Freedom of Belief Initiative, 2019 Report, p. 38, https://bit.ly/3amAKQi.

1967 Hofmann, *Armenians in Turkey*, p. 31.

1968 Rumelili & Keyman "Enacting multi-layered citizenship," p. 72.

1969 Bulut, Minorities in Constitution Making in Turkey.

1970 "Minorities in Turkey Tagged by 'race codes,' Official Document Reveals," *Hürriyet Daily News*, 01.08.2013, https://bit.ly/3uAZzyi

document to the family's lawyer of that he would present it to the District Directorate of National Education in Sisli. The document commented that:

> "As per the referenced Law (No 5580, the Law on Private Educational Institutions), these schools are founded by the Greek, Armenian or Jewish minorities and guaranteed by the Treaty of Lausanne. And only students with Turkish citizenship from their particular communities are allowed to attend these schools."[1971]

The same Law states that it is obligatory for these schools to accept only the Turkish citizens, so the school needs to know whether either of the student's parents has changed his or her religion, name or sect. The confidential ethnic code is stored in the identity register, which has been in use since 1923. The ethnic code for Armenian citizens is 2, and as long as that code is '2' on the official record of the identity register for both parents, the school will accept the student.[1972]

Thanks to this document, it was revealed that ethnic codes were being used confidentially in the official identity register and citizens were being stigmatized and blacklisted. Although this was confirmed officially for the first time, no one was surprised. Ethnic codes are used for non-Muslim citizens, each of whom is given a code in their civil registry records. It would be hasty to conclude that Muslims are exempt from this coding practice. As this story shows, the lady with the Armenian ethnic background had an ID card, on the back of which "Islam" was written, before it was changed to Christianity.[1973]

According to the information given, there are five different ethnic codes. The ethnic codes of Greeks, Armenians, Jews, Assyrians and Others are 1, 2, 3, 4 and 5, respectively.[1974] When a citizen with a Greek ethnic background comes to the Turkish Civil Registry Office, he is coded as Code 1 without his knowledge or approval. Even if he changes his religion and name, his code remains, playing a crucial determining role in school enrolment procedures, scholarship decisions, military service or applications for a position in a government agency.[1975] The coding practice has no legal basis or support, which mean it is neither legal nor fair. according to Oran, "it is a code to eradicate the non-Muslim citizens. Even giving that number is an act of infringement."[1976] Moreover, the confidential

1971 Bulut, Minorities in Constitution Making in Turkey, Preamble.

1972 Ibid.

1973 Ibid.

1974 Orhan Kemal Cengiz, "Turkey's Secret 'Ancestry Codes' Track Non-Muslim Minorities," *Al-Monitor Turkey Pulse,* 08.082013, https://bit.ly/3shSW4b.

1975 Bulut, Minorities in Constitution Making in Turkey, Preamble.

1976 Ibid.

nature of coding practice makes it appear even more underhand. As a former deputy of the Peace and Democracy Party (BDP) Altan Tan reacts "The State illegally profiling its own citizens based on ethnicity and religion, and doing this secretly, is a big catastrophe."[1977]

Inequality and Discriminatory minority policies prove that equal citizenship rights for non-Muslims in Turkey are being violated. This indicates that non-Muslims have not been accepted as equal citizens. On paper, Turkey has taken steps to fight discrimination and ensure equality, in practice it remains far behind internationally accepted equality and non-discrimination standards.

4.11.4 The Right to Participation

Feelings of detachment or dissatisfaction with wider society may lead to lesser or greater participation, in turn affecting minority rights.[1978] Democratic regimes should provide an environment in which everyone has equal representation and equal access to political, economic and cultural rights.

In Turkey, the right to participate in cultural life has been interpreted as general participation in national culture, which for decades has meant Turkish culture, which has become the core of relevant official, political and legal issues.[1979] Armenians in Turkey, by contrast, generally exhibit low levels of mobilization for participating in the political, legal and social life of the State. Concerns that mobilization for their cultural rights would bring swift State repression have been passed down through generations and have had a paralyzing effect on Armenian culture and expression.[1980]

The fear of State persecution disincentivizes people from participation. As Gellman attests, fear of visibility, stemming from remembered persecution impedes the creation of civil society.[1981] Faced by various forms of discrimination, Armenians have dissociated their cultural and communal lives from the wider Turkish society,[1982] leading many Armenians to adopt strategic approaches to avoid discrimination, remaining inconspicuous, quiet and outwardly integrated

1977 "Minorities in Turkey Tagged by 'race codes,' Official Document Reveals," *Hürriyet* Daily News, 01.08.2013.

1978 Melissa Nobles, *The Politics of Official Apologies* (New York: Cambridge University Press, 2008), p. 36.

1979 Bayir, Minorities and Nationalism, p. 12.

1980 Gellman, Democratization and Memories of Violence, p. 7.

1981 Ibid, p. 100.

1982 Rumelili & Keyman, "Enacting multi-layered citizenship," p. 72.

(not to say assimilated) into mainstream society. The continued persecution of the Armenian community reinforces the idea that it is better to blend into Turkish society than it is to stand out as Armenian.[1983]

When it comes to participation, Armenians fall into two groups. Integrationists see the resolution of community problems in the context of Turkey's larger democratic project, viewing themselves as agents of democracy rather than representatives of an ethnic community. According to Paylan: "We are radical democrats, and we have everyone sitting at our table. This is why we have to struggle for LGBT rights, for the Armenians, the Kurds, and the Alevis. We have to offer equality to every identity."[1984] Here is where the second group diverge. Isolationists believe that the carrying out a 'democratic project' in Turkey by members of a minority group is unrealistic and exposes the community to a nationalist backlash with lethal consequences.

4.11.4.1 Political Participation

Historically, since the establishment of the Republic of Turkey, Turkish elites never recognized the right of Armenians to articulate political demands, to voice its distinct political identity or to participate in any political process.[1985] Even today, Armenians as minority group have no civil and political representation.

On individual basis, there has been some progress for Armenian individuals for political participation in Turkey, reflected in the election of MPs from minority backgrounds including the Armenian, Roma, Syriac and Yezidi communities in June and November 2015. In the 2015 parliamentary elections each of HDP, CHP, and AKP included an ethnically Armenians in their electoral list and for the first time Armenians have been elected in the Turkish Parliament since 1961.[1986] In addition, in local elections, Armenians become candidates, but they are often not supported by the larger Armenian community.[1987] Instead it is their own personal initiative. Armenians as a community do not mobilize themselves to nominate candidates or to participate in political life. Even when they do

1983 Gellman, Democratization and Memories of Violence, p. 127.

1984 Nanore Barsoumian, "The Road Ahead: An Interview with Garo Paylan," *The Armenian Weekly*, 01.07.2015. http://armenianweekly.com/2015/07/01/the-road-ahead.

1985 Cheterian, *Open Wounds: Armenians*, pp. 36-37.

1986 Bardakci et al., Religious Minorities in Turkey, p. 157.

1987 Personal Interview with Ms. Celina Doğan, former member of Turkish Parliament, current member of Shishli Municipality Council in Istanbul, the interview was held in Istanbul on 18.02.2020.

participate, there is no legal guarantee that minorities will be represented in government bodies, and when the State notices that candidates are not supported by their community, it feels no obligation to consider them or include them in the decision-making processes.[1988]

With three Armenian MPs among their ranks, Armenian integrationists attempted to shift the focus of the discourse from 'narrow' parochial issues to larger issues of democratization in Turkey. Rumelili and Keyman suggest that "by locating demands for equal national citizenship at the centre of their negotiation of minority and national citizenship rights, Turkey's Armenians are making significant contributions to the democratization and pluralization of Turkish politics."[1989]

In addition, because of the limitations of the TPC, the struggle for Genocide recognition had been somehow replaced by the community's participation in the all-Turkish movement for civil rights, in which human and civil rights advocates from the middle and younger generations of Armenians are active.[1990] Younger Armenians see themselves as being in a position to teach their Turkish compatriots historical truths, and the search for roots and ethnic identities is a hot topic in Turkey.[1991]

But there is a price for such contributions, which generally does not figure in the discourse of liberal and progressive circles who support and benefit from such contributions. The costs to Armenians have ranged from coercive measures to lethal consequences. Meanwhile, the isolationists struggle – through perennial petitions to the government and State agencies or legal action where possible – to maintain what little has been left to the Armenian minority.[1992]

In this context, the historical evidence shows that Turkey's citizenship policies were civic republican. The citizenship law of 1928 gave citizenship to those residing in the Republic, but citizens' rights have become ethno-cultural, as ethnic groups develop various participation strategies based on the legal and political structure and its limitations. Turkish Armenians once hesitated to seek legal remedies or apply to State institutions for their grievances. Their experiences showed them that such attempts will not yield positive results. As much as

1988 Ibid.
1989 Rumelili & Keyman, "Enacting multi-layered citizenship," p. 80.
1990 Hofmann, *One Nation*, p. 100.
1991 Ibid, p. 81.
1992 Tchilingirian, "The 'Other' Citizens," p. 152.

possible, they want to settle their affairs without legal recourse, so they ignore the rights violations they occasionally encounter.[1993]

In a 2007 survey conducted by predominantly young Armenians of '*Nor Zartonk*',[1994] 97.6 % of Armenian participants said they were not active in politics, while and 97.4 % said they did not belong to any political party in Turkey.[1995] Meanwhile, those who are involved in politics have diverse ideological views. A number of Armenians support the CHP's secular and republican credentials and fear that the country's society might become even more dominated by Islam under the AKP. In contrast, the AKP is supported by a different group of Armenians due to the economic successes achieved under its leadership and its neoliberal orientation. These Armenians object to the CHP's past and the hostility towards minorities expressed by its radically nationalist wing. Noting the AKP's gradual policy shift, Armenians have started to turn away from the party in recent years. Following political developments since 2015, the AKP has lost a significant part of its supporters within the Armenian community. Since its foundation, the HDP, dominated by Kurdish activists but uniting the political left and ethnic and religious social minority groups, has become an alternative political force for Armenian voters.[1996]

For Armenians, there are rigid controls on who can speak on behalf of the community. The most influential actor is the Patriarchate, an autonomous actor that represents a conservative force with values that are not in line with many younger Armenian activists. Although State officials prefer the position of the Patriarch in relations with the Armenian society and in official protocol, the representational power and responsibility of the Patriarch has come under closer scrutiny in recent years.[1997] Today, various views have emerged as to whether the Patriarch should remain only a religious leader or whether he should also act as the Head of the nation *(milletbaşı)* representing Armenian civil society. The Patriarch is the religious leader of only the Apostolic Armenians, and civil representation would not be acceptable to different denominations or those who

1993 Özdoğan & Kılıçdağı, *Hearing Turkey's Armenians*, p. 29.

1994 By 2020 the case may have improved slightly, but as there are no available data, 2007 data are used here.

1995 "'Being a Minority in Turkey' Survey Results in English," *Nor Zartonk* Foundation, 2007, https://bit.ly/3sPSKbH.

1996 Bardakci et al., Religious Minorities in Turkey, p. 157.

1997 Ibid.

are Muslims or atheists. Being Armenian is not based solely on religion and denomination.

There is a lack of representation for non-Muslims in general and Armenians in particular in a variety of State institutions. It is rare[1998] to see Armenians involved at State institutional level.' Even the Minority Issues Review Committee[1999] (*Azınlık Sorunları Değerlendirme Kurulu*) does not conform to democratic norms as it does not include members from non-Muslim communities.[2000] It is not possible to accept such a result in contemporary participatory democracies.

In any case, as Mneesha argues, reminding the Turkish State of the wrongs they have done gives communities more power than before in the decision-making process. This form of cultural resilience affects local, national and international political participation, and offers the promise that minority citizens need not continue to be marginalized.[2001] The resistance in and partial return of Kamp Armen, an orphanage originally belonging to the Gedikpaşa Armenian Protestant Church is a good example. With its 'Let Kamp Armen be returned to the Armenian people' slogan, the movement was led by '*Nor Zartonk*', an activist group of Istanbul youths mostly comprised of Armenians. After weeks of protests to get the owner to return the grounds over to the Armenian church, Armenian youth occupied the space.[2002] During the six months of resistance in 2015, the group's visibility increased in the Turkish political arena and the Armenian diaspora.[2003] Armenians were encouraged to become more involved in the struggle for democracy and Human Rights in Turkey. This includes taking part in dialogue with political parties and fighting for rights and freedoms in Turkey.

1998 For example, Etyen Mahcupyan, a well-known ethnic Armenian writer, was appointed as chief adviser to Prime Minister Ahmet Davutoğlu. See "Etyen Mahçupyan appointed Turkish PM's Senior Advisor," *Armenpress*, 25.10.2014, https://bit.ly/389GcDq.

1999 Established on 5.1.2004 by Prime Ministerial Order No. 3530.

2000 Özdoğan & Kılıçdağı, *Hearing Turkey's Armenians*, p. 18.

2001 Gellman, Democratization and Memories of Violence, p. 202.

2002 Hrag Papazian, "Between Gezi Park and Kamp Armen: The Intersectional Activism of Leftist Armenian Youths in Istanbul," *Turkish Studies*, 18:1 (2017), p. 57.

2003 Ibid.

4.11.4.2 Economic Participation

Historically, Armenians along with Greek and Jews minorities, participated effectively in rapidly expanding sectors of the economy of the Ottoman Empire, for instance in banking, foreign trade with the west, finance. They were also prominent professionals such as medical doctors, pharmacists, engineers and lawyers.[2004] However the Young Turk regime as well as the Republicans, aimed at forming a national Turkish Muslim businessmen class at the expense of the non-Muslim minorities by pursuing economic and demographic Turkification policies. For example, wealth taxes were used to dominate Armenian business owners. Despite these policies, relatively speaking, the economic situation for most Armenians in Turkey is far better than their situation within the political, legal and administrative sectors.[2005] Economically, Armenians are comparatively well-off. Armenians in Istanbul are now members of the middle and business classes and have higher levels of material security than many other minority groups in Turkey.

Despite the history of financial discrimination against minorities, Armenians and particularly Armenian foundations inhabit a robust economic niche that they do not want to lose by challenging the State.[2006] Nevertheless, their right to participate in the economic life of the State has often threatened by either State led discriminatory policies or anti-Armenian campaigns in 1990s when Armenian industrialists and members of Trade associations received anonymous faxed letters demanding: "Don't do business with Jews and Armenians!."[2007]

4.11.4.3 Social Participation

What really mattered in Lausanne Treaty was that socioeconomic participation in internal minority issues through guaranteeing minority rights were guaranteed.[2008] Meanwhile, rights of participation in the broader society were often seen as a 'Trojan Horse', aimed at assimilating minority identities.[2009] Civil society in Turkey was historically weak due to state-centric ideology that granted the State a sovereign role in society and prioritizing collective interests over

---

2004 Eligür, "Ethnocultural nationalism and Turkey's non-Muslim minorities," p. 2.
2005 Bardakci et al., Religious Minorities in Turkey, p. 158.
2006 Gellman, Democratization and Memories of Violence, p. 121.
2007 Hofmann, Armenians in Turkey Today, p. 20.
2008 Konstantinos Tsitselikis, "A Surviving Treaty," p. 294.
2009 Ibid.

the individual.[2010] During the 1990s, the number and activities of civil society organizations grew due to various dynamics, such as the increasing impact of globalization.[2011] More recently, Armenians have put a great deal of effort into increasing their level of social participation. For example, as a response to President Erdogan's call to support a campaign to address COVID-19, the Armenian Patriarch donated his last 5 salaries,[2012] and the Armenian Foundations Union donated 500 000 Turkish Lira to fighting the virus.[2013]

Dialogue about memory is a tool that can expand participation for citizens. For Armenians, such dialogue plays a role in the reassertion of non-Turkish identity as a fundamental right of Turkish citizenship. The political elite, Turkish and Armenian intellectuals and civil society organizations were persuaded to open public discussion on taboo issues involving the Genocide, Armenian minority rights, Armenian-Turkish diplomatic relations and the impact of the Armenian diaspora.[2014] New spaces of historical knowledge are constantly being created in Turkey. In 2005, an academic conference on the 1915 events brought together an array of social scientists and historians to discuss the effect of 1915 and ethnic pluralism on Turkey's democratization.[2015] These and other sites of historical memory show that although Armenian memories of violence have not yet produced robust narratives, they may yet find new avenues of expression. Today, Aras Publishing and the Hrant Dink Foundation are two leading organizations working to remedy the lack of knowledge on Armenian society. The State can, through the Ministry of Culture, support institutions that are promoting Armenian history and culture.

In realistic terms, dialogue within select communities will not in itself change political behavior. A wide swathe of Turkish society exists outside the dialogue, opposing it. The claim here is more subtle – that dialogue serves as a window through which Armenians can see other ways of conducting relationships with each other. As Gellman argues, dialogue is the first step to engaging alternative ontologies.[2016] Strikingly, the debates on the Genocide at State and society

---

2010 Grigoriadis, Ioannis. N, Trials of Europeanization Turkish Political Culture and the European Union (New York: Palgrave Macmillan, 2009), p. 44.

2011 Ibid, pp. 46-50.

2012 *Jamanag* newspaper, 01.01.2020, https://bit.ly/3afMCQs.

2013 Özgür Altuncu, "*'Biz bize yeteriz Türkiyem' dediler,*" (We are enough for us my Turkey they said,) *Hurriyet*, 05.04.2020, https://www.hurriyet.com.tr/ekonomi/biz-bize-yeteriz-turkiyem-dediler-41486631.

2014 Kaya and Harmanyeri, Tolerance and Cultural Diversity, p. 24.

2015 Gellman, *Remembering violence*, p. 787.

2016 Ibid, p. 777.

levels have been good examples of the rising tolerance for Armenian ethnic and cultural rights. One such case was the controversial conference on 'Ottoman Armenians during the Demise of the Empire' held at Istanbul Bilgi University in. Despite protests, the conference became a good indicator of eradicating biased views on Armenian issues.[2017]

It seems there are still huge gaps to fill to move beyond tolerance and build social relationships based on human rights, citizenship, equality and non-discrimination. To achieve socio-economic participation, the antipathy between civic citizenship and ethnic origin should be reduced through compromise between the two poles of loyalty to the nation and devotion to the State.[2018] The participation of citizens in the democratic process is achieved through belonging to associations which can pursue common objectives collectively.[2019] Armenian society should explain its views and their basis to society and should listen to the other social groups which face similar problems of discrimination. The fear of losing social achievements and their high economic status encourages most of Istanbul's Armenians – even in the context of the social and political liberalization processes in the 2000s – to retain their strategic behavior and avoid ethno-cultural or ethno-political activities or demands.[2020] In this context, Armenians in Istanbul show high rates of assimilation and low rates of mobilization for cultural rights. They have clung to institutional guarantees from the Lausanne Treaty and rely on elite bargaining through the Patriarchate. However, Armenians have recently become more vocal in protesting their repression.[2021]

Finally, the generation gap and participation challenges become more evident within Armenian foundations. One side is formed by established officials, mostly elderly men who are conservative and pro-government. The other comprises younger members of the community, who insist on deeper reforms and more democracy within the church and foundations. They accuse the established elites of being unclear, power-obsessed, authoritarian, and of not doing enough to preserve Armenian culture, language and identity[2022]

2017 See Ayhan Kaya, "Turkey-EU Relations: The Impact of Islam on Europe," in *Yearbook of Muslims in Europe*, Jorgen Nielsen, Samim Akgönül, Ahmet Alibašic, Brigitte Maréchal, & Christian Moe eds., Vol. 1 (Leiden: Brill, 2009), pp. 384-386.

2018 Tsitselikis, "A Surviving Treaty," p. 308.

2019 See Guide on Article 11 of the European Convention on Human Rights, Freedom of assembly and association, CoE, 31.05.2020, para.107.

2020 Bardakci et al., Religious Minorities in Turkey, p. 155.

2021 Gellman, Democratization and Memories of Violence, p. 188.

2022 Bardakci et al., Religious Minorities in Turkey, p. 153.

4.12 The Turkish State's Obligations towards Armenian Minority Rights

Turkey's obligations and duties under international law to respect, protect and fulfill human rights also include minority rights.[2023] Turkey's obligation to respect and not interfere to the enjoyment of Armenians' rights in Turkey, its obligation to protect Armenian individuals and groups against human and minority rights abuses or violations as well as its positive action to facilitate the enjoyment of basic human and minority rights will be the focus of this section's examinations.

4.12.1 Respecting the Rights of Armenian Minority in Turkey

> "To see such a small minority as a threat means they don't have self-confidence. If you have self-confidence, why should you be afraid of a 0.1 percent minority?" Dikran Altun[2024]

From the minority perspective, the right to enjoy their own identity and culture, to use and be educated in their ethnic language, the right to religion, the preservation of their community assets and properties and opportunities for cultural production are seen as a litmus test for their collective rights. But for Turkey, the administration of language, religion, education, and culture has been yet another instrument of homogenization.[2025] ECRI recommended that the authorities respect impartiality in regulating religion, abolish discriminatory regulations and implement ECtHR rulings.[2026]

According to minorities law expert Murat Cano, in 1930s a security unit consisting of representatives from the General Directorate, the Ministry of Interior, the Intelligence Office and the foreign ministry was established, the function of which was to monitor the activities of minorities, especially Greeks and Armenians. It set out policies regarding minority communities' properties and controlled how much property minorities had and supervised their commercial

2023 UNOHCHR Official Page, International Human Rights Law, 2019, https://bit.ly/3gyycQu.

2024 Thomas De Waal, Great Catastrophe: Armenians and Turks in the Shadow of Genocide (Oxford: OUP, 2015), p. 251.

2025 Tchilingirian, "The 'Other' Citizens," pp. 126-127.

2026 Human Rights Council, "Summary of Stakeholders' submissions on Turkey Report of the Office of the United Nations High Commissioner for Human Rights," UN Doc. A/HRC/WG.6/35/TUR/3 para. 32.

transactions. In addition, to observe the activities of minorities, the Sub Commission of Minorities was founded by secret governmental decree in 1962.

In other words, the entire apparatus of the Turkish State is involved in running the affairs of minorities – in this case the Armenian community, which constitutes less than 0.1 % of the population. Institutions involved include the President's office, the Ministries of Interior, Justice, Culture, National Education and the Foreign Ministry, the National Intelligence Agency (MIT), military intelligence agencies, the national and Istanbul police agencies and scores of local government bodies. As Hrant Dink once said: "It is difficult to understand why every time a member of a minority has contact with a State agency, they come face-to-face with security forces, that is to say, with the police."[2027] However, there are some good practices recently put into action by the Turkish government in terms of respecting the rights of the Armenians in Turkey.

4.12.1.1 Good Practices

Recently, the government has dropped its mandatory 'verification of identity' to determine students' eligibility for Armenian schools. Under a new law (June 28, 2015) eligibility is decided by school principals, who are then responsible for registering a student. The MoE also simplified enrolment in minority schools. Students can now attend minority schools through a parental declaration and the school's consent.

Apart from insisting that all members of leadership bodies are Turkish citizens, the government no longer interferes in appointments below the level of the head of the religious community.[2028] Another important development is the removal of religious notation from the new chip-enabled national identity cards. However, the information contained in the chip does include a field for religion, and people can record their religion in this field if they wish. The Directorate of the Office of Identity Cards stated that information related to belief is considered sensitive and protected under Personal Data Protection Law[2029] – although

2027 Hrant Dink, "The Taste of Being a Minority" *in Contrasts and Solutions in the Caucasus*, Ole Høiris & Sefa Martin Yürükel eds. (Aarhus-Oakville: Aarhus University Press, 1998), p. 439.

2028 Mine Yildirim, "Turkey: Why State Interference in the Election of Chief Rabbi, Greek Orthodox and Armenian Patriarchs?," Forum 18, 11.08.2010, http://www.forum18.org/archive.php?article_id=1477).

2029 The Law No. 6698 on the Protection of Personal Data was published in the Official Gazette on 7 April 2016 and numbered 29677.

certain institutions can access this information. The information can in some circumstances still make people vulnerable to discrimination.[2030] On the other hand, the following sub-sections discuss the main areas where the government interferes and disrespect the rights of Armenians in Turkey.

4.12.1.2 Interference and Disrespect of Armenian Rights in Turkey

According to State law, only Armenian children could attend Armenian Schools, but they had to observe Muslim national holidays as well as their own.[2031] Turkey has not yet established an educational system that respects children's freedom of thought, religion and conscience or parents' right to raise their children in line with their religious views. Despite judgments by the ECtHR regarding mandatory 'Religious Culture and Ethics' courses, elective religion courses do not reflect Turkey's diversity. As schools offer packages containing religion courses, many students have to take elective religion courses they would not otherwise choose.[2032] In 1937, the MoE decided to appoint vice-principals to supervise administrative and financial transactions in minority schools.[2033] Law No.6581 in 1955[2034] specified that "Turkish[language] and Turkish Culture lessons" be taught by Ministry-appointed teachers.[2035] Currently, the vice principal position causes a duality in which culture course teachers led by the vice-principal, and contract-based teachers led by the Armenian principal are two separate groups. Recently, the State appointed teachers and sometimes vice principals are among those who the Armenian schools propose. These people mainly come from minority backgrounds.[2036]

In addition, State does not allow teaching Armenian history at Armenian schools and obliges to teach other subjects except Armenian language and Religion in Turkish. Armenian textbooks require translation into Turkish for official approval.

2030 Human Rights Council, "Summary of Stakeholders' submissions on Turkey Report of the Office of the United Nations High Commissioner for Human Rights," UN Doc. A/HRC/WG.6/35/TUR/3 12.11.2019, para.31.

2031 Ekmekcioğlu, *Recovering Armenia*, p. 125.

2032 "Pursuing Rights and Equality," Monitoring Report on the Right to Freedom of Religion or Belief in Turkey 2019, pp. 5-38.

2033 The practice was abandoned in the 1948-1949 school year but reintroduced in 1962.

2034 Law No. 6581 "Turkish and Turkish Culture Teachers at Minority Schools" adopted in 27.05.1955.

2035 While culture course teachers that are assigned by the State work as civil servants, other teachers work as employees of a private institution.

2036 Personal interview with Ms. Silva Kouyoumdjian, principal of *Getronagan* Armenian High School Armenian in Istanbul, the interview was held in Istanbul on 16.02.2020.

Moreover, almost all activities initiated by Armenian schools need State approval. Even the principal to one of the Armenian schools had to get a permission from the State to conduct an interview regarding this thesis.

Turkey's authorities do not respect the State's duty to neutrality and impartiality in religious matters, resulting in structural discrimination against religious minority groups,[2037] in particular issues relating to funding, places of worship and religious education. Nevertheless, Freedom of worship continues to be generally respected, although the Venice Commission recommendations on the community status of religions in Turkey have yet to be implemented.[2038] Requests by Christian communities to open places of worship and training for clergy remain pending. Hate speech and crimes against Christians and Jews continue.[2039]

The right to religious freedom encompasses the expectation that believers can associate without State intervention. The State is not allowed to determine whether beliefs or their expression are legitimate.[2040] USCIRF charges Turkey with interfering in minority religions, highlighting 'societal discrimination', violence, restrictions on attire, anti-Semitism and infringement on the property rights of religious minorities. Religious minorities are targeted because most religious and ethnic minorities are viewed with suspicion by some ethnic Turks. In Istanbul until 2020, repairs to Armenian structures required government permission, which was not always granted. Rebuilding is not tolerated, and church and community property is often sequestered by invoking the right of eminent domain.[2041]

With regards to freedom of expression slight changes were made in 2008 as part of the EU accession process, in particular regarding the Minister of Justice's authorization before judicial proceedings to trigger Article 301 of TPC. Although the later continues to be used[2042] against those the State perceives as 'traitors'. During times

---

2037 ECRI, "Report on Turkey, Fifth Monitoring Cycle" ECRI Secretariat Directorate General II - Democracy, CoE, 2016, para.a.89-90.

2038 Opinion on the Legal Status of Religious Communities in Turkey and the Right of the Orthodox Patriarchate of Istanbul to use the adjective "Ecumenical" adopted by the Venice Commission at its 82nd Plenary Session (Venice, 12-13.03.2010), p. 15.

2039 European Commission, Progress Report on Turkey, SWD (2019) 220, p. 31.

2040 Guide on Article 11 of the European Convention on Human Rights, Freedom of Assembly and Association, First edition – 31.12.2019, para. 201.

2041 Dickran Kouymjian, "When Does Genocide End? The Armenian Case," presented at Sonoma State University 11.03.2003 p. 11., https://bit.ly/38bcNJ3.

2042 Well-known figures charged under Article 301 include Nobel Prize-winning author Orhan Pamuk; author and activist Elif Şafak and murdered Turkish-Armenian journalist Hrant Dink.

of crisis, religious leaders of the Greek and Armenian communities are expected to publicly declare loyalty to the State, and to condemn foreign governments and legislatures of States or institutions who recall past and present persecution of non-Muslims in Turkey.[2043] Associations must use Turkish in their correspondence with State institutions, as well as in their internal records.[2044]

Another area of interference is related to foundation properties. Article 40 of Lausanne Treaty gives non-Muslim minorities the right "to enjoy security in law like other Turkish nationals, equal rights to establish, manage and control any charitable, religious and social institutions, schools and other establishments for education, with the right to use their own language and to exercise their own religion freely therein."[2045] Based on the Lausanne Treaty, Armenians of Turkey can ensure solidarity within their society.[2046] However, new laws prevented foundations from acquiring new property, even through donations, and properties they had acquired by donation or purchase since 1936 were expropriated. Armenians were severely damaged by discriminatory legal restrictions imposed upon minority foundations in the 1970s, 1980s and 1990s, with more than 1,400 assets belonging to Armenian Foundation were retrospectively classified as illegal acquisitions and confiscated by the State.[2047]

In reference to the interference in the internal affairs of foundations, one of the many problems is the fact that foundations cannot be managed with full autonomy and that their activity is restricted, because of the attitudes of State authorities. Troubles in the internal administration of foundations and discriminating attitudes within Armenian society can also negatively affect the effective operation of these institutions.[2048] The most striking problem regarding freedom of association is that the right has been effectively suspended since 2013, when the GDF repealed provisions on the election of board members and announced that new provisions would replace them.[2049] No new regulations on election

2043 Hofmann, *Armenians in Turkey*, p. 32.

2044 Article 31 of Law No.5253, 04.11.2004.

2045 See Lausanne Peace Treaty, https://bit.ly/2MMYjZa.

2046 USCIRF, "2012 Annual Report," p. 4.

2047 Raffi Bedrosyan, "Revisiting the Turkification of Confiscated Armenian Assets," *The Armenian Weekly*, 17.04.2012, https://bit.ly/2IWey4c.

2048 Raffy Bedrosyan, "Pandora's Box for Istanbul Armenians," *The Armenian Mirror Spectator*, 25.05.2020, https://bit.ly/3nsla9J.

2049 Özlem Ertan, "Foundations in Search of Justice," *Agos* newspaper, 16.11.2007.

procedures[2050] for non-Muslim foundations has been published since 2013,[2051] meaning that foundations cannot hold elections for board members. The government insists community foundations elections cannot take place without a government-drafted election regulation.[2052]

Meanwhile, State bureaucracy also interferes in the governance of non-Muslim foundations. Regulations guiding the election or appointment of religious leaders are drawn up by the communities themselves, but the Ministry of Interior can approve, deny or change them if they are deemed incompatible. The lack of an effective legal framework for religious foundation enforces dependency on political will, which is not compatible with the norms enshrined in the ECHR.[2053] In Turkey, no religious community has legal personality, so they cannot form legal entities and are therefore dependent on State authorities.[2054] The Turkish State claims that preparations for a regulation which will address the difficulties faced by non-Muslim minorities is currently in hand.[2055]

Minority communities that are permitted to maintain community foundations may own their places of worship, but the State frequently fails to acknowledge this.[2056] Turkey asserts that because some Christian churches are the property of the individual saints after which they are named, they cannot be returned to their rightful owners. The State, therefore, seizes them. If the State considers that a foundation has not held regular elections, it can declare the foundation defunct and seize its property, despite the fact that State policies work against

2050 The Law introduced the provision that community foundations "shall be managed by committees elected by their members," without clarifying how these elections might be carried out. Foundation elections were thus held 4-yearly, and any member of the Armenian community living in Istanbul could join the board of directors. In 1972, a new practice was introduced which held that community members not living near the foundation should not be elected to its administration. This practice meant that there were insufficient foundation directors, as fewer people lived near the foundations. In 2008 Article 29 of the Foundations Regulation enabled the declaration of a wider constituency in İstanbul and Anatolia.

2051 European Commission, Progress Report on Turkey, SWD (2019) 220, p. 39.

2052 Yildirim, "Minority foundations."

2053 Ibid.

2054 Ibid.

2055 Human Rights Council, "Working Group on the Universal Periodic Review, National report submitted in accordance with paragraph 5 of the annex to Human Rights Council Resolution 16/21 Turkey," UN Doc. A/HRC/WG.6/35/TUR/1 para.70.

2056 Block, "Judicialization and Implementation," pp. 152-153.

foundations holding regular elections.[2057] These apparently deliberate loopholes authorize discriminatory intervention by the State, which becomes a political issue, playing into decisions regarding the restitution of religious properties. In 2006 President Ahmet Necdet Sezer, a staunch secularist, stated that no special status should be granted to religious foundations, as this has already been granted in Article 101 of the Civil Code[2058] and the Lausanne Treaty.[2059] Throughout the Republican era, State interference with minority religions was reinforced by a new approach aimed at weakening these organizations.[2060] Lastly, a 2018 regulation obliges associations to disclose their membership to the authorities, although it violates constitutional guarantees to freedom of association and the right to privacy.[2061]

4.12.1.2.1 Interferences in the Armenian Patriarchate Affairs

The Synod and the Secular Committee were closed following the 1960 military coup. A Consultative Committee was established in its place in 1990, which was dissolved in 1997. The Turkish government justified the ban, saying that Turkey is a secular country and that such a committee would 'cause unrest'.[2062] In 1987, Bishop Mutafyan was charged with violating the country's Statutes on the preservation of historical buildings by repairing the leaking roof of a balcony at the Armenian Patriarchate. In 1986, Mutafyan was accused of sending two Swedish 'spies' to eastern provinces to collect stories on the Armenian Genocide. A confidential report revealed showed that Mutafyan was under surveillance 'for his Armenian nationalist inclinations'.[2063]

2057 Ibid.

2058 Inter alia, the Article states that the "Formation of a foundation contrary to the characteristics of the Republic defined by the Constitution, Constitutional rules, laws, ethics, national integrity and national interest, or with the aim of supporting a distinctive race or community, is restricted."

2059 Ertan, "Foundations in Search of Justice."

2060 Christopher Sheklian, "Promises of property: religious foundations and the justice and development party's ambiguous attitudes towards religious minorities," *Turkish Studies*, 20:3 (2019), p. 8.

2061 Ibid, p. 36.

2062 Tchilingirian, "The 'Other' Citizens," p. 144.

2063 Ibid.

4.12.1.2.1.1 State Interference in the Election of Patriarchs

Despite Turkey's international human rights obligations, the State interferes in the ways some religious communities – particularly the Armenians – elect their leaders, and Armenian Apostolic leaders are chosen with government permission as religious leaders of the Apostolic community which does not exist and are not recognized in law.[2064] The election of the Armenian Patriarch lacks legal certainty and is to a great extent outside the control of the religious community. The process of application for State permission to elect the religious leader is not legally required but is the established practice.[2065] The possible consequences of not applying for permission might include non-recognition of the religious leader by the State and withholding permission to wear religious clothing outside of places of worship. The government determines whether an election is permissible and when it can take place, and the chosen leader must be trusted by the government.[2066] On one hand it is difficult to understand the need for State involvement in the process, but on the other the lack of legal certainty explains the Armenian Church's need to ensure State cooperation.[2067] In the Republic period there have been six elections for a new Armenian Patriarch, and the State has interfered regarding the timing of the election or the election rules every time.[2068]

In 1961 the government enacted a decree (No. 511654),[2069] specifying Patriarchal election rules. It emphasized that this was a one-off process that would not create any future legal precedent. According to this election directive, which was based on 1863s 'National Constitution'[2070] of Armenians, Patriarchal elections

2064 Yildirim, "Turkey: Why State Interference."

2065 Ibid.

2066 Ibid.

2067 Yildirim, "Turkey: Why Can't Armenians Elect a Patriarch?," Forum 18, 15.02.2018, https://bit.ly/3nrKgpb.

2068 Ibid.

2069 A proposal came to the National Assembly of Turkey in 1949 stipulating that the patriarch is just a religious figure who cannot represent the community. Accordingly, only clergymen can elect him, and laymen cannot interfere in the electoral process. This proposal was withdrawn before ratification.

2070 Whether this 'National Constitution' applies in modern Turkey is unclear. The 'National Constitution' enshrines extensive rules on the internal management of the Armenian community, including the election of a new Patriarch. The non-religious administrative organs that are referred to in the Regulation were also annulled during the Republic. Hence, whether and to what extent the 'National Constitution' is legally binding remains unclear.

were to be undertaken in two phases. In the first, the electorates elect their lay delegates in each constituency, and the Spiritual Council designates the spiritual delegates. The assembly of delegates, consisting mostly of civilians (6/7), elected the Patriarch among the bishops of the Spiritual Council members who themselves or their fathers should be citizen of Turkey. In 1990 and 1998, elections were realized through the technical renewal of the 1961 decree. In 1999, responding to the Special Rapporteur's request for information on State interference,[2071] Patriarch Mutafyan replied that the Turkish Republic had intervened in the election of the Armenian religious leader. He noted that his election had met obstacles because of the hostility of a police chief in the Governor's office but that the authorities in Ankara had resolved the situation.[2072]

Because of this ambiguity, the Armenian Patriarchate had been in crisis since 2007 when the Patriarch Mesrop Mutafyan was diagnosed with a neurological disease that left him in a coma.[2073] Many disputes occurred between then and his death in 2019. Some claimed that a new Patriarch could not be elected until the current one dies, others argues the opposite.[2074] The Patriarchate applied to the State in December 2009 to elect a co-Patriarch to serve alongside Mutafyan until his death, then made a second application in January 2010 to elect a new Patriarch.[2075] The Governorate of Istanbul ruled that elections could not take place with Mutafyan still alive, and with no precedent in place, a deputy Patriarch was appointed to discharge his duties until his death.[2076] The Patriarchate elected

2071 UN Economic and Social Council, "Civil and Political Rights, Including Religious Intolerance, Commission on Human Rights Fifty-fifth session Item 11 (b) of the provisional agenda," UN Doc. E/CN.4/1999/5, p. 25.

2072 UNGA Document, "Interim Report of the Special Rapporteur of the Commission on Human Rights on the elimination of all forms of intolerance and of discrimination based on religion or belief Addendum 1 Situation in Turkey," 11.08.2000, UN Doc. A/55/280/Add.1 para. 90.

2073 According to Armenian Apostolic Church tradition, a Patriarch must either die or resign from his position before the election of a successor can be held.

2074 The 1863 'National Constitution' does not stipulate what to do when a patriarch falls ill; it only sets out the procedure to be followed when a patriarch dies or resigns. There are no Turkish laws on the issue either, but the Turkish Ministry of the Interior has repeatedly interfered with the nomination and selection process.

2075 *T.C. Icisleri Bakanligi* (Republic of Turkey Ministry of the Interior), Response to Oral Question (7/15743), submitted by Turkish Grand National Assembly. 26.11.2010, B.05.0.I LI.00.60001.164.02/9.16/6254.

2076 Ibid.

Aram Ateshian on 1 July 2010,[2077] excluding lay people from the process.[2078] The common perception was that the government had appointed a Patriarch, and despite objections, the deputy Patriarch was given the permission to wear religious attire outside places of worship, showing that the government considered the deputy Patriarch equal to the Patriarch himself, thus ignoring petitions to elect a new Patriarch.[2079]

In 2016, the Clerical Council retired Patriarch Mesrop Mutafyan on the grounds that he had been unable to perform his duty for 7 years, initiating the election of a new Patriarch. The State's obstruction which followed illustrates the challenges faced in this process. Immediately following the announcement of the election of Locum Tenens[2080] (*Deghabah*) which is necessary to initiate the election of the Patriarch, the Istanbul Governorship told the Patriarchate that "legally it is not possible to start the election process."[2081] claiming the process could cause divides within the community.[2082] Since then, the Armenian community has repeatedly appealed for dialogue with the State and judicial remedies to allow elections. In 2018 the State again blocked the election of a new Patriarch. The Istanbul Governorship intervened again. As a result, the Armenian Patriarchate's Clerical Council felt compelled to back down, annul its 2017 election of

2077 Rumelili & Keyman, "Enacting multi-layered citizenship," p. 75.

2078 Kılıcdagi, "Social and political roles of the Armenian clergy," p. 545.

2079 Özdoğan & Kılıçdağı, *Hearing Turkey's Armenians*, p. 60.

2080 The spiritual leader of Germany's Armenians, Archbishop Bekdjian was elected. When the Archbishop objected to the State's interference to annul his election in March 2017 as Locum Tenens of the Patriarchate, Ankara Administrative Court ruled in December 2019 that since the new Patriarch had now been elected, there was no reason for the case to be reviewed. The decision was appealed and is awaiting a ruling. For further information see: *İstanbul Ermeni Patriği Mutafyan'in Vefati Ve Yeni Patrik Seçimi Süreci Yorum No.*2019/30, (The Death of Istanbul Armenian Patriarch Mutafyan and the Election Process of the New Patriarch Comment No.2019/30,) *Avrasya İncelemeleri Merkezi* (Center For Eurasian Studies), https://bit.ly/38as6Cy and Mine Yildirim "Turkey: Constitutional Court Judgment on Armenian Patriarchal Election – A Precedent?," Forum 18, 25.03.2020, https://bit.ly/3uW7AiT.

2081 *"Valilik'ten seçime müdahale,"* (Election intervention from the Governorship,) *Agos* newspaper, 15.03.2017, http://www.*Agos*.com.tr/tr/yazi/17957/valilikten-secime-mudahale.

2082 Meanwhile, Archbishop Ateshian did not resign from his position as Patriarchal Vicar-General until the Clerical Council removed him from his position on 28.06.2017.

a Locum Tenens (temporary leader) and acknowledge the authority of the Patriarchal Vicar-General, Archbishop Aram Ateshian.

In 2019 the CC based on the individual application made by two local Armenians[2083] ruled that State interference was unnecessary in a democratic society, a precedent that is relevant for future similar cases of interference in the internal affairs of religious communities, particularly those the State considers Lausanne Treaty minorities. The CC noted that the election of a religious leader constitutes a form of manifestation of religion and, as such, is protected under the Constitution. The CC found that measures that led to the appointment of a Patriarchal Vicar-General (in 2010) occurred not as a result of a process that took place within the competing civilian and spiritual initiatives in the Armenian community, but as a result of "State pressure that was unconstitutional."[2084] As a result, the CC concluded that there has been interference in the Armenian community's right to freedom of religion or belief, a freedom that is guaranteed under Article 24 of the Constitution.[2085] It is worthwhile to mention that an important finding in CC's judgment concerns the legality of the restriction. The CC indicated that public authorities have the authority to organize the election of the Armenian Patriarch under the 1863 Regulation and practice in subsequent elections.[2086]

However, the CC ruled that according to Article 13 of the Constitution, fundamental rights may only be restricted by law and in the present case, a "legal provision that can prevent arbitrary actions by public authorities, that will enable persons to know the law, that is accessible, foreseeable and absolute is absent. As a result, the restriction cannot be considered as being prescribed by law."[2087]

In summary, the CC found that the State has not been able to demonstrate a pressing social need that overturn the "spirit of Armenian traditions" and the "Armenian community's will." Hence the interference in the applicants' right to freedom of religion or belief by refusing the call to organize Patriarchal elections cannot be considered compatible with the requirements of a democratic society,

---

2083 Application to Turkish CC. No.2014/17354, 2014.

2084 *Anayasa Mahkemesi "Din özgürlüğü ihlali" kararının gerekçesini açıkladı*, (The Statute of the Constitutional Court should have been declared "in violation of religious freedom"), *Agos* newspaper, 10.07.2019, https://bit.ly/2O5ivpJ.

2085 Ibid.

2086 Yildirim, "Turkey: Constitutional Court Judgment."

2087 *Anayasa Mahkemesi "Din özgürlüğü ihlali" kararının gerekçesini açıkladı*," (The Statute of the Constitutional Court should have been declared "in violation of religious freedom"), *Agos* newspaper, 10.07.2019, https://bit.ly/2O5ivpJ.

and Article 24 of the Constitution had thus been violated.[2088] The CC notes that restrictions cannot be considered as being prescribed by law, and found that the State has not been able to demonstrate a pressing social need that overrides the spirit of Armenian traditions and the Armenian community's will. Patriarch Mashalian welcomed the judgment, adding that "it should be taken into account in the preparation of directives for elections in the future."[2089]

Nevertheless, there is very important element regarding the timing of the verdict that should be discussed here. The application was lodged in 2014, but the CC did not rule until May 2019, two months after the passing of Patriarch Mesrob Mutafyan. In other words, the judgment came when the State's arguments that an election could not be held did not exist anymore. the judgment did not result in rectifying the injustice the Armenian community experienced. It also ended the possibility for an application to be made to the ECtHR. Therefore, the timing can be interpreted as a tactic from the CC to avoid contradicting State practice in situations where domestic practice contradicts human rights standards. The impact of this decision remains to be seen. A crucial finding in the judgment relates to the legality of the restriction.

4.12.1.2.1.2 The Election of the New Patriarch

After CC's May 2019 judgment, authorities continued to interfere in the election process of the new Patriarch following the death of Patriarch Mutafyan two months earlier. The interference was against the legally binding nature of CC judgments under Article 153 of the Constitution.[2090] The Armenian community formed an Election Steering Committee (*Mütesebbis Heyet*) to start the process of electing the 85th Patriarch. However, the Interior Ministry sent a directive for the election which indicated that the future Patriarch should be only "from among the class of bishops of the Armenian Patriarchate of Istanbul,"[2091] meaning, those who are directly serving in Istanbul. In other words, The Interior Ministry added a new restriction reducing the number of eligible candidates to

---

2088 Yildirim, "Turkey: Constitutional Court Judgment."

2089 Ibid.

2090 Inter alia, Article 153 of the Constitution states: "Decisions of the Constitutional Court.... shall be binding on the legislative, executive, and judicial organs, on the administrative authorities, and on persons and corporate bodies."

2091 "İstanbul Ermeni Patrikliği Patrik Seçim Talimatnamesi (Tam Metin)," (Istanbul Armenian Patriarchate Patriarch Election Instructions (Full Text)), *Hyetert*, 23.09.2019, https://bit.ly/3pgpGbO.

two, since only two out of 14 candidates were Turkish Armenian bishops who were serving in Turkey at that time. This was a direct contradiction to CC's Judgment. The Steering Committee, nevertheless, did nothing to challenge the State imposed restrictions in the selection criteria of the new Patriarch.[2092] Only couple of members resigned from the committee and two Armenians, appealed to the Administrative Court in October 2019, objecting to the Interior Ministry's interference in the Patriarchal elections then in preparation.

However, the Administrative Court has yet to give a verdict.[2093] While interviewing the newly elected Patriarch, he was trying to justify the State interference by referring that this practice of interference in selection of high religious leaders (Catholicos in the case of Republic of Armenia) is also a common practice in Armenia. So why it should be a problem here? This argument is unacceptable, since the assumingly unlawful practice of another country, should not justify the same practice in another country.

In the same line with the Patriarch, Celina Doğan thinks that it is normal for the State to interfere in the elections of the Patriarch. It was the Ottoman Sultan who established the Patriarchy, and it is unimaginable to think that the modern State will not interfere. In addition, when Armenians internally are not united, they have different and contradictory opinions on some issues (including the election of the Patriarch), and they cannot agree on common issues, at this point, it is anticipated and sometimes even requested from the State to intervene.

As General Comment No. 22 of the HRC states, the freedom to manifest religion or belief may be exercised "either individually or in community with others and in public or private" [and includes] the practice and teaching of religion or belief [which also] includes acts integral to the conduct by religious groups of their basic affairs, such as the freedom to choose their religious leaders, priests and teachers."[2094] If States interfere in this right, it is the obligation of the State to demonstrate, among others, that this restriction is prescribed by law, pursues a legitimate aim to protect public safety, order, health or morals, or the fundamental rights and freedoms of others and is proportionate to the aim pursued.[2095] Based on the analyzes above this is not the case in Turkey. In contrary, the government publicly interferes, which violates its international human rights

2092 Yildirim, "Turkey: Constitutional Court Judgment."

2093 Ibid.

2094 HRC, "CCPR General Comment No. 22: The right to freedom of thought, conscience and religion (Art. 18)," 30.07.93, UN Doc. CCPR/C/21/Rev.1/Add.4, para. 4.

2095 Yildirim, "Turkey: Why Can't Armenians Elect a Patriarch?"

commitments to allow religious communities to select their leaders freely and without State interference.[2096]

In addition, the lack of a permanent by-law[2097] regulating Patriarchal elections will pose problems in the next elections leaving it to the initiative of the political will and the bureaucracy, and allowing the variables such as political positions and characters of those involved in the solution of the problem to step in. It should be viewed as a democratic guarantee for the Patriarchate to have legal status and for the Armenian society to have an election by-law with which to conduct healthy Patriarchal elections.

4.12.2 Protecting the Rights of Armenian Minority in Turkey

"The State always leaves open wounds."[2098]
"Armenians are an ever-precarious entity in Turkey."[2099]
"I do not feel safe in this country."[2100]

Turkey's problematic relationship with protecting minorities is obvious in its refusal to adopt internationally binding instruments that reaffirm minority rights. Turkey is often opposed to the protection of minority rights through reservations to internationally binding documents. By those reservations, Turkey claims the right to interpret and apply these provisions in accordance with the related provisions and rules of the Constitution of the Republic of Turkey and the Treaty of Lausanne.[2101]

Turkey's nationalism is a significant factor for its legal system's failure to protect minorities. Critics blame civic nationalism for concentrating on the majority's identity as the founding element and its marginalization of minorities.[2102]

2096 Yildirim, "Turkey: Why State Interference?"

2097 It is worthwhile to mention that in the past petitions were made for a permanent statute for patriarchal elections to reduce bureaucratic obstacles and to avoid problems experienced with the authorities at every election period. These petitions were either rejected or left unanswered. For instance, a draft for the patriarchal election by-law had been submitted to relevant authorities left unanswered. In 2006, a proposal of an organization model for the patriarchate with legal entity was also not answered. In Özdoğan & Kılıçdağı, *Hearing Turkey's Armenians*, pp. 75-78.

2098 Ayla Jean Yackley, "Armenian migrants in Turkey live in shadow of century-old massacre," Reuters, 24.04. 2016, https://reut.rs/3nIMtwp.

2099 Ekmekçioğlu, *Recovering Armenia*, p. 15.

2100 Personal interivew with Kalayci.

2101 Bayir, Minorities and Nationalism, pp. 11-12.

2102 Ibid, p. 6.

The legal defence of nationalism is legitimized by the concept of equality before the law and non-distinction and the legal myth of the 'difference-blind State' in relation to minorities.[2103] In current international law the protection of minorities is mainly enjoyed by the individual members of minorities, but not as a group. However, although the rights bearers are individuals, the obligations attributed to States are considered 'collective in nature'.[2104] Turkish higher courts and national discourse stands against group dimensions of minority rights, failing to offer adequate protection to non-Turkish and non-Muslim citizens, while insults and hate speeches against groups have not been considered worthy of prosecution.

Today, although minority protection is inherent to democracy and not the latter's counter pole,[2105] a democracy does not automatically guarantee minority protection.[2106] Protection requires special measures, polices and laws and Turkey's current endeavors seem to fall short of this. Turkey cites its 9-th Development Plan to protect minority cultures,[2107] but closer examination demonstrates that its culture policies are confined to promoting 'national culture'.[2108] In its submission to CERD, Turkey claims that it "adheres to the legacy of multi-faith tolerance and cultural pluralism."[2109] Although this seems limited to the 'religious tolerance' rhetoric, as the text does not mention the maintenance of unique cultures and practices of diverse groups. The principle of non-discrimination, however, is rarely protected or enforced by practice. HRC finds out that State Party's "legislation on discrimination is not comprehensive, thereby failing to protect against discrimination on the grounds enumerated in the Covenant,"[2110]

2103 Ibid.

2104 Ana Filipa Vrdoljak, "Self-determination and Cultural Rights," in *Cultural, Human Rights*, Francesco Francioni & Martin Scheinin eds. (Leiden: Martinus Nijhoff, 2008), p. 61.

2105 Henrard, Devising an Adequate System, p. 299.

2106 Athanasia Spiliopoulou Â kermark, *Justifications of Minority Protection in International Law London* (The Hague, and Boston, MA: Kluwer Law International, 1997), pp. 31-32.

2107 See 9th National Development Plan in Turkey 2007-2013, https://bit.ly/3bhctew.

2108 Bayir, Minorities and Nationalism, p. 12.

2109 CERD Committee, Turkey State Report (2007), UN Doc. CERD/C/TUR/3; para.127.

2110 HRC, "Concluding Observations on the Initial Report of Turkey Adopted by the Committee at its 106th Session" (15 October - 2 November 2012), UN Doc. CCPR/C/TUR/CO/1., Section C. para.8.

and asks Turkey "to ensure that reliable public data is collected on cases of discrimination and their outcomes."[2111]

Hate crime legislation does not match international standards.[2112] Attacks, threats, and intimidation still occur,[2113] and very few perpetrators face punishment.[2114] CERD remains concerned about hate crimes against non-Muslim communities, and about hate speech in the media, including in TV series and films.[2115] The CERD Committee recommends that the State party take steps to prevent and combat such attitudes, including through information campaigns and education of the general public.[2116] In addition, HRC recommends that "the State party should intensify its efforts to effectively prohibit hate speech violating Article 20 of the Covenant, and to ensure that relevant criminal law provisions and policy directives are effectively implemented."[2117]

While noting that some cases had been addressed, CERD remained concerned at the low number of cases of hate crimes brought before domestic courts.[2118] In addition, it stated that persons belonging to minority groups did not enjoy equal economic, social and cultural rights to the majority.[2119] Meanwhile, the ECRI asked Turkey to ratify Protocol No.12 of the ECHR.[2120]

Amendments to Law No. 6529[2121] states that anyone discriminating against a minority based on differences of language, race, nationality, color, gender,

---

2111 Ibid, para. 9

2112 European Commission, "Key findings of the 2019 Report on Turkey."

2113 For example, "Another Armenian Church in Istanbul Attacked," *Asbarez* newspaper, 29.05.2020, https://bit.ly/30eN7aV.

2114 European Commission, "Key findings of the 2019 Report on Turkey."

2115 CERD Committee, "Seventy-fourth session 16 February – 6 March 2009, Consideration of Reports Submitted by States Parties under Article 9 of the Convention: Concluding Observations of the Committee on the Elimination of Racial Discrimination," 16.06.2009, UN Doc. CERD/C/GMB/CO/14, para.13.

2116 Ibid.

2117 HRC, "Concluding Observations on the Initial Report of Turkey adopted by the Committee at its 106th session," (15 October - 2 November 2012), UN Doc. CCPR/C/TUR/CO/1. para.22.

2118 CERD Committee, "Concluding Observations on the Combined Fourth to Sixth Periodic reports of Turkey," 2016, UN Doc. CERD/C/tur/CO/4–6, para.8.

2119 Ibid, para. 31.

2120 ECRI, "Report on Turkey, Fourth Monitoring Cycle, ECRI Secretariat Directorate General II - Democracy, CoE, Dec. 2010, p. 9.

2121 Law No. 6529 dated 02.03.2014 to amend various Acts with the purpose of advancing the Fundamental Rights and Liberties.

disability, political view, philosophical belief, religion or sect faces one to three years in prison.[2122] However, the law does not define hate crime, and anyone who has been discriminated against must prove the reason for that discrimination. It is almost impossible to prove a hate crime under such circumstances, and many crimes go unpunished, and the majority of the proceedings result in acquittal.[2123] There is no legislation regarding hate speech in Turkish Law.[2124]

In the context of Article 216 of TPC, since degrading someone on the ground of ethnicity is not a crime, the Supreme Court considers that calling somebody 'Armenian' in a disparaging sense constitutes slander, the accused is attempting to resurrect memories of persecution and Genocide.[2125] In addition, the Treaty of Lausanne provides only modest protection, with dominant Turkification policies minimizing the power of the Treaty. Anti-Armenian textbooks targeting Armenian and minorities, continue to be published. In September 2014, academics, intellectuals, artists and journalists publicly condemned the practice of "open hatred and hostility" towards Armenians in Turkish schoolbooks.[2126]

Although many Armenians do not see a direct threat from the State, they are threatened by the ultranationalist racist circles as well as in the hate speech and discourse towards Armenians.[2127] It seems there are no rigid legal mechanisms to protect Armenians against such threats. In contrary, some Armenians believe that the State intentionally does not protect the Armenians from threats. For example, in the case of Anti-Armenian protests during the recent 2020 September war in Artsakh, an Armenian Journalist thinks that:

> "the police could stop these convoys immediately, on the grounds that they are disturbing public order but the fact that they managed to storm both Kurtulus and Kumkapi is evidence of how little the authorities care. If people were organising a rally in support of LGBTQ rights or the pro-Kurdish HDP party [Editor's note: The People's

2122 See Article 122 of TPC.

2123 Fethiye Chetin, Personal email communication with the author, 20.2.2020.

2124 See Article 122 of TPC.

2125 Bayir, Minorities and Nationalism, p. 236.

2126 "Investigation Launched into Police March in Roma Neighbourhoods in Western Turkey," *Hurriyetdailynews.com*, 15.07.2015, https://bit.ly/3rhfd1r.

2127 Personal interview with His Beatitude Patriarch Sahak II Mashalian, Armenian Patriarch of Constantinople, the interview was held in Istanbul on 16.02.2020. and "Armenians feel uneasy in Turkey, says Turkish MP," *Arab News*, 02.10.2020, https://bit.ly/30hfQvD and Ayla Jean Yackley, "War in the Caucasus hits close to home for Turkey's Armenians," Eurasianet, 21.10.2020, https://bit.ly/3uUTwpV.

> Democratic Party], it would have been shut down immediately and there would have been numerous arrests."[2128]

In addition, as a reason for Stat's inaction to prevent and to stop the threats towards Armenians, Paylan argues: "The government is using this conflict for domestic consumption. Armenian-origin citizens have become scapegoats and the object of rising racism and hate speech."[2129] Others even believe that this policy of not preventing anti-Armenian sentiments and rhetoric is directly linked to the Armenians Genocide:

> "The current anti-Armenian rhetoric and acts of intimidation and war are directly linked to the Armenian Genocide. Above all, Azerbaijani and Turkish aggression against Armenia now is the continuation of the Armenian Genocide, and Turkey is continuing its genocidal anti-Armenian policies by supporting Azerbaijan by all means, including military aid and guidance."[2130]

Nevertheless, in some rare cases, the Turkish legal system addresses anti-Armenian incidents. In the case Sevag Sahin Balikci's murder, a soldier of Armenian descent, the court concluded that the perpetrator, another soldier, had killed him by accident, and that there was evidence of prior racial conflicts between the two.[2131] Balıkçı was killed in southeast Turkey on April 24, 2011, the 96th anniversary of the Armenian Genocide. Expert reports found the defendant, Kıvanç Ağaoğlu, was at fault and sentenced him to 4 years, 5 months and 10 days in prison. The Balıkçı family appealed the case, and the court ruling was overturned on procedural grounds. A retrial began on February 8 at Kozluk Penal Court of First Instance. At the retrial, a witness who was also serving in the military stated that Ağaoğlu deliberately killed Balıkçı, but then changed his statement. In the retrial he told the court that he changed his statement under pressure. The defendant was sentenced to 16 years and 8 months in prison. Garo Paylan commented: "I attach importance to this. At last, we have seen that a hate crime against Armenians in the country resulted in a court sentencing the defendant."[2132]

2128 Belayachi, "Turkish ultranationalists storm Armenian neighbourhoods."

2129 Nanore Barsoumian, "Sharp Rise in Hate Speech Threatens Turkey's Armenians," *The Armenian Weekly*, 08.10.2020, https://bit.ly/3bY9c2Y.

2130 Ibid.

2131 ECRI, "Report on Turkey, Fifth Monitoring cycle," ECRI Secretariat Directorate General II - Democracy, CoE 29.06.2016, para. 55.

2132 Pinar Tarcan, "Sevag Balıkçı Case: Defendant Sentenced to Prison for 'Conscious and Reckless Killing'," *Bianet*, 13.01.2020, https://bit.ly/37fwAY8.

On the other hand, it seems, Armenians in Turkey generally refrain from taking legal steps to protect their rights.[2133] Sevan thinks that when Armenians demand their rights, they become a threat and target.[2134] State authorities create difficulties for Armenian institutions that apply for legal mediation. Such organizations have been threatened by State officials if they did not withdraw court cases filed against the State.[2135]

Seeking legal remedy leads to even bigger problems on a group level. Fighting collectively for institutional rights is harder than fighting for individual rights.[2136] Even in the case of individual claims, often plaintiffs demand remain unaddressed, as was the case when Cilina Doğan filed a case against women harassment, but the judge indirectly told her that the law will not be implemented because she is an Armenian.[2137] In addition, religion is a big political actor within the Armenian community. If people want to communicate with the Turkish government, they often do so through the Patriarchate, which has particularly been the channel for the older generation to petition government.[2138]

With reference to the protection of foundation properties, in the early 2000s some reforms began to be adopted on this regard. From 2002, religious community foundations could once more acquire immovable property to meet their religious, charitable, social, educational, health, and cultural needs through the permission of the GDF.[2139] Nevertheless, the acquisition was tied to authorization by the GDF, and restrictions introduced on 24 January 2004, caused new problems. Offering the mandate to the GDF meant endorsing the repressive practices and violations of the former Foundations' Administration. The Regulation imposed a requirement that decisions regarding property acquisition be made "upon the receipt of opinion from relevant ministries, public institutions

2133 Rumelili & Keyman, "Enacting multi-layered citizenship," p. 72.

2134 Personal interview with Mr. Sevan Degirmendjian, teacher, journalist, activist and the manager of member of Turkish Parliament Garo Paylan, the interview was held in Istanbul on 18.02.2020.

2135 Özdoğan & Kılıçdağı, *Hearing Turkey's Armenians*, p. 114.

2136 Ibid, p. 29.

2137 Personal interview with Ms. Celina Doğan, former member of Turkish Parliament, current member of Shishli Municipality Council in Istanbul, the interview was held in Istanbul on 18.02.2020.

2138 Gellman, Democratization and Memories of Violence, pp. 119-120.

2139 Block, "Judicialization and Implementation," p. 153-154.

and organizations when necessary."[2140] In the end, only 20 % of applications filed between 2003 and 2004 for the return of approximately 2250 seized properties were considered due to bureaucratic obstacles.[2141]

In 2008 Law No. 5737 on Foundations[2142] repealed Law No. 2762 on Foundation, allowing religious communities to apply for the return of confiscated properties.[2143] In addition, the new law gives community foundations the right to acquire property (Article 12), receive in-cash and in-kind donations from organizations in Turkey and abroad provided the GDF is notified (Article 25), and set up economic enterprises and companies (Article 26). However, a positive response has been received for only 10 % of the applications made to the GDF as of November 2008 under provisional Article 7 of the Law on Foundations, by the Armenian foundations for the return of 262 immovable properties which had been seized within the framework of the 1936 Declaration practices.[2144]

For the first time in history, the law allowed a member elected by the foundations to sit in the Foundations' Assembly, the supreme organ of the GDF (Article 41). This legal basis cleared the path to establish a 'joint pool'. After lengthy discussions, consensus was reached to establish the Inter Foundation Solidarity and Dialogue Platform (VADIP), in April 2009 to maximize the material and spiritual assets of the community among Armenian community foundations. VADIP envisages the return of some of the properties of community foundations that were seized between the 1960s to the present (Provisional Article 7). Later on, this platform has been developed into the Armenian Foundation Association "*Ermeni Vakiflar Birliği*." However, this platform is a consultancy platform and has no legal status and authority over foundations, which creates problems in terms of accountability and responsibility.[2145] In addition, in August 2011, Erdogan passed a new order allowing individuals or institutions to apply for the restitution of properties that were not specifically described during registration

---

2140 Law No. 4771 on Act amending various Acts of 2002 and see Reyna, Y. and E.M. Zona No, *Son Yasal Düzenlemelere Göre Cemaat Vakıfları* (Community Foundations According to the Latest Legal Regulations) (Istanbul: Gözlem Yayınları, 2003), p. 127.

2141 Özdoğan & Kılıçdağı, *Hearing Turkey's Armenians*, p. 76.

2142 Law No. 5737 on Foundations, adopted on 26.02.2008.

2143 Block, "Judicialization and Implementation," p. 154.

2144 Özdoğan & Kılıçdağı, *Hearing Turkey's Armenians*, p. 76.

2145 *VGM-en Lousapanoutioon*" (Clarifications from VGM), *Jamanag* newspaper, 01.07.2020, https://bit.ly/34jukOc.

in 1936. Unlike the 2008 law, the new arrangement allowed applicants to receive compensation for properties that were sold to third parties.[2146]

Some judicial decisions on property rights have also been reversed, to the detriment of minority foundations, such as the returning of the Sanasaryan Inn back to the State. As one of the historic *hans* (inns) of Istanbul, Sanasaryan Han is one of the most important of all the seized properties of the Armenian community in Turkey. The Armenian Patriarchate launched a legal action in 2014.[2147] The Civil Court eventually rejected the case on the grounds that it was not within its jurisdiction. Following this, the Patriarchate approached the CC. In 2017 that rejection was overturned, underscoring the fact that the actions leading up to the seizure were illegal.[2148]

But the actual percentage of properties that have been returned is small, and the return of properties in ECtHR cases[2149] is likely because of the judgments themselves or the 2011 reforms. The judgments have been quite clear, indicating in most cases, that individual measures include the return of the property or monetary compensation. Though the properties have been returned, the Council of Ministers is reluctant to close these cases, probably because the requisite general measures have not been implemented. There are still no barriers to government expropriation of religious minority properties, and the structural problems on this issue are not yet fully addressed.[2150]

The Jewish, Armenian and Greek Orthodox communities are now in danger of losing properties because of a law that states that 'extinct' properties – buildings

2146 Regulation on the Implementation of Article 11 of Law of Foundation No. 5737, Official Gazette No.28071, entered into force in 01.10.2011.

2147 This is the first time that the legal personality of the patriarchate was recognized *de jure* by the State. See European Commission Progress Report on Turkey 2018.

2148 Uygar Gültekın, "Historic decision on Sanasaryan Han," *Agos* newspaper, 26.02.2018, https://bit.ly/3r5APha.

2149 The Samatya *Surp Kevork* Armenian Church, School, and Cemetery Foundation Board of Directors filed their case with the ECtHR in 2002 citing the 1974 case law that ruled that such organizations did not have permission to obtain immovable properties because the 1936 constitutive documents did not include the property. The Court ruled unanimously that Turkey must reregister the Şişli properties in the Land Registry in the foundation's name within three months of the final judgment of the case. If it failed to do so, Turkey would be required to pay the foundation €600,000. The case spent 74 months waiting for the ECtHR's judgment and afterwards Turkey has returned the property. A similar case regarding the Armenian *Surp Pırgic* Hospital alleged an infringement on their peaceful enjoyment of property.

2150 Block, "Judicialization and Implementation," p. 175.

that have had a prolonged absence of clergy or lay persons – revert to the government.[2151] In addition, since 2013 Armenian minority foundations are not able to conduct elections for their boards due to the absence of regulations for the elections. Despite promises to do so, the State has still not promulgated new regulations to replace those repealed in 2013 that would have allowed the election of foundation board members.[2152] The government insists community foundations elections cannot take place without a government-drafted election regulation.[2153] Legally, nothing prevents the GDF from producing the Regulation, nor is there any legally justifiable explanation for the GDF's failure to produce it. Indeed, Turkey has a positive obligation in international law to ensure that both community foundations and belief communities can fully exercise the right to freedom of religion and belief and to freedom of association, as the CoE's Venice Commission pointed out in March 2010.[2154]

The laws governing foundations have undergone various iterations since the founding of the Turkish Republic. This appears to indicate that, if there is sufficient momentum, changes can be (and have been) made to the constitution, laws and bureaucracy.[2155] However, the predominant element that has remained in each version of these laws is an underlying restriction on the right to association—particularly as it applies to religious minorities.

In this context, the Armenian Catholicosate of Cilicia (headquartered in Antelias, Lebanon) filed a lawsuit on April 25, 2015, against the government of Turkey seeking the return of its historic seat in Sis which was confiscated in 1921. The lawsuit was filed in Turkey's CC because the claim raised property rights

2151 International Coalition for Religious Freedom: Religious Freedom World Report: Turkey, 2001, P. 2.

2152 Yildirim, "Turkey: Minority Foundations Still Cannot Hold Elections."

2153 The Foundations Law also stated that the GDF would draw up and publish regulations for board elections within six months. It published a Foundations Regulation (one month late) on 27.09.2008, so community foundations began organising elections. However, on 19.01.2013 the GDF repealed Articles 29-33 of the regulations governing community foundation elections. Since then, whenever foundations have asked the GDF for permission to hold board elections, the GDF's standard response has been that the Regulation on Foundations is being prepared, and foundations will have to wait for these specific Articles to be finished.

2154 Opinion on the Legal Status of Religious Communities in Turkey and the Right of the Orthodox Patriarchate of Istanbul to use the adjective "Ecumenical" adopted by the Venice Commission at its 82nd Plenary Session (Venice, 12-13.03.2010).

2155 Block, "Judicialization and Implementation," p. 136.

issues for which lower courts would not have jurisdiction, but the Catholicosate decided to appeal directly to the ECtHR in Strasbourg in 2016, as Turkey's CC had decided to refer the case to a lower court. The referral of the Catholicosate's lawsuit to a lower court in Turkey is critical in view of the requirements of the ECtHR that before any case is brought to the ECtHR, all local legal remedies must first be exhausted, starting with the lowest court and ending with the highest court of the country being sued.[2156] The case did not pass the admissibility criteria of ECtHR and referred the case back as not all legal remedies had been exhausted. In July 2019, the Catholicosate of Cilicia, restarted the process by, filing a case in the 2nd Kozan Court of First Instance against the Kozan Municipality and the Turkish State treasury for the return of the Catholicosate.[2157] By the time of writing this section, the case was pending at the same court and a hearing date has not been decided. In summary, although many confiscated properties have been returned, hundreds of cases remain unresolved, buried in bureaucracy and legal disputes.[2158]

4.12.3 Ensuring the Rights of the Armenian Minority

> "The Treaty of Lausanne, for us, was like taking half out teeth away. In general terms, Lausanne recognized minorities, but it did not provide details for our survival, and the life is in the details. Therefore, our existence is now mainly dependent on Turkish laws."[2159]

4.12.3.1 Good Practice

Recently Turkey has demonstrated some positive developments in terms of fulfilling minority rights. Since 2009, improvements in education have taken place, such as the inclusion of Kurdish, Adyghe, Arabic and Laz language courses in the curriculum.[2160] This symbolizes the State's recognition of ethnic and

---

2156 Harut Sassounian, "European Court Finds Catholicosate's Suit Inadmissible and Cannot be Appealed," *Asbarez* newspaper, 24.10.2017, https://bit.ly/3aityov.

2157 "The Catholicosate of Cilicia Renews Its Demand for The Return of its Historical Religious Centre in Cilicia (Kozan, Turkey)," official website of Holy See of Cilicia, 24.08.2019, https://bit.ly/3p3OyV7.

2158 Tchilingirian, "The 'Other' Citizens," p. 152.

2159 Personal Interview with Ms. Celina Doğan, former member of Turkish Parliament, current member of Shishli Municipality Council in Istanbul, the interview was held in Istanbul on 18.02.2020.

2160 Kenan Çayır, "Citizenship, nationality and minorities," p. 526.

language-based differences in Turkey. Overall, as Lacin and Kenan argue "the AKP's understanding of religious freedom is compatible with the constitutional treatment of free exercise and non-discrimination on the basis of religion."[2161] The *Surp Giragos* Church, the largest Armenian church building in the Middle East, is often damaged in clashes, and since the summer of 2015, access to the church and worship in it have not been possible.[2162] The restoration of the church is being carried out using public funds, and repairs that began in April 2019 are expected to be completed in one year.[2163] Many places of worship have been renovated and reopened following renovation, and the Malatya Municipality rebuilt the Armenian cemetery in 2013, and the Istanbul Metropolitan Municipality has made plans to construct a new church.[2164]

In addition, in neighborhoods where Armenians have a noticeable presence, they are being invited to municipality events. Sometimes municipalities support Armenian cultural events by providing halls or public transport buses.[2165] The State has supported some Armenian newspapers, but it is not done systematically by law or regulations. "It all depends on the political will of the State" argues Degirmendjian.[2166] During religious ceremonies, security forces are present to protect the churches, and whenever a foreign country recognizes the Armenian Genocide the security alert is increased in Armenian Churches.[2167]

Regarding issues arising from immovable properties of non-Muslim minority foundations. In recent years, the Turkish government has taken an unprecedented step in returning $1 billion worth of formerly confiscated properties to minority

2161 Oztig and Aydın, "The AKP's Approach toward Non-Muslim Minorities."

2162 "Pursuing Rights and Equality Monitoring Report on the Right to Freedom of Religion or Belief in Turkey," Norwegian Helsinki Committee Freedom of Belief Initiative, 2019 Report, p. 24, https://bit.ly/3amAKQi.

2163 Ibid.

2164 CERD Committee, "Reports Submitted by States Parties under the Article 9 of the Convention Combined Fourth to Sixth Periodic Reports of States Parties due in 2013 Turkey," February 10, UN Doc. CERD/C/TUR/4–6. 2014. Para. 27.

2165 Personal interview with His Beatitude Patriarch Sahak II Mashalian, Armenian Patriarch of Constantinople, the interview was held in Istanbul on 16.02.2020.

2166 Personal interview with Mr. Sevan Degirmendjian, teacher, journalist, activist and the manager of member of Turkish Parliament Garo Paylan, the interview was held in Istanbul on 18.02.2020.

2167 Personal Interview with Ms. Celina Doğan, former member of Turkish Parliament, current member of Shishli Municipality Council in Istanbul, the interview was held in Istanbul on 18.02.2020.

religious groups.[2168] Overall, between 2003 and 2014, 1029 immovable properties have been registered in the name of community foundations belonging to non-Muslim Minorities.[2169] The implementation of the Law on Foundations has proceeded, with churches and synagogues allowed to benefit from free utilities in the same way as mosques.[2170] In 2010, Erdogan stated that non-Muslim minorities have the right to maintain and practice their identities and culture,[2171] and advised municipalities to protect non-Muslim cemeteries.[2172] Meanwhile, the issue of the Armenian Genocide can now find a platform for discussion in Turkey. Minorities can repair their churches and land-seizing incidents have decreased during the last decade.

4.12.3.2 Lack of State Support to Ensure the Rights of Armenian Minority in Turkey

Despite the good practices presented above, state-imposed difficulties on the Armenian community continue to have institutional, legal, and political implications. The two main defining institutions of the Armenian community, the church and the school, remain in a poor situation, facing administrative and financial problems and targeted by nationalists. As one young Armenian academic in Istanbul commented: "The future of the Armenian community in Turkey is bleak, not only because of the political and legal environment, but because social and career opportunities are not satisfactory."[2173]

One ongoing problem is the return to Armenian foundations the properties that are worth millions of dollars. This is vital for the community to assure its survival and help it develop and modernize. In the absence of State assistance, Armenian institutions rely on individual donations and major fundraising efforts. In recent years donations have declined considerably due to the global economic downturn and regional conflict. The income the community would gain from the possible return of hundreds of confiscated properties would provide a secure financial future.[2174] The community is also struggling to preserve its inherited

2168 Turan Kayaoğlu, "Getting Turkey Back on Track to Democracy, Human Rights, and Religious Freedom," *Review of Faith & International Affairs*, 14:2 (2016), p. 17.
2169 ECRI, Report on Turkey, 2016. Appendix: Government's Viewpoint.
2170 Kerem Karaosmanoğlu, "Re-imagining Minorities in Turkey: Before and after the AKP," *Insight Turkey* 12:2 (2010), p. 203.
2171 Official Gazette, No: 27580, *Genelge* (Circular), 13.05.2010, https://bit.ly/3c2VtYK.
2172 Karaosmanoğlu, "Re-imagining Minorities in Turkey," p. 203.
2173 Tchilingirian, "The 'Other' Citizens," p. 155.
2174 Ibid.

values, resources and assets. Revised laws and government initiatives described above can provide a fertile ground for making Turkish society at large aware of minority concerns and expectations.[2175]

In April 2014 the ECtHR commented that "there is a positive obligation incumbent on the State to put in place a system of recognition which facilitates the acquisition of legal personality by religious communities"[2176] However, religious minorities still lack full legal status and minorities whose rights are enshrined in the Lausanne Treaty face difficulties, such as restrictions on the right to train clergy.[2177] Cemeteries and the right to burial in accordance with one's beliefs, as well as the allocation of land for cemeteries, neither reflects the diversity of beliefs in Turkey nor meets the demands of its minorities. The establishment of cemeteries and the transport and burial of corpses are municipal obligations, but related applications made to municipalities do not always receive positive responses, and there are discrepancies between provinces. Meanwhile, the State body that was responsible for confiscations – GDF – has been given control of restitution and compensation. The absence of any independent valuation or review process increases the possibility that fair compensation may not be paid.[2178]

Meanwhile, the ECRI recommends that the authorities remove any racist material or that encourages stereotypes, intolerance or prejudice against minority groups from textbooks, which take their present shape and content as a result of a comprehensive curriculum reform of 2005.[2179] Despite rewriting, textbooks do not include any radical change in terms of their presentation of ethnic minorities.[2180] A close analysis of textbooks shows that they still assume that citizens are of Turkish ethnicity and are practising Muslims. The narrative either dismisses or ignores anyone who speaks a minority language or practises a religion other than Islam. Thus, the textbooks maintain the ethno-religious conception of the national identity.[2181] The textbooks omit information on the history and culture of minorities, and students are not informed about different cultures and social

2175 Ter-Matevosyan, "The Armenian Community and the AKP, Finding Trust under the Crescent," *Insight Turkey,* 12:4 (November 2010), p. 108.

2176 Magyar Keresztény Mennonita Egyház and Others V. Hungary, Application No.70945/11 et al, 08.09.2014 http://hudoc.echr.coe.int/eng?i=001-142196.

2177 Kayaoğlu, "Getting Turkey Back on Track," p. 18.

2178 Mine Yildirim, "What Does Turkey's Restitution Decree Mean?," Forum 18, 06.10.2011, https://bit.ly/3sPhVv8.

2179 ECRI, Report on Turkey 2016, para. 38 and 88.

2180 Çayır, "Citizenship, nationality and minorities," p. 519.

2181 Ibid, pp. 527–528.

communities that are part of these lands. Such a construction of citizenship and collective identity pushes minority groups outside the borders of collective identity. School textbooks need further revision to remove discriminatory elements against minority groups.[2182] It is important to give society the message that differences are legitimate and can coexist.

As of 2015, the Ministry of Religious Affairs was paying the salaries of nearly 120,000 Sunni religious officials, but refuses to pay the salaries of any other religious officials, in spite of an appeal by some Armenian Church Foundations.[2183] Meanwhile the media is dominated by big media holdings concentrating on increasing profits, and alternative and minority media, such as the newspapers *Taraf* and *Agos* depend on limited financial means to operate with in a repressive legal and political order.[2184]

4.12.3.3 State Support to Armenian Schools

Armenian society in Turkey finds it hard to shoulder the financial burden of their schools. The fact that they have to admit students who are unable to meet their education costs results in budget deficits for schools and dealing with these deficits is becoming harder.[2185] State support would mean that the salaries of Armenian teachers could be paid by the State,[2186] as there are only around 400 teachers – other than the culture course teachers who are State funded anyway. There is a serious shortage of minority class teachers because of lack of training, which should be carried out by the State.

Another problem is related to the infrastructure of the Armenian schools. For example, there is a risk of earthquakes in Istanbul, and Armenian School buildings are old and need renovations. Armenian foundations do not have sufficient

---

2182 European Commission, "Commission Staff Working Document, Turkey 2019. Report Accompanying the Document," p. 32.

2183 US Department of State, "2016 Report on International Religious Freedom – Turkey." Bureau of Democracy, Human Rights, and Labor 15.08.2017, p. 16. https://bit.ly/3sSqAgw.

2184 Yılmaz & Soyaltın, "Zooming into the 'Domestic,'" p. 18.

2185 Özdoğan & Kılıçdağı, *Hearing Turkey's Armenians*, p. 42.

2186 The number of teachers in Turkey, according to data from the 2018-2019 academic year, were 1,077,307. See Esra Ülkar, "*ERG Raporuna Göre: 92 bin Öğretmene Daha Ihtiyaç Var*," (According to the ERG report: 92 thousand more teachers are needed), *Hurriyet* newspaper, 28.11.2019 https://bit.ly/385hKDc.

resources to strengthen the buildings or make them safe and there is rarely any State support to ensure the safeties of the people utilizing these buildings.[2187]

The departments of Armenian Language and Literature in the universities[2188] are insufficient in terms of both quality and quantity. In most cases these Armenian studies produce literature in line with the official denying discourse of the Armenian Genocide or manipulating the history.[2189]

In addition, there is a need for an up-to-date Armenian Language and Literature textbook for teaching Armenian language at primary education and secondary levels that follows contemporary pedagogical methods. However, the process of preparing these books is difficult one that involves many bureaucratic hurdles.[2190] Armenian Migrant children initially were unable to enrol in Armenian schools due to their illegal status and the Law on Private Education Institutions which stipulates that only members of a minority group who are nationals of the Republic of Turkey can study in Armenian schools.[2191] Changes made to the Private Education Institutions Law[2192] in February 2011 enabled Armenian children to continue their education in Armenian schools as guest students, but these children cannot be awarded diplomas.[2193]

Granting rights and freedoms to Armenian schools would not be enough, and the State should provide operational and financial support to engage these rights. Minority group children will only benefit from educational policies if

---

2187 Personal Interview with Ms. Celina Doğan, former member of Turkish Parliament, current member of Shishli Municipality Council in Istanbul, the interview was held in Istanbul on 18.02.2020.

2188 In 1992, an Armenian Language and Culture Department was officially established within Ankara University's Faculty of Language and History-Geography, with a master's program since 2001 and a doctorate program since 2010. Armenian Language and Literature departments were established in Erciyes University, Kayseri, in 2010, and Trakya University, Edirne. In 2011, classes in Eastern Armenian began to be taught at Kadir Has University in Istanbul. Also, in Istanbul, Bogazici University, which had added a class in "Examination of Turkish Works Written in Armenian Script" in 2008, began offering classes in Western Armenian. In *Armenian Studies Past to Present* (Istanbul: Hrant Dink Foundation, 2018), p. 41.

2189 Ibid.

2190 Özdoğan & Kılıçdağı, *Hearing Turkey's Armenians* p. 41.

2191 Article 5/C/1 of Law on Private Education Institutions No.5580, 2007.

2192 Law of Private Education Institutions (Özel Öğretim Kurumları Kanunu), No. 5580, promulgated in Official Gazette 26434, 14 February 2007.

2193 Umut Uras, "Armenian Immigrants Look for a Better Life in Turkey," *Al Jazeera*, 20.04.2015, https://bit.ly/3mw3RmU.

they successfully combine identity affirmation and development, and inclusion-oriented content. States, however, tend to find it very hard to follow this double objective in practice.[2194]

Last but not least, similar to Lebanon, official documents or laws are not translated into Armenian by the authorities and Armenians cannot apply or submit documents in Armenian to government institutions. For example, there are no formal application forms for any official submission in Armenian. This not only prevents the language to be integrated within the larger society and keeps its usage only internally, but it also discourages Armenianss to use the language. Contrary to Lebanon using Armenian, is not a common practice in public spaces (e.g., on shop signs).

The State should provide support, in terms of positive discrimination according to the Treaty of Lausanne, to prevent the erosion of Armenian identity, langauge and culture. Effective and non-biased departments of Armenian Language and Culture should be established in universities to keep the Armenian Language and culture alive.

4.12.3.4 Recognizing the Armenian Genocide

Recognizing the Armenian Genocide can be considered one of the first and foremost steps to ensure the Rights of Armenians in Turkey. Recognition implies reparation; these acts are intimately interconnected. Turkey may continue denying the Armenian Genocide by blocking initiatives aimed at its recognition, but it cannot deny the very fact that almost two million Armenian citizens were forcibly driven from their homes in 1915, under the pretext of relocation to avoid intercommunal clashes and for strategic reasons because of war, leaving behind them thousands of churches, monasteries, schools, hospitals, and community and private properties.[2195]

On surface, it was assumed that State officials now started using more conciliatory language. On Armenian Genocide Memorial Day (24 April) the government offered condolences to the Armenian community for the 'inhumane' violence, stating that it was both peoples' responsibility to re-establish ties and do the utmost for friendship and peace.[2196] In 2019 Erdogan wrote: "This year as

2194 Spilipoulou-Åkermark, "Minority Education–Torn in Contradictions?," *European Yearbook of Minority Issues*, 9:1 (2010), p. 228.

2195 Aram I Keshishian. "The Armenian Genocide: From Recognition to Reparations," *International Criminal Law Review*, 14:2 (2014), p. 234.

2196 ECRI, Report on Turkey, 2016, para.34.

well, I remember with respect the Ottoman Armenians who lost their lives under harsh conditions of the WWI and offer my sincere condolences to their grandchildren."[2197] He referred to the Genocide as a "massive humanitarian crisis" which he implied was a normal occurrence "during any other empire's disintegration period." He briefly praised the "great contributions" of Armenians to the Ottoman Empire, speaking of the "free" and "equal" Armenian citizens of his country today who play "important roles" in society "as they did in the past."[2198]

Meanwhile, the Turkish Foreign Ministry issued the following statement in response to US President Donald Trump's 2019*Medz Yeghern* (Great Crime) message[2199]:

> "We reject US President Donald Trump's statement dated 24 April 2019 with regard to the events of 1915. This statement, based on the subjective narrative fictionalized by Armenians, is of no worth. Distortion of history for domestic political considerations can never be accepted. We remember the pain of more than 500,000 Muslims slaughtered by Armenian rebels in the same period and invite President Trump to be fair. Turkey stands behind its proposal to establish a Joint Historical Commission to shed light on all aspects of the events that took place 104 years ago. Radical Armenians, who want to ensure their responsibilities in the events of 1915 are overlooked, do not show the courage to respond positively to this proposal. On this occasion, we commemorate with respect Muslims, Christians, Jews, and all other Ottoman communities who lost their lives during the collapse of the Ottoman Empire."[2200]

By taking this stand, many argue that the government was trying to manipulate history by putting the perpetrators and victims in one category and continuing its denial policies. Moreover, on 24 April 2019 Erdogan tweeted:

> "The relocation of the Armenian gangs and their supporters, who massacred the Muslim people, including women and children in eastern Anatolia, was the most reasonable action that could be taken in such a period. The doors of our archives are wide open to all seeking the truth."[2201]

2197 "Turkish Prime Minister Mr. Recep Tayyip Erdogan published a message on the events of 1915," Ministry of Foreign Affairs of Turkey, 2019, https://bit.ly/3sUXWem.

2198 Nanore Barsoumian, "When Erdogan Apologizes," *The Armenian Weekly*, 09.05.2019, https://bit.ly/30dzk4e.

2199 "Statement by the President on Armenian Remembrance Day 2019," US Embassy in Armenia, 2019, https://bit.ly/3lHGMOc.

2200 "No: 113, 24 April 2019, Press Release Regarding the Statement by the U.S. President Donald Trump on the events of 1915," Ministry of Foreign Affairs of Turkey, 2019, https://bit.ly/32TpshT.

2201 Ibid.

This was one of his many tweets referring to the "events of 1915,"[2202] and was rejected by the Ministry of foreign Affairs of Armenia who made the following statement:

> "The reference to the victims of the Genocide as "Armenian gangs and their supporters" is insulting and deplorable. The justification of the Armenian Genocide planned and perpetrated by the Ottoman government as "relocation," and further qualifying it as "a most reasonable act" is particularly shocking and attests to the intent to destroy in whole or in part the Armenian population of Ottoman Turkey, a national, ethnical and religious group as defined by the Convention on the Prevention and Punishment of the Crime of Genocide. Furthermore, Turkey has consistently tried to introduce a religious dimension to its denialist narrative, which is beyond contempt."[2203]

Recognising the Armenian Genocide and ensuring proper reparation is one of the main responsibilities of the Turkish State, not only for the sake of Armenian minority in Turkey and victims and survivors of the Genocide, but also for the legitimacy of Turkish State and its democracy, rule of law and human rights record.

There are two categories of harm that was done through the Armenian Genocide: those whose impact cannot be substantively remedied, and those that can at least be partially remedied through present action. The former might be characterized as 'permanent damages,' and the latter as 'material damages'.[2204]

4.12.3.4.1 Punishment

The first reparative measure, a criminal judicial process applied to perpetrators, can no longer be acted on, as no adult perpetrators of Genocide remain alive. Although some convictions were obtained and records were produced, the judicial process begun after WW1 was not successful, as many perpetrators were tried *in absentia* or allowed to escape, whilst others received light or commuted sentences.[2205] Many involved in the Genocide went on to become important

2202 Barsoumian, "When Erdogan Apologizes."

2203 "Statement of the Ministry of Foreign Affairs of the Republic of Armenia on the commemoration of the Armenian Genocide," official website of MFA of Armenia, *27.04. 2019*, https://bit.ly/3lQEkVC.

2204 Theriault et al, "Resolution with Justice Reparations for the Armenian Genocide," p. 20.

2205 Vahakn Dadrian, "A Textual Analysis of the Key Indictment of the Turkish Military Tribunal Investigating the Armenian Genocide," *Journal of Military and Political Sociology*, 22:1(1994), pp. 125-162 at pp. 126-127.

members of Turkish government and influenced the ideology of post-Genocide Turkey.[2206]

4.12.3.4.2 Recognition, Apology, Education, and Commemoration

These measures require an admission of all aspects of the Genocide to ensure meaningful knowledge and engagement with the historical record, and to promote global awareness. Recognition should include the acknowledgment of what occurred and the roles of named perpetrators and perpetrator classes. Acknowledgment should specify complete details of injuries inflicted and the short- and long-term impacts on Armenians as individuals and as a group. The Turkish government should publicly and fully recognize the Genocide, and acknowledgment should include education in the facts of the Genocide to support better relations with Armenians.[2207]

The Turkish government should make an official apology to the Armenians for the Genocide and its subsequent denial. The apology should be linked to other components of the reparations package, to give the apology full and sincere meaning. Memorialization of the Genocide through days of remembrance, restoration of Armenian place names, museums and inclusion in Turkish textbooks will help keep the Genocide in the Turkish historical memory in a way that supports a continuing commitment against its legacy. Each of these measures is fully within the power of Turkey to implement. However, the Turkish government expends resources on denial and other harmful measures, such as the recent decision to stablish a state-led institution to deny the Armenian Genocide,[2208] to blockade Armenia's borders and support Azerbaijan in its activities against Armenia.[2209]

2206 Akçam, *A Shameful Act the Armenian Genocide and the Question of Turkish Responsibility* (New York: Henry Holt and Company, 2006), pp. 306-312, 340-344, 362-364. In addition, for detailed account of this continuity drawing on these and other analyses, see Avedian, "State Identity, Continuity, and Responsibility," pp. 807-809.

2207 Theriault et al, "Resolution with Justice Reparations for the Armenian Genocide," p. 123.

2208 "Erdogan Calls for Crackdown on Armenian Genocide Recognition Efforts," *Asbarez* newspaper, 18.07.2020, https://bit.ly/2NzBckI

2209 Theriault et al, "Resolution with Justice Reparations for the Armenian Genocide," p. 124.

4.12.3.4.3 Rehabilitation of Turkey

The government's denial campaign expands embedded attitudes, practices, and structures reflecting the ideology that drove the Armenian Genocide. Anti-Armenian prejudice is rampant in Turkey, leading to the public denigration and discrimination against Armenians, as well as violence. Turkey must alter attitudes, practices and laws so that prejudice is no longer embedded in Turkish culture and political institutions and practices. Rehabilitation can be achieved through recognition and apology and the process of making material reparations.

4.12.3.4.4 Return of Property and Compensation for Property, Death and Suffering

The Genocide dramatically reduced the Armenian population and dispersed it globally, while the physical and psychological effects permanently reduced the size, viability and vibrancy of the Armenian community. Compensation should be made for all Genocide-inflicted deaths as well as physical and psychological suffering, sexualized violence and forced labor. Land, buildings, and other property must be returned if not destroyed, and must be compensated for if unavailable. For all possessions for which reparations are indicated, compensation for lost use of a possession from its expropriation to the present is also required. In practical terms, return and compensation are the most complex and challenging aspects of the reparations. It will be necessary to determine which Turkish entity will be responsible for providing them, and to decide precisely which Armenian individuals and institutions will receive material reparation which is beyond the scope of this thesis to discuss.

Moreover, for the Armenians in Turkey, coming to terms with history should not be limited to the Genocide of 1915. There is a vast gap of knowledge in Turkey about the culture, history, arts and literature of Armenians because information has been destroyed or ignored by the State. Coming to terms with Armenian history means supporting studies to close this information gap. The State, through the Ministry of Culture, must support institutions that work on promoting Armenian history and culture.[2210]

2210 Özdoğan & Kılıçdağı, *Hearing Turkey's Armenians*, pp. 117-118.

4.12.3.5 *Other Steps Required from the State to Ensure the Rights of Armenian Minority*

To comply with contemporary standards of international human rights, Turkey must withdraw its reservations to various UN Covenants and sign the UNESCO Convention Against Discrimination in Education and the CoE's FCPNM as well as the Language Charter. The application of 'reciprocity', which goes against contemporary human rights, and suspension of minority rights should be abandoned.

Narratives which contain discriminatory discourse against Armenians should be removed from history textbooks, and equality with the majority should be observed, and clergy education should be encouraged. In addition, Historical Armenian churches must be restored and opened for worship, with their administration transferred to the Armenian Patriarchate, which should become a legal entity. Without legal personality judicial applications become meaningless. Turkey should thus provide legal status to religious foundations, offer non-Muslim minorities the opportunity to attain civil service, bureaucratic and military careers, provide the opportunity for children to learn their mother tongues in public schools, and recognize all minorities within Turkey. The government and bureaucracy should put equal citizenship into practice and give material support to Armenian schools and cultural institutions, preparing projects to prepare Armenian language teachers and fully eliminate obstacles that prevent foundations from acquiring property.[2211]

Other specific demands include the right to unlimited ethno-cultural development, financial support for non-religious Armenian institutions and for the preservation of historical and cultural heritage as an integral part of the Turkish State's cultural heritage.[2212] Armenian representatives need to be included in the Minority Issues Review Board to address non-Muslim minority issues. Legislative arrangements should be made to coordinate the joint election of foundation administrators as well as to facilitate the maintenance of foundations according to the Treaty of Lausanne. Meanwhile, the media, intellectuals, civil society organizations and relevant initiatives has to raise awareness on discrimination

---

2211 Fatih Öztürk, "Introduction to Minority Issues in Turkey – The Constitution – Making Process and EU Integration," *International Journal of Arts & Sciences*, 5:2 (2012), pp. 200-201.

2212 Bardakci et al., Religious Minorities in Turkey, p. 161.

policies and practices as week as on hate speech and to impart knowledge to the public about the Armenian culture and the history of Armenians in Turkey.

4.13 Armenians in Turkey and International/Regional Human Rights Mechanisms

Armenians in Turkey are reluctant to involve themselves in international human rights mechanisms. They fear repercussions and do not believe in the effectiveness of international mechanisms. However local minority elites dedicated to advancing the rights of marginalized groups have contributed significantly to democratization in Turkey. Turks who join Armenians to form solidarity coalitions, and intellectuals, academics, journalists and NGO workers have a capacity to discuss issues in ways that resonate with international audiences, frame the discourse of their communities and connect their cause to the international community.[2213]

Armenians take little part in International Human Rights Mechanisms, and different views within the Armenian community regarding the role of the EU affect the improvement of their rights. However, they concede that the negotiations with Brussels laid certain foundations for later developments. In addition, the ECtHR in Strasbourg is considered an important factor in the struggle for better rights, as it has repeatedly reached verdicts in favor of the Armenian community and the Turkish government is legally bound by its decisions.

Many Armenians believe that transformative change needs to be affected through domestic actors.[2214] The Patriarch has the following argument in this regard:

> "We want to voice our own issues, but by doing so we do not want to disgrace our country where we live. International organizations have issues with Turkey, and they utilize or misuse our claims to achieve their own political agendas. This has been the case throughout our history. We should learn from this history. The solutions to our problems must be sought in Ankara and nowhere else. In other words, when international organizations promote our rights, they do not ease our issues. In fact, they make them even more complex."[2215]

2213 Gellman, Democratization and Memories of Violence, p. 19.

2214 Bardakci et al., Religious Minorities in Turkey, p. 147.

2215 Personal Interview with His Beatitude Patriarch Sahak II Mashalian, Armenian Patriarch of Constantinople, the interview was held in Istanbul on 16.02.2020.

Nevertheless, the international community needs to be more engaged in helping the Armenian community improve its legal status and play a larger social and political role in Turkey.

4.14 The Role of the Republic of Armenia and Armenian Diaspora in Promoting Armenians' Rights in Turkey

The Armenian State established in 1918 was short-lived because of the Kemalist victory in the Turkish–Armenian War and the Bolshevik invasion in 1920.[2216] When the Soviet Union collapsed in the early 1990s, Armenia declared its independence on 21 September 1991 and Turkey was one of the first countries to recognize re-independence of Armenia. The border was briefly open, although only selected people and goods were allowed to across. An armed conflict over Artsakh, between Azerbaijan on one hand and Armenia and Nagorno Karabakh region on the other hand ended with a tenuous ceasefire in 1994, and Turkey sealed the land border with Armenia in 1993 in solidarity with Azerbaijan.[2217]

Turkey's official position is that the reopening of the land border is subject to return of non-recognized Republic of Nagorno Karabakh to Azerbaijan, the recognition of Turkey's borders by Yerevan, the abandonment of Armenia's international campaign for recognition of the Genocide.[2218] The Genocide part was also mentioned in the 2009 unratified protocol between Turkey and Armenia which by casting doubt on the fact of Genocide referred to the creation of intergovernmental commission to examine the events of 1915.[2219] Scholars of Genocide criticized this detail. According to Professor William Schabas, of the International Association of Genocide Scholars (IAGS) "Acknowledgement of the Armenian Genocide must be the starting point of any impartial historical commission, not one of its possible conclusions."[2220]

In 2015, Erdogan was invited by the Armenian president, Serzh Sargsyan, to attend the Genocide commemoration ceremony on 24 April in Yerevan.

2216 Bishku, "The Interactions and Experiences of Armenians," p. 439.

2217 Laura Batalla Adam, "Turkey's Role in the South Caucasus: Can Peace be Achieved?," *Turkish Review*, Kerim Balci ed., 3:3 (2013), p. 241.

2218 Ibid.

2219 See Protocol on the Establishment of Diplomatic Relations between the Republic of Turkey and the Republic of Armenia, http://www.mfa.gov.tr/site_media/html/zurih-protokolleri-en.pdf.

2220 "Open Letter of IAGS president to President Serzh Sargsyan and to Prime Minister Recep Tayyip Erdogan of October 8, 2009," *Asbarez* newspaper, 13.10.2009.

However, Erdogan did not accept the invitation and to divert international attention on the centennial commemoration of the Armenian Genocide advanced its Gallipoli commemorations to the same day.[2221]

Nevertheless, Turkish and Armenian citizens are free to cross the border through Georgia; visas are acquired on arrival.[2222] To add to the paradox, there is an Armenian representative in Turkey, a delegation to the Organization of the Black Sea Economic Cooperation in Istanbul. During the COVID-19 pandemic, many Armenians found themselves stranded in Turkey, and both countries cooperated for their return.[2223]

It should also be stated that the political preferences of Armenians in Armenia, Armenians in Turkey and Armenians in the diaspora could be different. The most important aspect of Armenia for many Armenians in Turkey is that former is a readily available source of language and culture, a source that could be used in various ways, such as visits, cultural activities, and teacher exchanges. In this context, the Hrant Dink Foundation launched many initiatives, for instance the Turkey-Armenia Travel Grant[2224] to increase direct contacts and cooperation between two neighboring countries' people, the Turkey-Armenia Fellowship Scheme in cooperation with Gyumri Youth Initiative Centre to promote experience sharing between two countries[2225] as well as Turkey-Armenia Journalists' Dialogue Programme to strengthen ties between journalists from Turkey and Armenia and to contribute to the establishment of direct and accurate channels of communication and news reporting across the two countries.[2226]

However, there is no available information on the subject, and all interviewees confirmed that there is no coordination between Armenians in Turkey and the Armenian State to allow the latter to promote the current minority rights of Turkish Armenians either within or outside Turkey by using international human rights mechanisms. In fact, most of the traditional Armenian elite do not

---

2221 Constanze Letsch, "Turkey Eclipses Centenary of Armenian Massacre by Moving Gallipoli Memorial," *The Guardian*, 16.04.2015, https://bit.ly/3r1kUQZ.

2222 Seferian, "The final frontiers," p. 264.

2223 "Armenia MFA Comments on Statements of Turkish Side Amid Fight Against COVID-19," *Armen Press*, 13.04.2020, https://armenpress.am/eng/news/1012024/.

2224 "Turkey-Armenia Travel Grant," Hrant Dink Foundation official website, 10.05.2020, https://bit.ly/38f6R1C

2225 "Turkey-Armenia Fellowship Scheme," Hrant Dink Foundation official website, 10.05.2020, https://bit.ly/3aeXVMx

2226 "Turkey-Armenia Journalists' Dialogue Programme," Hrant Dink Foundation official website, 10.05.2020, https://bit.ly/3re9Lwu.

condone such involvement by the Armenian Republic because they fear internal pressure and repercussions.

Nevertheless, Armenia has recently been more active in raising awareness and advocating for the rights of minorities in Turkey using international human rights mechanisms. One recent example is the recommendation made by Armenia in the UPR of Turkey to properly investigate and effectively prosecute racist hate speech and discriminatory statements directed at minorities such as Armenians, Kurds and Roma.[2227]

Meanwhile, many Armenians in Turkey try to distance themselves from the actions of the Armenians in the diaspora whose main focus is the Genocide recognition and reparation by Turkey.[2228] This is because of fears for internal repercussions and pressures from the State and the Turkish society. A recent example was a speech by Erdogan calling the Armenian and Greek Lobbies in the diaspora "evil powers" that Turkey will continue to fight.[2229] Therefore, some members of the established Armenian community in Istanbul sometimes warn leftists Armenians or converts not to listen to the Armenian diaspora's propaganda, pressuring Turkey to accept the Genocide.[2230] However, it should be emphasized that in Turkey the issue of the Armenian Genocide cannot be properly solved by excluding, threatening and demonizing the Armenian diaspora. This is because the vast majority of traditional Armenian diaspora members are successors of Armenian Genocide survivors, and it is their legitimate right and duty to be involved in this process. Finding ways for this involvement is another issue that can be discussed beyond the scope of this thesis.

Armenians in diaspora, despite their historical affinities, have seldom developed any collaborative coordination regarding the political position of minorities in Turkey.[2231] Although Armenians of Istanbul recently started to engage with pan-Armenian activities and have relationships with the Associations of Istanbulaite Armenians "*Bolsahayeru Miyutioon*" across the west, there is still a

---

2227 Human Rights Council, "Universal Periodic Review, Forty-fourth session, 15 June-3 July 2020, Agenda item 6 Report of the Working Group on the Universal Periodic Review,"24.03.2020, UN Doc. A/HRC/44/14

2228 Suciyan, The Armenians in modern Turkey, p. 33.

2229 Siranush Ghazanchyan, "Erdogan lashes out at Armenian, Greek lobbies," Public Radio of Armenia, 12.05.2020, https://en.armradio.am/2020/05/12/erdogan-lashes-out-at-armenian-greek-lobbies/.

2230 Özgül, "From Muslim Citizen to Christian Minority," p. 12.

2231 Bishku, "The Interactions and Experiences," p. 447.

huge lack of communication and information between the Armenians in today's Turkey and the Armenians in diaspora.

Turkey and Armenia, Turks and Armenians (wherever they are) have to deal with the traumas of their twentieth century events through dialogue and acknowledging historical wrongdoings, since these two States and their peoples, both at home and in the diaspora, live side by side as they did so for centuries in the past.[2232]

4.15 Concluding Remarks on the Rights of Armenian Minority in Turkey

The negative connotation of minority status in Turkey derives from the Ottoman *millet* system, where non-Muslims were thought of as subordinates in the hierarchical Ottoman society. These *millet* rights were later seen as privileges, due to their incompatibility with modern state-logic of uniformity among all citizens.[2233] Minorities have been considered as deliberate creations rather than facts of history, and their rights are portrayed as group-specific societal divisions, leading to the territorial fragmentation of the State.[2234] In the process of consolidating the nation-state, Turkey considered that unity was best achieved through uniformity, assimilation and homogenization, and Turkification was seen as the only viable political and legal policy in the management of diversity.

Turkey had been built according to the concept of oneness since the founding of the Turkish Republic. To 'Turkify' everyone, ethnic or religious differences were ignored and hate speech was normalized by consequent governments.[2235] The narrow Kemalist definition of national identity was the primary reason behind Turkey's restrictive approach towards minorities. In this context, both the official and societal stances concerning minorities were shaped by the perception of minorities as 'threats' to the integrity of the State, a second-class citizen and a tool of foreign interference.[2236]

2232 Ronald Grigor Suny & Fatma Müge Göçek, "Introduction: Leaving it to Historians," in *A Question of Genocide: Armenians and Turks at the End of the Ottoman Empire*, Suny, Göçek & Naimark eds. (UK: OUP, 2011), p. 1.

2233 Bayir, Minorities and Nationalism, p. 261.

2234 Ibid.

2235 Meltem Naz Kaso, "Minority groups face increasing discrimination in Turkey," *Zaman* newspaper, 20.03.2014.

2236 Block, "Judicialization and Implementation," p. 127.

With minorities considered as threats to the "indivisible unity of the State and of the nation,"[2237] prior to the EU reforms, the denial of legally not-recognized minorities was Turkey's official policy. Turkey's reservation to Article 27 is void and invalid because it contradicts the object and purpose of the Treaty. By limiting the scope of Article 27, minority groups are denied rights as individuals or as members of a group. This undermines the interdependent rights in the ICCPR, thus undermining the recognition of those rights.[2238] Turkey cannot exclude or modify Article 27 because it would violate the *jus cogens* norm,[2239] the object of which is to create legally binding standards for human rights in a framework of obligations. Finally, the impact of the reservation may involve Turkey violating the *jus cogens* norm of non-discrimination, even if Article 27 does not reflect a peremptory norm.

In addition, the rights provided by Lausanne Treaty to recognized non-Muslim minorities were often violated or at least not fully implemented. This thesis confirms Oran's observation that stresses three categories of Lausanne Treaty violations: restrictions in education (Arts. 40 and 42/3), language (Art. 40) and minority religious foundations (Art. 42/3).[2240] The reasons for such restrictive minority policies were grounded in Turkish nationalism and identity, which were constructed during the early years of the Republic. While some laws adopted in the Republican period restricted the exercise of the positive minority rights provided for in the Treaty of Lausanne, rarely legal arrangements have been made that directly take these rights under guarantee.[2241]

However, reforms to the previous minority rights policies changed the picture at the turn of the twenty-first century.[2242] The AKP went some way towards recognising minorities.[2243] Caught between fulfilling the conditionalities of the Copenhagen Criteria and maintaining its official assimilation policy, the government enacted a series of reforms granting minorities long denied language and property rights. Nevertheless, the government carefully avoided any official recognition of traditionally non recognized minority identities and made things

2237 Yilmaz, Minority Rights in Turkey, p. 32.
2238 Phillips, "The (In-)Validity of Turkey's Reservation," pp. 90-92.
2239 Ibid.
2240 Ibid, pp. 30-31.
2241 Özdoğan & Kılıçdağı, *Hearing Turkey's Armenians*, p. 109.
2242 Yilmaz, Minority Rights in Turkey, p. 33.
2243 Bardakci et al., Religious Minorities in Turkey, p. 87.

prohibitively difficult by attaching restrictive conditions to rights issues and giving bureaucrats authority in adopting secondary legislation.

Although a number of positive steps were taken, structural problems remain due to the prevalence of nationalistic perceptions of minorities. As argued above, the scope and effects of reform remain limited, many important problems remain unresolved, and new regulations are often implemented very slowly or counteracted in practice.[2244] It is easy to get the impression that the government's advances in minority rights are strategic acts aimed at preventing any further worsening of Turkey's image globally and its relationship with the EU, which has deteriorated in recent years.[2245] Some critics believe that recent reform initiatives are lip-service to the EU and that only serve to increase potential votes for the AKP.[2246]

Turkey's laws fail to protect many minorities from physical attack, hatred and animosity, and Turkish legislation specifically protects 'Turkishness' and emphasizes the protection of Turkish identity for its legally and formally equal citizens. If one group's problems are given priority in a pluralist society, the governance of that society cannot be considered democracy.[2247] Democratic governance demands that the State maintains an equal distance from such differences and does not prioritize any of them. It also implies that the State embraces all groups and guarantees minority rights so minorities can form strong and sustainable communities.[2248]

The AKP governments outlook seems to indicate the party's orientation toward Ottoman political premises, which granted non-Muslims generous rights but placed them on a lower status than Muslims. Turkey is increasingly being referred to as a 'police State', especially since the Gezi protests of 2013, and because of this, Turkey is losing credibility in terms of its democratization.[2249] Recent increases in Islamism nationalist and authoritarian policies[2250] reflect the fact that Turkey has been ruled by a single-party authoritarian government, creating tension among its citizens and threatening basic human rights. Moreover, there

2244 Ibid, p. 88.

2245 Ibid.

2246 Özdoğan & Kılıçdağı, *Hearing Turkey's Armenians*, p. 109.

2247 Bayir, Minorities and Nationalism, p. 243.

2248 Bernhard J.G. Reitsma, "Strangers in the Light: The Challenges of Being a (Christian) Minority in an Islamic Context," *Journal of Reformed Theology*, 2 (2008), p. 222.

2249 Gellman, Democratization and Memories of Violence, p. 97.

2250 See Ihsan Yilmaz and Galib Bashirov, "The AKP After 15 Years: Emergence of Erdoganism in Turkey," *Third World Quarterly*, 39:9 (2018).

is anti-minority rhetoric in in Turkish school textbooks, a negative framing of minority issues in the media.[2251]

In this context, legally recognized Armenians of Turkey have rights as members of a non-Muslim community derived from the Treaty of Lausanne and as citizen. The ethnic, national, and linguistic identities are not recognized. Armenian migrants and non-Christian Armenians are also not legally recognized as minority and hence they are not entitled to claim their minority rights. Armenians have experienced decades of prejudice, ignorance and intimidation. They faced restrictions on several minority rights to varying degrees in parallel to the changes in the political climate, despite the official acknowledgment of specific minority rights such as the right to maintain the ownership of the property held by the Armenian foundations, the right to freely observe religious activities, and to issue publications and conduct education in their own language under the 1923 Lausanne Treaty.[2252]

Recent political and social developments following the failed military coup in 2016 have destroyed many Armenians' political hopes for the time being.[2253] The Turkish identity has become more authority-oriented and state-centered. In other words, the State and society find it impossible to accept Armenians as citizens with equal rights.[2254] Despite some legal reforms over the last two decades, the negative approach of the administration, bureaucratic obstacles and unlawful judicial decisions reinforce the oppression and result in the violation of minority rights.

Turkey's policy of repressive measures towards Armenians resulted in steadily decreasing numbers.[2255] Armenians suffer from the fact that their existence is discounted and excluded. On one hand, their history is neglected, distorted and erased, and on the other their contemporary presence has been excluded from the public sphere. In recent years, a minority within the community has struggled to change this situation. Firstly, by establishing a counter-memory to ideological narratives that dismiss and deny Armenians' historical presence and legacy, and secondly by campaigning for a return of signs and symbols of Armenian-ness.[2256]

2251 Bardakci et al., Religious Minorities in Turkey, p. 19.

2252 "Committee for Monitoring Minority Rights: Minorities in Turkey," Human Rights Association-Turkey, (Istanbul), 02.06.1996, p. 3.

2253 Papazian, "Between Gezi Park and Kamp Armen," p. 60.

2254 Özdoğan & Kılıçdağı, *Hearing Turkey's Armenians*, p. 223.

2255 Ter-Matevosyan, "The Armenian Community and the AKP," p. 99.

2256 Papazian, "Between Gezi Park and Kamp Armen," p. 66.

The current situation of Armenians in Turkey falls below the lowest international standards for human and minority rights in some areas. There are still many unresolved problems facing Turkey's Armenian community. Armenians constantly face threats for their physical existence and security, they are directly being targeted and somehow treated as 'hostages' whenever negative developments take place in the context of wider geopolitical situation in the region and particularly in the context of Turkish-Azerbaijani vs. Armenian State relationships.

Armenian institutions remain deprived of legal rights enabling them to establish an effective internal administration. There is a shortage of religious leaders, and limitations to self-government in schools and churches. Meanwhile, the numbers of qualified Armenian teachers in Armenian schools are not sufficient and there is a lack of education in the Armenian native language and Armenian history in schools. As Degirmendjian believes, it seems that today it is almost impossible to govern Armenians only through the Patriarch. Armenians feel they are not represented in the eyes of the State.[2257] Many Armenians complain from the inability to act as a single and united community, since there is no legal recognition to the community *per se*. In addition, there is lack and inability of having united vision about the future of the community and many Armenians believe that in 50 years' time Armenians will become like today's Greeks in Turkey, around 2-3000 people.

Many Armenians see the development of an Islamic, nationalist and authoritarian government since 2010 as a setback to their situation as Turkish citizens. The suppression of protest movements, increased persecution of political opponents and restrictions on the freedom of press have led to renewed anxieties and fears. Some Turkish Armenians appear more willing to emigrate, but others still feel a strong connection to their homeland and try to come to terms with the social and economic conditions as much as possible and refrain from most political entanglements and activities.

The repression of minority identities may encourage assimilation into the ethnic majority because the cost of maintaining a separate identity becomes too high. This is true for the Armenian citizens of Turkey, where official negation of memories perceived as fundamental to their group identity has resulted in self-silencing. The contemporary violence against Armenians in Istanbul has

---

2257 Personal interview with Mr. Sevan Degirmendjian, teacher, journalist, activist and the manager of member of Turkish Parliament Garo Paylan, the interview was held in Istanbul on 18.02.2020.

reinforced this sense of minority vulnerability. Notable recent instances include the assassination of Hrant Dink in 2007, attacks on elderly Armenian women in Istanbul in 2013 and nationalist marches through Istanbul's Armenian and Kurdish neighborhoods in 2015, which included the chanting of slogans like "We will turn these districts into Armenian and Kurdish graveyards."[2258]

This thesis concludes that the Turkish law has not set up an adequate system to protect minorities groups against discrimination, assault, and prejudice.[2259] Armenians are enduring systematic inequality and discrimination in the public life, civil service and military service. Armenians are considered 'traitors' or 'foreigners' in their homes and lands, and it is no surprise that the Armenian community has become silent, reclusive and fearful.[2260] When fighting discrimination, the concept of 'tolerance' of the Armenians as a group under 'custodianship' is demeaning. Such concepts themselves support hierarchies and reinforce pre-existing inequalities between different social groups. Tolerance here implies condescension. A discourse aiming to prevent discrimination should instead be built on universal concepts such as equal citizenship, justice, freedom and human rights.[2261]

In addition, the State interferes almost in every sphere of Armenian institutional life, particularly in the internal affairs of minority religious foundations. CC judgments set precedents and ought to be considered as guidelines for other courts when considering similar cases. While judgments include important findings related to the State's unjustified interference in the internal affairs of the Armenian community, it also raises questions about whether the CC closes the door to international supervision.[2262]

Inclusive citizenship, participation in the public life of the State and equal representation can be considered as vital elements of a democracy. However, this requires that democratic regimes should have the institutional basis to protect elements of democracy. Armenians' demands for equal citizenship, equal participation and respect for their Armenian identity have increased in the new millennium. But despite protests and legal battles, the majority of the Armenian society of Turkey is passive to participate in the political, economic and social

2258 "Armenian-Populated Districts of Istanbul Attacked," *Asbarez* newspaper, 10.09.2015, https://bit.ly/3pjcFhp
2259 Bayir, Minorities and Nationalism, p. 6.
2260 Tchilingirian, "The 'Other' Citizens," p. 124.
2261 Özdoğan & Kılıçdağı, *Hearing Turkey's Armenians*, p. 33.
2262 Yildirim, "Turkey: Constitutional Court Judgment."

life on a State level.[2263] This is why, it can be argued that there is a need for new legal and political setting that supports and fulfill essential rights of democracy and also discourages the exclusion of minorities from society and participation in public life.

In this context, admitting to past mistakes is vital to the to the Armenians' present and future. Spotting and highlighting violations and holding responsible parties accountable for their crimes represents not only a collective form of healing but also shows a desire for trust and peaceful coexistence.[2264] The recognition of Armenian Genocide is one of the key challenges to Turkey's democratization. Diplomatic statecraft needs to move from policies of denial towards a more dialogic style of diplomacy informed by empathy. This last stage can be completed by reconciliation only when the crimes are recognized, and victims are acknowledged.[2265]

In addition, it is no longer sufficient for the government to limit itself to removing the barriers that make it difficult for Armenians to keep their identities and cultures alive. Direct government support is vital for the survival of the Armenian education and culture. Meanwhile, the disturbing anti-Armenians atmosphere which prevails in broad sections of society need to be countered through revision of history textbooks and inclusive education aimed at reducing ethnic and religious prejudice.

Based on the above arguments, it can be concluded that the Armenian existence, identity, and culture in Turkey face clear and imminent threat of extinction and the State as part of its international obligations should act urgently by legally providing mechanisms to respect, protect and fulfill the rights of Armenians in Turkey. Many unresolved problems face the Armenian community which have been discussed at length in this chapter, and any progress that has been made will not prevail without a more concerted effort to re-examine the long-established course of homogenization, which Turkey should consider to reverse.

Reform laws require a radical transformation of the dominant social mentality, and the official rhetoric is vital for changing prejudices against minorities. Turkey's multicultural heritage is yet to be embraced at the highest State level. Paying lip-service to religious tolerance will not make the government credible – deeds go much further than words. Only then would the Turkish State restore

2263 Ibid, p. 114.

2264 "Why Hafıza Merkezi?," *Hafiza Merkerzi*, 2020, https://hakikatadalethafiza.org/en/why-hafiza-merkezi/.

2265 Aybak, "Geopolitics of Denial: Turkish State's 'Armenian Problem,'" p. 138.

a sense of civic pride in its citizens and empower all minorities with a sense of entitlement as full citizens with equal constitutional rights. In other words, the Constitution should include provisions that will guarantee the survival and existence of different cultural groups.

After assessing the Turkish legal system in light of current International and European laws for respect, protection and fulfilling of Minority rights it can be argued that Turkey's position regarding to minority issues has been unmoving and defensive, falling far behind international and European laws regarding minority rights. Turkey should remove its reservations on minority rights from international treaties and sign/ratify other minority rights relevant treaties such as the UNESCO Convention against Discrimination in Education, the FCPNM and the Charter on Minority or Regional Languages of the CoE. These steps would pave the way for an adequate and modern legal system for minority protection.

Turkey has a two-hundred-year history of reforms being forced upon it from abroad, which perhaps partially explains its reluctance to accept them,[2266] but at the same time this should urge Turkish officials to revisit their official policies and try to come in compliance with internationally accepted norms. In any case, minority communities should be protected from political manipulation in the context of Turkey's foreign and internal affairs.

In terms of initiatives, the State has to provide more confident practices. Legal reforms can only manifest themselves if the process of reform is conceived as a sustained structural transformation. The State should maintain an equal distance from all religions and should include legal guarantees for minority rights. These reform efforts also need to be complemented by further improvements in the fields of education, the political participation of minorities, the media, minority languages, religious education, property rights, the right to association and peaceful assembly, and prohibition of discrimination.

2266 Hofmann, Armenians in Turkey Today, p. 45.

5. Comparison between Lebanese and Turkish Minority Rights Regimes

Lebanon and Turkey have similar historical roots when it comes to minority rights. For centuries both countries were part of the Ottoman Empire and minorities living in these territories were subject to the same *millet* system. Interestingly enough, although both countries inherited and incorporated some aspects of the *millet* system after establishing their republics, Turkey tried to enforce homogenized version of secularism for decades, while Lebanon based its social contract on a *Millet*-like sectarian basis.

In the context of minority rights, Lebanon and Turkey have many similarities. Both States are multicultural, multireligious and multilinguistic. They play host to legally recognized and unrecognized minorities with legal and socio-political implications and there is lack of clear numbers or statistics on minorities for political reasons. Both countries share a history of internal conflicts, instability, receiving refugees and a current economic, political and financial crisis.

Lebanon and Turkey both acknowledge and give precedence to international law when they contradict national laws. In both countries the source of minority rights is not the constitutions. In Lebanon it is the National Pact and the Tai'f Agreement, while in Turkey it is the Treaty of Lausanne. Neither constitution even mentions the word 'minority' in its text. At an international level, Lebanon and Turkey have the same obligations when it comes to international human rights law, despite the fact that Turkey has made reservations to Article 27 of ICCPR, and Article 30 of CRC and Lebanon has not ratified the optional protocol for CEDAW. Both countries are members of the OIC and have legal obligations of varying degrees of sophistication, since the current Statutes of European mechanisms (EU, CoE, OSCE) are incomparable with the Arab Region human rights mechanisms. Turkey is part of the CoE's ECHR, and decisions made by the ECtHR are legally binding for Turkey, and Lebanon ratified the ACHR but the ACtHR still is not functioning.

Minorities face severe challenges in terms of preserving their existence, identity, enjoying equality and non-discrimination and participation in the political, economic, and cultural life of both States due to a lack of legal guarantees. In other words, both countries have developed regimes that are inconsistent with current international human rights laws on minority regimes and fall way behind the current standards of international minority rights protection.

When it comes to the Armenians, in both countries Armenians face almost similar challenges to varying levels and in different proportions, especially when it comes to the right to equality and non-discrimination. For instance, in both countries, Armenians are often considered foreigners or outsiders, despite the fact that in the case of Turkey, most of what is now its eastern part was once the Armenians' indigenous homeland. However, the perception of Armenians as strangers in their own homes and lands are the mostly highlighted by the problems they have experienced in Turkey. In the case of Lebanon, the Armenians' presence dates back centuries, and they have successfully integrated themselves into Lebanese society over the last 120 years.

There is an overall lack of well-established legal mechanisms to protect their rights in cases of violation, which means in both countries minorities face uncertainty about the present, a constant decline in numbers, a tend towards emigration and lack of a united vision.

In addition, both countries host significant centers for the Armenians all over the world. Lebanon has the headquarters of the Holy See of Cilicia and the Armenian Catholicosate of Catholic Armenians, while Istanbul has one of the two Patriarchates of the Armenian Church.

In today's Turkey, Armenian institutions are deprived of strong legal basis that would enable them to establish an effective internal administration, and they struggle at both local and regional judicial level for the property ownership rights of their foundations, as well as in increasing their participation in civil society initiatives to exercise their citizenship rights and for the democratization of Turkey. In Lebanon, although some associations like *Homenetmen* – established in Istanbul back in 1918 and banned in Turkey since the early 1920s – effectively continue their function and host their headquarters in Bourj Hammoud, they lack systemic State support. The Armenian minority in Lebanon finds it very difficult to pursue and to protect their rights through judicial channels and are forced to address these challenges through political communications and compromises, as they are frozen out of judicial procedures that are more strongly influenced by political developments.

Beside the similarities, there are differences in minority regimes in the following areas. Firstly, the legal criteria of those who are considered minorities are different in each country. In Lebanon, the Tai'f Agreement recognizes only six Christian sects as minorities: Syriac Orthodox, Syriac Catholics, Latin Catholics, Assyrian Catholics, Chaldean Catholics and Coptic Orthodox. Combined, these groups have only one of the national parliament's 128 seats.[2267] There are

2267 See Lebanon's 2017 Parliamentary Election Law.

obstacles to the recognition of the Dom and Bedouins,[2268] Kurds, Syrians and other minorities. The Lebanese State does not consider the Tai'f Communities (Sunnis, Shia, Druze, Maronite, Catholics, Greek Orthodox or Armenians) as minority communities, but as national communities.[2269] This means that legally speaking, Armenians are not considered minorities in the eyes of Lebanese Legal System, but rather they are recognized only as a religious community and not as an ethnic, national and linguistic minority. However, regardless of how Armenians are identified, they are a minority group under international law because they meet the objective and subjective criteria of being a minority and should be entitled to minority rights under international human rights law. Being a minority is a fact rather than a definition, and minorities are defined as groups with separate linguistic, ethnic or cultural characteristics who seek to maintain and emphasize their identity – which is the case for Armenians in Lebanon.

Armenians in Lebanon are recognized as a community (Tai'f community), in Turkey there is no such recognition, and even the Patriarchate which was established by the Ottoman Sultan has no legal statues. In Turkey, the legal concept of a minority refers simply to 'non-Muslim' citizens. The concept derives from the Lausanne Treaty, which is considered as the source of official policy regarding minority rights, with the 'non-Muslim' phrase interpreted as meaning 'prominent non-Muslim communities' (Armenians, Greeks and Jews), minorities that were under the protection of the League of Nations when the Treaty was signed.[2270] Turkey still rejects the international definition(s) of minorities on the basis of race, language or religion, and denies Kurds, Alevis and other minorities their rights.[2271] Non-Christian Armenians and migrant Armenians are also not recognized as minority by the State.

The Turkish CC has only ever defined 'minorities' using the TEP-1980 judgment, as "citizen groups who [are different] from the majority in terms of language, religion, race, etc. and who have the legal rights to pursue their [different] being."[2272] In the CC's view, this minority definition has two components: objective

2268 CESCR, "Concluding Observations on the Second Periodic Report of Lebanon," 24.10. 2016, UN Doc. E/C.12/LBN/CO/2, 2016, para. 64.

2269 Personal interview with Mr. Shant Vartanian, newly appointed Lebanese diplomat, the interview was held in Beirut on 15.09.2018.

2270 Dressler, "Historical Trajectories," p. 16.

2271 Yılmaz, Minority Rights in Turkey, p. 28.

2272 Constitutional Court Verdict TEP (Türkiye Emekçi Partisi, Proletarian Party of Turkey), 08.05.1980.

differences and the recognized status of a minority.[2273] While recognizing ethnically or religiously different groups in a country, the CC considers that the mere existence of such groups is not sufficient to grant them differentiated special rights. The CC makes it clear that being different through ethnicity, religion and language, or being smaller than the majority does not qualify a group as a minority. The CC has added another dimension to the recognition of a minorities by asserting that rules on minorities in Turkey are governed by international treaties, so minority status cannot be granted by domestic law alone. In the CC's opinion, no minority groups exist in Turkey other than those mentioned in the Lausanne Treaty.[2274]

In Lebanon, the participation of the Armenians in the public life of the State is to some extent guaranteed by Tai'f Agreement, despite growing instances of violation of this guarantee. Three Armenian political parties (*Tashnagtsutioon, Henchagian* and *Ramgavar*) run in Lebanon along with a wide network of cultural, youth, educational, social, health and sport organizations functioning under the umbrella of each political party. Individual Armenians often have to be supported by Armenian institutions to gain access to public employment or benefit from opportunities, creating significant obstacles and raising questions on transparency and professionalism. Communities are empowered to a higher level than individuals when it comes to the right to participate in the public life of the State, which is not the case in Turkey. In Turkey, no such mechanisms or guarantees exist – since the establishment of Turkish Republic in 1923 all Armenian parties who initially were actively engaged in the Ottoman Empire's political life were banned. Today, there is no single Armenian political party functioning in Turkey and indeed there are unwritten rules that prevent the participation of Armenians in the public life, including employment as civil servants.

The personal affairs of Armenian minority members in Lebanon are governed by religious laws and courts, but in Turkey this practice has been on hold since the 1920s and is governed by the civil law of the Turkish State. Lebanon provides a wide margin for Armenian communities to manage their internal affairs and to a great extent does not interfere in the internal affairs of the Armenian community. However, Turkey systematically violates its obligation not to interfere in the Armenians' internal affairs. The rate of physical threats towards Armenians in Turkey is higher and Armenians are not as safe as they are in Lebanon. Turkey has a strong central government structure and retains a powerful control

2273 Bayir, Minorities and Nationalism, p. 203.
2274 Ibid.

of State administration, while Lebanon suffers from weak or insufficient State institutions.

Last but not least, despite the recent reports warning that Western Armenian language is deteriorating in both countries, relatively speaking the proficiency level and the extent of using it as a mother tongue on a daily basis seems to be better in Lebanon compared to Turkey. As indicated earlier, in Lebanon most of Armenians' and their institutions daily and internal administrative language is still Armenian, while this is not the case for plenty of Armenians in Turkey and Turkish language has become the dominant language for many.

It seems that minority rights in Lebanon and Turkey have insufficient legal foundation, and that ethno-cultural diversity does not exist in either country for its own sake. In other words, in both countries minority rights are not solely perceived as fundamental human rights. In Lebanon they act as a balancing tool between diverse communities against a background of insufficient State involvement and a lack of solid social contract based on the concepts of citizenship and human rights. In Turkey, the protection of minorities has been relegated to the realm of foreign affairs rather than being seen as a fundamental aspect of human and minority rights. The Turkish State views minority rights claims as a mechanism through which foreign powers can interfere with Turkey's sovereignty, and minority rights are understood as being begrudgingly granted privileges or exceptions rather than legitimately conferred rights.

On the basis of these considerations, the successful preservation of Armenian existence and identity in Lebanon and Turkey to date can be considered either as a result of both countries' unresolved search for a solution to the socio-political problems raised by their societies, or as a temporary condition in their search for legitimacy both internally and externally.

6. Conclusions

At international and regional levels, there is still a challenge to come up with an agreed definition for the term 'minority'. The current approach in international law to define minorities in a given State is inclusive and needs to be established by both subjective and objective criteria and does not depend on State recognition. In addition, the formulation of minority rights as individual rather than collective rights is reflected in the current universal mechanisms for their implementation.[2275]

Minority rights can generally be laid out under four headings: the right to existence, the right to identity, the right to equality and non-discrimination and the right to effective participation.[2276] Historical contexts help us to understand the inadequacy of existing mechanisms dealing with human rights violations against minorities. Although there has been a growth of acceptance and protection of 'special' rights for minorities since the emergence of Article 27 of the ICCPR, States remain reluctant to grant more than minimal rights to minorities. The current regulations are weak because they include many escape clauses, leaving too much discretion to States; regulations avoid the recognition of clear State obligations regarding minorities, and do not substantially acknowledge or protect the essential group dynamics of minorities. Many UN and European mandates are advisory and lack legally binding obligations.

European standards, however, have slightly stronger levels of enforceability. The ECtHR case laws, the provisions of the FCPNM and the Language Charter are legally binding. The monitoring mechanisms of FCPNM and the Language Charter are often political in nature and lack the ability to impose any sanctions on States that do not abide by them.

In terms of Arab State legislation and charters, however, overriding concerns include religion and society, and many States have not yet reached international standards for their entire populations, let along minority groups. Until agreement has been reached on the focus of human rights issues, it is almost obvious that some degree of conflict will continue, and Armenians along with other minorities in the Arab world will remain vulnerable to mistreatment. The standards and legal values of both the OIC and the LAS are weaker and fall a

2275 See Section 2.1 above.

2276 See Section 2.3 above.

long way short of international standards. There is an urgent need to strengthen human rights mechanisms both in OIC and the LAS.

The arguments described in the chapters above lead this thesis to conclude that legal frameworks on minority rights are firstly essential and secondly insufficient. UN and European frameworks lack legally binding implementation mechanisms and Arab States' own frameworks are ill-focused and misapplied. Dedicated and specialized institutional mechanisms need to be put in place at all levels to facilitate legislative and policy development and the design, implementation and monitoring of minority-related programmes.

In the final analysis, the soft approach toward minority rights, demonstrated by international or regional organizations such as the OSCE, which emphasises partnership, dialogue and cooperation, is one way forward, but sometimes there is no substitute to hard law. In addition, as long as the implementation of minority rights at the universal level remains subject to numerous escape clauses, weak monitoring mechanisms and only quasi-judicial review, political pressure remains one of the most effective avenues for addressing minority grievances and improving the record on minority protection. There is no one-size-fits-all solution to minority issues. Each country has a unique set of historical and contemporary circumstances that create different conditions and opportunities for addressing problems relating to minorities. This is true for Lebanon and Turkey. Each has its unique historical and contemporary conditions and contexts that have been discussed in the relevant chapters to better understand the current legal regimes in both countries vis-à-vis minorities.

The central research question addressed by this thesis was the examination of the extent to which the rights of Armenian minorities to exist, to enjoy their own culture, to profess and practice their own religion, and to use their own language, in community with the other members of their group, as well as their right to participation in public life are respected, protected and fulfilled in Lebanon and Turkey. The thesis examined local Statutes and practices towards Armenian minorities in Lebanon and Turkey in order to determine how the actual situation accords with national, regional, and international human rights law in both countries.

With regards to Lebanon, the thesis concludes that Lebanon's legal and constitutional treatment of diverse communities is intensely entrenched in regional religious tradition and directly linked with the conditions that lead to the establishment of the Lebanese State. Similar to many aspects of the *Millet* System, the French mandate in Lebanon established a political system that offered remarkable constitutional spaces and political conditions for the reconstruction of a post-Genocide Armenian community in Lebanon. Lebanese Armenians can be differentiated from other Armenian diasporas through political representation, cultural production, religious centers, and it remains the only country outside Armenia where Armenian political parties have seats in parliament.

Given the sectarian nature of Lebanese society and its governance, Armenians have been able to maintain many aspects of their identity. The autonomy under which Armenians manage their religious, educational, cultural and family affairs and the Lebanese context, which encourages communal political representation, provides the pillars upon which Armenian cultural distinction has been constructed since the 1920s. However, these spaces of communal autonomy are closely connected to weaknesses and difficulties at the core of the Lebanese State, which takes only a minimal role in protecting and fulfilling the minority rights of Armenians. There are insufficient and ineffective State institutions and legal practices in place within Lebanon to guarantee and ensure the rights of minorities as defined by international human rights law.

Lebanon is facing its worst crisis since the end of civil war. An accumulation of government mismanagement, corruption, lack of basic services, economic instability, financial collapse, and external interference have driven the devastating crises of Lebanon. The crises have contributed to a growing wave of anger and frustration that lead to widespread protest movement pushing for large scale political and legal reforms, little of which has seen significant progress for the last two years.[2277] The crises directly and negatively impact all Lebanese communities and specially the vulnerable ones who need further support, including.

Lebanon lacks a sustainable model to ensure equality and non-discrimination. Freedom of choice is restricted when political positions are predetermined according to communities and voters must choose candidates from Muslim or Christian groups. Those in power do not always represent the opinions of their community and are often returned to power by electoral majorities from other communities, raising the issue of democratic representation. Lebanon's structural difficulties make it very hard to accommodate social change within the system of confessional representation.

Although there have been modest improvements in human rights provision and governance in Lebanon, the analyzes of the thesis led to the conclusion that there is still a pressing need for further progress as there are many shortcomings in its implementation. The principal challenge continues to be establishing a systematic human rights approach, strengthening rule of law and citizenship

2277 Lewis Sanders IV, "Lebanon faces its worst crisis since the civil war," *Dw.com*, 08.07.2020, https://bit.ly/3bniiHD.

values as well as the achievement of equal participation, equal opportunities in economic, social, cultural, civil and political rights. Removing reservations from international human rights treaties (Article 2.2 of CERD and Articles 9/2, 16.1 and 29.1 of CEDAW), accepting individual complaints procedures of UN treaty bodies and most importantly reforming structural discrimination in religious family courts and introducing civil marriage as an option to all Lebanese citizens can be an entry point for larger reforms.

In this context it is hard to believe that the current form of political confessionalism in Lebanon, the State will be able to play an active supporting role towards any minority group including the Armenian culture in the country. However, it is possible that should the national Lebanese debate on political confessionalism become unblocked, some form of synthesis can be found, reconciling the need to preserve cultural autonomy for ethno-cultural groups with that of endowing the Lebanese State with the necessary power to intervene effectively in support of its cultural traditions. Therefore, it could be argued that Lebanon's future lies more in the realm of political negotiation, rather than in legal prescription.

In accordance with the Tai'f Agreement, Lebanon needs to overcome political confessionalism in favor of a common Lebanese citizenship based on rule of law and human rights. It needs to prevent religion (or sect) from being used as an 'entry ticket' to societal recognition and political position. Replacing a quota-based system designed to anchor diversity with a more consistently implemented rights-based approach to promoting diversity (including legally recognizing all those minority communities not recognized by the State) may actually be a more promising long-term approach to preserving the Lebanese legacy of multi-ethnic and multireligious coexistence.

While recognizing that the Lebanese consociational arrangement gave the Armenians remarkable opportunities to preserve their identity, this thesis cannot reach any clear-cut conclusions to present the Lebanese system as a successful and sustainable model for the protection of minority rights. The evolution of Lebanon's approach to ethno-cultural diversity, including minority rights, has been dictated mainly by State's need for stability, its political system and its political leadership, rather than by a recognition of the value of cultural diversity and minority/human rights *per se*.

The Armenian community in Lebanon has lost much of its strength because of the civil war, the ongoing economic and political crises and migration flows. However, it can be argued that the Lebanese State poses no existential or physical threat towards Armenians because of their national, ethnic, religious or linguistic background, and the State complies with international human rights law in terms of respecting Armenians' minority rights, although it cannot effectively protect them due to the inherent weakness of its State institutions and the lack of legal or judicial mechanisms to ensure Armenians' rights. Armenians need to be proactive, prepared and organized if they want to claim their rights locally and internationally, and must fight attempts to undermine those rights.

In the final conclusion, it seems that minority rights are not legally well founded in Lebanon, and ethno-cultural diversity exists not for its own sake, but because the stability of the State cannot be maintained without it until a more solid form of legitimacy based on cross-cultural allegiances and cleavages can be found. How long this temporary condition can last, and how legal and institutional change might affect the future of the Armenian community in Lebanon is hard to tell. In the meantime, the Armenian minority – while still enjoying non-interference by the State and freedoms to maintain its identity – faces severe challenges in terms of collective and institutional existence and development.

The Armenian minority in Lebanon urgently needs systematic State protection and the promotion of its rights to exist collectively, institutionally and sustainably, to preserve its identity, to fully enjoy equality and non-discrimination as well as to effectively participate in the political, social and economic life of the State.

In reference to Turkey, the minority rights regime in Turkey is derived from the Ottoman *millet* system, where non-Muslims were thought of as subordinates in the hierarchical Ottoman society as well as the Treaty of Lausanne signed in 1923. It seems that Turkish State's default position is to view any minority rights claim as a mechanism through which foreign powers can interfere in its sovereignty rather than legitimately conferred rights. Turkey's legal system has failed to protect minorities from physical attacks, hatred and animosity, while Turkish legislation has specifically protected 'Turkishness' and heavily emphasized the protection of Turkish identity even among its legally and formally equal but ethnoculturally diverse citizens.

Over the last two decades, caught between the conflicting goals of fulfilling the minority protection conditionality of the Copenhagen criteria and maintaining its official identity policy based on the assimilation of all cultural differences, Turkey has chosen to engage itself in an unattainable effort to achieve both. To realise the former, the government has enacted a series of constitutional and legislative reform laws implicitly granting religious, ethnic and linguistic minorities some of their long-denied language rights and making some progress towards protecting the previously violated property rights of non-Muslims. To achieve the latter, the government has carefully avoided any explicit reference in the letter and spirit of any reform laws that might suggest the official recognition of minority identities. It has also made it prohibitively difficult for minorities to exercise their limited rights by attaching restrictive conditions to them and by conferring on bureaucrats a virtually unchecked authority in adopting secondary legislation.

In other words, this thesis has found that policies pursued by the AKP and the living conditions experienced by Turkey's minorities continue to remain ambivalent and are characterized by a constant mixture of apparently conflicting improvements and measures taken against the minorities. The Treaty of Lausanne lags far behind the contemporary understanding of minorities and human rights. The new regime of minority rights that appeared on Europe's agenda in the 1990s has a more comprehensive context than the minority rights envisaged in international treaties signed after WWI, including the Treaty of Lausanne. The view that civil, political and social as well as cultural rights of citizenship should be taken under guarantee has become an indispensable part of the contemporary minority governance.

Turkey's reservation to Article 27 of ICCPR is void because it contradicts the object and purpose of the Treaty. Moreover, Turkey cannot exclude or modify Article 27 because it would violate the *jus cogens* norm,[2278] the object of which is to create legally binding standards for human rights in a framework of obligations. By limiting the scope of Article 27, minority groups are denied rights as individuals or as members of a group. This undermines the interdependent rights in the ICCPR, thus undermining the recognition of those rights.[2279] Finally, the impact of the reservation may involve Turkey violating the *jus cogens* norm of non-discrimination, even if Article 27 does not reflect a peremptory norm. In this context, Turkey needs to adhere to the treaties and conventions on minority and human rights to which it is a party, lift its reservations, and behave according to international conventions related to minorities – even those to which it is not yet a party, such as the UNESCO Convention against Discrimination in Education, FCPNM, and the Charter on Minority or Regional Languages of the CoE.

When it comes to the rights of Armenians in Turkey, Turkish-nationalist demographic engineering went from the marginalization of Armenians to Genocide, with the fate of the victims depending on a heavily Turkified national identity and the contingencies of international politics. In this context, Armenians have experienced decades of ignorance, prejudice and intimidation in Turkey, despite the fact that they are legally recognized and possess rights as citizens of Turkey

---

2278 Phillips, "The (In-)Validity of Turkey's Reservation," pp. 90-92.
2279 Ibid.

and as members of a non-Muslim community. The Lausanne Treaty has not been fully implemented due to the restrictive interpretations of the State as well as violations of its Articles on education, language and minority religious foundations.

In terms of their right to existence, Armenian individuals and institutions are subject to hate speech, intimidation, threats, and sometimes physical attacks, while Armenian institutions remain deprived of legal rights that would enable them to establish an effective internal administration. Armenians feel they are not represented in the eyes of the Turkish State, and many complain that they are unable to act as a single or a united community, since there is no legal recognition of community *per se*. Repressive measures show the Republic's policy towards the Armenians, resulting in a steady decrease in numbers, threatening the very existence of the Armenian community. Moreover, their history is neglected, distorted and erased, and their contemporary presence is excluded from the public sphere or under constant threat. There is anti-minority rhetoric in in Turkish school textbooks, a negative framing of minority issues in the media and difficulties with the restoration and protection of Armenian churches and historical sites.

This thesis reaches to a conclusion that the situation of Armenians in Turkey falls below the lowest international standards for human and minority rights in some areas. There are still many unresolved problems facing Turkey's Armenian community, such as the continues threats to their physical existence, lack of restitution of confiscated properties that have been sold to third parties, a shortage of priests, and limitations to self-government in schools and churches. There is a shortage of teachers in Armenian schools and a lack of education in the Armenian native language and Armenian history in schools. There is also systematic discrimination against employing Armenians in the civil service, and they have no right to hold political office as minority representative.

Armenians' demands for equal citizenship and respect for their identity have increased in the new millennium, but despite protests and legal battles, the majority of Armenian society of Turkey is passive and does not choose to participate in the political, economic and social life at State level. Therefore, it is vital to empower all minorities, including Armenians as full citizens with constitutional rights and guarantees to ensure their full participation in the political, economic, cultural and social life of the State.

In reference to Turkey's obligation to respect the rights of the Armenians, it seems that the Turkish State interferes with almost every sphere of Armenian community life. In theory, CC judgments set precedents and should guide other courts when considering analogous cases. While recent judgments include important findings related to the State's unjustified interference in the internal affairs of the Armenian community, they also raise questions about whether the CC is in fact closing the door to international and regional judicial mechanisms like the ECtHR.

With regard to Turkey's obligation to protect the rights of Armenians, the thesis concludes that Turkish legislation has failed to create an adequate system for the protection of not only Armenians, but also diverse groups against assaults and discrimination. Apart from a few cases, the courts' jurisprudence has mostly failed to achieve minority protection. Over the decades, the Turkish State has institutionalized segregation and discrimination against the Armenian community, increasingly tightening the boundaries of the Armenian community. The notion of Armenians as traitors or foreigners in their own homes and historical lands, is one of the biggest problems the Armenians encounter in modern Turkey. Under these circumstances the community has become reclusive, silent, and fearful.

Confronting the past is important to the present and the future. Recognizing violations and rendering them visible, holding responsible parties accountable for their crimes and institutionalizing justice not only facilitates collective healing but also encourages mutual trust and the desire for peaceful coexistence. The recognition of the Armenian Genocide and reconciling with Armenia and Armenians are now one of the key challenges to Turkey's ongoing process of democratization.

In terms of State obligation to fulfill the rights of Armenians, this thesis concludes that it is no longer sufficient for the Turkish government to limit itself to removing the barriers that make it difficult for Armenians to keep their identities and cultures alive. Direct and systematic government support is vital for the survival of Armenian education and culture. Meanwhile, the disturbing anti-Armenian atmosphere that prevails in broad sections of society ought to be countered through education aimed at reducing ethnic and religious prejudice. This must include a revision of history textbooks as well as appropriate normative and practical measures on a legal, political, and social level. The general aim should be to encourage and achieve respect toward the minorities as well as to effect political, social and cultural equality, effective participation in public life, free development and the promotion of their identity.

The thesis also studied the extent to which Armenians are aware of their rights and to what degree they are involved in human and minority rights activities and mechanisms both locally and internationally. It can be argued that in Lebanon, traditional Armenian political parties and religious institutions are actively engaged in claiming, protecting and ensuring the rights of their communities locally with the help of official stakeholders through negotiation, constant communication discussions and compromises. This should be continued also through more active involvement in legal or judicial mechanisms and through international human rights mechanisms. There is a significant lack of information and knowledge about international human rights laws and mechanisms within the Lebanese Armenians, and second, there is a hesitancy to engage with international human rights mechanisms to raise Armenian concerns in international arenas to avoid blame and confrontations at local levels. Armenians generally try to address their challenges through internal and local channels, and since human rights mechanisms in the Arab world have not been developed and do not function effectively, there is almost no involvement by Lebanese Armenians in any Arab human rights mechanisms.

In Turkey Armenian individuals and foundations, as well as the Patriarchate, are well aware of their rights at a local level and are also aware of the violations that have been committed and the mechanisms to address these violations. They advocate for their rights as much as the State imposed and social restrictions allow. But at a general level, Armenians in Turkey are reluctant to involve themselves in international human rights mechanisms. They fear repercussions and do not believe in the effectiveness of these international mechanisms. Armenians therefore take little part in international human rights initiatives and have different views within the Armenian community regarding the role of the EU and European human rights mechanisms in protecting and ensuring their rights. However, Armenians concede that negotiations with Brussels have laid certain foundations for future developments. In addition, the ECtHR in Strasbourg is considered an important factor in the struggle for better rights, as it has repeatedly reached verdicts in favor of the Armenian community and the Turkish government is legally bound by its decisions.

Regarding the role of the Republic of Armenia in protecting and promoting the rights of the Armenians in Lebanon, it should be noted, that Armenia and Lebanon have well stablished inter-state relationships dating back to the 1990s. Armenia tries to support the Armenian community in Lebanon as much as its limited resources allow and contributes to the peacekeeping efforts between Lebanon and Israel through deploying Armenian peacekeeping forces in UNIFIL. Joint programs between Armenian institutions in Lebanon and institutions within the Armenian State itself are aimed at protecting the Armenian language, history and literature. Although these initiatives are not funded or supported by the Lebanese State, the Armenian community enjoys the full respect of the Lebanese government in such matters, in line with international requirements on host State attitudes towards minority rights.

The role of the Armenian State in promoting the rights of the Armenians in Turkey is minimal, since no official inter-state relations exist between the two countries. Although Armenians in Istanbul have recently started to engage with pan-Armenian activities and have initiated joint cultural exchange projects, there is still a general absence of communication or information sharing between the Armenians in Turkey and the Armenians in the Republic of Armenia or the wider Armenian diaspora. There is no coordination between Armenians in Turkey and the Armenian State to allow the latter to promote the minority rights of Armenians in Turkey either within or outside Turkey by using international human rights mechanisms. In fact, most of the Armenian elite in Istanbul, do not condone such involvement by the Armenian Republic because they fear internal pressure and repercussions. Nevertheless, Armenia has recently been more active in raising awareness and advocating for the rights of its minorities in Turkey through the use of international human rights mechanisms. One recent example was the recommendation made by Armenia in the UPR of Turkey to properly investigate and effectively prosecute racist hate speech and discriminatory statements directed at minorities including Armenians, Kurds and Roma.[2280]

Turkey and Armenia, and Turks and Armenians wherever they may be, need to deal with the traumas of twentieth century events, through dialogue, acknowledging historical wrongdoings and initiating a reconciliation process through legal and social channels that results in proper restitution, remedy and reparations as well as the normalization of inter-state relationships. This is because these two States and their peoples, both at home and in the diaspora, live side by side as they have done for centuries in the past. Furthermore, a well-established inter-state relationship between Armenia and Turkey could remarkably improve the situation of the Armenian minority in Turkey, contribute to international peace and enhance the security and stability of the entire region.

In conclusion, the Armenian identity and culture in Lebanon and Turkey – and indeed their very existence in both countries – face threats of extinction in different degrees. The reduction of the Armenian presence in the Middle East comes with the threat of the evaporation of Armenian civilization and the disappearance of its language and culture. The Armenians are a vulnerable minority and surviving as a minority in a threatening environment is only possible in the

2280 Human Rights Council, "Universal Periodic Review, Forty-fourth session, 15 June-3 July 2020, Agenda item 6 Report of the Working Group on the Universal Periodic Review," 24.03.2020, UN Doc. A/HRC/44/14.

context of a strong community as well as State guarantees founded in international human rights law. Therefore, both Lebanon and Turkey must offer urgent support and guarantees to respect, protect and fulfill the rights of Armenians within their territories. Many unresolved problems face the Armenian community which have been discussed at length in this thesis, and any progress that has been made will not continue without a more concerted effort to re-examine the long-established course of sectarianism in Lebanon and homogenization in Turkey. Reform laws require a radical transformation of the dominant social mentality, and changes to the official rhetoric are vital when it comes to improving the rights of minorities.

In States like Lebanon and Turkey, where internal tensions run high or where the rule of law is not adequately established and the social relationships are threatened, as well as in States whose governments are not interested or deliberately avoid their international obligations, the rights of minorities remain vulnerable, marginalized and do not meet international standards, and this is very much the case for Lebanon and Turkey. It is clear that in order to significantly improve the lives of all minorities, including the Armenians, Lebanon and Turkey need further democratization, strengthening the rule of law and human rights mechanisms and preventing religious-conservative majoritarianism, sectarianism and increasing levels of authoritarianism.

Bibliography

1. Laws/Regulations/Decrees/Case Laws

Act No. 430 of March 3, 1340 (1924) on the Unification of the Educational System in Turkey.

Additional protocol on the Rights of Minorities to the European Convention on Human Rights. 19 January 1993, Doc. 6742, 1403-15/1/93-2-E.

African Charter on Human and Peoples Rights. http://www.humanrights.se/wp-content/uploads/2012/01/African-Charter-on-Human-and-Peoples-Rights.pdf.

AGBU Mission. 15 September 2020, AGBU official website. https://www.agbu.am/en/about-2/mission.

APCHR. Internal Regulations, adopted by Resolution 6826, Regular Session 1285 of the Council of Ministers of Foreign Affairs, September 2007.

Application by Levon Berç Kuzukoğlu and Ohannes Garbis Balmumciyan to Turkish CC. No.2014/17354, 2014.

Application of the Convention on the Prevention and Punishment of the Crime of Genocide (Bosnia and Herzegovina v. Serbia and Montenegro), 26 February 2007, ICJ, Merits, I.C.J. Reports 2007.

Arab Charter on Human Rights (2004). The League of Arab States. 22.05.2004, reprinted in 12 Int'l Hum. Rts. Rep. 893 (2005), entered into force on 15.03.2008.

ARF Programme (*Dzrakir Hay Heghapokhagan Tashnagtsutian*). Published by the 27-th General Assembly of ARF, 1998.

Articles adopted in first reading by the Third Committee of the Conference for the Codification of International Law in 1930 (Yearbook of the International Law Commission, 1956, Vol. II, p. 225).

Beirut Declaration on The Regional Protection of Human Rights, published by the Cairo Institute for Human Rights Studies and the Association for the Defence of Human Rights and Liberty. Beirut, Lebanon, 2003, https://bit.ly/354ATEY.

Beyoğlu Civil Court Decision (3. Asliye Hukuk Mahkemesi), Esas No: 2007/106, Decision No: 2007/197.

Cairo Declaration on Human Rights in Islam. U.N. GAOR, World Conf. on Hum. Rts., 4th Sess., Agenda Item 5, 05.08.1990, U.N. Doc. A/CONF.157/PC/62/Add.18 (1993). https://www.refworld.org/docid/3ae6b3822c.html

Canada: Immigration and Refugee Board of Canada. “Lebanon: Situation of Christians, including treatment by society and authorities; treatment of Christians by Hezbollah and Al-Qaeda; State protection (2011-2013).” 6.01.2014, LBN104728.E, https://bit.ly/2NElbYF.

CEDAW Committee. Concluding Observations and Recommendations - Report of the Republic of Lebanon, 2015, UN Doc. CEDAW/C/LBN/CO/4-5.

— — —. Concluding Observations of the UN Committee on the Elimination of Discrimination against Women, Lebanon, 33rd session, July 2005, UN Doc. CEDAW/C/LBN/CO/2.

— — —. Concluding Observations on the Combined Fourth and Fifth periodic reports of Lebanon, 2015, UN Doc. CEDAW/C/SR.1345 and 1346.

— — —. Consideration of reports submitted by States Parties under Article 18 of the Convention on the Elimination of All Forms of Discrimination Against Women, Third periodic report, Lebanon, July 7, 2006, UN. Doc. CEDAW/C/LBN/3.

— — —. General Recommendation No.21, Equality in Marriage and family relations (1994), UN Doc. HRI/GEN/1/Rev.9.

— — —. General Recommendation No. 25, on Article 4, paragraph 1, of the Convention on the Elimination of All Forms of Discrimination against Women, on Temporary Special Measures, Thirtieth session, 2004.

— — —. Summary record (partial) of the 1346th meeting, CEDAW/C/SR.1346, 06.11.2015.

CERD Committee. Combined Twenty-third and Twenty-fourth Periodic Reports Submitted by Lebanon under Article 9 of the Convention, due in year 2018, 29 January 2019, UN Doc. CERD/C/LBN/23-24.

— — —. Committee on the Elimination of Racial Discrimination considers the report of Lebanon. UN OHCHR official website, 11.08.2016, https://www.ohchr.org/EN/NewsEvents/Pages/DisplayNews.aspx?NewsID=20366&LangID=E

— — —. Concluding Observations on the Combined Fourth to Sixth Periodic Reports of Turkey. 2016, UN Doc. CERD/C/Tur/CO/4–6.

— — —. Concluding Observations on the Combined Eighteenth to Twenty-second Periodic Reports of Lebanon, 05.10.2016, UN Doc. CERD/C/LBN/CO/18-22, and 28.04.2004, UN Doc. CERD/C/64/CO/3.

— — —. Concluding Comments on Turkey 2009, 24.03.2009, UN Doc. CERD/C/TUR/CO/3.

— — —. Consideration of Reports Submitted by State Parties Under Article 9 of the Convention: Concluding Observations of the Committee on the Elimination of Racial Discrimination Lebanon, 28.04.2004, UN Doc. CERD/C/64/CO/3.

— — —. General Recommendation No. 32, The Meaning and Scope of Special Measures in the ICERD, 24 September 2009, UN Doc. CERD/C/GC/32.

— — —."Implementation of the ICERD, Article 7: "Teaching, Education, Culture and Information as Means of Eliminating Racial Discrimination, New York, United Nations, 1985.

— — —. Jewish Community of Oslo et al. v. Norway, Communication Application No.30/2003, U.N. Doc. CERD/C/67/D/30/2003 (2005).

— — —. "Monitoring racial equality and non-discrimination." UNHCR official website, August 2020, http://www2.ohchr.org/english/bodies/cerd/.

— — —. Reports Submitted by States Parties under the Article 9 of the Convention Combined Fourth to Sixth Periodic Reports of States Parties due in 2013 Turkey, 10.02.2014, CERD/C/TUR/4-6.

— — —. Reports Submitted by States Parties Under Article 9 of the Convention, sixteenth Periodic Reports of States parties due in 2002, UN Doc. CERD/C/383/Add.218, November 2003.

— — —. Seventy-fourth Session 16 February – 6 March 2009, Consideration of Reports Submitted by States Parties under Article 9 of the Convention: Concluding Observations of the Committee on the Elimination of Racial Discrimination, 2009, UN Doc. CERD/C/GMB/CO/14.

— — —. Turkey Report (2007) to the CERD. UN DOC. CERD/C/TUR/3.

CESCR. Concluding Observations on the Second Periodic Report of Lebanon, October 2016 UN Doc. E/C.12/LBN/CO/2.

— — —. General Comment No. 13: The Right to Education (Art. 13), UN Doc. E/C.12/1999/10 (Twenty-first session, 1999).

— — —. General Comment No 14: The Right to the Highest Attainable Standard of Health (Art. 12) 11 August 2000, UN Doc. E/C.12/2000/4.

— — —. General Comment No. 17: The Right of Everyone to Benefit from the Protection of the Moral and Material Interests Resulting from any Scientific, Literary or Artistic Production of Which He or She is the Author (Art. 15, Para. 1 (c) of the Covenant), 12.01.2006, UN Doc. E/C.12/GC/17.

— — —. General Comment No. 20: Non-discrimination in Economic, Social and Cultural Rights (art. 2, para. 2 of the International Covenant on Economic, Social and Cultural Rights), 2 July 2009, UN Doc. E/C.12/GC/20.

— — —. General comment No. 21: Right of everyone to take part in cultural life (Art. 15, para. 1a of the Covenant on Economic, Social and Cultural Rights), 21.12.2009, UN Doc. E/C.12/GC/21, https://www.refworld.org/docid/4ed35bae2.html.

———. List of issues in relation to the second periodic report of Lebanon, 20 July 2016, E/C.12/LBN/Q/2/Add.1.

———. The right to take part in cultural life: comments / submitted by the International Labour Organization, 09.05.2008, UN Doc. E/C. 12/40/12.

Charter of the United Nations, see http://www.un.org/en/sections/un-charter/chapter-i/index.html.

Code of Armenian Prelacy of Lebanon. www.armprelecylb.org, https://bit.ly/2Wy57dJ.

Commission on Human Rights on The Elimination of all Forms of Intolerance and of Discrimination. Interim Report of the Special Rapporteur of the Commission on Human Rights on the elimination of all forms of intolerance and of discrimination based on religion or belief Addendum 1 Situation in Turkey, 11.08.2000, UN Doc. A/55/280/Add.1.

Committee on The Protection of The Rights of All Migrant Workers and Members of Their Families Concluding Observations on the Initial Report of Turkey, 2006, UN Doc. CMW/C/TUR/CO/1.

Conference on Yugoslavia Arbitration Committee, 'Opinion No. 1', 31 *International Legal Materials* (1992) p. 1496; Conference on Yugoslavia Arbitration Committee, 'Opinion No. 2', 31 *International Legal Materials* (1992) p. 1498.

Constitution of Republic of Armenia adopted on *Adopted on 27.11. 2005*, https://www.president.am/en/constitution-2005/.

Constitution of Republic of Lebanon of 1926 with Amendments through 2004, OUP, Translated by Fouad Fahmy Shafik (constitution) and Abed Awad (Law No.462).

Constitution of Republic of Turkey, Turkey's Constitution of 1982 with Amendments through 2017, constituteproject.org/constitution/Turkey_2017.pdf?lang=en.

Constitutional Court of Turkey. "Din özgürlüğü ihlali" kararının gerekçesini açıkladı (Constitutional Court announces the reason for the "violation of freedom of religion" decision.") 10.07.2019, http://www.agos.com.tr/tr/yazi/22652/anayasa-mahkemesi-din-ozgurlugu-ihlali-kararinin-gerekcesini-acikladi.

Constitutional Court Rules of Procedure of Turkey. Published in the Official Gazette, 12 July 2012 – 28351.

Constitutional Court of Turkey, Verdict TEP (*Türkiye Emekçi Partisi*, Proletarian Party of Turkey), 08.05. 1980.

Convention [IV] Respecting the Laws and Customs of War on Land, Article 3, in James Brown Scott (ed.), The Hague Conventions and Declarations of 1899 and 1907. New York, NY,USA: OUP, 1915.

Convention on the Rights of the Child adopted and opened for signature, ratification and accession by UNGA Resolution 44/25 of 20 November 1989, entry into force 2 September 1990, in accordance with Article 49.

Convention on The Prevention and Punishment of The Crime of Genocide adopted by Resolution 260 (III) A of the UNGA 09.12.1948.

Copenhagen European Council 12 And 13 December 2002 Presidency Conclusions, https://www.consilium.europa.eu/media/20906/73842.pdf

Council of Europe, Collective Complaints Procedure - European Social Charter, (Council of Europe Publication, 2017).

— — —. European Charter for Regional or Minority Languages- 1992.

— — —. Explanatory Report for the Framework Convention for the Protection of National Minorities. European Treaty Series - No.157, Strasbourg, Council of Europe Publication, 1.11.1995.

— — —. Explanatory Report to the European Charter for Regional or Minority Languages. European Treaty Series No.148. Strasbourg, Council of Europe Publication, 5.11.1992.

— — —. Framework Convention for the Protection of National Minorities -1992.

— — —. Factsheet on the Framework Convention for the Protection of National Minorities, CoE official website, https://www.coe.int/en/web/minorities/fcnm-factsheet.

— — —. Monitoring the implementation of the Framework Convention for the Protection ofNational Minorities, CoE official website,https://www.coe.int/en/web/minorities/monitoring.\

— — —. Parliamentary Assembly Additional Protocol on the Rights of Minorities to the European Convention on Human Rights, 1993.

Council of Ministers of Foreign Affairs of LAS. Decision No.7790, 7 September 2014.

Court of Cassation in Lebanon. June 25, 1965, p. 117; al-ʿAdl, 2001, ruling of 29.03.2001.

CRC Committee. Consideration of Reports Submitted by States Parties under Article 44 of the Convention Concluding Observations: Turkey, UN Doc. CRC/C/TUR/CO/2-3, 2012.

— — —. General Comment No. 1: Article 29 (1), The aims of education, 17.04.2001, UN Doc. CRC/GC/2001/1.

— — —. General Comment No. 11: Indigenous People and their Rights under the Convention, fifth session, UN Doc. GRC/C/GC/11, 2009.

Decision No. 1/95 of the EC-Turkey Association Council Of 22 December 1995 on Implementing the Final Phase of The Customs Union (96/142/Ec).

Decision No. 5/1997 of Court of Cassation of Lebanon (Dissenting Opinion of Judge Mounah Mitri).

Decision No. 7/1985 of Court of Cassation of Lebanon.

Decision No. 9/1991 of Court of Cassation of Lebanon (Plenary assembly).

Decision No. 9/1991 of Court of Cassation of Lebanon.

Decision No. 25/1996 of Court of Cassation of Lebanon.

Decision No. 176 of French High Commissioner in Lebanon of 1939/8/19.

Decision No. 355 of French High Commissioner in Lebanon, 1940/12/18.

Decision No.1811 of French High Commissioner in Lebanon, May 1940 in Lebanon.

Decisions of the Constitutional Council in Lebanon 07.08.1994.

Decisions of the Constitutional Council in Lebanon 18.09.1995.

Decisions of the Constitutional Council in Lebanon 10.05.2001.

Decision of Turkish CC No:94/2 of 16.6.1994, in Official Gazette, 30 June 1994.

Decree No. 15 of 1925 on Lebanese Nationality.

Decree No. 60 Law and Regulations of 1936 on Religions in Lebanon.

Decree No.703 Amending Certain Laws and Decrees for the Purposes of Compliance with the Amendments to the Constitution, 3rd repeating Official Gazette dated 9 July 2018 and numbered 30473, Turkey.

Decree No. 7855 Law of the Judicial Organization Law in Lebanon, 1961.

Decree No.15215 of 27-9-2005 and its amendments, the appointment of holidays and official occasions in Lebanon.

Decree No. 511654 on Patriarchal election rules adopted in 1961 in Turkey.

Document of the Copenhagen Meeting of the Conference on the Human Dimension of the CSCE: https://bit.ly/2P3rMv4.

Doha Agreement 'On the Results of the Lebanese National Dialogue Conference, UN Doc. S/2008/392, https://bit.ly/34PpLJf.

ECHR. Guide to Article 8 of the European Convention on Human Rights, the right to respect private and family life, home and correspondence, Updated on 31 August 2019.

— — —. Guide on Article 11 of the European Convention on Human Rights, Freedom of assembly and association, Council of Europe, 31.05.2020.

ECtHR Case. Apostolidi and Others v. Turkey, Application No.45628/99, § 64, 27.03.2007.

— — —. Barankevich v. Russia Final, Application No.10519/03 Final, Eur. Ct. H.R. (Oct. 26, 2007).

———. Baylac-Ferrer and Suarez v. France, Application No.27977/04, 25/09/2008.

———. Belgian Linguistics, Application No 1474/62, 23 July 1968.

———. Bulgakov v. Ukraine, Application No. 59894/00, 2007.

———. Chauvy and Others v. France, Application No. 64915/01, 29 June 2004.

———. Fokas v. Turkey, Application No. 31206/02, § 30, 29.09.2009.

———. Garaudy v. France, Application No. 65831/01, 24.06.2003.

———. Güzel Erdagöz v. Turkey, Application No. 37483/02, 21.10.2008.

———. Hasan and Chavush v. Bulgaria, Application No. 30985/96, 2000.

———. Kokkinakis v. Greece, Application No. 14308/88, 25.05.1993.

———. Kozacıoğlu v. Turkey [GC], Application No. 2334/03, 19 02.2009.

———. Lehideux and Isorni v. France, Application No. 55/1997/839/1045, 1998.

———. Magyar Keresztény Mennonita Egyház and Others V. Hungary, Application No.70945/11 et al., 08.09.2014.

———. Mentzen v. Latvia, Application No.71074/01, 2004.

———. Mesut Yurtsever and Others v. Turkey, Application nos. 14946/08, 21030/08, 24309/08, 20.01.2015.

———. Monnat v. Switzerland, Application No.73604/01, 2006.

———. Nacaryan and Deryan v. Turkey, Application Nos.19558/02 and 27904/02, § 30, 08.01.2008.

———. Perinçek v. Switzerland, 15.10.2015, Application No. 27510/08.

———. Sejdic and Finci v Bosnia and Herzegovina, Application Nos. 27996/06 and 34836/06, Merits, 22.12.2009.

———. Sidiropoulos and Others v. Greece (57/1997/841/1047), Application No. 26695/95 10 July 1998.

———. Syllogos Ton Athinaion v. The United Kingdom, Application No. 48259/15, 31.05.2016.

———. Thlimmenos v Greece, Application No. 34369, 1997.

———. Ulusoy and Others v. Turkey, Application No. 34797/03, 03.05.2007.

———. Young, James and Webster v. The United Kingdom, Application No. 7601/76; 7806/77, 1982.

ECRI. Appendix: Government's Viewpoint, Observations of the Turkish Government on ECRI's Fifth Report on Turkey, 2016.

———. Conclusions on the Implementation of the Recommendations in Respect of Turkey Subject to Interim Follow-Up, adopted 03.04.2019, Published 6 June 2019.

— — —. "Leaflet". 2019, https://rm.coe.int/leaflet-ecri-2019/168094b101.

— — —. Report on Turkey, fifth monitoring cycle ECRI Secretariat Directorate General II - Democracy, Council of Europe, 29 June 2016.

— — —. Report on Turkey, fourth monitoring cycle ECRI Secretariat Directorate General II - Democracy, CoE, Dec. 2010.

Emek Partisi vs. Yargıtay Cumhuriyet Başsavcılığ (Labor Party vs. Supreme Court of Appeals Prosecution Office) in Turkey, Official Gazete:26.6.1998/ 23384.

EU Charter of Fundamental Rights: https://eur-lex.europa.eu/legal-content/EN/TXT/?uri=CELEX:12012P/TXT.

EU-Turkey Association Agreement (the "Ankara Agreement"), 12 September 1963, https://www.europarl.europa.eu/delegations/en/d-tr/documents/eu-texts

European Commission. Key findings of the 2019 Report on Turkey, European Commission - Countries insights, Brussels, 29.05.2019.

— — —. Turkey 1999 Regular Report, Brussels, 13.10.1999.

— — —. Turkey 2000 Regular Report, Brussels, 08.11.2000.

— — —. Turkey 2001 Regular Report, SEC (2001) 1756, Brussels, 2001.

— — —. Turkey 2002 Regular Report, SEC (2002) 1412, Brussels, 2002.

— — —. Turkey 2003 Regular Report, SEC (2003) 1426, Brussels, 2003.

— — —. Turkey 2004 Regular Report, SEC (2004) 1201, Brussels, 2004.

— — —. Turkey 2005 Progress Report, SEC (2005) 1426, Brussels, 2005a.

— — —. Turkey 2006 Progress Report, SEC (2006) 1390, Brussels, 2006a.

— — —. Turkey 2007 Progress Report, SEC (2007) 1436, Brussels, 2007.

— — —. Turkey 2008 Progress Report, SEC (2008) 2699, Brussels, 2008.

— — —. Turkey 2009 Progress Report, SEC (2009) 1334, Brussels, 2009.

— — —. Turkey 2010 Progress Report, SEC (2010) 1327, Brussels, 2010.

— — —. Turkey 2011 Progress Report, SEC (2011) 1201 final, Brussels, 2011.

— — —. Turkey 2012 Progress Report, SWD (2012) 336 final, Brussels, 2012.

— — —. Turkey 2013 Progress Report, SWD (2013) 417 final, Brussels, 2013.

— — —. Turkey 2014 Progress Report, SWD (2014) 307 final, Brussels, 2014.

— — —. Turkey 2015 Progress Report, SWD (2015) 216 final, Brussels, 2015.

— — —. Turkey 2016 Progress Report, SWD (2016) 366 final, Brussels, 2016.

— — —. Turkey 2018 Progress Report, SWD (2018) 153 final, Brussels, 2018.

— — —. Turkey 2018 Progress Report, SWD (2019) 220 final, Brussels, 2019.

European Commission for Democracy Through Law (Venice Commission). ‘Opinion on the amendments to the constitution adopted by the Grand National Assembly on 21 January 2017 and to be submitted to a national referendum on 16.04.2017’, www.venice.coe.int/webforms/ documents/ ?pdf=CDL-AD(2017)005-e.

— — —. “Report on Non-Citizens and Minority Rights.” adopted by the Venice Commission at its 69th plenary session (Venice, 15-16.12.2006), CDL-AD (2007)001para. 13.

— — —. Opinion on the Legal Status of Religious Communities in Turkey and the Right of the Orthodox Patriarchate of Istanbul to use the adjective “Ecumenical” adopted by the Venice Commission at its 82nd Plenary Session (Venice, 12-13.03.2010).

European Convention on Human Rights and Fundamental Freedoms, Council of Europe 04.11.1950.

European Council Directive 2000/43/EC of 29 June 2000 implementing the principle of equal treatment between persons irrespective of racial or ethnic origin, https://bit.ly/35V2fuN.

EU Network of Independent Experts on Fundamental Rights. Thematic Comment No.3 on “The Protection of Minorities in the EU.” 25.04.2005.

European Social Charter, 18.10.1961 ETS No.035.

Gusevs Viktors (Latvian) Petition 0714/2013, European Parliament Document, 31.03.2014, https://bit.ly/35XrLzy.

Hamazkayin Educational and Cultural Association Bylaws: https://www.hamazkayin.com/en/bylaws/.

Helsinki European Council 10 And 11 December 1999 Presidency Conclusions, https://www.europarl.europa.eu/summits/hel1_en.htm

Homenetmen Statutes. 2019, https://www.homenetmen.org/upload/pdf/Homenetmen-General-Bylaw-Ganonakir-2019.pdf

HRC. Ballantyne, Davidson, McIntyre v. Canada, Communications Nos. 359/ 1989 and 385/1989, UN Doc. CCPR/C/47/D/359/1989 and 385/1989/Rev.1 (1993).

— — —. CCPR General Comment No.18: Non-Discrimination, adopted at the Thirty-seventh Session of the Human Rights Committee, on 10 November 1989, UN Doc. CCPR/C/21/Rev.1/Add.1.

— — —. CCPR General Comment No.22: The right to freedom of thought, conscience and religion (Art. 18), 30.07.93, UN Doc. CCPR/C/21/Rev.1/Add.4.

— — —. CCPR General Comment No.23: Article 27 (Fiftieth session, 1994), Compilation of General Comments and General Recommendations adopted by Human Rights Treaty Bodies, U.N. Doc. HRI/GEN/1/Rev.1 at 38, 1994.

— — —. CCPR General Comment No. 24 (52): on Issues Relating to Reservations Made upon Ratification or Accession to the Covenant or the Optional Protocols thereto, or in Relation to Declarations under Article 41 of the Covenant." 04.11.1994, UN Doc. CCPR/C/21/Rev.1/Add.6.

— — —. CCPR General Comment No. 29: Article 4: Derogations during a State of Emergency, 2001m UN Doc. CCPR/C/21/Rev.1/Add.11.

— — —. CCPR General Comment No. 31: The Nature of the General Legal Obligation Imposed on States Parties to the Covenant, 26.05.2012 UN Doc. CCPR/C/21/Rev.1/Add. 13.

— — —. Concluding Observations on the Third Periodic Report of Lebanon, 09.05.2018. UN Doc. CCPR/C/NBN/CO/3.

— — —. Concluding Observations on the Initial Report of Turkey Adopted by the Committee at its 106th Session (15 October - 2 November 2012), UN Doc. CCPR/C/TUR/CO/1.

— — —. Consideration of reports submitted by States Parties under Article 40 of the Covenant, UN Doc. CCPR/C/LBN/3, 28.12.2016.

— — —. 'Initial Reports of States Parties: Turkey'. April 2011, UN Doc. CCPR/C/Tur/1.

— — —. Ivan Kitok v. Sweden, Communication No.197/1985, CCPR/C/33/D/197/1985 (1988), para. 9.8.

— — —. Lubicon Lake Band v. Canada, Communication No.167/1984 (26.03.1990), UN Doc. Supp. No.40 (A/45/40) at 1 (1990).

— — —. Sandra Lovelace v. Canada, Communication No.24/1977: Canada 30/07/81, UN Doc. CCPR/C/13/D/24/1977.

Human Rights Council. Compilation prepared by the Office of the United Nations High Commissioner for Human Rights in accordance with paragraph 15 (b) of the annex to Human Rights Council Resolution 5/1 and paragraph 5 of the annex to Council Resolution 16/21, August 2015, A/HRC/WG.6/23/LB/N/2.

— — —. Compilation prepared by the Office of the High Commissioner for Human Rights in accordance with paragraph 15 (b) of the annex to Human Rights Council Resolution 5/1, 02.09.2010, UN Doc. A/HRC/WG.6/9/LBN/2.

— — —. National report submitted in accordance with paragraph 5 of the annex to Human Rights Council Resolution 16/21, Lebanese Republic, 25.09.2015. UN Doc. A/HRC/WG.6/23/LBN/1.

———. National report submitted in accordance with paragraph 15 (a) of the annex to Human Rights Council Resolution 5/1 Lebanese Republic, UN Doc. A/HRC/WG.6/9/LBN/1 2015.

———. "Note by the Special Rapporteur on Minority Issues, Rita Izsák, on preventing and addressing violence and atrocity crimes targeted against minorities." UN Doc., A/HRC/FMI/2014/2 https://bit.ly/2RlhtFr.

———. Report of the Independent Expert on Minority Issues, Gay McDougall, Thirteenth Session, 07.01 2010, UN Doc. A/HRC/13/23.

———. Report of the Special Rapporteur on Freedom of Religion or Belief on His Mission to Lebanon, 30 November 2015, UN Doc. A/HRC/31/18/Add.1.

———. Report of the Working Group on the Universal Periodic Review-Lebanon, 22.12.2015, UN Doc. A/HRC/31/5.

———. Resolution 6/15, Forum on Minority Issues, 28.09.2007 UN. Doc A/HRC/RES/6/15.

———. Resolution 18/23 Forum on Minority Issues, 10.04.2012, UN Doc. A/HRC/RES/19/23.

———. Summary of Stakeholders' submissions on Turkey Report of the Office of the United Nations High Commissioner for Human Rights, 12 November 2019, UN Doc. A/HRC/WG.6/35/TUR/3.

———. Universal Periodic Review, Report of the Working Group on the Universal Periodic Review, Forty-fourth session, 15 June-3 July 2020, Agenda item 6, 24.03.2020, UN Doc. A/HRC/44/14.

———. Working Group on the Universal Periodic Review, Thirty-Fifth Session 20–31 January 2020 National report submitted in accordance with paragraph 5 of the annex to Human Rights Council Resolution 16/21, Turkey, 2020 Un Doc. A/HRC/WG.6/35/TUR/1.

———. Working Group on the Universal Periodic Review, Thirty-fifth Session 20 31 January 2020 Compilation on Turkey, Report of the Office of the United Nations High Commissioner for Human Rights, A/HRC/WG.6/35/TUR/2.

———. Working Group on the Universal Periodic Review Thirty-fifth session, Summary of Stakeholders' submissions on Turkey Report of the Office of the United Nations High Commissioner for Human Rights, 2020, UN Doc. A/HRC/WG.6/35/TUR/3.

International Covenant on Civil and Political Rights (ICCPR). Adopted by UNGA Resolution 2200A (21) on 16.12.1966.

International Covenant on Economic, Social and Cultural Rights. Adopted by UNGA Resolution 2200A (21) on 16.12.1966.

International Convention on The Elimination of Racial Discrimination (CERD) (1965). Adopted and opened for signature and ratification by UNGA Resolution 2106 (20) of 21.12.1965.

International Human Rights Instruments. Compilation of Guidelines on the Form and Content of Reports to be Submitted by States Parties to the International Human Rights Treaties, Addendum, May 2003, UN Doc. HRI/GEN/2/Rev.1/Add.2.

International Law Commission. Draft Articles on Responsibility of States for Internationally Wrongful Acts, with commentaries, 2001, UN DOC A/56/10 2:1: https://bit.ly/2KtkjnC.

— — —. "Guide to Practice on Reservations to Treaties." 2011, UN Doc. A/66/10/Add.1.

Intervention Request Submitted by Municipality of Anjar to the Court of First Instance in Bekka, 01.10.1997.

Istanbul Ermeni Patriği Mutafyan'in Vefati Ve Yeni Patrik Seçimi Süreci Yorum No.2019/30, (The Death Of Istanbul Armenian Patriarch Mutafyan And The Election Process of The New Patriarch Comment No.2019/30,) Avrasya İncelemeleri Merkezi (Center For Eurasian Studies), https://avim.org.tr/tr/Yorum/ISTANBUL-ERMENI-PATRIGI-MUTAFYAN-IN-VEFATI-VE-YENI-PATRIK-SECIMI-SURECI.

Izsák Rita. "Minority Issues in the First Cycle of the Universal Periodic Review (UPR) An analysis by the UN Special Rapporteur on Minority Issues." UNOHCHR, 2014, https://bit.ly/38C7Kmv.

— — —. "Report of the Special Rapporteur on Minority Issues, Human Rights Council Thirty-fourth session." 2017, UN Document, A/HRC/34/53.

LAS Council. Resolution No.5437, 1994.

— — —. Resolution No.6089, 12.03.2001.

— — —. Resolution No.6302, 24.03.2003.

Law No. 40/63 on Property Rights in Lebanon, 02.11.1963.

Law No. 120 CUP's *Cemiyetler Kanunu* (Association Law) of 1909.

Law No. 422 on Protection of Children in Violation of the Law or Exposed to Danger in Lebanon, 2002.

Law No. 553 Regulating Religious Sects in Lebanon, 24.07.1996.

Law No. 648 Law on Political Parties in Turkey, 13.07.1965.

Law No. 671 (The Hat Law) in Turkey 25.11.1925.

Law No. 2596 Relating to Prohibited Garments in Turkey, 1934.

Law No. 2762 for Foundations passed on: 05.06.1935.

Law No. 2935 State of Emergency Law in Turkey, 25.10.1983.

Law No. 4771 on Act amending various Acts of 2002 in Turkey, 08.08.2002.

Law No. 5237 Turkish Panel Code, Official Gazette 12/10/2004 No. 25611.

Law No. 5253 Association Law of Turkey, 04.11.2004.

Law No. 5442 Provincial Administration Law in Turkey, 10.06.1949.

Law No. 5580 of Private Education Institutions in Turkey, promulgated in Official Gazette 26434, 14 February 2007.

Law No. 5737 on Foundations in Turkey, adopted on 26.02.2008.

Law No. 5759 of 30.04.2008 to amend the New Turkish Criminal Code No. 5237 dated 26.09.2004.

Law No. 6216 on The Establishment and Rules of Procedure of The Constitutional Court of Turkey, March 2011.

Law No. 6328 on the Ombudsman in Turkey, Official Gazette dated 29.06.2013 and no. 28338.

Law No. 6529 to amend various Acts with the purpose of advancing the Fundamental Rights and Liberties in Turkey, 02.03.2014.

Law No. 6581 "Turkish and Turkish Culture Teachers at Minority Schools" 27.05.1955.

Law No. 6698 on the Protection of Personal Data, published in the Official Gazette on 7 April2016 and no. 29677, Turkey.

Law No. 6701 Law on Turkish Human Rights and Equality Institution. 20.4.2016. Published in the Official Gazette dated 20/4/2016 numbered 29690.

Law on Cultural Autonomy for National Minorities in Estonia, adopted in 1925.

Law on the Rights of Christian and Jewish Communities' Religious Authorities in Lebanon, 2.04.1951.

Lebanese Chamber of Deputies. Act No.62/16 of 19 October 2016 establishing an independent National Human Rights Commission including a Committee on the Prevention of Torture in Lebanon.

— — —. Act No.28 on access to information adopted in February 2017.

— — —. Act No.62/2016 establishing an independent National Human Rights Commission.

— — —. Resolution, 03.04.1997 Recognizing the Armenian Genocide.

— — —. Resolution, 11.05.2000 Recognizing the Armenian Genocide.

Lebanese Code of Civil Procedure, Legislative Decree No.90/83.

Lebanese Ministry of Education. Haykaliya jadida li al-taʿlim fi lubnan, (New Structure for Education in Lebanon), Ministry of Education Publication, 1995.

Lebanese Panel Code, Legislative Decree No. 340, 1943-03-01.

Legal Committee of Anjar Land Dispute. "*Hagirj Deghegutioon Aynjari Hoghayin Hartsin Veraperyal.*" (Summary Information of Anjar Land Dispute), Lebanon, a summary report, 2007.

Mandate of OSCE: http://www.osce.org/hcnm/107878.

Marrakesh Declaration. Executive Summary of the Marrakesh Declaration on the Rights of Religious Minorities in Predominantly Muslim Majority Communities 25th-27th January 2016, http://www.marrakeshdeclaration.org/files/Bismilah-2-ENG.pdf.

Norwegian Helsinki Committee Freedom of Belief Initiative. 2019 Report Pursuing Rights and Equality: Monitoring Report on The Right to Freedom of Religion or Belief in Turkey, Norwegian Helsinki Committee Freedom of Belief Initiative, 2019.

Official Gazette in Turkey No.25173, 19.07.2003. Amendment to the Law on Construction in Turkey.

— — —. No: 27580, Genelge (Circular), 13.05.2010, https://www.resmigazete.gov.tr/eskiler/2010/05/20100513-17.htm.

OIC Charter. https://www.oic-oci.org/page/?p_id=53&p_ref=27&lan=en.

OSCE. Office for Democratic Institutions and Human Rights (ODIHR), Turkey, Early Presidential and Parliamentary Elections, 24 June 2018: Final Report, 21.09.2018, https://www.osce.org/odihr/elections/turkey/397046.

— — —. The Bolzano/Bozen Recommendations on National Minorities in Inter-State Relations & Explanatory Note. OSCE Publication, June 2008.

— — —. The Graz Recommendations on Access to Justice and National Minorities. OSCE publication, November 2017.

— — —. The Hague Recommendations Regarding the Education Rights of National Minorities. OSCE publication, October 1996.

— — —. The Lund Recommendations on the Effective Participation of National Minorities in Public Life. OSCE Publication, 1999,

— — —. The Oslo Recommendations Regarding the Linguistic Rights of National Minorities. OSCE Publication, February 1998.

Ottoman Law on Associations. Provided and translated by the International Center for Not-for-Profit Law, https://bit.ly/327oX0B.

Parliamentary Electoral law of Lebanon - 2017, International Foundation for Electoral System, 2018, https://bit.ly/2X19jTl.

Parliamentary Human Rights Committee of Lebanon. "National Action Plan for Human Rights in Lebanon 2014-2019." https://bit.ly/2K7yezy.

Permanent Court of International Justice, Advisory Opinion in the Greco-Bulgarian communities' case, advisory opinion No.17, July 31, 1930, Series B.

Presidential Decree 4340. The official website of the Presidency of Council of Ministers of Lebanon, 31.01.2019, https://bit.ly/36WOvkO.

Prime Ministerial Order No. 3530 of Turkey, 5.1.2004.

Protocol on the Establishment of Diplomatic Relations between the Republic of Turkey and the Republic of Armenia, http://www.mfa.gov.tr/site_media/html/zurih-protokolleri-en.pdf.

Ratification status of the Arab Charter of Human Rights, https://bit.ly/2REAuEg.

Ratification of 18 International Human Rights Treaties. at https://indicators.ohchr.org/.

Recommendations of the Forum on Minority Issues on Rights to Education, Seventy-fifth session, August 2009, UN Doc. A/HRC/10/11/Add.1.

Regulation on the Implementation of Article 11 of Law of Foundation No. 5737, Official Gazette No.28071, entered into force in 01.10.2011.

Republic of Armenia National Security Strategy (approved at the session of National Security Council at the RA President office on 26.01.2007). https://www.mfa.am/filemanager/Statics/Doctrineeng.pdf.

Republic of Armenia Statistical Committee. "Report of Statistical Committee of Republic of Armenia Permanent Population of the Republic of Armenia as of October 1, 2020." 2020 https://www.armstat.am/file/Article/nasel_01.10.2020.pdf.

Reservation of Turkey to Article 27 of ICCPR in the official website of UNOHCHR, https://treaties.un.org/Pages/ViewDetails.aspx?src=TREATY&mtdsg_no=IV-5&chapter=4&clang=_en#EndDec.

Reservations to the Convention on the Prevention and Punishment of the Crime of Genocide. May 28, 1951, Advisory Opinion, International Court of Justice, ICJ Reports 1951, pp. 15-69.

Rome Statute of The International Criminal Court: https://www.icc-cpi.int/NR/rdonlyres/ADD16852-AEE9-4757-ABE7-9CDC7CF02886/283503/RomeStatuteng1.pdf.

Statute of the International Court of Justice (1945) https://www.un.org/en/charter-united-nations.

T.C. Icisleri Bakanligi [Republic of Turkey Ministry of the Interior]. Response to Oral Question (7/15743) submitted by Turkish Grand National Assembly. 26 November 2010. B.05.0.I LI.00.60001.164.02/9.16/6254.

Tai'f Agreement Text, Paragraph G, Political Reform, https://bit.ly/34Pmutr.

Treaty of Amsterdam amending the Treaty on European Union, the Treaties establishing the European Communities and certain related acts - Contents, Official Journal C 340, 10/11/1997. https://bit.ly/362JLZD

Treaty of Berlin. Treaty between Great Britain, Germany, Austria, France, Italy, Russia, and Turkey for the Settlement of Affairs in the East: Signed at Berlin, July 13, 1878 -Article 16, https://archive.org/details/jstor-2212670/page/n11.

Treaty of Lausanne. Treaty of Peace with Turkey Signed at Lausanne, July 24, 1923.

Treaty of Lausanne VIII. Declaration of Amnesty, www.mfa.gov.tr/viii_-declarat ion-of-amnesty.en.mfa.

Treaty of San Stefano. The Preliminary Treaty of Peace signed at San Stefano March 1878.

Treaty of Sevres. The Treaty of Peace Between the Allied and Associated Powers and Turkey Signed at Sevres August 10, 1920: https://wwi.lib.byu.edu/index.php/Section_I,_Articles_1-260.

Treaty on European Union. Title I: Common Provisions - Official Journal 115, 09/05/2008 P. 0017 – 0017.

Türkiye Büyük Millet Meclisi Zabıt Ceridesi (Turkish Parliament Minutes Journal) 18.11.1920.

Turkey's reservation to CRC and Article 29(C) of CRC: https://treaties.un.org/Pages/ViewDetails.aspx?src=TREATY&mtdsg_no=IV-11&chapter=4&clang=_en#EndDec.

Turkish Committee for Monitoring Minority Rights. "Minorities in Turkey." Human Rights Association, Istanbul, 02.06.1996.

UN Commission on Human Rights. Resolution 1995/24 Rights of persons belonging to national or ethnic, religious and linguistic minorities, ESCOR Supp. (No.4) at 92, 1995 U.N. Doc. E/CN.4/1995/24.

— — —. Resolution 2005/79: Rights of persons belonging to national or ethnic, religious and linguistic minorities." 21.04.2005, UN Doc. E/CN.4/RES/2005/7921.

— — —. Report of the Ad Hoc Working Group of Experts on Southern Africa. February 28, 1969, UN Doc. (E/CN.4/984/Add.18).

UN Declaration on the Elimination of All Forms of Intolerance and of Discrimination Based On Religion Or Belief, Proclaimed by UNGA Resolution 36/55 of 25 November 1981, https://www.ohchr.org/EN/ProfessionalInterest/Pages/ReligionOrBelief.aspx.

UN Declaration on the Rights of Persons Belonging to National or Ethnic, Religious and Linguistic Minorities. Adopted by UNGA Resolution 47/135 of 18.1992 https://www.ohchr.org/EN/ProfessionalInterest/Pages/Minorities.aspx.

UN Document. Guidance Note of the Secretary-General on Racial Discrimination and Protection of Minorities, UN Document, 2013, see https://www.ohchr.org/documents/Issues/Minorities/GuidanceNoteRacialDiscriminationMinorities.pdf.

UN Economic and Social Council. Report of the Third Session of the Sub-Commission on the Prevention of Discrimination and the Protection of Minorities to the Commission on Human Rights (30.01.1950), UN Doc. E/CN.4/358 and E/CN.4/Sub.2/119.

— — —. Commentary on the Working Group on Minorities to the UN Declaration on the Rights of Persons Belonging to National or Ethnic, Religious and Linguistic Minorities, 04.04.2005, UN Doc. E/CN.4/Sub.2/AC.5/2005/2.

— — —. Commission on Human Rights Fifty-fifth session Item 11 (b) of the provisional agenda, Civil and Political Rights, Including Religious Intolerance, UN Doc. E/CN.4/1999/58.

— — —. "Report of the Independent Expert on minority issues". Gay McDougall, 06.01.2006, UN Doc. E/CN.4/2006/74.

— — —. "Study on the rights of persons belonging to national or ethnic, religious and linguistic minorities". E/CN.4/Sub.2/384/Rev.1, 1979.

UNESCO's Constitution. UNESCO Official Page, 2019, https://bit.ly/2JeAfMz.

UNESCO. Convention Against Discrimination in Education 1960.

— — —. Convention on the Protection and Promotion of the Diversity of Cultural Expressions 2005.

— — —. Convention for the Safeguarding of the Intangible Cultural Heritage 2003.

— — —. Submission for the Universal Periodic Review of Turkey, para. 15. Contribution of UNESCO to Compilation of UN Information (to Part I. A. and to Part III - F, J, K, and P): Turkey, 2015, Universal Periodic Review (21st session) https://www.refworld.org/docid/54c109484.html.

— — —. Declaration on Race and Racial Prejudice, 27 November 1978.

— — —. Recommendation on the Safeguarding of Traditional Culture and Folklore, 15 November 1989.

UNGA. Basic Principles and Guidelines on the Right to a Remedy and Reparation for Victims of Gross Violations of International Human Rights Law and Serious Violations of International Humanitarian Law, GA Resolution 60/147, 16.12.2005.

— — —. Elimination of All Forms of Religious Intolerance- Situation in Turkey, Note by the Secretary General, UN Doc. A/55/280/Add.1, para. 62 Sixty-second session Item 72 (b) of the provisional agenda.

— — —. Implementing the responsibility to protect Report of the Secretary-General 2009 UN Doc. A/63/677, https://www.un.org/ruleoflaw/files/SG_reportA_63_677_en.pdf.

— — —. Legal Interim report of the Special Rapporteur of the Commission on Human Rights on the elimination of all forms of intolerance and of discrimination based on religion or belief, UN Doc. A/55/280/Add.1, August 2000.

— — —. Resolution. 16.09.2005, UN DOC A/60/L.1.

— — —. Resolution 60/251, 03.04.2006, UN Doc. A/RES/60/251.

— — —. Resolution adopted by the General Assembly [Part C of General Assembly Resolution 217 (III). International Bill of Human Rights] 217 C (III). Fate of Minorities, 10.12.1948, UN Doc. A/RES/3/217 C.

— — —. World Summit Outcome, Resolution adopted by the UNGA on 16.09.2005, UN Doc. A/RES/60/1.

UN Guide for Minorities. Pamphlet No. 4. The Minorities and The United Nations: Human Rights Treaty Bodies and Complaint Mechanisms.

— — —. Pamphlet No. 7 Minority Rights under the European Convention on Human Rights.

— — —. Pamphlet No. 11. The protection of the Rights of Minorities and the UN Educational, Scientific and Cultural Organization.

— — —. Pamphlet No. 12 "Protection on Refugees who belong to Minorities: The UN High Commissioner for Refugees."

UNDP. Marginalised Minorities in Development Programming: A Resource Guide and Toolkit., New York: UNDP publication, May 2010.

— — —. Lebanon Gender Justice & The Law. USA: UN Publication, 2018.

UNGA & UNSC Implementing the Responsibility to Protect: Accountability for Prevention, 10 August 2017, UN Doc. A/71/1016 –S/2017/556.

UNICEF. Implementation Handbook for the Convention on the Rights of the Child, third ed., UNICEF, 2007, https://www.unicef.org/Implementation_Handbook_for_the_Convention_on_the_Rights_of_the_Child.pdf.

— — —. Mission Statement. https://www.unicef.org/about/who/index_mission.html.

UNIFIL Mandate. The official website of UNIFIL, https://unifil.unmissions.org/unifil-mandate.

Universal Declaration of Human Rights. 10.12.1948.

Universal Islamic Declaration of Human Rights. Adopted by UNGA Resolution 217 A on 19.09.1981, http://www.alhewar.com/ISLAMDECL.html.

UNOHCHR. Compilation on Turkey Report of the Office of the UNHCHR, UN Doc. A/HRC/WG.6/35/TUR/2, 12 November 2019, para. 3.

— — —. International Human Rights Law. 12.12.2020, https://www.ohchr.org/en/professionalinterest/pages/internationallaw.aspx.

— — —. Minority Rights: International Standards and Guidance for Implementation. New York, Geneva: Human Rights Publication 10:3 2010 http://www.ohchr.org/Documents/Publications/MinorityRights_en.pdf.

— — —. Promoting and Protecting Minority Rights: A Guide for Advocates. New York, 2012, http://www.refworld.org/pdfid/5289ce5b4.pdf.

— — —. 'Report on The Impact of The State of Emergency on Human Rights in Turkey, Including an Update on The South-East: January-December 2017', March 2018, www.ohchr.org/Documents/Countries/TR/2018-03-19_Second_OHCHR_Turkey_Report.pdf>.

— — —. Report of the OHCHR. Human Rights Council, Sixteenth session, 2010.

— — —. The Ratification Status of Lebanon. As of July 2020: https://bit.ly/2S3hy1v.

— — —. Working Group on Minorities. 2020, https://www.ohchr.org/EN/Issues/Minorities/Pages/TheformerWGonMinorities.aspx.

UN Working Group on Minorities. Report on its third session, UN Doc. E/CN.4/Sub2/1997/18,10 July 1997.

US Department of State. "2007 Report on International Religious Freedom – Turkey." Bureau of Democracy, Human Rights, and Labor 14.09.2007, https://www.refworld.org/docid/46ee679269.html.

— — —. "Annual Report on International Religious Freedom 2008." https://2001-2009.state.gov/g/drl/rls/irf/2008/108476.htm.

— — —. "2011 Report on International Religious Freedom – Lebanon." Bureau of Democracy, Human Rights, and Labor 30.07.2012, https://bit.ly/2NyCZ7b.

— — —. "2016 Report on International Religious Freedom – Turkey." Bureau of Democracy, Human Rights, and Labor 15.08.2017, https://www.refworld.org/docid/59b7d82a13.html.

— — —. "2018 International Religious Freedom Report – Lebanon." Bureau of Democracy, Human Rights, and Labor, https://bit.ly/36T6gRI.

— — —. "2019 Report on International Religious Freedom: -Turkey." Bureau of Democracy, Human Rights, and Labor, https://bit.ly/3qgyC23.

USCIRF. 2012 Annual Report, p. 4, https://bit.ly/2OxGOwF.

Vienna Convention on The Law of Treaties. No.18232, Vienna, 23.05.1969.

Violations by Article and by State, ECHR Official page, 2020, https://echr.coe.int/Documents/Stats_violation_1959_2019_ENG.pdf.

Written statement of the Government of the United States of America. Reservations to the Convention on the Prevention of Genocide, 28 May 1951, ICJ, Advisory Opinion, I.C.J. Pleadings, p. 25.

2. Books /Articles /Journals/Reports

Abramson, Scott. "Lebanese Armenians; A Distinctive Community in the Armenian Diaspora and in Lebanese Society." *The Levantine Review*, 2:2 (Winter 2013) pp. 188-216.

Açıkgöz, Betül & Erdogan Keskinkılıç. "The Renunciation of Minority Rights and the Making of the 1926 Civil law: *Mahzar*s Penned by Non-Muslim Minorities." *Middle Eastern Studies*, 54:1 (2018) pp. 68-93.

Adam, Laura Batalla. "Turkey's Role in the South Caucasus: Can Peace Be Achieved?" In *Turkish Review*, Kerim Balci ed., 3:3 (2013).

Agos Newspaper. "Nufusumuz Hizla Azaliyor" (Our population is decreasing rapidly), 7.02.2020.

Ahmed Tawhida, & Israel de Jesús Butler. "The European Union and Human Rights: An International Law Perspective." *European Journal of International Law*, 17:4:1 (September 2006), pp. 771–801.

Akçam, Taner. *A Shameful Act: The Armenian Genocide and the Question of Turkish Responsibility*. New York: Metropolitan Books, 2006.

— — —. & Umit Kurt. *The Spirit of the Laws: The Plunder of Wealth in the Armenian Genocide*. New York: Berghahn Books, 2015.

Âkermark, Athanasia Spiliopoulou. *Justifications of Minority Protection in International Law*. London, The Hague, and Boston, MA: Kluwer Law International, 1997.

Akgönül, Samim. *The Minority Concept in the Turkish Context: Practices and Perceptions in Turkey, Gr Orthodox Patriarchate of Istanbul and France* (trans. Sıla Okur). Boston: Brill Publishing, 2013.

— — —. "Religious Minorities." in *The Routledge Handbook of Turkish Politics*, Alpaslan Özerdem, Matthew Whiting eds. New York, Routledge, 2019.

Aktar, A. *Varlik Vergisi ve Turklestirme Politikalari* (Capital Levy and "Turkification" Policies). Istanbul: Iletisim Publication, 2000.

Aktürk Şener. "One nation under Allah? Islamic multiculturalism, Muslim nationalism and Turkey's reforms for Kurds, Alevis, and non-Muslims." *Turkish Studies*, 19:4 (2018) pp. 523-551.

Alenius, Kari. "'The Birth of Cultural Autonomy in Estonia: How, Why, and For Whom?." *Journal of Baltic Studies* 38:4 (Dec. 2007), pp. 445-462.

Alexandris, Alexis. *The Greek Minority of Istanbul and Greek-Turkish Relations (1918-1974)*. Athens: Centre for Asia Minor Studies, 1994.

Altinay, Ayse Gul. *The Grandchildren: The Hidden Legacy of 'Lost' Armenians in Turkey*. New York: Routledge, 2017.

Aprahamian, Sima. "Armenian Identity: "Memory, Ethnoscapes, Narratives of Belonging in the context of the Recent Emerging Notions of Globalization and its Effect on Time and Space." *Feminist Studies in Aotearoa Journal*, 60 (1999) pp. 1-25.

Aras, Bülent & Şule Toktaş. "The EU and Minority Rights in Turkey." *Political Science Quarterly* 124:4 (2010), 697–720.

Arbatli, Cemal Eren & Gunes Gokmen. "Minorities, Human Capital and Long-Run Development: Persistence of Armenian and Greek Influence in Turkey." *CESIFO Working Paper* No.6268 Category 12.12.2016.

Arjomand, Saïd Amir. "The Constitution of Medina: A Sociolegal Interpretation of Muhammad's Acts of Foundation of the Umma." *International Journal of Middle East Studies*, 41:4, (2009) pp. 555-575.

Armenian Forum. "Neglecting Armenian Monuments, Turkey Violates Lausanne Treaty." 17 August 2000.

Armenian International Magazine. August-September 1994.

Armenian Patriarchate. Official Calendar booklet of the Armenian Patriarchate, 2019 Publication, 2019.

Artinian, Vartan. *Osmanlı Devleti'nde Ermeni Anayasasının Doğuşu, 1839-1863*. (The Birth of the Armenian Constitution in the Ottoman State 1839-1863), Istanbul, Aras Yayıncılık, 2004.

Augustyn Adam. "Treaty of Sèvres." *Britannica*, February 2021, https://www.britannica.com/event/Treaty-of-Sevres.

Aukerman, Miriam J. "Definitions and Justifications: Minority and Indigenous Rights in a Central/East European Context." *Human Rights Quarterly*, 22:4 (November 2000), pp 1011-1050.

Avedian, Vahagn. "State Identity, Continuity, and Responsibility: The Ottoman Empire, the Republic of Turkey and the Armenian Genocide." *European Journal of International Law*. 23:3 (August 2012), pp. 797–820.

Avsharian, Roupen. "The Tai'f agreement and the Lebanese Armenians." In *Armenians of Lebanon: From Past Princesses and Refugees to Present-Day Community*, Aida Boudjikian, ed., Beirut: Haigazian University and the Armenian Heritage Press, 2009.

Aybak, Tunç. "Geopolitics of Denial: The Turkish State's 'Armenian Problem.'" *Journal of Balkan and Near Eastern Studies*, 18:2 (2016) pp. 125-144.

Ayşe, Parla & Ceren Özgül. "Property, Dispossession, and Citizenship in Turkey; or The History of the Gezi Uprising Starts in the Surp Hagop Armenian Cemetery." *Public Culture* 28(3/80) (2016), pp. 617–653.

Aztag Newspaper, 03.04.1956.

— — —. 08.10.1975.

— — —. 13.10.1975.

— — —. 23.10.1975.

— — —. 09.01.1976.

— — —. 17.01.1976.

— — —. special issue, January 1994, p.92.

— — —. 28.03.2017.

Babikian, Christine. "L'identité Arménienne: Le cas Libanais." [The Armenian identity: The Lebanese case]. Paper presented at the Présence de L'arménie [The presence of Armenia] conference. Retrieved January 14, 2003, from Saint Joseph University (pp.1-8). History Department. Beirut, Lebanon.

Ballais, J. L., M. Al Amrawy, M. Al Dbiyat, L. Charbel, B. Geyer, L. Mezedjri. "The Place of the French Language in Arabic-Speaking Mediterranean." In *Handbook of the Changing World Language Map*. Brunn S., Kehrein R. (eds.). Cham: Springer, 2018.

Baillie, Lauren C. "Protection of Religious Minorities in Europe: The Council of Europe's Successes and Failures." *American University International Law Review*, 23:3 (2007), pp. 617-645.

Bali, Rifat. "Politics of Turkification During the Single Party Period." In *Turkey Beyond Nationalism*. Kieser, Hans Lukas ed., London: I.B. Taurus, 2006.

Balakian, *Grigoris. Armenian Golgotha: A Memoir of the Armenian Genocide, 1915-1918.* Peter Balakian & Aris Sevag (trans.). New York, USA: Albert A. Knopf, 2009.

Bardakci, Mehmet, A. Freyberg-Inan, C. Giesel, & O. Leisse. *Religious Minorities in Turkey: Alevi, Armenians, and Syriacs and the Struggle to Desecuritize Religious Freedom*. UK: Palgrave Macmillan 2017.

Barkey, Henry. "One Year Later, the Turkish Coup Attempt Remains Shrouded in Mystery." *Washington Post*, 14 July 2017.

Bartrop, Paul & Steven Leonard Jacobs. *Modern Genocide: The Definitive Resource and Document Collection* [4 volumes], Oxford: ABC-Clio, 2015.

Baskin, Oran. "The Minority Concept and Rights in Turkey: The Lausanne Peace Treaty and Current Issues." In *Human Rights in Turkey*, Zehra F. Kabasakal Arat ed., Philadelphia, PA: University of Pennsylvania 2017.

Bassiouni, Mahmoud Cherif. *Crimes against Humanity: Historical Evolution and Contemporary Application*. UK: Cambridge University Press, 25 Apr 2011.

Bayar, Yeşim. "In Pursuit of Homogeneity: The Lausanne Conference, Minorities, and the Turkish Nation." *Nationalities Papers*, 42:1 (2014) pp. 108-125.

Bayır, Derya. *Minorities and Nationalism in Turkish Law*. London: Ashgate Publishing, 2013.

Bebrioghlu, Murat. *Osmanli Devletinde Gayrimulslim Nizamnameleri*, (Non-Muslim Regulations in the Ottoman Empire,) Cahit Klukeci ed., Istanbul, Kişisel Yayinlar, 2008.

Bedoyan, Hratch. "The Social, Political, and Religious Structure of the Armenian Community in Lebanon." *The Armenian Review*, 32:2 (1979).

Belge, Ceren. "Friends of the Court: The Republican Alliance and Selective Activism of the Constitutional Court of Turkey." *Law and Society Review*, 40:3 (2006), pp. 654-655.

Bennafla, Karine. "A land appropriation conflict that reveals and produces borders: the case of Anjar." (Lebanon, Bekaa plain), *Cultures & Conflicts* [En ligne], 73 Printemps 2009.

Bishku, Michael B. "The Interactions and Experiences of Armenians and Jews in the Ottoman Empire and Republic of Turkey from the Young Turk Revolution of 1908 to the Present." *Nationalism and Ethnic Politics*, 23:4 (2017) pp. 431-452.

Bjørnlund, Matthias. "'A Fate Worse Than Dying': Sexual Violence During the Armenian Genocide." In *Brutality and Desire: War and Sexuality in Europe's Twentieth Century*. Dagmar Herzog ed. New York, USA: Palgrave Macmillan, 2009, pp.16 58.

Blake Janet. *Intangible Cultural Heritage - Working Definitions*. Italy: UNESCO, March 2001.

Blau, Judith & Mark Frezzo. *Sociology and Human Rights: A Bill of Rights for the Twenty-First Century*. Pine Forge Press, 2011.

Block, Allison. "S. Judicialization and Implementation of Religious Minority Rights in Turkey: Case Studies from the European Court of Human Rights." Doctoral Thesis, Johnson-Shoyama Graduate School of Public Policy, 2018.

Bogaards, Matthijs. "Formal and Informal Consociational Institutions: A Comparison of the National Pact and the Tai'f Agreement in Lebanon." *Nationalism and Ethnic Politics*, 25:1 (2019) pp. 27-42.

Bolsajian, Monique. "The Armenian Diaspora: Migration and Its Influence on Identity and Politics." *Global Societies Journal*, 6 (2018) pp. 30-40.

Boustani, Marwa, Estella Carpi, Hayat Gebara, & Yara Mourad. "Responding to the Syrian Crisis in Lebanon: Collaboration between Aid Agencies and Local Governance Structures." *Working Paper* September 2016, produced by IIED's Human Settlements Group, 2016 pp. 1-44.

Boyadjian, Maral Dikran. "Ethnic Identity and Psychological Well-Being among Fourth-Generation High School Students in Lebanon." MA Thesis, Beirut: American University of Lebanon, Beirut, 2005.

Bozorgmehri Majid. "The Human Rights in OIC, A Gradual Movement but in Progress." *Journal of Politics and Law*; 10:2 (2017), pp. 43–62.

Braude, Benjamin ed. *Christians and Jews in the Ottoman Empire: The Abridged Edition*. USA: Lynee Rienner, 2014.

Bulut, Eduard Alan. *Minorities in Constitution Making in Turkey*. UK: Cambridge Scholars Publishing, 2017.

Çağaptay Soner. *Islam, Secularism and Nationalism in Modem Turkey: Who Is a Turk?*. London: Routledge, 2005.

Capotorti, Francesco. "The Protection of Minorities under Multinational Agreements on Human Rights." *Italian Yearbook on International Law*, (1976).

Calfat, Natalia Nahas. "The Frailties of Lebanese Democracy: Outcomes and Limits of the Confessional Framework." *Contexto Internacional* 40:2 (May/Aug 2018) pp. 269-293.

Çarıkcı, Alaettin. "The Art of Memory: The Remembrance of the Armenians in Turkey." Dissertation, University of Leiden, 2016.

Carpi, Estella. "Lebanon and Its Linguistic Wandering: On the Road to Language De-essentialization." University of Sydney, 2014.

Carrera, Sergio Elspeth Guild, Lina Vosyliūtė Ceps, & Petra Bard Ceps. "Towards a Comprehensive EU Protection System for Minorities." *Policy Department C: Citizens' Rights and Constitutional Affairs European Parliament*, 2017.

Candar, Tuba. *Hrant Dink: An Armenian Voice of the Voiceless in Turkey*. New York: Routledge, 2017.

Caruso, Ugo & Rainer Hofmann, eds. *The United Nations Declaration on Minorities*. Leiden, The Netherlands: Brill Nijhoff, 2015.

Castellino, Joshua & Kathleen A. Cavanaugh. *Minority Rights in the Middle East*. Oxford: OUP, 2013.

Çayır, Kenan. "Citizenship, Nationality and Minorities in Turkey's Textbooks: From Politics of Non-recognition to 'difference multiculturalism." *Comparative Education*, 51:4 (2015).

Cheterian, Vicken. *Open Wounds: Armenians, Turks and a Century of Genocide.* UK: OUP, 2015 Press.

———. "The Last Closed Border of the Cold War: Turkey–Armenia." *Journal of Borderlands Studies*, 32:1 (2017), pp. 71-90,

———. "Book Review, The Armenians in Modern Turkey: Post-Genocide Society, Politics and History, by Talin Suciyan." *International Affairs*, 93:4 (July 2017), pp. 972–973.

Çolak, Yilmaz. "Language Policy and Official Ideology in Early Republican Turkey." *Middle Eastern Studies*, 40:6 (2004), pp. 67-91.

Collings, Deirdre ed. *Peace for Lebanon? From War to Reconstruction.* London: Lynne Rienner, 1994.

Council of Europe. "Cultural Rights in the Case-law of the European Court of Human Rights." Research Division of ECtHR, 2011 (updated 17 January 2017).

Claudio Corradett. *Philosophical Dimensions of Human Rights: Some Contemporary Views.* Rome: Springer Science & Business Media, 29 Oct 2011.

Crăciunean, Laura-Maria. "The European Court of Human Rights' Approach to Cultural Rights and Cultural Diversity." *Revista Română de Drept Comparat* (February 2013).

Craven, Matthew C.R. "The European Community Arbitration Commission on Yugoslavia." *British Yearbook of International Law,* 66 (1996).

Crawford, James. *The International Law Commission's Articles on State Responsibility: Introduction, Text and Commentaries, United Nations. International Law Commission.* UK: Cambridge University Press, 2002.

Crow, Ralph E. "Religious Sectarianism in the Lebanese Political System." *The Journal of Politics*, 24:3 (Aug 1962), pp. 489-520.

Dadoyan, Seta. B. *The Armenian Catholicosate from Cilicia to Antelias.* Antelias: Armenian Catholicosate of Cilicia, 2003.

Dadrian, Vahakn N. "A Textual Analysis of the Key Indictment of the Turkish Military Tribunal Investigating the Armenian Genocide." *Journal of Military and Political Sociology,* 22 (1994), pp. 125-162.

———. "Children as Victims of Genocide: The Armenian Case." *Journal of Genocide Research* 5:3 (2003), pp.421-437.

———. *The History of the Armenian Genocide.* New York: Berghahn Books, 2003- first published in 1995).

Dakessian, Antranig. "Lebanon". Armenian Diaspora Survey." *Armenian Diaspora Survey*, 2019 https://www.armeniandiasporasurvey.com/Lebanon.

Darbinyan, Asya & Rubina Peroomian. "Children: The Most Vulnerable Victims of the Armenian Genocide." In *Plight and Fate of Children During and*

Following Genocide, *"Genocide: A Critical Bibliographic Review"* book series, Samuel Totten ed., Vol. 10. New Brunswick, USA: Transaction Publishers, 2014, pp. 57-83.

Darbinian, Roupen. "In Retrospect: A Glance at the Last Thirty Years." *Armenian Review*, 6:3–23 (1953), p. 62.

Daudet, Yves & Kishore Singh. *The Right to Education: An Analysis of UNESCO's Standard-setting Instruments*. France: UNESCO, 2001.

Davison, Roderic. "Nationalism as an Ottoman Problem and the Ottoman Response." In *Nationalism in a Non-national State: The Dissolution of the Ottoman Empire*, William W. Haddad & William Ochsenwald ed. Columbus: Ohio State University Press, 1979.

De Waal, Alex. "Darfur and the Failure of the Responsibility to Protect." *International Affairs* 83:6 (2007), pp. 1039–1054.

De Waal, Thomas. *Great Catastrophe: Armenians and Turks in the Shadow of Genocide*. Oxford: OUP, 2015.

De Witte, Bruno & Eniko Horvath. "The Many Faces of Minority Policy in the European Union." In *Synergies in Minority Protection: European and International Law Perspective*, Kristin Henrard & Robert Dunbar eds. UK: Cambridge University press, 2008.

Dekmejian, Hrayr. "The Armenian Diaspora." In *The Armenian People: From Ancient to Modern Times*, Richard G. Hovannisian ed., Vol. 2. New York: St. Martin's Press, 1997.

Der Ghoukassian, K. "Lebanon in My Mind. The Civil War and the Centrality of the Lebanese-Armenian Community in the Making of the Armenia Diaspora Nationalism." In *Armenians of Lebanon: From Past Princesses and Refugees to Present- Day Community*, A. Boudjikian ed., Beirut: Haigazian University, 2009, pp. 411-429.

Der Karabetian, Aghop & Emma Oshagan. "Ethnic Orientation of Armenians in Lebanon." *The Armenian Review* 30:2 (1977).

Der Nersessian & Vahramian. *Aght'amar*. Millan: Oemme Edizioni, 1974.

Derderian, Katharine. "Common Fate, Different Experience: Gender-Specific Aspects of the Armenian Genocide, 1915-1917." *Holocaust and Genocide Studies* 19:1 (2005), pp. 1-25.

Deri, Mehmet. *Türkiye'de Azınlıklar ve Azınlık Okulları: Rum-Yahudi Ve Ermeni Cemaatleri* (Minorities and Minority Schools in Turkey: Greek-Jewish and Armenian communities). Istanbul: IQ Kültür Sanat Yayıncılık, 2009.

Deschenes, Jules. "Proposal Concerning a Definition of the term 'Minority'." UN Doc. E/CN.4/Sub.2/1985/31.

Dink, Hrant. "The Taste of Being a Minority." In *Contrasts and Solutions in the Caucasus*, Ole Høiris & Sefa Martin Yürükel eds. Aarhus-Oakville: Aarhus University Press, 1998.

Dogan, Ilhan & Osman Can. "Minorities in Turkey and in the EU." In *Deutsch-Türkisches Forum für Staatsrechtslehre III*, Otto Depenheuer ed., Münster: LIT Verlag, 2006, pp. 49–54.

Doğu, Ergil. "Identity Crises and Political Instability in Turkey." *Journal of International Affairs* 54:1 (Fall 2000), pp 43-62.

Dolgunsöz, Emrah. "Language Policies and Multilingual Education in Minority Schools in Ottoman Empire: Outcomes and Future Insights." *Idil* 3.12 (2014), pp. 97-108.

Donabedian-Demopoulos, Anaid. "Middle East and Beyond - Western Armenian at the Crossroads: A Sociolinguistic and Typological Sketch." In *Linguistic Minorities in Turkey and Turkic-speaking Minorities of the Periphery*, Christiane Bulut, Harrazowitz Verlag eds. 2018.

Dressler, Marcus. "Historical Trajectories and Ambivalences in Turkish Minority Discourse." *New Diversities* 17:1 (2015), pp. 9–26.

Dunbar, Robert. "Minority Language Rights in International Law." *The International and Comparative Law Quarterly*, 50:1 (Jan 2001), pp. 90–120.

Eblighatian, Melkon. *Kaghtagayanen Khorertaran* (From the Refugee Camp to Parliament), Vol. 2 Aleppo: Cilicia Publishing House 2005.

Educational Centre for Research and Development. "General Objectives of the Curricula and their Details." Beirut, 1997.

Ekmekcioğlu, Lerna. "Republic of Paradox: The League of Nations Minority Protection Regime and the New Turkey's Step-Citizens." *Int. J. Middle East Stud*, 46 (2014), pp. 657–679.

— — —. *Recovering Armenia: The Limits of Belonging in Post-Genocide Turkey*. Stanford, CA: Stanford University Press, 2016.

Ekmekji, Arsenian Arda. "Revisiting Artin in Beirut How Armenians Are Viewed in Lebanon." *Arab Stereotyping Conference*, Haigazain University, November 2001, https://bit.ly/38KlnQN.

El Machnouk, Saleh "Electoral System Reform in Lebanon: Dilemmas of a Consociational State." *Ethnopolitics*, 17:1 (2018).

Eldem, Edhem. "A Shameful Debate? A Critical Reassessment of the 'Torossian Debate.'" *Journal of Genocide Research*, 19:2 (2017), pp. 258-273.

Eligür, Banu. "Ethnocultural Nationalism and Turkey's Non-Muslim Minorities during the Early Republican Period." *British Journal of Middle Eastern Studies*, 46:1 (2019), pp. 158-177.

Ertan, Özlem. “Foundations in Search of Justice.” *Agos* Newspaper, 16.11.2007.

European Parliament. “Workshop Expansion of the Concept of Human Rights: Impact on Rights Promotion and Protection.” *Policy Department, Directorate-General for External Policies*, 2018.

Feroz, Ahmad. *The Young Turks: The Committee of Union & Progress in Turkish Politics, 1908–1914*. Oxford: OUP, 1969.

Fink, Carole. The League of Nations and Minority Question.” *World Affairs*, 157:4 (Jan. 1995), pp. 197-205.

— — —. “The Minorities Question at the Paris Peace Conference.” In *The Treaty of Versailles: A Reassessment After 75 Years*, Manfred Franz Boemeke, Gerald D. Feldman, Elisabeth Gläser eds. USA: Cambridge University Press, 1998.

— — —. *Defending the Rights of Others: The Great Powers, the Jews, and International Minority Protection, 1878–1938*. Cambridge: Cambridge University Press, 2004.

Fox, Graham. “The United Nations Forum on Minority Issues and its Role in Promoting the UN Declaration on the Rights of Persons Belonging to National or Ethnic, Religious and Linguistic Minorities.” In *The United Nations Declaration on Minorities an Academic Account on the Occasion of its 20th Anniversary (1992-2012),* Ugo Caruso and Rainer Hofmann eds. Leiden, The Netherlands: Brill Nijhoff, 2015.

Freedom House. *Turkey in Transit - Democratisation in Turkey*. New York: Printed in Hungary, 2008.

Fuller, Joseph V. *Papers Relating to the Foreign Relations of the United States, 1915, Supplement.* Washington: US Government Printing Office, 1928.

Gellman, Mneesha. “Remembering Violence: The Role of Apology and Dialogue in Turkey’s Democratization Process.” *Democratization*, 20:4 (2013), pp. 771-794.

— — —. *Democratization and Memories of Violence: Ethnic Minority Rights Movements in Mexico, Turkey, and El Salvador.* New York: Routledge, 2017.

Geukjian, Ohannes. “The Policy of Positive Neutrality of the Armenian Political Parties in Lebanon during the Civil War, 1975-90: A Critical Analysis.” *Middle Eastern Studies* 43:1 (Jan 2007), pp. 65-73.

— — —. “From Positive Neutrality to Partisanship: How and Why the Armenian Political Parties Took Sides in Lebanese Politics in the Post-Tai’f Period (1989–Present).” *Middle Eastern Studies*, 45:5 (September 2009), pp. 739–767.

— — —. “An Ignored Relationship: The Role of the Lebanese Armenian Diaspora in Conflict Resolution (1975–90).” *Middle Eastern Studies*, 50:4 (2014), pp. 554-567.

— — —. *Lebanon after the Syrian Withdrawal: External Intervention, Power-Sharing and Political Instability*. New York: Routledge, 2016.

Giesel, Christoph. "Status and Situation of the Jews in Turkey: Historical Lines of Development and Contemporary Circumstances in the Context of Socio-political Transformations." *Elektronik Siyaset Bilimi Araştırmaları Dergisi/ Electronic Journal of Political Science Studies*, 5:2 (2014), pp.1–32.

Gilbert, Geoff. "The Council of Europe and Minority Rights." *Human Rights Quarterly*, 18:1 (February 1996), pp. 160-189.

Göçek, Fatma Müge. "The 2007 Assassination of Hrant Dink through the Lenses of History." *Memory and Emotions* 70:2 (2018), pp. 149-163.

Goner, Ozlem. *Turkish National Identity and Its Outsiders: Memories of State Violence in Dersim*. New York: Routledge, 2017.

Grafton, David D. "Religious Minorities in the Diversity of Islamic Thought." In *Routledge Handbook of Minorities in the Middle East*, Paul S. Rowe ed. London: Routledge, 2019.

Goltz, Gabriel. "The Non-Muslim Minorities and Reform in Turkey." In *Turkey Beyond Nationalism: Towards Post-Nationalist* Identities, Hans Lukas Kieser ed. London: I. B. Tauris, 2006.

Grigoriadis, N., Ioannis. "On the Europeanization of Minority Rights Protection: Comparing the Cases of Greece and Turkey." *Mediterranean Politics* 13:1 (2008) pp. 23-41.

— — —. *Trials of Europeanization Turkish Political Culture and the European Union*. New York: Palgrave Macmillan, 2009.

Guibert, Nolwen & Sun Kim. "Compensation for the Armenian Genocide: A Study of Recognition and Reparation." In *The Armenian Genocide Legacy*, Alexis Demeridjian, ed. Palgrave Macmillan, 2016, pp. 102-113.

Gust, Wolfgang ed. *The Armenian Genocide: Evidence from the German Foreign Office Archives, 1915-1916*. New York, USA: Berghahn Books, 2014.

Hafner, Gerhard. "Human Rights of Minorities." In *All Human Rights for All Vienna Manual on Human Rights*, Manfred Nowak Karolina M. Januszewski & Tina Hofstätter eds. Vienna-Graz: Intersentia, 2012, pp. 462-466.

Hammami, Fida. "The Arab Charter on Human Rights: The Task Still Unfinished." *Irish Centre for Human Rights National University of Ireland Galway*, 2013.

Hammarberg, Thomas. Review Report on Human Rights of Minorities, *Council of Europe*, CommDH, 2009.

Hanioğlu, Şükrü M. *Preparation for a Revolution: The Young Turks (1902-1908)*. Oxford: OUP, 2001.

Harik, Judith. “Shaykh al-’Aql & the Druze of Mount Lebanon: Conflict and Accommodation.” *Middle Eastern Studies*, 30:3 (July 1994), pp. 461-486.

Harris, David J. “Collective Complaints under the European Social Charter: Encouraging Progress?” *International Law and Power: Perspectives on Legal Order and Justice*. Essays in Honour of Colin Warbrick, Kaikobad, K.H. & M. Bohlander eds. 2009.

Hayward, Susan. “Understanding and Extending the Marrakesh Declaration in Policy and Practice.” *United States Institute of Peace*, September 2016, https://bit.ly/381tkyv.

Henrard, Kristin. *Devising an Adequate System of Minority Protection: Individual Human Rights, Minority Rights and the Right to Self Determination International Studies in Human Rights*. The Netherlands: Martinus Nijhof Publishers, 2000.

— — —. “The Added Value of the Framework Convention for the Protection of National Minorities; the Two Pillars of an Adequate System of Minority Protection Revisited.” In *The Framework Convention for the Protection of National Minorities: A Useful Pan-European Instrument?*. Antwerp: Intersentia, 2008.

— — —. *The Interrelation between the Right to Identity of Minorities and their Socio-economic Participation*. Boston: Brill Publishing, 2013.

— — —. “The European Court of Human Rights, Ethnic and Religious Minorities and the Two Dimensions of the Right to Equal Treatment: Jurisprudence at Different Speeds.” *Nordic Journal of Human Rights*, 34:3 (2016), pp. 157-177.

Henrard, Kristin & Robert Dunbar. *Synergies in Minority Protection: European and International Law Perspectives*. Cambridge: Cambridge University Press, 2008.

Hewsen, Robert H. *Armenia: A Historical Atlas*. Chicago: University of Chicago Press, 2001.

Hilpold, Peter. “The League of Nations and the Protection of Minorities – Rediscovering a Great Experiment.” *Max Planck Yearbook of United Nations Law*, 17:1 (2013), pp.87-90.

Hoff, Anne-Christine. “Turkey Turns on Its Christians.” *Middle East Quarterly*, (Summer 2018), Middle East Forum online platform, https://www.meforum.org/7243/turkey-turns-on-its-Christians.

Hofmann, Rainer. “The Framework Convention for the Protection of National Minorities: An Introduction.” In *The Rights of Minorities in Europe, A Commentary on the European Framework Convention for the Protection of National Minorities*, Marc Weller ed., New York: OUP, 2007.

Hofmann Tessa. *Armenians in Turkey Today: A Critical Assessment of the Situation of the Armenian Minority*. Brussels: The Forum of Armenian Associations in Europe, 2002.

— — —. *One Nation, Three Sub-Ethnic Groups: The Case of Armenia and Her Diaspora*. Yerevan: 2011.

Holslag, Anthonie. *The Transgenerational Consequences of the Armenian Genocide: Near the Foot of Mountain Ararad*. Switzerland: Palgrave Macmillan, 2018.

Houry, Nadim. "Time for an Anti-discrimination Law." *Human Rights Watch*, 16.12.2012.

Hovannisian, Richard G. "The Historical Dimensions of the Armenian Question, 1878-1923." In *The Armenian Genocide in Perspective*, Richard G. Hovannisian ed. USA: Transaction Books New Brunswick, 1986, pp. 19-41.

— — —. ed. *The Armenian Genocide in Perspective*. USA: Transaction Books, 1986.

— — —. ed. *Remembrance and Denial: The Case of the Armenian Genocide*. Detroit, MI, USA: Wayne State University Press, 1999 pp.113-145.

— — —. ed. *The Republic of Armenia*, 4 Vols. Berkeley, USA: University of California Press, 1971-1996.

Hrant Dink Foundation. "Armenian Studies Past to Present." Istanbul, 2018.

Hsieh, Jolan. *Collective Rights of Indigenous Peoples: Identity-Based Movement of Plain Indigenous People of Taiwan*. New York: Routledge, 2006.

Hudson, Michael. C. "Trying Again: Power-Sharing in Post-Civil War Lebanon." In *International Negotiation*, 1997 (1).

Human Rights Watch. "Unequal and Unprotected Women's Rights under Lebanese Personal Status Laws." *Human Rights Watch Publication*, 2015.

Hüfner, Klaus. How to File Complaints on Human Rights Violations, A Manual for Individuals and NGOs. *German Commission for UNESCO and the United Nations Association of Germany*, 2010.

Hyusisyan, Varduhy. "Armenians in Lebanon After Israeli Invasion in 2006: A Community Under Threat of Vanishing." American University of Armenia, Political Science and International Affairs Program (MPSIA), 2008, p. 20, https://bit.ly/2Q4s0nJ

International Commission of Jurists. *Arab League's Human Rights Court Will Not Bring Justice to Victims of Violations*. Press Release, 2014.

— — —. "The Arab Court of Human Rights: A Flawed Statute for an Ineffective Court." 2015.

International Criminal Court. "Report on Preliminary Examination Activities 2018." https://bit.ly/2Oievyp.

International Institute for Democracy and Electoral Assistance. "Global State of Democracy 2019." 19.11.2019, https://www.idea.int/sites/default/files/publications/the-global-state-of-democracy-2019.pdf.

Işık, Tarik. "Türk Halkı Bir Tek Kendini Sever." [Turkish People Only Love Themselves], *Radikal*, 02.05.2011.

Jabareen, Yousef T. "Toward Participatory Equality: Protecting Minority Rights under International Law." *Israel Law Review*, 41:3 (Winter 2008), Cambridge University Press, 19.03.2012, pp. 635–676.

Jabarian, Appo. "Hariri Hijacks Armenian Seats in the Lebanese Parliament." *USA Armenian Life Magazine*, June 2019, https://bit.ly/36EfLox.

Jamanag Newspaper, "VGM-en Lousapanoutioon" (Clarifications from VGM). 1 July 2020, https://bit.ly/34jukOc

Jebejian, Arda. "Changing Ideologies and Extralinguistic Determinants in Language Maintenance and Shift Among Ethnic Diaspora Armenians in Beirut." School of Education University of Leicester, 2007.

— — —. "Patterns of Language Use among Armenians in Beirut in the Last 95 Years." *Haigazian Armenological Review* 31:1 2011. 8, (2011), pp. 453-469.

Kadıoğlu, Ayşe, "The Twin Motives of Turkish Nationalism." In *Symbiotic Antagonisms Competing Nationalisms in Turkey*, Ayşe Kadıoğlu & E. Fuat Keyman, eds. Salt Lake City: University of Utah Press, 2011, pp. 33–55.

Kaiser, Hilmar. "The Armenians in Lebanon during the Armenian Genocide." In *Armenians of Lebanon: From Past Princesses and Refugees to Present-Day Community*, Aida Boudjikian, ed., Beirut: Haigazian University & Armenian Heritage Press, 2009.

Kalpakian, Seta. "The Dimensions of the 1958 Inter-communal Conflict within the Armenian Community in Lebanon." Thesis, American University of Beirut, 1983.

Karaosmanoğlu, Kerem. "Re-imagining Minorities in Turkey: Before and after the AKP." *Insight Turkey* 12:2 (2010).

Kardeş, Selahattin. *Tehcir v Emval-i Metruke Mevzuatı* (in Turkish) (2nd ed.), (2012).

Kaso, Meltem Naz. "Minority Groups Face Increasing Discrimination in Turkey." *Zaman Newspaper*, 20.03.2014.

Kaya, Ayhan. "Turkey-EU Relations: The Impact of Islam on Europe." In *Yearbook of Muslims in Europe*, Jorgen Nielsen, Samim Akgönül, Ahmet Alibašic, Brigitte Maréchal, & Christian Moe. eds., Vol. 1. Leiden: Brill, 2009, pp. 377-402.

———. "Multiculturalism and Minorities in Turkey." In *Challenging Multiculturalism Book Subtitle: European Models of Diversity*, Raymond Taras ed. (Edinburgh University Press, 2012).

———. *Europeanization and Tolerance in Turkey: The Myth of Toleration*. England, Basingstoke: Palgrave Macmillan, 2013.

Kaya, Ayhan & Ece Harmanyeri. *Tolerance and Cultural Diversity Discourses in Turkey*. Istanbul: European Institute Istanbul Bilgi University, 2010.

Kaya Mehmed S. "Turkey's Vain Struggle to Create a Homogeneous Nation." *Middle East Policy, Middle East Policy Council* 25:2 (Summer 2018), pp. 121-135.

Kayalı, Hasan. "The Young Turks and The Committee of Union and Progress." In *The Routledge Handbook ff Modern Turkey*, Metin Heper & Sabri Sayarı eds., (Abingdon: Routledge, 2012).

Kayaoğlu Turan. "Getting Turkey Back on Track to Democracy, Human Rights, and Religious Freedom." *Review of Faith & International Affairs*, 14:2 (2016), 14-22.

Keshishian, Aram I. "The Armenian Genocide: From Recognition to Reparations." *International Criminal Law Review*, 14 (2014), pp. 233-241.

Kevorkian, Raymond. *The Armenian Genocide: A complete History*. New York: I.B. Tauris, 2011.

Kevorkian Raymond & Paul Paboudjian. Les Arméniens dans l'Empire ottoman à la veille du Génocide, (Armenians in the Ottoman Empire on the eve of the Genocide), Paris: Arhis, 1992.

Khamis, Fawzi & Fadi Al-Aridi. *Protecting Children at Risk in Light of the Law and Jurisprudence in Lebanon*. Lebanon: Friedrich Ebert Stiftung, 2nd edition, L2011.

Kilinç Ramazan. *Alien Citizens: The State and Religious Minorities in Turkey and France*. UK: Cambridge University Press, 2019.

Kılıcdag, Ohannes. "Social and Political Roles of the Armenian Clergy from the Late Ottoman Era to the Turkish Republic Istanbul Bilgi University, Istanbul, Turkey." *Philosophy and Social Criticism* 43:4-5 (2017), pp. 539–547.

Klebes, Heinrich. "The Council of Europe's Framework Convention for the Protection of National Minorities." *Human Rights Law Journal*, 16:92 (1995) pp. 92-115.

Knop, Karen. *Diversity and Self-Determination in International Law*. Cambridge: Cambridge University Press, 2002.

Kotchikian, Asbed. "Between (Home) land and (Host)land: Lebanese-Armenians and the Republic of Armenia." In *Armenians of Lebanon: From Past Princesses and Refugees to Present-Day Community,* Aida Boudjikian, ed. Beirut: Haigazian University and the Armenian Heritage Press, 2009.

Kouymjian, Dickran. "Confiscation and Destruction: A Manifestation of the Genocidal Process." *Armenian Forum,* 1:3 (Autumn, 1998), pp.1-12.

— — —. "The Destruction of Armenian Cultural Monuments: Its Significance for World Heritage Preservation." In *Noah's Country A Roadtrip through Post-Genocide Armenia*, Judith Crispin ed., Sydney: T&G Publishing, 2015.

— — —. "When Does Genocide End? The Armenian Case." Fresno State University, 11.03.2003 http://www.fresnostate.edu/artshum/armenianstudies/documents/pdf/2003%20DK-201%20When%20Does%20Genocide%20End%20%20Sonoma-Armen%20Weekly-final.pdf.

Krikorian, Mesrob K. *Armenians in the Service of the Ottoman Empire: 1860-1908*. New York: Routledge, 2018. first published in 1978.

Krüger, Heiko. *The Nagorno-Karabakh Conflict: A Legal Analysis.* London: Springer, 2010.

Kuper, Leo. *International Action Against Genocide*. London, UK: Minority Rights Group, 1984.

Kurban, Dilek. *A Quest for Equality: Minorities in Turkey.* UK: Minority Group International, 2007.

Kurban, Dilek & Kezban Hatemi. *The Story of an Alien(ation): Real Estate Ownership Problems of Non-Muslim Foundations and Communities in Turkey*. Istanbul: TESEV Publications, 2009.

Kymlicka, Will. "The Internalization of Minority Rights." In *Global Minority Rights,* Joshua Castellino ed., Ashgate Publishing, 2011.

Kymlicka Will & Wayne Norman. "Citizenship in Culturally Diverse Societies: Issues, Contexts, Concepts." In *Citizenship in Diverse Societies*, Will Kymlicka & Wayne Norman eds. Oxford and New York: OUP, 2000.

Lattimer, Mark. "Minority Participation and New Constitutional Law." *International Journal on Minority and Group Rights* 12, 2/3 (2005), pp. 227–244.

Legal Committee of Anjar Land Dispute. "Aynjari Hoghayin Hartsin Himnagan Hankrvannere." (The Main Stages of Anjar Land Dispute), Lebanon, 2007.

Lijphart, Arend. *Patterns of Democracy: Government form and Performance in Thirty-six Countries*. New Haven, CT: Yale University Press, 2012.

Lippe, John M. Vander. *The Politics of Turkish Democracy: Ismet Inonu and the Formation of the Multi-Party System, 1938-1950*. New York: State University New York Press, 2005.

Lobba, Paolo. "Holocaust Denial before the European Court of Human Rights: Evolution of an Exceptional Regime." *The European Journal of International Law*, 26:1 (2015), pp. 237-253.

Lukas, KieserHans, Mehmet Polatel & Thomas Schmutz. "Reform or Cataclysm? The Agreement of 8 February 1914 Regarding the Ottoman Eastern Provinces." *Journal of Genocide Research*, 17:3 (2015) pp. 285-304.

Macklem, Patrick. "Minority Rights in International Law." *International Journal of Constitutional Law*, 6:3-4 (July-October 2008), pp. 531–552.

Magliveras, Konstantinos D. "Completing the Institutional Mechanism of the Arab Human Rights System, The Arab Court of Human Rights." *International Human Rights Law Review* 6 (2017) pp. 30-52.

Magliveras, Konstantinos D. & Gino Joseph Naldi. "The Arab Court of Human Rights: A Study in Impotence." *Revue Québécoise de droit international*, 29:2 (2016), pp. 147-172.

Maila, Joseph. *Prospects for Lebanon: The Document of National Understanding: A Commentary*. Centre for Lebanese Studies, Lebanon 1992.

Makdisi, Usama. "The Modernity of Sectarianism in Lebanon." *Middle East Report, Minorities in the Middles East: Power and Politics of Difference*, 200 (Fall 1996).

Maksudyan, Nazan. "Book Review:" The Armenians in Modern Turkey: Post-Genocide Society, Politics and History." by Talin Suchiyan, London: Tauris, 2016., in *Global affairs*, 2:2 (2016).

Maktabi, Rania. "The Lebanese Census of 1932 Revisited. Who Are the Lebanese?" In *British Journal of Middle Eastern Studies*, 26:2 (1999), pp. 219-241.

Malaeb, Bilal. "State Fragility in Lebanon: Proximate Causes and Sources of Resilience." *Commission on State Fragility Report*, University of Oxford and University of Southampton, 2017.

Mansour, Maya W. & Carlos Y. Daoud. *Lebanon The Independence and Impartiality of the Judiciary*. Denmark: Euro-Mediterranean Human Rights Network, 2010.

Marashlian, Levon. "Finishing the Genocide: Cleansing Turkey of Armenian Survivors, 1920-1923." In *Remembrance and Denial: The Case of the Armenian Genocide*, Richard G. Hovannisian ed., Detroit, MI, USA: Wayne State University Press, 1999.

Marchand, Laure & Guillaume Perrier. *Türkiye ve Ermeni Hayaleti: Soykırımın I · zinde Adımlar* (Turkey and the Armenian Ghost: On the Trail of the Genocide), Istanbul: İletişim Yayınevi, 2014, pp. 9-18.

Marko, Jose. "Equality and Difference: Political and Legal Aspects of Ethnic Group Relations." In *Vienna International Encounter on Some Critical Issues Regarding the Situation of National Minorities*, F. Matscher ed. 1997.

Marks, Susan. *The Riddle of All Constitutions: International Law, Democracy, and the Critique of Ideology*. UK: OUP, 2003.

Marmara newspaper, 23, 25 & 28.01.1988.

— — —. 26.3.1994.

Martirosyan, Anna. "A Review of: "(Re)Constructing Armenia in Lebanon and Syria: Ethno-Cultural Diversity and the State in the Aftermath of a Refugee Crisis. Nicola Migliorino." *Journal of Immigrant & Refugee Studies*, 7:1 (2009).

Mazower, Mark. "Minorities and the League of Nations in interwar Europe." *Daedalus*, 126:2, (Spring 1997) pp. 47-63.

Medda-Windischer Roberta. "The European Court of Human Rights and Minority Rights." *Journal of European Integration*, 25:3 (2003) pp. 249-271.

Messerlian Zaven. *Armenian Participation in the Lebanese Legislative Elections, 1934-2009*. Lebanon: Haigazian University Press, 2014.

Michalska, Anna. "Migrant Workers as 'New' Minority. Sociological and Legal Definition of Minority." In *The Role of the Nation-State in the 21st Century: Human Rights, International Organisations, and Foreign Policy: Essays in Honour of Peter Baehr P. Peter*, R. Baehr eds. Boston: Martinus Nijhoff Publishers, 9 Dec 1998.

Migliorino, Nicola. *(Re)Constructing Armenia in Lebanon and Syria Ethno-Cultural Diversity and the State in the Aftermath of a Refugee Crisis*. USA: Berghahn Publications, 2008.

— — —. "The Lebanese System and Armenian Cultural Diversity, in Armenians of Lebanon." In *Armenians of Lebanon: From Past Princesses and Refugees to Present-Day Community*, Aida Boudjikian, ed., Beirut: Haigazian University and the Armenian Heritage Press, 2009.

Miller, Donald E. & Lorna Touryan. *Survivors: An Oral History of the Armenian Genocide*. Berkeley, USA: University of California Press, 1993.

Minority Rights Group International. "Minorities and Indigenous People in Lebanon." May 2019, https://bit.ly/3n3Xh7D.

Morgenthau, Henry, *Ambassador Morgenthau's Story Reading*. Taderon Press/ Gomidas Institute, England 2000.

Morris, B., & Dror Se'eavi, *The Thirty-Year Genocide: Turkey's Destruction of Its Christian Minorities, 1894–1924*. Boston: Harvard University Press, 2019.

Mubasyaroh, Mubasyaroh, "Da'wah Model of Prophet Muhammad in Madina." *Qudus International Journal of Islamic Studies*, 2:1 (August 2016), pp. 47-62.

Müftüler-Baç, Meltem & Lauren McLaren. "Enlargement Preferences and Policy- Making in the European Union: Impacts on Turkey." *Journal of European Integration* 25:1 (2003), pp. 17–30.

Munt, Harry. *The Holy City of Madina: Sacred Space in Early Islamic Arabia.* New York: Cambridge University Press, 2014.

Musgrave, Thomas D. *Self Determination and National Minorities.* Oxford: Clarendon Press, 1997.

Mwakagali, Mpoki. "International Human Rights Law and Discrimination Protections, A Comparison of Regional and National Responses." *Brill Research Perspectives in Comparative Discrimination Law*, 1:2 (2018), pp. 1-78.

Nalbantian, Tsolin. "Fashioning Armenians in Lebanon, 19461958." PhD Dissertation, Columbia University, New York, 2011.

— — —. "Going Beyond Overlooked Populations in Lebanese Historiography: The Armenian Case." *History Compass* 11/10 (2013), pp. 821–832.

— — —. "Articulating Power through the Parochial: The 1956 Armenian Church Election in Lebanon." *Journal of Middles East and North Africa Migration Studies*, 1:2 (2013) pp. 41-72.

— — —. "Armenians in the Middle East: From Marginalization to Everyday." In *Routledge Handbook of Minorities in the Middle East*, Paul S. Rowe ed., London, Routledge, 2019.

Nasrallah, Fida. "Syria after Ta 'if: Lebanon and the Lebanese in Syrian Politics." In *Contemporary Syria: Liberalization between Cold War and Cold Peace*, E. Kienle ed., London: British Academic Press, 1994, pp.132–138.

Nefes, Türkay Salim. "Understanding Anti-semitic Rhetoric in Turkey Through the Sèvres Syndrome." *Turkish Studies*, 16:4 (2015).

— — —. *Political Roots of Religious Exclusion in Turkey.* Oxford: Parliamentary Affairs, OUP, 2017.

Nicolas, Leila. *Minority Rights in Arab Levant: Between Extremism and the Envisioned Future Regional System.* New York: Fordham University, June 2016.

Nobles, Melissa. *The Politics of Official Apologies.* New York: Cambridge University Press, 2008.

Nowak, Manfred. *UN Covenant on Civil and Political Rights: CCPR Commentary* (revised 2nd ed.). Kehl am Rhein: Engel, 2005.

— — —. "An Introduction to the UN Human Rights System." In *All Human Rights for All, Vienna Manual on Human Rights*, Manfred Nowak Karolina M. Januszewski & Tina Hofstätter eds. Vienna-Graz: Intersentia, 2012. pp. 65-66.

Nowak, Manfred, Karolina M. Januszewski, & Tina Hofstatter eds. *All Human Rights for All, Vienna Manual on Human Rights.* Vienna-Graz: Intersentia, 2012.

— — —. "Human Rights of Specific Groups." In *All Human Rights for All, Vienna Manual on Human Rights,* Manfred Nowak Karolina M. Januszewski & Tina Hofstätter eds. Vienna-Graz: Intersentia, 2012.

Ntina, Tzouvala. "'These Ancient Arenas of Racial Struggles': International Law and the Balkans, 1878–1949." *European Journal of International Law*, 29:4 (November 2018) pp. 1149–1171.

Ofeish, Sami A. "Lebanon's Second Republic: Secular Talk, Sectarian Application." *Arab Studies Quarterly*, 21:1 (1999), pp. 97–116.

Oktem, Emre. "Turkey: Successor or Continuing State of the Ottoman Empire?." *Leiden Journal of International Law, Cambridge* 24:3 (Sep 2011) pp. 561-583.

Ömer, Turan. "The Armenian Question at the Lausanne Peace Talks." In *The Armenians in the Late Ottoman Period*, Turkkaya Ataov, ed. Ankara: Turkish Historical Society, 2001.

Onar, Nora Fisher & Mehmet Özgüneş. "How Deep a Transformation? Europeanization of Greek and Turkish Minority Policies." *International Journal on Minority and Group Rights*, 17:1 (2010), pp. 111–136.

Onaran, Nevzat. *Cumhuriyet'te Ermeni ve Rum Mallarinin Turklestirilmesi (1920-1930) Emvali Metrukenin Tasfiyesi – II.,* (Turkification of Armenian and Greek Properties in the Republic (1920-1930) Liquidation of Abandoned Property – II). Turkey: Evrensel Publications, 2013.

Özdoğan, Günay Göksu & Ohannes Kılıcdagı. *Hearing Turkey's Armenians: Issues, Demands and Policy Recommendations.* Turkey: Tesev Publication, 2012.

Özgül, Ceren. "From Muslim Citizen to Christian Minority: Tolerance, Secularism and Armenian Return Conversions in Turkey." Dissertation, The City University of New York, 2013.

— — —. "Legally Armenian: Tolerance, Conversion, and Name Change in Turkish Courts." *Comparative Studies in Society and History* 56(3) (2014), pp. 622–649.

Ozil, Ayşe. "Whose Property Is It? The State, Non-Muslim Communities, and the Question of Property Ownership from the Late Ottoman Empire through the Turkish Nation State." *Journal of the Ottoman and Turkish Studies Association*, 6:1 (Spring 2019), pp. 211-235.

Özkırımlı, Umut. "The Changing Nature of Nationalism in Turkey: Actors, Discourses, and the Struggle for Hegemony." In *Symbiotic Antagonisms: Competing Nationalisms in Turkey*, Ayşe Kadıoğlu & E. Fuat Keyman eds. Salt Lake City: The University of Utah Press, 2011.

Özkurt, Fatma Zeynep. "The impact of EU conditionality on democratisation in Turkey: institutional transformation and policy (re)formation of minority rights, freedom of expression, the military and the judiciary." PhD thesis, University of Nottingham, 2013.

Oztig, Lacin Idil & Kenan Aydın. "The AKP's Approach toward Non-Muslim Minorities: Constructivist and Rationalist Insights." *Alternatives: Global, Local, Political*, 42:2 (2017) pp.59-73.

Ozturk, Ahmet Erdi. "Turkey's Diyanet under AKP Rule: From Protector to Imposer of State Ideology?" *Southeast European and Black Sea Studies* 16:4 (2016) pp. 619-635.

Öztürk, Fatih. "Introduction to Minority Issues in Turkey – The Constitution – Making Process and EU Integration." *International Journal of Arts & Sciences*, 5:2(2012), Melikah University, Turkey.

Özyürek, Esra. "Convert Alert: German Muslims and Turkish Christians as Threats to Security in the New Europe." *Comparative Studies in Society and History* 51:1 (2009), pp. 91–116.

Palermo, Francesco & Natalie Sabanadze, *National Minorities in Inter-State Relations*. Boston: Brill, Nijhoff, 2011.

Papazian, Hrag. "*Türkiye'deki üç farklı Ermeni kimliği.*" (Three Armenian identity in Turkey). *Agos* Newspaper, 2016.

— — —. "Between Gezi Park and Kamp Armen: The Intersectional Activism of Leftist Armenian Youths in Istanbul." *Turkish Studies*, 18:1 (2017), pp. 56-76.

Papikian, Arpine "The Impact of Religion on the Preservation of Armenian Identity in Lebanon." Georg-August-Universität Göttingen, Göttingen Thesis, 2017.

Patrick, Dumberry. "Is Turkey the 'Continuing' State of the Ottoman Empire under International law?." *Netherlands International Law Review*, 59:2 (Aug 2012) pp. 235-259.

Patton, Marcie J. "Constitutionalism and Political Culture in Turkey." In *Political Culture and Constitutionalism: A Comparative Approach*, Daniel P. Franklin & Michael J. Baun eds. New York and London: Armonk, 1995.

Pejic, Jelena. "Minority Rights in International Law." *Human Rights Quarterly* 19:3 (1997), pp. 666-85.

Pellet, Alain. "The ILC Guide to Practice on Reservations to Treaties: A General Presentation by the Special Rapporteur." *European Journal of International Law, 24* (2013) pp 1061-1097.

Phillips, Alan. "The Framework Convention for the Protection of National Minorities: A Policy Analysis." *Minority Rights Group International,* (2002) pp. 1-16.

Phillips, Thomas James. "The (In-)Validity of Turkey's Reservation to Article 27 of the International Covenant on Civil and Political Rights." *International Journal on Minority and Group Rights* 27 (2020) pp. 66-93.

Pikulicka-Wilczewska Agnieszka & David B. MacDonald. *Identity Politics in the Age of Genocide*. New York: Routledge, 2007.

Picard, Elizabeth. *Lebanon, a Shattered Country*. New York and London: Holmes, 1996.

Pearson, Javaid Rehman. *Education*, (second ed.), Brunel: Brunel University, Pearson Education, 2010.

Petričušić, Antonija. "The Rights of Minorities in International Law: Tracing Developments in Normative Arrangements of International Organizations." *Croatian International Relations Review*, 11:38-39 (2005), pp. 47-57.

Raissouni, Mohammed. "Rights of Minorities in Islam, Report of the 9th Regular Session of the OIC Independent Permanent Human Rights Commission" OIC, 2016, https://bit.ly/3lkPOAR.

Ramaj, Erjona. "Binding International Norms, Jus Cogens." *European Journal of Sustainable Development*, 5:3 (01.10.2016), pp. 318-324.

Randa Nucho, Joanne. "Becoming Armenian in Lebanon." In *Middle East Report, No.267, Christians: Egypt, Iraq, Lebanon, Palestine* (Summer 2013), pp. 32-36.

Rasuly-Paleczek, Gabriele, & Maria Six-Hohenbalken. "Migration and its Impact on Armenia A field practice." Research Paper, University of Vienna, 2017.

Reilly, Benjamine. "Electoral Systems for Divided Societies." *Journal of Democracy*, 13 (2002), pp. 156–170.

Reitsma, Bernhard J.G. "Strangers in the Light: The Challenges of Being a (Christian) Minority in an Islamic Context." *Journal of Reformed Theology* 2 (2008), pp. 211-227.

Reyna, Yuda, & Ester M. Zonana. *Son Yasal Düzenlemelere Göre Cemaat Vakıfları*. (Community Foundations According to the Latest Legal Regulations), İstanbul: Gözlem Publication 2003.

Rishmawi, Mervat. "The Arab Charter on Human Rights and the League of Arab States: An Update." *Human Rights Law Review* 10:1 (2010), pp. 169-178.DOI: https://doi-org.uaccess.univie.ac.at/10.1093/hrlr/ngp043 Published: 10.02.2010.

Robinson, Nehemiah. *The Genocide Convention: A Commentary*. New York, NY, USA: Institute of Jewish Affairs, 1960.

Romano, David. "The Kurds in the Middle East." In *Routledge Handbook of Minorities in the Middle East*, Paul Rowe ed. London: Routledge, 2019.

Roscini, Marco, "Establishing State Responsibility for Historical Injustices: The Armenian Case." *International Criminal Law Review* 14:2 (2014), pp. 291-316.

Rosting, Helmer. "Protection of Minorities by the League of Nations." *The American Journal ofInternational Law*, 17:4 (Oct. 1923), pp. 641-660. Published online by CambridgeUniversity Press: 04 May 2017.

Rowe, Paul S. "The Sheep and the Goats? Christian Groups in Lebanon and Egypt." In *Nationalism and Minority Identities in Islamic Societies*, M Shatzmiller ed. Montreal: McGill-Queens UP, 2005.

— — —. ed. *Routledge Handbook of Minorities in the Middle East*. London: Routledge, 2019.

Rumelili, Bahar & Fuat Keyman, "Enacting Multi-layered Citizenship: Turkey's Armenians' Struggle for Justice and Equality." *Citizenship Studies*, 20:1 (2016), p. 70.

Russell, David & Nadim Shehadi. "Power Sharing and National Reconciliation: The Case of Lebanon." In *Power Sharing: New Challenges for Divided Societies*. London: Pluto Press, 2005, pp. 138-152.

Sahraoui, Hassiba Hadj. "Modernising the Arab Charter on Human Rights." *Yearbook of the International Commission of Jurists*, (2004), pp. 339-348.

Salhani, Maron. "The Armenian 'Signifier' in the Culture and Arts of the Land of the Cedars." In *Haygagan Inknutian Khntirner 21-rt Tarum* (Issues of Armenian Identity in 21 Century), Yerevan: Yerevan State University, 2014.

Sanjian, Ara. "Armenians and the 2000 Parliamentary Elections in Lebanon." Armenian News Network/Groong, 2000.

— — —. "The Armenian Minority Experience in the Modern Arab World." *Bulletin of the Royal Institute for Inter-Faith Studies*, 3 (1) (2001) pp. 149-179.

— — —. "Armenians and the 2009 Parliamentary Elections in Lebanon." Armenian News Network / Groong, 29.06.2009.

Sanjian, Avedis K. "The Sanjak of Alexandretta (Hatay): Its Impact on Turkish-Syrian Relations (1939-1956)." *Middle East Journal*, 10:4 (Autumn, 1956), pp. 379-382.

Sarafian, Ara. *United States Official Records on the Armenian Genocide, 1915-1917*. Princeton, USA: Gomidas Institute, 2004.

Schabas, William A. *Preventing Genocide and Mass Killing: The Challenge for the United Nations*. UK: Minority Rights Group International, 2005.

— — —. "Origins of the Genocide Convention: From Nuremberg to Paris." *Case Western Reserve Journal of International Law*, 40:1 (2007-2008), pp. 35-55.

— — —. *War Crimes and Human Rights: Essays on the Death Penalty, Justice, and Accountability*. London: Cameron May 2008.

Schahgaldian, Nikola B. *The Political Integration of an Immigrant Community into a Composite Society: The Armenians in Lebanon, 1920-1974*. New York: Columbia University, 1979.

Schwellnus, Guido. "Much ado about nothing? Minority Protection and the EU Charter of Fundamental Rights." Web papers on Constitutionalism & Governance beyond the State, No 5, 2001.

Seferian, Nareg. "The Final Frontiers: The Various Borders between Armenia and Turkey." *Turkish Review*, 3:3 (2013), pp. 258-264.

Sfeir, Myriam. "Arda Arsenian Ekmekji, An Armenian-Lebanese Academician Recounts." *Al-Raida*, 20:101-102 (Spring/Summer 2003), pp.71-73.

Sheklian, Christopher. "Promises of Property: Religious Foundations and the Justice and Development Party's Ambiguous Attitudes towards Religious Minorities." *Turkish Studies*, 20:3 (2019) pp. 403-420.

Shuayb, Maha. "Human Rights and Peace Education in the Lebanese Civics Textbooks." *The Centre for Lebanese Studies*, Lebanon, 10:1 (2015), pp. 135–150.

Siebenrock, Hanna. "The Enforceability of Human Rights in the States of the Arab League"(Diploma-Thesis, Institut für Europa - und Völkerrecht, 2018).

Simonian, Hovann ed. *The Hemshin: History, Society and Identity in the Highlands of Northeast Turkey*. New York: Routledge, 2007.

Šmihula, Daniel. "National Minorities in the Law of the EC/EU." *Romanian Journal of European Affairs*, 8:3 (September 2008), pp. 51-81.

Sözer Hande. *Managing Invisibility: Dissimulation and Identity Maintenance among Alevi Bulgarian Turks*. Boston: Brill, 2014.

Spilipoulou-Åkermark, S. "Minority Education–Torn in Contradictions?" In *European Yearbook of Minority Issues* (2010).

Suciyan, Talin. *The Armenians in Modern Turkey: Post-Genocide Society, Politics and History*. London: I. B. Tauris, 2016.

Suksi, Markku. "Personal Autonomy as Institution Form, Focus on Europe Against the Backdrop of Article 27 of the ICCPR." *International Journal on Minority and Group Rights*, 15:2 (2008) pp. 157-178.

Suleiman, Michael W. *Political Parties in Lebanon: The Challenge of a Fragmented Political Culture*. Cornell University Press, 1967.

Suny, Grigor Ronald & Fatma Müge Göçek. "Introduction: Leaving It to Historians." In *A Question of Genocide: Armenians and Turks at the End of the Ottoman Empire*, Suny, Göçek & Naimark eds. USA: OUP, 2011.

Swiss Confederation Government. *The Human Rights Council: Practical Guide*. 2018, https://www.eda.admin.ch/dam/eda/en/documents/publications/InternationaleOrganisationen/Uno/Human-rights-Council-practical-guide_en.

Tanielian, Jirayr. *Lipananahay Tebrotze: Tiver yev Mdoroumner* (The Armenian Schools in Lebanon, Some Data and Some Ideas). Lebanon, 2002.

Tanielian, Melanie. *The War of Famine: Everyday Life in Wartime Beirut and Mount Lebanon (1914-1918).* UC Berkeley: University of California, 2012.

Tashjian, Yeghia. "The Origin, Success and Failure of the Lebanese-Armenian "Third Force" during the Intra-communal Cold War (1956-1960)." *New Eastern Politics*, 2018, https://bit.ly/2PHZrMY.

Taşpinar, Ömer. *Kurdish Nationalism and Political Islam in Turkey: Kemalist Identity in Transition.* New York and London: Routledge, 2004.

Tavani, Claudia. *Collective Rights and the Cultural Identity of the Roma: A Case Study of Italy.* Boston: Martinus Nijhoff Publishers, 3 Sep 2012.

Tchilingirian, Hratch. "The 'Other' Citizens: Armenians in Turkey Between Isolation and (Dis)Integration." *Journal of the Society for Armenian Studies*, 25 (2016), pp. 123-155.

Teokmechian Zohrap. "Trkakan Despanatan Batsats Date." (The lawsuit filed by the Turkish Embassy,) *Zartonk Newspaper*, 20.05.2016.

Ter-Matevosyan, Vahram. "The Armenian Community and the AK Party: Finding Trust under the Crescent." *Insight Turkey*, 12:4 (2010), pp. 93-111.

Ter-Matevosyan, Vahram, Hamazasp Danielyan, Serge-Varak Sisserian, Nina Kankanyan & Nayiri Shorjian, "Institutions and Identity Politics in the Armenian Diaspora: The Cases of Russia and Lebanon." *Diaspora Studies*, 10:1 (2017).

Theriault, Henry C., Alfred de Zayas, Jermaine O. McCalpin, Ara Papian, "Resolution with Justice Reparations for the Armenian Genocide: The Report of the Armenian Genocide Reparations Study Group." March 2015.

Thompson, Richard H. "Ethnic Minorities and the Case for Collective Rights." *American Anthropologist, New Series*, 99:4 (Dec 1997) pp. 786-798.

Toggenburg, Gabriel. "A Rough Orientation through a Delicate Relationship: The European Union's Endeavours for (its) Minorities." European integration Online Papers 4, 2000.

Toktaş, Şule. "EU Enlargement Conditions and Minority Protection: A Reflection on Turkey's Non- Muslim Minorities." *East European Quarterly* 40:4, (2006), pp. 489–518.

Tørhaug, Hilde. "Lebanese Political Identity Exploring Sovereignty and Democracy in Lebanon through Norm Socialisation Processes." Institute for Statsvitenskap, University of Oslo, 2004.

Traboulsi, Fawwaz. "A History of Modern Lebanon - Second Edition." *Pluto*, England, (2012).

Trenz, Hans J. "Reconciling Diversity and Unity - Language Minorities and European Integration." *Ethnicities* 7:2 (2007), pp. 157-185.

Tsitselikis, Konstantinos. "A Surviving Treaty: The Lausanne Minority Protection in Greece and Turkey." In *The Interrelation between the Right to Identity of Minorities and Their Socio-economic Participation*, Kristin Henrard ed. Boston: Brill Publishing, 2013.

Turner, Nicholas & Nanako Otsuki. *The Responsibility to Protect Minorities and the Problem of the Kin-State*. United Nations University, Japan, 2010.

Uğur, Umit Ungor. "'Turkey for the Turks' Demographic Engineering in Eastern Anatolia, 1914–1945." In *A Question of Genocide: Armenians and Turks at the End of the Ottoman Empire*, Ronald Grigor Suny, Fatma Müge Göçek, & Norman M. Naimark eds. Oxforf, New York: OUP, 2011.

— — —. "The Armenian Genocide: A Multi-Dimensional Process of Destruction." *Global Dialogue*, 15:1 (Winter 2013), pp. 97–106.

Uğur, Umit Ungor & Mehmet Polatel. *Confiscation and Destruction: The Young Turk Seizure of Armenian Property*. London: Bloomsbury Publishing, 2011.

Ulusoy, Kıvanç. "Turkey's Reform Effort Reconsidered, 1987–2004." *Democratization*, 14(3), (2007), pp. 472–490.

Ümit, Kurt. "Legal and Official Plunder of Armenian and Jewish Properties in Comparative Perspective: The Armenian Genocide and the Holocaust." *Journal of Genocide Research the Armenian Genocide After 100 Years: New Historical Perspectives* 17:3 (2015), pp. 305-326.

— — —. "The Plunder of Wealth through Abandoned Properties Laws in the Armenian Genocide." *Genocide Studies International*, 10:1 (Spring 2016), pp. 37-51.

— — —. "The Political Micro-Economy of the Armenian Genocide, 1915-1922." *Journal of Balkan and Near Eastern Studies*, 20:6 (2018), pp. 618-638.

UN. *Final Clauses of Multilateral Treaties: Handbook*. New York, NY, USA: United Nations, 2003.

UN War Crimes Commission. *History of the United Nations War Crimes Commission and the Developments of the Laws of War.* (London: United Nations War Crimes Commission. His Majesty's Stationery Office, 1948). (English translation).

Ustun, Mustafa Tayfun. "The History of the Armenian Community in Lebanon: From 'Refugee Camps' to 'Neighbourhoods'." *International Journal for Social Sciences*, 5:9 (January 2017), pp. 93-108.

Vizi, Balázs. "Introduction to the Special Issue on Territoriality Language Rights and Minorities – European Perspectives." *International Journal on Minority and Group Rights* 23 (2016) pp. 423-427.

Von Bieberstein, Alice. "Surviving Hrant Dink: Carnal Mourning under the Specter of Senselessness in Post-Ottoman Topologies: The Presence of the Past." In *The Era of the Nation-State*, Nicolas Argenti ed., New York: Berghahn Books, 2019.

Vrdoljak, Ana Filipa. "Self-determination and Cultural Rights." In *Cultural, Human Rights*, Francesco Francioni & Martin Scheinin eds. Leiden: Martinus Nijhoff, 2008, pp. 41-78.

Wael, Allam. "The Arab Charter on Human Rights: Main Features." *Arab Law Quarterly*, 28:1 (2014), pp. 40-63.

Walter, Posch. "Crisis in Turkey: Just Another Bump on the Road to Europe?" *Institute for Security Studies Occasional Paper* 67, Paris, (2007) pp. 1-54.

Weller, Marc. *Universal Minority Rights: A Commentary on the Jurisprudence of International Courts and Treaty Bodies*. UK: OUP, 2007.

— — —. ed. *The Rights of Minorities in Europe, A Commentary on the European Framework Convention for the Protection of National Minorities*. New York: OUP, 2007.

Wivel, Klaus. *The Last Supper: The Plight of Christians in Arab Lands*. New York: New Vessel Press, 2013.

Wolff, Robert Lee Wolff & Harry Williams Hazard eds. "*The later Crusades, 1189-1311*, XVIII: *The Kingdom of Cilician Armenia*." (1969), pp. 630-659.

Wright, Jane. "Minority Groups, Autonomy, and Self-Determination." *Oxford Journal of Legal Studies*, 19:4 (Winter, 1999).

Yacoubian, Choulhadjian Vera. "The Politics of the Armenians in Lebanon: 1975-1989." Thesis, Lebanon: Lebanese American University, 2003.

Yeğen, Mesut. "Citizenship and Ethnicity in Turkey." *Middle Eastern Studies*, 40:5 (2004), pp. 682–708.

Yildirim, Mine. "The Collective Dimension of Freedom of Religion or Belief in International Law: The Application of Findings to the Case of Turkey." Dissertation, Finland: Abo, 2015.

— — —. *The Collective Dimension of Freedom of Religion: A Case Study on Turkey*. New York: Routledge, 2017.

Yılmaz, Altuğ. *Müslümanlaş(tırıl)mış Ermeniler* (Islamized-Islamatized Armenians). Istanbul: Hrant Dink Foundation, 2015.

Yilmaz, Ihsan & Galib Bashirov. "The AKP After 15 Years: Emergence of Erdoganism in Turkey." *Third World Quarterly*, 39:9 (2018) pp. 1812-1830.

Yilmaz, Gözde. "Exploring the Implementation of Minority Protection Rules in the 'Worlds of Compliance': The Case of Turkey." *Perspectives on European Politics and Society*, 13:4 (2012), pp. 408-424.

— — —. *Minority Rights in Turkey: A Battlefield for Europeanization*. New York: Routledge, 2017.

Yilmaz, Gozde & Diğdem Soyaltın. "Zooming into the 'Domestic' in *Europeanization: Promotion of Fight against Corruption and Minority Rights in Turkey*." *Journal of Balkan and Near Eastern Studies*, 16:1 (2014) pp. 11-29.

Young Civilians and Human Rights Agenda Association Ergenekon Is Our Reality. Ankara: Young Civilians and Human Rights Agenda Association, eds., 2010.

Yumul, Arus. "'Azınlık Mı Vatandas¸ Mı?'" [Minority or Citizen?] *in Türkiye'de Çoğunluk ve Azınlık Politikaları: AB Sürecinde Yurttaşlık Tartışmaları* [Majority and Minority Politics in Turkey: Citizenship Debates in EU Process]. Istanbul: TESEV Publication, pp. 2005, pp.101–21.

Ziegler, Karl Heinz, "The Peace Treaties of the Ottoman Empire with European Christian Powers." In *Peace Treaties and International Law in European History*, Randall Lesaffer ed. Cambridge: Cambridge University Press, Cambridge, 2004, pp. 338-364.

3. Online Sources

"9th National Development Plan in Turkey 2007-2013." Turkish Prime Ministry, 2007, http://www.sbb.gov.tr/wp-content/uploads/2018/11/Ninth_Develo pment_Plan_2007-2013.pdf.

Agos Newspaper. "Erdogan Threatens Armenian Citizens Once Again." 04.05.2015, http://www.agos.com.tr/en/Article/15565/erdogan-threatens-armenian-citizens-once-again.

— — —. *Nufusumuz Hizla Azaliyor* (Our Population Is Declining Rapidly), 07.02.2020,

— — —. "Valilik'ten seçime müdahale." (Election intervention from the Governorship), 15.03.2017, http://www.agos.com.tr/tr/yazi/17957/valilikten-sec ime-mudahale.

Ajroudi, Asma & Alia Chughtai. "Lebanon Elections 2018: Politics as Usual." AL Jazeera, 02.05. 2018 https://bit.ly/2I9Q98U.

Akın, Fehmi. "The Approach of the Ottoman Empire to Armenians within the Context of The Regulation of the Armenian Nation Dated 1864." Marmara University, 2008 https://bit.ly/2lSQRyd.

AKP political Group 2007. "Prime Minister and Chairman of the AKP Recep Tayyip Erdogan's Speech to his Political Group." 13.11. 2005,

Alechkevitch, Dmitri. "The Copenhagen Document and minority rights in 20 years of the Copenhagen Document." *OSCE Magazine*, 2, 2010, https://bit.ly/2R9ur9g.

Arar, Khaled. "The Armenians and the Awqaf confirm that they Have Documents Proving the Ownership of Anja." *Al-Diyar Newspaper*, 04.11.1997 https://bit.ly/36M3ldA.

Ararad Newspaper. "Why Do They Migrate from Motherland?." 2-8 July 2006.

Armenian Catholicosate of Cilicia. "Sunday Schools." 2019, https://bit.ly/2X2rBDJ.

"Armenians feel uneasy in Turkey, says Turkish MP." Arab News, 02.10.2020, https://www.arabnews.com/node/1743071/middle-east.

Armenian Mirror Spectator. "Pashinyan Visits Lebanon, Meets with Leadership." 2018, https://bit.ly/2O2EGZI.

Armenian Weekly Magazine. "Open Letter of IAGS president to President Serzh Sargsyan to Prime Minister Recep Tayyip Erdogan of 08.10., 2009." 12.10.2009. http://www.agaonline.org/de/aktionen/detail.php?newsId=333.

— — —. "Religious Minorities in Turkey: 'An Endangered Species'?" 12.04.2012 https://armenianweekly.com/2012/04/12/religious-minorities-in-turkey-an-endangered-species/.

— — —. "Turkish Flags Spark Controversy at Homenetmen Lebanon Basketball Game." 10.01.2017, https://bit.ly/2qF8dRm.

Armenpress. "Armenia MFA Comments on Statements of Turkish Side Amid Fights Against COVID-19." Armenpres.am. 13.04.2020, https://armenpress.am/eng/news/1012024/.

— — —. "Etyen Mahçupyan appointed Turkish PM's Senior Advisor." Armenpres.am. 25.10.2014, https://bit.ly/389GcDq

Asbarez Newspaper. "*Aram Gatoghigos yev Pakradouni Ge Merjen Lipanani Hamyanki Iravunke Khlelu Portse.*" (Aram Catholicos and Pakradouni Reject the Attempts to Violate the Rights of Armenian Community), 18.10. 2018, https://bit.ly/2KaAzd1.

— — —. "Armenian-Populated Districts of Istanbul Attacked." 10.09.2015.

http://asbarez.com/139676/armenian-populated-districts-of-istanbulattacked

— — —. "Tripoli Decides to Name Square after Sultan Abdul Hamid." 27.04. 2006, https://bit.ly/2X1hr6B.

Asfour, Lana. "Lebanon's divorce and child custody laws 'discriminate against women." The New Arab, June 2015, https://bit.ly/2IjpYhF.

Attarian, Hourig. "Armenian Schools and Education in Lebanon: Fostering A New Culture of Learning, Teaching and Practice." Gulbenkian Foundation, 2014, https://bit.ly/2pXDEWY.

Australian Human Rights Commission. "What is the Universal Declaration of Human Rights?" https://bit.ly/2Xm2YC7.

Ayman, Ibrahim. "History suggests Marrakesh Declaration no guarantee of religious freedom." Religious News Service, 01.02.2016, https://www.religionnews.com/2016/02/01/history-suggests-marrakesh-declaration-no-guarantee-religious-freedom-commentary/.

Azernews. "Anti-Armenian Protests Continue in Beirut." 02.052019, https://bit.ly/2C8kGzo.

Aztag Newwpaper. "*Azkayin Inknoutian Amrabentman Fond. 25 Timumi Entarachum Hulis Amsevan Entatskin. 15 Amsia Hashvegshir`270 Baraka.*" (National Identity Strengthening Fund. 25 Application Processed During July 15- Month Balance: 270 cases), 04.08.2018, http://www.aztagdaily.com/archives/403838.

— — —. "Haghortakrutioon." (Statement), 18.10. 2018, https://bit.ly/2NDbZDL.

— — —. "*Hayasdani Hanrabedutian 100 Amyagin Nvirvadz Mayis 28 Boghodayin Anvanagotchutioon yev Houshartsani Patsum.*" (Dedicated to the 100th Anniversary of the Republic of Armenia - "May 28" Avenue Naming and Opening of the Monument,) 17.07.2018, http://www.aztagdaily.com/archives/401264.

Bahout, Joseph. "Lebanon's Tai'f Agreement: Limits of Sect-Based Power Sharing." paper, Carnegie Endowment for International Peace, 2016, https://bit.ly/2C3zhMy.

Balian Arsho. "*Marash Taghamasi Norokutian Dzrakire Shudov Girakordzevi.*" (Marash District Renovation Project to Be Implemented Soon,) Aztag Newspaper, 09.07.2016, http://www.aztagdaily.com/archives/423401.

Banda, Maria. "Protecting R2P From Misuse." Opencanada.org, 2014, https://bit.ly/2QqNpI8.

Barsoumian, Nanore. "Sharp Rise in Hate Speech Threatens Turkey's Armenians." The Armenian Weekly, 08.10.2020, https://armenianweekly.com/2020/10/08/sharp-rise-in-hate-speech-threatens-turkeys-armenians/.

— — —. "The Road Ahead: An Interview with Garo Paylan." The Armenian Weekly Magazine, 01.07. 2015. http://armenianweekly.com/2015/07/01/the-road-ahead.

— — —. "When Erdogan Apologizes." Armenian Weekly Magazine, 09.05.2019, https://armenianweekly.com/2019/05/09/when-erdogan-apologizes/.

"Baudelaire Ndong Ella H.E. "Preventing and addressing violence and atrocity crimes targeted against minorities." Statement by the President of the Human Rights Council, Geneva, 25 November 2014.

BBC. "Lebanon: Why the country is in crisis." 05.08.2020, https://www.bbc.com/news/world-middle-east-53390108.

Bedrosian, Hamo. "*135 Dari Arach – Khrimian Hayrign u Berlini Vehajoghove.*" (135 years ago, Khrimian Hayirg and Berlin Conference), Asbarez Newspaper, 02.01.2014, https://hairenikweekly.com/2014/01/02/16507.

Bedrosyan, Raffi. "Revisiting the Turkification of Confiscated Armenian Assets." The Armenian Weekly, 17.04.2012, https://bit.ly/2IWey4c.

Bedrosyan, Raffy. "Pandora's Box for Istanbul Armenians." Armenian Mirror Spectator, 25.05.2020. https://mirrorspectator.com/2020/05/25/pandoras-box-for-istanbul-armenians/.

Belayachi, Djamel. "Turkish ultranationalists storm Armenian neighbourhoods in Istanbul as fighting rages in Nagorno-Karabakh." France 24, 15.10.2020, https://observers.france24.com/en/20201015-turkish-ultranationalists-storm-armenian-neighborhoods-istanbul-fighting-rages-nago.

Berkley Center for Religion, Peace, and World Affairs. "Religion and Conflict, Case Study Series Lebanon: The Persistence of Sectarian Conflict." 2013, https://bit.ly/2rthiwR.

Blua, Antoine. "Turkey Threatens to Expel Armenian Immigrants Amid Genocide Row." Radio Liberty, 17.03.2010, https://bit.ly/3scSG6B.

Britanica. "Hamidian massacres, Ottoman and Armenian History." Britanica.com, 2020,https://www.britannica.com/topic/Hamidian-massacres.

Brown, Chris. "State and Nation in Nineteen Century International Political Theory." LSE Research Online, April 2006, http://eprints.lse.ac.uk/745/1/Chapter8_Introduction.pdf.

Cengiz, Mahmut. "How the Corruption Investigations Of 2013 Still Shape Turkey's Bleak Future." Vocal Europe, 21.12.2017, https://bit.ly/2JnWEYq.

Cetin, Fethiye. ""Armenia Did Not Seem to Be Strange to Me…" Interview with Fethiye Çetin" Noravank Foundation, 04.05.2009.

— — —. Personal email communication with the author, 20.2.2020.

Cetıngulec, Tulay. "Does Turkey care about cultural diversity?" Al-Monitor Turkey Pulse, 17.08.2015, https://bit.ly/3qcQbzd.

Collelo, Thomas. "The National Pact" in Lebanon: A Country Study, Washington: GPO for the Library of Congress." 1987, https://bit.ly/34OYKWs.

Cumhuriyet Newspaper. "Erdogan: Bana çok daha çirkin şeyler söyleyenler oldu, Ermeni dediler!" (Erdogan: they said even uglier things to me, they said [I am] Armenian!), 16.08.2014.

— — —. "Hrant Küçükgüselyan'ın yargılanmasına başlandı." (The trial of Hrant Kucukguselyan has begun), 03.10.1981.

Current History: A Monthly Magazine of The New York Times, Volume 5, (February 1917) pp. 822-824).

Diario Armenia. “The Armenian electorate proved its strength. Three of the four ARF nominees - Hagop Bagratuni, Hagop Terzian and Alexander Matossian - were elected.” 07.05.2018, https://bit.ly/328lJd6.

Dinken.com. “Agos’un önüne ırkçı pankart.” (Racist banner in front of Agos), Dinken.com, 23.2.2014, http://www.diken.com.tr/agosun-onune-irkci-pankart/.

Doghramadjian, Hagop. “Diaspora Focus: Lebanon.” The Armenian Weekly, 19.05.2017 https://bit.ly/2PGoeB4.

Economist. “How Genocide denial warps Turkish politics.” 07.11.2019, https://www.economist.com/europe/2019/11/07/how-Genocide-denial-warps-turkish-politics.

— — —. “When the Music Stops: Lebanon’s economy has long been sluggish. Now a crisis looms.” 30.08.2018, https://econ.st/2FD0tV.

Erbal, Ayda. “Expanded Version: Lebanese Elections and Lebanese-Armenian Politics.” The Armenian Mirror-Spectator, 17.05.2018, https://bit.ly/3rQeEvJ.

“Erdogan Calls for Crackdown on Armenian Genocide Recognition Efforts.” Asbarez Newspaper, 18.07.2020, http://asbarez.com/194788/erdogan-calls-for-crackdown-on-armenian-Genocide-recognition-efforts/.

Freemuse Artsfreedom Online Platform. “Lebanon: Song touching ‘The Armenian question’ banned.” 03.05.2010, https://freemuse.org/news/lebanon-song-touching-the-armenian-question-banned/.

“ESCWA Warns: More Than Half of Lebanon’s Population Trapped in Poverty.” UN Economic and Social Commission for Western Asia, 19.08.2020, https://bit.ly/3ikj4Xt.

France24. “Fifty years ago: Black September for PLO.” 15.09.2020, https://bit.ly/2LWrYyC.

— — —. “‘All of them means all of them’: Lebanon protest slogans.” 21.10.2019, https://bit.ly/3jTz7wk.

— — —. “Lebanese PM Announces Government’s Resignation Over Beirut Blast.” 10.08.2020, https://www.france24.com/en/20200810-live-lebanese-pm-announces-government-s-resignation-over-beirut-blast.

Gapreilian, Sisak. “Armenian Troops Start Lebanon Mission.” Radio Freedom of Armenia, Azatutyun.am, 27.11.2014, https://bit.ly/2K7f2Sj.

Ghazanchyan, Siranush. “Erdogan lashes out at Armenian, Greek lobbies.” Public Radio of Armenia, 12.05.2020, https://en.armradio.am/2020/05/12/erdogan-lashes-out-at-armenian-greek-lobbies/.

— — —. “Garo Paylan submits inquiry to Turkish Parliament on 105th anniversary of Armenian Genocide.” Public Radio of Armenia, 24.04.2020, https://

en.armradio.am/2020/04/24/garo-paylan-submits-inquiry-on-armenian-Genocide-to-turkish-parliament/.

Gültekin, Uygar. "Historic decision on Sanasaryan Han." Agos Newspaper, 26.02.2018, http://www.agos.com.tr/en/Article/20265/historic-decision-on-sanasaryan-han

Hafiza, Merkezi. "Why Hafiza Merkezi." 15.05.2020, https://hakikatadalethafiza.org/en/why-hafiza-merkezi/.

Harutyunyan Aneta. "Lebanese people love Armenia through local Armenian community and definitely want to see the country – minister." Armenpress, 22.02.2018, https://bit.ly/2UvWhwT.

Hauer, Neil. "Middle East's Armenians in Retreat." Asia Times, 10.09.2019, https://bit.ly/2Wx73mO.

Haugbolle, Sune. "The Historiography and the Memory of the Lebanese civil war." SciencesPo, 25.10.2011, online paper, https://bit.ly/2SXX0Vi.

Hrant Dink Foundation. "Turkey-Armenia Fellowship Scheme." 10.05.2020, https://hrantdink.org/en/activities/projects/turkey-armenia-relations-programme/turkey-armenia-fellowship-scheme/270-turkey-armenia-fellowship-scheme.

— — —. "Turkey-Armenia Journalists' Dialogue Programme." 10.05.2020, https://hrantdink.org/en/activities/projects/turkey-armenia-relations-programme/dialogue-groups/328-turkey-armenia-journalists-dialogue-programme.

— — —. "Turkey-Armenia Travel Grant." 10.05.2020, https://hrantdink.org/en/activities/projects/turkey-armenia-relations-programme/turkey-armenia-travel-grant/226-turkey-armenia-travel-grant.

— — —. "Western Armenian Program." 10.05.2020, https://hrantdink.org/en/activities/projects/western-armenian-program/246-bati-ermenicesi-programi-2.

HRW. "Questions and Answers:" Turkey's Constitutional Referendum." 2018, https://bit.ly/2ViHcPA.

— — —. "Lebanon Events of 2018." online Report, 2018 https://bit.ly/338B8vy

— — —. Proposed Arab Court of Human Rights: An empty vessel without substantial changes to the draft Statute." 2014, hhttps://bit.ly/2YhmfVW.

Hürriyet Daily News. "Minorities in Turkey tagged by 'race codes,' official document reveals." August 2013, https://www.hurriyetdailynews.com/minorities-in-turkey-tagged-by-race-codes-official-document-reveals-51849.

— — —. "Investigation launched into police march in Roma neighbourhoods in western Turkey." 12.07.2015, https://bit.ly/357hxPb.

Hyetert Newspaper, "Istanbul Ermeni Patrikliği Patrik Seçim Talimatnamesi (Tam Metin)." (Istanbul Armenian Patriarchate Patriarch Election Instructions (Full Text)), 23.09.2019, https://bit.ly/3pgpGbO.

Ibrahim, Roula. "Arman Lebnan Yankaridoun." (Armenians of Lebanon are becoming extinct), Al-Akhbar Newspaper, 13.10.2018, https://bit.ly/2RWMgsJ.

Index Mundi. "Lebanon Demographics Profile 2018." July 2020, https://bit.ly/2AhnVVa.

International Coalition for Religious Freedom. "Religious Freedom World Report: Turkey." 2001, wysiwyg://102/http://www.religio...freedom.com/wrtpEurope/turkey.htm.

International Criminal Court official website. "Situation Under Investigation." September 2020, https://www.icc-cpi.int/pages/situation.aspx.

Irish Examiner, "Turkish police 'treated alleged killer as a hero." 03.02.2007, https://www.irishexaminer.com/world/crime/turkish-police-treated-alleged-killer-as-a-hero-24553.html.

Jamanag Newspaper. 01.04.2020, https://bit.ly/3afMCQs.

Jewish Virtual Library. "Reports on Religious Freedom: Lebanon." 2003, https://bit.ly/2MiWkv1.

Johnson, Constance. "Iraq/ICC: Investigation of ISIL Crimes Urged by Religious Minority." 30.09.2015, https://bit.ly/2LNbRTx.

KAICIID International Dialogue Center. "Secretary General Welcomes Declaration on the Protection of Religious Minorities from Marrakesh Conference." 27.01.2016, https://www.kaiciid.org/news-events/news/kaiciid-secretary-general-welcomes-declaration-protection-religious-minorities.

Kandaharian, Shahan. "Around 10,000 Syrian Armenians moved to Armenia and 8,000 to Lebanon." News.am, 11.102013 https://bit.ly/2NyTKza.

Kuyumciyan, Baruyr. "Hrant Dink School students dream of a real classroom." Agos Newspaper, 13.03.2015, http://www.agos.com.tr/en/Article/10865/hrant-dink-school-students-dream-of-a-real-classroom.

Ladoian, Hagop. "*Entunely Che*." (Not acceptable), Aztag Newspaper, 14.09.2019, https://bit.ly/34UgNul.

Lesaffer, Randall. "The Congress of Vienna (1814-1815)." Oxford Public International Law, http://opil.ouplaw.com/page/congress-vienna-1814-1815.

Letsch, Constanze. "Turkey eclipses centenary of Armenian massacre by moving Gallipoli memorial." The Guardian,16.04.2015, https://www.theguardian.com/world/2015/apr/16/turkey-armenia-1915-centenary-gallipoli-massacre-Genocide.

Melkonyan, Rouben. "Armenia did not seem to be strange to me…": Interview with Fethiye Cetin. Noravank Foundation, 04.05.2009, http://www.noravank.am/en/?page=theme&thid=1&nid=1793.

Mient, Jan Faber. "R2P is misused." 2011, https://bit.ly/35fC3uN.

Minority Rights Group International. "Linguistic rights, Minority Rights Group." June 2020, https://minorityrights.org/law-and-legal-cases/linguistic-rights/.

— — —. "Turkey, Current Issues." 2020 https://minorityrights.org/country/turkey/.

— — —. "World Directory of Minorities and Indigenous Peoples – Lebanon." June 2008, https://bit.ly/2QbwKb8.

Navoyan, Vahram. "On the Modern Challenges." Noravank Foundation, 19.09.2013, https://bit.ly/2WZX2ie.

News.am. "Nikol Pashinyan and Saad Hariri discuss Armenia-Lebanon ties." 20.10.2018, https://bit.ly/2CBnxAU.

Nicholson Robert. "Lebanon's Discontent Has Religious Roots." Wall Street Journal, 31.10.2019 https://on.wsj.com/2NElkvf.

Nor Zartonk Foundation. "Being a Minority in Turkey' Survey Results in English." 2007. http://www.norzartonk.org/files/survey 2007.pdf.

Norwegian Helsinki Committee Freedom of Belief Initiative. "Pursuing Rights and Equality Monitoring Report on the Right to Freedom of Religion or Belief in Turkey-2019." 30.08.2019, https://inancozgurlugugirisimi.org/wp-content/uploads/2019/08/Report_Turkey_ENG_web.pdf.

Open Society Foundation. "The Arab League and Human Rights: Challenges Ahead." Regional Seminar held in Cairo on 16-17.02.2013, Open Society Foundations-Arab Regional Office, the Swedish International Development Cooperation Agency (SIDA), Irish Aid and the Norwegian Ministry of Foreign Affairs, https://www.fidh.org/IMG/pdf/rapport_lea_uk-lddouble.pdf.

Operational Portal Refugee Situation. "Registered Syrian Refugees." 2020 https://data2.unhcr.org/en/situations/syria/location/113.

Orhan, Kemal Cengiz. "Turkey's Secret 'Ancestry Codes' Track Non-Muslim Minorities." Al- Monitor Turkey Pulse, 08.082013, https://bit.ly/3shSW4b.

Öz, Deniz. "Armenians Fleeing Syria Say it is Like Another Genocide." Ahval News, 28.11.2018, https://bit.ly/3o8ZmQA.

Pan Armenian net. "Erdogan supporters chant anti-Armenian slogan at rally in Turkey." 17.10.2016, https://www.panarmenian.net/eng/news/223362/.

Patience, Martin. "Lebanon protesters' euphoria gives way to despair." BBC, 16.10.2020, https://www.bbc.com/news/world-middle-east-54554278.

Patrick J. McDonnell. "Armenians in Lebanon keep their culture, memory of heroic 1915 battle alive." Los Angeles Times, 24.04.2015, https://lat.ms/2Q7xJsU.

Pikulicka-Wilczewska, Agnieszka. "No "Velvet Revolution" for Lebanese Armenians." Open Democracy. 28.06.2018, https://bit.ly/34giNfZ.

Rishmawi, Mervat. "The league of Arab States Human Rights Standards and Mechanisms." Open Society Foundation, 2015, http://www.cihrs.org/wp-content/uploads/2015/12/league-arab-states-manual-en-20151125.pdf.

Sanders, Lewis IV, "Lebanon faces its worst crisis since the civil war." Dw.com, 08.07.2020, https://www.dw.com/en/lebanon-faces-its-worst-crisis-since-the-civil-war/a-54094075.

Sassounian, Harut. "Istanbul Armenians Document Violations of Minority Rights in Turkey." Asbarez Newspaper, 04.03.2011, http://asbarez.com/93867/istanbul-armenians-document-violations-of-minority-rights-in-turkey/.

— — —. "European Court Finds Catholicosate's Suit Inadmissible and Cannot be Appealed." Asbarez Newspaper, 14.10.2017, https://bit.ly/3aityov.

Saudi Press Agency. "Arab League Secretary General Welcomes Saudi Arabia's Ratification on the Statute of Arab Court for Human Rights." 24.06.2016, https://www.spa.gov.sa/viewfullstory.php?lang=en&newsid=1513644).

Scheinin, Martin. "Turkey's Derogation from Human Rights Treaties – An Update." Ejil Talk Blog of the European Journal of International Law, 18.08.2016, https://www.ejiltalk.org/turkeys-derogation-from-human-rights-treaties-an-update/

Secretariat General of the Turkish Republic for EU Affairs. "Political Reforms in Turkey." Ankar, 2007, https://www.ab.gov.tr/files/pub/prt.pdf.

Serkan, Demirtaş. "Justice Minister vows greater freedoms through new Human Rights Action Plan." Hurriyet Daily News, 20.12.2019, https://bit.ly/3qe0mEx.

Shemmassian Vahram L. "The Settlement of Musa Dagh Armenians in Anjar, Lebanon, 1939-1941." Asbarez Newspaper, 02.01.2015, Special Issue, https://bit.ly/2CzUv50.

Simavoryan Arestakes. "Armenian Catholics in Turkey." Noravank Foundation, 01.03. 2010, http://www.noravank.am/eng/Articles/detail.php?ELEMENT_ID=4404.

Stockholm Center for Freedom. "Statistics Show that Turkey is the Top Violator of European Rights Charter." 10.04.2020, https://bit.ly/3i7dbgc.

Tarcan, Pinar. "Sevag Balıkçı Case: Defendant Sentenced to Prison for 'Conscious and Reckless Killing'." Bianet, 13.01.2020, http://bianet.org/english/minorities/218523-sevag-balikci-case-defendant-sentenced-to-prison-for-conscious-and-reckless-killing.

The Daily Star. "Turkish peacekeepers Arrive for Mission in South Deployment comes despite vocal opposition from Armenian community." 21.10.2006.

The Guardian, "Kurdish leader Abdullah Ocalan declares ceasefire with Turkey." 12.03.2013, https://www.theguardian.com/world/2013/mar/21/pkk-leader-ocalan-declares-ceasefire

The New York Times. "Armenia Denounces Lausanne Treaty; Note to the Powers Formally Reserves All Grants Under the Treaty of Sèvres." September 12, 1923.

The official website of AGBU Lebanon. http://agbulebanon.org/.

The official website of Agos Newspaper: http://www.agos.com.tr/en/home

The official website of Armenian Catholicosate of Cilicia. "The Catholicosate of Cilicia Renews Its Demand for The Return of Its Historical Religious Centre in Cilicia (Kozan, Turkey)." 24.08.2019, https://bit.ly/3p3OyV7.

The official website of the Armenian Patriarchate in Istanbul. http://www.turkiyeermenileripatrikligi.org/site/.

The official website of the Presidency of Religious Affairs in Turkey. https://www.diyanet.gov.tr/tr-TR/Kurumsal/Detay//3/diyanet-isleri-baskanligi-temel-ilke-ve-hedefleri.

The official website of Bourj Hamoud Municipality: https://www.bourjhammoud.gov.lb/ar.

The official website of Bolsahay.com.

The official website of Directorate General of Foundation in Turkey. https://www.vgm.gov.tr/foundations-in-turkey/foundations-in-turkey/cemaat-community-foundations.

The official website of the Embassy of Republic of Armenia to Lebanon. "Armenian Community in Lebanon." 2020, https://bit.ly/2K8TOni.

The official website of the European Commission against Racism and Intolerance (ECRI). https://bit.ly/2DG00Q2.

The official website of the European Social Charter. https://bit.ly/306Ak8l.

The official website of Goguikian Foundation. https://www.goguikianfoundation.org/.

The official website of Haigazian University. http://www.haigazian.edu.lb/.

The official website of Haytert.com. https://hyetert.org/

The official website of Hrant Dink Foundation. https://hrantdink.org/en/about-us/vission-mission.

The official website of HREIT. http://ennhri.org/our-members/turkey/.

The official website of Human Rights Council. https://www.ohchr.org/en/hrbodies/hrc/pages/home.aspx.

The official website of Jamanak Newspaper. http://www.jamanak.com/.

The official website of Marmara Newspaper. http://www.normarmara.com/.

The official website of Marrakesh Declaration. http://www.marrakeshdeclaration.org/about.html.

The official website of Armenian MoFA. https://www.mfa.am/en/.

The official website of MFA of Armenia. "Statement of the Ministry of Foreign Affairs of the Republic of Armenia on the commemoration of the Armenian Genocide." 27.04.2019. https://bit.ly/3lQEkVC.

The official website of MFA of Turkey. http://www.mfa.gov.tr/%C4%B0nsan-haklar%C4%B1.en.mfa.

The official website of MFA of Turkey, Human Rights. http://www.mfa.gov.tr/%C4%B0nsanhaklar%C4%B1.en.mfa.

The official website MFA of Turkey. "Turkish Prime Minister Mr. Recep Tayyip Erdogan published a message on the events of 1915." 2019. http://www.mfa.gov.tr/turkish-prime-minister-mr_-recep-tayyip-erdogan-published-a-message-on-the-events-of-1915.en.mfa

The official website of Nor Zaronk: https://www.norzartonk.org/.

The official website of the OHCHR's Indigenous Peoples and Minorities Section. https://www.ohchr.org/EN/Issues/Minorities/Pages/OHCHRIndigenousPeoplesMinoritiesSection.aspx.

The official website of the Ombudsman Institution in Turkey: https://www.ombudsman.gov.tr/English/index.

The official website of OSCE High Commissioner on National Minorities. http://www.osce.org/hcnm.

The official website of the Government of Republic of Armenia. "Speeches by Karen Karapetyan and Saad Hariri during the official dinner given in honour of RA Prime Minister." 13.03.2018, https://bit.ly/3bwR95j.

The official website of the OSCE High Commissioner on National Minorities. http://www.osce.org/hcnm.

The official website of Ramgavars. 2020, http://ragmamoul.net/en/.

The official website of the Regional Office of the Middle East and North Africa of OHCHR. https://www.ohchr.org/EN/Countries/MenaRegion/Pages/MenaRegion20122013.aspx

The official website of the Responsibility to Protect. https://bit.ly/2OkQqag.

The official website of the Special Rapporteur on Minority Issues. UNOHCHR, 2020 shorturl.at/BCGP2.

The official website of the Supreme Council of the Lebanese and Syrian Evangelics. www.scevanchurch.org evangelical council https://bit.ly/324JuCX.

The official website of the UN High Commissioner for Refugees (UNHCR). https://www.unhcr.org/.

The official website of UNOHCHR. "Human Rights Bodies - Complaints Procedures, Complaining about Human Rights Violations." September 2020, https://www.ohchr.org/en/hrbodies/tbpetitions/pages/hrtbpetitions.aspx.

— — —. Official website of Turkey. https://www.ohchr.org/EN/Countries/ENACARegion/Pages/TRIndex.aspx.

The official website of UNESCO, UNESCO Atlas of the World's Languages in Danger. http://www.unesco.org/languages-atlas/index.php.

The official website of UNOHCHR. http://www.ohchr.org/EN/HRBodies/HRC/Pages/AboutCouncil.aspx.

The official website of UNOHCHR, UN Treaty Bodies Database, the ratification status by country or by treaty, Lebanon, 06.01.2021, https://bit.ly/3gRrxCZ

Transparency International Global Coalition against Corruption. "Corruption Perceptions Index." 12.12.2020, https://www.transparency.org/en/cpi/2019/results/lbn.

Trtrian, Gasia. "Tashnag: Last Armenian Party Left Standing in Vote Aftermath." Daily Star, 11.05.2018, https://bit.ly/36SFRnm.

Turkish Daily News. "Lawyer Cano: 'The State withholds documents from its courts.'" 10.02.2001, http://www.hurriyetdailynews.com/lawyer-cano-the-state-withholds-documents-from-its-courts.aspx?pageID= 438&n=lawyer-cano-the-state-withholds-documents-from-its-courts-2001-02-10.

Ülkar, Esra. "ERG raporuna göre: 92 bin öğretmene daha ihtiyaç var." (According to the ERG report: 92 thousand more teachers are needed,) Hurriyet, 28.11.2019. https://bit.ly/385hKDc.

Uras, Umut. "Armenian Immigrants Look for a Better Life in Turkey." Al Jazeera 20.04.2015, http://www.aljazeera.com/news/2015/04/armenian-immigrants-life-turkey-150420070803126.html.

US Embassy in Armenia. "Statement by the President on Armenian Remembrance Day 2019." 2019, https://bit.ly/3lHGMOc.

US Holocaust Memorial Museum. "The Armenian Genocide (1915-16): Overview." 2021, https://bit.ly/3pdbDqa.

US Library of Congress, Legal Research Guide. "Lebanon, Introduction to Lebanon's Legal System." 2020, https://bit.ly/2Miq1II.

US Mission to OSCE. "On the Marrakesh Declaration and Freedom of Religion or Belief." 03.03.2016, https://osce.usmission.gov/on-the-marrakesh-declaration-and-freedom-of-religion-or-belief-statement-at-the-pc/.

Van Der Stoel, Max. "Keynote Address of Max Van Der Stoel CSCE High Commissioner on National Minorities at the CSCE Human Dimension Seminar on "Case Studies on National Minority Issues: Positive Results." Warsaw, 1993, http://www.osce.org/hcnm/38038?download=true.

Vohra, Anchal. "Lebanon Is Sick and Tired of Syrian Refugees." ForeignPolicy.com, July 2019, https://bit.ly/36Ovelf.

Williams, Mark. "Turkey-based Armenian publisher Aras Publishing takes Publishing House of the Year award, 2019." The New Publishing Standard, 26.01.2019, https://thenewpublishingstandard.com/2019/01/26/turkey-based-armenian-publisher-aras-publishing-takes-publishing-house-year-award/.

Yackley, Ayla Jean. "Armenian migrants in Turkey live in shadow of century-old massacre." April 2016, https://www.reuters.com/Article/us-turkey-armenia/armenian-migrants-in-turkey-live-in-shadow-of-century-old-massacre-idUSKCN0XL059.

— — —. "War in the Caucasus hits close to home for Turkey's Armenians. "Eurasianet, Oct 21, 2020, https://eurasianet.org/war-in-the-caucasus-hits-close-to-home-for-turkeys-armenians.

Yildirim, Mine, "Turkey: Constitutional Court Judgment on Armenian Patriarchal Election – A Precedent?" Forum 18, 15.03.2020, http://www.forum18.org/archive.php?Article_id=2556.

— — —. "Turkey: Minority foundations still cannot hold elections." Forum 18, 05.03.2019, http://www.forum18.org/archive.php?Article_id=2459.

— — —. "Turkey: Why can't Armenians elect a Patriarch?" Forum 18, 15.02.2018, https://bit.ly/3nrKgpb.

— — —. "Turkey: Why State interference in the election of Chief Rabbi, Greek Orthodox and Armenian Patriarchs?" Forum 18, 11.08.2010 http://www.forum18.org/archive.php?Article_id=1477).

— — —. "What does Turkey's Restitution Decree mean?" 06.10.2011, http://www.forum18.org/archive.php?Article_id=1621.

Yildiz, Murat. "'They are scared': Armenians flee Istanbul amid anger over Nagorno-Karabakh." Middle East Eye, 11.11.2020, https://www.middleeasteye.net/news/turkey-armenians-istanbul-flee-anger-nagorno-karabakh.

YouTube. "Raphael Lemkin, creator of word "Genocide", referring to Armenian Genocide." 29.04.2020, https://www.youtube.com/watch?v=F57pgpr_jdw

Zannier, Lamberto. "Keynote Speech by OSCE High Commissioner on National Minorities on the occasion of the launch of the Graz Recommendations on Access to Justice and National Minorities." 14.11.2017, https://bit.ly/2Rbxxtc.

Zaman Newspaper, "Turkey Criticized for not Signing Charter on Minority Languages." 23.06.2010.

— — —. "Ultra-nationalist group targets Turkey's Armenians." 28.11.2012.

4. Personal Interviews

Ainteblian, Khajag. Member of the Board of Trustees for the Armenian "Haratch Kalousd Gulbenkian" school in Anjar, the interview was held in Anjar on 05.10.2018.

Avakian, Vicken. Director of Radio Voice of Van, former principal of Levon and Sofia Hagopian Armenia College, Zarehian Seminary Teacher, writer, member of Homenetmen Central Committee, the interview was held online on 15.09.2018.

Balian, Arsho. Editor of Aztag Newspaper, the interview was held online on 05.08.2018.

Danzikyan, Yetvart. Chief Editor of Agos Newspaper, the interview was held in Istanbul on 19.02.2020.

Degirmendjian, Sevan. Teacher, journalist, activist and the manager of member of Turkish Parliament Garo Paylan, the interview was held in Istanbul on 18.02.2020.

Doğan, Celina. Former member of Turkish Parliament, current member of Shishli Municipality Council in Istanbul, the interview was held in Istanbul on 18.02.2020.

Haidostian, Paul. President of Haigazian University, Community and Religious leader of Armenian Protestant Community in Lebanon, the interview was held in Beirut on 17.09.2018.

Havatian, Yesayi. Member of the Legal Committee of Anjar land dispute, the interview was held in Anjar on 05.102018.

Kalayci, Arno. Lawyer, founding member of Nor Zartonk Foundation, the interview was held in Istanbul on 17.02.2020.

Keshishian, Aram I. Catholicos of the Armenian Orthodox Church, Holy See of Cilicia, the interview was held in Antelias on 21.09.2018.

Khederian, Simon. Lawyer at the Armenian Orthodox Religious Court, the interview was online held on 26.08.2018.

Kotchikian, Asbed. Senior Lecturer, Global Studies, Boston University, the interview was held online on 10.10.2018.

Kouyoumdjian, Silva. Principal of Getronagan Armenian High School Armenian in Istanbul in, the interview was held in Istanbul on 16.02.2020.

Mashalian, Sahak II. Armenian Patriarch of Constantinople, the interview was held in Istanbul on 16.02.2020.

Pakradouni, Hagop. Armenian Member and Secretary of Lebanese Parliament and chairperson-representative of the Central Committee of the Armenian Political Party ARF-Tashnagtsutioon in Lebanon, the interview was held in Beirut on 19.09.2018.

Sanjian, Ara. Lebanese Armenian historian, lecturer at Michigan University, the interview was held online on 10.10.2018.

Sarkisyan, Tatevik. Journalist, historian based in Turkey, the interview was held in Istanbul on 19.02.2020.

Seropian, Vagharshag. Secretary at the Armenian Patriarchate in Istanbul, interview was held in Istanbul on 16.02.2020.

Tashjian, Yeghia. Expert in political relations and research, founder of New Eastern Politics Bloc, the interview was held online on 08.09.2018.

Vartanian, Shant. Newly appointed Lebanese diplomat, the interview was held in Beirut on 15.09.2018.

Völkerrecht, Europarecht und Internationales Wirtschaftsrecht

Herausgegeben von Peter Hilpold und August Reinisch

Band 1 Florian Razesberger: The International Criminal Court. The Principle of Complementarity. 2006.

Band 2 Christian Wimpissinger: Steuerliche Verlustverrechnung nach EG-Recht. 2006.

Band 3 Christina Knahr: Participation of Non-State Actors in the Dispute Settlement System of the WTO: Benefit or Burden? 2007.

Band 4 Daniela Kröll: Toward Multilateral Competition Law? After Cancún: Reevaluating the Case for Additional International Competition Rules Under Special Consideration of the WTO Agreement. 2007.

Band 5 Georg Nolte / Peter Hilpold (Hrsg.): Auslandsinvestitionen – Entwicklung großer Kodifikationen – Fragmentierung des Völkerrechts – Status des Kosovo. Beiträge zum 31. Österreichischen Völkerrechtstag 2006 in München. 2008.

Band 6 Irmgard Marboe: Die Berechnung von Entschädigung und Schadenersatz in der internationalen Rechtsprechung. 2009.

Band 7 Peter Neumann: United Nations Procurement Regime. Description and Evaluation of the Legal Framework in the Light of International Standards and of Findings of an Inquiry into Procurement for the Iraq Oil-for-Food Programme. 2008.

Band 8 Kirsten Schmalenbach / Wolfgang Benedek (Hrsg.): Von Terrorismusbekämpfung bis Klimaschutz. Beiträge zum 32. Österreichischen Völkerrechtstag 2007 in Altaussee. 2008.

Band 9 Stephan Wittich / August Reinisch / Andrea Gattini (Hrsg.): Kosovo – Staatsschulden – Notstand – EU-Reformvertrag – Humanitätsrecht. Beiträge zum 33. Österreichischen Völkerrechtstag 2008 in Conegliano. 2009.

Band 10 Peter Hilpold (Hrsg.): Das Selbstbestimmungsrecht der Völker. Vom umstrittenen Prinzip zum vieldeutigen Recht? 2009.

Band 11 Peter Hilpold / Christoph Perathoner (Hrsg.): Immigration und Integration. Völkerrechtliche und europarechtliche Antworten auf eine zentrale Herausforderung der Zeit. 2010.

Band 12 Claudia Alfons: Recognition and Enforcement of Annulled Foreign Arbitral Awards. An Analysis of the Legal Framework and its Interpretation in Case Law and Literature. 2010.

Band 13 Peter Hilpold / Walter Steinmair / Christoph Perathoner (Hrsg.): Rechtsvergleichung an der Sprachgrenze. 2011.

Band 14 Werner Schroeder / Jelka Mayr-Singer (Hrsg.): Völkerstrafrecht, Rechtsschutz und Rule of Law. Das Individuum als Herausforderung für das Völkerrecht. Beiträge zum 34. Österreichischen Völkerrechtstag 2009 in Tramin/Südtirol. 2011.

Band 15 Werner Petritz: Vor dem Aus? Der Vertrag über die Nichtweiterverbreitung von Kernwaffen. Funktion und Relevanz anhand zweier Beispiele. 2012.

Band 16 Kirsten Schmalenbach (Hrsg.): Aktuelle Herausforderungen des Völkerrechts. Beiträge zum 36. Österreichischen Völkerrechtstag 2011. Unter Mitarbeit von Lando Kirchmair. 2012.

Band 17 Ruth Steger: Staatenimmunität und Kriegsverbrechen. Das IGH-Urteil im Verfahren Deutschland gegen Italien vom 03.02.2012. 2013.

Band 18 Christoph Vedder (Hrsg.): Völkerrecht 2012. Richterliche Praxis und politische Realität. Beiträge zum 37. Österreichischen Völkerrechtstag 2012. Unter Mitarbeit von Manuel Indlekofer. 2013.

Band 19 Wolfgang Benedek / Hans-Peter Folz / Hubert Isak / Matthias C. Kettemann / Renate Kicker (Hrsg.): Bestand und Wandel des Völkerrechts. Beiträge zum 38. Österreichischen Völkerrechtstag 2013 in Stadtschlaining. 2014.

Band 20 Andrea Bockley / Ursula Kriebaum / August Reinisch (Hrsg.): Nichtstaatliche Akteure und Interventionsverbot. Beiträge zum 39. Österreichischen Völkerrechtstag 2014 in Klosterneuburg. 2015.

Band 21 Caroline U. Amann: The EU Education Policy in the Post-Lisbon Era. A Comprehensive Approach. 2015.

Band 22 Karl Edlinger: Die völkerrechtliche Klassifizierung bewaffneter Konflikte. Konflikttypen, Abgrenzungen sowie Rechtsfolgen und deren Auswirkungen auf die Planung und Durchführung militärischer Operationen. 2016.

Band 23 Elisabeth Parteli: Pressefreiheit und Persönlichkeitsschutz. Ein Leitfaden für die journalistische Praxis. Das Spannungsverhältnis zwischen der Freiheit der Äußerung und dem Schutz der Persönlichkeitsrechte unter besonderer Berücksichtigung der Abgrenzung von Tatsachenbehauptung und Werturteil der Rechtsprechung des Europäischen Gerichtshofs für Menschenrechte zu Artikel 10 EMRK. 2017.

Band 24 Anna Fischer: Sezession im Völkerrecht – Faktisches Phänomen oder reale Utopie. Die Geschichte eines Prinzips im Lichte eines unglücklichen Präzedenzfalls. 2017.

Band 25 Ruth Steger: Aut dedere aut iudicare. Inhalt und aktuelle Entwicklungen rund um die völkerrechtliche Verpflichtung zur Strafverfolgung oder Auslieferung. 2017.

Band 26 Dominik Brunner: Der „DARIO“ - Artikelentwurf über die Verantwortlichkeit Internationaler Organisationen. 2018.

Band 27 Mona Mairitsch: UNESCO-Welterbe auf nationaler Ebene: Verpflichtungen und Herausforderungen. Am Beispiel Österreichs. 2019.

Band 28 August Reinisch / Astrid Reisinger Coracini (Hrsg.): Zurück zu den Quellen des Völkerrechts. Beiträge zum 44. Österreichischen Völkerrechtstag 2019 in Rust am Neusiedlersee. 2021.

Band 29 Kyfork Aghobjian: The Rights of Armenian Minorities in Lebanon and Turkey under National and International Law. 2022.

www.peterlang.com

www.ingramcontent.com/pod-product-compliance
Ingram Content Group UK Ltd.
Pitfield, Milton Keynes, MK11 3LW, UK
UKHW021830100926
8556IPUK00004B/255

9 783631 888483